INTERNATIONAL GOVERNMENT

CLYDE EAGLETON

PROFESSOR OF INTERNATIONAL LAW
NEW YORK UNIVERSITY

THIRD EDITION

THE RONALD PRESS COMPANY · NEW YORK

Library of Congress Catalog Card Number: 57–6803

*To the Inspiring Memory
of My Father*

PREFACE

The Charter of the United Nations provided that it should be reviewed at the end of its first decade and for such a purpose many studies of that experience have been made. Important developments have been taking place in that institution; behind it, equally as important changes are taking place in the relations between the nations of the world; even the law of nations is in revolutionary ferment. A new epoch is beginning for the community of nations.

Thus, a revision of this book has become desirable, and a Third Edition is offered. It follows the same plan and has the same purposes as before; I am convinced that these purposes are still justifiable and even more so today.

The reader will better understand the selection of the materials included in this book if he will bear in mind that I am not concerned with international relations in general, but with the slowly evolving constitutional law and organization of the community of nations, developing toward international, or world, government. I would not argue with anyone who disputes the title of the book; it would be a dispute as to the definition of government.

For the large university, which can offer several courses in the international field, this book furnishes the preliminary training for advanced courses in International Law and International Organization, or serves as the single course in the field which many students desire to take for general information.

For the smaller college, which can offer but one course, it does not go too far toward technical international law, or wander too far into the very broad field of international relations—economic, political, psychological, diplomatic, etc. It may be used for a one-term course or for a full-year course.

For the general reader, increasingly concerned with the United Nations and the search for international peace and security, the book offers a rounded survey of the forces and developments in which he is interested. Though the book is well documented, in order to enable the student to pursue his investigation of particular points, I have tried to achieve a presentation not too technical for the interested reader to follow. I should be happy if it found readers outside the class-rooms, and I think that it might be useful to speakers and discussion leaders.

The literature of this field is growing large, and an effort has been made to reduce the number of citations while at the same time offering ample guidance for further study. The student should read carefully the introductory remarks to the Bibliographical Abbreviations below.

I have again to thank Dr. Hans Aufricht, of the International Mone-tary Fund, who, as in earlier editions, has generously put at my dis-posal his wide knowledge of international law and organization. My colleague, Professor Waldo Chamberlin, has read the chapters on the United Nations and his unexcelled knowledge of the practical opera-tion of that institution has saved me many errors. If, in my effort to keep this book within a reasonable number of pages and a reasonable price, there are faults to be found with it, they cannot be blamed; the responsibility is entirely mine.

Clyde Eagleton

August 10, 1956

CONTENTS

PART III

BIBLIOGRAPHICAL ABBREVIATIONS

The list of abbreviations given below contains only materials to which reference is most often made; it is not intended as a full bibliography. Where a short title is encountered in the footnotes, the full title may be found by turning to this list.

Citations for such a wide range as is covered in this volume may become annoying to the reader, and an effort is made in this edition to reduce them, particularly in the latter part of the volume, dealing with international organization. Attention is here called to a number of materials which will rarely be cited, but which the student should keep constantly in mind if he wishes to pursue a topic at more length. The *Annual Review* summarizes each year the activities and problems of the United Nations. The series of volumes by the *Brookings Institution* result from a large research in anticipation of the conference for review of the Charter, and, when complete, will constitute the most thorough study of the United Nations. *Bishop, Briggs,* and *Fenwick,* while often cited, can be referred to more frequently for international law. The *Yearbooks* of the United Nations and of the International Court of Justice contain full current information as to those organizations; the latter has valuable bibliographies. The journal *International Organization* is indispensable; it keeps up-to-date as to the activities of all international organizations, and has bibliographies particularly useful for documentary material. The *Repertoire* and *Repertory* are official and highly analytical summaries of the practice of the United Nations in relation to the various articles of the Charter. They contain many useful tables. The annual *Report by the President to Congress* summarizes the activity of the United Nations and the attitude of the United States toward its various phases. The *Staff Studies,* by the staff of the Senate Foreign Relations Committee, are compact and authoritative. The annual volumes instituted by the World Peace Foundation and now continued by the Council on Foreign Relations (*Doc. Am. For. Rel.*) provide much documentary material; and the annual volume issued by the Council on Foreign Relations (cited below as *Survey*) provides critical analysis of American foreign policy. Goodrich and Hambro, and Kelsen, cover the constitutional law of the United Nations; it would be burdensome to cite them at every point. Finally, the annual report of each international organization, or organ of the United Nations, is a current summary of information and a guide to further study.

LEAGUE OF NATIONS. League of Nations documents are usually cited by the number on the lower right hand corner of the document. Guides to these documents are Marie J. Carroll, *Key to League of Nations Documents Placed on Public Sale*, four volumes covering 1920-33 (Boston, World Peace Foundation) and a fifth volume for 1934-36 (Columbia University Press), and the compact and useful guide by Aufricht, cited below.

UNITED NATIONS. The documentation of the United Nations is already large and will increase steadily; few libraries have it well enough organized for convenient use. Within it is material dealing with almost every human activity. Each organ has its *Official Records;* each document has its letter designation (e.g., A/— for the General Assembly; E/— for the Economic and Social Council); many of the documents are also printed as supplements to *Official Records.* There are some indexes, but there is no easy way to locate material. See Carol Carter Moor and Waldo Chamberlin, *How to Use United Nations Documents* (New York University Press, 1952).

International law cases referred to in the text are listed in the index.

A.J.	American Journal of International Law. Published by the American Society of International Law. 1907–.
Annals	The Annals of the American Academy of Political and Social Science.
Annuaire	Annuaire de l'Institut de Droit International. 1873–.
Annual Digest	Annual Digest of Public International Law Cases; being a selection from the decisions of international and national courts and tribunals. London, 1919–.
Annual Review	Annual Review of United Nations Affairs. New York, 1949–.
Aufricht	Hans Aufricht. Guide to League of Nations Publications: A Bibliographical Survey of the Work of the League, 1920-1947. New York, 1951.
Ball and Killough	M. Margaret Ball and Hugh B. Killough. International Relations. New York, 1956.
Bishop	W. W. Bishop, Jr. International Law: Cases and Materials. New York, 1953.

Borchard — E. M. Borchard. The Diplomatic Protection of Citizens Abroad, or, The Law of International Claims. New York, 1915.

Brierly — J. L. Brierly. The Law of Nations: An Introduction to the Law of Peace. 4th Ed. Oxford, 1949.

Briggs — H. W. Briggs. The Law of Nations: Cases, Documents and Notes. Revised Ed. New York, 1952.

Brookings, *Organization* — Waldo Chamberlin and Clyde Eagleton. The United Nations: Organization, Functions and Procedures. Washington: The Brookings Institution, not yet published.

Brookings, *Peace and Security* — L. M. Goodrich and A. P. Simons. The United Nations and the Maintenance of International Peace and Security. Washington: The Brookings Institution, 1955.

Brookings, *Proposals* — Francis Wilcox and Carl Marcy. Proposals for Changes in the United Nations. Washington: The Brookings Institution, 1956.

(Four further volumes are planned to complete an over-all appraisal of the United Nations.)

B.Y.I.L. — British Yearbook of International Law. London, 1920—.

Cheever and Haviland — D. S. Cheever and H. F. Haviland. Organizing for Peace: International Organization in World Affairs. Boston, 1954.

Com. Prog. Cod. — Documents of the Committee for the Gradual and Progressive Codification of International Law (League of Nations). Also found in *A.J.*, 20, Special Numbers for July and October, 1926.

C.S.O.P. — Commission to Study the Organization of Peace: Research Affiliate of the American Association for the United Nations. Various reports and studies. New York.

Dept. of State Bull. — The Department of State Bulletin. United States Department of State. 1939—.

Dept. of State Pub. — The Department of State publications are numbered consecutively and also subdivided into numbered series. Washington, Government Printing Office.

Dickinson, *Cases* — E. D. Dickinson. The Law of Nations. New York, 1929.

Dickinson, *Equality* — E. D. Dickinson. The Equality of States in International Law. Cambridge, Mass., 1920.

Doc. Am. For. Rel. — Documents on American Foreign Relations. Annual volume. Boston: World Peace Foundation, 1939-51. Since 1952, published by the Council on Foreign Relations, New York.

Eagleton, *Analysis* — C. Eagleton. Analysis of the Problem of War. New York, 1937.

Eagleton, *Forces* — C. Eagleton. The Forces That Shape Our Future. New York, 1945.

Eagleton, *Responsibility* — C. Eagleton. The Responsibility of States in International Law. New York, 1928.

Fauchille — P. Fauchille. Traité de Droit International Public. Tome I (in three Parts, or volumes); Tome II. Paris, 1923-25.

Fenwick — C. G. Fenwick. International Law. 2nd Ed. New York and London, 1934.

Foreign Affairs — Foreign Affairs. Published quarterly by the Council on Foreign Relations, Inc., New York, 1921–.

Goodrich and Hambro — L. M. Goodrich and E. Hambro. Charter of the United Nations. Commentary and Documents. 2nd Ed. Boston, World Peace Foundation, 1949.

Hackworth — G. H. Hackworth. Digest of International Law. 9 Vols. Washington: Government Printing Office, 1940-44.

Hague Acad. — Académie de Droit International. Recueil des Cours. (One volume, 1923; several volumes per year thereafter. Numbered consecutively and by years.) Paris.

Hall — W. E. Hall. A Treatise on International Law. 8th Ed. by A. Pearce Higgins. Oxford, 1924.

Hearings — Hearings before the Committee on Foreign Relations, United States Senate, Seventy-ninth Congress, First Session, on the Charter of the United Nations for the Maintenance of International Peace and Security. Washington, Government Printing Office, 1945.

Hearings, *Charter Review* — Hearings before a subcommittee of the Committee on Foreign Relations. Revision of the United Nations Charter. Eighty-first Congress, Second Session. Washington: Government Printing Office, 1950.

Howard-Ellis — C. Howard-Ellis. The Origin, Structure and Working of the League of Nations. Boston, 1928.

Hudson, *Cases* — M. O. Hudson. Cases and Other Materials on International Law. 2nd Ed. American Casebook Series. St. Paul, 1936.

Hudson, *Court* — M. O. Hudson. The Permanent Court of International Justice. A Treatise. New York, 1943.

Hudson, *International Legislation* — M. O. Hudson. International Legislation. A Collection of Multipartite International Instruments of General Interest, beginning with the Covenant of the League of Nations. 9 Vols. Washington, Carnegie Endowment for International Peace, 1931-45.

Hudson, *World Court Reports*	M. O. Hudson. World Court Reports. A Collection of the Judgments, Orders and Opinions of the Permanent Court of International Justice. 4 Vols. Washington: Carnegie Endowment for International Peace, 1934-43.
Hyde	C. C. Hyde. International Law, Chiefly as Interpreted and Applied by the United States. 2nd Revised Ed. 3 Vols. Boston, 1945.
I.C.J.	International Court of Justice. Reports, paged by years, and Yearbooks.
Int. Con.	International Conciliation. Monthly. Numbered Series. New York: Carnegie Endowment for International Peace.
Int. Organ.	International Organization. Quarterly. Boston: World Peace Foundation, 1947–.
Jessup	P. C. Jessup. A Modern Law of Nations: An Introduction. New York, 1948.
Kelsen	Hans Kelsen. The Law of the United Nations: A Critical Analysis of its Fundamental Problems. London: Institute of World Affairs, 1950. Supplement, Recent Trends in the Law of the United Nations. Consecutively paged. 1951.
L.N.T.S.	League of Nations. Treaty Series.
L. of N. Doc.	Documents issued by the League of Nations, cited usually by the catalog number on the lower right hand corner of the document.
McNair	A. D. McNair. The Law of Treaties. British Practice and Opinions. New York, 1938.
Mander	L. Mander. Foundations of Modern World Society. Stanford, 1947.
Mexican Cl. Com.	Claims Commission, United States and Mexico. Opinions of Commissioners under the Convention Concluded September 8, 1923, between the United States and Mexico. February 4, 1926, to July 23, 1927. Washington: Government Printing Office, 1927.
Miller	D. H. Miller. The Drafting of the Covenant. 2 Vols. New York-London, 1928.
Moore, *Arbitrations*	J. B. Moore. History and Digest of the International Arbitrations to which the United States has been a Party. . . . 6 Vols. Washington: Government Printing Office, 1898.
Moore, *Digest*	J. B. Moore. A Digest of International Law. . . . 8 Vols. Washington: Government Printing Office, 1906.

O.J.	Official Journal. League of Nations.
Oppenheim	L. L. Oppenheim. International Law. A Treatise. 2 Vols. 4th Ed. by A. D. McNair. London, 1928.
Ottlik's *Annuaire*	Annuaire de la Société des Nations. Preparé sous la direction de G. Ottlik. Genève, 1920-38.
Palmer and Perkins	N. D. Palmer and Howard C. Perkins. International Relations: The World Community in Transition. Boston, 1953.
P.C.I.J.	Permanent Court of International Justice. Series A, Judgments; Series B, Advisory Opinions; later, Series A/B.
Phillimore	Sir Robert Phillimore. Commentaries upon International Law. 3rd Ed. 4 Vols. London, 1878-89.
Pol. Sci. Q.	Political Science Quarterly. New York, 1886–.
Pol. Sci. Rev.	The American Political Science Review. Published by the American Political Science Association. 1907–.
Postwar Preparation	Postwar Foreign Policy Preparation, 1939-1945. Department of State Publication, 3580, General Foreign Policy Series 15. Washington, 1950.
Proc. Am. Soc.	Proceedings of the American Society of International Law. Washington, 1907–.
Ralston	J. H. Ralston. International Arbitration from Athens to Locarno. Stanford, 1929.
Ray	J. Ray. Commentaire du Pacte de la Société des Nations selon la Politique et la Jurisprudence des Organes de la Société. Paris, 1930. With annual supplements entitled La Politique et la Jurisprudence de la Société des Nations.
R.D.I.	Revue de Droit International. Paris, 1927–.
R.D.I. (Genève)	Revue de Droit International, des Sciences Diplomatiques et Politiques. Genève, 1923–.
R.D.I.L.C.	Revue de Droit International et de Législation Comparée. Bruxelles, 1874–.
R.D.I.P.	Revue Générale de Droit International Public. Paris, 1869–.
Repertoire	Repertoire of the Practice of the Security Council 1946-51. United Nations. St/PSCA/1. Cales No. 1954. VII. 1.
Repertory	Repertory of Practice of United Nations Organs. Volume 1: Articles 1-22 of the Charter. Volume II: Articles 23-54 of the Charter. Volume III: Articles 55-72 of the Charter. Volume IV: Articles 73-91 of the Charter. Volume V: Articles 92-111 of the Charter. Index Volume. United Nations, Sales No. 1955. V. 2.

Report to Congress Report by the President to the Congress, on US Participation in the UN. Annual volume. Separately numbered Department of State publications.

Report to the President Charter of the United Nations: Report to the President on the Results of the San Francisco Conference by the Chairman of the United States Delegation, the Secretary of State. Department of State Publication No. 2349. Washington: Government Printing Office, June 26, 1945.

Research in International Law Research in International Law. Nationality, Responsibility of States, Territorial Waters. Harvard Law School, 1929. Found also in *A.J.* XXIII (1929), Special Supplement, with same pagination.

Research in International Law. I. Diplomatic Privileges and Immunities. II. Legal Position and Functions of Consuls. III. Competence of Courts in Regard to Foreign States. IV. Piracy. V. Piracy Laws of Various Countries. Harvard Law School, 1932. Found also in *A.J.* XXVI (1932), Sec. 2, April for I and II, July for III, October for IV and V, with same pagination.

Research in International Law. I. Extradition. II. Jurisdiction with Respect to Crime. Harvard Law School, 1935. Found also in *A.J.* XXIX (1935), Sec. 2, January and April for I, July for II, with same pagination.

Research in International Law. III. Law of Treaties. Harvard Law School, 1935. Found also in *A.J.* XXIX (1935), Sec. 2, October, with same pagination.

Research in International Law. I. Judicial Assistance. II. Rights and Duties of Neutral States in Naval and Aerial War. III. Rights and Duties of States in Case of Aggression. Harvard Law School, 1939. Found also in *A.J.* XXXIII (1939), Extra Number, June for I, July for II, October for III.

Ross Alf Ross. A Text-Book of International Law. With an Introduction by J. L. Brierly. London, 1947.

Rousseau Charles Rousseau. Droit International Public. Paris, 1953.

Satow Sir Ernest Satow. A Guide to Diplomatic Practice. 2 Vols. London, 1922.

Sibert Marcel Sibert. Traité de Droit International Public. Le Droit de la Paix. 2 Vols. Paris, 1951.

Sohn Louis B. Sohn. Cases and Other Materials on World Law. The Interpretation and Application of the Charter of the United Nations and of the Constitutions of Other Agencies of the World Community. Brooklyn, 1950.

Staff Studies	United States Senate. 83rd Congress, 2d Session. Subcommittee on the United Nations Charter. 1954-55.
	—— Review of the United Nations Charter: A Collection of Documents. Doc. No. 187.
	Staff Study No. 1: The Problem of the Veto in the United Nations Security Council.
	Staff Study No. 2: How the United Nations Charter Has Developed.
	Staff Study No. 3: The Problem of Membership in the United Nations.
	Staff Study No. 4: Representation and Voting in the United Nations General Assembly.
	Staff Study No. 5: Pacific Settlement of Disputes in the United Nations.
	Staff Study No. 6: Budgetary and Financial Problems of the United Nations.
	Staff Study No. 7: Enforcement Action Under the United Nations.
	Staff Study No. 8: The International Court of Justice.
	Staff Study No. 9: The United Nations and Dependent Territories.
	Staff Study No. 10: The United Nations and the Specialized Agencies.
	Staff Study No. 11: Human Rights, Domestic Jurisdiction and the United Nations Charter.
	Staff Study No. 12: The Status and Role of the Secretariat of the United Nations.
	The Staff Studies are now collected into one volume, Doc. No. 164.
Survey	Survey of American Foreign Relations. Published for the Council of Foreign Relations. (Annual volume.) New Haven, 1928-31. Continued under the title The U.S. and World Affairs. Annual Volume 1931–. New York.
Svarlien	Oscar Svarlien. An Introduction to the Law of Nations. New York, 1955.
Temperley	History of the Peace Conference of Paris. 6 Vols. London: Institute of International Affairs, 1920-21.
Ten Years of World Cooperation	League of Nations. Ten Years of World Cooperation. Secretariat of the League of Nations. 1930.
UNCIO Doc.	Documents of the United Nations Conference on International Organization, San Francisco, California, April 25–June 26, 1945. Published in cooperation with the Library of Congress by the United Nations Information Organizations. 15 Vols. and index. New York. (Documents will be cited by the document numbers.)

U.N. Doc.	Documents issued by the United Nations, cited by document number or other designation.
U.N.T.S.	United Nations Treaty Series.
Walters	F. F. Walters. A History of the League of Nations. 2 Vols. New York, 1952.
Wertheimer	E. F. Ranshofen-Wertheimer. The International Secretariat. A Great Experiment in International Administration. Washington: Carnegie Endowment for International Peace, 1945.
Wheaton	H. Wheaton. Elements of International Law. 8th Ed. by R. H. Dana. London, 1866.
Williams	Sir John Fischer Williams. Chapters on Current International Law and the League of Nations. London, 1929.
Wright, *Mandates*	Quincy Wright. Mandates and the League of Nations. Chicago, 1930.
Wright, *Study of War*	Quincy Wright. A Study of War. 2 Vols. Chicago, 1942.

PART I

There is, and has been for many centuries, a community of nations. Its members have been steadily pushed into closer cooperation by certain forces, primarily of economic interdependence and, more recently, the fear of war. Though the states which are its members claim to be sovereign and unlimited, they nevertheless submit to rules of law which have grown up through usage or which they have accepted in treaties. In the earlier stages of this community, relationships between states were usually bilateral; but many of these relationships were of interest to all states, and rules and procedures were developed which applied equally to all. Institutions of the community as a whole were much later in appearing.

While the term "community of nations" is still correct, it will appear in later parts of this volume that there is a trend today toward a community of peoples, rather than of states. The foundations of the community of nations are apparently being rebuilt.

Chapter 1

THE COMMUNITY OF NATIONS

1. EARLY GROWTH

In one sense, there has always been a community of nations. Nations are grouped human beings, and the gregarious instinct, as well as the other forces which draw individuals together, also brings groups of individuals together. There have always been some meeting points of common interest: some trade, some emigration, some hospitality to or protection for aliens, some wars. Behind such things, humanity has had certain instincts or feelings in common and has been united in its struggle with the forces of nature. The same forces to which political scientists ascribe other forms of political organization have led also to international organization. Man, said Aristotle, is a social animal; this instinct of sociability has led him through various forms of associations, at first in tribes and clans, later as peoples or nations; and now the movement is toward organization of all peoples in the world..

GREEK. While rules of international law may be found as far back as 500 B.C. or before, the clans and tribes of the ancient world were for the most part isolated and jealous of each other. Raids were more common than trade, and no right of existence on the part of other groups was recognized. "It is well known," says Oppenheim, "that the conception of a Family of Nations did not arise in the mental horizon of the ancient world."[1] In the exceptional culture of the Grecian peninsula, the idea of universal empire was disregarded, its groups of separate but homogeneous peoples offering the nearest resemblance to the international society of today. Arbitration was known amongst them, and rules for the alleviation of warfare, as well as the ancient principles which upheld the sanctity of treaties and of ambassadors. The institution of the guest-friend provided for the admission and protection of aliens. Toward international organization Greece contributed nothing more than the amphictyonies, or religious associa-

[1] Oppenheim, I, p. 55. (Refer to the list of bibliographical abbreviations above). See also Cheever and Haviland, Chap. ii; Palmer and Perkins, pp. 15 ff.

tions. But her history offers a compelling illustration, exceptional in those times, of the forces which draw together independent states which have interests in common.

ROMAN. It was long before a similar community of independent states again appeared, for the Roman state was a vast empire, allowing little room for interstate relationships.[2] A universal law, the *pax Romana* of which the apostle Paul boasted, "civis Romanus sum," did prevail; but it was the law of one state reaching individuals within that state, and not a law governing states themselves. Out of this, however, grew one contribution of great importance to international law, the *jus gentium*, in which there is a revived interest today.[3] Aliens in Rome were tried before the *praetor peregrinus* according to their own laws. In the effort to ascertain these laws, Rome accumulated the rules and customs of all nations; and from these could be derived the fundamental rules of law accepted by all peoples: *jus autem gentium omni humano generi commune est.* The *jus gentium* was a fertile source of international law in its formative period. Mention should be made also of the *jus fetiale*, which provided rules for the beginning and ending of wars, for heralds, treaties of peace and the like, and for the prosecution of claims against other states.

RISE OF NATION STATES. The theory of a universal empire continued long after the fall of the Roman Empire. It was maintained on the one hand by the Church, on the other hand by the Holy Roman Empire. Feudalism and the Church stood in the way of the idea of the state, without which the modern community of nations would not be possible. In the rivalry of this period, universalism could not survive and a shocking era of decentralization followed, out of which nations began gradually to shape themselves. As early as the Treaty of Verdun in 843, this process had started, and the idea of a universal state diminished until the abdication of Francis II in 1804 formally dissolved the Holy Roman Empire. As nation states grew stronger, the power of the Empire and of the Papacy decreased. From feudalism were borrowed the ideas of territorial control and personal allegiance. Machiavelli exalted the power of the state, and Bodin contributed a doctrine of sovereignty. The Thirty Years' War was a period of transition from one system to another—a period of great confusion. The success of the

[2] In her early history, however, Rome was one of a community of nations. C. Phillipson, *International Law and Custom of Ancient Greece and Rome*, 2 vols. (London, 1911), I, pp. 107-8; also Fenwick, p. 11. And Cicero spoke of a *civitas gentium.*

[3] Article 38(1c) of the Statute of the International Court of Justice: "the general principles of law recognized by civilized nations."

Reformation put an end, practically speaking, to the supremacy of both the Empire and the Papacy; and from this time forward variety and individualism became possible, and separate nations became firmly established.

So long as the theory of universal empire continued there could be nothing but internal law; there could be no law between states, for there could be only one state. Not until the legal right of independent coexistence of states was admitted could there be a community of nations, with laws and customs based upon common needs and interests. This recognition, political and legal, was given by the Peace of Westphalia, in 1648. Article 5 of the Treaty of Osnabrück, one of the treaties which constituted that famous Peace, reads:

That there be an exact and reciprocal equality amongst all the Electors, Princes and States of both Religions, conformably to the State of the Commonweal, the Constitution of the Empire, and the present Convention: so that what is just of one side shall be so of the other, all violence and force between the two Parties being forever prohibited.[4]

And the signatories were bound to maintain all the provisions of the Peace. While the Treaty concerned members of the Empire primarily, there could be little question that if the Empire admitted the independence of its members, the independence of states outside the Empire, such as France and England, which had long ago asserted their freedom, would go unchallenged.

The Peace of Westphalia is therefore regarded as laying the foundations of the modern international society. "Implicitly, if not by its definite provisions, the Peace of Westphalia created what was in effect a new society of nations and gave to that society a fundamental law."[5] Nationalism and personal sovereignty remained the dominant forces, distinctly particularist in character. The principle of territorial jurisdiction was established, each state being supreme within its own territory. From this independence flowed equality, for all states were equally sovereign and were now recognized as such in a binding treaty.

BALANCE OF POWER. But no one of them was ever again to be permitted to prevail over the others. The only salvation of each lay in the admission of a legal right of independence on the part of the others. Thus began the principle, or practice, of "balance of power," which was to dominate the politics of Europe during the following centuries. The principle was not a new one, for Polybius had said many centuries before, "Nor ought such a force ever be thrown into one hand as to

[4] Quoted by R. B. Mowat, *The European States System* (London, 1923), p. 16.
[5] Fenwick, p. 18.

incapacitate the neighboring states from defending their rights against it."[6] The balance of power was not a principle of international law, although the Peace of Utrecht spoke of "the establishment of a just peace for Christendom by a just equilibrium of power." It was no more than an expression of the principle of self-preservation, a practical solution of a problem; and it may be said that it has doubtless safeguarded weak states and has certainly prevented any one Power from attaining permanent hegemony in Europe. The principle of community action was thus recognized, though in its most vague form and with the most rudimentary means of expression. It was only when the whole community was threatened, as by a Napoleon, that the disjointed machinery of the balance of power set to work. We shall see later how it developed into the Concert of Europe and finally into the closer cooperation of the League of Nations and the United Nations.

OBSTACLES AND AIDS. Various obstacles hindered the development of a community of nations during this period. Peoples were ruled by monarchs whose dynastic and personal ambitions shaped policy; Machiavellian diplomacy was the order of the day. Later, when democracies replaced autocracies, the situation was little better; for democratic nationalism upheld state sovereignty as strongly as the king had upheld personal sovereignty and was as selfish and whimsical in expression as any king. It was a period of low ebb for international law. Treaties were disregarded; Frederick the Great observed that he acted first and then found lawyers to justify his actions. This was the time of the Wars of Succession, of the violation of the Pragmatic Sanction, of the partition of Poland. The heterogeneous character of the states which had sprung from the soil of feudalism added to the difficulty, for there were political organizations of every sort and belief, aligning Catholic against Protestant, monarchy against democracy, eastern against western Europe. Colonial rivalries, in the days of the mercantile theory, produced bitter struggles. And as serious as any difficulty was the lack of communications, which made acquaintanceship slow and bred fear based upon ignorance.

On the other hand, these very elements of conflict compelled states to seek agreement upon rules of behavior; and there were important consolidating forces at work. The sequence of Renaissance and Reformation produced a "European republic of letters," which meant a certain community of thought and ideals, and which had one striking advantage over our own day—a common language, for all educated

6 Quoted by J. B. Scott, in E. A. Walsh, *The History of International Relations* (New York, 1922), p. 100; and see F. L. Schuman, *The Commonwealth of Man* (New York, 1952), p. 34.

men could speak Latin. The itinerant student, even the itinerant professor, was unconcerned with national boundaries. Christianity also developed the community of thought; it taught a common morality; its international force was exhibited in the so-called "Truce of God"; it helped develop the widespread code of sportsmanship in arms which was called chivalry. The unifying effect of the Crusades was enormous. After them came an amazing expansion of commerce, and men were drawn together by a much more compelling force than culture—that of pecuniary gain. Colonial and trade rivalries produced many conflicts, so many, indeed, that rules for commercial intercourse became essential. Thus appeared the early codes of maritime law, such organizations as the consular service or the Hanseatic League, and such rules as those for title to newly discovered lands, boundaries, and similar matters. The reduction of the number of states after the feudal period aided in the development of the community, as did their proximity and necessary contacts in the close quarters of Europe. This also helps to explain why the community of nations found its beginnings in Europe. And at the end of the eighteenth century, new forces made their impression with incalculable results. The American and French revolutions enhanced the importance of the individual and made democratic nationalism possible. Some degree of popular control over policy became practicable, and the needs of individuals provided a greater constant in organizing the community. The way was prepared for a community of peoples rather than of states. With the liberation of the individual, with freedom of thought encouraged by education and developing intelligence, a philosophy of international relationships began to appear—a philosophy of interest within the comprehension of the average individual.

2. THE PRESSURE OF INTERDEPENDENCE

During the nineteenth and twentieth centuries two great forces developed which were to change habits of life all over the world. These were interdependence, primarily economic, and, consequent upon this interdependence, the changing character of war. Human beings have been pushed together by these forces in an effort to build international laws and organizations, which could help them to solve these new problems and relieve them from the increasing dangers appearing in modern warfare.

INDUSTRIAL REVOLUTION. The Industrial Revolution, with its incredibly far-reaching effects, was of transcendent importance in the growth of law and government, both in the domestic and in the international fields. It has made not only individuals, but nations utterly dependent upon each other. First among its effects, doubtless, was the improvement of communications, without which other effects could scarcely have been felt. Many new inventions (e.g., movies, radio, aviation) have brought peoples so much closer together that the world is now, in effect, only a fraction of its former size. Information is disseminated throughout the world at such instantaneous speed that peoples know each other better, and the effects of fear or hate founded upon ignorance are being steadily diminished—though they are far from gone!

But the effects of the Industrial Revolution go much deeper, reaching down to those motives of individual self-interest which dominate human action. It became possible for individuals to acquire large fortunes, and, since money is able to earn profits, the capital reserves thus accumulated sought investment. Such investments could often more easily, or more profitably, be sought in foreign lands, and this caused investigation of conditions in foreign lands and, in general, a greatly increased interest in them. The interest was mutual; the more highly developed industrial country needed raw materials from abroad and foreign markets in which to sell, while the less developed country was eager to sell its raw materials and was forced to rely on the industrial country not only for necessary machinery and manufactured articles, but also for the technical skills necessary for the utilization of its natural resources. If the capitalist in the more advanced country desired to put his money to work, the industrialist of the newer country needed financial aid and was as eager to borrow as was the capitalist to lend. To carry on this essential exchange, individuals had to go from one country to another, and governments naturally took an interest in the movement of their citizens. And so rules of international law for the protection of aliens and their property, as well as international institutions, both official and unofficial, were added to the methods developed by private enterprise for economic exchange. Interdependence has progressed at such a rapid rate that even individuals, caught up as they are within the system, scarcely realize that the day of individual self-sufficiency is gone. It is not surprising that the realization comes more slowly to nations.

It may be worthwhile, then, to take a moment to reflect upon the changes which have occurred in American life since the beginning of our history and thus illustrate the effects of this interdependence.[7]

---

[7] In earlier editions of this book, the effects of interdependence were more fully illustrated than seems necessary today. The reader is now referred to the author's book, *The Forces That Shape the Future* (New York, 1945).

The farmer can still get a drink of milk for himself, but the city dweller—and by now a majority of us are city dwellers—depends upon the efforts of perhaps a million persons for the delivery of a bottle of milk to his door each morning.

This is not exaggeration; it is an authentic illustration of the effects of interdependence. Suppose we take a dairy farmer in Connecticut or upstate New York, who contributes to the milk supply of New York City. To raise the food for his cows, agricultural implements, fertilizer, seed, and other things are needed, and to supply each of these needs we must go back to factories and business firms. The milk, when ready, is picked up by a truck, and the truck represents not only the trucking company that operates it, but a great automotive industry that makes the trucks, and a great oil industry that supplies the fuel. The milk is carried to a railway for transportation to New York City, and this involves the hundreds of thousands of employees of the railway; it is characteristic of the system that it is impossible to pick out two or three of them and say that they were the ones who delivered the milk. When it reaches New York, it is put through various processes and bottled; this brings in not only the men at work at the dairy station, but thousands of others who make the machinery, the bottles, the paper caps for the bottles, or who see that the milk is in good sanitary condition. The milk is then delivered from door to door by small vehicles, horse or auto, and these require stables or garages, as well as more manufacturers. Finally, the bill collector comes around, and behind him are the manufacturers and printers and distributors of paper and ink and pencils and typewriters![8]

The average individual believes that he gains by having the things of life supplied for him through such joint and specialized endeavor; and to this end he is willing to give up more and more of his personal self-sufficiency and to trust more and more of his affairs to the increasing machinery of law and governmental administration. But there is more than willingness involved; he cannot do otherwise, granted the complicated economics of modern life. He could not, in any large city, have even that vital necessity, a drink of water, but for a governmental organization involving perhaps hundreds of millions of dollars and a great staff for maintenance. Individual liberty is more and more cut down; the government must set up restraints and safeguards around the individual, so that other individuals may be assured that they will not suffer from their dependence upon him. Not every man can carry his own weights and measures with him; not every man is enough of a chemist to know whether the food or drugs that he buys are adulterated or not. If he did know, other people might not trust his knowledge or his measures, and would demand that they be inspected and examined and a license issued. And so, while we complain of the diminishing range of our individual liberty, we constantly demand more protection from the government, and upon it our security and happiness have come to depend.

[8] Eagleton, *Forces*, pp. 10-11.

INTERDEPENDENCE OF NATIONS. Similarly, if not to the same degree, peoples in the various states of the world have come to depend upon each other, and the prosperity and safety of one is affected by what others do. Foreign policy is affected by such pressures. But for their overseas trade the English people would starve in a few weeks; at the beginning of World War II, the British Food Minister noted with pride that the food stocks had been built up to such an extent that England could carry on for three or four months if cut off from the rest of the world. It was because of such dependence that Britain for so long felt it necessary to maintain a colonial empire and a powerful navy and to base her policy upon control of the seas. The United States, on the other hand, being comparatively self-sufficing, could—until recently—adopt a policy of isolation. Foreign policy must now be interested in such things as oil, the struggle for which rivals the explorations of and competition for new lands of three centuries ago; a similar struggle has now started for uranium.

Manifestly, in this sort of a world, regular and secure means of communication and movement are of importance for carrying on the trade upon which—rather than upon numbers of soldiers—the strength of a nation depends. Uncooperative nationalism makes it difficult to provide such assurance. The tariff, for example, has long been an international issue, and today various other types of restriction on trade have been devised. When the McKinley Tariff Act was put into effect by the United States, twelve hundred workers in the pearl button factories of the city of Vienna were laid off. The Smoot-Hawley tariff evoked official protests from thirty-three foreign states, the French Government observing that it would do as much harm to the province of Britanny as if the province had been devastated by a war. The complaints and retaliation aroused by recent United States restrictions upon the importation of Swiss watches or foreign cheeses are beginning to make the American people aware that such restrictions deprive the foreigner of dollars, so that he cannot buy from the United States such needed things as agricultural machinery. Efforts to build up regulations and machinery to assure a safer and more equitable exchange of goods and resources between nations have made little headway.[9]

The world is far smaller than it used to be. A war could be fought and won in Europe, a century or so ago, before news of it reached the United States; indeed, the battle of New Orleans was fought a fortnight after the Treaty of Ghent was signed, and it was a month later before the news arrived that the war had ended. Today, news is trans-

[9] See the discussion of the ITO, GATT, and the OTC, in Chap. 13 below.

mitted so rapidly that an American, listening to his radio, can hear what a foreign statesman says before the people in the rear of the hall where he speaks can hear him. Two centuries ago it required weeks of travel to cross the American continent or the Atlantic Ocean; today, it is possible to reach almost any part of the world within a day.

In this smaller world, peoples anywhere in the world are thrown together and depend upon each other. The factories, and the persons who are supported by them, must draw their materials from all over the world; the more industrially advanced a state is, the more it depends upon other parts of the world. The United States has vast natural resources; it is perhaps the most self-supplying large state in the world, and the proportion of its needs from abroad is small as compared with its total trade. But these needs include such things as vanadium or manganese, without which our precision machinery could not operate; or tungsten, without which "the whole TVA development would be useless"; or rubber, without which we would be pushed back to the "horse and buggy days." Scientific invention may provide substitutes, but materials for the substitutes must also be found; if making synthetic rubber exhausts our petroleum supply, we are forced to search the world over for oil.

And on the other hand, other peoples depend upon us, or upon each other, and cannot therefore permit any state to close its doors against trade. The mere enforcement of a law or administrative regulation in one country may discourage investment in that country and decrease the value of the stocks of a company in another state. International exchange works so poorly that there may be a huge surplus of butter or potatoes or meat in the United States while people are starving in other countries. It becomes more and more difficult to draw a line between domestic and foreign affairs; the effect of laws adopted or policies pursued within one country must be measured in terms of what its effects will be in another country.[10]

While economic forces are doubtless the most impressive and compelling factors in the life of prosperity-loving human beings, international interdependence is revealed elsewhere as well. Science, art, and culture transcend all boundary lines and are only slightly hindered by linguistic differences. The railway, the telephone, the airplane, the

[10] The above brief survey may be supplemented by reading J. B. Condliffe, *The Commerce of Nations* (New York, 1950); John B. de Mille, *Strategic Materials* (New York, 1947); P. T. Ellsworth, *The International Economy: Its Structure and Operation* (New York, 1950); Leith, Furness and Lewis, *World Minerals and World Peace* (Brookings Institution, 1943); Eugene Staley, *World Economy in Transition* (Council on Foreign Relations, 1939). These will lead into many other materials, covering matters for which there is not room in this volume.

automobile, atomic energy, or any one of a thousand important inventions and discoveries are each the joint product of men of various nationalities whose knowledge has been combined for the benefit of mankind. Modern inventions and methods are almost at once known throughout the world; it was impossible for the United States to prevent the Soviet Union from developing the atomic bomb. The exchange of students and teachers and scientific journals, the instant publication of new discoveries in the newspapers or by announcement over the radio, keep all peoples in touch with the latest improvements. Without such exchange of knowledge the progress of civilization would be incalculably slower. Resurgent nationalism seeks to keep to itself such knowledge; the United States, in the wave of fear of communism, refuses to grant visas or passports to or from this country to scientists on the least suspicion of sympathy with communism. Not only is the effort to prevent exchange of knowledge practically impossible, but it is self-defeating, and scientific associations in this country have protested strongly against such restrictions on movement.

Many other illustrations could be offered of the great growth of international intercourse: the multitudes of tourists who visit other countries each year; missionaries; mutual aid in disasters; marriages, such as the thousands contracted by GI's in Germany, England, and Japan. All such connections build up the feeling that human beings, wherever located, are part of one family and that it would be a dire loss for them to be deprived of exchange and intercourse, and that protection for such interchange should be assured by the community of nations.

It has been necessary to emphasize this situation of mutual dependence, for it is the foundation upon which the structure of modern society must be built. It is the appearance of this factor which marks the modern epoch and gives hope that the community of nations will, through sheer necessity, establish the laws and governmental machinery which it so badly needs. No state is able to live alone, or alone to fight a war today; an individual can no longer feel confident that his state can, of itself alone, protect him in his needs. For that purpose, his state has become inadequate; it must now reach out for aid into law and organization outside itself. It will be long before the effects of this situation will be worked out; it is hard to overcome centuries of belief that one's state is the final form of organization and that it must operate independently of any outside controls. Nationalism is still strong; indeed, it has been resurgent, assertive, and aggressive since World War II. It has also been fearful.

3. THE PRESSURE OF WAR

The scientific development and interdependence above described have changed the character of war and made it so terrifying an instrument that fear of war has now become a compelling pressure leading toward government within the community of nations. Interdependence called for rules and institutions; war calls additionally for executive power and for the physical force necessary to contravene the use of physical force by a state. The consequences of modern war upon the life of the individual are only slowly being realized by the average citizen. It is necessary to pay some attention to these effects, not only because they stir people to action, but also because of their influence in shaping international government.

Compared with today, war a century ago was not very harmful. It was carried on by small numbers of professional soldiers and the bulk of the population hardly knew that their country was engaged in war, except for increased taxes, or unless the battle swept near them and foraging soldiers took some of their possessions.[11] Other nations were unconcerned. Today, however, war reaches every person and every thing, not only in the countries at war but in other countries. More than this, it can hardly be fought except upon a totalitarian basis, and it therefore endangers democracy and private enterprise and, more broadly, undermines the bases of our civilization. It has become so enormous that preparation must be made for it continuously. It has spread into many fields and has become so varied an operation that, to use a bon mot attributed to Clemenceau, "war is too serious a matter to let it be directed by military men." Certainly, the professional knowledge of a military man a century ago is irrelevant today; and scientists and technicians must work steadily to keep a nation's knowledge of war-making devices ahead of that of its rivals. Industrialists, business managers, experts of all kinds must pool their knowledge and keep steadily at work so as to be ahead, or at least up to date, when the next war comes. As this is written, the government voices its concern at the lack of scientifically trained men, and the newspapers are full of advertisements calling for such persons. War now tends to become universal, totalitarian, and permanent—a continuing process involving economic penetration, fifth columns, terrorism, confusing propaganda, and psychological warfare on many fronts.

Thus, what we used to think of as peacetime, following a war, no longer exists; war and preparation for war occupies a large part of the

---

[11] The total military force of the United States, during the war of 1812, was 17,000 men; in the Mexican War, 4,400; in the Spanish-American War, 18,700. See Wright, *Study of War*, I, p. 662.

resources and energies of a nation at all times. Civil defense is now a peacetime term for guarding against war, and classrooms are posted with notices as to the refuge to be sought when the bombs begin to fall. The United States has become painfully conscious of the word "security"; freedom of movement, of thought, of almost anything, is now in time of "peace" more closely constricted than ever before in time of war.[12] The ramifications of modern war are continuously reaching further into our lives and ideals and habits of thought.

PERSONS. A modern army must be counted in millions instead of thousands, and it is no longer a small professional caste, but the whole population, most of whom must have special training for the tasks they are expected to perform. Such training cannot be postponed till the war starts; the United States was able to postpone training in the past two wars because the British Navy could protect us during our months of preparation. This will not be possible again; indeed, the United States will probably be the object of first attack. Volunteering cannot solve the problem; it can be met only by compulsory military training in time of peace. Whether the numbers in uniform will be greater than ever or whether it will be a push-button war is still being debated, but one can be sure that, whether for army or other war service, every man, woman and child will be called upon to contribute to the war effort. It is said, according to various estimates, that anywhere from twenty-five to fifty persons must be working to keep one man at the front supplied. Factories of all sorts must be converted to war production, transportation provided, communications developed. The girl who works in a factory producing the new missiles of war, the scientist in his laboratory, the coal miner or the oil worker, the railway man or the merchant mariner—any one of them may in fact contribute as much toward winning a war as the soldier at the front.

Such persons are logically subject to attack. International law attempted, with some success in the past, to differentiate between the combatant and the noncombatant and to protect the latter, but this distinction cannot be maintained when all are contributing to the war effort. Much less can it be maintained with weapons of mass destruction. It is useless to talk of the immorality of such weapons or to seek to outlaw them, for the fear that someone else might use them compels each state to be prepared with them—each state, that is, which is able to do so. If war is to be the instrument through which a state protects its vital interests, then that state must equip itself with the most effective weapons of war. A modern war is not to be won by a few thousand men in uniform on a few acres of battlefield; it is won by

[12] This is somewhat beside the point since no one, including the courts, has been able to say what war is. See § 130 below.

breaking the morale of a whole people. Mass destruction, fear and outrage, danger and starvation, these are the weapons of modern war; and they are directed not against uniformed soldiers only, but against whole populations. It is difficult to realize the inhumanity of this kind of war and very difficult for a democracy to realize that it must pursue courses outrageous to its own instincts if it is to win the war.

THINGS. Another rule of international law has been wrecked by the character of present-day war. The law of war was once able to maintain that private property was to be protected; that it was not subject to capture, but must be paid for; and that it was not subject to destruction, unless for military exigency—e.g., a house in the midst of a battlefield. But today, military exigency covers complete robbery and devastation. This, too, is logical, according to the peculiar logic of war, for modern war requires and uses all things. No state can supply itself with the vast and varied amounts of materials which it must have. The more materials a state can acquire by seizure from enemy people—or from neutrals!—the more it strengthens itself and weakens the enemy. A German plant producing ball bearings was one of the principal objectives of Allied air attack; oil refineries in Rumania were another, and it did not matter that they were owned by American companies.

It was once legitimate to fire only upon a "fortified town" or a "military objective"; private property was protected by the law of war. Today, anything may be a military objective—a power plant, a railway junction, a bridge, a dam, a factory, even a school or a hospital if the objective is to weaken enemy morale. Such things may be more important than forts or ships, though destruction of private property is particularly important at sea. There was once a distinction between contraband and noncontraband goods, the former being those things used in making war. But now, everything is used in making war. Blockade no longer covers merely a port; a whole continent is now blockaded, from a distance, and egress as well as ingress is prohibited. It was once forbidden to sink a ship without warning and without saving the lives of those on board. But the airplane or submarine cannot obey such a rule, and now the ship must be destroyed, not only to prevent its cargo reaching the enemy, but also to prevent its future use by the enemy. Even ships carrying food are destroyed, for the sooner the population can be starved, the sooner the war will end. During the World Wars, the shipbuilding industry was hard put to it to build ships faster than they were sunk. The destruction on land and sea was incredible.

NEUTRALS. The area of war was once confined to the belligerents, and indeed to small portions of their territory; other states could legally and actually remain neutral. But the law of neutrality, like practically all else of the law of war, was destroyed by the past few wars and one may confidently assert now that it is an obsolete status.

In the long struggle to maintain a balance between the rights of the belligerent and the rights of the neutral, the former gained steadily, for he was armed, fighting desperately, and willing to take risks, whereas the defenseless neutral sought only to avoid fighting. If the neutral should fight for his rights—as the United States twice has done—he lost his neutrality and became involved in war; if he did not fight for his rights—which was our situation before Pearl Harbor—he lost steadily in economic strength, was rendered more vulnerable through loss of possible allies and by the increasing strength of the belligerent, and was finally brought into the war under the most disadvantageous conditions.[13]

A few states were able to remain neutral in the past war, but only because the belligerents found it an advantage to have them as neutrals. The state which remains neutral suffers about as much as the belligerents, except as to lives lost. Neutrals may trade only as the belligerents wish, may receive only what is permitted to come to them, may suffer from lack of food or other supplies as much as the belligerents. The belligerent nation needs supplies and a strategic area within which to operate. It is little concerned by the feelings of the neutrals. No state can fight a war solely upon the basis of its own resources; it must reach outside. Thus war is no longer restrained within the territory of the belligerents. It sweeps over boundaries like a forest fire; World War II, though it originated in eastern Europe, pulled in the Spahis of North Africa and the Papuans of New Guinea. The situation of small neutral states is dangerous not only to themselves but to other states and to the community of nations as a whole. Their efforts to remain neutral, and their weakness, leave exposed the flanks of their larger neighbors; twice the insistence of Belgium and the Netherlands has led almost to the defeat of those attacked by Germany through these states. The question is thus raised, and not only for small states, whether a state can be permitted to remain neutral when such a status aids an aggressor and endangers the peace and safety of the entire community of nations. The American people have apparently learned that lesson. Hardly two decades ago they were taking refuge behind the "neutrality legislation"; nowadays, they are criticizing India and others for their "neutralism."

TOTAL WAR. Any war requires centralized direction, but in a modern war, which makes use of all persons and all things, the government must take control over everything. Hitherto, rigorous con-

[13] Eagleton, *Forces*, pp. 39-40; see also C. G. Fenwick, *American Neutrality: Trial and Failure* (New York University Press, 1940); and see § 134 below.

trol has been required only for the army, but the last two wars have taught us that all the resources of a nation, human or material, must submit to the same sort of rigorous control. Since these resources cannot be readied after war starts, a government must train those needed for warmaking—not merely soldiers—organize production, reserve ample materials, keep ahead of technological advance. It must do these things in what used to be called peacetime, and this means that it must exercise powers which it was formerly permitted to use only during war. We cannot afford to trade so freely, since economic resources are important weapons; we cannot permit an enemy to build up his war potential from our resources, as we did for Germany and Japan, and so we forbid trade in many things with the Soviet Union and with Communist China.

This necessary extension of governmental control raises questions of another sort. Is democracy able to survive this sort of war without becoming totalitarian itself? The American people are traditionally opposed to compulsory military training in time of peace, and to governmental controls such as are needed to prepare for war, and to regimentation of their lives and thinking in general; yet these things have come upon them. To enable such things to be done, the people must be stirred up to a fearful vigilance; and this may be dangerous, as was shown by the wave of McCarthyism which dominated the country and made it unsafe for one to express one's thoughts openly, or to associate with unjustly accused friends or even relatives, and which restricted freedom of movement through passport control by inferior officials, against which there was no recourse until the courts at length intervened. If democracy adopts the totalitarian methods which war requires, it can hardly remain a democracy; if it fails to do so, its national existence may be ended by the next war adventurer. The danger is now greatest to the United States, for it is now clear to any aggressor that he must first get the United States out of the way, presumably by overwhelming surprise attack. In these days of A-bombs and H-bombs, this might mean annihilation.

Finally, there is to be noted the incredible cost of modern war, a cost so large as to be incomprehensible to the average person, and a cost as great to the victors as to the vanquished. In time of peace, the United States has paid out thirty-five billions of dollars a year in preparation for war. At the same time, the people find it difficult to supply needed schools, and Congress is unwilling to provide help—which could be provided in ample quantities from the above sum—for underdeveloped countries. Norman Angell pointed out years ago that there was no profit in war;[14] the lesson is much more plain to see

[14] In a little book still well worth reading; Norman Angell, *The Great Illusion*.

nowadays. A defeated state is no longer able to pay in reparations what it cost to defeat him; and nations do not find any gain in conquest, in annexing and ruling a resentful national group.

The above situation makes urgent the question of whether war is not too dangerous and costly a method of settling differences between states. This feeling is spreading, and it is sometimes urged that nations should cease preparing for war; indeed, most of the states of the world are unable to make such preparation. In a later chapter in this volume, it will be maintained that there are some things worth fighting for; yet the prospect of war with modern instruments and the possibility of global catastrophe make one hesitate at the conclusion. There is, however, an alternative, the same one to which individuals have turned for centuries past; it is expressed in the title of this book and is the justification for the title and the book. To this development we now proceed.

4. DEVELOPMENT OF COMMUNITY ORGANIZATION

The law and the institutions of the community of nations have developed because of the pressures of interdependence and war, mentioned above, and they have operated with cumulative force in recent years.[15] The conflicts, to which the essential intercourse between states leads, result gradually in the formation of rules, since law is ever the product of the resurgent pressure of mutual and conflicting desires and interests. These concessions by sovereign states are inspired by self-interest; a national group will make a concession only when forced to, or when shown an advantage for the group. This is the law of nature, the law of self-preservation; but nations have been slow in recognizing that self-preservation may be achieved as well, or better, through co-operation as through conflict. It is through the coercive experience of the wastefulness of continuous strife, through the realization that there is gain for all in submission to general rules of intercourse, that law and government appear. The law and government of the community of nations have been much slower in evolving, because this community was much later in appearing (until nation states had been consolidated); this was because of the slower development, waiting upon the Industrial Revolution, of the interdependence which had earlier been

---

[15] This may be illustrated by reference to *International Agencies in Which the United States Participates*, and *Participation of the U.S. Government in International Conferences*, Dept. of State Pubs., Nos. 2699 and 3031. See also *The Yearbook of International Organizations*, published by the Union of International Associations (Brussels).

realized among individuals, and psychological conditioning over centuries to the effect that there could be no higher form of human organization than the state for the protection of individual human beings. The force of international interdependence has shown results increasingly, leading to rules of law, to diplomatic and consular machinery, and now into a steadily increasing number of international organizations.

CHARACTERISTICS OF THE COMMUNITY OF NATIONS. The development of this community of nations has given to it certain distinctive characteristics. In the first place, it is universal, for it covers the whole world. It matters little that one state does not like another and refuses to shake hands with it; this does not remove the hard fact that the other state is on this earth and that it cannot be entirely avoided. "Coexistence" is unavoidable. Until rocket transportation to other planets is put upon a practicable basis, the community of nations will have no coordinate bodies with which to deal, no rivals to serve as a check or spur, no common enemy against whom it must unite in self-defense.

The community of nations at first included only a few states in Western Europe, and non-Christian states were excluded. Gradually other states were admitted. The states of the Western Hemisphere came in as heirs of European civilization, but other non-European states were admitted slowly and upon conditions, most of them subject to the limitations of exterritoriality. Japan was early relieved of this burden, and the prestige of defeating Russia gave her rank as a Great Power. Others, such as Turkey (1923), more slowly satisfied the standards of the community. There is now a practically universal community bound together by customary international law and treaties; it was greatly widened after World War II, when half a billion people, in a number of new states, came in. Both the League of Nations and the United Nations (Article 2, paragraph 6 of its Charter) have attempted some control over nonmembers, but it remains generally true that no state can be bound by the obligations of the United Nations unless it has voluntarily accepted membership therein. There are thus two communities, one within the other, with two systems of law. The possibilities of conflict between the two are much reduced by the fact that by far the greater part of the states in the world are now Members also of the United Nations.

The basic unit of international society has thus far been the state, of which there is an uncertain number—depending upon how one defines a state.[16] They differ in many ways. Some are large in area or popula-

---

[16] There are now (1956) seventy-six Members of the United Nations and others which seek and deserve admission. For various others, statehood is claimed. A list of eighty-nine states is given in Palmer and Perkins, Appendix I, p. 1223.

tion; others are tiny in comparison. Every type of political system is to be found in this community; most of them today would call themselves democratic no matter how autocratic and totalitarian they are in fact. They differ also in economic strength, in geographic location, in race, religion, language, social ideals—a most heterogeneous group. There are certain characteristics, however, which each has, or should have: a territorial base; a presumably stable organization, or government, of the people thereon; some homogeneity of political ideals; common aims. Each may claim equality with all others before the law of the community; and each must have independence, though just how much independence remains uncertain.

The condition of membership in the broader community of nations is submission to its rules and the assumption and maintenance of rights and duties therein. This, of course, is a statement of principle, and the reader may conclude, after finishing this volume, that there is little substance to it in practice. He would be wrong, though he would find much ground for cynicism in the conduct of states. The economic and other forces of interdependence of which we have spoken lead states to submit, as inevitably as they have led individuals to submit, to law and government. The greater the self-sufficiency of a people, the more abounding its supply of natural resources and its ability to exploit them, the longer may be its resistance to these compelling forces, but ultimately it must join in cooperation with other states and agree upon common rules and common efforts: this has been the experience of the United States. *Hodie mihi, cras tibi;* if a state refuses to make a concession for the group, it cannot expect the group to do anything for it. There are common needs to which all must bow: no matter how high national pride may soar, it must submit, for example, to the rules of the Universal Postal Union or deprive itself, to its own great loss, of vital means of communication. This is the practical situation, and it leads to juridical results.

Manifestly, the state is not submerged, in a legal sense, beneath these rules of the community of nations. However little may be its actual weight in the community, however near to bankruptcy or to absorption by an aggressor, it still claims "sovereignty" and its independent personality. We are still far from the *civitas gentium* of which Cicero spoke and from the universal state of which Wolff dreamed; the system is rather a free society of states united only by common needs and solidarity of interests. Each people continues its separate existence (until some other people overthrows it!), develops its own personality, shapes its own political physiognomy. Each is given exclusive jurisdiction within its own territory and provides such internal machinery and rules as pleases it, provided only that it satisfy the few obligations demanded of it by the community. Independence and equality are not eliminated; on the contrary, following the well-known paradox of government, submission to the rules of the community of nations secures for each state a greater degree of liberty and equality than would be possible through its own unaided efforts. Many states, in fact, could not exist without such support.

The community of nations still operates upon the principle of voluntary cooperation among independent states who acknowledge no master above. This is its characteristic feature: the ability to undertake cooperative measures of administration or control without a unified authority above to give orders. This peculiarity, which will be encountered over and over again, is illustrated by the word "international"[17]—international law is a law *between* states rather than one imposed by an authority above. The community of nations does not extirpate nationalism; on the contrary, it is founded upon nationalism. There is no superior political power which can require submission from any state. The nation state is the basic unit of the community, and the growth of the community depends upon the collective satisfaction by its members of their common needs. There is no necessary conflict between nationalism or patriotism, and internationalism; on the contrary, intelligent patriotism recognizes that national advancement is more securely to be obtained by cooperative community action than by depending upon its own might.

5. SOVEREIGNTY AND POWER POLITICS[18]

The preceding sentence would not be accepted by some persons, and it leads into discussion of the "doctrine of sovereignty." It is a dis-

[17] The word was apparently first used by Jeremy Bentham in 1780. It does not appear in dictionaries before 1876, and as late as 1909 the Century Dictionary defined it as "forcing a somewhat disorganized or weak state to submit to the combined control of protection of several stronger nations." J. C. Faries, *Rise of Internationalism* (New York, 1915), p. 11, citing Fitzedward Hall, *Modern English*, p. 317. However, Victoria had long before employed the Latin form, preferring *jus inter gentes* to *jus gentium*.

[18] There are innumerable writings on the doctrine of sovereignty, from which a few titles are here listed: H. E. Cohen, *Recent Theories of Sovereignty* (Chicago, 1937); E. D. Dickinson, "A Working Theory of Sovereignty," *Pol. Sci. Q.*, 42 (1927) and 43 (1928); J. W. Garner, "Limitations on National Sovereignty in International Relations," *Pol. Sci. Rev.*, 19 (1925); R. G. Hawtrey, *The Economic Aspects of Sovereignty* (London, 1930); H. Kelsen, *Das Problem der Souveränität und die Theorie des Völkerrechts* (Tubingen, 1920); H. J. Laski, *The Foundations of Sovereignty and Other Essays* (New York, 1921); J. Maritain, *Man and the State* (Chicago, 1951); C. H. McIlwain, *Constitutionalism and the Changing World* (London, 1939); Q. Wright, "Fundamental Problems of International Organization," *Int. Con.*, 369 (1941).

cussion which involves on the one hand legal theory and on the other hand power politics.

LEGAL THEORY. A survival of the era of personal monarchy, the doctrine of sovereignty was transferred, when democracy supplanted autocracy, from the personal monarch to the state. The authorship of the doctrine is generally credited to Jean Bodin (1576), who defined it as the "puissance absolue et perpétuelle d'une république." But Bodin's purpose was to bring up the state from its position of subordination; he never subordinated international law to territorial sovereignty. Neither did Grotius nor Vattel, who, like Bodin, admitted sovereignty but reconciled it with international law through principles of natural law. The doctrine of internal sovereignty was of great stabilizing value in the contest between kings and feudal lords.

In Germany, however, the doctrine of external sovereignty was built up until it wrecked the Hague Conferences and made contempt of international law. Hegel the philosopher, Treitschke the historian, and Jellinek the jurist constituted a triumvirate which dealt blows to international law from which it has never recovered. To Hegel, the state was supernatural and *sui generis*, and law could be nothing but the will of the state. Treitschke, accepting this, admitted that the state could be bound by treaties, but subject to the principle *rebus sic stantibus;* thus a treaty was only a sort of moral obligation, to be abandoned at any time the state wished. Jellinek defined state sovereignty as the innate quality of a state through which it can become legally bound only by its own volition, and promulgated his theory of autolimitation. Pushing this line of thought to the extreme, Lasson was able to conclude that the relations between states are more a matter of mechanics than of law—the bigger must overwhelm the smaller. From this it follows unavoidably that war is the ultimate judge between right and wrong, so far as two sovereign states are concerned.

Granted its premise, that the state is an end in itself, absolute and irresponsible, this sort of logic is inexorable and it is for this reason that the doctrine must be rejected *in toto*. It states an impossibility: the coexistence of more than one absolute and unlimited power within one juridical system is a contradiction in terms.[19] Furthermore, the facts of practice do not support the doctrine.

In their efforts to evade the anarchy to which this logic leads and to reconcile theory with practice, the supporters of the doctrine of sovereignty have put forward various modifications. Aside from such evasions as that a fictitious or theoretical sovereignty may be admitted,

[19] Williams, pp. 13-22; Palmer and Perkins, pp. 62-68; Cheever and Haviland, pp. 12-13.

though a real one does not exist; or that sovereignty is incompatible with submission to a concrete will but not incompatible with submission to a legal order, there are two principal attempts to modify the harshness of the doctrine. One of these asserts that international law is law only when incorporated as part of national law; the other is the theory of autolimitation, which asserts that a state can be bound only through its own will but that, once having given its consent, it remains permanently bound. It will be necessary to discuss both of these under the heading of international law but it may be observed at this point that (as to the former) if international law is no more than national law, then it can be changed at the will of any state, which is untrue in fact; and (as to the latter), if a state is really sovereign and unlimited and can be bound only by its own consent, then it can at any time, even after having given its consent, modify or reject the rule, which is equally untrue in fact.

SOVEREIGNTY IN PRACTICE. It is to be doubted that support could ever have been found for the Hegelian theory, since the Peace of Westphalia or before. No state since that time has ever been entirely free from external control. The doctrine of sovereignty presumed omnipotence, but there can be only one highest, and such a situation has not existed since the fall of the ancient universal empires. We shall see later[20] that states are only relatively independent; that domestic law is constantly subordinated to international law; that states regularly make reparation for violations of that law; and that they may sometimes be compelled to submit to the will of the community. No state today would maintain that it can reject international law or that it can do whatever it wishes in the community of nations. Never, in diplomatic correspondence or otherwise, is it asserted that a state is independent of the rules established by the community. Along with sovereignty now goes responsibility and the term now means, in its external sense, no more than the sphere of relative external freedom from control and exclusive internal jurisdiction permitted to it by the community of nations.

The concept of sovereignty represents, in the international community, precisely the same difficult problem which the idea of individual liberty has always presented within the state.[21] No fixed and immutable boundary line can ever be drawn for government. The group must interfere with the freedom of action of the individual to the extent that group-needs require, and this varies. In the community of nations, growing interdependence and the realization of

[20] Refer to Chap. 3 below.
[21] See the discussion of Article 2(7) of the Charter of the United Nations, pp. 302-3 below.

the mightily increasing danger of war are leading to more and more extension of control by the group, to greater and greater diminution of national freedom. The degree of limitation varies with the case and the time. Sovereignty is not a unit, which a state has or does not have; it is a relative term. One state may have more independence than another, and no state can do as it wishes simply because it is a sovereign state.

The above discussion of sovereignty is in terms of a legal theory, the logic of which cannot be maintained in the face of facts. Nevertheless, the word still carries weight with statesmen and peoples, who wish to reserve for their respective states as much freedom from external limitation as possible. This desire, put into the Charter of the United Nations in the term "sovereign equality" in Article 2, paragraph 7, greatly impedes the development of international law and organization. It is a natural enough feeling, with centuries of tradition behind it, and it leads into a vicious circle hard to break. States have more "individual liberty," or "sovereignty," than have individuals within their respective governments and, since they are unwilling to make the community of nations strong enough to give its members the aid and protection which they need, each is forced to build up its own strength in whatever way it can and strive to advance its own interests, in rivalry with others, by whatever means it can find—frequently contrary to law or morality.

6. NATIONALISM AND POWER POLITICS

It does not follow from this situation—which is believed to be a transitional one—either that "sovereignty must be abolished" or that sovereignty is so fixed an institution that "power politics" must be the rule of life and that international government is therefore impossible.

"Power politics" is a vague phrase which has come to have a menacing connotation; it is sometimes set forth as alternative to international government, so that the latter would be impossible until power politics should be eliminated. Actually, however, power is an aspect of all human relationships, whether between individuals or groups of individuals, such as nations. Continuous power struggles go on between interest groups in all phases of life; they are present in the Women's Home Missionary Society of the church, or the student fraternity in the university, or in local, national, or international matters. There is power politics within a system of government as well as outside of law. It is precisely the function of law and government to hold these struggles for power within certain rules by which the game is to be played; they are not eliminated, but certain extreme manifestations of the struggle, such as the use of violence, are prohibited. Within states, the strength of the community is organized to see that the rules of the game are observed; there is an authority above, backed by overwhelming force. Among nations, there is no such superior authority and, while the law of nations has been surprisingly well observed, there are large fields of competition and dangerous methods which are not covered by that law. In such gaps a balance of power has been historically sought, often through bloody conflict.

To many persons, this seems inevitable, and they conclude that solutions can be found only in terms of the use of power by one state against another. The school of thought represented by the so-called "realists"[22] apparently regards such a lawless world as inevitable; to the especially patriotic ones, it may seem preferable. This is extreme and unjustified pessimism; it leaves no alternative to the anarchy and wars of the past; it denies the human experience of need for and development of law in their relations with each other. Most, if not all, of the states of the world have national power quite inadequate to give them the protection they need and the means to satisfy their desires; indeed, there are today only two states in the world who can feel secure in their national strength, and if they were to come into conflict they would cancel each other out. It is difficult to see why this school of thought should be called "realistic"; it is so only in describing the present situation, but it makes no provision for the future.

It is undoubtedly true that nationalism, which nourishes and expands sovereignty, is strong today; its importance in present political development can hardly be exaggerated.[23] Nationalism is a feeling, a force, which has in the past freed human beings and set up democracies to improve their lives, and which has also produced totalitarian regimes and the utmost in oppression and brutality. It has tremendous appeal, especially to colonial and backward peoples, who do not realize that national independence for them may mean stepping out of the frying pan into the fire. The cry for "national self-determination," as we shall later see, is now leading to a cleavage in the United Nations

[22] See Hans J. Morgenthau, *In Defense of the National Interest* (New York, 1951), and other writings; George F. Kennan, *American Diplomacy, 1900-1950* (Chicago, 1951); T. V. Kalijarvi and associates, *Modern World Politics* (New York, 1956), p. 8. See also, from another viewpoint, H. W. Briggs, "Power Politics and International Organization," *A.J.*, 39 (1945).

[23] The discussion in Palmer and Perkins, Chap. ii, with many quotations and citations, is very helpful. Two of the best works concerning nationalism are C. J. H. Hayes, *The Historical Evolution of Modern Nationalism* (New York, 1948), and Hans Kohn, *The Idea of Nationalism* (New York, 1944).

and is being abused by the Soviet Union and others for the purpose of producing unrest and disorganization in the community of nations. Like war, to which it leads, nationalism is an instrument of great strength which needs to be kept under careful restraint and control. It depends upon power, thus far, for the achievement of its ends, and so long as each national group is free to seek its ends through power, in jealous rivalry with others, there will be anarchy and violence among nations. Palmer and Perkins properly conclude that "nationalism, whatever its form, makes peace forever insecure and that therefore means must be found to transcend nationalism, or at least to counteract the noxious effects of totalitarian nationalism. Here we have squarely posed a great problem of our age."[24]

Power politics is always with us, and must be reckoned with. It is possible, however, to control and channel the use of power, and today, men are demanding that this be done. For centuries, the state has been accepted as the highest form of human organization, *ne plus ultra*. Today, however, the forces of interdependence and war have made the state inadequate to serve the purposes for which it was created. The state is not an end in itself, not a divine institution; it was created and is maintained to serve the needs of human beings. If it is insufficient to care for his needs, man will demand more, and he is in fact doing so now. He demands that the irresponsible use of power by sovereign states be regulated, as the abuse of power by individuals has been regulated. He knows that the only realistic answer is that of the experience of the past, which means collective security, backed by law. It is normal human nature that he should want the power of others to be limited but to keep his own powers; and it is slow work for him to come out from centuries of belief that the state is his best protection and that he must not allow outsiders to interfere with it. To such hesitant patriots it needs to be pointed out that the organized community of nations could hardly interfere with him or his state more than is now possible for any state sufficiently powerful, through intervention, war, and conquest!

The alternatives are not absolute. One cannot say "abolish sovereignty," but it is possible to limit certain rights and powers now claimed by sovereign states. The term "sovereignty" will doubtless continue to be useful in political science, not in the sense of absolute and irresponsible power, but as indicating an extent of jurisdictional control and freedom of decision, limited by international law and treaty, which is the qualification for membership, as a legal person, of the organized community of nations.

[24] Palmer and Perkins, p. 56.

On the other hand, one cannot merely assert that power is reality and that to "expect states at their present stage of development to accept any international code as binding is wishful thinking." States do accept such codes, almost every day. The answer must be sought somewhere between the two extremes; progress in political development is always slow and gradual and world government is not to be expected overnight. Power and its use will always be a problem, but it can and will, ultimately, be brought under law and government in the community of nations, as it has between individuals.

Chapter 2

INTERNATIONAL LAW

7. DEVELOPMENT OF INTERNATIONAL LAW

The bond which holds together the loose structure of international society is international law. *Ubi societas, ibi jus.* In any community there must be rules for the guidance of its members; they are necessary to avoid continuous conflict of interests and desires. The principles laid down in the law of nations, and the theories attaching to its formation and interpretation, furnished the constitutional foundations for the inchoate organization of the community of nations; later, the Covenant of the League of Nations and the Charter of the United Nations added to this constitutional structure. It is in the sense of constitutional development in the community of nations that international law is surveyed in this volume, rather than for the purpose of learning the law in a technical or professional sense. This chapter is devoted to the nature of the law and its development in practice; having considered this, we shall be better able to answer the usual skeptical question: "Is there any such thing as international law?"

ORIGINS.[1] The law of nations appeared as a result of much the same forces that have produced law anywhere else. Human beings learn, ultimately, and sometimes in a very hard way, that it is more profitable to solve their continual conflicts by adherence to rules rather than by fighting. Law is not so much an edict issued from above, the rational process of a legislative authority, as it is an evolutionary process whose statement by a proper authority, or merely by custom, is a recognition of this process. Since law is the product of the necessity of reconciling clashing forces and ambitions, it was natural that, out of the welter of feudal conflict and the terrible wars which marked the establishment of nation states, efforts should have been made to build a law between these states. They were manifested first in codes of

---

[1] J. Hosack, *The Rise and Growth of the Law of Nations* (London, 1882); G. Butler and S. Maccoby, *The Development of International Law* (London, 1928); A. Nussbaum, *A Concise History of the Law of Nations* (New York, 1947); Svarlien, Part I.

sea law. The peculiar character of the unpossessable seas, and their function as highways of commerce for all nations, produced early efforts in this direction. The rivalry of commercial enterprise and later of colonial empire intensified the need. For unknown periods, rules had been in process of customary development, and in the fifteenth century they began to be collected and published. The most famous of these collections is the *Consolato del Mare*, which, published about the time of Columbus' discovery of America, stated the law of the Mediterranean Sea. There were other codes, which cannot always be given precise dates. The Amalfitan Tables are said to go back to the eleventh century; the Laws of Oleron, for western Europe, to the twelfth; the Laws of Wisby, for the Baltic states, to 1288; the Maritime Law of the Hanseatic League to 1614; the so-called Rhodian Sea Law, which may be apocryphal, was first published in 1561.

Explorations and colonial claims later gave rise to many new problems. The whole question of title by discovery had to be adjusted, and with it the question of proper boundary lines. To these problems the Roman Law principles relative to private property were applied with more or less success. Once colonies were established, and the possibilities of lucrative trade were realized, a great field of competitive effort appeared. Restrictions were placed by each nation upon trade with her colonies, and as a result of the conflicts thus engendered the development of the law of neutrality was begun. It is not surprising that there was great disregard for international law when it is recalled that the law was as yet hardly formed, much less established, and that the states of Europe were all engaged in desperate and bloody struggles to maintain their new and hard-won independence. But while Frederick the Great called upon the jurists to justify his thefts, while Poland disappeared, and while Maria Theresa *pleurait et prenait toujours*, adjustments in international law were being made by conference and by treaty. Above all, writers were beginning to lay down the rules and establish standards to which states would be called upon to adhere.

WRITERS. Indeed, it is to writers, rather than to statesmen, that international law owes the formulation of its basic principles. It is true that they did not have the authority to decree the law, nor did any one else have such authority. Writers could and did suggest rules to meet the needs of the new situation; they could, by their teachings, impress upon states the need for law to govern their conduct; and they could, in the absence of legislative bodies and records, state what the law was as revealed in customary practice, and how it could be improved. To modern readers, their works bear little resemblance to law. They were forced to search for evidence and justification in Roman, canon, and natural law, and sought precedents in history, classics, and even in mythology. Much of their work has been abandoned, but it was of great importance in setting out guideposts and in arousing public interest, and especially in insisting that natural justice limits the state as well as individuals.

The horrors of the Thirty Years' War stirred Grotius to write his famous treatise, and he has deservedly been given the title of the father of international law. But there were writers before his time who cannot be overlooked and to whom modern thought is nowadays returning. In the middle of the fourteenth century, Legnano, of Bologna, wrote (though it was not published until 1477) *De bello, de represaliis, et de duello*. It is not difficult to understand why these early writers paid so much attention to the law of war, and it is greatly to their credit that they should have attacked the problem of the existence or justification of war, as well as the methods of conducting war. In 1557, Vitoria, a Dominican monk of Salamanca, Spain, wrote thirteen *Relectiones theologicae*, of which the sixth was entitled *De jure belli*. Vitoria was the first to employ the phrase *jus inter gentes*, the Latin equivalent of international law, and was the first to think of a community of nations based upon reason and sociability.[2] *De jure et officiis belli*, by Ayala, provost of the Spanish armies in the Netherlands, is of less importance. The great Spanish Jesuit, Suarez, published in 1612 his *Tractatus de legibus ac Deo legislatore*, in which he first distinguished between reason and custom as sources of international law, a distinction followed ever since. Of him Westlake says:

> . . . But Suarez has put on record with a master's hand the existence of a necessary human society transcending the boundaries of states, the indispensableness of rules for that society, the insufficiency of reason to provide with demonstrative force all the rules required, and the right of human society to supply the deficiency by custom enforced as law, such custom being suitable to nature.[3]

Perhaps the greatest of pre-Grotian writers was Albericus Gentilis, professor of Civil Law at Oxford University, who wrote in 1598 his *De jure belli*, a work which was the source of the first and third books of Grotius. He is regarded as one of the founders of the historical school of international jurists, but he did not discard the law of

[2] Dr. Scott suggests that Vitoria, rather than Grotius, should be regarded as the founder of international law. J. B. Scott, *Francisco de Vitoria and His Law of Nations* (Oxford University Press, 1934), p. 3. This view is severely criticized by Nussbaum, *loc. cit.*, p. 309.

[3] J. Westlake, *Chapters on The Principles of International Law* (Cambridge, 1894), pp. 27-28. On pp. 26-27 he translates a famous passage from Suarez.

nature. He lacks the broad humanitarianism and the idealism of Grotius, and has not had such a widespread appeal as the latter.

Grotius.[4] The unrestrained license of war and the anarchy of his day, so Grotius tells us, led him to write his famous *De jure belli et pacis*, which appeared in 1625, in the midst of the bloody Thirty Years' War. It is a work of amazing erudition and broad knowledge, and because of its idealistic support of humanitarian principles it gained a tremendous following among those of his day who felt that some restraint ought to be put upon the barbarous practices of the time. Gustavus Adolphus is said to have slept with a copy of it beneath his pillow. Grotius admitted that he owed much to his predecessors, particularly to Gentilis, but his was by far the most scholarly and systematic presentation. He drew from many sources, primarily from natural law—the dictate of right reason—but he also supported his views by precedent and thus brought in positive law, or practice. The fundamental principles which he laid down are still the foundation of international law; indeed, that law is today returning to some of Grotius' principles, which it had for a time disregarded.

Grotius accepted the dogma of sovereignty, but he considered it to be restrained by natural law; in his mind, a state was not above all law. His distinction between just and unjust wars is again becoming important. His disregard for neutrality, which follows from his belief that all states should support the just cause, is now being justified in terms of collective security. Recent trends support the importance which he gave to the individual. He was criticized for identifying the law of nature with the *jus gentium*, but the recent revival of natural law[5] is proving that he was not far wrong. All in all, as one must say in the field of political science "back to Artistotle," so one must say in the field of international law "back to Grotius."

Post-Grotian Writers. The most popular of the followers of Grotius was Vattel, who is more often quoted than Grotius himself. He did not claim originality and admitted that he built upon the work of another disciple, Wolff; but Vattel popularized international law. His influence has been great, but sometimes misleading. Where Grotius

[4] Grotius, or Hugo van Groot, was born in 1583, at Delft, Holland, where his tomb is now a shrine for those interested in international law. He wrote Latin verses at the age of nine and became a Doctor of Laws at the University of Leyden at the age of fifteen. Because of his religious views, he was imprisoned for life in 1619, but escaped in a trunk, with the help of his wife. He was the Swedish Minister to France from 1634 to 1645, and died there. He was a poet, philosopher, historian, and mathematician, as well as jurist and diplomatist. His book had forty-five Latin editions before 1748, and there have been innumerable translations.

[5] See pp. 36-37, 40-41, below.

had used natural law as a bar to irresponsible sovereignty, Vattel let down that bar and emphasized the independence and equality of states and their fundamental rights and duties. He cannot be called entirely a natural lawyer, since he also appealed to precedents, but his reasoning was a priori. What he sought in practice was not so much a customarily established rule, as evidence to support his own preconceived belief as to what the rule should be.

Other followers of Grotius include: Zouche, of Oxford, whose work Fauchille called the first treatise on international law, properly so named, and who is regarded as one of the founders of the positivist school; Pufendorf, the leader of the natural law group; Bynkershoek, of Holland, whose *De dominio maris* gave us the rule of the three-mile limit for territorial waters; and Wolff, whose books, popularized by Vattel, taught the *civitas maxima*.

The development of international law has more recently been aided by the work of various organizations. Two of them appeared as a result of the interest inspired by the arbitration of the *Alabama* claims: the Institut de Droit International, a selective body which includes most of the great international lawyers; and the International Law Association, an organization of broader membership, with branches in many countries. In many states, there are national organizations, such as the American Society of International Law, which publish periodicals. There are also endowed bodies, such as the Carnegie Endowment for International Peace or the World Peace Foundation. Unfortunately, the interest of such bodies, and of foundations, has turned to politics and to organization rather than law, in recent years.

During the nineteenth century there was a tremendous growth of the law through customary practice and treaty making and the influence of many writers.[6] American precedents began an important development of the law of neutrality. While an attempt (at Brussels in 1874) to build a code for land warfare, based upon the model of the famous rules prepared by Lieber for the United States armies in the Civil War, was a failure, actually the rules were observed to a great extent in practice. Treaties against slave trading were executed until slave trading was put upon almost the same footing as piracy, as a rule of customary law. Increased trade and intercourse led to the building of a widespread law for the protection of aliens and of their property. Territorial jurisdiction was more closely defined, and arrangements developed through which states could help each other in the exercise of this jurisdiction, such as extradition, or the rules of private inter-

---

[6] Many of these writers are listed in the Bibliographical Abbreviations at the beginning of this volume.

national law. Arbitral tribunals were called upon to an increasing degree, and their decisions established invaluable precedents. Furthermore, the need for rules to regulate the increasingly intricate intercourse of nations produced the beginnings of a method of international legislation by means of law-making conferences and treaties. At the Congresses of Vienna and Aix-la-Chapelle, for instance, the rank of diplomatic agents was established, and here, as well as later, arrangements were made for traffic on international rivers. Various rules were recognized for the conduct of war, such as the Geneva Convention of 1864 which established the Red Cross, the Declaration of St. Petersburg which regulated the use of explosive bullets, and the numerous conventions agreed upon at the Hague Conferences. Scientific study, for the most part unofficial, presented new problems and offered solutions, and an increasingly intelligent public opinion began to interest itself in a problem which it slowly recognized as having an important influence upon the fortunes of individuals.

Two wars of modern character in the twentieth century have practically wrecked what used to be a large part of any text of international law—the laws of war and neutrality. New methods of warfare rendered old rules out-of-date and they were deliberately disregarded. As a result, it has been freely asserted—without considering the large body of international law for peacetime—that the law of nations is impotent and useless. As to this, it must be observed that war is the antithesis of law.[7] The two cannot live together. When two or more states are permitted to build up powerful military forces and hurl them at each other in a life-and-death struggle, it is too much to expect that the nice etiquette of war laid down at a peaceful conference table should be observed. The effort must now be directed against the use of war or, to put it in other words, to bring the use of force under the rule of law.

8. TERMINOLOGY

International law, as the term is generally used, means international public law, which is the subject of our present discussion and ordinarily the only subject of discussion in the texts of international law. It is the law dealing with the legal relations between states as states; it covers those cases in which a state claims that another state

[7] "Talking about the laws of war is almost as sensible as preaching about the chastity of prostitution." Howard-Ellis, p. 321; see also p. 352.

has violated international law.[8] There are, however, some collateral terms which must be understood.

INTERNATIONAL PRIVATE LAW. International private law, or conflicts of law, concerns those situations in which an individual has rights or obligations under the domestic laws of different states, resulting in a conflict between the two legal systems applied to the case. A set of customary principles has grown up by means of which domestic courts resolve such conflicts. It is ordinarily said that it is entirely a matter of domestic law, yet Justice Gray once said that:

International law in its widest and most comprehensive sense—including not only questions of right between nations, governed by what has been appropriately called the law of nations, but also questions arising under what is usually called private international law, or the conflict of laws, and concerning the rights of persons within the territory and dominion of one nation, by reason of acts, private or public, done within the dominions of another nation,—is part of our law . . .[9]

At present, it is unfortunately true that a state cannot be held responsible before an international tribunal for its failure to observe the principles of international private law. There seems to be no good reason, however, why it should not ultimately become a branch of international law, as binding upon states as any other rules of international law, and this viewpoint increasingly appears in current writings.

ADMIRALTY LAW. A similar situation exists for admiralty law, which takes care of conflicts arising on the high seas, and between ships of different nationalities. Its rules are probably as well observed as if they were binding international law. Since they do involve international legal relations, it would seem that admiralty law should also be accepted as binding upon domestic courts, with the state held responsible for failure to observe its rules. But again, as in the case of "conflicts of laws," it is discretionary with a state whether it will observe these rules or not.

INTERNATIONAL ADMINISTRATIVE LAW. Attention should also be called to a new development within the field of international law, to what might be called international administrative law. Such are the rules, usually conventional (by treaty), for postal service and other international communications, or for traffic on international rivers, or for international copyrights, or for the civil service of international organizations. They cannot be compared to municipal ordinances as

---

[8] This is the usual statement, based upon the assumption that only states can be subjects of international law. But, as will be seen in Chap. 5 and elsewhere below, individuals and international organizations as well as states may have rights and duties under international law.

[9] *Hilton v. Guyot*, 159 U.S. 163 (1894); and see Fauchille, I, pp. 5-6.

to source, but they are comparable as to nature. This is a rapidly widening field and deserves classification as a part of international law.[10]

POLICY. A continuing policy is sometimes confused with law. The fact that it is long maintained and well respected seems to give it the character of enforceable law. Doubtless the best illustration is the Monroe Doctrine, long maintained by the United States and observed by other states. However, it has been denied to be law by these same states, and Presidents of the United States have been careful to assert that it is a policy of the United States alone. Were it a rule of international law, it would be susceptible of interpretation and application by the community of nations, and in consequence would doubtless have been abandoned earlier.

9. SOURCES OF INTERNATIONAL LAW[11]

The foundation of international law, in the sense of the force which led to its statement, is the universal craving for justice; but this justice must have human interpretation. The international lawyer has three sources upon which he can call to show that a principle of law has been established, and he must turn to various evidences to substantiate his claim. No rule may be regarded as valid unless it can be shown to be derived from a treaty, or from a custom as valid as law, or, in the absence of one of these, from "general principles of law."

TREATIES. The most tangible of these, the most concrete before a court, is the treaty; but how far treaties establish rules of law it is difficult to say. Not every treaty purports to lay down a rule. The ordinary bilateral treaty is legally binding, but only on the parties which signed it; it does not intend to lay down a general rule of conduct for all nations, though it may do so for the parties. The question may be raised whether, if precisely the same rule were found in bilateral treaties among all states, each with all others, this would not amount to a rule of customary law applicable to all states. Technically, the answer would be no, for each state would be bound only to the other state party to the treaty, and a state might be willing to continue its treaty with some states but not with others. Practically, the answer would be yes; even if a treaty should lapse, a state could ask, and through comity would probably receive, the benefit of the rule.

---

[10] Another new field, international criminal law, is now beginning to take shape. See § 30, below.

[11] Most of the textbooks expatiate at length upon this subject. See Bishop, pp. 14-40; Briggs, pp. 43-52; Brierly, pp. 39-47; Hyde, I, pp. 10-14; J. G. Starke, "Treaties as a Source of International Law," *B.Y.I.L.*, 1946, p. 344; R. R. Wilson, *The International Law Standard in Treaties of the United States* (Cambridge, 1953).

In this sense, the treaty would be an evidence of customary law rather than a source itself of law.

But today, hundreds of treaties are being made with definite legislative intent. As a source of law, in this sense, the treaty is weak, since states which do not sign are technically not bound by a rule upon which practically all of the community of nations may have agreed. This situation is due to the lack of efficient legislative machinery— one of the worst defects of the community of nations.[12]

CUSTOM. The chief source of international law is custom, the source of most law. As a community develops, rules gradually evolve through custom. They are tested by experience, applied and interpreted by courts, and may be finally put into statute form by legislative act. The last process is not essential. The Anglo-Saxon common law, with whose growth international law finds an analogy, is in large part still unwritten. Such a law has the advantage of flexibility, but the defect of vagueness, and it is difficult at times to say whether or not it has reached a point at which it may be relied upon as law. This is particularly true of international law, where not many precedents are available. A continuing practice does not alone make law. Customary law in a legal sense means something more than mere usage; it means a usage felt to be obligatory upon those under its incidence. It may be criticized because it is slow in its development, because it is difficult to fill its gaps, and because the line between custom and customary law is not clearly drawn. On the other hand, Anglo-Saxon lawyers claim for it that it is more responsive to current demands than is a fixed written law.[13]

"GENERAL PRINCIPLES OF LAW." To use a discredited term, the law of nature is a third source of international law. It is not the natural law of two or three centuries ago, as taught by Hobbes and Pufendorf and others, an entirely subjective law discarded by political philosophers because of the lack of authoritative determination. It appears in much more ancient form. Again we must return to Aristotle, who said "Natural law is that which has authority among all men," and to Cicero and Gaius, who asserted that the *jus naturale* and the *jus gentium* were one and the same. Grotius has been much criticized for identifying the two, but recent thinkers are inclined to credit him more than his critics.[14]

---

[12] This will be discussed at greater length in Chap. 8, below.

[13] See Kopelmanas, "Custom as a Means of the Creation of International Law," *B.Y.I.L.*, 1937, p. 127; also J. L. Kunz, in *A.J.*, 47 (1953), p. 662; and M. O. Hudson in *U.N. Doc.* A/CN. 4/16.

[14] "In effect, they were the same set of rules looked at from a different point of view; for rules which were everywhere observed, i.e., *jus gentium*, must surely be

There has always been something behind stated law—a reservoir upon which judges could call in emergency. Our own courts have been forced at times to admit that there were no precedents, and to fall back upon common sense and justice.[15] This reservoir was known to the earlier philosophers as *recta ratio*, right reason. But, since there was no authority to determine what was right reason, modern thinkers have sought a more satisfactory foundation in objective principles which can be judicially ascertained. It is nothing new for a judge to resort to fundamental principles when specific rules and precedents are lacking. In many treaties of arbitration, the arbiter was instructed to seek his decision according to the principles of justice, equity, and the law of nations; and authoritative statement is now found in Article 38 of the Statute of the International Court of Justice:

> The Court shall apply:
> 1. International conventions . . .
> 2. International custom . . .
> 3. The general principles of law recognized by civilized nations . . .

What are these "general principles of law recognized by civilized nations" but the old *jus gentium?* This new law of nature has a more substantial foundation than the older one; like the *jus gentium*, it embraces principles which may be judicially proved by reference to the various legal systems of the nations. There is no doubt that pure positivism, rejecting reason and accepting only practice, is no longer regarded as sufficient, and that it is respectable for a judge to fill in gaps in the stated law and to keep pace with changing social conditions, by appeal to fundamental principles judicially ascertainable. Such recourse is naturally more often necessary in so incomplete a system as international law.

---

rules which the rational nature of man prescribes to him, i.e., *jus naturale*, and vice versa." Brierly, p. 11.

For recent studies in the law of nature, see Brierly, § 2; H. Lauterpacht, "La théorie du droit naturel," *Hague Acad.*, 18 (1927), p. 263; L. Le Für, "Le droit naturel et le droit rationnel ou scientifique," *R.D.I.*, 1 (1927), pp. 658-98; F. Pollock, "History of the Law of Nature: A Preliminary Study," *Columbia Law Review*, 1 (1901), pp. 11-32, 2 (1902), pp. 131-43; J. S. Reeves, "Influence of the Law of Nature on International Law in the United States," *A.J.*, 3 (1909), pp. 547-61; Rousseau, p. 889; Williams, Chap. i; A. Verdross, in *Hague Acad.*, 52 (1935).

15 "We think the case in hand is not so governed by authority but that it may be dealt with upon principle," J. Cardozo, in *Sokoloff v. The National City Bank*, 239 N.Y. 165 (1924): "It remains for us to determine whether the result of the present judgment is contrary to common sense and justice," J. Lehman, in *Russian Reinsurance Co. v. Stoddard*, 240 N.Y. 163 (1925). Similarly, in international law, *Eastern Extension . . . v. U.S.*, Nielsen's *Report*, p. 75; *Cayuga Indians Claim, ibid.*, p. 307.

10. EVIDENCES

To find a rule of international law, then, one must go back to treaties, to custom, or to general principles. Of these, customary law is most difficult to prove. A treaty is a tangible document, where the rule may be seen upon inspection, even though difficulties of interpretation may arise. A "general principle of law," as, for example, that contracts must be observed and executed, may sometimes be sought out in the statutes or judicial decisions of the various states. But the task appears more difficult when one is asked to prove a rule of customary international law. How should one go about building up a brief?

To the Anglo-Saxon lawyer, accustomed to the customary rules of the common law, the task would not seem unusual. In international law the procedure is much the same, although more difficult perhaps, because fewer precedents are available and because they are not so easily accessible. In general, the object is to show that the rule offered has actually been accepted in practice as binding by the community of nations. To this end, evidences must be sought in various places.

JUDICIAL DECISIONS. Doubtless most important as evidence would come judicial decisions.[16] It is necessary, however, to distinguish between decisions of an international court and those of domestic courts. The former are more acceptable as evidence upon the assumption that the judges are more independent and impartial, and better qualified to pass upon questions of international law. Actually, of course, such an assumption depends upon the standing of the court. Arbitral tribunals have not always succeeded in obtaining the best type of judges, for voluntary selection by states has been the rule, and states have tried to pick judges favorable to themselves. Furthermore, the tribunal has often been restricted by the *compromis d'arbitrage*, which states the procedure, and even the law to be followed (as in the famous Three Rules of the Treaty of Washington, according to which the *Alabama* Arbitration was decided), as well as the limits of the jurisdiction of the tribunal. It was an advance over this haphazard procedure when a panel of distinguished judges was provided in the old Hague Tribunal. The community of nations now has, in the International Court of Justice, a court of high standing, whose decisions may be regarded as of the greatest authority in proving such rules of law as have been covered by its judgments.

16 As Briggs observes (pp. 48-49), judicial decisions may also be a source of law. See H. Lauterpacht, *Development of International Law by the Permanent Court of International Justice* (London, 1934); E. Hambro, *The Case Law of the International Court of Justice* (Leyden, 1952).

The decisions of national courts, while furnishing by far the greatest number of precedents, are necessarily controlled by the laws of the state and are apt to be vitiated by national bias, as well as being less authoritative because the judges are not usually so well-trained in international law. Decisions of national prize courts are looked upon with justifiable suspicion, in spite of such conscientious judges as Lord Stowell.[17] Decisions may be affected by national policy, or by an attitude taken by the particular state concerning a particular rule of international law, for example, the attitude of certain Latin American states toward the Calvo Clause. Nevertheless, while they must be critically assessed, domestic court decisions offer valuable evidence and constitute the most voluminous and accessible material.

STATE PAPERS. The practice of states may be sought also in official acts and documents which reveal the views of individual states and which, taken together, may establish a community viewpoint. The legislation of a state may thus be taken to represent the views of a state. Like bilateral treaties, however, a statute may or may not state what is regarded as law by its authors. It may, like the Neutrality Act of 1794, or the Truman statement concerning the Continental Shelf in 1945, lay down what the United States thinks should be the proper rule of international law; and this may ultimately be accepted as law by the community.

More valuable, doubtless, is the diplomatic correspondence of states, particularly that in which a point of law is argued. Presumably, the arguments advanced against another state are arguments which would be admitted by the plaintiff state when employed against itself; in any case, it is fair to cite such arguments against the state which used them.[18]

[17] Who said: "I trust that it has not escaped my anxious recollection for one moment what it is that the duty of my station calls for from me;—namely, to consider myself as stationed here, not to deliver occasional and shifting opinions to serve present purposes of particular national interest, but to administer with indifference that justice which the law of nations holds out, without distinction to independent states, some happening to be neutral and some to be belligerent." *The Maria*, 1 C. Robinson 350 (1799). See also H. Lauterpacht, in *B.Y.I.L.*, 1929, p. 65; and *U.N. Doc.* A/CN. 4/6.

[18] Moore's *Digest of International Law* (supplemented now by Hackworth's *Digest*) constitutes the most convenient summary of such materials issued by any state. Among other valuable sources are the *Foreign Relations* volumes published by the United States; the *British and Foreign State Papers*, a monumental and invaluable source of information; the *Archives Diplomatiques* of France, and the *Staatsarchiv* of Germany. In the publications of the League of Nations and the United Nations a new source of material is to be found. Especial attention is called to the replies of governments to the League of Nations questionnaires for the 1930 Codification Conference, and to the drafts issued by the International Law Commission of the United Nations.

WRITERS. Finally, the views of publicists, jurists and text writers are frequently referred to by tribunals. Such men have presumably made a thorough study of precedents, and according to their respective authority the result of their studies will be referred to as evidence in courts of law. The Supreme Court of the United States has, however, made a necessary distinction, in that "such works are resorted to by judicial tribunals, not for the speculation of their authors concerning what the law ought to be, but for trustworthy evidence of what the law really is."[19] On the other hand, such speculation may be of value in setting guides for the development of international law. It is the scientific function of the scholar to offer his interpretation of what he finds. Of greater authority than an individual voice are the views reached, after debate, by scientific societies, such as the Institut de Droit International, the International Law Association, or the Harvard Research in International Law.

11. SCHOOLS OF THOUGHT

It has been customary to classify writers on international law into three schools: natural lawyers, positivists, and eclectics or Grotians, who draw from both. In the first group belong those writers, such as Pufendorf, who relied solely on natural law and denied validity to custom or even to treaty. But few in this school have gained repute. On the other hand, there were as few who went to the other extreme, founding their systems entirely upon positive practice, denying any authority to a law of nature. The majority fall into the group of eclectics, and the real dividing line is as to whether a writer—while relying upon both natural law and practice—tends more toward one than toward the other.

NATURAL LAWYERS. The difficulty with natural law was its subjective character. There was little practice or custom upon which the earlier writers could rely. They were forced, therefore, to build upon a theoretical foundation. International law owes to natural law its beginning, and owes to it, also, the conception—without which international law could never have been realized—that even sovereign states are subject to law. Thus states were subjected to a natural order, and a law was asserted which, if difficult to ascertain, was none the less binding upon them. To the medieval lawyer, the law of nature was to be ascertained by appeal to right reason, the reasoning of the best minds. He was aided in his search by Roman and canon law. But it

[19] Justice Gray, in *Paquete Habana*, 175 U.S. 700 (1899).

was still rather a strain upon human credulity to permit even the best mind to extract from the labyrinth of its mental processes a rule of action which should control others—at any rate, until it should be determined who was the possessor of the best mind.

The fact that natural lawyers could not always agree among themselves easily gave rise to suspicion that there was no fixed law of nature. And indeed, since this law could consist only of general principles, the only means of obtaining rules was to see how the principles were actually worked out in reference to a particular set of circumstances—and this meant interpretation by means of actual practice. The words of Maine are still true, that "the grandest function of the law of nature was discharged in giving birth to modern international law," but the offspring has denied its parent's teachings and has sought other support. The law of nature, as taught by Pufendorf, has for the most part been abandoned; but, as we have seen, it has been lately revived in more modern garb.

POSITIVISM. As the natural law school became discredited, the pendulum swung in the other direction, and publicists asserted that only those rules could be regarded as law which could be shown in the practice of states. This group is known as the positivist, or historical, school, since its evidences and authority are sought in historical records. The positivists have been found mostly in Germany, England, and the United States. The earliest writer who deserves the title is probably Gentilis, who dissociated law from theology and ethics. But even Gentilis found the *nuda historiarum recitatio* fruitless. The daily doings of states, good or bad, juridical or political, consented to or imposed upon, furnish no satisfactory source of law, no matter how often repeated. Stagnation is the inevitable result of a system in which there is no appeal to reason. "Custom," Westlake points out, "had introduced bad rules as well as good ones."[20] To avoid this difficulty, positivists attempted to base all rules upon the consent of states, a consent which must often be assumed, and which has no support in their logic. It was impossible for them to be consistent; indeed, there are very few of them who do not somewhere deny their fundamental premise, that the consent of the states, which they claim to be above any authority, is necessary to law. In one way or another they admit an authority outside of the state, for without this admission it would be impossible to establish the binding force of international law upon states. Positivism, by its own witness, cannot stand alone. The tendency during this period has been toward positivism; now it is swing-

[20] J. Westlake, *Chapters on the Principles of International Law* (Cambridge, 1894), p. 27.

ing back toward natural law. But neither can do without the other. Naturalists must admit that practice affords the only human interpretation of their principles; positivists must admit that reason must be added to practice before it can be called law.

The positivist doctrine, insofar as it is based on the theory of consent, has been vigorously assailed by the "Vienna School" and others in recent years.[21] These writers in general assert a "monist" conception, to the effect that all law, national or international, constitutes one system, in which international law is supreme. The binding force of international law, therefore, is the same as that of any other law, and requires no separate defense. This school of thought is criticized as giving insufficient consideration to the actual practice of states.

12. THEORY OF CONSENT[22]

In proving a rule of international law it has usually been held necessary to show the consent of states to that law, and this leads us into a very difficult theoretical discussion. It has been seen that an unqualified doctrine of sovereignty is unacceptable. Nevertheless, it is still upheld even in the Charter of the United Nations, and its effects are far from being weeded out. One of these effects, vital in its results upon international law itself, we must now consider.

If a state is sovereign, then it cannot be bound without its own consent. This would mean that unanimous consent must be obtained before a rule of international law could be established for the community of nations; actually, however, no rule of international law could be proved to have received the formal assent of all nations, or of any large number of them; nor can this ever be done until machinery is set up for that purpose. International tribunals do not seek to ascertain whether the state accused had ever registered its consent to the rule under discussion, but rather to ascertain what has been the practice of the community. A rule of general acceptance cannot be denied by a state on the plea that history discloses no acceptance of the rule by that state.

In the face of this actual situation, the bald statement of the corollary of sovereignty, that a state could not be bound without its own

---

[21] See H. Kelsen (the founder of the Vienna School), *Das Problem der Souveränität und die Theorie des Völkerrechts* (Tubingen, 1928); also his *General Theory of Law and State* (Cambridge, Mass., 1945); J. L. Kunz, "The Vienna School and International Law," *New York University Law Quarterly Review*, 10 (1933-4), p. 370; Ross, p. 59; A. Verdross, *Die Verfassung der Völkerrechtsgemeinschaft* (Wien und Berlin, 1926); J. C. Starke, "Monism and Dualism in the Theory of International Law," *B.Y.I.L.*, 1936, pp. 66-81.

[22] Briggs, pp. 21-22, with numerous references.

particular consent, was untenable and positivists sought to evade the issue. It was not difficult to admit that a state entering the community of nations must accept the laws in existence at that time; this is a fair rule and is maintained; but if a state were really sovereign and unlimited by external authority, it could disavow any rule at any time. It was necessary, therefore, to assume consent not only on the part of new members for old rules, but also on the part of all members for all rules, including new ones. And so the theory of tacit consent appeared, by which it was assumed that after a rule had survived for an indefinite time without formal opposition, it was agreed to by all members. It was asserted that consent, once given, could not be revoked.

This is unsatisfactory to the logical mind. States are bound because they have agreed to be bound, but why is this agreement binding? If a state is really sovereign, and dependent only upon its own will, why must it continue to be bound by a rule to which it has once given its consent but which at a later date runs contrary to its will? Triepel and others sought the answer in a fundamental norm, or in the maxim *pacta sunt servanda*. But if there is no power above the state, from what source does even this fundamental rule derive authority to bind the illimitable state? If a state is to be bound, it must be by a compelling force from the outside; to say that it is obligated through its own consent means that no obligation exists. The doctrine of autolimitation is, as Hobbes would put it, to make a thing depend upon itself. One cannot lift oneself by one's own bootstraps.

"It is quite impossible," says Brierly, "to fit the facts into a consistently consensual theory."[23] Either there is no sovereignty (in the absolute sense) or there is no international law; the two are irreconcilable. Actually, however, there are rules which do effectively limit the power of the state. No one would deny this today. But once it is admitted that there is a power outside the sovereign state and able to limit that state, then the doctrine of sovereignty is nullified, and with it the theory of individual consent.

CONSENT OF COMMUNITY. The sources and evidences which influence the international judge reveal the will of the community rather

[23] Brierly, p. 38; and see as to the theory of consent, J. L. Brierly, "Le fondement du caractère obligatoire du droit international," *Hague Acad.*, 1928, III, pp. 467-549; P. E. Corbett, *Law and Society in the Relations of States* (New York, 1951); M. O. Hudson, "The Prospect for International Law in the Twentieth Century," *Cornell Law Quarterly*, 10 (1925), p. 429; R. Pound, "Philosophical Theory and International Law," *Bib. Viss.*, 1 (1923), pp. 71-90; J. B. Scott, "The Legal Nature of International Law," *A.J.*, 1 (1907), pp. 831-66; W. W. Willoughby, "The Legal Nature of International Law," *A.J.*, 2 (1908), pp. 357-65; W. W. Willoughby, *Fundamental Concepts of Public Law* (New York, 1924), p. 283.

than of each individual state. This, it must be emphasized, is the actual situation, aside from any theoretical argument over sovereignty. "Nor is it to be admitted," said Justice Story in the case of *La Jeune Eugenie*, "that no principle belongs to the law of nations, which is not universally recognized, as such, by all civilized communities, or even by those constituting, what may be called, the Christian States of Europe."[24] It is the consent of the group which must be established, rather than the consent of each individual state. It is not permissible, nor is it done in practice, for a state to refuse to meet its obligations with the declaration that it had never given its consent to a rule well established, or that it had decided to change its mind and revoke its consent once given.

How the will of a political group is to be expressed is, in each case, a matter of the machinery and methods provided. It is usually, but not always, a matter of majority rule. In the United States, the Constitution may be amended by a minority of the people, through a very complicated machinery for expressing the group will. The *vox populi* is never a determinate mathematical calculation. The machinery of the community of nations is not the best for ascertaining the wishes of the community, but the layman may console himself by reflecting upon the task of a judge called upon to interpret the unwritten common law in its earlier days. That judge was able to find his way, and international judges as well are blazing a trail. It may not be possible to say how many years a rule must continue, or how many states are required, to establish the consent of the community to a rule of customary law, but international tribunals have usually been able to determine, to the satisfaction of the community, whether or not a rule has met with acceptance.

RELATIONSHIP OF MUNICIPAL TO INTERNATIONAL LAW.[25] It has been maintained by some that only those international rules may be called law which are accepted and applied within a state; and that, since they derive from domestic law and are applied by domestic courts, they are really domestic law. Such a statement is obviously incorrect as regards cases tried by international tribunals, but it is equally untrue as to cases tried by the courts of a state.

[24] 2 Mason 448 (1822).
[25] See Bishop, pp. 69-78; Briggs, pp. 60-64; Hyde, I, § 5; H. Kelsen, "Les rapports de système entre le droit interne et le droit international public," *Hague Acad.*, 1926, IV, pp. 231-326; Ruth Masters, *International Law in National Courts* (New York, 1932); E. D. Dickinson, in *University of Pennsylvania Law Review*, 101 (1952-1953); H. Triepel, *Völkerrecht und Landesrecht* (Leipzig, 1899); J. Westlake, "Is International Law a Part of the Law of England?" *Law Quarterly Review*, 22 (1906), pp. 14-26; Q. Wright, *The Enforcement of International Law through Municipal Law in the United States*, (University of Illinois Social Science Studies No. 5, 1916).

It is an accepted principle that the customary law is binding upon all states and must therefore be enforced when necessary within a state by the courts of that state. To admit that international law is ultimately dependent upon domestic law and courts, or that municipal law may override international law, would be to deny international law outright, and no state makes such a denial. As a matter of actual practice it may easily be shown that (1) a state must have domestic laws which will enable it to carry out its obligations under international law;[26] (2) that it cannot have laws—not even its constitution—which conflict with international law;[27] (3) that decisions of its domestic courts, putting its own law above international law, are not final but may be reviewed and reparation demanded by an international tribunal;[28] and (4) that international law reaches beyond the authority of a state, and may enable it to do something which otherwise it could not do.[29]

In several modern constitutions, international law has been made a part of municipal law; the same result has been reached in repeated decisions of American courts: "International law is part of our law and must be ascertained and administered by the courts of justice of appropriate jurisdiction, as often as questions of right depending upon it are duly presented for their determination."[30]

A domestic court is, however, instructed by its own national legislation or Constitution, and may therefore be required to put its own law first. What of such possible conflicts? The first duty of every state is to provide laws and machinery which will enable it to meet

26 See *U.S. v. Arjona,* 120 U.S. 487 (1886); "Jurisdiction of the Courts of Danzig," *P.C.I.J.,* Series B, 15. "And whereas Her Britannic Majesty cannot justify itself for a failure in due diligence on the pleas of insufficiency of legal means of action which it possessed. . . ." *Alabama Award,* F. Wharton, *A Digest of the International Law of the United States,* 3 vols. (Washington, 1887), III, p. 633.

27 "There could be no question that national laws must yield to the law of nations if there was a conflict," Umpire Plumley in the *Aroa Mines* case, Ralston, *Venezuelan Arbitrations,* p. 344; and see the Gentini case *ibid.,* p. 725; Cutting case, Moore, *Digest,* II, p. 235; and others quoted in Eagleton, *Responsibility,* p. 64; *Research in International Law,* Responsibility of States, Article 2. "In such a case a treaty is superior to the Constitution which latter must give way," Montijo case, Moore, *Arbitrations,* p. 1440.

28 "The defense of res adjudicata does not apply to cases where the judgment set up is in violation of international law," Moore, *Digest,* VI, p. 694. The Supreme Court of the United States has on several occasions been reversed by international tribunals; Root, in *A.J.,* 3 (1909), p. 535; J. H. Ralston, *Law and Procedure of International Tribunals* (Stanford, 1926), § 179.

29 A state could not under its own laws seize a pirate of another nationality on the high seas, but is authorized to do so by international law.

30 *Paquete Habana,* 175 U.S. 700 (1899). See also the *Nereide,* 9 Cranch 423 (1815); the *Charming Betsy,* 2 Cranch 117-118 (1804). Quotations from some of the newer constitutions are given in Bishop, p. 68, and Briggs, p. 58.

its international obligations. How a state does this is of no concern to international law; it is free to organize and rule itself as it pleases. But if the state fails to meet these international obligations because of a conflict between its own laws and the law of nations, or if its courts are unable to give effect to the latter, that state becomes responsible to the state whose rights have been violated. Internally, the court may proceed with the utmost correctness according to its own laws, and may, even with perfect propriety according to those laws, violate international law. In so doing, however, it comes into conflict with a superior law, and must make reparation for the injury it has produced. A court often says that it is unable, under its domestic laws, to give relief, and that reparation must be sought through diplomatic channels. The fact that a domestic court collides with international law, far from settling the matter, simply establishes the responsibility of the state for the violation of international law.[31] Just as a law of a member state in the United States must give way before a power delegated to the national government, so no national law or court decision can stand up against the law of the community of nations. It is only those who regard the state as sovereign, and above all law, who find difficulty with this proposition, and they are forced to bow to the facts of practice.

13. IS INTERNATIONAL LAW TRUE LAW?

There can be no doubt that international law has been, and still is, shockingly inadequate for the needs of the community of nations. To admit that it is violated at times is not of great significance, for many legal systems suffer more frequent violation.[32] It has been defective in many ways. It has had neither judge, nor legislator, nor policeman. The greater part of international relations did not come within its jurisdiction at all—such matters as the control of war, the pacific settlement of disputes, the vast problems of international economics, of imperialism and self-determination. It might be able to offer decisions on such matters, but only if states voluntarily brought them before international tribunals.

It is proper to observe, at this point, that if international law is weak and defective, this is not its fault, but the fault of the peoples who make it what it is. Law, as was said earlier, is a product of social con-

[31] This is the situation which proponents of the "Bricker amendment" reject, or fail to comprehend.

[32] "I venture to say that international law is on the whole as well obeyed as municipal law," J. B. Moore, *International Law and Some Current Illusions* (New York, 1924), p. 300.

sciousness. It does not just grow by itself; its failure is the failure of those who do not give it the support which would make it stronger and more effective.

AUSTINIAN DEFINITION. An especial responsibility rests upon the American people, in this respect, as the strongest nation in the world; and among them upon lawyers, who have in the past given little support to international law. The domestic lawyer is apt to deny to international law the character of true law because of the influence upon him of the Austinian definition of law, in which he was earlier trained. Austin held that law proper was a command from a determinate authority; that law was a rule of conduct laid down for an intelligent being by an intelligent being having authority over him. As to this, it is to be observed in the first place, that the definition was made for individuals within a state, before it was ever conceived that there could be a community of states with a government of its own. Again, the definition was founded upon the prevailing doctrine of sovereignty, which is now, at any rate for external purposes, obsolete. But even as a description of municipal law, says John Bassett Moore, "it is not sufficiently comprehensive, since it would, for instance, exclude a large part of constitutional law, much of which, like a considerable part of international law, is not enforced by courts by means of specific penalties."[33] And Professor Brierly, of Oxford University, calls it "a misleading and inadequate description even of the law of a state; it does not, for instance, account for the existence of the English Common Law."[34] The School of Historical Jurisprudence of Savigny and Maine taught that custom precedes law and remains the essence of it, and that the true test of law is recognition of law as a binding rule and observance of law as such. Even among legal philosophers, no one seems today to know what law is, but, says Hershey, in summary indictment, "It is now generally agreed that the Austinian view of law is formal, narrow, arbitrary, unhistorical and unphilological."[35]

There is certainly a body of rules of conduct for states, rules generally accepted as binding. They are interpreted and applied by courts, both domestic and international, which call them law. They are argued by states in their correspondence and before tribunals as law, and the decisions of these tribunals are as faithfully observed as are the decisions of municipal courts. In only one respect does interna-

[33] J. B. Moore, *International Law and Some Current Illusions*, p. 292. On p. 294 he adds: "the world has come to regard the rules governing the intercourse of nations as constituting a system of law, for the maintenance of which even the use of coercion is justified."

[34] Brierly, p. 49.

[35] Hershey, *Essentials of International Public Law and Organization* (New York, 1927), p. 7.

tional law fail to measure up even to the Austinian definition: that is, the lack of a superior authority having power over states below it. But, says Hyde, "It is no longer seriously or widely maintained that the existence of law is necessarily dependent upon the presence of a power to enforce it."[36]

Whether international law is true law or not depends upon one's definition of law, but the factual situation remains the same. Conduct within the society of nations is in fact controlled by rules which are determined and applied by courts, which may be enforced by external coercion, and which are accepted as law by those to whom they apply. "It may be fairly doubted," says Hall, "whether a description of law is adequate which fails to admit a body of rules as being substantially legal, when they have received legal shape, and are regarded as having the force of law by the persons they are intended to guide."[37]

SANCTIONS. "That society," says Professor Hyde, " does not as yet, however, itself undertake to make hard the way of the transgressor by fixing penalties and enforcing them, powerful forces, nevertheless, unceasingly operate to produce respect for international law."[38]

What are these forces?[39] In one group, we may put such forces as the "moral conscience of mankind," public opinion, etc. These are powerful forces, more effective than the policeman in securing respect for law, forces which nations fear. But they are forces which apply as well to matters entirely outside of law, to rules of etiquette, or sports, or religion, as well as to rules of a political character. They can hardly be classified as juridical sanctions. Habit is always a strong factor in observance of law. Reciprocal needs are another; a state observes the law on one occasion because it hopes to be able to invoke that law upon another occasion, and does not wish to set a precedent which can be used against it.

In the earlier texts of international law it was customary to insert a few pages, as a sort of a bridge between the law of peace and the law of war, descriptive of the methods by which coercion could be applied. These methods were treated not so much as sanctions as preliminaries of war, or as means of retaliation or of self-help. They were usually divided into amicable and non-amicable methods. Under the former were placed good offices, mediation, arbitration and the

[36] Hyde, I, p. 15. "In my opinion, a law may be established and become international, that is to say, binding upon all nations, by the agreement of such nations to be bound thereby, although it may be impossible to enforce obedience thereto by any given nation party to the agreement." *The Prometheus*, 2 Hong Kong Law Reports 217 (1906).

[37] Hall, pp. 14-15.

[38] Hyde, I, p. 15.

[39] See E. Root, "The Sanction of International Law," *Proc. Am. Soc.*, 1908, p. 14.

like; under the latter, retaliation, reprisals, "pacific blockade" and others. These methods shaded off gradually into the final recourse, the *ultima ratio regis*, war itself. All of them, including war itself, could be used at any time, without illegality; and there was no judge to say, when one of them was employed by a state against another state, whether it was for the legitimate maintenance of a right or for a less worthy purpose. International consolidation has proceeded at such a rapid rate as to make this classification obsolete. Amicable methods, so-called, belong under (and will be discussed later as part of) the machinery for the pacific settlement of international disputes. Non-amicable measures are rapidly being taken over by the community, to be used only under its authority, for the enforcement of its rules, and so should be discussed under the new heading of sanctions.

Until international society was organized upon a basis of collective responsibility, a nation could protect its rights only through its own efforts. These efforts might or might not extend so far as that technical status known as war. Short of war, there were a number of possibilities. The first step would usually be the breaking off of diplomatic relations. This could be followed by various other pressures such as retaliation, reprisals, embargo, blockade, or even forcible intervention in, or invasion of, the offending state. Such measures of compulsion were not regarded as war, and could therefore be accepted as non-hostile, unless they were taken up as war by the state challenged. Resistance on the basis of war produced a complete change in the law of peace, bringing into effect the laws of neutrality and of belligerent warfare, and producing great inconvenience through the burdens placed upon non-participants. These were inconveniences to be avoided if possible, and more so were the direct consequences of war to the defeated party. Reprisals or intervention thus went often unchallenged, so as not to convert the situation into the legal status of war.

These measures of self-help, which included war itself, were and are unsatisfactory. They may be used in the cause of justice, to enforce a legal right, but they may equally well be used for selfish purposes.[40] States are unwilling to give them up until they are assured of better means of enforcing their rights, and it may be said in defense of these measures that they have often served as a protection for international law. They have, therefore, played a useful part, but it is doubtless correct to deny to them the quality of juridical sanctions. When all is said and done, self-help is merely the exercise of might, which may or

[40] "Thus if war ensues because of the breach of international law, or because of fidelity to the principles of that law, the consequences may prove in fact to be identical," and for that reason "the fear of war is not to be deemed a sanction possessed of a legal character." Hyde, I, p. 15.

may not be also right. It does not express the will or represent the authority of the community of nations. Can it be said, then, that there are international juridical sanctions? Before answering this question, it must be recalled that international society is now divided into an inner and an outer circle. The outer circle is the older community of nations, inchoate and unorganized, resting upon customary law and having no sanctions beyond morality and self-help. This is not to deny that the wider community has a true law and that the law is obeyed to a remarkable degree. But it lacks a sense of collective responsibility, and it does not have sufficient organization to protect itself against the exceptional lawbreaker.

COMMUNITY SANCTIONS. Within the inner circle, represented first by the League of Nations, and now by the United Nations, true juridical sanctions are available. The essential point of difference is that machinery is here provided by which the community may determine illegality and may decide upon means of coercion to be employed in the name of the community against the offender. The action here taken is not unilateral, the irresponsible action of one state against another, but the action of an organized political group. These new sanctions will be examined later in this volume, but we may note at this point that they may only be employed against a breach of the peace and not against any other violation of international law; and that, in practice, the operation of the enforcement action of the United Nations depends, as it did in the case of Korea, upon the voluntary cooperation of Member states. We are still far from enforceable law, from the *civitas maxima*, from world government.

14. THE CURRENT REVOLUTION IN INTERNATIONAL LAW

The interdependence of peoples, discussed above, exerts constant pressure for law among nations; at the same time, the deadlocking effect of ideological conflict and the appearance of new nationalisms, each proudly asserting its sovereignty, now slow up the needed development. In the face of cold war, nations turn—as they have always turned in the face of war—to military and political action rather than to law. The first purpose of law is, usually, to protect the life and property of the members of the community to which it applies, through the requirement that disputes be settled by law and not by the use of force. This, however, has not been true of international law;[41]

[41] See the remarkable study by Julius Stone, *Legal Controls of International Conflict* (New York, 1954).

nations have preferred to depend upon their own strength—a dangerous delusion in days when a war could mean annihilation for all.

There are many new nations, and many new problems. These new nations are not satisfied with the old international law; they had no share in making it, and they feel that they are exploited under it. Their pressure is felt in such terms as "human rights," or "economic sovereignty," or "self-determination"; these will be noticeable at many points in the following pages. They demand new law, but at the same time they jealously hug their sovereignty to their bosoms and show themselves unwilling to submit to law; in the United Nations, where they have a voting majority, they always prefer political action to legal methods or to resort to the Court. There is much inconsistency; the same states which vigorously assert their own sovereignty have no hesitancy in pushing the United Nations into invading the sovereignty of others. The reserved field of domestic jurisdiction is constantly under attack by states who would resist any intervention whatever into their own affairs.

Thus, international law is in a state of upheaval; the very foundations upon which it was built are being changed. The sovereign immunities of state agents and property are being diminished, and it becomes more and more possible to sue a state. The importance of the state is diminished, too, by the increasing recognition of other entities as subjects of international law. Formerly, only a state could be a legal person; now, international organizations are, and individual human beings increasingly gain that status. Attention indeed is being concentrated upon the individual and his rights and, though many of the states which demand international protection for the rights of individuals would not permit such protection within their own territories, there is no doubt that the individual, rather than the state, is becoming the foundation of international law. After all, it is he, and not the state, which is the unit of human society.

The upheaval is being felt in many fields. Even the sanctity of the high seas is being challenged—on the one hand, to extend national jurisdiction far beyond the long accepted three mile limit and, on the other hand, to set up international regulation for conservation of the resources of the sea. The exclusive territorial jurisdiction of states is proving inadequate to restrain crime, and an international criminal law and jurisdiction are being developed. Most important of all, but far behind, is the effort to bring under control the use of force by states and to substitute for settlement of disputes by force, settlement by law.

These changes are made difficult by the theory of consent and by the lack of legislative procedures through which new international law can be made. Not only has no progress been made in this direction, but states seem wholly uninterested in the need. Treaties, the only way by which new law can be promptly made, are being signed by the hundred; only a small part of them are ratified and by a small number of states for each treaty. The temper of the times is against law, yet nations must have law, and they keep striving to develop it. The development is full of inconsistencies, and the United Nations, as we shall see, is torn by the conflict between law and politics.[42]

[42] For current viewpoints and theories concerning international law, see among others: J. Americano, *The New Foundations of International Law* (New York, 1947); H. W. Briggs, "New Dimensions in International Law," *Pol. Sci. Rev.*, 46 (1952); P. E. Corbett, *Law and Society in the Relations of States* (New York, 1951); E. D. Dickinson, *Law and Peace* (Philadelphia, 1951); Jessup; G. Lipsky, ed., *Law and Politics in the World Community* (Berkeley, 1953); Myres McDougal, "Intertional Law, Power and Policy: A Contemporary Conception," *Hague Acad.*, 82 (1953), p. 137; H. Morgenthau, *Peace, Security, and the United Nations* (Chicago, 1946); H. A. Smith, *The Crisis of the Law of Nations* (London, 1947); Kurt Wilk, "International Law and Global Ideological Conflict," *A.J.*, 45 (1951), p. 649; Q. Wright, *Contemporary International Law: A Balance Sheet*, (New York, Doubleday Short Studies in Political Science, 1955).

PART II

Who are the members of this community of nations, and what is their legal status? It has generally been said that they are states; but today, other entities are claiming some status under international law. In past practice, a group obtained status through recognition bestowed by other members; now it is sought through membership in the United Nations. How does a member acquire title to territory, or transfer it; and how does it know its boundaries? Many rules, or principles of international law—with many uncertainties also—have been developed as to the rights and duties of membership, and especially as to the control (jurisdiction) which members may exercise over persons and things, in and outside their territories. And what is the position under international law of the individual human being?

Chapter 3

MEMBERSHIP

TITLE TO TERRITORY

A political organization, like a biological organism, may be born, grow, reach majority, suffer from illness or external forces, and finally, perhaps, die. It may grow or weaken, not only in area, population, industrial strength, and military power, but also in its authority and influence in the community of nations. In terms of international law, such developments involve acquisition of title to territory, boundaries, recognition, continuing personality of the state and state succession, and legal rights and duties in the various stages of development.

15. MODES OF ACQUIRING TERRITORY[1]

DISCOVERY AND OCCUPATION. Title to territory has often been taken through discovery of hitherto unoccupied lands. Originally, discovery was regarded as sufficient, but it came to be regarded as establishing merely an inchoate title, with occupation necessary to make it permanent. What is meant by unoccupied territory, *terra nullius*, has never been quite clear, for almost always some people were living upon the land. Possession by uncivilized tribes was usually disregarded,[2] but even land claimed by a Great Power, when abandoned or not maintained by it, might be claimed by another state. The arbitration between the United States and the Netherlands over Las Palmas Island illustrates, to an attenuated degree, the difficulties of

---

[1] Briggs, pp. 239-51; J. Goebel, Jr., *The Struggle for the Falkland Islands* (New Haven, 1927); M. Khadduri, "Iran's Claims to the Sovereignty of Bahrayan," *A.J.*, 45 (1951), p. 631; N. L. Hill, *Claims to Territory* (New York, 1945); M. F. Lindley, *The Acquisition and Government of Backward Territory in International Law* (London, 1926).

[2] *Johnson and Graham's Lessee v. M'Intosh*, 8 Wheaton 543 (1823): *The Fama*, 5 C. Robinson 106 (1804).

determining what is needed to establish legitimate occupation.[3] Conflicts in Africa led to an agreement, at the Conference of Berlin concerning the Congo, that claims to territory should be notified to other Powers, and that "there should be established an authority sufficient to cause acquired rights to be respected."

While various potential boundary disputes remain in South America and elsewhere, the limited extent of unoccupied territory makes this method of claiming title of less importance today. Activities in the Antarctic area, however, raise interesting questions as to the application of the rule. Occupation, in this situation, must be regarded as the manifestation of intention to maintain possession, and the establishment of a temporary base where permanent occupation is impracticable might be regarded as sufficient evidence of such intention.[4]

CESSION. Title to territory may, in the second place, be acquired through a number of forms of cession. States are rarely found in generous enough mood to make gifts of territory. Exchanges are almost as rare, but may be illustrated by the trading of Bessarabia for the Dobrudja, or of the island of Heligoland for African territory. The usual methods of cession are purchase or conquest. Many instances of the former are to be found in the history of the United States, from the Louisiana Purchase to that of the Virgin Islands. Cession may also result from defeat in war, formerly confirmed by treaty. Though money payments were made to Mexico in 1848 for areas now part of the United States, and to Spain for the Philippines, these areas should be regarded as cession through conquest rather than as cession through purchase. That the treaty of cession is made under duress does not invalidate the title thus conferred, so long as war is not illegal.

CONQUEST. Technically, title by conquest must be distinguished from title by cession following conquest, in that the inhabitants of the subjugated territory pass under the control of the conqueror without a treaty. Nowadays, it may be doubted whether conquest gives title in either case. This depends upon whether one agrees that war has become illegal, and also therefore its consequences, such as conquest.

[3] The opinion of the arbitrator may be found in *A.J.*, 22 (1928), p. 867; see also Bishop, p. 265, and Briggs, p. 239. The Clipperton Island award, similar in nature, is in *A.J.*, 26 1932), p. 390.

[4] See T. W. Balch, "The Arctic and Antarctic Regions and the Law of Nations," *A.J.*, 4 (1910), p. 265; Bishop, pp. 274-80; R. Dollot, "International Law Relating to the Polar Regions," *Hague Acad.*, 75 (1950); Hackworth I, § 67; Hyde, § 104; D. H. Miller, "Political Rights in the Arctic," *Foreign Affairs*, 4 (1925), p. 47; E. Plischke, "Trans-polar Aviation and Jurisdiction over Arctic Air Space," *Pol. Sci. Rev.*, 37 (1943), p. 999; G. Smedal, *Acquisition of Sovereignty over Polar Areas* (Oslo, 1931); Naval War College, *International Law Situations* (1937), p. 69.

"One must hope," said Oppenheim, "that the time will come when war will disappear entirely, but, as long as war exists, subjugation will also be recognized."[5] There is no doubt that international jurisprudence has recognized title based upon conquest—indeed, there is little territory held by any state which was not acquired through conquest— but there are now powerful trends against such recognition in the future.[6] As far back as 1890 a Pan-American congress adopted a resolution that "conquest shall never hereafter be recognized as admissible under American public law"; and Project No. 30 proposed by the American Institute of International Law laid down the rule, "In the future, territorial acquisitions obtained by means of war or in presence of an armed force, to the detriment of any American republic, shall not be lawful."[7] Article 10 of the Covenant of the League of Nations, had it been positively interpreted and enforced, would have made conquest impossible.

On January 7, 1932, Secretary of State Stimson announced that the United States "does not intend to recognize any situation, treaty, or agreement which may be brought about by means contrary to the covenants and obligations of the Pact of Paris. . . ." The "Stimson Doctrine" was adopted by the Assembly of the League of Nations, and again reaffirmed in a note from nineteen American republics at the time of the conflict between Bolivia and Paraguay.[8] The United States has on several occasions—e.g., in the case of the Baltic states, or Austria —refused to recognize a title to territory acquired by force. The Atlantic Charter rejected aggrandizement; the Charter of the United Nations obligates Members not to use force in any manner inconsistent with the Charter; the Nuremberg Tribunal held aggressive war to be a crime; and the United Nations employed military force to halt aggression in Korea.

Thus, the trend is strongly against recognition of title to territory acquired by conquest. Parallel with this is the strong reaction against colonial empire, and the revival of the cry for "self-determination." The American Declaration of Independence speaks of the "consent of the governed" and Rousseau's theory of popular sovereignty moved in the same direction. Napoleon III and Italy employed the

---

[5] Oppenheim, I, p. 463.

[6] *The Foltina*, 1 Dodson 450 (1814); *Fleming v. Page*, 9 Howard 603 (1850); *Brunell v. U.S.*, 77 Fed. Supp. 68 (1948). See, for a survey of this subject tending to say that conquest is illegal, M. M. McMahon, *Conquest and Modern International Law* (Washington, 1940).

[7] *A.J.*, 20 (1926), Special Supplement, p. 384. The Sixth Conference of American States, at Havana in 1928, adopted a resolution that "All aggression is considered illicit and as such is declared prohibited." *A.J.*, 22 (1928), p. 357.

[8] *Survey*, 1932, pp. 195, 217, 301; Hyde, I, §§ 109C, 109F; Bishop, pp. 642-43.

plebiscite on several occasions, but the idea was coldly received elsewhere until President Wilson, at the Peace Conference in 1919, asserted that "no right anywhere exists to hand peoples about from sovereignty to sovereignty as if they were property," and included in the famous Fourteen Points the principle "that in determining all such questions of sovereignty the interests of the populations concerned must have equal weight with the equitable claims of the government whose title is to be determined." The practical application of such a principle is, however, extremely difficult, especially in the absence of an international government strong enough to prevent the use of force and with authority to determine the rights of the peoples concerned. Several plebiscites were allowed by the Peace Conference of 1919, as in Eupen and Malmédy, the Saar Basin, and Upper Silesia, and there have been a few others. The fact that a plebiscite was granted as an act of conquerors, rather than as a matter of right, makes it impossible to speak of a right to have a plebiscite under international law.[9]

ACCRETION. New territory may also be added through the natural process of accretion. The term applies to an extension of land due to alluvial deposits brought down by rivers or through the working of the sea. This apparently includes other natural forces within territorial waters, such as the appearance of a volcanic island. Artificial extension of the land through dikes seems permissible. Where such accretion pushes the land out, territorial waters are measured anew from the island or other extension.[10]

PRESCRIPTION. This has been asserted as ground for title in international as well as in domestic law. It refers to long-continued possession, in the face of legal title held earlier by another: "It is a principle of public law, universally recognized, that long acquiescence in the possession of territory, and in the exercise of dominion and sovereignty over it, is conclusive of the nation's title and rightful authority."

Leases do not give de jure title, but they are frequently nothing more than disguised cessions, practically conferring sovereign control upon the lessor. Similarly, spheres of influence and areas under administrative control, such as Bosnia and Herzegovina under Austria until they were formally annexed in 1908, may mean effective control without title. New types of spheres of influence are appearing today, such as the eastern European satellites of the Soviet Union, or the bases set up by the United States in various foreign areas.

9 See, as to plebiscites, Sarah Wambaugh, Monograph on Plebiscites (New York, 1920). Self-determination has had a renascence under the United Nations where it constitutes a very difficult problem. See § 128 below.
10 The Anna, 5 C. Robinson 373 (1805); Bishop, p. 281.

16. BOUNDARIES[11]

THE "HINTERLAND." There naturally arose, in connection with the vast areas of newly discovered territory, the question of the extent to which the claim could legitimately reach. Could a man who had just set foot upon a few inches of land thereby claim for his state the entire continent upon which he stood? Obviously not, if occupation and actual possession were necessary to render title by discovery valid. On the other hand, it was hardly reasonable to allow later arrivals to claim territory up to the back fences of settlers who had already arrived. There was long debate over the principles to be applied. According to one theory, the discoverer was entitled to all lands necessary for his security. This theory was disputed by those who argued that a claim should not be permitted to extend beyond the material limits within which the government could make its authority felt. And how much land was necessary for security until a reasonable time for achieving effective occupation had elapsed? The original charters granted by the British Crown to colonists in America granted the land from sea to sea, and this claim was vainly maintained later by the United States in the "54° 40' or Fight" controversy over the Oregon country. There was also the theory of determination by natural boundaries, such as a mountain divide or watershed.

While the rule of effective occupation was ultimately admitted, there was not sufficient law to adjust such disputes, and settlement was usually made through treaty and compromise fixing artificial boundaries. During the nineteenth century the arena was transferred from America to Africa and competition became keen as the amount of unclaimed territory decreased, until the Berlin Conference in 1885 laid down rules as to notification and effective occupation. The question is by no means dead, for boundary disputes may yet appear whose solution will depend upon earlier claims.

MARITIME BOUNDARIES. The seaward boundaries of states are especially difficult to ascertain, because of the configuration of the coastline. The needs of self-defense, fishing and such rights, exercise of jurisdiction for certain purposes, combined in earlier days to produce extravagant claims. About the beginning of the eighteenth century,

---

[11] On boundaries, see Bishop, p. 291; also S. W. Boggs, *International Boundaries: A Study of Boundary Functions and Problems* (New York, 1940); Norman Hill, *Claims to Territory in International Law and Relations* (London, 1945); T. H. Holden, *Political Frontiers and Boundary Making* (London, 1916); Stephen B. Jones, *Boundary Making; A Handbook for Statesmen, Treaty Editors and Boundary Commissioners* (Carnegie Endowment, Washington, 1945); P. de Lapradelle, *La frontière. Etude de Droit International* (Paris, 1928).

Bynkershoek laid down the famous rule of the cannon shot limit—
terrae dominium finitur ubi finitur vis armorum. The range of the
gunshot in those days was calculated at three miles, and this distance,
rather than the range of guns, has been most widely accepted in practice, though some states claim a few miles more.

A distinction must be made between the three miles of sea along the
coast, which is regarded as part of the actual territory of a state and
under its sovereignty (with exception made for innocent passage),
and extension of jurisdiction for certain purposes beyond this limit.
The United States for various purposes, and other states for even more
varied purposes, have at times exercised jurisdiction as far as twelve
miles. Modern circumstances of life, such as the greater speed of
vessels, longer range of guns, radio communication, traffic problems,
pollution of waters, as well as the pursuit of smugglers and boot-
leggers, have led to assumption of jurisdiction beyond three miles in
many cases. Various proposals have been made for extending territorial waters beyond three miles or for permitting jurisdiction beyond
this limit. The League of Nations Codification Conference in 1930
was unable to reach agreement; and the International Law Commission
of the United Nations is still uncertain.[12]

In the case of bays and gulfs, it is especially difficult to establish the
coast line from which territorial waters are to be measured. The
logical effect of the application of this rule would be to include behind
the coast line such indentations as are not more than six miles across,
but national defense, or even control of traffic, may require more. It
is hardly to be expected that the United States would deny herself,
for example, control over Chesapeake Bay, and our courts have maintained such jurisdiction.[13] Norway, with deep indentations of her coast
line, argued that the territorial waters boundary need not follow the
sinuosities of the coast but that their external boundary should be
measured parallel to the principal direction of her coast line. Her claim
was rather generously upheld in 1952 against England in the Fisheries
Case before the International Court of Justice.[14]

A strait separating two states is usually divided by a middle boundary line. If it is entirely within a state, but more than six miles wide,

12 The documents prepared for the 1930 Conference contain invaluable materials on
this subject. See Acts of the Conference for the Codification of International Law, III,
Minutes of the Second Committee (1930, V. 16). The International Law Commission
has been unable to go further than to say that no state need recognize a claim beyond
three miles, and that more than twelve miles is forbidden. U.N. General Assembly,
Official Records, Tenth Session, Supplement No. 9 (A/2934).

13 The Alleganean, Moore, Arbitrations, p. 4332; North Atlantic Coast Fisheries,
Scott, Hague Court Reports (London, 1916), p. 146.

14 I.C.J. Reports, 1952, p. 114.

conventional arrangements will have to be made; indeed, such arrangements are necessary where the strait is a highway between seas. Artificial waterways, though under the control of one state, must be adjusted to international needs, as the United States found in the case of Panama Canal tolls.[15]

RIVER BOUNDARIES. When a river touches upon two or more states, very difficult problems may arise. A river wholly within a state, such as the Mississippi, is entirely subject to the control of that state. Where a river flows between two states, the boundary set by jurisprudence is the *thalweg*, or center of the main navigable channel.[16] Each state has a general right of navigation, and a particular right of jurisdiction out to the *thalweg*. If by a gradual process of erosion or accretion, the channel is changed, the boundary line follows it; but a sudden diversion of the channel leaves the territorial boundary where it was.[17]

Though not a boundary question, it is convenient at this point to mention the new and important questions arising in connection with rivers which flow from one state to another. The right of navigation upon such rivers has long been a problem. The state at the mouth of such a river has an enormous advantage and such states have been compelled to admit navigation through their territory. From the time of the Congress of Vienna, it may be said that international law supports a right of innocent navigation of such rivers, but geographic and other influences have made it necessary to draft conventional arrangements for each river separately. In some cases, such as the Rhine and the Danube, quite a jurisprudence has appeared and administrative institutions have been created, with a considerable degree of supervision over navigation.[18] Part XII of the Treaty of Versailles greatly extended the principle of freedom of fluvial navigation, but Soviet control over the Danube since World War II has badly set back the principle in that area.

New uses of international rivers are now coming to the fore and, with them, new questions. Irrigation, generation of hydro-electric

[15] As to the Suez Canal, see Charles B. Selak, Jr., "The Suez Canal Base Agreement," *A.J.*, 49 (1955), p. 487.

[16] *Louisiana v. Mississippi*, 202 U.S. 1 (1906).

[17] *Arkansas v. Tennessee*, 246 U.S. 158 (1918); and see the "Chamizal Boundary Dispute," *A.J.*, 5 (1911), p. 785. In the latter case, the United States rejected an arbitral award, but has since arranged with Mexico for administration of Rio Grande River problems through a joint river commission; Bishop, p. 296; Briggs, p. 258; Hackworth, I, p. 409.

[18] See the cases before the Permanent Court of International Justice, in Series B, No. 14 and Series A, No. 23. They are named international rivers, says Oppenheim, "because freedom of navigation in time of peace on such rivers in Europe and on many of them outside Europe for merchantmen of all nations is recognised by international law," Oppenheim, I, p. 373. See also Hyde, I, p. 562.

power, flood control, and such things are becoming of great importance, especially for underdeveloped countries. Modern machinery and methods make possible vast enterprises for diversion and storing of water and, when a state undertakes such an enterprise, it may do harm to other states on the river—what are the rights of each to the water? The increasing importance of the matter appears in the disputes between India and Pakistan (Indus river-system), between Iran and Afghanistan (Helmand River) and over the Jordan and Nile rivers. There have been few cases upon which to build international law, but analogous precedents may be found in disputes between the States of the United States. [19]

LEGAL PERSONALITY

17. MEMBERS

Having inquired as to the physical makeup of states, we have next to ask concerning their organization and character and whether and why they are entitled to be called members of the society of nations.

We are concerned here with the broader community of nations, rather than the inner circle of the League of Nations and now the United Nations. It may properly be regarded as a universal body, in the sense that it has grown from the Christian community of Western Europe to cover the whole world; all peoples, however primitive, are so far under the control of recognized members of the community that the latter can be regarded as responsible for them. There are, however, constant changes in these entities; new ones appear, and questions arise concerning their rights and duties in the community.

Being a member of the community of nations signifies acceptance of obligations and the holding of rights under the law of that community, and in this sense, a member is spoken of as a "legal person" or as a "subject of international law." It has usually been said that states alone can be subjects of international law (though this statement cannot now be made with much certainty) and there are some writers who maintain that the mere fact of being physically present as a state automatically means membership in the community, with correlative rights and duties.[20] Even if this was true, it would still be necessary to ascertain

---

[19] For a survey of this problem, see *U.N. Doc.* E/ECE/136 (1952), and the Report of the 46th Biennial Conference of the International Law Association (Edinburgh, 1954); also, Bishop, pp. 295-300; Briggs, pp. 263-77.

[20] See Bishop, pp. 232-34, quoting Lauterpacht; and Briggs, pp. 113-15.

which of the various human organizations on the earth are entitled to be called states. The more generally accepted view, maintained in practice, is that membership, or status as a subject of international law, should be open only to those properly qualified. In any case, it becomes necessary to ask by what criteria and procedure and authority the determination is made that an entity[21] is a state, or otherwise a subject of international law.

STATES. The political scientists usually define a state as a group of people having a fixed territory, an organized government exerting control over the area, and independence. People and territory would seem to be essential to the definition, and also a political organization which can speak externally for the state and internally administer justice.[22] Various human groups might measure up to the definition thus far—some universities, for example, have territory, population, and government with discipline over members. But they do not possess what is regarded as the chief requisite—independence from external control, which is said to distinguish the state from any other human organization.

Independence, however, is also a word of uncertain meaning in practice. If it indicates absolute freedom from external control, then no political group could be a member of the community of nations, for none has such unlimited freedom of action. Independence is a relative term; it is not a unit, or an attribute, which a state does or does not have. One state may have more than another and none is entirely free. It becomes necessary, therefore, to examine practice and the theoretical classifications which have been suggested.

18. CLASSIFICATIONS

Writers who have attempted to classify the members of the community of nations have found themselves embarrassed by the confusing wealth of plan and structure which the tide of political evolution has cast up. As Lawrence says, "the classificatory skill of jurists

[21] For example, the Organization of American States; the United Nations; certain territorial entities listed as members of specialized agencies such as the Postal Union; or an individual human being. See Sibert, I, pp. 118-55; Rousseau, p. 77; Jessup, *passim*. The Statute of the International Court of Justice says that states only may appear before it. See *U.S. v. Kusche,* 56 Fed. Supp. 201 (1944); U.N. General Assembly Resolution 289 (IV); Bishop, p. 169; Briggs, p. 66.

[22] Rousseau suggests that responsibility, the assumption of obligations to maintain internal order and external faith, is a more true characteristic of the state than is independence or sovereignty. Ch. Rousseau, "L'Independance de l'Etat dans l'ordre international," *Hague Acad.,* 73 (1948), pp. 171-253.

toils far behind the constructive ingenuity of statesmen."[23] Using one or another set of terms, however, they have usually arrived at a three-fold division into sovereign, part-sovereign, and dependent states.[24] Even among the writers who uphold the doctrine of sovereignty, the classification of part-sovereign is admitted, thus destroying their claim that sovereignty is indivisible and rendering it useless as a test of membership.

So-Called Sovereign States. Most of the states commonly recognized as members of the community are so free from external control that they may be called independent, but in no case is there complete freedom. "In a strict sense," says Hyde, "no member of the international society is or can be independent."[25] There are in fact numerous limitations upon them aside from the equal incidence of international law. Neutralized states are unable to make war, or cede territory, or enter into certain types of treaties. Belgium, for example, after 1839, was unable to sign the treaty guaranteeing the neutrality of Luxembourg, or the Hague Convention Limiting the Employment of Force for the Recovery of Contract Debts. And it must be noted that if neutralization is a limitation upon the neutralized state, it is also a limitation upon those states, actually including the most powerful states of the world, who signed the treaty of collective guarantee. Again, certain states are limited in their treatment of minority groups within their control, or as to freedom of transit; and such conditions on membership had been earlier imposed by the Treaty of Berlin upon the Balkan states.

There are some so-called sovereign states whose independence is little more than fictitious. Cuba, for a time, was able to send and receive diplomatic agents, make treaties, and be a member of the League of Nations, though she was bound by a treaty with the United States which guaranteed her independence, forbade her to make treaties which might impair her independence, or to alienate any of her terri-

[23] T. J. Lawrence, *Principles of International Law* (7th ed.; London, 1923). "For international purposes, however, this classification is immaterial," Hall, p. 23; and see Hyde, I, § 13; Fenwick, p. 353; Bishop, pp. 170-218; Briggs, pp. 65-97; Svarlien, Chap. vi.

[24] "The Community of nations is found to be composed of states which enjoy full membership and of other states which enjoy but partial membership. Of those which enjoy full membership some few are subject to restrictions which, while qualifying the enjoyment of their rights, do not limit their status of full membership." Fenwick, pp. 85-86.

"Au point de vue de la souveraineté, on peut classer les différents Etats du globe en trois catégories: *souverains, protégés, vassaux.*" Fauchille, I, p. 257.

Ross prefers the term "self-governing," which means "when and in so far as it is the highest legal power in relation to its individual members." He then distinguishes between "fully self-governing, partly self-governing, and non-self-governing." Ross, p. 15.

[25] Hyde, I, p. 43.

tory for colonization or for military or naval purposes, or to contract a debt beyond the ordinary revenues of the island. The United States was given "the right to intervene for the protection of Cuban independence, the maintenance of a government adequate for the protection of life, property and individual liberty, and for discharging the obligations with respect to Cuba imposed by the Treaty of Paris on the United States, now to be assumed and undertaken by the Government of Cuba."[26] A similar relationship existed between England and Egypt. Many such arrangements have been discarded, as has that with Cuba; but new ones appear. The Byelo-Russian and Ukrainian Socialist Soviet Republics are completely under the control of the Soviet Union which, however, proclaims their independence; they are separate voting members of the United Nations, but they do not exchange diplomatic envoys with other states. Hungary, Poland, Czechoslovakia and the Balkan states are still nominally independent; others such as Tibet or Viet Nam appear to be falling into the same anomalous situation as other satellites of the Soviet Union. Do they have independence in a measure which entitles them to international personality?

It appears, then, that members of the community of nations may have drastic limitations upon their freedom of action, may submit to a large degree of control by other states, and may nevertheless retain their membership. The leading powers of the world may be subject to similar, perhaps lesser, restrictions. Germany, upon entering the League of Nations, objected to the performance of military duties under the Covenant on the ground that her war-making power was limited by the Treaty of Versailles. The United States, because of her comparative isolation and ample resources, is probably more nearly an independent state than any other state in the world, but she, like all states, is limited by all her treaties. "In fact," says Hyde, "the whole body of treaties to which a State is a party betokens a check upon legislative freedom."[27]

So-Called Part-Sovereign States. Among states classified as part-sovereign could be found some which had as much share in the rights

---

[26] The treaty may be found in Malloy, I, p. 362. It was abrogated by a new treaty concluded in 1934 (48 Stat. at Large 1682).

A treaty of 1936 recognized Egypt as a sovereign and independent state and formed an alliance between England and Egypt, leaving to the former rights for the protection of the Suez Canal. See *B.Y.I.L.*, XVIII, p. 79; *A.J.*, 31 (1937), Document Section, p. 77. This arrangement, too, has now been discarded.

[27] Hyde, I, p. 209. "These limitations exist. There is abundant evidence that in one form or another they will become more important in the future. Little advantage can be derived from attempting to subordinate them to theories which tend to deny or distort their true significance." Dickinson, *Equality*, pp. 278-79.

of the community as others listed as full-sovereign. Bulgaria, for example, was, by the Treaty of Berlin and until 1908, a tributary principality under the suzerainty of the Sultan; yet she had the right to make war and treaties, and her delegates attended the Hague Conference of 1899. English courts recognized dependent Indian states as sovereign and granted their rulers sovereign immunities, but no third state would have thought of conceding to them even a qualified membership or voice in the community of nations.[28] Protectorates have the one common element, "the prohibition of all foreign relations except those permitted by the protecting state."

There are now no personal unions (unless the British Commonwealth be so regarded), such as that existing between Hanover and England until 1837, or between Belgium and the Congo Free State until 1909; nor real unions, such as the union between Norway and Sweden until 1905, or that between Austria and Hungary until World War I disintegrated it. Likewise, the terms suzerain and vassal have become obsolete.

The federal state produces some questions. There is no doubt as to the capacity of a federal state for membership in the community of nations, but the rights of its member states are insignificant. Some members of the former German Empire had the right of legation and of treaty-making, and some of the cantons of Switzerland enjoy a very limited right to make treaties. Whatever the legal status, there is little doubt that, should such a treaty be violated, protests and reclamations would be directed to the central government of the federal state. The member states of the United States have no international personality whatever.

THE BRITISH COMMONWEALTH OF NATIONS. There are organizations which, exemplifying the prolific ingenuity of constructive statesmanship, cannot be classified at all. One of the most interesting of these developments, not only because of its novelty but because of the lessons to be drawn from it for international organization, is the British Commonwealth of Nations. The constitutional development within the Empire has proceeded at such a rapid rate of decentralization that each of the self-governing Dominions is now practically independent. Each Dominion is free to make its own treaties and to send and receive diplomatic agents, and does so. The development of Dominion independence has been constitutional, rather than international, and

28 *Mighell v. Sultan of Johore*, L.R. (1894) 1 Q.B. 149. As to protectorates, see *King v. Earl of Crewe*, L.R. (1910) 2 K.B. 576; T. Baty, "Protectorates and Mandates," *B.Y.I.L.*, 1921-22, pp. 109-21; F. Despagnet, *Essai sur les protectorats* (Paris, 1896); G. W. Rutherford, "Spheres of Influence: An Aspect of Semi-Suzerainty," *A.J.*, 20 (1926), pp. 300-25; Sibert, I, p. 158. A number of former protectorates, such as Tunis or Cambodia, now seek independence.

foreign states have accepted in practice this development, without formal recognition of independence. If Britain is willing for Canada to send a diplomatic agent, or to make a treaty, the United States will receive the agent and sign the treaty. For all practical purposes, the Dominions are independent; technically, in international law, their status may still be debatable. The Report of the Inter-Imperial Relations Committee of 1926 described the situation thus: "They are autonomous Communities within the British Empire, equal in status, in no way subordinate one to another in any aspect of their domestic or external affairs, though united by a common allegiance to the Crown, and freely associated as members of the British Commonwealth of Nations."[29] The Netherlands and France attempted a similar development for some of their colonies, but the current wave of "self-determination" outstripped them.

THE PAPACY. The pope was for centuries a temporal sovereign of great importance, until the Italian Law of Guarantees of 1871 reduced his temporal power to insignificance. However, his own protests against such a unilateral act, together with certain privileges left to him, such as inviolability of the few acres in which he resided and the right of legation and of treaty-making (concordats), made it possible to debate interminably his international position. In February, 1929, the Lateran Accord was signed, including three documents: a political treaty, a concordat, and a financial agreement. According to Article 2 of the first document: "Italy recognizes the sovereignty of the Holy See in the field of international relations as an attribute that pertains to the very nature of the Holy See, in conformity with its traditions and with the demands of its mission in the world." In Article 24, however, "With regard to the sovereignty pertaining to it in the field of international relations, the Holy See declares that it wishes to remain and will remain extraneous to all temporal disputes between nations, and to international congresses convoked for the settlement of such

[29] "The committee are of opinion that nothing would be gained by attempting to lay down a Constitution for the British Empire . . . considered as a whole, it defies classification and bears no real resemblance to any other political organization which now exists or has ever yet been tried." This report is the nearest approach to a constitution for the present system. It was made to the Imperial Conference of 1926, and is found in *British Parliamentary Papers*, 1926, Cmd. 2768, quoted in Hudson, *Cases*, pp. 26-27; Bishop, p. 182.

There is an extensive literature on this subject. Many citations are given in Hyde, I, p. 53; Oppenheim, I, pp. 193-200. Reference may be made particularly to P. J. N. Baker, *The Present Juridical Status of the British Dominions in International Law* (London, 1929); W. Y. Elliott, *The New British Empire* (New York, 1932); H. D. Hall, *The British Commonwealth of Nations: a Study of Its Past and Future Development* (London, 1920); A. B. Keith, *Responsible Government in the Dominions*, 3 vols. (Oxford, 1912); R. B. Stewart, *Treaty-Making Procedure in the British Dominions*, *A.J.*, 32 (1938), p. 467.

disputes, unless the contending parties make a joint appeal to its mission of peace; nevertheless, it reserves the right in every case to exercise its moral and spiritual power. In consequence of this declaration, the State of the Vatican will always and in every case be considered neutral and inviolable territory."[30] "Vatican City" was thus recognized—by Italy—as a sovereign state; and some other states (not the United States) have since entered into diplomatic relations with it. It can only be said that Vatican City possesses some degree of international personality, though not so much as other members of the community—not enough, for example, to enable it to participate in a conference or join the United Nations.[31]

MANDATES AND TRUST TERRITORIES. Another perplexing development was the mandates system of the League of Nations, now transformed into "trusteeship" under the United Nations. The idea originated in reaction against the habit of seizing territories as a result of conquest in war, and substituted therefore the principle that "the well-being and development of such peoples form a sacred trust of civilization." The territory from which the mandates were created was taken from Germany and Turkey and distributed to mandatory powers in 1919. These powers were to report annually to the Council of the League, and a Permanent Mandates Commission was set up to oversee the administration of the mandates. There were thus political communities, "renounced" according to the Treaty of Versailles in favor of the Allied Powers and by them distributed among themselves as mandatory states, each responsible in an uncertain and varying degree for its conduct in the mandated territory. Much ingenuity has been expended in trying to locate sovereignty in these entities.[32]

There are many other anomalous situations. By Article 102 of the Treaty of Versailles, the Free City of Danzig had its own government, but its foreign relations and customs were to be supervised by Poland, and it was "placed under the protection of the League of Nations."[33] By an agreement of 1923, the city of Tangier became an international

---

[30] The treaty may be found in A.J., 23 (1929), Supplement, p. 187.

[31] As to the status of the Papacy, see R. Bompard, Le pape et le droit des gens (Paris, 1888); C. G. Fenwick, "The New City of the Vatican," A.J., 23 (1929), p. 214; A. P. Higgins, "The State of the City of the Vatican," B.Y.I.L., 1929, p. 214; J. L. Kunz, "The Status of the Holy See in International Law," A.J., 46 (1952), p. 308. The question of diplomatic relations between the United States and the Holy See is discussed in American Bar Association Journal, 38 (1952), p. 471.

[32] These entities are discussed in more detail in §§ 98-101 below. See Wright, Mandates, in general; and the advisory opinion of the International Court of Justice on the International Status of South West Africa, I.C.J. Reports, 1950, p. 128; and Bishop, p. 187.

[33] See the case of the Polish Postal Service in Danzig, P.C.I.J., Series B, No. 11; also Series B, No. 15, and Series B, No. 18.

zone; its statute was revised in 1945.[34] The status of the North American Indian tribes was described by Chief Justice Marshall as "domestic dependent nations."[35] The status of a revolutionary *de facto* government will be considered below. Whether the League of Nations possessed an international personality of its own was much debated among writers. The United Nations is clearly a legal person, according to the International Court of Justice,[36] but is it a member of the community of nations, or a community of nations itself?

From the above collection of illustrations it is apparent that no state has unlimited freedom from external control, and that no two states have the same amount of independence. Nor can there be found any standard amount, or measure, of independence required for membership in the community of nations. Manifestly, independence does not furnish a sufficiently accurate test for such membership. "Independence," says Hyde, "is not essential"; and he adds: "If independence be regarded as a necessary possession of a State of international law, the existing practice of treating as subjects or persons of that law various types of so-called dependent States is incapable of explanation."[37] A state may apparently exist without being regarded as an international person,[38] and, on the other hand, entities not commonly regarded as states have been admitted to membership in international organizations.

If independence is not a sufficient test for membership in the community of nations, what is? The United Nations is now faced with this problem and has made some effort to solve it, but it cannot be said that an answer is yet found. A Member of the United Nations must, under the Charter, be regarded as a state. During the controversy over Indonesia, Australia argued that, since the Netherlands had negotiated an agreement with the Indonesian Republic, the latter was a sovereign state; the Netherlands maintained that it was a colony. Indonesia was admitted to the United Nations and now is undoubtedly a state and a legal person.[39] Libya, a former Italian colony, was set up by the United Nations as a state, though it was economically and militarily unable to stand alone. Vigorous efforts have been made in

[34] *A.J.*, 23 (1929), Document Section, p. 235; G. H. Stuart, *The International City of Tangier* (Stanford, 1931).

[35] *Cherokee Nation v. Georgia,* 5 Peters 1 (1831).

[36] In the case of Reparations for Injuries Suffered in the Service of the United Nations, *I.C.J. Reports*, 1949, p. 176.

[37] Hyde, I, p. 22, note 6.

[38] *Wulfsohn v. Russian Socialist Federated Republic,* 234 N.Y. 372 (1923); *Salimoff v. Standard Oil Co. of New York,* 262 N.Y. 220 (1933); Bishop, pp. 214, 234, 245; Briggs, pp. 148, 165.

[39] U.N. Security Council, Second Year, *Official Records,* pp. 1620 ff.; Bishop, pp. 175 ff.; Sohn, pp. 745-62.

the General Assembly to gain independence for Tunis, Morocco, and Cyprus, though unsuccessfully. On the other hand, Hyderabad, a well-organized and wealthy princely state in India, claimed autonomy under the India Independence Act of 1947, and India asserted that Hyderabad was a domestic matter. The Security Council did nothing, and India took Hyderabad by force.[40] The plea of the Republic of the South Moluccas for independence from Indonesia cannot obtain a hearing before the United Nations; and Communist China, in full control over a vast area and population, is not admitted to the United Nations. By what criteria are such apparently inconsistent decisions reached?

These answers were of course political ones. Criteria for reaching such judgments have not been provided in international law, nor have procedures for giving or enforcing judgment. The recent revival of "self-determination," however, has led in the United Nations to some effort to establish criteria by which it can be decided whether a claimant group is, or is entitled to be, self-governing or independent. A committee prepared a list of "factors" to be taken into account in determining whether a colonial power was properly guiding a non-self-governing territory toward self-government. In this approach (adverse to colonial powers) standards were set high, and many recognized states could not measure up to them.[41] In general, two criteria have been most often stated in debates, though neither Members nor United Nations bodies have observed them in practice: Ability to stand alone, with effective control over the area; and ability and willingness to meet international obligations.

19. RECOGNITION[42]

In practice, the test of membership has been recognition, an individual political decision by each other member. The organized com-

[40] C. Eagleton, "The Case of Hyderabad before the Security Council," *A.J.*, 44 (1950), pp. 277-302.

[41] The list of factors is to be found in an annex attached to General Assembly Resolution 742 (VIII); it is printed in Appendix IV (see below) in this volume as the nearest approach to an answer to this important question, though far from being complete as yet. See also the standards enunciated by the League of Nations with regard to independence for the mandated territory of Iraq, *L. of N. Doc.* VI.A.1 (1931), quoted in Briggs, p. 75.

[42] As to recognition of independence, see Bishop, pp. 219-33; Briggs, pp. 99-117; C. A. Berdahl, "The Power of Recognition," *A.J.*, 14 (1920), p. 519; J. Goebel, Jr., *The Recognition Policy of the United States* (New York, 1915); M. W. Graham, *The Diplomatic Recognition of the Border States* (Berkeley, 1933, 1935, 1941); J. G. Hervey, *The Legal Effects of Recognition in International Law* (Philadelphia, 1928); H. Lauterpacht, *Recognition in International Law* (New York, 1947); H. L. Stimson, *The United States and Other American Republics*, Dept. of State Pub. No. 156 (1931).

munity of nations does not act; each state decides for itself whether to shake hands with the neophyte and admit it to fellowship. The result is a haphazard and unsatisfactory process of admission as a result of which a political entity may be regarded as a member of the society of nations or as a subject of international law by some states and not by others.

Before taking up the practice of recognition, we must pause to consider the conditions under which a group may develop to the point of being considered for membership. A combination of members previously recognized, such as Texas and the United States, or the various units which made up Italy, may result in a new member whose status does not require recognition. On the other hand, a member may divide peaceably and by mutual agreement, as did Norway and Sweden, or as a result of war, as in the case of the Balkan states, usually with no need for recognition beyond the treaty made. When a new political entity appeared in territory not hitherto regarded as measuring up to the standards of Western civilization, such as Liberia, or when an older state under the same disadvantage sought to be recognized, recognition was usually obtained through negotiation.

REVOLUTION. Where a group claims independence as the result of secession or of violent revolution, difficult readjustments are involved. There are two types of *de facto* governments, said Mr. Justice Field:

> One of them is such as exists after it has expelled the regularly constituted authorities from the seats of power and the public offices and established its own functionaries in their places, so as to represent in fact the sovereignty of the nation. . . . The other kind of *de facto* governments, to which the doctrines cited relate, is such as exists where a portion of the inhabitants of a country have separated themselves from the parent state and established an independent government. The validity of its acts, both against the parent state and its citizens or subjects, depends entirely upon its ultimate success.[43]

The former process does not create a new state, but merely replaces the previous government within a state; the latter process creates a new state, potentially a member of the community of nations. In the case of revolutionary change, it appears that three possible stages of recognition are admitted in practice: insurgency, belligerency, and independence.

INSURGENCY. A group fighting for political rather than for personal or selfish purposes may be recognized as insurgents, thus lifting it slightly higher than pirates or criminals, punishable under criminal

[43] *Williams v. Bruffy*, 96 U.S. 176 (1877). See also the *Tinoco Claim*, 1 *I.A.A.* (U.N.), p. 369.

law.[44] It has been the rule that other states must prevent any aid from their territories reaching rebels within a friendly state; any intervention on behalf of the rebels was illegal. The rule of nonintervention in such matters has been shaken in recent years. The Soviet Union found ways of supporting, within a foreign country (e.g., Czechoslovakia), those who would change its government into one more amenable to the Soviet Union; the Arab League announced support for the rebels in Algeria against France. On the other hand, the United Nations did not hesitate to intervene in support of a revolutionary movement against the Netherlands in Indonesia, in spite of objections based upon the "domestic jurisdiction" clause of the Charter. In this case, the United Nations—through political rather than legal action—set aside the old rule of international law; in the case of Czechoslovakia, the Soviet Union maintained self-righteously that she did not intervene, and at the same time accused the United States of intervention in the domestic affairs of other states, such as Korea, Formosa, and Viet Nam.

BELLIGERENCY. A stage higher than insurgency is recognition of belligerency, which produces important legal changes. When a revolutionary government has achieved control over a certain territory and when the range of its operations is such as to affect third states, the latter—or the parent state—may concede to the insurgents the rights of a belligerent. This means that the law of war is to be applied as if between two independent states, and that the recognizing third states agree to assume the duties of neutrals.[45] The new belligerent may now avail itself of the right of search, seizure for contraband, and blockade and it may claim for its military the rights of soldiers in time of war; it also assumes responsibility for adherence to the laws of war. The question of recognition of belligerency is sometimes embarrassing to outside states, for their citizens may suffer until this step is taken, while on the other hand they may antagonize the parent state by premature recognition. Where the parent state has recognized the belligerency of the rebels, as the United States tacitly did when President Lincoln declared the Confederate ports blockaded, other states need not hesitate to recognize. In general, the step should be considered as a recognition of a factual situation rather than as an expression of sym-

[44] *The Three Friends*, 166 U.S. 1 (1897). A thorough discussion of the status of insurgency is provided in Briggs, pp. 998-1004; see also Bishop, pp. 262 ff., and Hackworth, VII, pp. 166 ff.

[45] See Hackworth, I, § 52; Hyde, I, p. 199; Bishop, p. 261; for the Spanish Civil War, N. Padelford, *International Law and Diplomacy in the Spanish Civil Strife* (New York, 1939).

pathy. It concedes a certain amount of international personality, for the revolutionary party thus becomes a subject of the laws of war and neutrality.

INDEPENDENCE. The third stage is the recognition of *de jure* independence, with full admission to membership in the community of nations. The justification for the use of recognition must be found in this admission. A state may exist and carry on a certain amount of intercourse with other states without having been recognized. There is no direct bar, in the absence of recognition, to ordinary commercial intercourse between individuals. But the damage to prestige, the lack of the ordinary diplomatic and consular channels, the absence of machinery and of the protection furnished by treaties, and the risk to individuals in a commerce not subject to the ordinary protection given to citizens abroad, may easily result in great detriment to the unrecognized state. On the other hand, the state which refuses recognition may suffer to such an extent that it may sacrifice its scruples and its desire to maintain legal principles for commercial gain, as did some states when they recognized the Union of Soviet Socialist Republics.

It is this difficulty, doubtless, which explains the attempted distinction between *de facto* and *de jure* recognition. The former seems to be a sort of a stop-gap arrangement, a *modus vivendi*, permitting commercial intercourse without necessarily restoring full diplomatic intercourse. *De facto* recognition is apparently revocable, but during its continuance it seems to differ little in legal effect from *de jure* recognition.[46] But the only test of membership in the community of nations upon a permanent basis is *de jure* recognition.

RECOGNITION OF GOVERNMENTS. There seems to be little difference in practice or principle between recognition of a new state (e.g., Israel, in 1948) and the recognition of a new government within a state. The latter is more frequent; it raises the question whether a state finds the new government acceptable to speak on behalf of the state within which it has come to power. The question does not usually arise from a constitutional change of government within a state; it is usually the result of violent overthrow of the preceding government. Refusal to recognize a government does not extinguish the recognition given to the state which it purports to represent. For fifteen years the United

[46] Illustrations of *de facto* recognition are said to be found in the attitude of the United States toward the Carranza regime in Mexico in 1915 (which became *de jure* recognition in 1917); or of England toward the new government of Russia in 1921; or the hasty recognition by the United States of the new state of Israel in 1948. *Dept. of State Bull.*, XVIII, p. 673. See *Oetjen v. Central Leather Co.*, 246 U.S. 297 (1918); *Luther v. Sagor*, L.R. (1921), 3 K.B. 532. Hyde, I, p. 193, and Brierly (1949 ed.), p. 131, suggest that there is no legal difference between the two types of recognition.

States refused to recognize the new government of Russia while maintaining that the state of Russia continued to have certain obligations to it.

Similarly, the United States has for some years refused to recognize the Communist government of China, which controls the entire mainland, while continuing to recognize the Nationalist government as the legitimate government of all China, though it holds only Formosa and some adjacent islands. This situation has produced much confusion of thought in the United States. To most Americans communism was obnoxious and the conduct of Communist China was immoral, and they were therefore unwilling to face the fact that it existed and was in control in China. At the same time, they demanded that it live up to standards of international law, and the United States was put into the anomalous position of demanding performance of legal duties from a government to which it denied legal status, and with whom it had to talk through a third party. This absurd situation is partly the result of the whole process of recognition, and partly the result of the habit which Americans have of deciding on foreign policies according to their likes or dislikes. John Bassett Moore spoke of the "preposterous and mischievous supposition that the recognition of a government implies approval" of that government, which supposition, he said, was contrary to elemental principles of international law.[47] Secretary-General Lie complained of, though he admitted, the unilateral right of each state to refuse to recognize a new government, which, he thought, was a right to be differentiated from the right of representation in United Nations organs; he complained also because the United Nations did not have the authority to recognize or refuse to recognize a new government.[48]

METHODS OF RECOGNITION. Recognition may be either collective or individual. The former method is exceptional and due usually to political considerations motivating the making of a peace treaty. Collective recognition, as the Secretary-General complained, is not a right which belongs to the United Nations but it could be argued that each Member has, under the Charter, certain legal obligations toward all other Members and that, consequently, admission as a Member estab-

[47] Quoted in Briggs, pp. 129-30. He quotes also Secretary of State Acheson, who said in 1940: "We maintain diplomatic relations with other countries primarily because we are all on the same planet and must do business with each other." See Arthur Dean, "United States Foreign Policy and Formosa," *Foreign Affairs*, 33 (1955), p. 360; Q. Wright, "The Chinese Recognition Problem," *A.J.*, 49 (1955), p. 360.

[48] Memorandum of March 8, 1950, *U.N. Doc.* S/1466, quoted in part in Bishop, pp. 227-28. Debates in the United Nations as to the criteria for determining which government should represent a Member are summarized by Dr. Liang in *A.J.*, 45 (1951), p. 689.

lishes the admitted state in relation to other Members as a legal person —which is, in principle, the significance of recognition in international law. However, recognition is ordinarily an individual action on the part of each state, which offers the accolade when and how is pleases.[49]

Recognition may be explicit and formal, or it may be implicit and informal. It may come through proclamation or statement in a treaty or other such definite act; or it may be tacit, through some procedure which can only be undertaken with another subject of international law, such as the making of a treaty with it, or the sending and receiving of diplomatic agents.[50] Recent practice indicates the possibility of conditional recognition; but recognition, once given, appears to be final and cannot be withdrawn; diplomatic relations may be broken off, but this does not affect legal status.

STANDARDS. There is no right to demand, and no duty to grant, recognition,[51] nor are there any criteria set by the community of nations for the guidance of members in granting recognition. Each state decides for itself, arbitrarily, though it may have evolved some principles of its own. In the development of the recognition policy of the United States, three principles have been followed. At first, the only requisite element was stability: "It is sufficient for us to know that a government exists capable of maintaining itself; and then its recognition on our part inevitably follows."[52] Later, however, emphasis was laid upon the ability and willingness of the new government to meet its international obligations, and this was the reason offered for the refusal of the United States to recognize the Soviet government.[53] In

[49] Mr. Warren Austin, representative of the United States, said to the Security Council in 1948, with regard to recognition of Israel, "I should regard it as highly improper for me to admit that any country on earth can question the sovereignty of the United States of America in the exercise of that high political act of recognition. . . ." U.N., Security Council, Third Year, *Official Records*, No. 68 (294th Meeting), p. 16.

[50] The United States gave recognition to the Soviet Union by exchange of notes stating certain agreements made. See Hackworth, I, pp. 298-405; *Survey*, 1933, p. 290. Six formulas for granting recognition are listed by Bishop, p. 220.

[51] The contrary is maintained by some writers. Thus Hall says: "Theoretically a politically organised community enters of right into the family of states and must be treated in accordance with law, as soon as it is able to show that it possesses the marks of a state," Hall, p. 103. See also H. Lauterpacht, *Recognition in International Law* (New York, 1947). *Contra*, Hyde, I, p. 55; Fauchille, I, No. 203; Oppenheim, I, § 71.

[52] Mr. Buchanan, Secretary of State, to Mr. Rush, 1848, Moore, *Digest*, I, p. 124; see also Hackworth, I, § 33.

[53] "Some speak as though stability was all that was necessary. What, however, would avail mere stability in the prosecution of a policy of repudiation and confiscation? In the case of Russia, we have a very easy test of a matter of fundamental importance, and that is of good faith in the discharge of international obligations." The obligations in which Russia had failed, according to Secretary Hughes, were repudiation of debts, confiscation of property, and attempts to stir up revolution in other countries. *A.J.*, 17 (1923), p. 297; Hyde, I, p. 45.

1913, President Wilson inaugurated a radical change, adopted by the Central American republics, who agreed not to recognize "any other government which may come into power in any of the five Republics as a consequence of a coup d'etat or a revolution against a recognized Government, so long as the freely elected representatives of the people thereof have not constitutionally reorganized the country."[54] This was an unworkable policy, and it was abandoned by Secretary of State Stimson, who in 1931 said that the policy was to base recognition, "not upon the question of the constitutional legitimacy of the new government, but upon its de facto capacity to fulfill its obligations as a member of the family of nations."[55]

LEGAL EFFECTS. The legal effects of recognition and nonrecognition have produced a complicated jurisprudence, much too complicated for study here.[56] For the most part, the effects of failure to recognize are political or practical, but occasionally a legal problem arises which causes embarrassment or loss. The rule seems to be firm that an unrecognized state cannot sue in the courts of the state which refuses recognition. It is for the executive department to grant or refuse recognition and the courts are bound by its decisions. When recognition is given, its effects are retroactive and validate the acts from the beginning of the recognized government. In general, both recognizing and unrecognized states may suffer in commercial relations because of the lack of diplomatic agencies to further and protect trade.

To sum up, recognition is at present an arbitrary, unilateral, and haphazard proceeding which could and should be made much more useful. If it means anything at all, it should mean that the state recognized is regarded by the recognizing state as qualified for legal membership in the community of nations and entitled to rights and duties under international law. It should be a means of protecting the law of the community and should not be sacrificed for purposes of emotion, or political or commercial profit. It could be much more valuable as a collective procedure of the community as a whole, rather than of members individually, through which a state should pass before admission to rights and duties of membership. Perhaps it would be better

54 *Conference on Central American Affairs* (Washington, Government Printing Office, 1922-23), p. 287; Hackworth, I, p. 188.

55 Secretary Stimson's address was printed as Dept. of State Pub., No. 156 (1931). See also Taylor Cole, *The Recognition Policy of the United States since 1901* (New Orleans, 1928); G. H. Hackworth, "The Policy of the United States in Recognizing New Governments During the Past Twenty-five Years," *Proc. Am. Soc.*, 1931, pp. 120-31.

56 For this, see especially the editorial notes in Briggs and cases and citations therein given.

to say that if the community of nations was properly organized, recognition would no longer be necessary.[57]

20. CONTINUING PERSONALITY AND STATE SUCCESSION[58]

SUCCESSION OF GOVERNMENTS. When a member has been admitted to the community of nations, with determinate boundaries within which to exercise jurisdiction, its character as a member remains unchanged until the termination of its existence. This is true regardless of modification in its internal organization, and regardless also, in general, of increase or diminution in its territorial area.[59] A violent change of government therein may involve the need of recognition for the new government, but does not affect the rights or obligations of the state which it serves: it merely raises the question whether the community of nations regards the new government as properly qualified to act with authority and propriety for its state. Treaties continue to be binding, and financial obligations must still be met; property rights are unaffected, and claims for damages due to violations of international law continue. "A state neither loses any of its rights, nor is discharged from any of its duties, by a change of form in its civil government. The body politic is still the same, though it may have a different organ of communication."[60]

It sometimes happens that decrease in territorial area may make it physically impossible for a state to discharge its obligations. This is notably true of obligations of a local nature, connected with territory now alienated. Sometimes the generally weakened resources of a state do not permit it to meet its financial obligations. In such a situation, special arrangements must be made by convention, as was done in Article 254 of the Treaty of Versailles. The Allies laid down the rule that "the partition of the pre-war debt of the German Empire and

[57] See Bishop, p. 234; Briggs, p. 66; and in *Proc. Am. Soc.*, 1950, p. 169; and Jessup, p. 44.

[58] On this topic: E. J. S. Castrén, "Recent Aspects of the Succession of States," *Hague Acad.*, 78 (1951), p. 385; E. H. Feilchenfeld, *Public Debts and State Succession* (New York, 1931); M. Huber, *Die Staatensuccession* (Leipzig, 1898); A. B. Keith, *The Theory of State Succession, with special reference to English and colonial law* (London, 1907); J. L. Kunz, "Identity of States under International Law," *A.J.*, 49 (1955), p. 68; A. N. Sack, *Effets des transformations des Etats sur leurs dettes publiques et autres obligations financières* (Paris, 1927); Wilkinson, *The American Doctrine of State Succession* (Baltimore, 1934).

[59] *The Sapphire*, 2 Wallace 164 (1871). See Bishop, pp. 193-95; Briggs, Chap. iii; Hackworth, I, 387.

[60] Chancellor Kent, as quoted in J. B. Scott, *Cases in International Law* (St. Paul, 1922).

the German states will be made in proportion to the contributory power of the ceded territories," and the article above cited did in fact provide a complicated mathematical ratio for such payments.[61]

SUCCESSION OF STATES. But there may be succession of states as well as of governments. A state's existence, as an independent member of the community, may be terminated in a number of ways. While it could possibly result from physical causes, it is usually a political process. Thus, an independent state may be absorbed by one or more states, voluntarily as in the case of Texas, or involuntarily through forcible annexation or incorporation, as in the case of the Transvaal or South African Republic or as in the notorious case of Poland. A state may disappear as the result of division into several states, as happened to the Holy Roman Empire and more recently to Austria-Hungary. When a state dies the problem of inheritance arises, and rules in connection with this problem are put under the title of "State Succession."

State succession may be either universal or partial: universal when a state is entirely absorbed by a state or states; partial, when only part of a state is affected, either by becoming incorporated into another state or by becoming independent. Universal succession is illustrated by the annexation of Texas to the United States, or by the division of Poland between three states. Partial succession is illustrated by the addition of California, a part of Mexico, to the United States, or by the successful revolt of a portion of a state which thereby becomes independent as, for example, the secession of the United States from the British Empire.

Such transfers of territories raise important and perplexing questions as to the succession of rights and duties. There is much dispute over the law of state succession: we can only suggest a few general principles, all of which are probably open to debate. That some rights and some obligations are passed on to the receiving state is not doubted, but just which ones they are, in a given set of circumstances, may be difficult to ascertain. Not all treaties of a defunct state are binding upon its successor. It would be unfair to pass on alliances, or personal affairs of a monarch. Treaties of a political character are excluded and there is debate as to whether commercial treaties and treaties of extradition should be inherited. Sovereign control, together with all public property, passes to the receiving state, but subject to obligations.[62] Contracts in general should be maintained, at any rate those beneficial to the locality. A British court refused to return funds

---

[61] Hyde, I, §§ 124-25, 130.
[62] *U.S. v. Prioleau*, 2 Hemming and Miller 59 (1865).

confiscated by the Transvaal (South African) Republic during its struggle with Great Britain; the plaintiff was a citizen of Great Britain, and an alien might have been able to recover in an international tribunal.[63] That the debts were incurred by the conquered country in resistance to the conqueror should not invalidate the debt.

The conqueror undoubtedly may establish such laws as he pleases over acquired territory, but until he does the old laws remain in force and rights acquired under those laws remain undisturbed: "A cession of territory is never understood to be a cession of property belonging to inhabitants."[64] Citizenship and civic rights depend upon the law of the successor states.

The law of state succession needs revision and clearer statement. It is embarrassed not only by very great difficulties as to justice, but also by anachronistic conceptions of sovereignty and war. It needs to be stated in terms of better guarantees of the rights of the peoples transferred.

RIGHTS AND DUTIES

21. FUNDAMENTAL RIGHTS

The classic texts of international law devote much attention to the so-called fundamental rights of states. Most of these are now severely questioned, yet, as Oppenheim said, "it must be taken into consideration that under the wrong heading of fundamental rights a good many correct statements have been made. . . ."[65] The doctrinal development of international law has been largely derived from these "rights" and they still serve as goals.

It may be suggested that the chief of these "fundamental rights," existence, is a fact rather than a right. There is no right for a state to be born; at best, a state once in existence may claim the right to

---

[63] *West Rand Central Gold Mining Co. v. King*, L.R. (1905) 2 K.B. 391. "As the distinction was not based on arguments and was not approved by any other nation, it could not change the rules of law which existed when the decision was rendered." Feilchenfeld, *op. cit.*, p. 389.

[64] *U.S. v. Percheman*, 7 Peters 51 (1833). See Briggs, p. 236; and *P.C.I.J.*, Series B, No. 6, p. 30.

[65] Oppenheim, I, p. 235. See also Brierly, p. 35; Dickinson, *Equality, passim*; Fauchille, I, Pt. I, pp. 394-756; Fenwick, pp. 150-162; Hall, Chap. viii; Hyde, I, pp. 116-61; Moore, *Digest*, I, pp. 60-66; Westlake, *op. cit.*, pp. 293-303; A. P. Higgins, "The Duties of States," *Proc. Am. Soc.*, 1927, pp. 17-22; J. B. Scott, *The American Institute of International Law: Its Declaration of the Rights and Duties of Nations*, (Washington, 1916); *Draft Declaration on the Rights and Duties of States*, U.N. General Assembly, Fourth Session, *Official Records*, Supp. No. 10 (Report of the International Law Commission).

continue to exist. But the society of nations offers no guarantee, for it has not yet clearly made war or conquest illegal. Article 10 of the Covenant of the League of Nations was intended to protect "existing political independence," but it was not enforced; nor has the United Nations done more. There are no cases in which a tribunal has maintained the right of a state to continue to exist.[66]

SELF-PRESERVATION. Attached to the right of existence, and sometimes identified with it, is the primordial right of self-preservation. It is a natural right, widely recognized in all legal systems. But the protection of a state's existence raises questions which international society has not answered so well as has the state in the case of attack upon an individual. What, in the first place, is this existence which must be defended? Today, at any rate, there is little chance of a state being entirely extinguished as the result of attack. Not even in the bitterest moments of World Wars I and II was it proposed that the state of Germany should be eliminated, as a source of danger or for any other reason, nor has the Soviet Union obliterated the states brought under its control.

But there may be justifiable self-defense against lesser harm than death, and thus one arrives at the question: What interests of the state may properly be protected by force, in the name of defense? and What measures injurious to a state may be regarded as calling for self-defense? At this point, existence becomes confused with jurisdiction, with respect, and with other matters. Within the state there are laws and courts to determine what is legitimate self-defense; in the community of nations, each state determines for itself when it is fighting in self-defense.[67]

There can be no question of the right to take up arms against direct and illegal invasion. The defending state may even anticipate attack and invade the challenging state, provided the attack is imminent and certain; but of this each state is unfortunately its own judge. But the situation may be one in which the danger is less direct. Thus, in 1817, marauders used the Spanish territory of Amelia Island as a base of

[66] Indeed, Hyde says: "The right of a state to continue its life as such may be said to depend in a strict sense upon the effect of its conduct upon the international society. The welfare of that society may not require the maintenance of a particular State; its very extinction may be deemed for the general good." Hyde, I, p. 204.

[67] "Every nation is free at all times and regardless of treaty provisions to defend its territory from attack or invasion and it alone is competent to decide whether circumstances require recourse to war in self-defense." Secretary of State Kellogg, in note accompanying the Pact of Paris (1928). Secretary Stimson later sought to set limitations upon these words by denying to a state an unlimited discretion as to what constitutes self-defense; and Article 51 of the Charter of the United Nations does not leave to a state complete freedom in this respect. See Briggs, p. 985.

operations, and from it plundered commerce in American territory. There was no military action upon the part of Spain against the United States, no threat or even thought of attack; but in view of Spain's failure to restrain the marauders the United States attacked the island.[68] Likewise, when the United States failed to prevent Canadian insurgents from using her territory as a base of operations, British forces destroyed in American territory the ship *Caroline*, which had been used by the insurgents.[69] The principle was stretched further by the famous case of the seizure of the Danish fleet in 1807 by the British, to forestall its seizure by Napoleon. Writers have long been divided as to the legality of that act. But if it can be accepted as a proper act of self-defense, it is not a great step further to justify the German claim of self-defense in invading innocent and neutral Belgium. At what point is the line to be drawn?

We may carry the question further. How far is a state justified in employing the best weapon of self-defense, that is, offense, against indirect threats, such as mobilization, or even more remote threats, such as a steadily increasing army and navy? The Soviet Union regards the chain of bases built round it by the United States as evidence of the aggressive intent of this country; the American people, however, think of it as necessary for self-defense. Are NATO and SEATO and other such arrangements to be regarded as essential for the defense of the United States? Can Israel believe the assertion of Egypt that arms bought from the Soviet Union are solely for defense? It is the uncertainty of answers to such questions that has produced the great competition in armaments, the balance of power, military alliances, etc.[70]

Even further, in this age in which the very existence of one state may depend upon its ability to draw supplies from another state, would it be justifiable self-defense for one state to extort forcibly from another the supplies it needs or to defend itself by military action against high tariffs or other measures detrimental to it?

AGGRESSION AND DEFENSE. The difficulty of the situation lies in the fact that international society has not regarded attack upon one of its members as a crime against that society—though the Nuremburg Tribunal has now made such a declaration. War has not been made

[68] Moore, *Digest*, I, pp. 42, 173.

[69] *Ibid.*, II, § 217.

[70] "First. The Monroe Doctrine is not a policy of aggression; it is a policy of self-defense. . . . The Monroe Doctrine rests 'upon the right of every sovereign state to protect itself by preventing a condition of affairs in which it will be too late to protect itself.'" C. E. Hughes, quoted in *A.J.*, 17 (1923), pp. 615-19. NATO is explained in terms of Article 51 of the Charter; see § 159 below.

illegal.[71] If a state is to be allowed, on its own judgment, to undertake violent measures against another, the latter must equally be allowed to use its own judgment as to how it shall meet the danger it faces. It is not surprising, then, since the state is the sole judge of the necessity for defensive action, that the doctrine of necessity has been pushed to indefensible lengths, and that self-defense has, through abuse, served as an excuse for aggrandizement.

For whatever right of existence or self-preservation a state may have there is a corresponding responsibility. Each state owes to every other state the duty, correlative to the right, of respecting the other's right of self-preservation. It has the duty of preventing conspiracies, and perhaps propaganda, within its territories against other states with which it is on friendly terms. It must not allow its territory to be used as a base for espionage, or for the preparation of military or naval expeditions against other states. The famous *Alabama* Award illustrates the legal force of this latter duty. The state which does not restrain such acts injurious to another state cannot so readily complain if the latter state invades its territory to put down the danger with which it is menaced.

INDEPENDENCE. We have spoken of the importance of independence as a qualification for membership in the community of nations, and have noted that the term has relative significance—that some states may have more independence than others. There is, however, no certain guarantee in law of this so-called right. Article 10 of the Covenant of the League of Nations made an attempt at such a guarantee, but it was abortive. The Charter of the United Nations obligates Members, in Article 2, paragraph 4, to refrain from the use of force against the political independence of any state. Independence, once acquired, may now be better protected by law than in the past, but the community of nations is not yet strong enough to guarantee it as a right.

Nor is it an absolute right; there are correlative duties attached to the freedom of action claimed. The state has jurisdiction over aliens within its territories, but it must protect these aliens according to the requirements of international law. It may not permit its territory, much less its machinery of government, to be used against a foreign state. International law may even—as in the case of minorities—set certain standards for the treatment of a state's own citizens. From the viewpoint of international law, independence means little more than the quality of possessing machinery which, free from regular control or

---

[71] It may be argued that war has been made illegal by the Charter of the United Nations, but the Security Council is bound by no rules of law when it determines the existence of a breach of the peace.

direction by another state, can represent a state authoritatively in its dealings with the community of nations, and which can enforce international law and maintain international justice on behalf of the community within its borders. Insofar as independence relates to membership in the community of nations, an independent state would appear to be one which has been recognized.

INTERVENTION. In connection with independence, writers usually discuss intervention, and a doctrine of nonintervention has been built up which is regarded as the duty correlative to the right of independence. This duty is to refrain from the performance of any act which would violate the internal autonomy or the external independence of another state, such as the making of an arrest by one state within another, or interference in the conduct of the latter's foreign policy. Intervention has been described as "dictatorial interference by a state in the affairs of another state for the purpose of maintaining or altering the actual condition of things."[72] Any interference of an imperative character from the outside with the ordinary and legitimate conduct of its own affairs by a state could be regarded as intervention. The problem is a political rather than a legal one. The argument in cases of intervention is not upon a legal basis, nor before an international court; it would be difficult to show that a state could defend itself against intervention by judicial appeal. On the contrary, treaties have sometimes provided for intervention, and tribunals have rewarded the industry shown in intervening to protect legal rights by conceding to the intervening state a preferential position in the payment of reparation.[73]

For the dearth of evidence as to the legal character of the rule of nonintervention there is excellent reason. Aside from the political considerations which have motivated states in their failure to accept a rule of nonintervention, there are powerful reasons of a more legal nature. One of these is the legality of war. So long as war is not illegal, it is difficult to see how lesser acts of violence can be declared illegal. It has been seen already that the international community is still in the stage of self-help and that there is no common authority to compel the observance of rights. If, then, there should be taken away from states the right of self-help short of war—of which intervention is the most important method—they would be forced to fall back upon the far worse evil of war in order to maintain their legal rights. The objections to intervention are not so much due to its principle as to its abuse.

[72] Oppenheim, I, p. 262.
[73] See the Venezuelan Preferential Claims Case, Scott, *Hague Court Reports*, p. 441.

Intervention is simply a weapon, which may be the sword in the hand of justice, or a club in the hand of a thug. The society of nations cannot eliminate war or intervention until it provides some satisfactory substitute for the protection of rights.

From the viewpoint of developing international government, the question of intervention or nonintervention is one of fundamental importance,[74] and this is shown by the current difficulties of the United Nations with the question. A government, or law, must have a right to intervene; the problem within any state is to find the boundary line between the right of the government to interfere and the right of its subjects to be free from interference. The doctrine of non-intervention means protection for the sovereignty of individual members of the community of nations, and it was therefore put into Article 15, paragraph 8, of the Covenant of the League of Nations and into Article 2, paragraph 7, of the Charter of the United Nations. Strictly interpreted, the latter clause would make impossible almost any recommendation by the United Nations concerning the internal affairs of its Members. It has been the cause of much controversy and, though it involves interpretation of the constitution of the United Nations, it has in practice been handled through political vote rather than as a legal question. Members have seemed to regard intervention —in the form of a recommendation, rather than dictatorial interference—by the organized community of nations as more acceptable than intervention by a state; and they seem to favor a general recommendation more than one addressed to a particular state.[75]

The consistent maintenance of a right of intervention in the past, and the trends today within the United Nations, show that independence is not a fundamental legal right, in the sense that a state has a right not to be interfered with, no matter what it does. Certainly, a state is subject to the restrictions put upon it by international law, and until the community of nations itself takes over the task of protecting the rights of its members and forbids states to use force at will against other states, we cannot expect that states will give up intervention as a means of protecting their own rights.

[74] On the subject of intervention the following works, among many others, may be referred to: H. G. Hodges, *Doctrine of Intervention* (Princeton, 1915); E. C. Stowell, *Intervention in International Law* (Washington, 1921); P. Winfield, "The History of Intervention in International Law," *B.Y.I.L.*, 1922-23, pp. 130-49; P. Winfield, "The Grounds of Intervention in International Law," *B.Y.I.L.*, 1924, pp. 149-62; C. G. Fenwick, "Intervention: Individual and Collective," *A.J.*, 39 (1945), p. 645.

[75] See below, pp. 304-5; *Report of the United Nations Commission on the Racial Situation in South Africa*, U.N. General Assembly, Eighth Session, *Official Records*, Supplement No. 16 (A/2505); L. Preuss, "Article 2 (7) of the Charter of the United Nations and Matters of Domestic Jurisdiction," *Hague Acad.*, LXXIV, p. 553.

EQUALITY.[76] If there were such a thing as absolute sovereignty, then any sovereign state would be the equal of any other (though they would cancel each other out), and extravagant assertions of such equality have been made. Russia and Geneva have equal rights, said Chief Justice Marshall in an oft-quoted statement. How far such an assertion is correct depends upon the viewpoint from which one looks at equality. There are great inequalities in size, in economic strength, in military power, in influence within the community of nations and it is not difficult to find in such inequalities basis for an argument that there should also be inequality in legal rights.

States do not always have equality within international organization. The Concert of Europe was able to exert its will without legal opposition, and the primacy of the Great Powers has long been recognized. This primacy received legal confirmation in the establishment of the Council of the League of Nations, and again, in even more discriminatory fashion, in the Security Council of the United Nations, where it was a noticeable exception to the principle of "sovereign equality" laid down in Article 2, paragraph 1.[77] In international administrative bodies it is not unusual for voting strength to depend upon financial or colonial strength. It is in international conferences of a legislative character, perhaps, that the ancient principle of equality is best maintained, with unfortunate results, as we shall see, upon international legislation.

On the other hand, it is clear, and has been maintained in the courts, that all states are equally entitled to receive such protection as the law of nations offers for the rights they have. The rule that treaties are binding applies equally to all, and the rule that reparation should be made for an injury done in violation of international law in principle affords redress to the smallest as well as the largest of nations. If in practice this protection is not received, it is not due to any lack of approval for the legal principle of equality of rights, but because of the ineffective machinery for judgment and enforcement—a greater

---

[76] On the doctrine of equality of states: P. J. N. Baker, "The Doctrine of Legal Equality of States," *B.Y.I.L.*, 1923-24, p. 1; Dickinson, *Equality;* J. Goebel, Jr., *The Equality of States* (New York, 1923); A. Lande, "Revindication of the Principle of Legal Equality of States, 1871-1914," *Pol. Sci. Q.*, 62 (1947), pp. 258, 398; A. D. McNair, "Equality in International Law," *Michigan Law Review*, 26 (1927), p. 131; H. Kelsen, "The Principle of Sovereign Equality of States as a Basis for International Organization," *Yale Law Journal*, 53 (1944), p. 208; H. Weinschel, "The Doctrine of the Equality of States and its Recent Modifications," *A.J.*, 45 (1951), p. 417. See also *The Antelope*, 10 Wheaton 66, 122 (1825).

[77] It should be noted, on the other hand, that the irresponsible behavior of the majority of small states in the General Assembly of the United Nations is leading to consideration of methods of weighted representation therein.

defect in the international system than in domestic legal systems.

It is impossible to state satisfactory conclusions as to the equality of states in international law. States do not in fact have equal rights, nor do they have equality in the administration of the affairs of the community. And while theoretically the law of nations affords equal protection to all, the protection becomes fictitious when made to depend upon self-help, which reduces it to subordination to superior might. In this situation, the only hope of securing real equality depends upon the developing sense of community responsibility.

RESPECT. Closely allied to sovereignty and equality is the so-called right to respect. This would seem to be rather a matter of etiquette or comity than of law; yet, peculiarly enough, an imposing jurisprudence has been built up about it. Originally, this right was the result of monarchical or nationalistic pride, but today certain parts of it may be explained by the need of protection to be given to those carrying on the intercourse of states. The right to respect manifests itself in the requirement that neither the heads of sovereign states nor their diplomatic representatives or emblems shall be injured or insulted. They are entitled to immunity and special protection in foreign states, and many famous cases uphold this principle as one of law. When Mattueof, the ambassador of Peter the Great in England, was beaten by creditors, his master demanded the heads of those who had so mistreated him; and England was forced to send a special ambassador, bearing an engrossed copy of the Act of Anne which would make such injuries punishable in the future, to offer a formal speech of apology.[78]

A state must have criminal laws to punish those who commit such an injury, and it must make reparation, usually by formal apology, but sometimes even by pecuniary reparation, for the failure to protect the dignity of the foreign state. The line between a legal duty, entailing reparation, and mere ceremonial procedure is sometimes difficult to draw. The formalities of salutes to visiting men-of-war or dignitaries may or may not fall under the head of law. An apology is sometimes to be considered as a discharge of legal liability and sometimes as a response to the demands of etiquette. No agreement could be found as to the line between slander and legitimate criticism; and the language of diplomacy has become shamefully coarse and insulting.

INTERCOURSE. The assertion is often made, and more often denied, that there is a right of intercourse between states. Rather than a right, it would seem to be a fundamental element in community life around

---

[78] This case is found in Ch. de Martens, *Causes Célèbres* (Leipzig-Paris, 1827), I, pp. 47-74, along with many other cases of this type.

which certain rules of law have grown up. Certain methods of intercourse are usual in practice, and rules of positive law have grown up upon the assumption that these methods will be used. Thus, there is no legal right to send to or receive from another state diplomatic agents, but no state can afford to be without these agents of official international intercourse and a detailed system of rules for their protection has developed. Again, a state may refuse to allow entrance to aliens, or may deport them, but such a policy would prove too injurious to a state to be continued indefinitely. Upon the fact that aliens do travel between and reside in different states, a far-reaching code for their protection has grown up, from which a large part of international litigation arises. Or again, a state is free to set up almost any sort of barrier to trade and intercourse, against one or all states. She may prohibit trade entirely, or in certain articles, or with certain states; she may establish high tariffs against some or all states, so far as customary international law is concerned (though there are many treaty limitations); she may require passports and visas.

However, any one of these acts may bring protests or reprisals from other states, such as those which greeted the Smoot-Hawley tariff of 1930 in the United States. As this conflict of interests grows, the clamor for rules to ameliorate the situation becomes stronger, and in such conflicts is to be found the source of law.[79] The factual situation is such that, even though it may not be claimed as a legal right, it would be impossible for a state to forbid all intercourse with other states. One may say that there is no general right of intercourse but that, where a state permits intercourse, international law seeks to protect it. Or, one may say that there is a general right of intercourse, but that states are still free to impose severe restrictions upon the exercise of that right in the interest of national security and prosperity. The result is much the same.

JURISDICTION. The most important right—and duty—of a state is jurisdiction. It is solidly established in jurisprudence, so much so that a separate chapter must be devoted to it.

From the viewpoint of sovereignty, jurisdiction means internal sovereignty, exclusive control over all persons and things within its territory. There are, of course, restrictions, even upon the internal administration of a state, set by international law and they are constantly increasing in number as the needs of the community rise above the claims of the state. "The extent of both the right and the duty of a State to do justice within its own domain, as well as elsewhere, is also

[79] For such struggles, see the discussion of GATT and the ITO in § 121, below.

fixed by international law."[80] The jurisdiction of a state is simply the amount of control left to that state by the community of nations; or, if the statement be preferred, the powers reserved to the states after they have delegated to the community the exercise of certain powers. In practice, vast powers are left to the states, and the community interferes very little with their internal administration. It should be noted that the state not only administers its own affairs, but acts also as the agent of the community of nations to enforce international law within its territory.

22. DUTIES OF STATES

States have been concerned mostly with their rights, but there is an obverse side to every coin, and one side is as important as the other. For every right, there is a correlative duty, and for every wrong there should be a remedy. If a state has rights under international law, it must concede such rights equally to other states and must make reparation when it fails to do so. The rules of law are based upon reciprocity: *do ut des.*

RESPONSIBILITY.[81] Responsibility is the principle which claims the performance of these obligations and demands reparation for their non-performance. It must be set up against the rights enumerated.

The responsibility of a state may arise from its own act, through a governmental agent, causing injury to another state or to an alien; or it may, less directly, arise from the act of an individual within its control, causing injury to another state or to an alien.

Membership in the community of nations presupposes acceptance of the rules of the community. These rules permit to a state exclusive jurisdiction within its borders, with few limitations upon its exercise. But this very competence implies the acceptance by the state of responsibility for internationally illegal acts occurring within its control. If one nation concedes to another a monopoly of control within the boundaries of the latter, and so excludes itself from the possibility of

[80] Hyde, I, p. 440.

[81] On the subject of state responsibility, see Borchard, entire; E. M. Borchard, "Responsibility of States at the Hague Codification Conference," *A.J.*, 24 (1930), p. 517; *Com. Prog. Cod.*, Questionnaire No. 4, *A.J.*, 20 (1926), Special Number, p. 176; Eagleton, entire; A. Freeman, *The International Responsibility of States for Denial of Justice* (London, 1938); *Research in International Law*, Draft Convention on Responsibility of States; F. Garcia-Amador, "State Responsibility in the Light of the New Trends of International Law," *A.J.*, 49 (1955), p. 339. The International Law Commission is now working on this subject.

For cases, see Bishop, Chap. vii, and Briggs, Chap ix.

protecting its own rights therein, it can only be upon the understanding that the latter state will protect those rights and will assume responsibility for injuries done to the other state or its citizens. Thus the territorial control exercised by one state, and the protection exercised by another state over its nationals and interests abroad, become mutually corrective forces, whose interplay is regulated by international law.

While the state may be regarded, from the external viewpoint, as a unity, it is an abstract entity which can deal with other states only through state agents, individuals acting under its authority—though it may *be* injured in its personality, or dignity, as a state. The organization of a state and the apportionment of its powers among its various agents is not ordinarily a matter of interest to the law of nations. Whether the agent acts within or without his competence, whether he be a superior or an inferior agent, does not matter if through his act international law is violated. A state may injure another through the violation of its territorial jurisdiction, as in the case of the capture of the *Florida* within the waters of Brazil,[82] or by breaking a treaty, as in the case of the *Wimbledon*.[83] It may injure an alien through discrimination against him, or by denial of justice, or by other violation of the law for the protection of aliens. The state is not made a guarantor of alien life and property within its limits. For acts of individuals within its jurisdiction injurious to foreign states or to aliens, and even to a large extent for acts of its own agents injurious to aliens, it can be held responsible only if it has failed to use due diligence in preventing the injury, or if it has not put into satisfactory operation the local machinery for the redress of the injury.[84]

PENALTIES. Though the community of nations lacks formal sanctions, severe penalties may be assessed against states which fail to measure up to the international standard of justice. If a state which ordinarily measures up to that standard fails for some reason in a particular case, it will have to make reparation.[85] Consistent failure of this sort will lead the community to disregard local justice as administered in the guilty state, on the ground that its agencies of redress are not worthy of confidence. Other states, a stage further along, have

[82] *The Florida*, 101 U.S. 37 (1879); and see Moore, *Digest*, II, p. 367, and §§ 209-20.
[83] *P.C.I.J.*, Series A, No. 1.
[84] See below, § 34.
[85] As to the measure of damages, see Borchard, pp. 413-30; Eagleton, Chap. viii; C. Eagleton, "Measure of Damages in International Law," *Yale Law Journal*, 39 (1929), pp. 52-76; Hyde, I, §§ 298-99; H. E. Yntema, "Treaties with Germany and Compensation for War Damages," *Columbia Law Review*, 23 (1923), pp. 511-27, and 24 (1924), pp. 134-53.

been subjected to exterritorial jurisdiction, which is removed as ability to give proper protection to aliens is demonstrated. A step further, and the state unable to assure proper protection may find itself reduced to a protectorate; finally, as has been asserted in at least one case, the annexation or absorption of such a state is justified.[86]

Against such measures it is not a sufficient reply to assert that no sovereign state can be interfered with, or that the alien who goes to a state does so at his own risk. International interdependence calls for constant movement of persons from one state to another. Responsibility for such persons cannot be disclaimed on the charge that they seek personal gain. If a person goes to a foreign state for the purpose of making money, this is no more than the baker or the tobacconist is doing at home. In either case, the operation is essential for the satisfaction of the needs of the community, and should be protected by the law of the community. Both his own state and the state to which he goes may profit by the activities of the alien; the community of nations today could not afford to do without his services. There have been abuses of the efforts made to give him protection and the outcry against intervention and imperialism has often been justified, but the remedy should not be sought in surrendering the interests of the community, and their protection by international law, to the wishes of some sovereign state. The solution is rather to be sought in an international organization and law which can offer this protection upon the basis of impartial judgment and collective action in the name of the community. Sovereignty must give way to responsibility, and independence to interdependence. [87]

[86] "And, in the end, growing out of this very transaction, a system was created under which all property rights became so manifestly insecure as to challenge intervention by the British Government in the interest of elementary justice for all concerned, and to lead finally to the disappearance of the state iself. Annexation by Great Britain became an act of political necessity if those principles of justice and fair dealing which prevail in every country where property rights are respected were to be vindicated and applied in the future in this region." R. E. Brown Claim, American and British Claims Arbitration, Report of Fred K. Nielsen (Washington, Government Printing Office, 1926), pp. 198-99. See footnote 73, p. 83, above.

[87] Rousseau concludes his study of independence of states with the remark that if independence is the factor which characterizes the juridical status of the state, it must always be with the corrective, subject to the international responsibility of the state. The jurist may ask, he says, whether the sole worthwhile criterion of the state in international law is not to be found in the fact that a state assumes responsibility for illegal acts imputable to it. Ch. Rousseau, "L'independance de l'État dans l'ordre international," Hague Acad., 73 (1948), pp. 250-51.

Chapter 4

JURISDICTION

23. THE PROBLEM

Whether from a practical or a theoretical viewpoint, the jurisdiction of a state is one of the most important fields of international law and one of the most important divisions of international organization. In the law of jurisdiction is to be found the distribution of powers between the community of nations and its members, and the basis of legal relationships between these members.

Jurisdiction is both a right and a duty. Each state is free to work out its own standards and ideals of justice for its members; and this freedom international law concedes, with certain restrictions. This is one of the chief functions of the state, the *raison d'être* for the foregathering of that particular group of individuals. From their viewpoint, the administration of justice is, on the one hand, a duty internally, and, on the other hand, a right as against other states. But their state is also a member of the community of nations. From the community viewpoint, the state has a right to administer justice to its own members according to its own ideals; but it has also a duty of maintaining the law and the standards of the community within its range of jurisdiction.

In general principle, then, a state is free to organize itself as it sees fit for the administration of justice within its range of control. For this purpose a judicial system would seem to be essential, and it must be one which is able to give to aliens the justice which is required by the law of nations. But a state may set up such courts or other official bodies as it wishes, and these bodies exclusively determine the lawfulness of acts within that jurisdiction. No other state may pass upon their lawfulness; only when they appear to be in conflict with international law may an appeal be made from them, and then to an international tribunal and not to the courts of any other state.

The ordinary basis of the jurisdiction of a state is its own territory, within which it has more or less exclusive control; but the extension of international life and interdependence has led states to claim a legal control over persons or things outside their own territory, in various circumstances.[1] They found it necessary to extend their jurisdiction to cover their own nationals abroad, an extension justifiable by the bond of allegiance and by the duties owed by a citizen to his own state. Of course, and this is an important point, a state cannot arrest or try one of its own citizens in the foreign state; it is only when it has the individual or the thing within its own physical control that a penalty can be enforced.

The extension of a state's jurisdiction beyond this point has been resisted by Anglo-Saxon countries, but the intricacy of modern life is nevertheless pushing both practice and theory farther away from the territorial basis. It was not difficult to admit that a crime committed by a person abroad, which takes effect within a state, is punishable within that state, as, for example, shooting across a frontier. Nor was it difficult to assert that any person who commits acts abroad dangerous to the safety of a state should be liable to punishment if he should ever come within the grasp of the injured country. And from this it is not a far step to assess a penalty against anyone abroad, whether national or alien, who injures a citizen of a state. By now, with crime organized upon an international scale, the question of an international criminal jurisdiction has arisen.

The Report of the Research in International Law dealing with "Jurisdiction with Respect to Crime" lists so concisely the different principles upon which penal jurisdiction is claimed by states that it is quoted here in full:

These five general principles are: first, the territorial principle, determining jurisdiction by reference to the place where the offence is committed; second, the nationality principle, determining jurisdiction by reference to the nationality or national character of the person committing the offence; third, the protective principle, determining jurisdiction by reference to the national interest injured by the offence; fourth, the universality principle, determining jurisdiction by reference to the custody of the person committing the offence; and fifth, the passive personality principle, determining jurisdiction by reference to the nationality or national character of the person injured by the offence. Of these five principles, the first is everywhere regarded as of primary importance and of fundamental character. The second is universally accepted, though there are striking differences in the extent to which it is used in the different national systems. The third is claimed by most States, regarded with misgivings in a few, and generally ranked as the basis of an auxiliary competence. The fourth is widely, though by no means universally, accepted as

[1] "Far from laying down a general prohibition to the effect that states may not extend the application of their laws and the jurisdiction of their courts to persons, property, and acts outside their territory, it (international law) leaves them in this respect a wide measure of discretion which is limited only in certain cases by prohibitive rules; as regards other cases every State remains free to adopt the principles which it regards as best and most suitable." In the Lotus Case, *P.C.I.J.*, Series A, No. 10, p. 19.

the basis of an auxiliary competence, except for the offence of piracy, with respect to which it is the generally recognized principle of jurisdiction. The fifth, asserted in some form by a considerable number of States and contested by others, is admittedly auxiliary in character and is probably not essential for any State if the ends served are adequately provided for on other principles.[2]

Obviously some overlapping and many conflicts are possible with such varying theories and systems. A person may be subject to two jurisdictions, as for taxation, or nationality. It is usually true that the man who has been tried in a foreign state will not be tried again for that offense in his home state; but the individual may well be caught between the horns of a dilemma, while the two states vainly argue the question of jurisdiction. There is much confusion on the border lines, and serious studies are now being made to secure greater uniformity. The rules of jurisdiction, of long standing, cover most cases.

24. TERRITORIAL JURISDICTION

In a famous statement, John Marshall laid down the rule which has for many years been the foundation of the jurisdiction of states, that is, a territorial foundation:

The jurisdiction of the nation within its own territory is necessarily exclusive and absolute. It is susceptible of no limitation not imposed by itself. Any restriction upon it, deriving validity from an external source, would imply a diminution of its sovereignty to the extent of the restriction, and an investment of that sovereignty to the same extent in that power which could impose such restriction.[3]

Over all persons and all things within its territorial limits—with the few exceptions made by international law shortly to be noted—a state has exclusive jurisdiction. Its right to make and enforce laws within its boundaries is practically unlimited, and this right will be conceded by the courts of other states, which will usually refuse to sit in judgment over such acts.[4] It does not follow from this that rights given by the laws of one state will be respected in another state.[5] If injustice is

[2] *Research in International Law,* Jurisdiction with regard to Crime, p. 445.

[3] *Schooner Exchange v. M'Faddon,* 7 Cranch 116, 135 (1812).

[4] "Every sovereign state is bound to respect the independence of every other sovereign state, and the courts of one country will not sit in judgment on the acts of the government of another, done within its territory." *Underhill v. Hernandez,* 168 U.S. 250 (1897). The intricacy of modern business, however, sometimes demands such inquiry.

See Bishop, pp. 342, 418 ff., 455 ff.; Briggs, pp. 298 ff.; Hackworth, II, pp. 4 ff.

[5] For examples of such difficulties, see *Caldwell v. Van Vlissingen,* 9 Hare 415 (1851) and *Brown v. Duchesne,* 19 Howard 183 (1856), both involving patent rights; *Strathearn S.S. Co. v. Dillon,* 252 U.S. 348 (1920); *The Creole,* Moore, *Arbitrations,* 4375 (1853).

done by the refusal of the courts to act in such cases, relief must be sought through diplomatic action.

This exclusive jurisdiction comports certain obligations. Since one state cannot send its officials to protect its own citizens in a foreign state, the latter state must assume the responsibility for protecting those persons—a matter which will be considered below. It must also prevent injury to other states emanating from within its territory; it must not allow noxious fumes to cross from its territory into that of another state, nor permit filibustering expeditions or conspiracies to be prepared against other states; other questions are under consideration today, such as diverting the waters of an international river, or permitting propaganda broadcasting. The famous *Alabama* Award against England resulted from the failure of England to use due diligence in preventing the equipping of a privateer which could be used by the Confederacy against the North in the Civil War. In 1954, Costa Rica charged that Nicaragua was a base for the operation of a rebellion against her government and asked the intervention of the Organization of American States.[6]

In ordinary circumstances, no state may exercise jurisdiction within another state. It is not free to make an arrest or seizure therein. When a detachment from a German warship attempted to arrest deserters in a Brazilian port, and when the United States captured a Confederate vessel, the *Florida*, within Brazilian waters, it was admitted that the acts were illegal, and reparation was made.[7] Nor can one state set up a court within another state, nor recruit soldiers therein, as Citizen Genêt discovered in the early days of the American Republic.[8] Foreign military forces may not pass through a state without its permission. On the whole, the exercise of territorial jurisdiction is the highest manifestation of sovereignty and to interfere with it is illegal and may be regarded as insulting.

Territorial jurisdiction includes aliens. The alien owes temporary allegiance to the state of his residence and may be punished for failure therein.[9] Whether he is exempt when he violates local jurisdiction upon instructions from his own state is perhaps debatable, but this may

---

[6] See the *Trail Smelter* case between the United States and Canada, Dept. of State Pub., Arbitration Series No. 8. As to filibustering, Moore, *Digest*, III, pp. 178-80, VII, pp. 908, 917. Also, as to aid against neighbors, Corfu Channel Case, *I.C.J. Reports*, 1949, p. 4, and Greek Frontier incidents, *U.N. Doc.* S/360 and A/519. On broadcasting, J. B. Whitton, "Efforts to Curb Dangerous Propaganda," *A.J.*, 41 (1947), p. 899. On rivers and other things, J. Andrassy, "Les Relations Internationales de Voisinage," *Hague Acad.*, 79 (1951), p. 77.

[7] Moore, *Digest*, II, pp. 367, 587 and IV, § 623; Hackworth, II, p. 282.

[8] Moore, *Digest*, II, § 224.

[9] *De Jager v. Natal*, L.R. (1907) A.C. 326; the case of "Lord Haw-Haw," Bishop, p. 344; Hyde, I, § 219; and refer to § 33 below.

be maintained as a general rule. On the other hand, his own state may not arrest him in another state, except through extradition, and criminals may thus, to some extent, find refuge in foreign lands.

TERRITORIAL WATERS. The jurisdiction of a state extends out to the limits of its territorial waters, though within these waters it is slightly limited by international law.[10] It is difficult at times to discern whether these limitations, ordinary in practice, are set by comity or by international law. There is no doubt of the rule permitting innocent passage to foreign merchantmen through these waters. These ships must, however, and especially within a port, conform to local regulations as to pilotage, navigation, sanitation, etc. In matters involving internal order and discipline on board the vessel, even minor violations at local law, the local authorities do not usually interfere, leaving adjustment to the master of the vessel or to his state; but if the events on board are such as to disturb public order, the local state may assume jurisdiction. To what extent it will do so is apparently a matter for its own determination, and it is difficult to predetermine just how serious a breach of public order is necessary to inspire it to action. The practice of the United States is shown in the case of Wildenhus, who had committed murder on board a Belgian vessel in a New Jersey port. Over the protest of the Belgian consul, who sought a writ of habeas corpus, the New Jersey court tried the case, and its right to do so was upheld by the Supreme Court. French policy is more generous, leaving to the state of the ship a large degree of control. This was illustrated in the peculiar case of *Regina* v. *Anderson*, in which an American citizen committed murder upon a British vessel within French waters. The French courts did not try the case, and the American was convicted in a British court.[11]

In this case, the British court observed that either the United States or France could as well have taken jurisdiction. Thus concurrent jurisdiction is possible; and on the other hand, it is possible that the murderer could go untried, for lack of laws within one state authorizing his trial. In the famous case of *Queen* v. *Keyn*, the captain of a

---

[10] Concerning jurisdiction in territorial waters, see *Com. Prog. Cod.*, "Questionnaire No. 2, Territorial Waters," *A.J.*, 20 (1926), Special Number, pp. 62-147; Hyde, I, §§ 221-226; Hackworth, II, pp. 208-82; P. C. Jessup, *The Law of Territorial Waters and Maritime Jurisdiction* (New York, 1927); W. E. Masterson, *Jurisdiction in Marginal Seas* (New York, 1929); L. *of N. Doc.* C.351.M.145, 1930.V.14; *Research in International Law*, The Law of Territorial Waters; and refer to § 45 below.

[11] *Wildenhus* v. *U.S.*, 120 U.S. 1 (1887); *Regina* v. *Anderson*, 11 Cox, Criminal Cases, 198 (1868); *Chung Chi Cheung* v. *The King*, Judicial Committee of the Privy Council (1939) A.C. 60. As to French policy, see *The Sally and the Newton*, translated in Dickinson, *Cases*, p. 434, and comments in Jessup, p. 145. For other cases in this field, see Dickinson, *Cases*, pp. 433-512; Hackworth, II, §§ 139-40; Bishop, pp. 371 ff.; Briggs, pp. 333-46.

German vessel had been convicted by a British court of manslaughter because of a collision within the British three-mile limit. A higher court reversed the verdict for lack of jurisdiction, since no British statute had been provided authorizing the court to try such a case. The British Parliament at once remedied this defect by passing the Territorial Waters Jurisdiction Act of 1878.[12]

The concurrence or conflict of two jurisdictions often puts a shipmaster into embarrasing situations. A British court convicted a British master for false imprisonment because he had transported a banished person from Chile, an act authorized by the Chilean government, but illegal under British laws.[13] A similar difficulty was raised by the Eighteenth Amendment to the Constitution of the United States, which raised the question of enforcement on foreign vessels in territorial waters. In the case of *Cunard* v. *Mellon*, the Supreme Court upheld the right of the United States to prevent foreign vessels from bringing in liquor solely for the use of passengers and crew and even under seal. A foreign vessel might thus be deprived of such beverages for the entire voyage and in some cases was forced to violate its own state's laws where such laws required liquor to be carried for the crew.[14]

AIR. Is the atmosphere above a state to be included in its territorial jurisdiction? Little help is to be found in national jurisprudence in answering this question. The injury done by a signboard jutting out over a neighbor's land, or by a balloon falling into a field, is not to be compared with the great problems of military or commercial aviation or of atomic radiation, and their effects upon subjacent territory.[15]

Two principal theories appeared. One claimed that the sovereignty of the state over its own territory extended *usque ad coelum;* the other asserted that the air, like the high seas, was free to all. The high air, however, is a situation quite different from the high seas; and tragic recollections of war damages from the air left each state uncompromising in its desire for complete control over the air above. Article 1 of

---

[12] *Queen v. Keyn*, L.R. (1876) 2 Ex. Div. 63.

[13] *Regina v. Lesley*, 8 Cox, Criminal Cases, 269 (1860).

[14] *Cunard v. Mellon*, 262 U.S. 100 (1923). See *Cook v. U.S.*, 288 U.S. 102 (1933). This situation was adjusted, to some extent, by the treaty with England of January 23, 1924, which allowed liquor to be brought in under seal in return for the right to pursue suspected British vessels for a certain distance beyond the three-mile limit. *Treaty Series* (U.S.), No. 685; *A.J.*, 18 (1924), Supp., p. 127.

[15] As to aerial jurisdiction, see Bishop, pp. 285-91; Briggs, pp. 320 ff.; J. C. Cooper, *The Right to Fly* (1947); Fauchille, I, Pt. II, pp. 581 ff.; Hackworth, IV, pp. 357-91; A. K. Kuhn, "International Aerial Navigation and the Peace Conference," *A.J.*, 14 (1920), p. 369; Oliver Lissitzyn, *International Air Transport and National Policy* (1942); A. D. McNair, *The Law of the Air* (2nd ed., 1953); C. N. Shawcross and K. Beaumont, *Air Law* (2nd ed., 1951).

the Convention on Aerial Navigation of 1919 therefore read: "The High Contracting Parties recognize that every Power has complete and exclusive sovereignty over the air space above its territory"; but Article 2 allowed "freedom of innocent passage above its territory to the aircraft of the other contracting states, provided that the conditions laid down in the present Convention are observed."[16]

The principle thus enunciated has in general been followed ever since. The Convention of 1919 was superseded by the Convention on International Civil Organization of 1944 and other arrangements made since that time; there is now an International Civil Aviation Organization.[17] States have been reluctant to submit to a general multilateral treaty and a large part of international air transport is now carried on through bilateral arrangements between the states concerned. It remains true that each state has sovereignty over the air above, insofar as this is not limited by treaty arrangements, and that it has the right to admit, or to deny admission to, any plane; the air above is not like the high seas, free to all.[18]

RADIO. The same principles of national sovereignty apparently apply to radio communication. A state is free, legally if not actually, to prevent the passage of radio waves across its territory. Conferences were held at Berlin in 1903 and 1906. At the International Radiotelegraphic Conference at London in 1912 rules were laid down for communication from ship to ship and from ship to shore, absolute priority being given to SOS calls. The Washington Conference of 1927 extended the application of previous rules to all radio stations; and there were further conferences at Madrid (1932) and Cairo (1938). The chief problem was distribution of channels, but there are many other problems. In 1932 the International Telecommunications Union was set up, and it was reorganized in 1947 to become one of the specialized agencies of the United Nations.[19]

---

[16] The Convention may be found in *L.N.T.S.*, LVIII, p. 346, and in Hudson, *International Legislation*, I, p. 359.

[17] See § 114, below.

[18] New problems are constantly arising and each raises questions as to former freedoms, whether over the land or the sea. See Myres McDougal and N. A. Schlei, "The Hydrogen Bomb Tests in Perspective: Lawful Measures for Security," *Yale Law Journal*, 64 (1955), p. 648; O. Lissitzyn, "The Treatment of Aerial Intruders in Recent Practice and International Law," *A.J.*, 47 (1953), p. 559. U.S. weather balloons floating over the Soviet Union brought complaints from that state early in 1956. See Bishop, p. 374, note.

[19] See § 119 below; also Fauchille, I, Pt. II, pp. 633 ff.; Hackworth, IV, pp. 277 ff.; Hyde, I, § 192; O. Mance, *International Communications* (London, 1943); J. D. Tomlinson, *International Control of Radiocommunications* (Michigan, 1945).

25. LIMITATIONS UPON TERRITORIAL JURISDICTION

There are, as has been above noted, some limitations upon the absolute right of jurisdiction which a state enjoys in its own territory; and these limitations are important as revealing the extent to which international law has found it necessary to interfere with the control which a state has in its own territorial area. Some of these limitations are set by customary international law, such, for example, as the use of territorial waters or the protection of aliens; others, a rapidly increasing field, are set by treaty and include such things as the protection of minorities, the use of straits and canals, the navigation of rivers, or land and air transit. The latter are too variegated to study at this point and will be discussed in other connections; but it is necessary now to consider some of the more usual limitations, especially those set by customary international law.

SERVITUDES. Writers disagree widely as to what constitutes an international servitude and its significance.[20] It may, perhaps, be compared in some respects to an easement in domestic law. By most writers it is attached to territory, and there is much disagreement as to whether a servitude is a limitation upon sovereignty. Some writers, and an international tribunal in one important case, have even denied the existence of servitudes.[21] Such limitations are usually set by treaties, and it is difficult to see why some treaty limitations should be called servitudes while others are not.

IMMUNITIES. Doubtless the best established of the restrictions upon territorial control are the so-called diplomatic immunities and other such immunities attached to the sovereign state. These were formerly based upon the character of personal sovereignty, or upon the equal character of sovereign states, and the fiction of the exterritorial quality of the diplomat and his belongings was developed. Today they are justified by the needs of international intercourse and are measured by these needs.[22] The head of a state cannot be arrested or tried or other-

[20] As to servitudes, see Bishop, p. 301; Briggs, pp. 313-20; G. Crusen, "Les servitudes internationales," *Hague Acad.*, 1928, II, pp. 5-74; Dickinson, *Equality*, pp. 382-99; Fenwick, Chap. xvi; A. D. McNair, "So-called State Servitudes," *B.Y.I.L.*, 1925, pp. 111-27; P. B. Potter, "The Doctrine of Servitudes in International Law," *A.J.*, 9 (1915), pp. 627-41; H. D. Reid, *International Servitudes* (1932).

[21] It was denied by the Hague Tribunal in the North Atlantic Coast Fisheries Case, Scott, *Hague Court Reports*, pp. 159-60. For other cases, see Dickinson, *Cases*, pp. 382-99; Hudson, *Cases*, pp. 486-502; Scott, pp. 255-64.

[22] "It is perfectly clear that ex-territoriality is a fiction which has no foundation either in law or in fact . . . there are sound practical as well as theoretical reasons for abandoning the term 'ex-territoriality,' for the mere employment of this unfortunate expression is liable to lead to errors and to legal consequences which are absolutely inadmissible." *Com. Prog. Cod.*, "Diplomatic Privileges and Immunities," *A.J.*, 20 (1926), Special Number, p. 153.

wise subjected to jurisdiction within a foreign state; nor can his ambassadors, ministers, or other members of his diplomatic representation.[23] Consuls, however, are entitled to these immunities only for their official archives, but in practice they are given many privileges, often affirmed by treaties. The increasing number of diplomatic agents and their concentration at headquarters of international organizations, such as Geneva or New York, led to reconsideration of immunities and the present tendency is to limit them to those which are really essential to the performance of high diplomatic duties, and to reduce the number of those who are entitled to enjoy all privileges.[24]

ARMY. A foreign military force may not enter a friendly state without permission, and when such permission is given no jurisdiction will be taken by that state over members of the force, so long as they remain attached to it and under control of their officers. It has been maintained that members of a military force entering a state without its permission should be given no exemption but should be subjected to the ordinary laws of the land for offenses committed therein. While this results logically from exclusive jurisdiction, it is harsh logic; the individual has no opportunity for judging whether or not the expedition is justified by international law; he must obey and not reason why. When McLeod was arrested and tried in New York State for murder resulting from his participation in the *Caroline* episode, England emphatically demanded his release and Secretary of State Webster admitted the justice of the demand.[25]

PUBLIC VESSELS. Unlike an army, a foreign warship is assumed to have a right of entry into the territorial waters of any state, unless expressly prohibited. Within the territory of a foreign state it is exempt from jurisdiction, though it is expected to observe navigation, sanitary, and other such regulations. The vessel itself is inviolable and no one on board may be arrested. It is thus possible for a warship to give asylum to local offenders, a practice which is to be reprobated, although sometimes justified as a humanitarian measure. Members of the crew ashore have been held liable to local jurisdiction, though in ordinary practice those guilty of petty infractions of the law, such as drunkenness, are returned to their ship.

Other public vessels have consistently been granted the same im-

[23] This subject is further discussed in § 85 below, where citations may be found.

[24] As to international organizations, refer to § 85 below, and see Briggs, p. 793 ff.; Martin Hill, *Immunities and Privileges of International Organizations* (1947).

[25] Moore, *Digest*, II, pp. 25-26; Hyde, I, §§ 201-02; *Arce v. State of Texas*, 202 S.W. 951 (1918); *Horn v. Mitchell*, 223 Fed 549 (1915). The large numbers of American soldiers stationed in England and elsewhere during and after World War II led to special agreements, but the principle above stated was maintained.

munity.[26] The principle involved is, according to Hyde, "not the ownership or exclusive possession of a ship by a foreign sovereign, . . . but rather the appropriation and devotion of the vessel to the public service under governmental authority."[27] The use of such a vessel for commercial purposes does not necessarily deprive it of its public character.[28] Recently, however, the number of cases in which governments have undertaken enterprises distinctly business or commercial in character has brought this principle under heavy criticism. In such cases, to claim immunity would seem unfair in competition with private enterprises. But while courts have at times recognized the changed situation, they have consistently denied that it was within their power to change the law, and the rule seems still to be one of immunity.[29] To change it requires international legislation, a slow and difficult process, though some advance was recorded by the Brussels Conference of 1926. Seventeen states there agreed that vessels owned and operated by states, with their cargoes and passengers, should be subject to local jurisdiction, though nontrading public vessels and ships of war must be sued in their own countries. In 1952, the United States Department of State took the position that immunity should not be granted for private acts.[30] The status of state aircraft is not yet clear, though their immunities seem more restricted.

[26] The Sapphire, 11 Wall. 164 (1871); The Parlement Belge, L.R. (1880) 5 Prob. Div. 197. There are numerous recent cases, for which see Dickinson, Cases, pp. 594-621; Evans, pp. 232-61; Hudson, Cases, pp. 546-64; Scott, pp. 300-10. In general as to the immunities of public vessels, see Com. Prog. Cod., "Legal Status of Government Ships Employed in Commerce," A.J., 20 (1926), Special Number, pp. 260-78; J. W. Garner, "Immunity of State-Owned Ships Employed in Commerce," B.Y.I.L., 1925, pp. 128-43; A. D. McNair, "Judicial Recognition of States and Governments and the Immunity of Public Ships," B.Y.I.L., 1921-22, pp. 57-74; Bishop, p. 421.

[27] Hyde, II, p. 837.

[28] The Parlement Belge, L.R. 4 P.D. 129; Berizzi Bros. v. Pesaro, 271 U.S. 562 (1926); Compania Española v. Navemar, 303 U.S. 68 (1938); see also Annual Digest (1919-22), Case No. 105, where a South African court said "any use of a vessel for the purpose of obtaining revenue for the State is a public purpose, just as its use for the protection of the State is public."

[29] In a case involving one of the United States Shipping Board vessels, a German court said: "Admittedly proposals tending toward the abolition of the immunity allowed to state property serving private purposes, or tending towards, at least, a restriction of such immunity in the international law of the sea, have been finding increasing favor among competent authorities. But this development has not become so generally pronounced in the practice of international intercourse that one should deduce from it a legally valid change of the principles of international law cited above." The Ice King, translated in Hudson, Cases, pp. 557-58.

[30] The Brussels treaty is found in L.N.T.S., 176, p. 199; it is quoted in Briggs, p. 499. The statement of the Department of State is in Dept. of State Bull., XXVI, p. 984; it is quoted in Bishop, p. 434. See National City Bank of New York v. Republic of China, 348 U.S. 356 (1955); W. W. Bishop, "Immunity from Taxation of Foreign State Owned Property," A.J., 46 (1952), p. 239.

OTHER STATE PROPERTY. An analogous situation is found with regard to other property of a state. A sovereign cannot be sued in foreign courts and it thus becomes impossible to sue and attach his property.[31] The foreign sovereign may sue in a local court, but if he thus submits himself to jurisdiction, he must accept judgments with the conditions attached and must be prepared to allow suits for counterclaims.[32]

EXTERRITORIAL JURISDICTION. Another exemption, now practically extinct, is what is known as exterritorial or consular jurisdiction.[33] In various historical developments in centuries past, a state has been permitted, or has assumed the right, to administer justice to its own subjects in a foreign state. The practice was early abolished in Europe, but was long maintained in countries whose administration of justice was regarded as so different or so deficient as to justify it. As these states secured stability, or measured up to the international standard of justice, the restrictions were removed. Japan freed herself in 1899; the capitulations were abolished for Turkey by the Treaty of Lausanne in 1923; the United States and Great Britain were negotiating for the termination of their extraterritorial rights in China when World War II intervened.

To sum up, the exceptions to territorial jurisdiction are not widespread or of very great importance. On the understanding that it carries with it responsibility, the jurisdiction of states is being extended; but where it conflicts with the needs of the community it remains limited, or added limitations are imposed. Jurisdiction is more and more measured by the needs of the community of nations rather than by national claims to sovereignty, and its extension is in accordance with the use made by the community of the machinery of the state. How far this development will continue is now uncertain, but there are tendencies toward extending it beyond territorial limits and making jurisdiction concurrent or universal. To these developments we must now turn.

---

[31] *De Haber v. Queen of Portugal*, L.R. (1851) 17 Q.B. 196; *Vavasseur v. Krupp*, L.R. (1878) 9 Ch. Div. 351; *French Republic v. Jefferson County*, 200 Kentucky 18 (1923). See *Research in International Law*, Competence of Courts in regard to Foreign States; Bishop, pp. 434 ff.; Briggs, pp. 437 ff.

[32] *U.S. v. Prioleau*, 2 Hemming and Miller 559 (1865).

[33] The term "exterritorial" is used with several meanings. It has been applied to the vessels of a state on the seas, to diplomatic agents and property abroad, to criminal jurisdiction over aliens abroad, or to the special situation above described. See the *Report of the Commission on Exterritoriality in China* (Washington, Government Printing Office, 1926); L. Strisower, "L'Exterritorialité et ses principales applications," *Hague Acad.*, 1923, p. 233.

26. THE HIGH SEAS[34]

A second stage of jurisdiction is that exercised by a state over its own nationals abroad. International law interposes no objection to this extension of jurisdiction beyond the territorial limits of a state, though this sometimes produces complications which must be adjusted. Naturally, the first field of such jurisdiction is over nationals upon the high seas, but it has been widely employed to control them in foreign lands as well.

In ancient days the seas were free. With the appearance of the idea of sovereignty, states attempted to extend their sovereign control over parts of the sea. Venice claimed the Adriatic as her own, and England demanded recognition of her sovereignty over the English Channel and the North Sea. This control might exclude fishermen or even commerce, but usually it called merely for salute to the flag. But when Spain and Portugal, under authority of the Papal Bull of Demarcation, attempted to exclude all ships from large parts of the ocean, Queen Elizabeth I, disregarding consistency, asserted that the sea was by natural rights and by the needs of intercourse open equally to all. A famous controversy between writers followed. Grotius, in his *Mare Liberum*, fought for freedom of the seas, and he was answered by the Englishman, Selden, with *Mare Clausum*. It was not until the eighteenth century, with Bynkershoek and others to aid, that the views of Grotius prevailed. By the nineteenth century the extravagant claims of earlier centuries had disappeared, and the great body of salt water outside the territorial limits of states was free to all. This freedom, however, is now being challenged, as we shall shortly see.

Freedom of the seas means that no state has sovereignty over any portion of the seas beyond its territorial waters, and therefore, though with increasing exceptions, that no state can take jurisdiction over any but its own ships upon the high seas.

Upon the ocean, then, in time of peace, all possess an entire equality. It is the common highway of all, appropriated to the use of all; and no one can vindicate to himself a superior or exclusive prerogative there. Every ship sails there with the unquestionable right of pursuing her own lawful business without interruption; but, whatever may be that business, she is bound to pursue it in such a manner as not to violate the rights of others. The general maxim in such cases is, *sic utere tuo, non alienum laedas*.[35]

[34] As to jurisdiction on the high seas, consult F. W. Fulton, *The Sovereignty of the Sea* (Edinburgh, 1911); G. Gidel, *Le Droit International Public de la Mer*, 3 vols. (Paris, 1931-34); A. Pearce Higgins, "Le régime juridique des navires de commerce dans la haute mer," *Hague Acad.*, 1929, V, pp. 5-79; Jessup, *Territorial Waters*, Chap. ii; Piggott, *The Freedom of the Seas* (Oxford, 1919); P. B. Potter, *The Freedom of the Seas* (New York, 1924); *U.N. Doc.* P/CN.4/32, and A/CN.4/53.

[35] Justice Story, in the *Marianna Flora*, 11 Wheaton 1 (1826). For other cases as

A State may not acquire territory in the open sea, though it may apparently acquire sub-soil rights, as, for example, a mine or a tunnel extending out underseas.[36]

But freedom cannot be interpreted to mean lawlessness. In order to have some degree of control over ships on the seas, and also because of the personal bond between the state and its subjects, states are allowed jurisdiction over their own ships upon the seas. This was at first justified by the fiction of exterritoriality, but recent cases deny that a ship is "a floating bit of the territory of its state."[37] The basis of jurisdiction seems now to be national character. As Fenwick puts it: "Since it is necessary that some one state should exercise jurisdiction over the vessel, let the state which chooses to assume a degree of responsibility for the vessel by permitting it to fly its flag be the state whose law must be held to control acts done on board the vessel."[38] Each state, to this end, must have its own rules with regard to the registry of vessels under its flag, this giving the vessel national character. The law of the flag state, then, applies on board the vessel and covers crimes there committed and also such questions as marriage and nationality.[39]

While the control of a state over its own vessels provided some degree of order, the interests of the community of nations demanded more. The principle of the freedom of the seas is founded upon the need of intercourse between states, rather than upon the rights of any one state on those seas, and in order to protect this intercourse, rules have been laid down which do not leave vessels entirely free outside their national jurisdictions. There is, for example, the matter of collision between vessels of different states, and of salvage. To care for such matters as these there has grown up a body of maritime law which will be applied by the courts of any state in the same manner, thus constituting a sort of international law.[40] A Convention for the Safety of Life at Sea, of 1929, provides conventional authority for rules concerning collisions, seaworthiness of vessels, radio equipment, iceberg patrol, meteorological data, and such things.

---

to authority on the high seas, see Bishop, pp. 371 ff.; Briggs, Ch. v; Hudson, *Cases*, pp. 658-729.

[36] May a state set up an anchored base on the high seas, such as a radar or aviation station?

[37] *Lam Mow*, 19 Fed (2nd) 951 (1927); *Cunard v. Mellon*, 262 U.S. 100 (1923).

[38] Fenwick, pp. 191-92.

[39] As to the nationality of a child born on shipboard, see *Marshall v. Murgatroyd*, L.R. (1870) 6 Q.B. 30; *Lam Mow*, 19 Fed (2nd) 951 (1927). As to marriage, *Fisher v. Fisher*, 250 N.Y. 313 (1929).

[40] "When, therefore, we find such rules of navigation . . . accepted as obligatory rules by more than thirty of the principal commercial states of the world, we are constrained to regard them as in part at least, and so far as relates to these vessels, the law of the sea. . . ." *The Scotia*, 14 Wallace 170 (1872).

Visit and search of foreign vessels, in time of peace, has long been regarded as illegal. "No nation can exercise a right of visitation and search upon the common and unappropriated parts of the sea, save only on the belligerent claim," said Lord Stowell in 1817, and his judgment has been followed by American courts and strongly upheld by the political department of the United States.[41] Nevertheless, there have always been exceptions to the rule and it cannot be maintained in an absolute sense. Piracy, of course, has always been an exception; and if it be conceded that a suspected ship can be searched to determine whether or not it is engaged in piracy, or perhaps slave trade, then any ship can be so searched. Many treaties concede a right of search for protection of submarine cables or fishing, or with regard to arms traffic or for other purposes; and a state will not hesitate to visit and search when necessary for its self-defense, as did Spain in the case of the *Virginius*.[42]

CONTROL BEYOND TERRITORIAL WATERS. Such situations are most apt to be found in the seas adjacent to territorial waters. The three-mile limit is not so firmly established as tradition would have it be; this was revealed at the Conference for the Codification of International Law at The Hague in 1930, under the auspices of the League of Nations, and again in the work of the International Law Commission of the United Nations.[43] Many states, it appeared, claimed sovereignty over territorial waters to an extent of four, six, ten miles or even more. This claim must be distinguished from the numerous claims to jurisdiction (rather than sovereignty) for certain distances and for certain purposes. The United States almost from the beginning of its history has asserted a right to investigate for smuggling as far as twelve miles, and renewed that claim in the Tariff Act of 1922.[44]

41 The United States denied the right claimed by Great Britain to impress into her navy British seamen found on board foreign vessels, or to search for this purpose. Moore, *Digest*, II, p. 987. Later, during the Civil War, a British mail steamer, the *Trent*, carrying two Confederate agents, Mason and Slidell, was stopped by an American warship and the two men removed from it. Secretary of State Seward admitted the justice of the English protest and the two men were relased. See *British and Foreign State Papers*, LV, p. 602; Moore, *Digest*, VII, p. 768; and cases of *Le Louis*, 2 Dodson 210, 245 (1817); *The Antelope*, 10 Wheaton 66 (1825); the *Marianna Flora*, 11 Wheaton 1 (1826); *La Jeune Eugenie*, 2 Mason 409 (1822).

42 Moore, *Digest*, II, pp. 895-903.

43 *Com. Prog. Cod.*, Questionnaire No. 2, "Territorial Waters," found in *A.J.*, 20, (July 1926), Sp. Supp., p. 62; L. of N. Conference for the Codification of International Law, *Bases of Discussion*, II, Territorial Waters (1929.V.2.). See also *Research in International Law*, Territorial Waters, p. 243; and Report of the International Law Commission, General Assembly, Ninth Session, *Official Records*, Supp. No. 9 (A/2693).

44 49 U.S. Stat. 517, C.438 (1922); Bishop, p. 401; Briggs, p. 371.

The doctrine of hot pursuit illustrates another phase of this border problem. During the days of the Eighteenth Amendment in the United States, a Canadian rum-runner, the *I'm Alone*, was discovered ten and a half miles from shore and immediately fled to the high sea. She was pursued for some two hundred miles, warned, and finally sunk, with the loss of one life. The United States justified this act as having been begun within its territorial waters; since the treaty of 1924 gave her a right to search British vessels as far as twelve miles out therefore, it was argued, she could initiate pursuit within the twelve-mile, rather than the three-mile, limit. An arbitral tribunal, however, awarded fifty thousand dollars to Canada, without explaining why; apparently, it felt that the sinking of the vessel was too severe a penalty for the crime committed.[45]

CONTIGUOUS ZONES AND CONTINENTAL SHELF. Since the end of World War II there has been a rapid extension of claims to jurisdiction or to sovereignty in the waters contiguous to territorial waters; these claims reach far out into the hitherto sacred high seas. There have always been disputes over fishing; the effort of the United States to control seal fishing in the Bering Sea will be recalled; more recently, England and Norway took a dispute to the International Court of Justice, which upheld Norway in its claim to control fishing for some distance beyond a three-mile limit drawn parallel to a line which would not follow the sinuosities of the coast and would therefore include deep indentations.[46] Modern methods mean wholesale fishing in large fleets with canneries on board; and this leads, on the one hand, to resentment in adjacent nations against the intruding fishers and, on the other hand, to danger of extinction of an important food supply. The Japanese particularly have found themselves in trouble: Australia was roused by the extent of Japanese pearl fishing in her vicinity; California was aroused by Japanese fishing fleets in her accustomed waters; recently, Korea has drawn a line against them. The ability to drill for undersea oil has produced much interest in the subsoil of the sea; there are questions of laying cables and pipe-lines; there are coral and sponges and other resources of the sea over which competition will develop.

On September 28, 1945, President Truman issued two proclama-

---

45 Dept. of State Pub., Arbitration Series No. 2; Hackworth, II, pp. 703-08; G. G. Fitzmaurice, "The Chase of the *I'm Alone*," *B.Y.I.L.* (1936), p. 82. The doctrine of hot pursuit was admitted by the Canadian government in this correspondence; a leading case for the doctrine was a Canadian case, "The Ship North," *A.J.*, 2 (1908), p. 688.

46 *I.C.J. Reports*, 1951, Judgment of December 18, 1951, p. 116.

tions, one authorizing "conservation zones" for fishing, the other claiming the right to exploit subsoil resources of the sea as far out as the "continental shelf" extends. Both proclamations included the statement: "The character as high seas . . . and the right to their free and unimpeded navigation are in no way thus affected."[47] These stirred up some interest, but little opposition; but they furnished an opening wedge for other states which, unlike the United States, asserted sovereignty not only over subsoil but over the seas themselves for long distances. Peru, Ecuador and Chile reached an agreement claiming sovereignty for some two hundred miles into the South Pacific and under this claim laid a fine on a Greek fishing fleet (owned by Onassis, under the Panamanian flag) of three million dollars; some United States fishing vessels also were seized. A claim made by Argentina, it was reported, would include the Falkland Islands; the United Kingdom is seeking judicial determination of the claim; both she and the United States oppose such extension of sovereignty.

Many states now have regulations, or are displaying concern, over the seas contiguous to their shores, and consideration is given to international administration for the conservation of the resources of the sea. The ramifications are widespread; they involve such things as sponge gathering, whaling, hydrogen bomb experiments, naval manoeuvres, pollution of water, the right of United States flyers to patrol the seas near Communist China. The sanctity of the high seas is thus rudely shaken. Competition for the vast and hitherto unclaimed areas of the ocean is developing rapidly; on the other hand, the interest of the community of nations and the need for regulation is apparent. The International Law Commission is studying the problem, and a conference met in Rome in 1955 to study, in a technical sense, the "living resources of the sea."[48] It remains to be seen how the law concerning jurisdiction over the seas will develop.

[47] 10 Federal Register, pp. 12, 303, 304; quoted in Bishop, pp. 412-14, and in Briggs, pp. 377-84.
The term "continental shelf" refers to the slowly sloping land mass of a continent before it drops deeply into the sea. Its width varies. In general on this subject, see: J. W. Bingham, *Report on the International Law of the Pacific Coast Fisheries* (1938); S. Gutierrez Olivos, *Mar Territorial y Derecho Moderno* (Chile, 1955); L. Leonard, *International Regulation of Fisheries* (1944); M. W. Mouton, *The Continental Shelf* (The Hague, 1952); S. Riesenfeld, *Protection of Coastal Fisheries under International Law* (1942); Myres McDougal and N. A. Schlei, "The Hydrogen Bomb Tests in Perspective: Lawful Measures for Security," *Yale Law Journal*, 64 (1955), p. 648; and several articles in the *American Journal of International Law*, 45 (1951).

[48] Report of the International Law Commission, U.N. General Assembly, *Official Records*, Eighth Session, Supplement No. 9 (A/2456); more particularly the memorandum by Gidel (though it does not bear his name) *U.N. Doc.* A/CN.4/32, and one by Francois, A/CN.4/53. Comments by governments are in A/CN.4/19 (1950).

27. CONTROL OVER NATIONALS
IN FOREIGN LANDS

The extent to which control is claimed over nationals in foreign lands differs widely. Continental states do not hesitate to claim such control; thus, the French Code of Criminal Procedure provides that "Every Frenchman who, outside of the territory of France, is guilty of a crime punishable by French law, may be prosecuted and judged in France."[49] The insistence of states, who have such laws, upon the performance of military service by their nationals who have become naturalized in the United States, has led to many conflicts over the right of expatriation. Anglo-Saxon states have been more hesitant in claiming such jurisdiction because of their emphasis upon the territoriality of law. Nevertheless, says Hyde, "It is generally agreed that a State may punish its nationals for disobeying its commands while within a foreign country, notwithstanding the legal quality which the territorial sovereign may have annexed to the acts of disobedience."[50]

Legislation is in general presumed to be territorial,[51] but it may be specifically directed to acts committed outside the state. Earl Russell, in a famous case, was convicted in the British House of Lords, after a divorce granted in Nevada, for a bigamous marriage contracted in Nevada.[52] The right of the United States to levy an income tax upon its nationals abroad has been sustained by the Supreme Court of the United States; and that Court has held it legitimate to apply a statute against conspiracy to defraud to an act done in Brazil.[53] Other illustrations of jurisdiction over citizens abroad are acts concerning treason against a state, correspondence with foreign governments (Logan Act), slave trading, crimes committed by American consuls abroad, etc.[54] Such interpretations are necessary consequences of the intricacy of modern life, which makes it possible for a person in one state to injure a person in another state, without physical presence or contact. These claims of jurisdiction may lead to conflicts of law, and principles for the settlement of such conflicts are to be found in international private law, though it is difficult at times to distinguish between public and private law and there seems little reason why both should not be regarded as one field of law.

[49] Translated in Dickinson, *Cases*, p. 683; and see *ibid.*, pp. 671, 685.
[50] Hyde, I, pp. 802-803.
[51] Bishop, pp. 342-44; especially, Dickinson, *Cases*, p. 684.
[52] L.R. (1901) A.C. 446.
[53] *Blackmer v. U.S.*, 284 U.S. 421 (1932); *Cook v. Tait*, 265 U.S. 47 (1924); *U.S. v. Bowman*, 260 U.S. 94 (1922).
[54] See Dickinson, *Cases*, p. 691; *Research in International Law*, Jurisdiction with respect to Crime, found also in *A.J.*, 29 (1935), Supp., p. 519. Illustrative cases may be found in any casebook.

28. JURISDICTION OVER ALIENS ABROAD

Another field, more unsettled and debated, is the extension of jurisdiction to cover an offense committed, not by a citizen, and not within the territory of the state, but by an alien abroad. Pushed to its extreme, this theory would lead to the universality of criminal jurisdiction.

The right is clearly admitted in some cases upon the high seas. The doctrine of hot pursuit at times permits it. The most used illustration, however, is piracy. International law confers upon any state the right to arrest and punish any person guilty of piratical acts; and while each state may have its own statutes for this purpose, the right to take jurisdiction over a person of another nationality upon the high seas is exceptionally derived from the rule of international law. Piracy differs from the exercise of jurisdiction over aliens in foreign lands in that in the latter case, no arrest can be made abroad, and punishment may be administered to the alien only if he, or his property, comes within the territorial control of the state.[55]

Aside from such exceptional situations, there is much disagreement. That the exercise of jurisdiction over aliens abroad is illegal has been strongly maintained by the United States and by England. A well-known example is the *Cutting Case*. Cutting, an American citizen, had published in the United States what was regarded as a libel upon a Mexican citizen, and for this he was tried by Mexican courts. Emphatic representations were made by the United States against this action, upon the grounds that it was contrary to international law, that it was unsupported by existing legislation, and that the penal laws of a state can have no extraterritorial application, except to nationals. To this Mexico replied that her action was justified by international law, and she was able to cite the legislation of a number of states in her support. Since neither side surrendered its position and no international court passed upon it, the case is inconclusive.[56]

[55] The international crime of piracy is much more difficult to define than it appears to be. It must apparently be committed upon the high seas; if a pirate comes within the territorial waters of a state, he is subject to the domestic laws as is an ordinary criminal. It is not the absence of authorization which renders them pirates, for a state may engage in piracy. *The Helena*, 4 C. Robinson 3 (1801). Piracy is not merely robbery; but the purpose must apparently be private rather than political. See Hall, § 81; Oppenheim, I, p. 499; *Research in International Law*, Piracy; *In re Piracy Jure Gentium*, Judicial Committee of the Privy Council 1934; *A.J.*, 29 (1935), p. 140; *Com. Prog. Cod.*, "Questionnaire No. 6, Piracy," 1927.V.1, pp. 115-19, and answer of Rumania, pp. 201-22; and Report of the International Law Commission, General Assembly, Tenth Session, *Official Records*, Supp. No. 9, (A/2934), p. 6.

For cases, see Briggs, pp. 361-69; Dickinson, *Cases*, pp. 518-25; Hudson, *Cases*, pp. 692-705.

[56] Moore, *Digest*, II, pp. 228-42; and Briggs, pp. 571-75; Hyde, I, §§ 241-43.

There are exceptions, however, in the practice of the United States, and of England. An alien who commits perjury before an American consular official abroad is punishable.[57] The decision in the case of *Ford* v. *United States* would seem to extend the statute against conspiracy and fraud to aliens.[58] In England, the case of the *King* v. *Godfrey* concedes the right to extradite a person who was not present in Switzerland at the time that he obtained goods by false pretenses therein.[59]

The practice of Continental states reveals a wide and varying range of statutes applying to aliens abroad. Among crimes so covered are those against the safety of the state and against counterfeiting, and, with many varying conditions attached, offenses committed against subjects by foreigners abroad.[60] Continental writers defend this practice as strongly as Anglo-Saxon writers condemn it.

The case of the *Lotus*, before the Permanent Court of International Justice, brought the issue before an international tribunal. A collision occurred upon the high seas between a French ship, the *Lotus*, and a Turkish ship, the *Boz-Kourt*, and the latter was sunk with some loss of life. The officers of both ships were tried and convicted for manslaughter under the Turkish Penal Code, and France objected that such jurisdiction was illegal under international law. The Court refrained from saying that it was legal; but it denied that "international law prohibits a state from exercising jurisdiction in its own territory, in respect of any case which relates to acts which have taken place abroad, and in which it cannot rely upon some permissive rule of international law." The court remarked that while the territorial character of criminal law is fundamental, "it is also true that all or nearly all these systems of law extend their action to offences committed outside the territory of the State which adopts them."[61] The judgment did not satisfy partisans on either side. Anglo-Saxon writers maintain that it was decided on the theory, admitted by them, that a crime may take effect in another jurisdiction—e.g., a shot fired across a frontier, or, in this case, death produced on the Turkish vessel through negligence on

[57] *U.S. Rev. Stat.* § 1750.

[58] *Ford v. U.S.*, 273 U.S. 593 (1927). Expressions in *U.S. v. Bowman*, 260 U.S. 94 (1922), clearly leave the way open to apply the statutes therein cited to aliens, though the court does not speak to that point.

[59] *King v. Godfrey*, L.R. (1923) 1 K.B. 24. See the case of "Lord Haw-Haw," L.R. (1946). A.C. 347, and in *A.J.*, 40 (1946), p. 663.

[60] They are summarized in Moore, *Digest*, II, pp. 258-59, though much development has taken place since that time. See the French, Austrian, and Mexican codes quoted in Dickinson, *Cases*, pp. 671, 675, 691. The Turkish Penal Code, which in this connection is taken directly from the Italian, is found in the *Lotus Case*. See, in general, *Research in International Law*, Jurisdiction with respect to Crime.

[61] The *Lotus Case* stirred up a vast amount of discussion. P.C.I.J., Series A, No. 10.

the French vessel. Writers of the other school equally maintain that the judgment has cleared the way for the development of an international penal law.

29. EXTRADITION[62]

In the absence of universal criminal law, it is obvious that a criminal may take advantage of the numerous exclusive national systems and, merely by stepping across a border, find asylum in another state. To remedy this situation, the practice of extradition has grown up. Extradition refers to the delivery, by the state in which the accused person happens to be, and upon demand of the accusing state, of a person suspected of having committed a crime in the latter state. Fauchille asserts that the duty of extradition exists in customary international law; Oppenheim and others are as emphatic that it rests solely upon treaty.[63] Certainly, international law puts no obstacle in the way of a state which wishes to extradite in the absence of a treaty; but, since each state must determine for itself whether it is willing to trust the judicial system of the requesting state, and whether the crime for which extradition is asked is as serious as it is adjudged by the other state, it does not seem possible to assert a customary rule requiring extradition.

Treaties of extradition are so numerous as to make up for the absence of a customary rule. Certain general principles may be found in them. A person may not be tried for any crime other than that for which he was extradited; he has been surrendered on that specific condition.[64] A certain amount of evidence must be shown. Crimes are interpreted in accordance with the law of the state asking extradition; sometimes it must be a crime according to the law of both states. Political crimes are not ordinarily extraditable, though the difficulty of defining exactly what constitutes a political offense raises a number of problems.[65] There is disagreement also as to whether a state should

[62] On extradition in general see: *Com. Prog. Cod.*, "Report on Extradition," *A.J.*, 20 (1926), Special Supp., p. 243; Hackworth, IV, Chap. xii; Hyde, II, pp. 1012-64; J. B. Moore, *Extradition and Interstate Rendition*, 2 vols. (Boston, 1891); *Research in International Law*, Extradition; A. Rolin, "Quelques questions relatives à l'extradition," *Hague Acad.*, 1923, pp. 181-227.

[63] Fauchille, I, p. 994; Oppenheim, I, p. 565. In *Factor v. Laubenheimer* the Court said: "the principles of international law recognize no right to extradition apart from treaty," 290 U.S. 276 (1933).

[64] *U.S. v. Rauscher*, 119 U.S. 407 (1886). For other cases of extradition, see Bishop, pp. 366-70; Briggs, pp. 580-600; Dickinson, *Cases*, pp. 692-762.

[65] In the English case, *In re Meunier*, L.R. (1894), 2 Q.B. 415, it was held that crimes of anarchists, being directed against society as a whole, were not political crimes and were extraditable. See also *In re Castioni*, L.R. (1891) 1 Q.B. 149.

surrender by extradition one of its own citizens. States which provide for the punishment of their own citizens for certain crimes committed abroad may logically refuse to surrender them for trial for such crimes. The United States, however, which does not make this provision, stands ready in the interests of justice to surrender her own citizens. In the case of *Charlton* v. *Kelly*, the court rejected a plea that the extradition treaty with Italy rested upon a reciprocal basis, and that since Italy refused to surrender her citizens for trial in the United States, the United States should consequently refuse to extradite Charlton to Italy. Without such an interpretation, Charlton would have escaped punishment.[66]

30. THE QUESTION OF INTERNATIONAL JURISDICTION

In the preceding survey of national jurisdictions, it has been seen that there has been a constant effort to expand the jurisdiction of the state in order to give itself proper protection and to secure the proper repression of crime. Criminal methods and organization have steadily improved, and have become international in scope and operation, in such matters, for example, as counterfeiting or smuggling. To meet this development states have used the principles of nationality and of diplomatic protection to extend their control beyond territorial limits, first to their own citizens, and at length to aliens, for crimes committed abroad. Such extensions produced conflicts between various legal and jurisdictional theories, and the question arose as to whether further advance was possible without international agreement. Meanwhile, there had been in process a movement, attracting little attention until the *Lotus* case, which sought to create a universal criminal law and jurisdiction. Organizations were formed, journals published, and conferences held for this purpose.[67] The variety of proposals offered may be considered from the viewpoints of (1) individuals and (2) states.

The situation of individuals and the possibility of violations of international law by them will be considered in the following chapter.

---

[66] *Charlton v. Kelly*, 229 U.S. 447 (1913).

[67] There is an Association International de Droit Pénal, which published the *Revue International de Droit Pénal*. The ideas have been studied and more or less approved by the Institut de Droit International, by the Interparliamentary Union, and by the International Law Association; see the 31st Report (1922), the 33rd Report (1924) and the 34th Report (1926) of the I.L.A. Information and references may be found in V. V. Pella, "Toward an International Criminal Jurisdiction," *A.J.*, 44 (1950), p. 37; and in Historical Survey of the Question of International Criminal Jurisdiction (Secretariat memorandum), *U.N.Doc.* A/CN.4/7/Rev. 1.

Those who advocate an international criminal jurisdiction point to piracy and to violations of the laws of war and neutrality as well-established instances of the capacity of individuals to violate international law; they suggest also counterfeiting, slave trading, breaking of cables, traffic in arms and in women and children, etc., as matters proper to be included under international jurisdiction. These, they say, should be made internationally illegal and subject to punishment by any state (uniformity of law and penalty being established) or by an international court.

Certain crimes of war committed by individuals have always been regarded as illegal, and an unsuccessful attempt was made after World War I, under the Treaty of Versailles, to try the German Kaiser and other Germans for "a supreme offense against international morality and the sanctity of treaties, and for violations of the law of war." This feeling of outrage was greater after World War II; Hitler and Mussolini were extra-legally punished, but trials for many others were successfully carried through, the death penalty being exacted in some cases.

The principal crime which could be committed by a state would be aggressive war-making, which the Pact of Paris attempted to declare illegal; and more and more support has appeared for regarding it as an international crime. It is manifest that an international law and jurisdiction, with much strength behind it, would be needed to handle such a crime. Such legislation would collide violently with the long-accepted theory that a state can commit no crime, but this may be regarded as an anachronistic theory. The idea of a penalty against a state, while usually denied, is not entirely absent in practice and finds support in present-day thinking.[68]

In such a development, the idea of an international criminal court would naturally appear (the Treaty of Versailles provided for such a body to try the Kaiser, but it was never constituted). Before the Committee of Jurists which elaborated the Statute of the Permanent Court of International Justice, Baron Descamps proposed a court which should try crimes against international public order and the universal law of nations; it met with some favor in the committee, but was rejected by the Assembly of the League of Nations. The International Law Association approved in 1924 a plan for a court which should have jurisdiction over violations of international obligations of criminal character by citizens of one state, or by stateless persons, against

[68] See material gathered in C. Eagleton, "Measure of Damages in International Law," *Yale Law Journal,* 391 (1929-30), pp. 61-66; S. Glueck, *War Criminals—Their Prosecution and Punishment* (1944).

another state or its citizens, and over violations of the law of war.[69] A report was submitted in 1931 to the League of Nations, which adopted a resolution encouraging certain private organizations to continue their studies and submit them later for consideration.

Additional impetus was given to the idea of an international criminal law and court by the assassination of King Alexander of Yugoslavia in France in 1934, and by the more recent trials of war criminals following World War II. The former led to adoption by the League of Nations Assembly of a Convention for the Prevention and Suppression of Terrorism and of a Convention for the Creation of an International Criminal Court.[70] This Court was never established, but the International Military Tribunals established at Nuremberg and Yokohama may be regarded as international criminal courts, and around them rages a great debate among international lawyers.[71] A Charter for the International Military Tribunal was agreed upon by the Four Powers, and within it was stated the law to be followed by the Court:

A. Crimes against peace. Namely, planning, preparation, initiation or waging of a war of aggression or a war in violation of international treaties, agreements or assurances, or participation in a common plan or conspiracy for the accomplishment of any of the foregoing.

B. War crimes. Namely, violations of the laws or customs of war. . . .

C. Crimes against humanity. Namely, murder, extermination, enslavement, deportation and other inhumane acts committed against any civilian population, before or during the war; or persecution on political, racial, or religious grounds in execution of, or in conjunction with, any crime within the jurisdiction of the Tribunal, whether or not in violation of the domestic laws of the country where perpetrated.

Leaders, organizers, instigators and accomplices participating in the formulation or execution of a common plan or conspiracy to commit any of the foregoing crimes are responsible for all acts performed by any persons in execution of such plan.

Various questions were raised by this procedure. Could these four victor nations declare international law on behalf of the community

---

[69] *P.C.I.J.*, Advisory Committee of Jurists, *Procès Verbaux* of the Proceedings of the Committee (1920), pp. 49, 129, 498-515. Report of the 34th Meeting of the International Law Association (1926), p. 118, and 31st Report (1922), p. 76.

[70] Conference for the Repression of Terrorism, C.94.M. 47. 1938.V. The former convention was ratified by only one state, the latter by none, though 23 states had signed the former, and 13 the latter. *O.J.*, 1938, Sp. Supp. No. 193, p. 54. See A. Sottile, "Le Terrorisme International," *Hague Acad.*, 65 (1938), pp. 91-184 and bibliography.

[71] From the large literature dealing with this subject, reference may be made to *Trial of War Criminals*, Department of State Publication No. 2420; S. Gueck, *War Criminals—Their Prosecution and Punishment* (New York, 1944); Q. Wright, "War Criminals," *A. J.*, 39 (1945), p. 357.

It should be noted that these tribunals differ in character from the usual national military tribunals which try persons for violations of the laws of war.

of nations, and would it be *ex post facto* law? Is aggressive war finally made a crime? And is it clear now that individuals are subjects of international law and that they may appear before an international court? Do orders from a superior officer afford immunity? What effect would such precedents as here established have upon the conduct of statesmen and military men hereafter?

The "Nürnberg Principles" were approved by fifty-five states in the General Assembly of the United Nations and, under its instructions, the International Law Commission formulated them into rules of law—without, however, saying that they are law. The Genocide Convention, adopted by the General Assembly in 1948, has been ratified by a large number of states (not including the United States).[72] It regards as genocide "acts committed with intent to destroy, in whole or in part, a national, ethnical, racial, or religious group." The efforts in the United Nations to state "human rights" and provide against their violation looks toward an international jurisdiction, as do the attempts to define "aggression," or to state a code of "Offences against the Peace and Security of Mankind."[73] This interest led the Assembly, by Resolution 489(V), to set up a committee to draft a statute for an International Criminal Court, and it submitted such a statute to the Ninth General Assembly.[74] This effort seems a little premature, both as to law and jurisdiction, but there is little doubt that the effort will continue, because of current needs in an interdependent world.

[72] U.N., General Assembly Resolution 260 (III); *U.N. Doc.* A/810; Report of the International Law Commission, General Assembly, Fifth Session, Supp. No. 12 (A/1316), p. 11.

[73] Report of the International Law Commission, General Assembly, Ninth Session, Supp. No. 9 (A/2693), p. 9.

[74] Report of the 1953 Committee on International Criminal Jurisdiction, General Assembly, Ninth Session, Supp. No. 12 (A/2645).

Chapter 5

INDIVIDUALS

31. PERSONALITY IN INTERNATIONAL LAW

In accordance with a generally, though not universally, accepted interpretation of the concept of sovereignty, it has usually been said that states only can be subjects of international law, and that individuals can be no more than objects of that law, in the same category with ships, or horses or pigs, or other chattels. Says Oppenheim: "Subjects of the rights and duties arising from the Law of Nations are states solely and exclusively. An individual human being, such as a king or an ambassador, for example, is never directly a subject of International Law." Elsewhere he classifies individuals in the words: "Persons and things are *objects*, not *subjects*, of the Law of Nations."[1] According to Article 34 of the Statute of the International Court of Justice: "Only States may be parties in cases before the Court."

INTERNATIONAL LAW REACHES INDIVIDUALS. However, in a broad and indirect sense, international law has always sought to protect the individual. In its earlier natural law connections, the state was not regarded as irresponsible, and writers thought in terms of a law superior to the state and able to protect individuals against the state. Humanitarian intervention has been approved by writers and practiced by states. Treaties have contained provisions for the protection of minority groups within a state, and for peoples in mandated areas.

Further than this, however, individuals have long had relationships with international law which positivists have been embarrassed to explain. The positions of pirates, blockade runners, and contraband carriers have often been brought up for explanation. Piracy is unquestionably a violation of international law, but it is one for which no state is responsible, and for which the pirate himself must suffer the

---

[1] Oppenheim, I, pp. 21, 521; and see George Manner, "The Object Theory of the Individual in International Law," *A.J.*, 46 (1952), p. 428.

115

penalty.[2] Article 3 of the Treaty of Washington (unratified) in 1922 made members of submarine crews liable, as pirates, for violations of the law of war as therein laid down. The person who runs a blockade or carries contraband has violated international law and no state is responsible for his act; the duty set by international law is upon the individual rather than upon his state. The Supreme Court of the United States has held that counterfeiting is an offense against the law of nations; and it has found in that law rules which reach down to protect innocent fishermen.[3]

In such cases as these, it is argued, the individual does not come into contact with international law but with domestic law. It is a state, it is pointed out, which punishes the pirate, or which confiscates the blockade-running ship. This is the same argument which we have already condemned: that international law is law only when enforced by state action, and then it is state law. It evades the situation. The authority of the law against piracy on the high seas derives not from a state but from the community of nations. The law which the state executes is not its own law but international law. The pirate or the blockade runner, in fact, has a right not to be punished for what international law has not declared to be illegal.

It must be repeated that international law has not in the past developed its own agencies of execution. It has relied, for the most part, upon states and their machinery. It merely defines piracy and authorizes states to seize pirates, leaving the penalty to be set by the state. Not even this much liberty is allowed to states in the case of those who run blockades or carry contraband, for the penalty in these cases is closely guarded by the law of nations. If international law is part of the law of the land and must be applied by the courts of the land, it is difficult to understand how international law could fail to be applied to individuals during the process.

The community has the power, if it wishes, to deal directly with the individual, and in occasional instances it does so. The Danube and Rhine commissions, for example, are bodies which make regulations affecting individuals, and which can, through their own courts, enforce them directly upon individuals belonging to riparian states. Some of the older international administrative bodies were given power to

---

[2] "Piracy includes acts differing much from each other in kind and in moral value; but one thing they all have in common; they are done under conditions which render it impossible or unfair to hold any state responsible for their commission." Hall, p. 310. For discussion of piracy, and citations, see p. 108 above.

[3] *U.S. v. Arjona*, 120 U.S. 479 (1887); *Paquete Habana*, 175 U.S. 677 (1900); and, for England, *Emperor of Austria v. Day and Kossuth*, 2 Giffard 628 (1861).

fix rules binding upon member states or their nationals, and to enforce decisions upon individuals—e.g., the Sanitary Councils, or the Sugar Union.[4]

INDIVIDUALS BEFORE INTERNATIONAL TRIBUNALS. There have been a number of instances in which an individual was authorized to appear before an international tribunal. A Central American court functioned for a number of years with the right to hear complaints of individuals against states; it was not a successful experiment. The second Hague Conference (1907) proposed an international prize court which, had it been established, would have allowed jurisdiction over individuals.[5] There was considerable discussion in the Committee of Jurists which drafted the Statute of the Permanent Court of International Justice, but the Assembly of the League of Nations held that the time was not yet ripe for permitting individuals to appear before that court. A series of international courts, the Tribunaux Arbitraux Mixtes, was created to try claims of individuals arising under Article 297 of the Treaty of Versailles. These included claims of individuals against states, and the rights claimed were asserted by the tribunals to belong to individuals and not to their states.[6]

The theory of the exclusive personality of the state is so artificial in character that states and tribunals have found it difficult to maintain consistency.[7] According to present practice, an individual may present a claim only with the consent of his own state, which may sacrifice that claim to political or other exigencies. If supported, it is then regarded as the claim of the state, for only states can have rights under international law. Nevertheless, the tribunal must be satisfied that the individual is a national of the claimant state, and if the individual thereafter loses that nationality, the entire claim is lost—though in legal theory it is the claim of the state and should not be affected by anything that the in-

---

[4] See Chap. 7 below.

[5] As to the Central American Court of Justice, see p. 220 below, and A. de Bustamente, *The World Court* (New York, 1925), p. 74. As to the proposed prize court, J. B. Scott, *The Hague Conventions and Declarations of 1899 and 1907* (New York, 1918), p. 189. See also E. M. Borchard, "The Access of Individuals to International Courts," *A.J.*, 24 (1930), p. 359; S. F. Séfériadès, "Le problème de l'accès des particuliers à des juridictions internationales," *Annuaire*, 1929, II, p. 257.

[6] "It is the national who may express a desire for restitution, not the Government. Again, possession is to be restored to the evicted owner, not the Government." *Case of Ex'ors of F. Lederer, Recueil des decisions des tribunaux arbitraux mixtes institués par les traités de paix* (Paris, 1923-24), III, p. 768.

[7] Thus a Claims Convention with Spain in 1802 speaks of "excesses . . . by . . . individuals . . . contrary to the law of nations or to the treaty." Malloy, II, p. 1650. Awards are made by tribunals in the form: "The United States of America, on behalf of B. E. Chattin, $5,000."

dividual may do.[8] Frequently the money is awarded to the individual, but it is always paid to the state, and whether or not the individual will ever receive it depends upon the generosity of his state.[9] Again, the claim is argued upon the ground of the damage done to the individual, not to his state; and damages are measured by his loss, not by that of his state. Such situations are not only ridiculous inconsistencies in legal theory, but show disregard for human justice. The case of stateless persons who, since they have no state to represent them, have no possible access to an international court, is particularly shocking.

THE INDIVIDUAL AS A SUBJECT OF LAW. It is for the individual human being that law and government exist, and it is absurd to deny him access to the protection of international law. A large number of international lawyers have claimed for the individual a position in international law,[10] and an increasing number of organizations demand that the individual be given such protection. Thus, the Institut de Droit International at its 1929 session in New York adopted a Declaration of the International Rights of Man; and the American Law Institute issued a Statement of Essential Human Rights.[11] The opinion of the Nuremberg Tribunal, which the General Assembly of the United Nations

[8] "There must, then, be an individual who has a claim, and a British or American nationality; else we cannot take jurisdiction." Case of McHugh, Sherman and Brain, Moore, *Arbitrations*, p. 3279; see also *ibid.*, pp. 1465, 3063; J. Hanna, "Nationality and War Claims," *Columbia Law Review*, 45 (1945), p. 301.

[9] "A claimant, having a perfectly legal claim, is now dependent for relief primarily upon the political strength or influence of his nation, on its political relations with the country complained against and on the disposition and willingness of the Foreign Office to exert diplomatic efforts in his behalf. His claim becomes the plaything of politics and of their accidents. The government of the injured citizen is subjected to political pressure to espouse what may be a poor claim, and in prosecuting a claim is led to invoke the support of a whole people on behalf of a single citizen or corporation, a primitive and mediaeval form of collective revenge which survives in practically no other branch of public law." E. M. Borchard, "Responsibility of States for Damage done in their Territories to the Person or Property of Foreigners," *A.J.*, 20 (1926), p. 747; and see Williams, pp. 258-59, note 3.

[10] "Looking upon the individual as the real object of all law, it proclaims the necessity of rendering international law democratic by placing individuals in the first rank of its subjects. It is gradually gaining force and ground in all countries. It is followed by an ever-increasing number of jurists, of which the most prominent are: Schücking and Wehberg, in Germany; Kelsen and Verdross, in Austria; Saldana, in Spain; Basdevant, Duguit, de Lapradelle and Scelle, in France; Krabbe, in Holland; Mandelstam, in Russia; and Alvarez, Garner and Ralston, in America." Politis, p. 23, quoted by Q. Wright, *Research in International Law since the War* (Carnegie Endowment, Division of International Law, Pamphlet No. 51), p. 32. Wright adds to this list the names of Westlake, W. Kaufmann, Diena, Cavaglieri, Osawa, and Eagleton, and could have included himself. See also H. Aufricht, "Personality in International Law," *Pol. Sc. Rev.*, 37 (1943), p. 217; Jessup, *passim*; F. S. Dunn, "The International Rights of Individuals," *Proc. Am. Soc.*, 1941, p. 14; *Annals*, 243 (1946); C.S.O.P., *Fourth Report* (1943), Part III; *Int. Con.*, No. 426 (1946).

[11] *Annuaire*, 1929, II, p. 298.

later approved and recommended to be stated and adopted as law, said:

That international law imposes duties and liabilities upon individuals as well as upon states has long been recognized. . . . Crimes against international law are committed by men, not by abstract entities, and only by punishing individuals who commit such crimes can the provisions of international law be enforced.[12]

The emphasis in this trial was upon the duties of individuals, but the judgment clearly recognized individuals as subjects of international law.

32. THE UNITED NATIONS AND HUMAN RIGHTS

On the other hand, it is the rights of individuals that have been emphasized in the United Nations. The Charter states that one of the objects of that organization is "to achieve international cooperation . . . in promoting and encouraging respect for human rights and fundamental freedoms." For several years the effort of the United Nations to carry out this purpose moved along hopefully; it has now been caught up in the political currents of the "cold war" and, more particularly, in the extravagant attitudes of the anti-colonial majority in the General Assembly. As a result, it is stalled for the moment, but it will undoubtedly progress at a slower and more reasonable rate.[13]

The motivation which stirred up the current great interest in human rights was stated in the Preamble to the Declaration by United Nations of January 1, 1942: ". . . and to preserve human rights and justice in their own lands, and that they are now engaged in a common struggle against savages and brutal foes seeking to subjugate the world." The Latin American states were particularly interested and made several suggestions for amendment of the Dumbarton Oaks Proposals. A Panamanian "Declaration of Fundamental Human Rights and Freedoms" was offered at the first General Assembly of the United Nations; and the Ninth Conference of American States at Bogota in 1948 adopted an "American Declaration of the Rights and Duties of Man" which is probably the first official international statement in this field.

[12] From the judgment of the Tribunal as reprinted in *A.J.*, 41 (1947), Document Section, pp. 220-21. See *Ex parte Quirin*, 317 U.S. 1 (1942).

[13] There is large literature concerning human rights. See the United Nations Yearbooks on Human Rights, and the records of the Commission on Human Rights; also: R. Brunet, *La Garantie Internationale des Droits de l'Homme* (Geneva, 1947); J. F. Green, *The United Nations and Human Rights* (Brookings Institution, 1956); H. Lauterpacht, *International Law and Human Rights* (New York, 1950); J. Robinson, *Human Rights and Fundamental Freedoms in the Charter of the United Nations* (New York, 1946).

UNITED NATIONS DECLARATION OF HUMAN RIGHTS. The Commission on Human Rights called for in Article 68 of the Charter was established in 1946, with Mrs. Franklin D. Roosevelt as chairman. The United States favored a mere declaration of principles; the United Kingdom preferred a treaty; the important question of implementation remained in the background. The Universal Declaration of Human Rights was completed in June, 1948 and unanimously adopted by the General Assembly—with eight abstentions and two absences. The Preamble proclaimed it to be "a common standard of achievement"; and the chairman said: "It is not a treaty; it is not an international agreement. It is not and does not purport to be a statement of law or of legal obligation."[14]

The Declaration, which will doubtless be recorded among the great documents of history, contains thirty articles. It begins with the statement that "All human beings are born free and equal in dignity and rights"; and Article 2 asserts that "Everyone is entitled to all the rights and freedoms set forth in this Declaration, without distinction of any kind. . . ." Some of the articles deal with what are ordinarily called "civil rights," such as freedom of opinion and expression, of religion or of assembly; prohibition of slavery, inhuman punishment, arbitrary arrest, and interference with privacy; or the right to a presumption of innocence and to a fair trial. Other articles assert economic and social rights not so well recognized in past practice, such as the right to marry as one wishes, to social security, to work and to free choice of employment, to education, to rest and leisure. These could be accepted by all states as a "common standard of achievement," each state being free to pursue these objectives in its own way and as it was able.[15]

COVENANT(S) OF HUMAN RIGHTS. It might have been better, in retrospect, had delegates been content with a declaration which, though not law, could possibly have grown into customary law more easily than it could be adopted as law through treaty. However, enthusiasm was great, not least in the United States, and the Commission proceeded to work on a "Covenant of Human Rights," a treaty to be ratified by states. It ran immediately into the question whether the new social and economic rights could be stated as legal obligations. The United States strongly urged that it should contain only the well-known and accepted civil rights, and prophesied that the treaty would

14 U.N. General Assembly, Third Session, First Part, *Official Records*, Plenary, 180th Meeting, p. 860. The declaration was adopted by Assembly Resolution 217 (III), to which it is attached; it has been very widely reprinted.

15 Its effect may already be seen in various national constitutions, in laws, in treaties, and in cases before national courts. See The Impact of the Universal Declaration of Human Rights, *U.N. Doc.*, Sales No. 1953.XIV.1 (ST/SOA/5/Rev.1).

fail of acceptance if the other and less well-known rights were included. After various tergiversations, the Assembly instructed the Commission to prepare two covenants; it did so, and presented them in 1954.[16]

The debates and proposals revealed little heed for logic or for practicality; it was manifest that some of the proposals could not be put into effect by many states, including those who proposed them. The most faraway of these measures was the "right of self-determination," which is hard to conceive of as a right of an individual; yet by order of a majority in the General Assembly it was put into the Covenant. There were proposals also for "economic self-determination," for measures against the incitement of hatred and violence; enthusiasm spilled over into suggestions for other declarations for the rights of children, the rights of teachers, etc.

IMPLEMENTATION. The lack of realism in such proposals was revealed when it was sought to make provision for the enforcement of the rights stated. National sovereignty was far from being prepared to make the necessary submissions to international control. Article 2 of each Covenant denies self-executing character and merely obligates states to take steps, of their own choosing, toward realization of the rights stated; and Article 4 allows action in derogation of those rights in case of "public emergency." There was long argument over the "federal-state clause" which would limit the obligations of federal states to those steps possible to be taken under their constitutions; this was rejected and a Soviet motion was adopted specifically extending obligations to all parts of federal states.[17] Similarly, the Assembly ran roughshod over the "colonial clause," which would allow a state to exclude its colonies from the obligations. Such a struggle developed over the right of a state to sign the Covenant with reservations that no decision on this point could be reached.

How to deal with violations of human rights under the Covenants has thus far proved to be an insoluble problem. States are unwilling to permit individuals to bring complaints against them; it is, indeed, a revolutionary thought that an international organization should be

[16] U.N., Commission on Human Rights, *Report of the Tenth Session* (E/2573), p. 65.

[17] This claim on the part of federal states has arisen in various connections (e.g., the International Labour Organization). It is opposed on the ground that a state which is a member of the community of nations, entitled to rights and duties under the law of that community, should be able to speak for all parts of itself and to accept responsibility for those parts; it is not fair to unitary states, it is held, that they must assume full responsibility whereas a federal state could avoid some responsibilities by appealing to the distribution of powers under its constitution. See Yuen-li Liang, "Colonial Clauses and Federal Clauses in United Nations Multilateral Instruments," *A.J.*, 45 (1951), p. 108.

able to intervene to protect an individual against his own state. The Soviet states were unwilling to consider implementation of the Covenants in any form; the other larger states would hear of no more than examination of complaints submitted by other states; other states asked for hearing of complaints offered by individual complainants or by nongovernmental organizations. Australia proposed a court, and France a commission, before which individuals or nongovernmental organizations could bring complaints; there was also an Argentine proposal for a sort of attorney-general to examine complaints and to decide whether they should be considered by an international authority.

None of these measures of implementation have been acceptable and the general result of the pressure brought to bear has been to make acceptance of the Covenants themselves less probable. The obligations called for in the Covenants, aside from implementation, are sometimes quite radical and much time will be required before nations can adjust themselves to such thinking. Nevertheless, there can be little doubt that the efforts of the United Nations to carry out its Charter purpose in this respect have done much to increase recognition of the individual as a unit of society worthy in itself, and to improve the status of human beings everywhere. It is a gain that states have admitted, in the Declaration of Human Rights, that they will regard the rights therein stated as a "common standard of achievement" and will work toward their realization—even though each is left free to work in its own way. The pressure upon them will surely continue, but it is to be expected that progress will be slow. The same human beings who demand better status for themselves and for their fellows are unwilling to allow international supervision over their respective states to accomplish this end.

ATTITUDE OF THE UNITED STATES. The rather reckless enthusiasm for human rights led to unfortunate repercussions in the United States. A number of lawyers, more interested in constitutional law than in international law or the United Nations, became fearful that such agreements as the Genocide Convention or the Covenants of Human Rights would impose obligations upon the United States, or enable the federal government to take action internally, which, according to their views, would not be authorized by the Constitution.[18] Nation-

18 Is the Constitution so immutable that it must be upheld even if it stands in the way of great human progress? In this case, of course, it did not need to be changed, for no obligation could be imposed upon the United States by the United Nations except such as the United States was willing to ratify in a treaty. It was not necessary to amend the Constitution and hamstring the treaty-making power; a two-thirds vote in the Senate was required to accept the feared treaty and one-third of the Senate could thus kill it.

alists and isolationists joined in, and the "Bricker Amendment"—which would have subordinated the treaty-making power and international law to the Constitution and to Congress—was barely averted in a Senate vote. The "great debate" thus stirred up produced a surprising amount of antagonism to the United Nations. On April 6, 1953, Secretary of State Dulles announced that the Covenants of Human Rights would not be ratified by the United States, though this country would continue to study sincerely the development of human rights, in which it has always been interested.[19] There is little hope at present for adoption of the Covenants, but the influence of the Declaration will continue to be felt.

BY-PRODUCTS. The movement for human rights has many ramifications, some of them difficult to link with the movement. They cannot be studied here, but it may be noted that efforts have been made, and in some cases conventions signed, concerning: freedom of information;[20] prevention of discrimination;[21] protection of minorities;[22] genocide; status of women;[23] slavery and forced labor;[24] self-determination,[25] and other matters. Arguments based on human rights have appeared in various disputes before the United Nations, such as that concerning South Africa, or, under the peace treaties, that with Bulgaria, Hungary and Rumania, or that with regard to the death sentences in Greece.

Thus, a revolution is taking place in international law, the effects of which will reach into many fields. While progress has been made toward international protection of the individual, the community of nations has yet to establish a clear statement of his legal rights and duties. The "Nürnberg Principles" recognize the need of an international jurisdiction to control those who incite to aggressive war or commit inhumane crimes; the draft code of "Offences against the Peace and Security of Mankind," the attempt to define aggression, the

---

[19] *Dept. of State Bull.*, 28 (1953), pp. 580, 592.

[20] See General Assembly Resolution 59 (I); Report on Freedom of Information, *U.N. Doc.* E/2426; U.N. Conference on Freedom of Information, *Final Act*, E Conf. 6/79 (1948); *Report of United States Delegates to the United Nations Conference on Freedom of Information*, Dept. of State Pub. No. 3150 (1948).

[21] U.N. Commission on Human Rights, *Report of Second Session*, E/600; and *Report of Tenth Session*, E/2573.

[22] U.N. Subcommittee on Prevention of Discrimination and Protection of Minorities, *U.N. Doc.* E/CN.4/641 and other reports.

[23] Convention on the Political Rights of Women—History and Commentary, *U.N. Doc.*, Sales No. 1955.IV.17.

[24] Report of the Ad Hoc Committee on Slavery, *U.N. Doc.* E/1988; Report by the Secretary General, E/2357; Report of the Ad Hoc Committee on Forced Labour, E/2431.

[25] See § 128 below.

efforts towards an international criminal jurisdiction, all move in the same direction. The studies so far made with regard to control of atomic weapons likewise indicate the need for jurisdiction over individuals, and such jurisdiction is a key feature in the various plans offered in connection with the current movement for world government. It is not difficult for a student of the American federal system to conceive of the citizen as the subject of more than one law, having different and sometimes conflicting rights and duties as a citizen of the United States and coincidently as a citizen of a member state. It is much more difficult to transmute this understanding into the acceptance by national groups of an international central government, able to reach into a state and punish an individual therein, or to protect an individual against his own government.

33. LEGAL STATUS OF ALIENS

It is the individual abroad who comes most often into contact with international law. An extensive system of rules has been developed for the protection of the alien and, as intercourse between states grows, the importance of these rules increases steadily. Most international litigation arises today, not from injuries done by one state to another, but from injuries suffered by aliens.

RIGHT OF ENTRY. We have noted above the claim of some writers that a right of commerce, or intercourse, exists as between states. This is interpreted by some as giving to an alien the right to enter any state; others reach the same conclusion by deduction from the natural law principle of individual liberty. These writers do not, however, deny the power of a state to exclude certain types, or certain groups of aliens; at the most, the claim is that no state is free to exclude all aliens. This would seem to be a statement of fact rather than of law. No state could, under existing circumstances, isolate itself from other states.

It cannot be doubted that a state is free to exclude aliens, individually or by groups, and to admit only those whom it pleases to admit. This right has been emphatically affirmed by the Supreme Court of the United States,[26] and it has been put into effect in her increasingly stringent immigration laws. These laws no longer directly exclude racial or national groups, but lay emphasis upon political affiliation; they have always included, of course, restrictions concerning health

[26] *Chae Chan Ping v. U.S.*, 130 U.S. 581 (1889); *Nishimura Ekiu*, 142 U.S. 651 (1891). For cases as to admission and expulsion, see Briggs, pp. 525-38; Dickinson, *Cases*, pp. 828-42; Moore, *Digest*, IV, §§ 550-59.

and moral character.[27] Other countries have similar restrictions, more or less severe. International law affords no guarantee of the right of an individual to move from one country to another. Freedom of movement can no longer be said to exist in international intercourse (in spite of the Declaration of Human Rights); the individual must carry a passport and gather visas and be prepared to be stopped at any frontier.

Similarly, aliens, if admitted, may be expelled, though practice affords illustrations of some limitations upon the use of this right. If an alien is suddenly deported, to his material loss and without apparent justification for the abrupt action, his state would be justified in making diplomatic inquiry, and damages have been collected where the procedure of such a dismissal was shown to be arbitrary or unreasonable.

ALLEGIANCE. The alien, when admitted to a state, is subject to the jurisdiction of that state and owes a temporary allegiance to it.[28] He must obey its laws and submit to its penalties for breaking them. He must pay taxes and has been called upon to perform civic duties and military service. Aside from the deprivation of political rights, such as voting or holding office, his situation may be little different from that of a citizen. His civil rights will be much the same as those of his neighbors who are nationals, though various restrictions may be put upon him.[29] For such rights as he has, international law requires that he be given the same protection under domestic law as the national receives; indeed, he may have an advantage over the national, in that his state may intervene for him if the standard of justice in the state is low. The right of the alien to appeal to international law is a restricted one, as has been seen, but he may have a remedy against the state of his residence which nationals of that state do not have.

[27] The McCarran Act (cited below, footnote 46) has made it possible to restrict movement in and out of the United States almost as severely as can be done in any totalitarian state. Under it, an inferior immigration officer may prevent the entry of anyone on the mere allegation of charges which are not revealed and which the accused person has no opportunity to answer. The Department of State could in the same way refuse a passport to an American citizen, but judicial decisions are now easing that tyranny.

[28] *De Jager v. Attorney General of Natal*, L.R. (1907) A.C. 326; *Joyce v. Director of Public Prosecutions*, L.R. (1946) A.C. 347. See Bishop, p. 344.

[29] States of the United States have set some strong restrictions, some of which have been upheld by the Supreme Court and others denied. A number of States have forbidden orientals to own land or to practice a profession. In different localities, an alien may not own a dog, or a gun, or receive a license as a junk dealer, or to run a pool-hall, etc. See cases in Bishop, pp. 120-30; Briggs, pp. 532-38; Dickinson, *Cases*, pp. 850-61.

34. DIPLOMATIC PROTECTION OF CITIZENS ABROAD[30]

The exclusive jurisdiction of a state within its own borders is checked, as we have seen, by certain rights of protection accorded by international law to the status of an alien therein. The bond of nationality which unites a person to his own state is the basis for extension of both control and protection over him in foreign lands.[31] His status is evidenced by his passport. From the viewpoint of domestic law, the citizen may not ordinarily demand protection from his home state, as of legal right; but from the viewpoint of international law, his state may afford protection to him if it so pleases.[32] The extent of this protection and the procedure to be followed are regulated by international law.

LOCAL REMEDIES. The general principles of the responsibility of states have been outlined above, and we may now consider them more closely insofar as they relate to the protection of aliens. In general, the duties of a state in this respect may be described as prevention and punishment, as restraint and redress.

No state can guarantee the life or property of an alien. The American tourist who is robbed in Paris must appeal to French police and courts as would any Parisian, and he need not hope for an American warship to appear in response to his frantic appeals for justice.[33] The duty which international law requires of France is that it should give to the American as good an administration of justice as it would give to a Frenchman. This administration of justice should measure up to "a

[30] This is a large part of the subject of responsibility of states in international law, for which references were given on p. 88.

[31] However, in the recent case of Nottebohm, the International Court of Justice held that the right of diplomatic protection did not depend entirely upon domestic laws conferring nationality. *I.C.J. Reports*, 1955, p. 4.

[32] But, according to *Rev. Stat.*, § 2001, "Whenever it is made known to the President that any citizen of the United States has been unjustly deprived of his liberty by or under the authority of any foreign government, it shall be the duty of the President forthwith to demand of that government the reasons of such imprisonment; and if it appears to be wrongful and in violation of the rights of American citizenship, the President shall forthwith demand the release of such citizen. . . ."

But, under the Nottebohm decision (see the preceding footnote), an international tribunal may refuse to permit a state to protect a person who by its own law is a national of that state.

[33] The warship, it may be observed, is much less apt to be sent in the situation of today, when any local struggle may become a world war, fought with the terrible modern means of destruction, than in earlier days when England protected by force such a person as Don Pacifico, or the United States sent the Marines to Nicaragua.

certain reasonable standard of civilized justice," but usually the alien is entitled to the same protection as the national—no more, and no less.[34]

"DUE DILIGENCE." The state must have proper machinery for the protection of individuals within its borders, and the government must exercise "due diligence" in preventing or punishing injury to aliens. This does not mean that special protection must be given to them, unless special circumstances demand it, such an an anti-racial riot. There have been an undue number of such cases in the United States, in which insufficient protection was given to Chinese or Italians, as a result of which the United States was obliged to pay damages. Thus, at Rock Springs, Wyoming, a mob drove out all Chinese residents, killing twenty-eight, wounding eighteen, and destroying valuable property. The coroner returned a verdict of death from causes unknown! Such a burlesque on justice could not be maintained. There was neither protection nor punishment; and the United States paid at one time over $276,000 in behalf of Chinese citizens injured in this and other riots.[35] Damages were paid also in consequence of the well-known New Orleans riot of 1891, and for others. The principle involved was stated by Lord Palmerston in the case of *Don Pacifico:* "The Greek Government having neglected to give the protection they were bound to extend, and having abstained from taking means to afford redress . . . ," England was justified in demanding reparation.[36]

Mob cases usually involve the payment of damages, since there is usually sufficient warning to allow the government to take unusual precautionary measures. If, however, the situation is beyond the control of the usually adequate forces of government, the state cannot be held liable. Nor can it be expected to anticipate the secret or sudden outbursts of individual passion. In such cases, though the government may have been diligent enough in its precautionary measures, it may yet render itself liable through failure to take prompt and efficient action to apprehend and punish the offender. To allow his escape when he could have been captured, or to be dilatory or inefficient in prosecution, has often been considered by an international tribunal to be sufficient justification for an award. In the *Janes Case,* before the

[34] In reaction against claims regarded by them as unduly pressed, the Latin American states support the Calvo Doctrine, which asserts that in no case can an alien ask for better treatment than a national would receive. See Borchard, *loc. cit.,* p. 845; Eagleton, *Responsibility,* § 33; A. V. Freeman, *The International Responsibility of States for Denial of Justice* (London, 1938), pp. 469-89; Hyde, II, pp. 994-98; North American Dredging Co. Case, Claims Commission, U.S. and Mexico, *Opinions of the Commission* (Washington, 1927), p. 21.

[35] Moore, *Digest,* VI, pp. 822-36.

[36] *Ibid.,* p. 853.

Mexican Claims Commission, an award of $12,000 was made because "the Mexican authorities did not take proper steps to apprehend and punish the slayer of Janes"; and in another case the United States was directed to pay to a Mexican widow $10,000 because Texas courts had postponed the trial of the murderer of her husband, for one reason or another, from 1922 to 1927.[37]

"DENIAL OF JUSTICE." While lack of due diligence may bring liability, the ordinary basis of a claim is a "denial of justice." The duty of the alien, as has already been observed, is to seek redress in the local courts; and it is ordinarily true that he has no right to call upon his own state for aid or to expect pecuniary damages until these remedies have failed.[38] There are various ways in which such a failure may occur. It may result from the absence of machinery or laws through which redress is obtainable; from refusal of access to the courts; from delay, collusion, venality, anti-national bias, or other fault in judicial procedure (but not from mere error on the part of the court); from arbitrary interference by the executive or other authorities; from failure to execute the decree of the court. In the case of the *Salvador Commercial Company*, an American firm was fraudulently deprived of a concession, and when it attempted to appeal to local courts an executive decree arbitrarily blocked this means of redress. Local remedies being thus closed, it was held that Salvador was guilty of a denial of justice.[39] And in the *R. E. Brown Claim*, the tribunal said:

> All three branches of the government conspired to ruin his enterprise. The Executive department issued proclamations for which no warrant could be found in the Constitution and laws of the country. The Volksraad enacted legislation which, on its face, does violence to fundamental principle of justice recognized in every enlightened community. The judiciary, at first recalcitrant, was at length reduced to submission and brought into line a determined policy of the Executive to reach the desired result regardless of Constitutional guarantees and inhibitions.[40]

Awards have been given for such injuries as false arrest or inhumane treatment during imprisonment, but, for the most part, all claims are subordinated to the central rule that local remedies must have been

[37] Janes Case, Mexican Cl. Commission, p. 108; Galvan Case, *ibid.*, p. 408.

[38] This is believed to be the correct meaning of "denial of justice" as a technical term of international law. See C. Eagleton, "Denial of Justice in International Law," *A.J.*, 22 (1928), pp. 538-59. The term has, however, been employed in a wider meaning, so as to cover every internationally illegal act injurious to aliens. Hyde, II, pp. 909-17; Borchard, p. 330. See also A. V. Freeman, *The International Responsibility of States for Denial of Justice* (Longmans, 1938); O. Lissistzyn, "The Meaning of the Term Denial of Justice in International Law," *A.J.*, 30 (1936), p. 632.

[39] *U.S. For. Rel.*, 1902, p. 838.

[40] American and British Claims Arbitration Tribunal, *Report of Fred K. Nielsen* (Washington, 1926), p. 198.

exhausted before diplomatic interposition—the presentation of a claim on behalf of the injured individual by his state to the other state—is permissible. The result of this rule is a desirable tendency to consider denial of justice, in the sense above described, as the only foundation for an international claim on behalf of an injured alien.[41] As judicial systems (and other means of redress) in the various states become more and more trustworthy there will be less and less opportunity for the alien to appeal to his home state for aid.

However, we must now notice an increasing trend to provide means through which the alien individual may present his own claim on an international basis. He has been at the mercy of his own government; under the *Nottebohm* decision, even his own state may not be permitted to intervene on his behalf; and it is exceptional that an individual may be permitted to present his own claim before an international tribunal. On the other hand, it is increasingly recognized that the claim actually belongs to the individual; it is absurd to say, as is the practice, that he, or his state on his behalf, loses the claim because he has changed his nationality; damages are awarded in the name of the individual, even if to his state, and they are measured by the harm which he suffers, rather than that suffered by his state. Finally, there is the situation of the unfortunate stateless person, for whom there is no way to present a claim. Such considerations will doubtless be taken into account in the forthcoming study of state responsibility undertaken by the International Law Commission.[42]

35. NATIONALITY[43]

The national character of an individual is of vital importance to him. Whether his rights are his own or those of his state under existing international law, there are no procedural means by which they can be upheld except through a state. This national character is a nec-

---

[41] It may be observed that proper application of the rule of local redress may produce different results in different states. Thus an award against a policeman in the United States may be illusory, since the policeman may be unable to pay; whereas under administrative law systems, such as France, the state may accept liability for the act of its agent.

[42] See Chap. 3, footnote 81, above.

[43] On nationality, see, *Com. Prog. Cod.*, Questionnaire No. 1, also in *A.J.*, 20 (July, 1926), Special Number; *Bases of Discussion*, I, Nationality (1929.V.1.); *Acts of the Conference for the Codification of International Law*, I, Plenary Meetings (1930.V.-14.). Also, *Research in International Law*, Nationality; R. W. Flournoy and M. O. Hudson, *A Collection of Nationality Laws of Various Countries* (New York, 1929); C. Cogordan, *La Nationalité* (Paris, 1890); J. M. Jones, *British Nationality Law and Practice* (1947); E. S. Zeballos, *La Nationalité au Point de Vue de la Législation Comparée*, 5 vols. (1914-19).

essary qualification for admission to an international tribunal or for benefits under a treaty and its absence would deprive him of the usual method of redress—diplomatic interposition. International law doubtless requires protection for an alien, but procedurally he can invoke that protection only by appealing to his own state. Thus a person without national character is left entirely without protection.

Nationality is the bond which unites a person to a particular state. It is, so to speak, his card of membership, entitling him to the rights and duties of membership. Naturally, it is the state which decides who are to be its members, but if the state reaches too far in its claims it may collide with similar claims by other states, and thus arouse international problems. "In a broad sense," says Hyde, "international law limits the right of a State to impress its national character upon an individual, or to prevent that character from being lost or transferred. The freedom of action of each member of the family of nations is, however, wide."[44] It would be almost correct to say that international law makes no provisions as to nationality, leaving each state free to do what it wishes. It is, however, true that certain principles have been established in practice, and if a state should step beyond these its action would doubtless result in vigorous protest from other states. If for example the United States should by law declare all Canadians to be American nationals,[45] it is hardly to be expected that Canada would placidly accept the ruling, or that an international court would respect the claim of the United States to appear in behalf of Canadian subjects.

ACQUISITION OF NATIONALITY BY BIRTH. In the usual practice of states, nationality may be acquired either through birth or through naturalization. Citizenship through birth may result from being born within the territorial jurisdiction of a state, the *jus soli;* or from being born of the nationals of a certain state, no matter where, the *jus sanguinis.* The one depends upon the place of birth, regardless of parentage; the other depends upon parentage, regardless of the place of birth. A state may employ either or, in varying degrees, both of these principles. In the United States the Fourteenth Amendment makes all persons, born in the United States and subject to the jurisdiction thereof, citizens of the United States and of the state wherein they

44 Hyde, II, p. 1066.

45 The word "national" is usually employed, today, in the external sense, and thus as a term of international law; whereas the word "citizen" or "subject" now refers to internal character and rights. It is to be observed that a state may confer nationality without conferring the rights of citizenship internally. While a citizen is always a national, a national is not always a citizen. Persons in the territorial possessions of the United States are nationals, but they have, or may, become citizens only through act of Congress.

reside. An attempt was made, after several years of study, to clear up the confusion of nationality in the United States by passage of the Nationality Act of 1940, but it merely confounded the confusion; and the Act of 1952 not only failed to clarify the situation but added some elements of control of a fascist character.[46] Quotation of its provisions with regard to acquisition of nationality by birth is sufficient evidence of the confusion:

SEC. 301. (a) The following shall be nationals and citizens of the United States at birth:

(1) a person born in the United States, and subject to the jurisdiction thereof;

(2) a person born in the United States to a member of an Indian, Eskimo, Aleutian, or other aboriginal tribe: *Provided*, That the granting of citizenship under this subsection shall not in any manner impair or otherwise affect the right of such person to tribal or other property;

(3) a person born outside of the United States and its outlying possessions of parents both of whom are citizens of the United States and one of whom has had a residence in the United States or one of its outlying possessions, prior to the birth of such person;

(4) a person born outside of the United States and its outlying possessions of parents one of whom is a citizen of the United States who has been physically present in the United States or one of its outlying possessions for a continuous period of one year prior to the birth of such person, and the other of whom is a national, but not a citizen of the United States;

(5) a person born in an outlying possession of the United States of parents one of whom is a citizen of the United States who has been physically present in the United States or one of its outlying possessions for a continuous period of one year at any time prior to the birth of such person;

(6) a person of unknown parentage found in the United States while under the age of five years, until shown, prior to his attaining the age of twenty-one years, not to have been born in the United States;

(7) a person born outside the geographical limits of the United States and its outlying possessions of parents one of whom is an alien, and the other a citizen of the United States who, prior to the birth of such person, was physically present in the United States or its outlying possessions for a period or periods totaling not less than ten years, at least five of which were after attaining the age of fourteen years: *Provided*, That any periods of honorable service in the Armed Forces of the United States by such citizen parent may be included in computing the physical presence requirements of this paragraph.

(b) Any person who is a national and citizen of the United States at birth under paragraph (7) of subsection (a), shall lose his nationality and citizenship unless he shall come to the United States prior to attaining the age of twenty-three years and shall immediately following any such coming be continuously physically present in the United States for at least five years: *Provided*, That

---

[46] Public Law 414, 82nd Congress, Second Session, known as the McCarran Act. Its provisions concerning entry into this country, as well as its changes concerning nationality, have produced severe criticism and it is to be hoped that it will be modified.

such physical presence follows the attainment of the age of fourteen years and precedes the age of twenty-eight years.

(c) Subsection (b) shall apply to a person born abroad subsequent to May 24, 1934: *Provided, however,* That nothing contained in this subsection shall be construed to alter or affect the citizenship of any person born abroad subsequent to May 24, 1934, who, prior to the effective date of this Act, has taken up a residence in the United States before attaining the age of sixteen years, and thereafter, whether before or after the effective date of this Act, complies or shall comply with the residence requirements for retention of citizenship specified in subsections (g) and (h) of section 201 of the Nationality Act of 1940, as amended.

NATIONALITY BY NATURALIZATION. Naturalization, which is the acquisition of nationality through adoption by a state of a person who has no other claims to its citizenship, may be either collective or individual. In the former case, it may result from conquest or cession of territory, though in modern times the inhabitants are usually given the right by treaty to choose which nationality they prefer. In the latter case, a voluntary action, the individual renounces his former allegiance and, if he can meet the tests and qualifications set by the state to which he applies, he may swear allegiance to this state and secure a new nationality. It must be noted, however, that the state of his former allegiance may not be willing to give him up and, since each state makes its own laws in this respect, he may find himself with two nationalities.

DUAL NATIONALITY. The conflicts which may rise as a result of the various situations above described will doubtless have been noted. A person may have more than one nationality if his parents were within a foreign country when he was born—*jure sanguinis* and *jure soli;* or if he becomes naturalized but his former state continues to claim him (or even his children); or, in the case of a woman, through marriage to a foreigner. For a long time, the rule was clear that a woman took the nationality of her husband and automatically lost her former nationality.[47] In the United States, women, in their increasing independence, carried out a successful movement against the involuntary changes of citizenship forced upon them. As a result of powerful agitation by women's organizations the United States passed the Cable Act in 1922, under which marriage alone would not confer or terminate citizenship, though naturalization was made easier for the alien woman who married an American citizen.[48]

[47] *Mackenzie v. Hare,* 165 Cal. 776 (1913), 239 U.S. 299 (1915). See Bishop, pp. 329-30; Briggs, p. 485.
[48] Subsequent amendments have modified the procedure and put the alien, man or woman, who marries an American spouse upon a more equal footing. See the Nationality Act of 1952, above cited; also, Bishop, p. 329; Briggs, p. 485; Hackworth, III, § 247; Hyde, II, pp. 1114-21.

Loss of Nationality. Fundamentally, the principle at issue in cases of dual allegiance is the right of expatriation, that is, the right of an individual to break off at will the bond of allegiance to a state. Originally, it was generally maintained that allegiance was indissoluble, and this seems to have been admitted by the United States. But the pressure of immigration soon persuaded her to the other view, and Congress in 1868 asserted it in these words: "Whereas the right of expatriation is a natural and inherent right of all people, indispensable to the enjoyment of the rights of life, liberty, and the pursuit of happiness . . . ," therefore any official declaration denying the right of expatriation "is declared inconsistent with the fundamental principles of the Republic"; and all naturalized citizens of the United States, while in foreign countries, "are entitled to and shall receive from this Government the same protection of persons and property which is accorded to native-born citizens."[49] Unfortunately, the naturalized person's state had as much right to maintain its claim to him as had the United States to deny it; the Act of 1868 was a unilateral declaration having no force abroad. In this situation, that state would take jurisdiction which actually had the disputed national within its control. However, the principle of expatriation was vigorously asserted by the United States through diplomatic negotiation. A number of treaties were signed, embodying the compromise that a naturalized American who went back to his former state would be treated as an American citizen by that state for a term of two years, while the United States would not attempt to protect him beyond that period. Most modern writers uphold a theoretical right of expatriation, and it seemed well on its way to recognition as a principle of international law before 1914. Military exigencies during and following the first World War have produced a decided setback among states which are unwilling to lose needed human resources.

On the other hand, a number of states will terminate the national connection for various reasons, frequently as a penalty. The United States has tended to regard the bond with its natural born citizens as permanent, but the Act of 1952 declares that nationality may be lost by voluntary naturalization abroad, by taking an oath of allegiance to a foreign country or serving in its armed forces, or by treason against the United States or desertion from its armed forces.[50] Thus, it is possible for a person to have no nationality, or to be a national of a state which will not release him, but to which he is afraid to return or to call upon for protection; and the result of two world wars and of

[49] *Rev. Stat.* §§ 1999, 2000.
[50] The provisions of the Act of 1952 are actually much more complicated than this statement indicates.

various totalitarian regimes and ideological conflicts has been to create a large number of "stateless persons," refugees, and displaced persons.

ATTEMPTS AT CODIFICATION. Thus, tragic problems exist for many thousands of persons because of the laws and policies of the various states concerning nationality. An attempt was made, at the conference at the Hague in 1930, to secure some uniformity and to remedy injustices caused by the conflict of nationality laws. In spite of long and careful preparation, and in spite of the very conservative proposals made, little agreement could be reached. A Convention on Certain Questions Relating to the Conflict of Nationality Laws was signed, which recognized that "it is for each state to determine under its own laws who are its nationals"; and the wishes of those who sought international regulation found expression only in the statement that "this law shall be recognized by other States, in so far as it is consistent with international conventions, international customs, and the principles generally recognized with regard to nationality." Thus the problem of dual nationality remained unsolved; in fact, it was affirmed that "a person having two or more nationalities may be regarded as its national by each of the States whose nationality he possesses," and the consent of the state was required before he can renounce its nationality. However, there were not enough ratifications to make this agreement of importance. When the convention conceded the right of a state to refuse to give up its claim to a national, the United States, adhering to its belief in a right of expatriation, refused to sign the convention.

Two protocols were adopted by the conference, one providing that a person of dual nationality habitually resident in one of the two countries, should not be subject to military obligations in the other country; the other would eliminate a certain type of statelessness. Finally, a recommendation was adopted urging that a stateless person be admitted by the state whose nationality he last possessed. None of these agreements obtained enough ratifications to establish effective law.

The United Nations has continued the efforts to find solutions for the unfortunate persons lost in the maze of nationality laws. When the International Refugee Organization was ended, the United Nations appointed a United Nations High Commissioner for Refugees, though providing him with neither money nor authority. At that time there were about a quarter of a million persons labeled as refugees or displaced persons, and millions of others whose condition was uncertain and unhappy. Special bodies were created, the U.N. Relief for Palestine, and the Korean Relief and Rehabilitation Agency. Stateless persons, having no passport, cannot even travel to another state except through special arrangements; they are unknown to international law, further proof of the need for that law to reach down to individuals.[51]

The Declaration of Human Rights moves in this direction by providing (Article 15) that everyone has a right to a nationality and cannot arbitrarily be deprived of it or of his right to change it. It would be interesting to know how many states have changed their nationality laws accordingly; the United States has not. The Economic and Social Council initiated a study, carried on through the International Law Commission, which has now resulted in two alternative conventions, submitted for consideration by governments, one on "Elimination of Future Statelessness," the other on "Reduction of Future Statelessness."[52] Mention may also be made of the various efforts of the Commission on the Status of Women.

[51] As to refugees, see Louise W. Holborn, "The Legal Status of Political Refugees," *A.J.*, 32 (1938), p. 680; *Annuaire*, 1936; Sir John Hope Simpson, *The Refugee Problem* (1936); and in general the United Nations *Yearbooks*.

[52] A Study of Statelessness, *U.N. Doc.* E/1112 (1949); Report of the International Law Commission (Sixth Session), General Assembly, Ninth Session, *Official Records*, Supp. No. 9 (A/2693), pp. 2-8; Wm. Samore, "Statelessness as a Consequence of Conflict of Nationality Laws," *A.J.*, 45 (1951), p. 476.

Chapter 6

OFFICIAL INTERCOURSE BETWEEN STATES

36. NEGOTIATION

There has always been a certain amount of intercourse between different parts of the world; it was carried on for the most part by private individuals, and rules were developed by which their respective states could give them some protection. From the earliest days, there have been instrumentalities for communications between governments. There were heralds and special envoys; and the treaty was the binding and permanent record of agreements reached. The pressures of interdependence, described above, resulted in an enormous growth of such agents for international intercourse. As economic interests of states have become more and more political, states have become further involved, either through regulation of trade or by engaging in trade themselves. The services which a state now provides for its citizens are far more numerous than they once were, and each of these requires relationships with other states in fields formerly unknown to them—for example, health, education, agriculture, and now, atomic energy. Consequently, states have had to increase their means of communication with each other and are, with modern means of transmission such as radio and teletype and telephone, in practically continuous communication with each other. It may be noted also that these relationships, once almost exclusively bilateral, are now becoming increasingly multilateral.

Official intercourse between states represents their endeavor to reach amicable agreement upon matters of common interest. It is a process which never ceases and which calls for more and more machinery and rules and conferences, through which states may reach agreement and put it into legally binding form. Negotiations may be carried on directly by heads of states, but this is a procedure reserved for exceptionally important matters;[1] agents have usually been designated for this purpose. Ultimately it became necessary to establish permanent agents in the various countries, and thus the diplomatic and consular systems developed: the former to take care of the interests of the states, the latter to care for citizens or their interests abroad. The conference also appeared as a convenient means of handling matters of interest to a number of states.

Negotiations may eventuate in a treaty or other form of agreement among states. The treaty, originally bilateral in form and contractual in nature, is now being used, in multilateral form, to state new rules for members of the community of nations. A number of institutions of an administrative character have been set up to deal with matters of continuing common interest, usually of a technical nature, such as the Universal Postal Union and the specialized agencies. Means for the pacific settlement of disputes between states have evolved, though they fall far short of the needs in the community. Finally, over-all bodies have been established, in the League of Nations and the United Nations.

In this chapter the older means and methods of international intercourse will be briefly described—means which are of course still in use and on a far greater scale than ever before. The following chapters will take up the procedures for international legislation and administration, and for the settlement of disputes.

37. THE CONSULAR SYSTEM

Consular representation was the earliest continuing means for carrying on official international intercourse between states.[2] In view of the earlier theory that an alien should be handled according to the law of his own state rather than that of the state of his residence, it was desirable to send agents who could explain that law; such agents were to be found in ancient Greece and Rome. With the reinvigoration of trade about the thirteenth century, the office became important. Each

---

[1] President Wilson attended the Peace Conference of 1919; the meetings of President Roosevelt and President Truman with Churchill and Stalin to reach settlements after World War II are well known; President Eisenhower went to the "summit conference" at Geneva in 1955.

[2] In general, as to the position of consuls, see Briggs, pp. 812-35; *Com. Prog. Cod.*, "Legal Position and Functions of Consuls," *A.J.*, 22 (1928), Special Number, pp. 105-10; A. de Clercq and C. de Vallat, *Guide pratique des consulats* (5th ed., Paris, 1898); A. H. Feller and M. O. Hudson, *Diplomatic and Consular Laws and Regulations*, 2 vols. (Washington, 1933); Hackworth, IV, pp. 655-949; J. I. Puente, *The Foreign Consul: His Juridical Status in the United States* (Chicago, 1926); I. Stewart, *Consular Privileges and Immunities* (New York, 1926); *Research in International Law*, Legal Position and Functions of Consuls; E. C. Stowell, *Consular Cases and Opinions* (Washington, 1909).

state found it necessary to send out representatives to administer the commercial affairs of its citizens abroad. A representative might be elected by the national group in a foreign state or he might be sent out by the home state—at first to travel with a ship, later to reside in one place. However chosen, his function was to apply the law of his own state, usually to commercial problems; and the result was the building of commercial law, codified, as we have noted, in the *Consolato del Mare*. The system was carried by the Crusades to the Orient, where the "capitulations," or consular jurisdiction, continued long after it had been dropped, as to its judicial functions, in Europe.

Several important changes have developed to distinguish the older system from consular practice of our own day. In the first place, the doctrine that the alien carries with him his own law was supplanted by the rule of subjection to the jurisdiction of the state of residence. Naturally, the judicial functions of the consul disappeared in this process, except in countries of exterritorial jurisdiction. Again, it became the practice for a state to appoint its own consuls, and thus the *consules electi* disappeared. The development of the diplomatic service deprived the consul of some functions, and certainly diminished his prestige, but his essential task, the promotion of commerce, still remains.

ORGANIZATION OF THE CONSULAR SERVICE. Whereas the diplomatic service maintains only one office in a state, the consular service usually has offices at every important commercial center. Each state has its own organization and regulations. The typical official is the Consul, but there are supervisory officials, such as the Consul-General, and various grades of subordinate officers, as Vice-Consul, Deputy-Consul, or Consular Agent. Usually, nowadays, they are consuls *de carrière:* they are appointed by a state exclusively for the consular function, and are not permitted to engage in a business of their own. In less important places, a state may choose from the inhabitants individuals who are authorized to exercise certain consular functions. Each state is divided geographically into consular districts by the sending state, and the area of consular jurisdiction for each office is thus established.

Consuls derive their authority from both the sending and the receiving state; they are regarded as officers both of the state which appoints and the state which receives them. The authority of the receiving state is conferred upon the consul through the issuance to him of an *exequatur*, a document which recognizes his commission from his own state and permits him to exercise his consular functions within the receiving state. The *exequatur* may be refused or revoked without explanation. Authority from his own state is derived from his commission, issued in the United States by the President, with the consent of the Senate. He may or may not be put under the direction of his diplomatic officer in the state to which he is accredited. Since the Rogers Act of 1924, a foreign-service officer of the United States may be assigned to either diplomatic or consular functions. The consul is a representative of his state abroad and should therefore come under the control of the foreign office; at the same time he works in behalf of commercial and other interests and may receive instructions from other departments of the government. Whereas the diplomat represents the national interest, the consul promotes private trade and interests, which may, however, become a national interest (e.g., in the case of oil). It is not always easy to differentiate functions.

FUNCTIONS OF THE CONSUL. The work of a consul is varied and trying. A United States consul must promote the interest of American citizens within his jurisdiction, protect them in all acquired privileges, and facilitate trade relations. For his fellow-citizens abroad he must keep a record of permanent residents, certify to births, marriages, and deaths, attest wills, perform notarial functions, protect them against injustice in local courts or from unjust detention, and take charge of estates of deceased Americans. He has onerous duties with regard to shipping; he must receive the papers of American vessels arriving at his port, and deliver them to the master after the obligations to the crew have been discharged; issue bills of health to vessels clearing for his country; ship or discharge American seamen; adjust quarrels between master and crew; certify invoices and enforce customs regulations; and assist stranded vessels or stranded seamen. He provides visas for alien immigrants (as well as for other travelers), and watches over their numbers and qualifications; he arranges for the extradition of criminals; he observes the execution of commercial treaties. In behalf of citizens at home he maintains all possible contacts and acquires all possible information concerning local markets or materials, or other matters which might afford an apportunity for American business interests, which information he dispatches home in regular reports; he answers specific inquiries concerning addresses and business standing and other matters. In general, he attempts to promote American trade in his locality.[3] He is usually able to keep busy, and even to stir up

---

[3] "When written to directly by any firm and given a clear indication of the information wanted, consular officers will incorporate in their replies, addressed to the inquirer, data in regard to prevailing conditions in trade and industry, rates of applicable customs duties, imports and exports of various commodities prominently associated with the trade of their districts, the extent to which various goods are manufactured locally, the foreign competition to be met, prevailing prices, peculiarities of local trade practices, lists of firms engaged in the importation and sale of similar articles,

trade without resorting, as did O. Henry's consul, to scattering cockle-burrs among a barefooted population in order to create a demand for shoes.

A consul has no diplomatic character, and his privileges and rights under international law are debatable.[4] Usually, however, many such rights are given to him by treaty. While he himself is not inviolable, nor immune from local jurisdiction, his office and archives probably are; and he may demand free access to his fellow-citizens, and undisturbed communication with his own state. In practice, he is treated with respect and given every facility for the performance of his duties. He is a public official, but not a diplomat.

The status of the consul can be illustrated by the recent notorious case of Mme. Kasenkina, a Russian national who leaped from the third floor of the Russian consulate in New York, where the consul was attempting to hold her a prisoner. The consul complained that the police had entered his "extraterritorial" premises in order to investigate; the United States rejected his claim, informed him that he had exceeded his rights in holding Mme. Kasenkina, and revoked his *exequatur*. The Soviet government retaliated by closing its consulates in New York and San Francisco and rejecting United States consulates in Vladivostok and Leningrad.[5]

38. DIPLOMATIC INTERCOURSE[6]

Historically, the diplomatic system appears upon the scene later than the consular system. The earlier agents of diplomacy were transient ones. Diplomacy in the modern sense of the word began to take form between the Italian city-states about the fifteenth century. They had so many dealings with each other that they found it convenient to have permanent representatives always on watch. Other states imitated the practice, which developed further after 1648 when co-

---

suggested local agencies for the distribution of American goods, principal publications available for advertising, advertising rates, and local advertising agencies, etc." From the prefatory words to Publication No. 3 of the Department of State, *Consular Officers of the United States*, October 1, 1929.

[4] See Briggs, pp. 822-32; Hackworth, IV, pp. 699-806; Hudson, *Cases*, pp. 874-906.
[5] The case is described in Bishop, pp. 451-55.
[6] From the vast literature in this field, a few general references are here given: C. S. Blaga, *L'Evolution de la Diplomatie* (Paris, 1938); J. W. Foster, *The Practice of Diplomacy* (Boston, 1906); R. Genet, *Traité de Diplomatie et de Droit Diplomatique* (Paris, 1931); Sir E. Satow, *Guide to Diplomatic Practice* (London, 1932); A. Sereni, *The Italian Conception of International Law* (New York, 1943).

existent membership in the community of nations was recognized, and when dynastic, colonial, and commercial rivalries called for constant employment of diplomatic agencies.

The early methods of diplomacy were developed under the theories of Machiavelli; they were devious and subterranean, matching the motives and purposes of sovereigns. An ambassador, according to the famous bon mot of Wotton, was "an honest man sent to lie abroad for the benefit of his country"; and Bynkershoek asserted that ambassadors were nearly always spies. Etiquette and precedence, in those days of bitter rivalry between growing new states, were of primary importance; and many *causes célèbres* mark the historical struggle.[7] Diplomacy today has outgrown such early conceptions. It is less ceremonious, more open and more businesslike; an embassy must now include experts on economics and finance, on agriculture or education or other matters—all of which have become part of the political interest of a state.

RIGHT OF LEGATION. Since the act of sending or receiving a diplomatic agent by one state is regarded as recognition by it of the other state, it is usually true that only recognized members of the community of nations may exchange diplomatic agents. According to some writers, there is a *jus legationum*, a right to send and receive diplomatic agents. While the necessities of community life require this exchange, the undoubted legal rights of a state to refuse to receive an official sent for that purpose, or to break off diplomatic relations entirely at any time, seem to indicate that diplomatic representation is a practice rather than a right. A state in its own discretion may send diplomatic agents to, or receive them from, any political entity. Representation may be terminated through the breaking off of diplomatic relations by one state, by war, by revolutionary change of government, or by the extinction of a state.

ORGANIZATION OF THE DIPLOMATIC SERVICE. The organization of a state's diplomatic service begins with the head of the state who, in

[7] During the days of Louis XIV, for example, the rivalry between France and Spain led the Spanish ambassador in England to hire a number of persons to hamstring the horses and attack the servants of the French ambassador, after which the Spanish representative was able to take the leading place in the parade undisturbed. Louis XIV, however, by dire threats, forced the King of Spain to apologize and to concede precedence to France thereafter; and in celebration of this notable victory had a medal struck. Martens, *Causes Célèbres*, I, pp. 353-56. See also F. de Callieres, *De la Manière de négocier avec les souverains* (Amsterdam, 1716); Comte de Garden, *Traité complet de diplomatie* (Paris, 1833); J. W. Foster, *The Practice of Diplomacy* (Boston, 1906).

international law, speaks authoritatively for the state in its foreign relations. Such was, at any rate, the old rule: Jefferson, as Secretary of State, informed Citizen Genêt that the President, "being the only channel of communication between this country and foreign nations, it is from him alone that foreign nations or their agents are to learn what is or has been the will of the nation; and whatever he communicates as such, they have a right and are bound to consider as the expression of the nation, and no foreign agent can be allowed to question it. . . ."[8]

In these days of democratic control of foreign policy and of constitutional limitations upon the treaty-making power, it is incumbent upon a state seeking to make a treaty with another to investigate the constitutional authority given by that state to the agents with whom it is dealing. However, according to Jefferson's statement, which is a generally accepted principle, the word of the chief of state, giving assurance that constitutional requirements have been met, must be accepted by other states. It would be possible, thus, for a state to be bound internationally, even though the agreement made were internally in conflict with the constitution.[9] This is a particular problem in the United States, illustrated by the controversy over the "Bricker Amendment," though it had come up often enough before that controversy; other states have the same problem to a greater or lesser degree. On the one hand, it is highly important that there should be one voice able to speak authoritatively for the nation to other nations, and to bind the nation legally; if this is not provided, how can one nation trust and deal with another? On the other hand, the people of a nation are not willing to be bound by the word of the chief of state which does not represent their will. It is a difficult problem, and the responsibility would seem to lie with each state to guard itself against misuse of authority by its chief of state; manifestly, the other state cannot control that situation.

Each state maintains a department for the direction of its diplomatic agents abroad, usually called the Ministry of Foreign Affairs, but in

[8] Moore, *Digest*, IV, p. 670; see Hyde, II, p. 1215, note 5; E. S. Corwin, *The President's Control of Foreign Relations* (Princeton, 1917); Hackworth, IV, § 421; *U.S. v. Curtiss Wright*, 299 U.S. 304. Concerning democratic control of foreign policy, G. Almond, *The American People and Foreign Policy* (New York, 1950); T. Bailey, *The Man in the Street* (New York, 1948); W. Y. Elliott and a study group of the Woodrow Wilson Foundation, *United States Foreign Policy: Its Organization and Control* (New York, 1952); D. C. Poole, *Conduct of Foreign Relations under Modern Democratic Conditions* (New Haven, 1924).

[9] C. Fairman, "Competence to Bind the State to an International Engagement," *A.J.*, 30 (1936), p. 439.

the United States called the Department of State.[10] This department has general supervision over all the external relationships of the state, and, in general, such relationships must pass through its hands. It selects and distributes its representatives abroad, and instructs them in their duties. Such instructions may be independently formulated by the department or issued in accordance with directives which it receives itself from the chief of state or from the legislative body. The organization of such a department presents many difficulties. In a democratic age its dependence upon the legislature and upon popular control in general produces complications. It is hard to correlate the activities of various independent departments and direct them all through the channel of the foreign office; the United States has an amazing number of agents abroad, in foreign economic aid, Point 4 work, military activities, and for many other purposes. Some of the work is mere administrative routine, while some is public policy in its most rarefied form; some of the work calls for technical knowledge, and some for social poise. Upon the organization and support of the foreign office depends to a high degree the reputation of a state abroad.

FOREIGN SERVICE. The organization of the diplomatic service is based in the first place upon the classifications laid down at the congresses of Vienna and Aix-la-Chapelle. According to this classification, "diplomatic agents are divided into three classes: that of ambassadors, legates or nuncios; that of envoys, ministers, or other persons accredited to sovereigns; that of chargés d'affaires accredited to ministers for foreign affairs." There is little of practical value in these distinctions today, beyond establishing an order of precedence. Each state is free to send a representative of whatever rank it prefers, though rank actually depends upon reciprocity. Ambassadors and ministers receive from the head of their state letters of credence, which they present to the head of the state to which they are accredited; the chargé d'affaires is commissioned to the foreign minister only. Since a state is free to reject at will the person sent to it, the practice of *agréation* is observed; that is, inquiry is first made as to whether the person whose appointment is proposed will be acceptable.[11] A state is free also to

---

[10] See C. E. Hughes, "Some Aspects of the Work of the Department of State," *A.J.*, 16 (1922), p. 355; T. H. Lay, *The Foreign Service of the United States* (New York, 1925); J. L. McCamy, *The Administration of American Foreign Affairs* (New York, 1950); E. Plischke, *Conduct of American Diplomacy* (New York, 1950); G. Stuart, *American Diplomatic and Consular Practice* (New York, 1936); G. Stuart, *The Department of State* (New York, 1949); *Foreign Service: A Short Account . . .,* Dept. of State Pub. No. 3789 (1950).

[11] A well-known instance of refusal to accept is that of Keiley, who was rejected by Italy in 1885 because of a speech in which he had criticized the King of Italy for the invasion of the rights of the Pope. He was likewise rejected by Austria because "the

ask for the recall of a diplomatic agent who has become *persona non grata*, or even to dismiss him by handing to him his passports.[12]

The internal organization of an embassy or legation is determined by each state for itself. There are usually, below the chief of the mission, a number of secretaries; a legal advisor, called Counselor; various attachés, persons attached to the mission with diplomatic status for the purpose of studying particular problems, military, commercial, financial, etc.; and such clerks, interpreters, and others as are needed.[13] The diplomatic corps in a capital has a loose organization, the ambassador longest in residence there being the *doyen;* precedence is based upon seniority of residence at that capital, within each rank.

The ambassabor, or other diplomatic agent, is the spokesman for his country in the state to which he is accredited. A constant interchange of views is carried on, and sometimes more formal negotiations which may lead to a treaty. He and his staff gather information as to the policies, military strength, economic situation, public opinion, or any other matter which might be of service to his own government. He has the task of protecting the interests of his own state and of his fellow countrymen in the state where he is at work. The ambassador's purpose is to promote good relations, and to do this he must win the confidence of those with whom he has to deal. He should therefore be able to speak the language of the country and should understand and respect its customs. If he laughs at the idea of afternoon tea, he may offend; if he refuses to serve wine in France, or does serve it in a Moslem country, he may lose favor. He cannot gain good will by attempting to impose the customs of his own country upon the country to which he is sent. The task of a diplomat is a delicate one; it calls for some native characteristics and for quite a lot of training.

---

position of a foreign envoy wedded to a Jewess by civil marriage would be untenable and even impossible in Vienna." The United States recognized the right of Austria to refuse to accept Keiley, but for several years appointed no minister to Austria. Moore, *Digest*, IV, § 638.

[12] During the First World War the United States requested the recall of the Austro-Hungarian Ambassador, Dumba, and of the German military and naval attachés. For the famous case of Lord Sackville, British Ambassador to the United States, see Moore, *Digest*, IV, § 640.

[13] For many years, the foreign service of the United States was the prey of the spoils system, and only men of independent means could afford to take a post. Improvement began with the Rogers Act of 1924, which amalgamated the diplomatic and consular services, and provided remuneration which enabled our representatives to live. Subsequent legislation has improved their situation; there are post allowances and other perquisites, and many embassy buildings are now owned by the United States. Unfortunately, the morale of the foreign service was badly shaken by the unjust accusations made in the name of national security during the early 1950's. See W. P. Maddox, "The Foreign Service in Transition," *Foreign Affairs*, 25 (1947), p. 303; George Kennan, "The Future of our Professional Diplomacy," *ibid.*, 33 (1955), p. 566.

39. PRIVILEGES AND IMMUNITIES[14]

Chiefly in order to give him freedom in the performance of his important functions of preserving harmony between nations and to leave him unembarrassed in this respect, but partly also out of respect to his own state and to the principle *par in parem non habet imperium*, a diplomatic official is accorded certain privileges. The most important of these is inviolability and special protection. "The person of a public minister is sacred and inviolable. Whoever offers any violence to him not only affronts the sovereign he represents, but also hurts the common safety and well-being of nations; he is guilty of a crime against the whole world."[15] A similar protection must be given to his residence and property, and his correspondence with his own government must not be disturbed. He may display his flag or emblem, and worship as he pleases. He is allowed freedom of transit to or from his post, even though dismissed; and this freedom applies also to third states through which he must pass. Whether by law or by comity, he is accorded such privileges as bringing his baggage uninspected through the customs.

For the same reasons, a diplomatic official is immune from practically all jurisdiction on the part of the state to which he is accredited. The embassy itself may not be entered by local police without permission, though it is doubtful whether the rule would be respected in extreme cases, such as the use of the embassy as an asylum for a criminal.[16] The envoy himself may not be arrested or subjected to

[14] There is a large literature concerning diplomatic privileges and immunities—consult any good text of international law. Reference may be made to: *Com. Prog. Cod.*, "Questionnaire No. 3, Diplomatic Privileges and Immunities," reprinted in *A.J.*, 20 (1926), Special Number, pp. 148-75; *Research in International Law*, Diplomatic Privileges and Immunities; C. Eagleton, "The Responsibility of the State for the Protection of Foreign Officials," *A.J.*, 19, p. 293; R. Genet, *Traité de Diplomatie et de Droit Diplomatique* (Paris, 1931-32); C. J. B. Hurst, "Les immunités diplomatiques," *Hague Acad.*, 1926, II, p. 119; Ch. Morton, *Les privilèges et immunités diplomatiques* (Lausanne, 1927); E. Satow, *A Guide to Diplomatic Practice* (3rd ed., London, 1932). The International Law Commission of the United Nations has now begun study of this topic.

[15] *Respublica v. de Longchamps*, 1 Dallas 116; see Bishop, pp. 446-50; Briggs, pp. 748-811; Moore, *Digest*, IV, p. 622. Each state has laws providing special penalties for attacks of this sort. See *U.S. Rev. Stat.*, §§ 4062-4065. The famous case of Mattueof in England, which necessitated passing the Act of Anne (7 Anne, c. 12) illustrates the duty of a state, C. de Martens, *Causes Célèbres* (Leipzig, 1858-61), II, pp. 47-74. For other citations, refer to p. 99 above.

[16] Political asylum is upheld more in Latin America than elsewhere. In a recent instance, Haya de la Torre, a Peruvian politician, sought asylum in the Colombian embassy, which shielded him for several years. The case was heard three times by the International Court of Justice. *I.C.J. Reports*, 1950, pp. 266 and 395, and *ibid.*, 1951, p. 71. Similarly, the dictator Peron, unseated in Argentina, found asylum in Paraguay.

jurisdiction for any reason whatever, unless, as would probably happen in any serious matter, his state should waive immunity for him. In the case of Carlos Waddington, who had committed a murder, the Belgian government surrounded the Chilean embassy in order to prevent his escape, but did not arrest him until the Chilean government had waived immunity for him. The diplomat cannot be compelled to give evidence, though he may be authorized to do so by his own state. How far he is free from taxation is at present uncertain. These immunities extend to the diplomat's official staff, to his own family, and to his servants. In practice, such persons are registered with the foreign office of the place of residence, and their status may be easily ascertained by reference to the diplomatic list.

Exemption from local process does not leave the local state entirely unprotected, nor the diplomat himself entirely irresponsible. The purpose of immunities today is not to advertise the dignity of a monarch or of a state, but to maintain free from interruption the highly important business between states. The diplomat is expected to use his privileges for this purpose, and not for his own glorification. He is not free to violate the laws of the state to which he is accredited, although he cannot be punished by the law of that state for violations. As Hyde says: "the functions of a minister are not deemed to be curtailed by his respect for the local law; and his usefulness to his own country is increasingly regarded as dependent upon his possession of a reputation unblemished by any imputation of hostility or unfriendliness toward the state to which he is accredited."[17] In any serious case, his own state would usually waive immunity and leave him to be tried under the law which he has violated. Other penalties, however, are available to the injured state. An offending diplomat may be reported to his superiors who may impose upon him a penalty more severe than the local law provides. His recall may be demanded and, in extreme cases, he can be given his passports and escorted from the country. While abuse of diplomatic privileges sometimes occurs, the deterrents against abuse are powerful.[18]

As the sacrosanct character of the state has diminished, so have the privileges of its ambassadors. The quality accorded to the diplomat today is not so much inviolability as freedom from interference in the performance of his duties. Modern conditions have altered his situa-

[17] Hyde, II, p. 1266.

[18] Too many cases of speeding, for example might bring a protest from the state and this would indicate that his status as *persona grata* had been impaired. The result might be transfer to a lesser post, or dismissal from the service—a penalty far more severe than the local court could impose. See C. Hill, "Sanctions Constraining Diplomatic Representatives to Abide by the Local Law," *A.J.*, 25 (1931), p. 252.

tion. It is no longer necessary to maintain an entire quarter of a city exempt from national jurisdiction for the benefit of local diplomats; and not so many servants are needed, each with immunities, when a taxicab can be summoned at a moment's notice or a bath obtained merely by turning a faucet. The intricacy of modern business has created problems which the old mantle of the diplomat can hardly cover—for example, foreign exchange or radio communication or the control and taxation of shares of stock owned by him. The increase in the number and type of national agents abroad produces a disinclination on the part of states to extend further the peculiar privileges of a diplomat; it is often true that an agent sent by a state on a specific mission performs more important functions than the agent accredited as a diplomat. On the whole, the tendency seems to be to decrease the privileges as well as the number of those to whom these privilges belong—though increasing activity constantly swells the number. Dignity is now less important than getting the job done efficiently.

This seems to be particularly true of the growing numbers of a new type of diplomat, the international official who is either a member of the staff of, or the representative of a state to, an international organization. Such persons are engaged in multilateral diplomacy, which calls for methods different from those of the old bilateral diplomacy and more nearly resembling parliamentary negotiation, and is done in the brightest limelight. The privileges and immunities of such persons are based upon treaty and are usually limited to those necessary for the fulfillment of the purposes of the organization in which they participate. They raise many new problems, particularly for the state in which the headquarters of the organization is found.[19]

40. CONFERENCES[20]

A conversation between two diplomats in an embassy office, or even over a Cointreau at a sidewalk cafe, could be regarded as a conference,

[19] See Article 105 of the Charter of the United Nations, and § 85, below; also, Cheever and Haviland, pp. 819-21.

[20] See on this topic, *Com. Prog. Cod.*, "Procedure of International Conferences and Procedure for the Conclusion and Drafting of Treaties," *A.J.*, 20 (1926), Special Number, pp. 747-50; F. S. Dunn, *The Practice and Procedure at International Conferences* (John Hopkins Studies, 1929); R. G. Gruber, *Internationale Kongresse und Konferenzen* (Berlin, 1919); N. L. Hill, *The Public International Conference* (Stanford University Press, 1929); F. W. Holls, *The Peace Conference at the Hague* (New York, 1900); V. D. Pastuhov, *A Guide to the Practice of International Conferences* (Washington, 1945); E. Satow, *International Congresses*, Foreign Office Peace Handbooks, Hist. Sect., No. 151 (London, 1920).

but the term has, usually, a more formal and impressive connotation. A conference, or congress, is ordinarily a specially assembled meeting of the representatives of a number of states for the purpose of reaching agreement, through this more formal and more collective method of negotiation, upon matters of interest to that group; and matters of such importance are today usually of interest to most members of the community of nations.

Conferences were, before the creation of the League of Nations, impromptu and haphazard; they depended upon whether or not some state felt sufficient interest in a subject to assume responsibility for summoning and maintaining a conference to discuss it. While one could be summoned at any time, by any state, for any purpose, it was costly and risky to hold a conference. Except for a few public unions, there was no automatic or regular means of summoning or managing a conference. With the establishment of the League of Nations, conferences have become more regular, more numerous, and more efficient. A central secretariat makes possible the automatic calling of a conference to deal with a particular problem; it allows thorough preparation in advance, better management of procedure, and continuation of the effort after the conference has adjourned. A vast amount of business is thus conducted on behalf of the community of nations, which can not act through a legislature but must seek agreement among the sovereign states, its members.

Since the chief function of conferences today is the preparation of international legislation, discussion of the procedure of conferences is reserved for consideration in a later chapter.

41. TREATIES[21]

The work of the diplomat may proceed by conversations, without record, or perhaps with an *aide-memoire* to help recall what was said; it may be conducted through correspondence, and thus have a written record; or it may eventuate in a signed agreement, in legally binding

[21] As to treaties in general, see J. Basdevant, "La conclusion et la rédaction des traités et des instruments diplomatiques autres que les traités," *Hague Acad.*, 1926, V, pp. 539-643; L. Bittner, *Die Lehre von den völkerrechtlichen Vertragsurkunde* (Stuttgart, 1924); *Com. Prog. Cod.*, Report to the Council (1927.V.16); A. F. Frangulis, *Théorie et Pratique des Traités Internationaux* (Academie Diplomatique International, 8é Année); W. McClure, *International Executive Agreements* (New York, 1941); A. D. McNair, *The Law of Treaties* (New York, 1938); *Research in International Law*, Law of Treaties (1935); Q. Wright, "Conflicts between International Law and Treaties," *A.J.*, 11 (1917), p. 566.

The International Law Commission of the United Nations is now working upon the law of treaties. A draft report by Lauterpacht, Rapporteur, is to be found in *U.N. Doc.* A/CN.4/63.

form, generally called a treaty. The modern community of nations is built upon treaties, and the rule *pacta sunt servanda*, the most fundamental norm in international law, holds the system together. The treaty has been developed from an agreement between two states for their own purposes, until today it may be signed by most of the states of the world and embody rules or principles of the utmost importance to members of the community. This development represents the belief of these members, however slowly accepted, that it is through agreements, rather than through weapons, that progress is to be made.

POWER TO CONTRACT—INTERNATIONAL LAW. The validity of a treaty depends upon capacity to contract (which is a question both of international law and of domestic law) and upon execution of the document by the proper authorities and through the proper procedures. It is usually said that since states only are subjects of international law, only states can make treaties. In practice, states do sometimes make agreements which they call treaties with political bodies (e.g., an Indian tribe) which are not recognized as members of the community of nations. Whether an international court would interpret such treaties according to the rules of international law may be open to question and certainly such agreements must be distinguished from ordinary contracts made between states and individuals. But not every state has an unlimited capacity to make treaties. As Hall says, "All states which are subject to international law are capable of contracting, but they are not all capable of contracting for whatever object they wish."[22]

POWER TO CONTRACT—CONSTITUTIONAL LAW. This capacity is measured also by internal constitutional law. The head of the state is recognized by international law as the authority through whom such obligations are assumed by the state, but he may be restricted by his state's constitution. While on the one hand a state would not care to be bound by a treaty exceeding the constitutional limits of its treaty-making power, on the other hand it would not permit another state to pass judgment upon its constitution, nor would another state be so presumptuous. It would appear, then, that a state has only the duty of assuring itself that it is dealing with the authorities empowered by the constitution of the other state with the authority to make treaties; it has not the right to determine whether these authorities have exceeded their constitutional powers, internally. The responsibility for seeing to it that these officials do not exceed their authority must rest upon the state which authorizes them to act for it.[23]

[22] Hall, p. 380.
[23] See footnote 9, above.

This problem presents itself in particularly difficult form in the United States, whose Constitution says: "This Constitution, and the Laws of the United States which shall be made in pursuance thereof; and all Treaties made, or which shall be made, under the Authority of the United States, shall be the supreme law of the Land." This phrase "Authority of the United States" may be interpreted as meaning, within the limits of the Constitution, or as meaning, made by the authority designated in the Constitution. The former construction, if strictly adhered to, could render impossible a treaty which dealt with any matters reserved to the member states. In the case of *Missouri* v. *Holland*, however, the Supreme Court held valid, under a treaty with Canada, a statute formerly declared by it to be an unconstitutional assumption by Congress of power belonging to a State.[24] In the era of legislative treaties, upon which the United States is now entering, capacity to make such treaties will be of vital importance, for they deal with almost any imaginable subject. Both the United States and other states would suffer if the Constitution were interpreted to forbid making treaties in the field of labor, health, control of arms, trade, or atomic energy.

It is not clear whether a treaty in direct violation of a specific prohibition of the Constitution would be upheld by the Supreme Court. It would not be unreasonable to interpret the Constitution as purposely leaving the treaty-making power without stated limits, since it is impossible to foretell under what circumstances a treaty might have to be made—e.g., a treaty of peace after defeat in war. Doubtless the Supreme Court will expand the treaty-making power to meet the needs of the nation, just as it has done with the commerce power.[25] But it should always be remembered that a treaty properly made by the designated constitutional authorities of a state binds that state in international law, and that the state will be held responsible for violations of it.

RATIFICATION. Treaties are usually negotiated by persons commissioned by the chief of state for that purpose. In the days of Grotius, the plenipotentiary was given "full powers" through which he could,

---

[24] *Missouri v. Holland*, 252 U.S. 416 (1920); see also *Santovincenzo v. Egan*, 284 U.S. 30. Numerous citations are given to literature dealing with this question in Hyde, II, p. 1392.

While the United States has at times been unwilling to negotiate treaties which might seem to invade the reserved rights of States, Secretary Stimson said in 1932 that "the position that we did not have the constitutional powers to enter into a treaty providing for such control was not well taken." Hackworth, V, p. 21.

For British practice, see McNair, Chap. ii.

[25] See the remarks of former Chief Justice C. E. Hughes, in *Proc. Am. Soc.*, 1929, pp. 194-95.

by his own signature, bind his state. The modern constitutional requirement that the legislative body must approve the treaty has made such authority rare. The "full power" today refers to discretion in negotiation rather than power to bind. Signature by the plentipotentiaries signifies agreement to the terms and text of the treaty, which cannot thereafter be altered without the consent of all; and the treaty is usually dated from its signature. But the approval of the states themselves, evidenced through exchange of ratifications, is necessary in order to make the treaty a legally binding instrument.

If the requirement of ratification was justified at one time through fear that the sovereign might be betrayed by his agent, today its justification is found in the necessity of securing the approval of the people, in the democratic systems of this age. It has the virtue of preventing the conclusion of secret treaties binding the state to objectionable measures, but it also brings with it very great inconveniences, and the question is often raised as to whether there is a duty of ratification. Clearly there is no legal duty; otherwise, ratification would be useless. But there is certainly an obligation, founded in the convenience of the community of nations, to refuse ratification only for excellent reasons. When an envoy may be in direct communication with his chief executive upon all questions which may arise during negotiations, it is fair to assume that the treaty will be concluded in accordance with the wishes of that authority. However, ratification depends in many states upon another agency of the government. Where this situation exists, it is distinctly to the discredit of a state if its agencies are unable to agree; and its credit abroad is sure to suffer.[26]

Aside from such internal problems, states are in general dilatory in approving treaties, and this, granted the present need for treaties, particularly for those of a legislative character, makes development to meet the needs of the community of nations slow and difficult. It becomes the more difficult when one takes into account the practice of affixing reservations—a practice rendered notorious by the Senate of the United States.[27] A reservation attaches, for the state making it,

[26] The policy of the Senate of the United States, which must approve treaties before the President may proceed to ratification, has aroused much criticism. The House of Representatives has never failed in its moral obligation of providing the money and legislation necessary to make a treaty effective, though it could easily, if it followed the example of the Senate, demand an improper share in the treaty-making process. See Fleming, *The Treaty Veto of the Senate*; J. E. Harley, "The Obligation to Ratify Treaties," *A.J.*, 13 (1919), pp. 389-405; K. Colegrove, *The American Senate and World Peace* (New York, 1944); Q. Wright, "The United States and International Agreements," *Int. Con.*, No. 411 (1945), p. 379.

[27] Notorious is hardly too strong a word to use when one considers the reservations made to the Treaty of Versailles, for political party purposes, which kept the United States out of the League of Nations, the quite useless reservations made concerning

a condition or exception to the treaty and, in principle, it must be accepted by other signatories. The efforts, which included two international conferences, to meet the reservations of the United States Senate to adherence to the Permanent Court of International Justice probably required more time and effort than would have been necessary to negotiate a new treaty.

The problem of reservations was unsatisfactorily answered by the International Court of Justice in a case arising from the perplexity of the Secretary-General of the United Nations over reservations offered to the Genocide Convention. That convention was to come into effect with twenty ratifications, and the Secretary-General was unable to say whether a ratification accompanied by a reservation should be counted. He referred the question to the General Assembly, which debated it at length and then asked the Court for an advisory opinion, at the same time asking the advice of the International Law Commission. The two bodies gave divergent answers, and the Assembly approved the one from the Court, to the effect that any state could make a reservation, and that each other signatory could determine for itself whether it would accept the reservation offered. The result could be, in a multilateral treaty, a quite incomprehensible set of bilateral relationships among signatories.[28]

TERMINATION. A treaty may expire because the set time limit has been reached; and some provision is usually made in modern treaties, either for automatic expiration, or for denunciation upon notice given, or for renewal unless denied. Or it may be dissolved through the mutual agreement of its makers, either expressely or through conclusion of another treaty replacing it. There is much uncertainty as to which treaties survive a war.[29] If a treaty is violated by one party, the other party may declare it void.

In general, however, there is insufficient provision in the law of nations for the revision of a treaty which does not include in itself a method of termination. To supply this need the rule that circumstances alter cases has been argued: *Omnis conventio intelligitur*

---

adherence to the Permanent Court of International Justice, and the consistent reservations with regard to treaties of compulsory arbitration. The reservation unnecessarily added to the adherence to the "Optional Clause" of the Statute of the International Court of Justice, with regard to "domestic questions" was followed by other states, with damaging effect upon the compulsory jurisdiction of the court. See H. W. Malkin, "Reservations to Multilateral Conventions," *B.Y.I.L.*, 1926, p. 141; McNair, Chap. ix; H. D. Miller, *Reservations to Treaties* (Washington, 1919); M. Owen, "Reservations to Multilateral Treaties," *Yale Law Journal*, 38 (1928-29), p. 1086; also citations in footnote 26, above.

[28] *I.C.J. Reports*, 1951, p. 15.

[29] See cases in Bishop, pp. 147-56; Briggs, pp. 934-46; Dickinson, *Cases*, pp. 1112-22; Hudson, *Cases*, pp. 964-81.

rebus sic stantibus.[30] States have at times attempted to free themselves from an antiquated or burdensome treaty by reference to this principle. An unbending rule of *pacta sunt servanda* could block progress and lead to intolerable situations; on the other hand, a state cannot be permitted to violate its obligations and justify its violation by maintaining that circumstances are no longer the same as they were when the treaty was made. Lacking the consent of all parties, there appears to be no way to revise a treaty unless it contains within itself provisions for this purpose—except by a treaty after a war, which is legitimate so long as war is legitimate. Until the community of nations becomes better organized and able to intervene in such a situation, the argument of *rebus sic stantibus* can hardly be maintained; termination cannot be left to the unilateral judgment of a signatory. The Covenant of the League of Nations attempted to care for the situation by providing (Article 19) that the Assembly could advise reconsideration of treaties which had become inapplicable; but it found it impossible to apply this principle in practice. The Charter of the United Nations contains no such provision, except by implication in Article 14.

DURESS AND ILLEGAL NATURE. There appears to be no rule in international law, as there is in domestic law, which would make invalid a treaty signed under duress. If there were such a rule, a treaty of peace signed after defeat would not be valid. In the anarchy which war produces, such a rule could not stand; but the defeated state has the same opportunity to upset the treaty by war as the conqueror had to impose it by war—however satisfactory that may be. It is often asserted that a treaty established for purposes contrary to international law is illegal and not binding. Desirable as this may be, there seems little support for it in practice. Hall's statement that "a treaty is not binding which has for its object the subjugation or partition of a country" finds no substantiation in history.[31] Poland was partitioned. The United States has negotiated with Great Britain a treaty which sets aside a rule of law admitted in the same treaty—the three-mile limit. On the other hand, the Covenant of the League of Nations (Article 20) and the Charter of the United Nations (Article 103) both assert that the constitutional document prevails over any treaty inconsistent therewith.

[30] The rule was asserted by Russia in 1870 to escape certain clauses of the Treaty of Paris of 1856. As a result, the Powers agreed that "it is an essential principle of the law of nations that no power can liberate itself from the engagements of a treaty, nor modify the stipulations thereof, unless with the consent of the contracting powers by means of an amicable arrangement." See Hall, pp. 409-12; A. D. McNair, "La terminaison et la dissolution des traités," *Hague Acad.*, 1928, II, p. 463; H. Tobin, *The Termination of Multilateral Treaties* (New York, 1933).

[31] Hall, p. 383; and see Hyde, II, § 490; Oppenheim, I, p. 713; Fenwick, p. 330.

INTERPRETATION. In interpreting a treaty, the purpose is to seek out the agreed intention of its makers and this is often much more difficult than it would appear to be. The signatory parties may agree upon an interpretation, or they may submit the matter to an international tribunal. Various canons of interpretation have been laid down by publicists and in cases, some of them highly technical and refined.[32] In general, the rules should be those of common sense; treaties should be interpreted according to their reasonable rather than their literal sense; words should be understood in their usual meaning rather than hunting for special meanings; the whole must be considered rather than any part; and, where the text is ambiguous, the intention of the framers may be sought in the *travaux préparatoires*, the records of the negotiations.

The treaty, always an instrument of the greatest importance, has now even greater significance as the only instrument through which new international law can purposefully be made; it will be considered from this viewpoint in Chapter 8. For such important purposes as they serve, both the law and procedure for treaty-making is surprisingly inadequate. It is indeed difficult to define a treaty and to know whether or how it can be distinguished from other forms of international agreement, such as an exchange of notes. Much improvement is needed in these respects before the treaty can serve efficiently the purpose for which it is badly needed—that of peaceful change in the community of nations.

[32] As to the interpretation of treaties, see C. C. Hyde, "The Interpretation of Treaties by the Permanent Court of International Justice," *A.J.*, 24 (1930), pp. 1-19; McNair, pp. 163-306; R. R. Wilson, "Interpretation of Treaties," *Proc. Am. Soc.*, 1930, pp. 39-45; J. C. Yü, *The Interpretation of Treaties* (New York, 1927).

PART III

The next step toward international government was the appearance of institutions established by and acting in the name of the community of nations. These institutions were specialized, each dealing with a particular technical function; it was not until the League of Nations that an attempt was made to set up an over-all institution for the maintenance of peace and order among nations.

It is doubtless somewhat misleading to classify these developments under the usual categories of executive, legislative, and judicial, but for purposes of convenience the following three chapters are so arranged. Actually, the development was haphazard, and institutions and procedures were squeezed into whatever form the pressure of conflicting forces made possible. There was little advance toward executive organization, but definite progress in the administrative field. The greatest advance was probably that made in the means of settling disputes between nations; the least was in the field of making new law.

PART III

Chapter 7

INTERNATIONAL ADMINISTRATION

42. NEW NEEDS

Up to this point, our discussion of international intercourse has been concerned with the individual and independent action of states. There has been, thus far, no institutional character to this development, no integrated machinery representing the collective action of the entire community. Each state made its own arrangements with each other state separately, and dealt only with those with whom it was pleased to deal. To secure universal or even uniform action under such conditions was practically impossible. Any machinery set up for such a purpose was *ad hoc*.

Further development was essential, and under the pressure of common need new methods and institutions began to appear. These did not represent the particularistic aims and methods of separate states, but were rules and institutions characteristic of an integrated society. States pooled their efforts and worked through central organizations speaking the joint voice of all, rather than speaking in many discordant voices. Judicial machinery, at first irregularly constituted and rudimentary in character, slowly evolved into the highly respected Permanent Court of International Justice. International unions and other administrative bodies began to act in the name of the collective society. Instead of bilateral agreements, multifarious in character and innumerable in number, between pairs of states, conferences undertook to handle matters of interest to all in one meeting of all, and multilateral treaties were employed as the instrument of international legislation.

During the latter half of the nineteenth century and the early part of the twentieth, much progress was made. At the least, the fundamental problems and difficulties were uncovered, and in some cases significant advance was made toward solutions. The gains made were, however, quite incommensurate with the needs to be met. Individuals have not yet learned to think and plan intelligently upon an international basis, but

157

the pressure of international interdependence, now at its height, is
steadily forcing them out of exclusive faith in national sovereignty and
into acceptance of rules and procedures set up by the community of
nations. Economic losses are better teachers than textbooks, and the
two world wars of the twentieth century ruthlessly teach the need for
more efficient international government.

New problems appear every day. How can the resources of the sea
—fish, sponges, pearls, oil, etc.—be conserved except through international regulation? How can air traffic be safely carried on between
nations? The development of international rivers calls for administrative machinery. There are suggestions of international administration
over the subsoil of the deep seas, over Antarctic regions, or over the
airspace in which satellites will be circulating. The number of international organizations grows, bringing more administration in the
form of civil service, personnel, and management problems. Weather
forecasting, common measurements for screw threads and other things,
common terms for medical supplies—the needs for common action
are innumerable.

International organization cannot be effective until national
systems can be geared into it. The machinery of national governments
was originally built with only the domestic needs of the state in view,
and with no realization of the fact, now pressing heavily upon states,
that domestic efforts of all sorts depend, to an increasing degree, upon
situations external to the state. The national state has become, willy-
nilly, part of a wider system. The cogs of national governmental machinery do not fit into the wheels of the international system, and
both suffer from the resulting friction and inefficiency. Today, it is
the community of nations which suffers most; but already it is apparent that a state stands to lose greatly if it is unable to participate
rapidly and smoothly in international action. Conflict with national
constitutions appears in many forms. It may be that a proposed course
of procedure is in conflict with constitutional provisions and cannot
be adopted until the difficult process of constitutional amendment has
been carried through. The method of making treaties in a particular
state may be inefficient, and international legislation may be delayed
because of such incapacity, with resultant loss to that particular state.
The federal state, with its inability to bind its members, presents a peculiarly difficult problem. It is uncertain how far a chief of state may
bind his own state, nor is it clear what a treaty is in the law of each
state. In the ensuing pages, the effects of this situation will often be
seen, whether as to administrative, legislative, or judicial action. No
answer is available at present; but the student of international govern-

ment will have to devote much thought in the future to the reorganization of his own domestic government, so that it may fit in with and profit from the developing international government.[1]

43. DEVELOPMENT OF ADMINISTRATIVE FUNCTIONS

As law develops, it acquires a positive as well as a negative character. It not only prohibits certain acts, but it performs certain acts. It says not only "this must (or must not) be done by the citizen," but also, "this must be done *for* the citizen." The function of government is not merely to give commands to its citizens, but to perform services for them. In consequence, the machinery of government has been steadily increasing as its range of action necessarily widens. These newer services, contributing to health, prosperity, and so on, are largely technical and administrative in character. The increase of administration is the most marked characteristic of modern governments. New departments have been, and are being, steadily added, and each of them expands its activities continuously. These departments, with but few exceptions, found that they were incapable of coping with the problems which faced them within the confines of their territorial jurisdiction. The health of the nation, for example, could not be properly protected until international arrangements could be made to prevent the transfer of disease from other states. The departments of Commerce and Agriculture, and others, find it necessary to maintain many agents abroad, and encourage international agreements for the solution of their problems. Internal and external activities are inextricably mixed; even in Congressional debates the statement may be heard that it is no longer possible to keep foreign and domestic affairs in separate categories.

PRIVATE INTERNATIONAL ASSOCIATIONS. Within the state, much machinery had been created to perform the increasing functions of government; it appeared equally necessary to set up machinery to take care of the international phases of these functions. There has been a large response to this pressure in the form of private international associations. They range from the Olympic Games to the World Parliament of Religions; from the Red Cross to the International Railway

[1] In the United States, the procedure of treaty-making has been under heavy attack, and efforts have been made to develop a bipartisan foreign policy. In order for the nation to speak with one voice, it would be necessary to coordinate the shares of the various departments in the statement of foreign policy, and to coordinate the representatives of the United States in the various international organizations to which she now belongs. See, as to the general problem, the symposium in the *Pol. Sci. Rev.*, 38 (1944), p. 913; W. Y. Elliott and a study group of the Woodrow Wilson Foundation, *United States Foreign Policy: Its Organization and Control* (New York, 1952).

Union. There is an International Wine Office to encourage the use of wine, and an International Bureau against Alcoholism to discourage it. Legislators meet in the Inter-Parliamentary Union; businessmen in the International Chamber of Commerce; laborers in the International Association for the Legal Protection of Labor; students in the Students' International Union. There are associations for hotel-keepers, and associations for the deaf and dumb. Great business corporations, such as the Standard Oil Company, are international in their organization. A complete list of such bodies would mount up into the thousands; indeed, granted their independent action and often ephemeral character, it would be practically impossible to compile a complete list.[2] They do, however, cover almost every field of human activity, and illustrate in remarkable fashion the extent to which such human activities depend upon factors beyond national frontiers and call for international organizations.

PUBLIC INTERNATIONAL UNIONS. Private associations lead to official ones. To such private bodies states might send delegates, or offer subventions. In many of them now in existence, governments are members alongside of private individuals and corporations; in others, administrative departments of governments, such as railway administrations, may be members. The transition from purely private to purely official organizations is very gradual, and is often difficult to draw a boundary line. Such bodies as the European Conference on Time Tables, with delegates from states, from railway and steamship administrations, and from Pullman and air companies, defy classification. The International Agricultural Coordination Commission included in its membership the official Institute of Agriculture, various sections of the Secretariat of the League of Nations, the International Chamber of Commerce, the Institute of Intellectual Cooperation, and many private agricultural societies. The International African Institute lists as members "Governments, scientific organisations, learned societies, research institutions, business houses, missionary societies and private indi-

2 The Yearbook of International Organizations, 1951-52, lists 951 such organizations, of which 385 had appeared since 1944. This volume is published by the Union of International Associations, located at Brussels. Some fascinating titles are to be found in this list; for example, what is the International Liaison Committee for the Maximum Card? or Fleurop-Interflora? or the Mazdaznan Youth Movement? The International Magical Congress should not be overlooked, nor the Federation of Pelota Vasca.

See the various issues of La Vie Internationale, published at Brussels from 1908-9; the League of Nations, Handbook of International Organizations (Geneva, 1938); International Organizations in Which the United States Participates, Dept. of State Pub. No. 3655 (1949). A great deal of current information is provided in the Dept. of State Bulletin.

viduals." We shall soon encounter the difficulty of defining an international public union; the attempt to define a private international association has produced a number of learned dissertations, but no agreement.[3]

The purposes sought by these international associations may sometimes be best served by private bodies, sometimes by official bodies, sometimes by both. Efforts to regulate particular commodities in trade may be either public or private, or both, as in the case of sugar or coffee[4]; some bodies may ultimately become specialized agencies. The public international unions were created by differing groups to meet differing needs, and they have followed no set model; they have paid little attention to the juridical bases and classifications laid down by political scientists.[5] As "experiments in international administration," they vary widely as to function, institutions, authority, methods, and scope. To classify them is almost impossible; as Potter says, it would be as difficult to classify the pebbles on the beach.

For our purposes, the easiest approach is through function, and we shall survey the earlier administrative agencies under the headings: Transport; Communications; Cultural and Scientific; Economic; and

---

[3] See Guillois, "Les Associations Internationales," *R.D.I.P.*, 22 (1915), pp. 1-127; A. Normandin, *Du Statut Juridique des Associations Internationales* (Paris, 1926); Union des Associations Internationales, Publication No. 98, August, 1921 (Bruxelles).

[4] See M. B. Amzalak, "Le Café et le sucre au point de vue international" in *Hague Acad.*, 78 (1951); Palmer and Perkins, p. 258; E. S. Mason, *Controlling World Trade: Cartels and Commodity Agreements* (New York, 1946). The League of Nations made a study of Economic Aspects of International Industrial Agreements (E.736.1931. II. B.21).

[5] For classifications, see Burns, in *B.Y.I.L.*, 1926, p. 57; Kazansky, in *R.D.I.P.*, 9 (1902), p. 359; Neumeyer, in *R.D.I.* (*Genève*), 2 (1924), p. 349; Rapisardi-Mirabelli, in *Hague Acad.*, 1925, II, p. 367 *et seq.*; Woolf, *International Government*, pp. 169, 183.

On international public unions in general, see *Annuaire de la Vie Internationale*, 1905-7, Office Central des Institutions Internationales (Bruxelles), 1910-11; F. de Ruffini, "La protection internationale des droits sur les oeuvres litteraires et artistiques," *Hague Acad.*, 1926, II, p. 391; Descamps, *Les offices internationaux et leur avenir* (Bruxelles, 1894), Chaps. viii, xii; W. Kaufmann, "Les Unions internationales de nature économique," *Hague Acad.*, 1924, II, p. 181; F. Meili, *Die internationalen Unionen über das Recht der Weltverkehrsanstalten und des geistigen Eigentums* (Leipzig, 1899); G. Moynier, *Les bureaux internationaux des Unions universelles* (Genève, 1892); K. Neumeyer, "Les Unions internationales," *R.D.I.* (*Genève*), 2, 1924, pp. 16-40, 138-44, and 3 (1925), pp. 20-25, 102-8; M. Pilotti, "Les Unions d'Etats," *Hague Acad.*, 1928, IV, pp. 445-546; Poinsard, *Les Unions et ententes internationales* (Berne, 1901); A. Rapisardi-Mirabelli, "Théorie générale des Unions internationales," *Hague Acad.*, 1925, II, pp. 345-90; P. S. Reinsch, *Public International Unions* (Boston and London, 1911); P. S. Reinsch, "International Unions and Their Administration," *A.J.*, 1 (1907), pp. 579-623; L. Renault, "Les Unions internationales," *R.D.I.P.*, 3 (1896), pp. 14-26; B. Von Toll, *Die internationale Bureaux der allgemeinen völkerrechtliche Verwaltungsvereine* (Tübingen, 1910). The modern specialized agencies will be considered in Chap. 13 below.

Social. The large number of such bodies, even of those having an institutional character, renders impossible more than a summary survey.

44. TRANSPORT

WATERWAYS. Recalling the fact that in the channels of intercourse between states has been found the natural field for collisions and rivalry, and recalling also that it was here that the need for agreement was most effective in building up international solidarity, it is not surprising to find that in this field permanent organs of administrative character first begin to appear.

THE RHINE. We have already referred to the problem of the international river, the river which flows through more than one state. The admission of the general principle of territorial sovereignty in such a case as this may mean the exclusion from the sea of all commerce except that of the state which controls the river mouth. The two great river highways of Europe, the Danube and the Rhine, along the banks of which had marched the armies of barbarians, the Roman legions, and the Christian crusaders, had been disputed for centuries; and with the growth of trade, the adjustment of the many problems connected with their use became of pressing necessity. As far back as 1506 there was a treaty agreement providing for organized control of the Rhine; and many arrangements were made as to both rivers until more permanent principles were laid down by the Congress of Vienna. "The Congress of Vienna established the rule that international rivers—that is, rivers crossing or forming the boundary of more than one state—were to be administered for the benefit of the world commerce, but their administration and navigation were to be left in the hands of the riparian States."[6] Revisions were made of these provisions of the treaty which

[6] J. P. Chamberlain, *The Regime of the International Rivers: Danube and Rhine* (New York, 1923), CV, p. 29.

On international rivers, see also J. Blociszewski, "Le régime international du Danube," *Hague Acad.*, 1926, I, pp. 257-337; F. Corthèsy, *Etude de la Convention de Barcelone sur le régime des voies navigables d'intérêt international* (Paris, 1927); Ch. de Visscher, "Le nouveau régime international du Rhin," *R.D.I.L.C.*, 3rd Series, 1 (1920), pp. 80-85; J. Hostie, "Le Statut International du Rhin," *Hague Acad.*, 1929, III; A. Kasama, *La navigation fluviale en droit international* (Paris, 1928); G. Kaeckenbeeck, *International Rivers*, Grotius Society Publications, No. 1 (London, 1918); Sir Oswald Mance, *International River and Canal Transport* (1944); J. P. Niboyet, "Les tribunaux pour la navigation du Rhin et le pouvoir judiciaire de la Commission Centrale du Rhin," *R.D.I.P.*, 30 (1923), pp. 5-33; G. Sherman, "International Organization of the Danube under the Peace Treaties," *A.J.*, 17 (1923), pp. 438-59; H. A. Smith, *The Economic Uses of International Rivers* (1931); D. Sturdza, *Recueil de documents rélatifs à la liberté de Danube* (Berlin, 1904); G. Tarrius, *Les eaux industrielles internationales et leur réglementation internationale* (Perpignan, 1935); W. J. M. Van Eysinga, "Les fleuves et canaux internationaux," *Bib. Viss.*, 2 (1924), pp. 121-57.

applied at first only to the Rhine; but the machinery remained fundamentally the same. A Rhine Commission was set up to administer the principles of the treaty. It was composed of one member from each state bordering the Rhine, and each state had one vote, except in certain administrative matters, as to which, voting power was distributed according to the length of the river bank of each state. Its function was, in general, to prevent interference with navigability and to keep navigation moving according to its regulations. The necessity of uniform interpretation of these regulations called for judicial bodies, and so the "Rhine Courts" were established at convenient points on the river. These were local courts, with an appeal to a special court of appeal in each Rhine state, and their decisions were executory in the other states. Either party, however, might appeal to the commission instead of the national appeal court, and thus the application of the international agreement could come finally before an international tribunal.

In theory, changes in legislation were made by states; but a practice was accepted which deserves especial attention as the beginning of a flexible system which has since been put into almost universal use by public unions. In practice, regulations concerning navigation, licenses, and such matters, were adopted by the commission and accepted by states. To change the treaty itself, however, an international conference was necessary. Thus it is possible, in a union, to adjust regulations as rapidly as changing conditions demand, and not necessarily by unanimity, while the treaty remains the fundamental law, to be revised only by formal action.

THE DANUBE. The principles accepted at the Congress of Vienna were applied in the Treaty of Paris in 1856. Two commissions were set up by this treaty, the temporary European Danube Commission, to which the Great Powers and Turkey belonged, and whose function was to improve the navigation of the mouths of the river, and the Riparian Commission, composed of riparian states only, which was supposed to administer traffic on the river and to succeed to the European Commission's authority. However, the Riparian Commission was never put into operation, and the European Danube Commission gradually assumed complete control. The commission, to which Rumania, as a riparian state, was added when she became independent, was self-supporting through tolls and had an annual budget of about $400,000. It was authorized to undertake engineering works, to issue licenses, to fix and collect tolls and to levy fines. It had its own flag and diplomatic immunities and was neutralized. It was a remarkable example of the possibilities of international administration, independent of riparian states, able to impose its authority directly upon individuals, and efficient in operation.[7]

The development of international fluvial administration was advanced by the peace treaties at the end of World War I. Articles 354-362 of the Treaty of Versailles continued the previous organization and rules for the Rhine; and by Article 331, the Elbe, the Oder, the Niemen and the Danube were declared international rivers for which commissions and rules were provided. In the case of the Danube, in addition to continuing the European Danube Commission, Article 347 created an International Commission. The seat of the European Danube Commission was at Galatz, that of the International Commission at Bratislava; and the latter, like the former, had its own flag and privileges and immunities. The Danube was divided between them as the "maritime Danube" and the "fluvial Danube." A *Statut Definitif du Danube* was adopted at Paris in 1921; and a statute concerning the regime of navigable waters of international interest was annexed to the Barcelona Convention of 1921.[8]

World War II, however, wrecked this example of international river administration. Germany, under Hitler, denounced the clauses of the Treaty of Versailles with regard to rivers and made the denunciation effective with the occupation of Austria. After the defeat of Hitler, the Soviet Union called a conference at Belgrade in August 1948, at which it took the position of "the Danube for the Danubians," reaffirmed riparian sovereignty, declared former treaties void (without getting the consent of the signatories), excluded non-riparian states and put the Danube under the control of the riparian states, excluding Austria and Germany. In fact, the Danube is now under the control of the Soviet Union, and the great development of international law concerning rivers is badly set back.[9]

---

[7] P. Bailly, *Le Danube* (Paris, 1947); J. Blociszewski, "Le Régime international du Danube," *Hague Acad.*, 1926, I, p. 255; J. Duvernoy, *Le Régime international du Danube* (Paris, 1941); F. L. Hadsel, "Freedom of Navigation on the Danube," *Dept. of State Bull.*, 18 (1948), p. 787; H. Hajnal, *Le Droit du Danube International* (The Hague, 1929); Walker D. Hines, *Report on Danube Navigation*, League of Nations (C.444a. M.164a. 1925.VIII).

[8] See the next paragraph. A great deal of authoritative information is to be found in the case, Jurisdiction of the European Commission of the Danube, *P.C.I.J.* Series B, No. 14, in which Rumanian claims to riparian sovereignty were rejected. See also, G. Sherman, "The International Organization of the Danube under the Peace Treaties," *A.J.*, 17 (1923), p. 451.

[9] This development is summarized, with full documentation, by J. L. Kunz, "The Danube Regime and the Belgrade Conference," *A.J.*, 43 (1949), p. 104. Dr. Kunz remarks: "The Soviet Union fully enjoyed the 'mechanical voting' against which it thunders at Lake Success. There were no genuine negotiations at all." See *Dept. of State Bull.*, 19 (1948), p. 333; Rousseau, p. 399; Sibert, p. 807.

Barcelona Conference. The principle of freedom of communications and transit was affirmed in Article 23 of the Covenant of the League of Nations; and Article 338 of the Treaty of Versailles provided that the previous articles concerning international rivers were to be replaced by a later convention. Consequently, a committee of the Peace Conference was continued under the name of the *Commission pour l'étude de la liberté des communications et du transit*. This was taken over by the League of Nations, and was finally converted into the Advisory Commission of that body. The problem had become one of providing a uniform international regime for such rivers; and many new elements have now appeared, such, for instance, as hydraulic or electric power. Such a regime was established by the Conference of Barcelona of 1921, in the "Convention on the Regime of Navigable Waterways of International Concern."[10] It is correct to say that the principle of free navigation upon international rivers is a principle of international law.

Railways. Another group of means of communication obviously calling for international agreement is railways.[11] It is too much for impatient commerce calmly to endure, to require that passengers, and much more goods, shall be unloaded and reloaded at every frontier. But to permit direct passage through several states involved many problems, such, for example, as the division of labor and expenses involved in a single through ticket, or the more vital matter of a uniform gauge track upon which all trains could run. It was impossible for states individually to handle such matters and, after several attempts, a convention was signed at Berne in 1890 (revised in 1924) which created the International Union of Railway Freight Transportation. This office, according to Woolf, has more extended powers than any other international institution. The fundamental principle of the Convention was the obligation of the contracting states to transport through merchandise and to enforce this obligation upon their railways. To this end, the central office must necessarily be given a large degree of supervision. It arranges the settlement of accounts between

[10] Found in L. of N. *Treaty Series*, VII, pp. 36-63. See also F. Corthèsy, *Etude de la Convention de Barcelone sur le régime des voies navigables d'intérêt international* (Paris, 1927); Oppenheim, I, pp. 378-81.

[11] On railways, see P. Chavan, *Les communications internationales par voies ferrées et le problème de la souveraineté de l'état* (Lausanne, 1927); N. Droz, "L'Union internationale des chemins de fers," *R.D.I.P.*, 2 (1895), pp. 169-84; S. Raikowitch, *Le régime international des voies ferrées et la Société des Nations* (Paris, 1925); K. Stieler, *Die internationale Eisenbahnverband*, Völkerrechtsfragen, Pohl und Wenzel, Heft XI (Berlin, 1926); Sir Ralph Wedgwood and J. E. Wheeler, *International Rail Transport* (Oxford University Press, 1947). For the Pan American Railway Congress Association, see Dept. of State Pub. No. 3655, cited in footnote 2, above.

the various railway administrations, and has adequate power for the collection of debts. It does not merely advise, but gives decisions, upon the request of the disputants.

There are various other railway bodies more or less official in character—it must be remembered that railways in Europe are usually governmental enterprises. An International Conference for Promoting Technical Uniformity on Railways dates back to 1882. It has held a number of conferences, maintains a permanent bureau, and divides expenses among its eighteen member states according to the length of their railways. An International Railway Congress Association, founded at Brussels in 1885, is composed of companies and state railway administrations. There is a Committee for International Railway Transport, which was set up in 1902 to study legal problems; an International Railway Wagon Union (1921); an International Railway Union (1922) composed of railway administrations. In these organizations, sovereign states become associated with more humble bodies. In the European Conference on Time Tables (1923), for example, there assemble delegates of states, of railway and steamship administrations, and of Pullman and air companies. The Permanent International Association of Road Congresses (1908), which has in its membership fifty states and colonies, is subsidized by states, corporations, and individuals. A number of treaties concerning road transport were made under the United Nations in 1950 and thereafter.

AERIAL TRANSPORTATION. Finally, there remains to be considered the comparatively new field of aerial transportation. The Convention Relating to the Regulation of Aerial Navigation, signed at Paris in 1919, recognized "that every Power has complete and exclusive sovereignty over the air space above its territory," but each Power agreed to allow "freedom of innocent passage" to the aircraft of other contracting states which observe the conditions set down. Detailed regulations were provided as to marking and signals, traffic, licenses and medical certificates for pilots, meteorological information, customs, and similar matters. Clearly an administrative body was needed, and the convention provided for an International Commission for Air Navigation, located at Paris, and charged with many duties. It had a striking range of legislation in its power to change the regulations for aerial navigation by majority vote. In 1925 an International Conference on Private Law Affecting Air Questions created the Technical Committee of Legal Experts on Air Questions (CITEJA), in which forty-three states participated.[12] A convention signed at Warsaw in

[12] On aviation see Chap. 4, footnote 15, above and C. L. Bouvé, "The Development of International Rules of Conduct in Air Navigation," *Air Law Review*, 1 (1930),

1929 provided for the liability of the international air-carrier. A third Conference on Private Air Law was held at Rome in 1933, and a fourth at Brussels in 1938. The International Air Tranport Association, set up by private airline companies in 1945, replaced the earlier International Air Traffic Association, founded in 1919. Much of the activity above described is now absorbed in the International Civil Aviation Organization, which will be discussed in a later chapter.

Mention has already been made of the Organization of Communications and Transit of the League of Nations and of its work in co-ordinating the machinery and principles of river navigation. A similar task was undertaken by that body in other fields. The conference at Barcelona had adopted a general convention which asserted, on the part of signatories, the principle of freedom of transit (i.e., the right to utilize means of communications within all states) and the principle of equality of treatment. At the second General Conference of Communications and Transit, at Geneva in 1923, a similar task was accomplished for the regime of railways and for maritime ports, and other conventions were adopted as to electric and hydraulic power.

45. COMMUNICATIONS[13]

TELEGRAPHY. Telegraphy was introduced about 1840, and immediately became an international problem. In Europe several regional combinations were formed which, upon the initiative of France, were united, along with others, by the Convention of 1865, revised in 1875. It took the name of the Telegraphic Union in 1908. The first conference laid down the principles that wires should be open to the use of all, of cooperation between states, and of a base rate. In the battle between national sovereignty and common needs, the latter won, and an international bureau, the first of its kind, was set up at Berne to collect and distribute information and to prepare for conferences.

---

p. 1; K. Colegrove, *International Control of Aviation* (Boston, 1930); M. O. Hudson, "Aviation and International Law," *Air Law Review*, 1 (1930), p. 183, also found in *A.J.*, 24 (1930), p. 228; V. Little, "Control of International Air Transport," *Int. Organ.* 3 (1949), p. 29; O. J. Lissitzyn, *International Air Transport and National Policy* (New York, 1942); Sir Osborne Mance, *International Air Transport* (London, 1944); L. Tombs, *International Organization in European Air Transport* (New York, 1936); J. B. Van Zandt, *Civil Aviation and Peace* (Brookings Institution, Washington, 1944).

[13] On communications and transit in general, see M. Bourquin, "L'organisation internationale des voies de communications," *Hague Acad.*, 1924, IV, p. 163; Ch. de Visscher, *Le droit international des communications* (Paris, 1923); Ch. Dupuis, "Liberté des voies de communications. Relations internationales," *Hague Acad.*, 1924, I, p. 127; G. Hanotaux, *L'oeuvre de Barcelone* (Paris, 1922).

Three conferences have been held thus far dealing with radio-telegraphy. Reinsch tells us that it was at first a matter of exclusive private contracts, with the result that stations could not communicate with each other, no matter what distress there might be, unless the message was transmitted by the Marconi system. It was regarded as of nationalistic advantage for a state to have a monopoly on radio communication in this manner.[14] However, this position was partly surrendered at the Berlin Conference of 1906, and more fully at the London Conference of 1912. Provisions were made, applying to all wireless stations, requiring ship to ship or ship to coast communication and connection between local telegraph and coastal radio stations. In 1925 the International Broadcasting Union was set up by nine European countries, including both state and private broadcasting systems.

At the International Radiotelegraphic Conference of Washington, in 1927, the range of activity was defined as "the transmision by radio of writing, signs, signals, pictures, and sounds of all kinds by means of Hertzian waves," and it was extended to cover all stations, not merely maritime stations. This convention set up also an International Technical Consulting Committee. One of the difficulties of the conference, illustrating the problems of international organization, was the fact that in most cases the government operated the radiotelegraphic system, while in others, such as the United States, it was in private hands. The Telegraphic Union became the Telecommunications Union in 1934.[15]

POSTAL UNION. The best known of the Public Unions is the Universal Postal Union. During the Middle Ages, messages were carried by merchants, or by the messengers of monasteries, or others. As printing and commerce increased communications, governments took an interest in and protected such messengers. The Hapsburg Emperors turned over to the Taxis family the right to carry mails, and their system continued until 1867, when it was taken over by the Prussian Government, a natural step, since the postal service had become a public utility of the first order. Meanwhile, the reform of Sir Rowland Hill in England had introduced penny postage, involving the

---

[14] Reinsch, *Public International Unions*, p. 128; see also Woolf, *International Government*, pp. 212-16.

[15] On radiotelegraphy, see L. G. Caldwell, "The International Committee on Wireless Telegraphy," *Air Law Review*, 1 (1930), pp. 211-31; M. Davis, "International Radiotelegraph Conventions and Traffic Agreements," *ibid.*, pp. 349-75; A. Huth, *Radio Today*, Geneva Studies, XII, No. 6 (1942); I. Stewart, "The International Radiotelegraphic Conference of Washington," *A.J.*, 22 (1928), pp. 28-49; Sir O. Mance, *International Telecommunications* (1943); J. D. Tomlinson, *The International Control of Radio Communications* (Ann Arbor, 1945).

simple process of pasting on a stamp. But there was as yet no uniformity as between states. Each state had its own rates and its own weights; and the mathematical computations forced upon post offices were perplexing. The price depended upon the route taken, so that, to use Reinsch's well-known illustration, the cost of a letter sent from the United States to Australia would be 5 cents, 33 cents, 45 cents, 60 cents, or $1.02 per half ounce, according to the route by which it was sent. The situation was further complicated by the fact that a state might use its postal system as an income producer, and attempt to make a profit from other states. This was a game at which more than one could play.

A conference was held in Paris in 1863, upon the proposal of Postmaster-General Blair of the United States. Its purpose was simply to study the situation, and while it laid down no rules, it reached agreement as to principles. Meanwhile, Stephan in Germany had worked out a project by 1868, based upon the system among the German states; but the Franco-Prussian War delayed a conference until 1874. The Berne Conference simply brought to a head a great many proposals made by different persons. Agreement was reached upon a single postage rate (though some leeway was allowed each state), and upon a unit of weight. The principle that each administration should keep what it collected was adopted, though it has been the object of frequent attack since. An international bureau was created, and disputes were to be arbitrated. The Postal Union today embraces almost every area in the world.

The organization of the Universal Postal Union included congresses, conferences (now unused) and the bureau at Berne. Delegates have power to bind their governments to an unusual degree, and, in practice, ratifications are not awaited. The congress acts by majority vote, and, if ratifications are obtained to the signatures which make up this majority, others must accept the convention or withdraw. The Postal Union has the uncommon advantage of an automatic sanction which gives ample assurance that no state will withdraw.[16] Proposals may also be made between congresses, through the bureau, which submits them to governments for consideration. If a sufficient number of affirmative replies is received, the proposals are prepared by the Swiss Government as a diplomatic document, ready for signature. In such a case, unanimity is required for changes affect-

---

[16] "In one instance the French Government was strongly opposed to any change in a foreign postage rate, and its delegate announced that he would refuse to accept it. The proposed change, however, was adopted by a majority of votes; and the French Government, sooner than give up the incalculable advantages of membership in the Postal Union, promptly ratified the change." Sayre, *op. cit.*, p. 25.

ing organization or fundamental rules; a two-thirds majority for other provisions; and a majority if it is only a matter of interpreting the regulations.

The International Bureau of the Universal Postal Union is established at Berne, under the supervision of the Swiss Post Office. For the purpose of sharing expenses, members are divided into seven classes, of which the first class pays twenty-five units, and the seventh class one unit. The bureau has little authority, but its work is of much importance. It collects and distributes information which is essential; and for this purpose publishes a monthly magazine in four languages, a dictionary of post offices, a list of routes, and other such material. It makes investigations, handles interim proposals, and takes care of such matters as the loss of registered mail, or the division of sea transit charges. One of its most important functions is to interpret the convention at the request of a member. Disputes are submitted to the arbitration of two other postal administrations, one chosen by each disputant, a third being chosen if necessary by these two.

In the sense of having authority to compel obedience on the part of states, the Postal Union cannot be called government; but in the sense of performing an essential administrative function for members, its work must be classified as one of the most characteristic of governmental activities today.[17] The Universal Postal Union is now one of the specialized agencies.

46. SCIENTIFIC AND CULTURAL

Science, literature, and art are international in character. Discoveries, inventions, and scientific thought in general pass rapidly from one nation to another, and become part of advancing civilization (without such exchange, we would not have the auto, radio, atomic energy, and many other things which we enjoy today). National laws for their protection, such as for patents and copyrights, are ineffective beyond national frontiers. Indeed, nations seem to encourage, by tacit condonation, the violation of foreign patents or the pirating of literary works, while at the same time giving protection to their own scientists or writers within their jurisdiction.

INDUSTRIAL PROPERTY. The first efforts at international protection were initiated by private international association, and led to the crea-

[17] See R. L. Bridgman, *The First Book of World Law* (Boston, 1911), Chap. iv (for early documents); Reinsch, pp. 21-28; Sayre, pp. 19-25; J. F. Sly, "The Genesis of the Universal Postal Union," *Int. Con.*, No. 233 (October, 1927); Woolf, *International Government*, pp. 186-205; and the publications of the Union itself.

tion of the International Union for the Protection of Industrial Property, concluded in Paris in 1883, and revised frequently thereafter.[18] A prerequisite for membership is that the state shall have a special administrative service for patents. Periodic conferences are held, and an international bureau is established at Berne, under the supervision of the Swiss government, which performs the usual functions of liaison, information, and preparation for conferences. A peculiarity of this union is that it contains within itself limited unions for special purposes. The original union established the principle that a state should give to foreign inventors the same rights as it gives to its own, as to trademarks, patents, industrial designs or models, and rights against unfair competition. In addition, the arrangement of Madrid of 1891 provided, for such as signed, the registration of trademarks; and a similar arrangement of the same place and date was made for the repression of false indications of origin. There is also an International Association for the Protection of Industrial Property, founded in 1897 and located at Zurich.

COPYRIGHT. The position of writers and artists was equally precarious, and for many years efforts were made through bilateral treaties to protect their rights. After various preliminary conferences, a Convention for the Protection of Works of Art and Literature was signed at Berne in 1886 (revised at Rome in 1928). This convention, with subsequent revisions, gives to the author or artist not merely national protection, but a minimum international protection, and engages states to unify the formalities by which literary rights are established and to pursue and seize imitations, whatever the form of reproduction. The union has periodic conferences and a bureau at Berne, which is united with the Bureau for the Protection of Industrial Property. A great deal of effort has been devoted to the puzzling problem of the legal statement of such rights, and there appears to be a tendency toward grouping them all together under the heading of "scientific property."[19] There is now a United International Offices for the Protection of Industrial, Literary, and Artistic Property, located at Berne.

[18] On industrial property, see S. P. Ladas, *The International Protection of Industrial Property* (Harvard University Press, 1930); M. Ostertag, "International Unions for the Protection of Industrial, Literary and Artistic Property," *Michigan Law Review*, 25 (1926), pp. 1-17; S. Rathenau, "Die internationale Union zum Schütz des gewerblichen Eigentums nach deutschen Recht während des Krieges," *Z.V.*, 9 (1915), p. 63.

[19] On intellectual property, see E. Clunet, *Etude sur la convention d'Union internationale pour la protection des oeuvres littéraires et artistiques* (Paris, 1887); F. de Ruffini, "La protection internationale des droits sur les oeuvres littéraires et artistiques," *Hague Acad.*, 1926, II, pp. 391-569; S. P. Ladas, *The International Protection of Literary and Artistic Property* (New York, 1938). Refer also to § 113 (UNESCO), below.

WEIGHTS AND MEASURES. The first International Public Union, if it may be so identified, was the Geodetic Union, created in 1864, and now succeeded by the International Association of Geodesy, located in Paris. Triangulation for mapping purposes calls for the establishment of points of measurement in other countries, and also demands uniform terms. A Prussian official induced his government to call a conference for this purpose in 1864, and an association was established, located at Potsdam, and maintained for some time by the Prussian government. In 1886, it was internationalized, with an independent budget. It had a triennial conference, an annual commission, and a central bureau. After various conferences had studied the problem of uniform scale maps for the world, there was set up in 1913 the Central Bureau of the International Map of the World on a Millionth Scale. It is located in the Ordinance Survey Office at Chessington, Surrey, in England and has now mapped about 40 per cent of the land area of the world.

In a building at Sèvres, France, specially constructed for quiet and stability and under triplicate lock, are kept the standard metric measures by which a large part of the world weighs and measures the articles of daily use. It houses the International Bureau of Weights and Measures, established by a convention of 1875 at the request of the Geodetic Union for uniform measures. A convention of 1921 added to its duties that of finding uniform electrical measurements. A conference of delegates meets every six years, and the International Committee of Weights and Measures supervises the bureau.[20]

COUNCIL OF SCIENTIFIC UNIONS. Among the numerous conferences held at the end of World War I was one on International Scientific Organizations, held in London in 1918, which set up the International Research Council. This was reconstituted in 1931 under the name of the International Council of Scientific Unions. Twenty-nine states hold membership in it through national research councils, and thirteen others participate directly as governments. It includes ten scientific unions, as well as governments. The purpose of the council is to provide cooperation between scientific bodies. It is located at Cambridge, England, and is aided by UNESCO.

INTERNATIONAL HYDROGRAPHIC BUREAU. A postwar conference set up in 1921 a bureau whose purpose is to coordinate the hydrographic work of the various member states, for the purpose of making naviga-

---

[20] C. E. Guillaume, *La Création du Bureau International des Poids et Mesures et son Oeuvre* (Paris, 1927). In January 1948, new electrical units were added, concordant with the mechanical units. See Dept. of State Pub., No. 3655 (cited above), p. 117. In the same publication see p. 109, concerning the map, and p. 122, concerning the scientific unions.

tion safer, and to attain more uniformity in documents. It operates through a general conference, a bureau, and a secretary-general, and has a budget of 160,000 gold francs. The contributions of members are determined by the ship tonnage of each. It is located at Monaco. There is also an International Council for the Exploration of the Sea, and a similar body for the Mediterranean. Fishing constitutes an important food supply; as the need for fish increased and the supply diminished, states took up the study of the peripatetic fish quite seriously. Conferences were held at the beginning of the present century, and a convention in 1902 provided for conferences, a central committee, and a permanent bureau and laboratory at Copenhagen. The bureau studies biology, hydrography, and the plankton, the floating food supply of the fish.[21]

47. ECONOMIC

In view of the economic interdependence of nations, the need for cooperation in this field is manifest; it is unfortunately true, however, that nations find great difficulty in their efforts toward economic cooperation. Among the earliest of such efforts were the International Union for the Publication of Customs Statistics, set up in 1890 at Brussels, and the International Statistical Institute. The latter body goes back to 1853 for its beginnings, though it was not until 1913 that a permanent office was established at the Hague. It seeks to provide uniformity in the reporting of administrative and scientific statistics.

AGRICULTURE. In the field of agriculture we encounter the most vital of all economic interests—the food supply. The farmer has always held an isolated position, and agriculture has lagged far behind other economic development. It was this which attracted the attention of a Californian, David Lubin, who, believing that farmers in all lands have a common interest, conceived the idea that international organization would give to them more collective force and a better opportunity for ameliorating their condition. He peddled his idea industriously and finally gained the sympathetic attention of the King of Italy. The Italian government invited a conference which met at Rome in 1905 and established the International Institute of Agriculture. This institute had an elaborate organization, and almost all states belonged to it. Its members could choose to belong to one of five groups, in which the units ranged from sixteen units, with five votes, down to one unit, with one vote. Its functions were to collect

[21] See P. C. Jessup, "L'exploitation des richesses de la mer," *Hague Acad.*, 1929, IV, pp. 405-514; also, Dept. of State Pub., No. 3655, pp. 51, 129.

and distribute, as rapidly as possible, information as to agricultural methods, markets, prices and wages, plant diseases, and such matters of cooperation as insurance, credit, and common legislation.[22]

Various other bodies could be mentioned in the agricultural field, such as the International Seed-Testing Association, the International Society for the Study of the Chemistry of the Soil, the International Union of Forest Research Organizations, the Comité International du Bois, two or more bodies to deal with locusts, the International Commission on Agricultural Engineering, the International Commission on Agricultural Industries, and others. Some of these activities have now been taken over by the Food and Agriculture Organization.

COMMODITIES. A more recent development has been the creation of agencies to deal with one particular commodity.[23] The surplus of coffee, and consequent competitive efforts to dispose of it, led to negotiation among coffee producing states and to the establishment in 1940 of the Inter-American Coffee Board. The purpose of this board was to promote orderly marketing of coffee, and it had authority to increase or decrease the export quotas, so as to adjust supply to demand. Voting strength was based on export and import figures, the United States having twelve of the thirty-six votes, Brazil nine, Columbia three, and the other members one apiece. It was terminated in 1948.

Probably the most powerful of all the public unions, although it is now defunct, was the Sugar Union. The increased production of sugar after the discovery of the sugar beet, and the use of duties and bounties in the combat for markets, led to a desperate situation. Great Britain especially was affected and, after a vain effort with a few states, forced an agreement at Brussels in 1902, establishing a sort of customs union to equalize competition and aid consumption through the reduction of taxes. A bureau to collect information was established at Brussels, but there was also a commission to exercise constant supervision. This commission, composed of one delegate from each member state, could by majority vote order a change in the internal legislation of any signatory state, such as suppressing bounties, raising or lowering the tariff on sugar in that state, or preventing import from specified states. As the situation began to improve, however, states reverted to the old order and lost interest. Great Britain withdrew in 1913 and all others had formally withdrawn by September 1, 1920.[24]

22 See L. of N. Doc. 375.M.155, 1931.II.A; Hobson, The International Institute of Agriculture (1931).

23 See International Labour Office, Intergovernmental Commodity Control Agreements (Montreal, 1943); and p. 161 above.

24 On the Sugar Union, see D'Aulnis de Bourouill, La Convention rélative au régime des sucres (La Haye, 1902); N. Politis, L'Organization de l'Union Internationale des Sucres (Paris, 1904); Int. Organ., I, p. 384.

After the first World War, the sugar crisis reappeared, and led first to unofficial efforts (such as the Chadbourne Agreement of 1931) to improve the situation. In 1937, representatives of 22 sugar importing and exporting governments signed an International Sugar Agreement, under which a council and an executive committee were set up. Only the council can change the quotas agreed upon. Voting is proportioned according to the amount of sugar exported or imported. A small secretariat is maintained at London.

Efforts to adjust the trade in tin began in 1931, and an International Tin Study Group was set up in 1933. Its purpose was to limit the production and export of tin. An advisory committee concerning wheat, set up in 1933, became the International Wheat Council, with headquarters at Washington. Its purpose was to determine quotas and fix prices, but rapidly changing circumstances have forced it to reconsider the agreement made. A Rubber Study Group was established in 1944, which has thus far no permanent organization or regular meetings. Many other efforts are being made in the commodity field, such as the International Cotton Advisory Committee. In such groupings may be found the beginnings of new specialized agencies.[25]

48. HEALTH AND SOCIAL

HEALTH. If science is not stayed by national frontiers, much less is disease. Six times during the nineteenth century cholera and plague followed trade and pilgrimage routes into Europe, with terrible devastation. National administrations were impotent against it; a quarantine cannot be effective without notification that disease is on the way. In no situation is international cooperation so imperiously demanded, and many treaties mark the vain effort of national sovereignty to avoid international supervision.[26]

As far back as 1838, a health council was imposed upon Turkey, to establish a quarantine service at that crossroads. Various conferences and sanitary councils marked the effort to combat the continuing epidemics in Europe. In 1892, at Venice, an International Sanitary Convention was agreed upon, to be followed by many others. These require notification of the menace of disease, and prescribe measures for precaution and quarantine to be taken in ports, with regard to

[25] The United Nations now has a Coordinating Committee for International Commodity Arrangements, *U.N. Doc.* E./2763 (1955); see also *U.N. Doc.* Series E/CN. 13/. FAO also has such a committee.
[26] See Linden A. Mander, *Foundations of Modern World Society* (Stanford, 1947), Chap. i.

shipping, and in other ways. In more dangerous localities, sanitary councils were established with much authority. Turkey objected to the one at Constantinople as an interference with her national sovereignty, and it was ended in 1923. The Council at Alexandria was much more successful, and was credited with producing a 50 per cent improvement within one decade. There were others at Tangier, at Teheran, and for the Danube River. These bodies provided an international health administration which regulated shipping, disinfection, quarantine, hospitals, and which could, by majority vote and without appeal, penalize ship captains for failure to observe regulations.

In 1907 the International Office of Public Health was set up at Paris. It was given no power; its purpose was not to take the aggressive against disease. It was not placed under the League of Nations, but acted as an advisory body to the Health Organization of the League.[27] There are, however, a number of more or less official bodies dealing with other phases of health. An International Commission for the Decennial Revision of Nosological Nomenclature was created in 1900, whose purpose was to secure uniform terms and statistics concerning the causes of disease and death. It received a new lease of life when, in 1920, some forty governments adhered to it. Its funds were supplied for a time by the city of Paris; later by the League of Red Cross Societies. There was organized in 1927 an International Office for Epizootics, whose function is to coordinate research as to the contagious diseases of animals. It is supported by the governments of forty-six states and colonies. Various other health bodies exist, such as the International Bureau against Alcoholism and the International Union Against Tuberculosis. Many of these functions are now being handled by the World Health Organization.

SLAVERY. In various other social and humanitarian activities international administrative cooperation has been possible, more particularly since the organization of the League of Nations. The anti-slavery movement dates back to the Congress of Vienna, resulting in many treaties prohibiting the slave trade at sea, and finally in the Act of 1890, at the Brussels Conference, which organized two bureaus, one at Brussels and a Maritime Bureau at Zanzibar. In 1926 the League of Nations offered for signature a treaty whose purpose was to complete and develop the Brussels program. By this treaty states agreed to pro-

---

[27] The difficulties of international cooperation are illustrated by the refusal of Austria and Germany to support the Office of Public Health because it was located at Paris rather than at Berlin; and by the refusal of the United States to cooperate if it should be united with the League of Nations. As to the liquidation of the office and transfer to WHO, see Dept. of State Pub., No. 3655, p. 231; and Aufricht, p. 163.

hibit slavery in any form within their territories. The chief obstacle to its success has been the unwillingness of states to submit to international supervision.

There was an International Penal and Penitentiary Commission, founded at Paris in 1880, with its seat in Berne; its work has now been taken over by the United Nations. Its purpose was to collect information concerning prison systems and the repression of crime, for the guidance of governments. Several conferences to secure cooperation in dealing with international criminals were held from 1905 on, and in 1924, at Vienna, the International Criminal Police Department was organized. It was moved to Berlin in 1941, and to Paris in 1951.

An International Bureau for Enquiries regarding Relief to Foreigners may be traced back to 1907; and a proposal made by Senator Ciralao in 1921 led to the establishment of the International Relief Union at Geneva in 1927 to which thirty states were parties. The League of Nations and the International Labor Organization assisted in this work, and in 1930 the Intergovernmental Committee on Refugees was organized. These activities were taken over by the International Refugee Organization.

Many other organizations could be listed which perform social functions. There is—or was—an International Central Office for the Control of Liquor Traffic in Africa, an International Office for the Protection of Aborigines, an International Social Security Association, an International Union for Suppression of White Slavery, an International Association of Judges of Juvenile Courts, an International Office for the Protection of Nature, the United Nations Relief and Rehabilitation Administration, which served in the wake of World War II, and many others. Many of these functions are now served or coordinated by the Economic and Social Council of the United Nations, or by specialized agencies.

49. WHAT IS AN INTERNATIONAL ORGANIZATION?

The above survey of earlier international organizations is of course quite inadequate. There are hundreds of them, and more being created every year; the ones mentioned above are arbitrarily selected for purposes of illustration. Some of them are composed of private individuals, with no governmental participation; some are composed of governments only; some combine both or even include other international bodies. Some have authority, some have none; some have large staffs and budgets, most of them do not; some have a wide range of function, some are narrowly limited. Today, there are "specialized agencies," which will be studied in Chapter 8. Which of these various bodies should properly be called an "international organization"?

INTERNATIONAL PUBLIC UNIONS. In the earlier development of these international bodies, the term "international public union" was used, and various efforts have been made to define them. Even the word "international" is difficult to interpret. Does it refer to purpose or to membership? Is the Carnegie Endowment for International Peace, or the Standard Oil Company, international in character? If it must be international in purpose, must this purpose be one which interests the whole world, or could it apply to an agreement concerning a locality, e.g., the Danube River? The word "public" would seem to imply that the activities of the body are those of states, rather than of individuals; but how many states? And are individuals to be entirely excluded? Is the word "association" to be used for organizations of individuals, and "union" for those of governments? Such bodies should be non-commercial in character; is it to be excluded if it makes money, as the Danube Commission did?

Definition. Though there is disagreement as to the meaning of the term "international public union,"[28] there are perhaps four elements of a definition which, put together, distinguish international from other bodies. A public union, it seems clear, is based upon a treaty, and today one could say, upon a law-making multilateral treaty, rather than upon the bilateral or contractual type. A treaty can be made only by states, who are therefore necessarily included; but it does not follow that states cannot admit others than states into membership. As we have seen, modern treaties have admitted to a common organization individuals, corporations, international associations of various kinds, and branches of the League of Nations. In the face of such a development it does not seem possible to demand that states

[28] One of the first authorities upon public unions was the Russian, Kazansky, who demanded that unions have universality, organization, administration, contract, and states as members. See F. de Ruffini, *op. cit., Hague Acad.,* 1926, II, pp. 479-80.

According to Neumeyer (*R.D.I.,* Genève, 3, 1925, pp. 20-24) the essential elements of a public union are: (1) they are concerned with matter of internal law, but of general interest; (2) composed of states; (3) have a common organ or organs; (4) univesality of purpose and of membership; (5) autonomy.

Fauchille offers the following definition: "Les Unions internationales sont des conventions qui, au lieu d'intervenir entre deux ou trois Etats dont les intérêts spéciaux sont exclusivement pris en considération, sont conclues entre un assez grand nombre d'Etats qui se placent a un point de vue plus général, de telle sort que le reglement adopté par eux peut convenir aussi à d'autres Etats et être accepté par ceux-ci, et qui ont en outre entre eux des liens particulièrement étroits, se manifestant par des organes communs." *Traité,* I, Pt. 3, p. 453. If mere treaties are unions, it would be necessary to include in the list hundreds more than are usually named.

only shall be members of public unions; but one can insist that, in order to deserve the title of an International Public Union, the agreement establishing it should be an official treaty between states.

In the second place, an essential element, distinguishing the union from mere treaties for a common purpose, is permanent organization. The word "union" is sometimes applied to treaties which provide no organs, such as the Union to Combat Phylloxera, or the Iceberg Patrol in the Atlantic, or the Latin Monetary Union. The duties called for in these treaties are carried out by state agencies or even by a department of some one nation. It does not seem logical to call such a system a Union; if so, the term might have to include such treaties as those dealing with white slavery, or the Automobile Convention of 1909. Perhaps such bodies could be classed as the most rudimentary form of the Union.

In the third place, a union should be universal, in the sense that it should be open to the membership of all qualified states. Prerequisites may sometimes be demanded: for instance, a railway union could not well admit to membership a state whose railways were of a different width.

Finally, some criterion of purpose should be established, although it is difficult to state one. Clearly, a union is not legislative or judicial in purpose, though it may include either or both functions. It should be primarily for the *administration* of interests common to all states, but political decisions must also be made. This, however, contrary to the views of some, would not exclude an association whose interest is in a locality, such as the Danube River. Other states than those on the banks of the Danube may have an interest in it. Boats from the United States may desire to use it; and even if none do, the United States may have a great interest in seeing that goods going from or to her own ports have fair treatment en route through the Danube, or more broadly, in seeing that the Danube does not become a source of friction leading to war.

50. ORGANIZATION AND COMPETENCE OF UNIONS

ORGANIZATION. Even within the limits of the above criteria, there is the greatest variety of structure and organization among the unions. Some of them have only three or four members; the Postal Union claims hundreds. Most of them are composed of states only; but there is an increasing number with hybrid membership. They may include departments of government, such as a postal or railway administration, rather than the state itself; or groups of states united in other organizations, such as the International Agricultural Coordination

Commission; or private individuals or associations of individuals, as in the case of the European Conference on Time-Tables.[29] Several types of organs are in use. In practically all cases there is a periodic conference, essential for making the treaty originally and for revising it later; there may be an intermediate body, a council or commission or board, to make or revise the administrative regulations; there must be a bureau, or secretariat, to carry on routine work. The fundamental principles of the union are, however, usually subject to change only by a diplomatic conference, which is thus the legislative source for the union. The conference meets more or less regularly, sometimes annually, sometimes, as in the Union for Weights and Measures, every six years. The interval is not always a fixed time.

Except in the rare cases of organizations such as the Danube Commission or the sanitary councils, which were self-supporting, expenses are met by contributions from members. A frequent method of allocating such contributions is to divide the members into a number of classes, to which states are sometimes assigned, but from which they usually choose for themselves. States in each class then pay according to class, one paying perhaps six or seven times as much as another; but in such cases, voting power is correlatively increased. In other cases, payment is made according to population, as in the case of the Bureau of Weights and Measures, or according to the amount of commerce, as in the Bureau for Commercial Statistics; or according to the length of railways, or of coast line. Rarely do states make equal payments. Indeed, the theory of the equality of states is disregarded insofar as financial payments are concerned, and this has had its effect on the voting power of states. Where inequality of voting is not secured through classes for payments, it may be provided in another way, such as allowing extra votes for colonies. In most cases for administrative regulations, and in a number of cases for fundamental provisions, majority rule prevails in one way or another.

The most characteristic and essential organ of the union is the permanent central office, usually a commission or bureau, but sometimes called the central office. The commission, less frequent, is composed of delegates of states and is thus, to a degree, a diplomatic body, representative of sovereignty. The bureau is the more usual body, and more characteristically an administrative organ. It is independent of any state, but for purposes of convenience it may be put under the supervision of the state within which it is located, as is true of various unions located in Berne, and a number of others. While some problems may arise in these cases as to the recruitment or management of the

[29] This is of some importance since certain enterprises, such as railways or telegraph, may be government-owned in one country and in private hands in another.

personnel, there can be no interference by the local state with the international functions of the union. The personnel of a bureau is usually limited to a small number, perhaps not more than five or six, with typists or other such employees added as needed. The Union may provide its own rules for recruitment and advancement, or it may turn this task over to the state in which the bureau is located.

COMPETENCE. From the viewpoint of competence, or authority, there is not much to be said. The unions, it should be remembered, are administrative rather than executive in character. The treaty perhaps establishes certain duties for member states, but no authority for enforcement, no sanctions, are in most cases given to the bureau. It seems hardly worth while, then, to follow the division of Sayre, who spoke of organs with little or no power (in which class practically all would fall), organs with power of control over local situations, and organs with power of control over member states. A more useful classification would be: (1) those which, through research, statistics, or in other ways, supply information or machinery to meet a common need; (2) those whose task is also to gather information as to the measures taken in execution of obligations under the treaty; (3) those which have some administrative control over individuals, or over localities; (4) those which have control over states.

Some of the unions have more or less extensive judicial and legislative powers. The Postal Union Bureau may offer advisory opinions; some of the river commissions have their own courts. As to legislation, which will be discussed elsewhere, it has been possible in only a few cases to bind states by majority decision in the conference. The power of the bureau to make administrative regulations without consulting the member states is a legislative power worthy of emphasis, comparable to the issuance of orders by the Federal Trade Commission, or other domestic administrative body.

Is a union a mere society, or is it endowed with legal personality? If the latter, is it under international law or domestic law, and which domestic law? It is beyond the range of this work to enter into the complicated legal problems involved, but it may be recalled that there can be other persons at international law than states. If one looks at the union from the viewpoint of the law which created it and gave to it its power of action, it is a subject of international law. If one asks whether it can sue or be sued, whether it can hold property and by what title, the answers would be sought in the field of private international law. This, however, is merely existing practice; there is no reason why a treaty should not endow a union with the right to share in an international conference or appear before an international tribunal.

EVALUATION. There is general agreement as to the importance and value of these administrative bodies, whether as to their significance in international government, or as to their methods and accomplishments. They are, of course, inevitable, in one form or another. States often find themselves impotent to protect their own members without such cooperation, as is the case in matters of health, or of air navigation. Or they find it more useful and economical to take joint action, as for the publication of customs tariffs, or the establishment of postal and telegraphic communications. In some cases, the problem is one of *terrae nullius*, and can be handled in no other way, as, for example, the slave trade at sea, or fisheries. The unions have the advantage of permanence, of continuous activity, of technical study, and accumulating experience. They reduce the arena of political or diplomatic controversy by emphasizing technical solutions. As a result, they have developed some popular confidence in international administration. They have accustomed people to the idea of cooperation rather than of war for the solution of problems, and the lesson is already being applied in broader fields; the very placidity with which they pursue their appointed tasks—in contrast with friction in other international fields—is reassuring. It would be impossible to do without them today.

They have had, however, a haphazard organization, and there is much room for improvement. It is difficult to explain why some have been accepted while other needed ones have not appeared. Apparently, states have held the balance between the important, which could not be denied, and the unimportant, which did not matter. The haphazard creation of these bodies has meant a haphazard protection of community rights. There has been no central direction, no bureau of research or recommendation, no central agency to secure coordination, or to propose new functions, much less sufficient power. Authority is reserved to the diplomatic conference, with its inefficient procedure based upon the equality of states, and embarrassed by the necessity of political bargaining or by such exhibitions of national pride as caused Germany and Austria to reject the Public Health Office because it was not located at Berlin.

Some progress toward coordination was attempted under Article 24 of the Covenant of the League of Nations, and the effort is being carried on by the United Nations. The various administrative agencies of the United Nations system will be separately discussed in Chapter 13, below; at that point, some of the characteristic features of the new international administration will be surveyed.

Chapter 8

INTERNATIONAL LEGISLATION

51. THE MODERN PROBLEM

The sources of international law, as we have seen, are custom and treaty and, behind these, the "general principles of law recognized by civilized nations." Custom, in spite of its enormous importance, is not easily ascertainable as new law. At what point it crystallizes into law is hard to determine; as to this, and also as to the general principles of law, judges must decide. In the *Paquete Habana*, Justice Gray spoke of a custom going back for centuries; in the *Scotia*, the consent of thirty states was mentioned. But not all customs require centuries for their establishment; and it is doubtful whether the specific consent of thirty states to any customary rule of law could ever be shown. The judge must decide according to his idea of the consensus of opinion, rather than by the number of years or the number of states. Custom is not a satisfactory process for making new law.

As the need for new international law increased in many fields, means were sought by which this law could be more readily made. There could be little advance, however, for states still clung to the theory of consent, and subordinated any formal method of legislation to the rules of equality and unanimity. No legislative process can be effective when subjected to a *liberum veto;* and nations were slow to arrive at the stage of being willing to submit to a decision reached by majority vote. The Assembly of the League of Nations showed some trends toward legislative procedure, as does the General Assembly of the United Nations; but neither was given authority to make rules of law.

The treaty remained the only alternative, and upon it has fallen almost entirely the burden of making new international law. It is a vehicle which was never intended to carry such a load, and it has had to be stretched mightily to cover the legislative needs of the community of nations. A treaty which is intended to make law necessarily differs from the contractual, bilateral treaty. It calls for many signatures, and this requires, to secure necessary agreement, conferences and efficient conference methods. The drafting of such treaties is of a different type, and the securing of numerous ratifications—the evidence of the consent of the sovereign states—becomes another burden. The reservations which could be attached to a bilateral contract are annoying and destructive in a legislative act. Old rules as to interpretation or termination of treaties are inadequate for the necessary revision of legislative instruments. Questions arise as to supervision over the execution of legislative treaties, and as to their application to states which have not signed them. There has been a strong movement for the codification of international law; progress has been sought also through unification of national laws on particular subjects.

To such problems of international legislation this chapter is devoted.[1] Perhaps some improvement has been made, especially through the experience of organizations such as the International Labour Organization and the League of Nations, in the preparation of treaties. But it nevertheless remains true that, in the development of international government, the legislative function has been the most backward and is now the most inadequate for the needs of the community; and this will doubtless remain true so long as states put the right of individual national decision above the right of community decision. It should be noted at this point that no people have clung more closely to this right than the American people.

It is desirable to reiterate here what has been said previously, that it has become a matter of vital importance to fit the cogwheels of the national machinery of government into the cogwheels of the international machinery. The need is particularly great in the field of international legislation, and deficiencies of this sort go far to explain the difficulties of making new international law. It is unfortunately true, at times, that national constitutions, made primarily for domestic purposes, do not provide sufficient methods by which the state can legally be bound to international agreements. It is uncertain what agents are authorized to speak for the state, or how far their authority to bind the state extends. Where such authority exists, and the state accepts an obligation, machinery may be lacking by which the obligation can be put into internal effect. Even more embarrassing is the fact that the provisions of a constitution may be in direct opposition to the terms

---

[1] Not much has been written on this subject. See S. Engel, "On the Status of International Legislation," *A.J.*, 44 (1950), p. 739; T. Gihl, *International Legislation* (Oxford, 1937); M. O. Hudson, *International Legislation*, 9 vols. (New York, 1931-); Palmer and Perkins, p. 397. The volumes edited by Hudson are a collection of legislative treaties, but Vol. I contains an introduction which is still the best discussion of the subject.

of the international agreement. In result, desirable legislation may be blocked because of the unwillingness of the negotiators to act in contravention of their own constitutions; or the agreement may be accepted and thus precipitate a conflict between domestic and international law; or the constitution must be amended, which is frequently a very difficult task, necessarily delaying the process of international legislation. Apart from this problem of governmental mechanics, the reluctance of states to surrender positions or principles embodied in their law must be taken into account in the negotiation of international agreements.

THE MULTILATERAL TREATY. While a bilateral agreement may sometimes contain a rule of law, the modern development of legislative treaties has been in the direction of treaties signed by as many states as can be induced to sign. The treaties of Vienna (1815) and Paris (1856) are earlier instances of instruments including rules of law and accepted by a number of states. With the establishment of the League of Nations, the volume of such legislation increased steadily, demonstrating the importance of the multilateral treaty as an instrument for international legislation.[2]

This developing practice brings to our notice certain differences between the bilateral treaty of past use and the multilateral legislative treaty of today. The mere increase in the number of such treaties, and in the number of signatories to each, has led to improved means for making treaties. Multilateral treaties can hardly be made except in conferences and the conferences tend to adopt legislative procedure and to become periodic. The large number of signatories produces complications in the legal effect of the treaty as between the signatories and as concerns pre-existent treaties. Such a treaty is opened to acceptance by all states and signatories cannot, as in the case of bilateral treaties, choose their partners; consequently, some of the older implications of treaty-making become untenable. For example, it can hardly be maintained that signature by one party imports recognition of the sovereign independence of a state which later becomes a party.[3] Again, it may be asked whether the old rule, that the violation of a treaty in one part or by one signatory invalidates the whole treaty, should be applied to legislative treaties? A legislative treaty would seem, on the contrary, to imply the use of sanctions against the of-

[2] The League of Nations Treaty Series required more than a hundred volumes; and the United Nations Treaty Series already contains over a hundred and sixty volumes.

[3] The United States has, on various occasions, specified that its signature to a multilateral convention did not imply recognition of other signatories. See, for examples, Hyde, I, pp. 190-93.

fender, as is done when an individual violates a domestic law. It would be absurd to abrogate a law merely because it has been broken by one of the subjects to which it applies.

While the term "international legislation" may be used in a general sense, the process is of course far from being really legislative, since a treaty can bind only the parties which accept it. Some of the difficulties in this connection have been summarized by C. W. Jenks as follows:

> The requirement of ratification results in many laboriously negotiated instruments never coming into force or only coming into force after such delay and between a group of parties so arbitrary in composition that their value is greatly limited. It often happens that an instrument is brought into force only by allowing the parties to make reservations of so far-reaching a character that the instrument loses most of its value. The fact that instruments are binding only upon the parties . . . is doubly disastrous in its consequences in that it both accentuates the difficulty of bringing instruments into force and places quickly reached limits of effectiveness once they are in force for certain parties. The traditional conception of international instruments as creating relations between States alone is a fertile source of difficulties; it . . . limits the extent to which the provisions of instruments enure directly to the benefits of the individuals in the interest of whom they are frequently intended. There is often no provision for any organized international supervision over the application of the instrument . . . the position as regards the termination and modification of instruments is in very many cases quite unsatisfactory.

Mr. Jenks goes on to say that many of these weaknesses could be eliminated by the inclusion of appropriate provisions when the treaty is drafted, and therefore urges strongly an international legislative drafting bureau such as is nowadays provided for various parliamentary bodies.[4]

The purpose of the legislative treaty is not to make a bargain, as has usually been true of treaties in the past, but to state a rule. Its terms are general rather than specific. In its making, in its range of incidence, and in the general interest in its enforcement, it approaches statute law in character.[5] On the other hand, in order to deserve this character, the legislative treaty should not be subject to abrogation by individual states; it should be applicable to those states which are in a minority of opposition or of inertia; and it should provide means of change, or revision.

[4] C. W. Jenks, "The Need for an International Legislative Drafting Bureau," *A.J.*, 39 (1945), pp. 165-66; see also "The Conflict of Law Making Treaties," in *B.Y.I.L.*, 1953, p. 401.
[5] Wright points out that "law-making treaties frequently govern the day-to-day conduct of individuals and a wide range of administrative officials. Thus their proper execution requires the continuous operation of internal law, and states have tended to follow the example of the United States in giving them automatic effect as internal law within the territory." *A.J.*, 23 (1929), pp. 98-101.

52. CONFERENCE METHODS

For purposes of treaty-making by a group of states, the conference (or congress) has long been employed by the community of nations, although the purposes of the average conference of today are quite different from those of the conferences of a century ago. "On the one hand," says Dunn, "there is the traditional conception of the diplomatic congress of representatives of independent states, surviving from the time when international intercourse was chiefly confined to the relations of states as political units; on the other hand, there is the rapidly growing tendency to look upon international conferences as parliamentary assemblies, organized along the general lines of legislative bodies."[6] The conference resembles a legislative body in its purpose and output, in its composition, including technical experts and even unofficial representatives, in its increasing tendency toward periodicity or continuity, in its scientific preparation, and in its rules of procedure and voting. The vastly increased number of such conferences reveals the importance of this new legislative process.[7]

Conference procedure, however, had many defects and needed improvement. The defects were summed up by Hudson as follows:

In the first place, it was difficult to get any conference assembled to consider possible legislation. No central authority existed to convoke it, no machinery existed to be availed of, no personnel trained in the work of such conferences was at hand. The initiative usually fell to some single state, requiring careful preliminary negotiations and involving onerous responsibilities. A restrictive agenda had to be agreed upon and seldom was the necessary preparatory work done to assure successful collaboration. When once it was assembled, the issue of a single spasmodic conference was often in doubt. Not until various unions were established, did periodicity begin to appear. Even after the inauguration of the Hague Conferences, their continuance remained very precarious; the second Hague Conference was possible only after delicate negotiations, and in spite of its *voeu* it was still uncertain whether a third conference would be held when the clouds of 1914 enveloped all international cooperation in a haze of bewildering doubt.[8]

[6] F. S. Dunn, *The Practice and Procedure of International Conferences* (Baltimore, 1929), p. 188. He calls attention to the increasingly frequent substitution for the old diplomatic plenipotentiary of the technical expert, and even of unofficial agents. *Ibid.*, pp. 42-46.

[7] See S. E. Baldwin, "The International Congresses and Conferences of the Last Century as Forces Working toward the Solidarity of the World," *A.J.*, 1 (1907), pp. 565-78; M. Burton, *The Assembly of the League of Nations* (Chicago, 1941); R. G. Gruber, *Internationale Staatenkongresse und Konferenzen, ihre Vorbereitung und Organisation* (Berlin, 1917); N. W. Hill, *The Public International Conference* (Stanford University Press, 1929); O. Hoijer, *Les traités internationaux*, 2 vols. (Paris, 1928); V. D. Pastuhov, *A Guide to the Practice of International Conferences* (Carnegie Endowment, Washington, 1945); E. Satow, *International Congresses* (Foreign Office Handbooks, London, 1920).

[8] M. O. Hudson, "The Prospect for International Law in the Twentieth Century," *Cornell Law Quarterly*, 10 (1925), pp. 439-40.

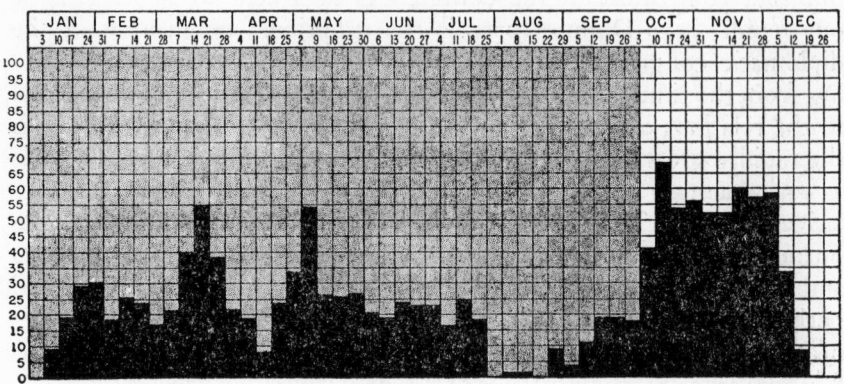

The existence of the central machinery of the new international organizations has produced many improvements. In the first place, meetings of the councils and assembly and other organs of these bodies, which must be regarded as conferences, are automatic and regular; no one state is required to take the risk of inviting a conference to assemble. If a state objects to one item on the agenda, there are many other items which it cannot afford to miss. There is no problem as to what states should be invited; all members are expected to attend, and a state cannot afford to be absent. The process is impersonal and automatic, and seeks the widest possible participation; thus conferences have become larger and tend toward universality. Much more adequate preparation can be made through the permanent secretariats of such intergovernmental organizations, and the important prerequisite of obtaining opinions and perhaps consent of governments—a sort of preliminary negotiation—can be more efficiently handled.

The permanence and continuity of these bodies make them far superior to an *ad hoc* conference, whose work is necessarily hasty and is for the most part wasted if it adjourns without having agreed

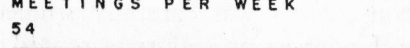
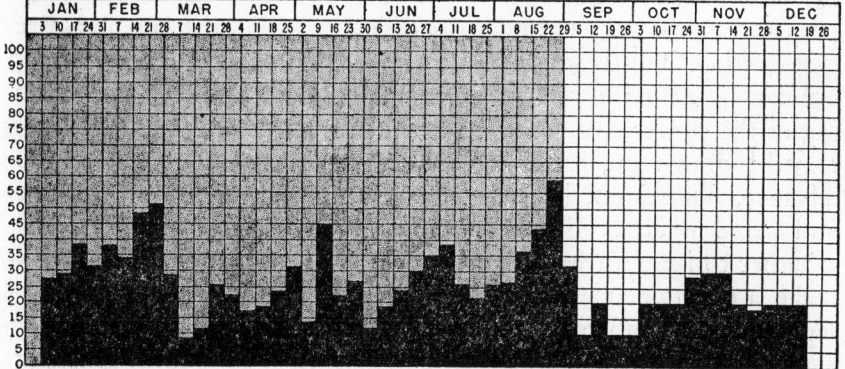

upon a draft. Debates in the General Assembly of the UN offer a test of public opinion as to whether a question is ripe for discussion. If sufficient agreement is revealed, the matter may be referred for study to a commission, or to a special committee of experts. The effort is not necessarily ended with adjournment, as in the case of an *ad hoc* conference; it may, if necessary, be carried on from year to year until it reaches fruition. The continuity provided by permanent machinery is of the greatest importance. If the assembly fails to reach agreement, its work is not wasted, for it will meet again and build upon what it has already accomplished. There is no problem as to whether states which have sent delegates to one conference will do so for the next one, for member states send delegates regularly. The membership is a fixed one, which can grow in experience, and which does in fact act under rules of procedure which more nearly resemble a parliamentary body than the old diplomatic conference. Nor does it have to await the pressure of a crisis to be summoned; it is regularly in session and can take up difficulties before they reach the critical state. And finally, such central machinery makes possible execution of, or supervision over the observance of, the agreements reached by the conference—something which could not well be done by the *ad hoc* type of conference.

INTERNATIONAL LABOUR CONFERENCE. The procedure for making international legislation through conferences was carefully studied by the International Labour Office. Under its procedure, a report is prepared on the subject under discussion, showing the law and practice existing. This is sent, together with a questionnaire, to the governments concerned; replies are expected six months before the opening of the conference. On the basis of these replies draft conventions may be drawn up, and submitted to governments four months in advance. Sometimes the first report is discussed in one conference and acted upon at the next conference. The conference decides whether to issue a treaty (convention) for ratification, or merely to make a recommendation to be adopted by states in their national legislations. Members are obligated by the ILO Charter to submit such conventions to the authorities in their own states which are competent to deal with them. Provision is also made for watching over the observance of accepted Labour Conventions, and economic sanctions may be taken (Articles 411-420) against a state which fails to measure up to its obligations. It is probably correct to credit the International Labour Organization with the most effective methods thus far devised for the preparation and promotion of international legislation, though these methods fall far short of what is needed in the field.

53. VOTING

The work of the international conference, and especially its legislative output, which necessarily eventuates in treaties, has long been embarrassed by the doctrine of sovereign equality.[9] It appears in various phases of the legislative process. Each state, no matter how small or how large, has claimed the same representation, the same voting power, the same right to obstruct through failure to ratify, as any

[9] Refer to Chap. 3, pp. 85-86, above, and citations there given. See also Margaret Burton, *The Assembly of the League of Nations* (Chicago, 1941); N. L. Hill, "Unanimous Consent in International Organization," *A.J.*, 22 (1928), pp. 319-29; D. P. Myers, "Representation in Public International Organs," *A.J.*, 8 (1914), pp. 81-108; C. A. Riches, *The Unanimity Rule and the League of Nations* (The Johns Hopkins Press, 1933); C. A. Riches, *Majority Rule in International Organization* (The Johns Hopkins Press, 1940); Sir J. F. Williams, "The League of Nations and Unanimity," *A.J.*, 19 (1925), pp. 475-88.

other state, and this in committees as well as in plenary sessions. The principle was again sanctified in the Charter of the United Nations which (Article 2, paragraph 1) bases the whole organization upon the "sovereign equality" of Members. The result was insistence by the Great Powers upon a right of veto, and students are now beginning to devote attention to schemes of differential voting power as a means of circumventing unanimity, and the veto.

The rule of equality was extended into the requirement of unanimity, which means that the *liberum veto* of any one state can defeat the measure under consideration. The most famous illustration of this was the refusal of Persia to accept a resolution interpretative of the Covenant of the League for which all other Members had voted.[10] But while the rule of equality has been sacredly maintained by the small states and given lip-service at least by the larger states, in practice it has long been overridden or evaded; from the viewpoint of convenience, of common needs, of community pressure toward progress, the rule is intolerable. "Insistence upon complete equality in the constitution and functioning of an international union, tribunal or concert is simply another way of denying the possibility of effective international organization."[11] Even at the Hague Conference, of which it was boasted that the doctrine of equality had achieved a great triumph, the Powers had their way. "It is abundantly clear," says Scott, "that the delegations at the Hague did not and could not possess equal influence in framing the conventions, and that, notwithstanding the principle of legal equality, the larger States either forced their views upon the Conference or by their opposition prevented an unacceptable proposition from being accepted."[12] The fiction of "quasi-unanimity" was developed, by which a majority of votes was treated as unanimity. In the minutes of the Second Hague Conference there is recorded: "adopted unanimously with the exception of two votes (United States and Great Britain) and one abstention (Portugal)." A majority vote allowed a proposal to be recorded, even if not passed, and thus brought it to the attention of the world.

---

[10] It should be noted, however, that in accordance with the practice of the assembly the president declared that the resolution was not rejected, since the assembly had not voted for the contrary interpretation—a procedure which illustrates the means found to evade the destructive effects of the doctrine of equality. *Records of the Fourth Assembly*, 1923, Plenary, p. 86.

[11] Dickinson, *Equality*, p. 336. "If, then, the world is ever to reorganize itself for the peaceful regulation of international affairs, that organization must provide for the essential inequality of states." L. S. Woolf, *International Government* (New York, 1916), p. 120.

[12] Quoted in Dickinson, *Equality*, p. 290, note 2. He calls attention in the pages following to the reaction against the principle of equality as employed at the conference.

In the public unions, regarded usually as politically unimportant, concession has been made to the greater importance of some states. Thus, in the Postal Union, the participation of colonies gave six votes to Great Britain, four to France, three to Germany, and two to the United States. Or, as in the case of the Institute of Agriculture, membership was classified, with a different number of votes assigned to each class. States may be assigned to a class, or may choose it, paying a proportionate share of the expenses; or the class may be determined by railway mileage, population, commercial importance, or other measure. In many of the unions or commissions a majority vote prevails on procedural matters, and in some cases for fundamental changes. The Sugar Commission could by majority vote compel a state to change its tariff laws. The governing body of the Universal Postal Union acted upon majority vote, and such a decision of its congress must be put into effect at once by postal administrations without awaiting ratification. In the Institute of Agriculture, two thirds of the membership constituted a quorum, and its decisions bound absent members. By the Convention of Air Navigation in 1919, five votes were assigned to each of the five Great Powers and one each to other states, with the specific intention of giving control to the Powers, a majority being sufficient for action.

At the Peace Conference at Paris in 1919, the Powers who had won the war took complete charge. A distinction was made from the beginning between the Principal Allied and Associated Powers and other states. The five Great Powers controlled everything; others were permitted to participate only insofar as their interests were involved. To each of the five Great Powers were apportioned five delegates; to Belgium, Brazil and Serbia, three each; one or two each to others. These arrangements, as well as the rules of procedure, were established by the five Great Powers in advance of the meeting. All chief officials came from these five states and they held a majority in each committee. The usual rights of equal states were completely disregarded. The Treaty of Versailles was put into effect, for example, in the face of China's refusal to sign. To criticisms of such methods the reply was that so vast a task could never have been accomplished if homage had been paid to antiquated methods based upon sovereign rights.

While Article 5 of the Covenant of the League of Nations provided for unanimity except where otherwise expressly stated, in practice there were many exceptions to the rules of equality and unanimity. Aside from such extrinsic forces as the disinclination to be found in a small minority and the desire to cooperate, there was a sort of gentlemen's agreement not to count abstentions as negative votes, thus making it possible to secure unanimity without consent having been given. Some highly important exceptions were made by the Covenant itself, which could be amended by a majority of states in the Assembly including the states represented on the Council.[13]

The United Nations Conference on International Organization at San Francisco was summoned by the Four Powers, who admitted equality of voting in principle but nevertheless accomplished their desires by sheer force of power, to which other states submitted. The rules of procedure of the conference provided for decisions by a two-thirds majority; and the rule of unanimity was abandoned for all organs of the new United Nations. It should not be forgotten, however, that such decisions (except some in the Security Council) do not bind members, and that ratification is still required for this purpose. In the General Assembly, where there is no veto to protect the larger states, the preponderance of small states, each with a vote equal to any other, has led to increasing study of "weighted voting."[14]

54. THE PROBLEM OF RATIFICATION

SIGNATURE. Thus the rule of unanimity, one of the chief embarrassments in international legislation, is being steadily hewed down, insofar as representation and voting in conferences is concerned. But the work of the conference is, after all, only tentative. If agreement is reached, a treaty is signed; but it must still be ratified. The modern significance of signature is somewhat uncertain. Apparently, it means nothing more than agreement upon a definite text, together with a willingness to submit this text to the government for consideration as to ratification. It certainly implies no obligation to ratify, but it perhaps means that ratification can be given later only to the text signed. It is a preliminary, and far from final, expression of the willingness of the state to be bound.

FAILURE TO RATIFY. But it is in the process of ratification, where the will of the sovereign state is finally expressed, that the chief difficulty is found. It has often been true that multilateral treaties, duly signed by delegates having plenipotentiary powers, have failed to secure enough

[13] Howard-Ellis lists 10 such exceptions, p. 124; Buell gives 7 for the Assembly and 13 for the Council, p. 668; Hill, p. 192, and in *A.J.*, 22 (1928), p. 327, note 33, gives the same list; Sir John Fischer Williams lists 12, and suggests a number of others, *A.J.*, 19 (1925), pp. 485-87.

[14] A thorough study of "The Role of the General Assembly and the Problem of Weighted Voting" is provided by Louis B. Sohn, in the Ninth Report (Charter Review Conference) of the Commission to Study the Organization of Peace (New York, 1955).

ratifications to go into effect.[15] By 1930, there were still sixteen states which had signed conventions at the Second Hague Conference but had failed to ratify a single one of the treaties they had signed; indeed, none of the fourteen conventions there signed was ratified by all of the states which had signed them.[16] The most remarkable example, perhaps, is that of the famous Geneva Protocol, which was unanimously adopted by the Assembly, actually signed by nineteen states, and ratified by none.[17] Many treaties have had to wait for years before securing enough ratifications to ensure validity.

The situation is no better under the United Nations; indeed, less attention has been paid to the need for securing ratifications to legislative instruments than under the League of Nations,[18] and practically no attention has been given to the problem in general. Examination of the status of some eighty United Nations treaties, about the beginning of 1954, shows that not one of them (an average being taken) was accepted by as many as half the Members. In many cases, signatures were given which were never confirmed by ratification. The Netherlands had the best record—fifty-three treaties ratified and fifteen signed; Venezuela the worst—three accepted and two more signed. Twenty-one of the Member states had accepted less than ten treaties each; fourteen others had acted in any way on less than ten each. Thus, over half the Members had a very poor record of action

[15] The number of ratifications required to put a treaty into effect varies, and is usually stated in the treaty. A disarmament treaty, for example, would probably require the consent of all states at the conference. In other cases, the treaty may go into effect as soon as any two states have signed, others having the right to add their ratifications later. The irregular process of ratification accounts for the custom of giving to a treaty its date of signature rather than of ratification. See McNair, Chaps. vii and viii.

[16] M. O. Hudson, "Present Status of the Hague Conventions of 1899 and 1907," *A.J.*, 25 (1931), pp. 114-17.

[17] According to a chart prepared by the Secretariat of the League of Nations, *Table Showing the State of Signatures, Ratifications and Accessions in Agreements and Conventions Concluded under the Auspices of the League of Nations up to September 1, 1930* (1930.V.18. Table 1). Over half of those who could have ratified the treaties before them had not acted at all with regard to them. For the Twenty-first List of this kind, see *Official Journal*, Special Supplement No. 193 (July 10, 1944). A supplement dated July 31, 1946 brings the record up to the end of the League, *ibid.*, Special Supplement No. 195.

The International Labour Conference had adopted, up to 1939, sixty-seven conventions. About a dozen members had failed to ratify all of them, and another dozen had ratified less than ten. *Constitutional Questions* (ILO, Montreal, 1946), p. 195.

For Latin American treaties, see the chart issued by the Pan American Union, *Status of the Pan American Treaties and Conventions*.

For United Nations treaties, see *U.N. Doc.* Series ST/LEG/3.

[18] The table referred to in the previous footnote was issued quarterly by the League of Nations in an effort to bring pressure to bear upon states dilatory in acting upon its treaties.

on treaties submitted to them for approval. The Latin American states had an average of action on eighteen treaties; the Soviet bloc on eighteen; the Near Eastern states on seventeen; Western European states on sixty-three; the United States on forty-seven. Many of the states most eager in proposing new things do not get around to ratifying them. It is impossible to tell how many inactions are due to opposition, how many to inertia, but manifestly most states will not accept new rules of law by ratifying treaties made for that purpose.[19]

ACCESSION. Modern practice provides for accession, or adhesion, by states, that is, for deposit of an instrument of acceptance which may be equivalent to both signature and ratification. Thus a treaty, which has been ratified and is in effect, may be opened to adhesion by other states; or a treaty which has been adopted in a conference (such as the General Assembly of the United Nations) could be opened to adhesion by any state, and go into effect as soon as it has received a stated number of accessions. This procedure has the advantage of making it possible for states not represented at the conference to accept the treaty, and thus widen the range of the application of the treaty. Accession under such conditions should be equivalent to ratification, but some states made a practice of acceding *ad referendum*. The utility of ratification after accession is not apparent.[20]

PROPOSALS. The delays and deadlocks in putting a treaty into effect led the League to make a special study of the problem. The committee appointed for this study accepted the principles that "the signature of an international convention on behalf of a country indicates an intention on the part of the Government of that country to make a fresh examination of the question with a view of putting the Convention into force as far as it is concerned"; and that, on the other hand, the interests of other contracting parties require that they know what is to be the fate and the territorial scope of the agreement. From a survey of the efforts made by the League, it concluded that League treaties were better ratified than treaties made outside the League. As means of

---

[19] The Report of the Secretary-General for 1955 noted that 118 treaties were open for acceptance and that 1,037 ratifications had been received. This would mean that each Member had, on average, ratified 17 of the 115 treaties.

[20] A resolution of the 8th Assembly of the League said:

"The procedure of accession to international agreements given subject to ratification is an admissible one which the League should neither discourage nor encourage.

"Nevertheless, if a state gives its accession, it should know that, if it does not expressly mention that this accession is subject to ratification, it shall be deemed to have undertaken a final obligation. If it desires to prevent this consequence, it must expressly declare at the time of accession that the accession is given subject to ratification." L. of N., *Records of the Eighth Assembly*, Plenary, p. 141.

improving the situation for the future it suggested that states be requested annually to give reasons for failure to ratify; that more preparatory work is needed, and that states should be educated to their responsibilities in the matter; that there should be a pledge, in accordance with the practice of the International Labour Office, to submit the treaty for approval by the proper authority within eighteen months; that another conference be called to consider the problem and make changes where a treaty is inoperative through lack of ratifications; that the time limit for signature be reduced; and that in some technical argeements ratification is not necessary at all.[21]

Such conservative suggestions were characteristic of the cautious steps necessary in dealing with sovereign states. The International Labour Organization, more concerned with humanity than with sovereign states, has gone further. The International Labour Office does the preparatory work and presents a draft treaty for consideration by the conference. When the conference adopts a draft convention or a recommendation by a two-thirds vote, all member states are obligated, by Article 405 of the Treaty of Versailles, to submit it to "the authority or authorities within whose competence the matter lies, for the enactment of legislation or other action." Thus, in the procedure of the Labour Organization, signature becomes a mere formality, or rather a collective act. A member state may be required to submit to its constitutional body a treaty which it has not been willing to sign, thus giving to the legislature (which is usually the competent authority) a chance to consider a treaty which the executive may never have been willing to negotiate. The rule of the majority here binds even those who do not sign.

A PROPOSAL TO ASSUME RATIFICATION. Mr. Philip Noel Baker has suggested the adoption of a rule that ratification be assumed on the part of a state which has signed, or in the case of a treaty which has been adopted by majority vote in the Assembly of the League of Nations, unless the treaty is specifically rejected within a fixed period of time.[22] The effect of such a procedure would be to put the burden of action upon the signatory states and to compel them to accept the responsibilities and duties of joint action within the community of

[21] The committee gives as reasons for the delay: (1) the complicated machinery of modern government; (2) shortage of parliamentary time; (3) necessity of new domestic legislation to put treaty into effect; (4) difficulties discovered after signature; (5) interdependence with other international instruments.

This committee reported that out of 39 League treaties, 26 were in force; and that 552 ratifications had been received while 553 signatures remained unratified. This was characterized as "not discouraging." The committee's report is found in *L. of N. Doc.*, 1930.V.11.

[22] In *B.Y.I.L.*, 1924, pp. 62-64.

nations. The sovereign right to refuse ratification would not be denied; a state would be compelled only to express an opinion. This does not seem unreasonable. Indeed, in such a society of voluntary cooperation as we now have, the most effective means of securing the attention to community business necessary for its advance is to provide an automatic penalty for failure to attend to that business. But nationalistic particularism is as yet too strong to hope that this proposal may be adopted at any time soon; and there is also an undoubted difficulty to be found in the variegated constitutional provisions within different states for the making of treaties. The most significant statement made by the special committee which investigated the problem was this: "The existence of a considerable number of international conventions constitutes today a permanent and regular feature of international life, and it is to be hoped that States will gradually adapt their administrative machinery and parliamentary procedure to the requirements of this situation which is still comparatively new."[23]

RATIFICATION NOT REQUIRED. Finally, it is to be noted that, in the case of some agreements, it is possible to dispense with ratification entirely.[24] This has been done in the case of some bilateral treaties, and much of the progress accomplished in the administrative unions has been in this fashion. It is often possible for governments to conclude agreements of technical or other character for which there is no constitutional requirement of ratification. An example was the Agreement concerning Transit Cards for Emigrants, of June 14, 1929. The League Committee above quoted recommends that "whenever the character of the contemplated agreement permits of the adoption of this procedure, it should be adopted, since, *ab initio*, it avoids the difficulty created by delays in ratification."

A step in the direction of more flexibility in the requirement of ratification was tried during the first years of the United Nations, through use of a formula by which a state could agree to be bound by an instrument (1) by signature without reservation as to acceptance, (2) by signature with reservation as to acceptance, followed by acceptance, and (3) by acceptance. Thus, states which were constitutionally able to bind themselves without formal ratification could do so, or could reserve the right to ratify; it was possible to accept a treaty quickly, and in one step, but no state was required to do so. However, this procedure was questioned in the Sixth (Legal) Committee of the General Assembly, and the committee unanimously

[23] Report of the Committee, Appointed to Consider the Question of the Ratification and Signature of Conventions Concluded under the Auspices of the League of Nations, 1930.V.11., p. 4.
[24] C. G. Fitzmaurice, "Do Treaties Need Ratification?" in *B.Y.I.L.*, 1935, p. 8.

voted against it. This does not necessarily end the use of the procedure, but it discourages change in the old ways to which states are accustomed.[25]

RESERVATIONS TO MULTILATERAL TREATIES.[26] If the necessity of ratification involves embarrassments, it must be said that international legislation is even more complicated by the possibility of reservations. Individuals are not permitted to say, concerning a domestic statute, that they individually refuse to accept it or that they accept it with reservation; but a state may insist, with regard to a legislative treaty, that it shall not be bound by such legislation except under reservations imposed by it. It may be argued that since a state is free to reject the treaty entirely, it may accept the treaty under such conditions as pleases it; but this, in the case of the modern legislative treaty, does not take into sufficient account the position of the other signatories. Marjorie Owen remarks (perhaps with some exaggeration), "Signatories may claim the moral advantage of a treaty while obviating all burdensome obligations by a timely reservation."[27] A treaty presumably states a common purpose, but reservations may completely destroy this unity of view. Legislation is far from real when its subjects are free to accept only such parts of it as they care to.

In order to settle the problem of the adherence of the United States to the Permanent Court of International Justice in accordance with the reservations which she attached to her adherence, the original signatories were forced to hold two international conferences, and no final decision was ever reached.[28] Perhaps the best illustration is to be found in the Pact of Paris of 1928. This treaty came into effect upon

25 "The Use of the Term 'Acceptance' in United Nations Treaty Practice" is summarized by Dr. Yuen-li Liang, in *A.J.*, 44 (1950), pp. 342-49.

26 See Chap. 6, pp. 151-52, above, and D. F. Fleming, *The Treaty Veto of the American Senate* (New York and London, 1930); Hyde, II, § 519A; H. W. Malkin, "Reservations to Multilateral Conventions," *B.Y.I.L.*, 1926, pp. 141-62; McNair, Chap. ix; D. H. Miller, *Reservations to Treaties, Their Effect, and the Procedure in Regard Thereto* (Washington, 1919); M. Owen, "Reservations to Multilateral Treaties," *Yale Law Journal*, 38 (1928-29), pp. 1086-1114; William Sanders, "Reservations to Multilateral Treaties at Ratification or Adherence," *A.J.*, 33 (1939), p. 488.

27 Marjorie Owen, *op. cit.*, p. 1087.

28 The Senate of the United States has acquired an unenviable reputation for attaching reservations to treaties. Various estimates have been offered as to the number of reservations made by the Senate. See *Cornell Law Quarterly*, 5 (1920), p. 247; *Yale Law Journal*, 38 (1928-29), pp. 1091, 1096-97. Reference has been made to the fantastic proposals for reservations which have appeared in the Senate. None, however, can equal the effective reservation offered by Salvador to the Convention on Treaties signed at Havana, February 20, 1928: "The delegation of Salvador not only casts its negative vote to Article 13, but it also votes against the convention and does not sign it." This is headed "Reservation of the Delegation of Salvador." *A.J.*, 22 (1928), Supp. p. 142.

ratification by the fifteen original signatories, several of whom accompanied signature with various restrictive statements. Other states accompanied their accessions with similar restrictive statements, and Russia declared that she refused to accept certain of the original restrictions. What, then, is the technical legal status of the pact? Is it valid between any states, without agreement among all parties? If so, between which states and to what extent?

Such questions are of especial importance for treaties intended to make law. Such a treaty is supposed to state a rule for the signatories, having the same meaning for all, but if each state can limit its acceptance as it wishes, the rule does not apply equally to all. The League of Nations devoted attention to the problem of reservations and suggestions were made ranging from prohibition of reservations or listing of permitted reservations, to holding another conference to consider the reservations attached to a treaty made at another conference. The opinion of the International Court of Justice, referred to above,[29] leaves freedom to each signatory to make reservations and to reject the reservations of others; the result of these possibilities could be complete confusion as to the applicability of the rule to the various signatories.

55. REVISION OF TREATIES

Another difficulty must be listed among those which hamper the process of international legislation. This, too, has been mentioned in an earlier chapter, where it was observed that the *clausula rebus sic stantibus* does not provide a solution, since there is no way of reaching an authoritative decision as to when circumstances have changed. It is especially a weakness in relation to international legislation, for here is involved the problem of "peaceful change." If there is no other way to change an unsatisfactory situation, it will be changed by the use of force, or by violation of the unsatisfactory obligation, and the result of such action is to weaken all treaties. All the efforts of the Holy Alliance were unable to maintain the provisions of the Treaty of Vienna, and it did not take Germany long to upset the Treaty of Versailles. It is ironical that, among nations, the only way to change a legal obligation in the absence of consent of all parties, is by war; the situation is only made worse when war is regarded as illegal!

Many treaties provide no means of change, but the modern trend is to include within the treaty a terminal date or means of change. Article 19 of the Covenant of the League of Nations was intended to meet the need for treaty revision; it had originally been part of Article 10,

[29] See Chap. 6, pp. 151-52, above.

which was criticized as perpetuating a *status quo*. In 1921, when a request came from Bolivia for reconsideration of her treaty with Chile, a Committee of Jurists reported upon the meaning of Article 19. They asserted that the modification of a treaty was a matter solely within the competence of the contracting parties, that the assembly was unable to modify any treaty, and that it could advise reconsideration of a treaty only when the conditions existing at the time of its conclusion had undergone so radical a change that it was beyond reasonable possibility to enforce it. In subsequent debates it was held that an agreement for obligatory arbitration could not be employed to compel revision of a treaty which included no means of revision; that only under Article 19 could a claim for revision be presented. At the Tenth Assembly, the Chinese delegation proposed a committee to examine the means of rendering the article more effective; but the only result was, after some opposition, a resolution conceding to each Member the right to raise the question of whether the assembly should proceed in accordance with Article 19—a decision which may have had political, but certainly had no legal, significance.[30]

I.L.O. In the International Labour Organization much more study has been given to the problem. It was originally said that the Governing Body should report as to the need of revision every ten years. Did this mean to wait ten years, or to report within ten years? The procedure seems to be that the Governing Body will decide whether or not to put revision of a convention upon the agenda of the conference; and the conference can add others only by two-thirds vote and by postponing discussion until the following year. There are other difficult questions, such as whether revision may be partial or total, and whether revision abrogates previous conventions, or leaves both new and old in existence and perhaps in conflict. The Labour Organization has made advance in securing discussion and even revision, but it has also realized that there is as much danger in instability due to periodic revision as in the lack of opportunity for revision.

The Charter of the United Nations contains no reference to revision of treaties beyond the words "regardless of origin" found in Article 14. A proposal by Argentina for revision of the peace treaty with Italy failed; and an Egyptian effort to obtain revision of its treaty of 1936 with England, flamboyantly presented to the Se-

---

[30] The bitter struggle over revision of the Peace Treaties was mostly responsible for the inability to make use of Article 19. As to Article 19, see Goellner, *La révision des traités sous le régime de la Société des Nations* (Paris, 1925); Ray, *Commentaire*, pp. 559-67; *Records of the Second Assembly* (1921), Plenary, p. 466; *ibid.*, Fifth Assembly (1924), Third Committee, p. 202; *ibid.*, Tenth Assembly (1929), Plenary, pp. 177-78.

curity Council, received no support.[31] Beyond occasional complaints regarding specific treaties made in debates, the matter of treaty revision has not appeared in the proceedings of the United Nations, and that organization has given no attention to the problem as a whole, or in general to the improvement of the means of international legislation. Respect for the sanctity of treaties is hard to maintain when unjust treaties must remain unjust.

56. CODIFICATION OF INTERNATIONAL LAW[32]

The word codification usually implies a legislative act, systematizing existing law, correcting defects and inconsistencies, and filling in gaps in order to secure a complete and correlated code of law upon the subject. Internal codification, difficult as it is, is probably simpler than the codification of the law of nations. The state has a legislature with power to act, known rules of law, courts to interpret them and, behind all, the pressure of the needs of national unity. In international law, the first problem is to ascertain and secure an agreed statement of existing rules. International law does not have unified action behind it, nor a central legislative authority to decree the new code; on the contrary, each state must be induced to give its consent, and reasons of national pride or political exigency may cause refusal. International law does not have behind it so much of precedent and experience as does domestic law. Indeed, its codification calls for formal agreement upon fundamental principles, never yet given by the entire community of nations, and the grouping of rules under these principles. The codification of international law, if it means anything at all, means systematic legislation.

UNOFFICIAL CODIFICATION. The first efforts at codification were made by private individuals. It was proposed by Jeremy Bentham as

[31] See the *Repertory*, I, p. 479; and the *Repertoire*, pp. 314-15.
[32] As to codification in general, see P. J. N. Baker, "The Codification of International Law," *B.Y.I.L.*, 1924, pp. 38-65; J. C. Bluntschli, *Das moderne Völkerrecht der civilisirten Staaten als Rechtbuch dargestellt* (Nordlingen, 1868); J. Constantinoff, *La codification du droit international et l'unification législative* (Paris, 1929); Ch. de Visscher, "La codification du droit international," *Hague Acad.*, 1925, I, pp. 329-455; D. D. Field, *Outlines of an International Code* (2nd ed., New York, 1876); P. Fiore, *International Law Codified and Its Legal Sanction* (English translation by E. M. Borchard, New York, 1918); M. O. Hudson, "The Progressive Codification of International Law," *A.J.*, 20 (1926), pp. 655-99; E. Root, "The Codification of International Law," *A.J.*, 19 (1925), pp. 675-84; J. B. Scott, "The Gradual and Progressive Codification of International Law," *A.J.*, 21 (1927), pp. 417-50; "Historical Survey of Development of International Law and Its Codification by International Conferences," *U.N. Doc.*, A/AC. 10/5, 29 April, 1947.

part of his scheme for perpetual peace, but his own contribution was in the form of principles moral rather than legal in character. The movement really began from the impetus furnished by the code of the laws of war, drafted by Francis Lieber in 1863, for the use of the armies of the United States in the Civil War. It was remarkably successful and was widely followed, and Lieber's own interest in the development of international law led to other attempts, such as Bluntschli's famous code, which appeared in 1868. In 1872 and 1876 David Dudley Field, a lawyer with experience in codifying the law of the state of New York, published his "Draft Outlines of an International Code." The interest inspired by the successful arbitration of the *Alabama* Claims led to the formation of the Institut de Droit International and of the Association for the Reform and Codification of the Law of Nations, now called the International Law Association. Both of these bodies made scientific studies of topics on international law, and their recommendations, while of no legal authority, have much weight. The same may be said of the work of the Research in International Law, which operated earlier under the auspices of the Harvard Law School.

CODIFICATION IN THE WESTERN HEMISPHERE. In the Western Hemisphere a great theoretical interest had long been in evidence. As far back as 1826 a congress had met at Panama, upon the suggestion of Colombia. At this congress codification was proposed, though without result. Another met at Lima in 1875, upon the invitation of Peru; and in 1888-1889 certain conventions of private international law were signed at Montevideo. In the latter year the United States, which had hitherto refrained from participation, initiated the series of Pan-American Conferences. At the first, it was agreed that the time for codification was not yet ripe. It was not until the Third Conference, at Rio de Janeiro in 1906, that a Committee of Jurists was actually appointed, composed of one delegate from each member state. It approved a gradual rather than global codification. The first World War having interfered, the committee was reconstituted at the Fifth Conference, which affirmed the principle that progress could be better made through the work of scientists than through diplomatic conferences and approved global codification for private international law, with separate conventions for public international law. Meanwhile, the American Institute of International Law had been created for the specific purpose of aiding in this work, and in 1924, at the request of Secretary of State Hughes, the Governing Board of the Pan-American Union asked the Institute to submit projects of international law to the Committee of Jurists. Thirty projects of public international law and an entire code of private international law were ready in 1925. They were studied by the Committee of Jurists and reduced to twelve, which were considered by the Sixth Conference of American States at Havana in 1928. Subsequent conferences multiplied agencies and committees, and the Mexico City Conference in 1945 reorganized them under the direction of the Inter-American Juridical Committee, which is an active working body.[33]

CODIFICATION BY THE LEAGUE OF NATIONS. Until the creation of the League of Nations, attempts at codification were haphazard and infrequent. Such an effort usually resulted, at first, from an acute problem which was adjusted as opportunity appeared, at a conference probably called for another purpose. Thus the rules for fluvial navigation and diplomatic rank were adjusted at the Congress of Vienna, and rules for contraband and blockade were laid down at the Congress of Paris in 1856. In the latter part of the nineteenth century, a few conferences were called for the specific purpose of legislating on certain topics, such as those which produced the Geneva Convention of 1864, to provide better care for wounded, or the Declaration of St. Petersburg, in 1868, forbidding the use of explosive bullets. The Hague Conferences of 1899 and 1907 enlisted public interest, and were more successful. In addition to a number of declarations, the First Hague Conference issued three conventions, one dealing with the Pacific Settlement of International Disputes, one with respect to the Laws and Customs of War on Land, and one concerning the adaptation of the Geneva Convention to naval warfare. The Second Hague Conference produced thirteen conventions, mostly dealing with the laws of war and neutrality.

At the time of the creation of the League of Nations, and again during the making of the Permanent Court of International Justice, the need of codification was suggested. Even during the war there had been demands from all corners of the earth for a third Hague Conference. After the war, however, there was a reaction against the Hague system which had failed to stop the war, and the Covenant as finally adopted contained not a word as to codification. In 1924, however, the

[33] As to codification in the Western Hemisphere, see A. Alvarez, *La codificacion del derecho internacional en America* (Santiago, 1923); A. S. de Bustamante, *The Progress of Codification under the Pan American Union* (Habana, 1926); Current Notes, by C. G. Fenwick, in *A.J.*, 47 (1953), pp. 292, 698; Pan American Union, "The Codification of International Law in the Americas," Law and Treaty Series, No. 20 (1946); J. B. Scott, "The Codification of International Law in America," *A.J.*, 19 (1925), pp. 333-37; "Conventions on Public International Law Adopted by the Sixth International American Conference," *A.J.*, 22 (1928), Supp., pp. 124-66; *Inter-American Conference on Problems of War and Peace*, Pan American Union, Congress and Conference Series No. 47 (Washington, 1945). See also Inter-American Juridical Committee, *Recommendations and Reports: Official Documents, 1942-1944* (Rio de Janeiro, 1945).

council was asked to set up a Committee of Experts for the Gradual and Progressive Codification of International Law, which was to prepare a provisional list of subjects, communicate them to members, study their responses, report to the council upon the topics which seemed sufficiently ripe, and upon the preparation for conferences to consider them. This committee assembled first in 1925 and selected several topics for the study of states. In 1926 it sent out seven questionnaires and three reports, and in 1927 it issued others.[34] Thirty-nine states replied, with more or less promptitude, and their responses were examined by the council. Upon its recommendation, the Eighth Assembly approved the appointment of a Preparatory Committee for the Conference, which had meanwhile been invited by The Netherlands to meet at The Hague. Three subjects were selected for the consideration of this conference: Nationality; Territorial Waters; and the Responsibility of States for Damage Caused in Their Territory to the Person or Property of Foreigners. The Preparatory Committee sent out a questionnaire to the governments, and upon their replies constructed Bases of Discussion rather than a draft treaty.[35]

On March 13, 1930, the Codification Conference assembled at The Hague. Forty-eight states were represented, and the delegates included some of the ablest international lawyers in the world. Nevertheless, it accomplished practically nothing.[36] One convention concerning certain questions of conflict of nationality laws and three protocols dealing with statelessness and military obligations in cases of double nationality were adopted. The Committees on Nationality and Territorial Waters presented reports, the Committee on Responsibility of States was unable even to agree upon a report.

Various reasons have been offered for this failure. It was said that

[34] These were really more than questionnaires. They were valuable scientific studies of the topic, though of varying quality, each presented by a subcommittee in which divergent views were often revealed. They are printed in L. of N. Doc., 1927.V.1. and 1928.V.4.; and are also printed in A.J., 20 (1926), Special Supp., and 22 (1928), Special Supp.

[35] See L. of N. Doc., 1928.V.1.; 1929.V.1.; 1929.V.2.; 1929.V.3.

[36] As to this conference, see E. M. Borchard, " 'Responsibility of States' at the Hague Codification Conference," A.J., 24 (1930), p. 517; R. W. Flournoy, "Nationality Conventions, Protocols and Recommendations by the First Conference on the Codification of International Law," ibid., p. 467; G. H. Hackworth, "Responsibility of States for Damage Caused in their Territory to the Person or Property of Foreigners," ibid., p. 500; M. O. Hudson, "The First Conference for the Codification of International Law," ibid., p. 447; and other articles in this volume. The reports of the conference itself are found in L. of N. Doc., 1930.V.14; 1930.V.15; 1930.V.16; 1930.V.17. The conference itself recommended more preparation and made other suggestions which may be found in the Final Act, 1930.V.7, p. 18. See also the discussion in Records of the Eleventh Assembly (1930), pp. 211, 565; and Observations by Governments, 1930.V.4.

experience was lacking for this particular type of a conference, and that too much had been attempted in too short a time. The failure may be summed up, however, as due to the unwillingness of states to make any concessions. A mile more or less of territorial waters does not involve the security or national honor of a state, yet each state clung to the limit set by its own laws; the criterion of acceptability was often whether the proposal conflicted or not with existing domestic laws. There were some political aspects involved—e.g., the Calvo Clause—and in such matters states are not so willing to subordinate their national attitudes as they are in matters such as health or communications.

CODIFICATION UNDER THE UNITED NATIONS. The debate over the meaning of the word "codification"—whether it is merely statement of existing law or the making of new law—arose again out of the effort to carry out Article 13 of the Charter of the United Nations, which makes it the function of the General Assembly to encourage "the progressive development of international law and its codification." An International Law Commission was set up, composed of fifteen experts elected by the General Assembly.[37] A statute was provided which differentiated between "progressive development"—that is, new law—and codification, "the more precise formulation and systematization of rules" in fields in which there was already much precedent. Subjects under the former heading must be approved by the General Assembly; under the latter heading the commission may choose its topics and chose Regime of the High Seas, Law of Treaties, and Arbitral Procedure, to which have more recently been added Diplomatic and Consular Privileges and Immunities, and Responsibility of States. Under the former heading, the General Assembly has unloaded upon the commission some of the pet ideas of delegates, such as Rights and Duties of States, formulation of "Nürnberg Principles," Offences against the Peace and Security of Mankind, or Definition of Aggression.

The product of the commission is of great value to international lawyers, but it cannot become law until ratified by states and, thus far, states have shown little interest in the work or willingness to alter their views or laws. The draft code for Arbitral Procedure put no further obligation upon states to submit to compulsory jurisdiction and sought merely to assure that the procedure of arbitration, once it was agreed to arbitrate, would work effectively. Nevertheless, these slight advances were severely criticized in the General Assembly by many

---

[37] The idea of a full-time and paid commission of experts was rejected as too costly by states which have no hesitation in spending billions in preparation for war. The experts are rewarded for their services by being paid expenses for the days on which they meet and work.

states; forty amendments were suggested, and the whole draft was sent back to the commission for reconsideration. This result, on the first of the codes submitted, is discouraging, not only to the commission, but to all who are interested in meeting the needs of the community of nations through peaceful change.

Meanwhile, there is a haphazard production, originating in almost any committee, but largely from those under the Economic and Social Council, or draft conventions on all sorts of subjects, such as road traffic, obscene publications, freedom of information, political rights of women. These are not referred to the International Law Commission; thus, more international law is being made in the Economic and Social Council than anywhere else. There is, in the United Nations, no systematic consideration of the legislative treaties which need to be prepared, and no regular procedure for putting such treaties as appear into proper form, or for submitting them to governments for approval. Procedure and product is haphazard.

Granted the current lack of interest on the part of states in the making of new international law and the lack of means of getting it adopted, a scientific statement of the law issued by the commission is probably as useful as the effort to obtain ratifications for a legally binding treaty-statement of law. Sir Cecil Hurst, indeed, argued that this type of work cannot be done on an official basis, since national political motives would influence voting, and that consequently, a group of experts should make recommendations and these recommendations should be left to grow into customary law through acceptance by tribunals.[38] Failure on the part of states to ratify treaties embodying the law might be regarded as rejection and thereby weaken even the long-accepted rules. The problem is illustrated by the distance between a Declaration of Human Rights and a Covenant of Human Rights.

Brief mention may be made of another possible contribution to international legislation. The resolutions adopted by the General Assembly and other organs, or in the specialized agencies, are, by the Charter, mere recommendations, having no legally binding effect; yet they occasionally contribute to the building of customary law. Thus the Declaration of Human Rights, and the approval of the "Nürnberg Principles" are already having their effect in national courts and legislation. The contribution thus made is small, but worthy of notice.[39]

[38] Sir Cecil Hurst, "A Plea for the Codification of International Law on New Lines," *Grotius Society*, October 16, 1946. See also the paper by Yuen-li Liang, in *Proc. Am. Soc.*, 1947.

[39] F. Blaine Sloan, "The Binding Force of a 'Recommendation' of the General Assembly of the United Nations," *B.Y.I.L.*, 1948.

57. UNIFICATION OF PRIVATE LAW[40]

Another process, connected with if not really part of international legislation, is the far-reaching movement toward securing uniformity in national legislation. The effort here is not to provide rules binding upon states, as does international public law, but to attain agreement among states so that each will enact laws within its own jurisdiction, applicable to individuals therein, in harmony with similar legislation within other states. The effort may be compared with that of the Conference of Governors who attempt to obtain uniform laws in the various states of the United States. The result is to put persons in different countries upon practically the same legal footing. When one considers the highly difficult field of Conflicts of Law—e.g., the possibility of being held to be married in one state and not in another, or the validity of a contract or bill of exchange in another state—the importance of this approach is not to be minimized.

The effort to unify private law may be carried on by associations of individuals, by diplomatic conferences, or by organizations within which governments, governmental administrations, great corporations, and private individuals are all members together. The purpose and function of many international public unions, as we have seen, is no more than the encouragement of such uniform laws. The unification of law may result from a treaty between states; from the pressure of individual citizens or organizations within their own states, working in conjunction with similar bodies in other states; or from meetings of members of parliaments who have agreed to converge their efforts in such a semi-official body as the Inter-Parliamentary Union. In this uncharted field, the ancient distinctions between public and private law become badly tangled, but international cooperation proceeds nevertheless.

One of the most important fields in which this work has been carried on is that dealing with instruments of commerce. As far back as 1874, The Netherlands invited a conference (which never met) to establish rules as to the competence of tribunals and the execution of foreign judgments. In 1910, thirty-five states met at The Hague to study such questions as bills of exchange, and continued the work at the Second Conference in 1912, which agreed upon regulations, a treaty, and a bureau. The war broke up this program, and it was renewed in 1923

[40] See J. Constantinoff, *La Codification du droit international et l'unification législative* (Paris, 1927); M. O. Hudson and A. H. Feller, "The International Unification of Laws concerning Bills of Exchange," *Harvard Law Review*, 44 (1931), pp. 333-77; F. A. Mann, "The Interpretation of Uniform Statutes," *Law Quarterly Review*, 62 (1946), p. 278; J. B. Moore, *International Law and Some Current Illusions* (New York, 1924), Chap. vii.

under the aegis of the League of Nations, becoming part of the vast economic activity of the League. In May, 1930, a convention was signed at Geneva providing for uniform laws among thirty-three states as to bills of exchange. Another field favorable to the unification of law is that of maritime law, in which much successful work has been accomplished. In 1897, the Comité Maritime International, an association of private individuals, met at Antwerp. It has held many meetings of its own and has led to several diplomatic conferences. In 1913 the secretary claimed that "more than three-quarters of the tonnage of the world is now regulated by uniform maritime law elaborated by the International Maritime Commission." Its work includes such matters as responsibility for collisions at sea, salvage, maritime mortgages, loans, safety of navigation, and similar matters. In 1926-1927, upon the invitation of the Italian government, an Institute for the Unification of Private Law was set up at Rome under the auspices of the League of Nations. Doubtless the most successful work which has been done in this field, however, is that of the International Labour Organization, which has put into effect various conventions calling for national legislation relating to conditions of labor.

CODIFICATION AND UNIFICATION. The relationship between the movement for codification of international law and the unification of national laws is uncertain. The latter will doubtless make more headway, because of the desire of states to retain control within their own hands, and also because of its especial appeal to legislative bodies, who can claim more participation and importance in such work than in that of codification. It thus represents a compromise, for, while the treaty-making authority must make the convention providing for unification, the laws must be put into effect by national legislatures. It has the further advantage that, even when efforts fail to eventuate in binding treaties, states may nevertheless adopt in their legislation the principles more or less agreed upon; and agreements may be made among a few states for this purpose if the effort fails among many. On the other hand, the method of unification does not measure up to treaty legislation for many purposes. Even under a convention, there may be room for divergences between systems of national legislation, which would leave the individual under dual control. And, since such laws are domestic laws, they are subject to change and to interpretation by domestic courts, which may enunciate differing views in different states. Finally, unification, like private international law in general, is defective in that there is no responsibility upon the state for its observance.

CONCLUSIONS. Some advance in international legislation has been achieved, in spite of the many anachronistic methods which still embarrass its progress. The necessities of international intercourse are slowly breaking down the obstructiveness of sovereignty and national pride, but they are still strongly with us. Insofar as preparation of conventions embodying new law is concerned, there has been great improvement. Conferences are much more often manned by experts rather than by diplomats, and they tend more to the use of parliamentary procedure. Public unions, the technical bodies of the League of Nations, and now the specialized agencies have learned to work more and more upon a scientific basis, more and more free from political prejudices. There have been significant improvements as to representation and efficient methods of work. Majority rule has become the usual practice in international organs and equality of voting is being questioned.

This improvement, however, is limited to methods of preparation, and states still cling rigidly to the theory of consent when it comes to being bound by new rules of law. It is hardly conceivable that states would agree to be bound by new rules adopted by majority vote and without individual ratifications, though this is permitted in some small matters. As long as this attitude persists, so long will the burden of persuading states to accept the new law fall upon the conference or other organ; it would be a large gain if this burden could be removed. International legislation remains the weakest part of the functioning of international government, and much more attention needs to be given to it, as a problem for solution, than is now being given.

Chapter 9

PACIFIC SETTLEMENT OF INTERNATIONAL DISPUTES

If it were possible in the study of international government to follow the usual separation into legislative, executive, and judicial functions, it would be proper to devote this chapter to the international judiciary. The community of nations has developed various methods for the peaceable adjustment of differences, but not all of these can be spoken of as judicial methods. Not until 1920 was a court (the Permanent Court of International Justice) established deserving of this characterization, and the phrase "judicial settlement" has been reserved to its work and that of its successor. Except for these courts, neither the League of Nations nor the United Nations has advanced much beyond the traditional principles and methods earlier developed by the community of nations for the pacific settlement of disputes. These principles and methods remain fundamental, and understanding of them, their defects and difficulties, is essential today.

58. DIPLOMATIC PROCEDURES

The term "pacific settlement of international disputes" was made famous by the convention of that name adopted at the First Hague Conference and revised at the Second Hague Conference. To the problem involved, however, earlier writers on international law gave but scant attention. It was usual to include a short chapter or so in the text, by way of transition from the law of peace to the law of war, in which were discussed amicable and non-amicable modes of settlement. The non-amicable methods are not instruments for the determination of justice or for pacific settlement, but rather instruments for coercive action, whether just or unjust. Amicable methods, on the other hand, deserve consideration here as the current means of settling conflicts between states.

DIPLOMACY. Always the first, and by far the most important, method of adjusting international differences is diplomacy. Foreign offices are constantly at work for this purpose, and in most cases agreement is reached if it is sincerely desired. For every case which breaks into public notice, or which calls for other than diplomatic correspondence, there are hundreds which are settled in the ordinary daily routine of chancelleries. Such negotiations may be carried on through oral or written communications between ambassadors and foreign ministers, or they may perhaps call for an international conference, and they may eventuate in a formal treaty or in a mere exchange of notes. It has been so established a practice that the diplomatic agents of the state should first take up consideration of the problem, that it has been asserted as a rule to be obeyed.[1] Such a requirement is found in the Covenant of the League of Nations, and in many treaties calling for arbitration or conciliation, in which other methods of settlement must await the failure of diplomatic negotiations; it is restated in Article 33 of the Charter of the United Nations. The force of the rule is shown by the condemnation visited upon Austria because of her ultimatum to Serbia in 1914, which forestalled the usual methods of diplomacy for the maintenance of peace.

GOOD OFFICES. "Good offices" is a term applied to the attempt of a third state to bring together two disputants in an effort to secure peaceable settlement. It is the least possible interference in a disagreement, and involves on the part of the state offering its good offices no suggestion of a solution and no participation in the negotiations through which a solution is reached. It may, however, lead to an invitation to offer a solution or to participate in negotiations, in which case the procedure is converted into one of mediation. The term is sometimes confused with the off-the-record discussion (French, *officieux*) of a matter which a state does not care to consider on a full diplomatic footing.

MEDIATION. Mediation goes a step further than good offices. The mediator proposes a solution, offers his advice, and in general attempts to conciliate differences. He has no right to impose his views, and the offer of mediation could therefore be regarded with suspicion before

---

[1] It may be difficult to say when diplomatic negotiations have failed. In the first *Mavromattis Case*, the Permanent Court of International Justice said that states are in the best position to judge the political reasons which may prevent diplomatic settlement. But "when negotiations between the private person and the authorities have —as in the present case—defined all the points at issue between the two Governments, it would be incompatible with the flexibility which should characterise international relations to require the two Governments to reopen a discussion which has in fact already taken place and on which they rely." *P.C.I.J.*, Series A, No. 2, p. 15; and see the dissenting opinions of Moore (p. 62) and of Finlay (p. 41).

the Hague Convention for the Pacific Settlement of International Disputes elevated it to a formal and accepted method of procedure. This convention gave to third states the right (but not a duty) to offer good offices or mediation, and the exercise of this right was not to be regarded as an unfriendly act. According to Article 4 of that convention, "the part of the mediator consists in reconciling the opposing claims and appeasing the feelings of resentment which may have arisen between the States at variance." It was further provided that such measures "have exclusively the character of advice, and never have binding force," and that they do not interrupt any warlike measures being taken. The effort of the mediator is to reach a settlement, and it tends toward compromise rather than toward legal solution. His role is clearly not that of a judge. Neither the offer of mediation nor the proposal for solution need be accepted by either disputant. Among the numerous cases of mediation may be mentioned that of the United States and Mexico between Salvador, Honduras, and Guatemala in 1906; the A.B.C. mediation between the United States and the Huerta regime in Mexico in 1914; or President Wilson's offer to the belligerents in World War I, in December, 1916.[2]

COMMISSION OF INQUIRY. Another method of pacific settlement was provided by the First Hague Conference. It rests upon the theory that many disputes could be settled if the facts of the case could be established. The Hague Conference therefore recommended that, in differences of opinion as to the facts, a commission of inquiry should be employed to elucidate the facts—provided it involved neither honor nor vital interests. The commission was to be set up by special agreement between the parties to the controversy, that is, after the quarrel had begun, and the report of the commission was to be limited to a statement of the facts, and in no way have the character of an arbitral award. It leaves the Powers in controversy freedom as to the effect to be given to such statement. The method was successfully used a few years later when the Russian fleet, on its way to Japan, fired upon some English fishing vessels off Dogger Bank in the North Sea. A commission was instituted, which reported that there were no Japanese vessels among the fishing boats. Russia paid reparation to England for this unjustifiable action when the facts had thus been ascertained.[3]

[2] As to good offices and mediation, see Fauchille, I, Pt. 3, pp. 518-31, with numerous examples; Hyde, II, p. 1561; Moore, *Digest*, §§ 1065-68. The Convention for the Pacific Settlement of International Disputes is found in Scott, *Hague Conventions and Declarations* (New York, 1918).

[3] On Commissions of Inquiry, see Bokanowski, *Les commissions internationales d'enquête* (Paris, 1908); A. Mandelstam, "La commission internationale d'enquête sur l'incident de la mer du Nord," *R.D.I.P.*, 12 (1915), pp. 161, 531; Ralston, Chap. xxvii;

KNOX AND BRYAN TREATIES. The success of the commission of inquiry in the above instance greatly increased interest in this method. At the second Hague Conference the six articles of the convention dealing with this subject were elaborated into twenty-eight, but without extending its range of operation at all. The United States and Great Britain set up in 1909 a joint commission for frontiers and waterways along the Canadian boundary. In 1911, Secretary Knox negotiated treaties which provided for submission to a mixed high commission of inquiry which was to make recommendations for settlement in advance of arbitration. They were a step toward changing the commission of inquiry into a commission of conciliation, but they were rejected by the Senate. The so-called Bryan Treaties in 1913 made much broader use of the commission of inquiry than had originally been proposed. They provided for permanent commissions, established in advance, to which must be submitted all disputes of any nature whatever, if diplomacy had failed, except where there was an obligation to arbitrate. A report was called for within one year, and until it was announced, there could be no war or hostilities. According to Bryan, the advantages of these treaties were that they allowed time for passions to cool and an opportunity to separate questions of fact from questions of national honor, and that they allowed time for world forces of peace to operate. The fundamental principles of the treaties were that the commission should be a permanent one; that inquiry should be applied to all quarrels; that hostilities are prohibited for a time; and that the recommendation has only its own intrinsic merit to commend it to acceptance. The right of the commission to suggest bases of settlement is implicit in the treaties. Twenty-eight such treaties, negotiated in 1913-1914, were ratified by the United States, and although forgotten for a time, were revived through the appointment of new commissioners by President Coolidge.

The principles of the Bryan Treaties were of some importance in the development of pacific settlement. The Central American Treaty of 1923 recognizes them, and they were applied also, with some limitations, in the Gondra Convention made at Santiago in 1923 between certain Latin-American states. The theory was recognized in Article 15 of the Covenant of the League of Nations, and in general is an important step in the tremendous growth of the method of conciliation.[4]

Scott, *Hague Court Reports*, p. 403. The United Nations commissions of investigation under Article 34 of the Charter have been used for a number of different purposes. See p. 520 below.

[4] As to the Bryan Treaties, see J. Efremoff, "La conciliation internationale," *Hague Acad.*, 1927, III, pp. 24-29; J. B. Scott, *Treaties for the Advancement of Peace between the United States and Other Powers* (Oxford, 1920).

59. ARBITRATION[5]

MEANING. Among pacific methods for the settlement of international disputes, arbitration has been by far the most useful. While there is still disagreement as to its precise definition, it seems safe to define it as the settlement of international disputes, according to legal rules and methods, by arbiters chosen by the disputant parties themselves. The word has sometimes been used in the broader sense of almost any kind of pacific adjustment. Indeed it is sometimes said that arbitration is nothing more than compromise, and that it has nothing to do with justice. This charge may perhaps have been true in its earlier stages. During the Middle Ages a prince, called upon to act as an arbiter, might perhaps prefer for safety's sake to favor in his decision the more powerful party, and there was little law to guide him even if he wished to use it. Even after the revival of arbitration in the nineteenth century there was hesitancy in regarding it as a judicial process. Ralston mentions the Mexican Commissioners of 1840 who asseverated that they were present, not to judge, but to resolve difficulties. And as late as 1907, Secretary Root asserted in his instructions to the American delegates to the Second Hague Conference that it had been a very general practice for arbitrators to act as negotiators rather than as judges. This, however, is the exception rather than the rule. In most cases where compromise has appeared in the award, it may be traced either to the authority for such procedure conferred in the *compromis*, or to the fact that the matter referred to arbitration was not suitable for judicial decision. The former situation may be illustrated by the *Delagoa Bay Case*, in which the arbitrators were instructed to do substantial justice, and not to concern themselves with technicalities; the latter by the *Casablanca Case*, in which political rather than judicial interests were at stake.

Today, there can be no doubt that arbitration is a legal procedure.

[5] As to arbitration in general, see K. Carlston, *The Process of International Arbitration* (New York, 1946); E. Descamps, *Essai sur l'organisation de l'arbitrage* (Bruxelles, 1899); W. Jully, "Arbitration and Judicial Settlement, Recent Trends," *A.J.*, 48 (1954), p. 380; A. Merignhac, *Traité théorique et pratique de l'arbitrage international* (Paris, 1895); J. H. Ralston, *The Law and Procedure of International Tribunals* (Stanford University Press, 1926); D. Schindler, "Le progrès de l'arbitrage obligatoire depuis la création de la Société des Nations," *Hague Acad.*, 1928, V, pp. 237-360. For reports of arbitrated cases, see A. de Lapradelle et N. Politis, *Recueil des arbitrages internationaux*, I (Paris, 1905), II (Paris, 1924); H. La Fontaine, *Pasicrisie Internationale; Histoire documentaire des arbitrages internationaux* (Berne, 1902); J. B. Moore, *History and Digest of the International Arbitrations to which the United States has been a Party*, 6 vols. (Washington, 1898); J. B. Moore, *International Adjudications*, 6 vols. (New York, 1929); J. B. Scott, *The Hague Court Reports* (New York, 1916); and reports of various claims commissions; U. N. Reports of International Arbitral Awards, 4 vols. up to 1956.

A study of decided arbitrations will show a vast majority decided according to legal rules. Most writers regard this as the proper aspect of arbitration. "Mediation," says Moore, "is an advisory, arbitration a judicial function. Mediation recommends, arbitration decides."[6] According to Hyde, arbitration means "an impartial adjudication according to law, and that before a tribunal of which at least a single member who is commonly a national of a state neutral to the contest acts as umpire."[7] The Hague Convention for the Pacific Settlement of International Disputes states that "international arbitration has for its object the determination of controversies between states by judges of their own choice, upon the basis of respect for law."

On the other hand, a distinction is now made between arbitration and judicial settlement. This distinction is found in Article 12 of the Covenant of the League, which was amended to require submission of any dispute likely to lead to a rupture to "arbitration or *judicial settlement* or to inquiry by the Council." The fact that this amendment was introduced as a result of the creation of the Permanent Court of International Justice suggests that the distinction is one of machinery rather than of principle; the essential difference would seem to be that the court, with its fixed personnel, seat, and procedure, is not so malleable in the hands of disputants as is the arbitral tribunal whose members, organization, procedure, and even rules of law to be used may be fixed by the *compromis d'arbitrage*. As helpful a statement as is available is that given by the Legal Section of the Secretariat of the League in a memorandum with regard to the creation of the court: "Arbitration is one judicial method of settling disputes. Now, arbitration is distinguished from judicial procedure in the strict sense of the word by three features: the nomination of the arbitrators by the parties concerned, the selection by these parties of the principles upon which the tribunal should base its findings, and finally its character of voluntary jurisdiction. The boundary line between the two kinds of judicial procedure cannot be definitely fixed."[8]

[6] Moore, *Digest*, VII, p. 25. See also the illuminating discussion by Judge Moore, in *International Adjudications*, Modern Series, I, "Historical and Legal Notes," pp. 15-91. It contains an exhaustive survey of all authorities.

[7] Hyde, II, p. 1581. He quotes Westlake, I, p. 354: "The essential point is that the arbitrators are required to decide the difference—that is, to pronounce sentence on the question of right. To propose a compromise, or to recommend what they think best to be done in the sense in which the best is distinguished from the most just, is not within their province, but is the province of the mediator."

[8] Advisory Commission of Jurists, *P.C.I.J.*, Documents Presented to the Commission relating to Existing Plans for the Establishment of a Permanent Court of International Justice, p. 113. For a discussion of the distinction between arbitration and judicial settlement, see J. Garnier-Coignet, "Procédure judiciaire et procédure arbitrale," *R.D.I.*, 6 (1930), pp. 123-47.

PROCEDURE. Arbitrations, in past practice, have been instituted by a bilateral treaty, called the *compromis d'arbitrage*, signed by the parties to the dispute. The *compromis* states the question to be answered, names the arbitrators or the method by which they are to be selected, provides for a place of meeting, expenses, rules of procedure, and even the rules of law to be used. It may require decision according to strict rules of international law; it may, as in the case of the Three Rules of the Treaty of Washington by which the *Alabama* Claims were decided, state the rules themselves; or it may allow the use of equity, or of natural justice, or authorize the judge to act as *amiable compositeur*, or mediator. In the last case, as Politis comments, it may be practical, but it is not arbitration. The parties before the tribunal are technically states only, but in fact they often include individuals whose claims are being presented by their states, and whose nationality must be established before the state is permitted to plead for them. Each state is represented by an agent and by counsel, and argument is usually written, in the form of memorials, case, countercase, etc. The *compromis* is the charter of the tribunal, although the tribunal may determine its own competence under the terms of the *compromis*.

The selection of judges is one of the most important and also one of the most criticized elements of arbitral procedure. Formerly, appeal was made most often to sovereigns, a procedure which had the advantage of choosing a judge not representative of either party. But the sovereign was incompetent himself to determine legal questions, and was forced to call upon his legal advisers, persons who would never, perhaps, have been selected as arbitrators. Furthermore, the sovereign was inclined to decide upon a political basis, calculated according to his own interests. The tendency has therefore been to choose experts—but preferably an expert who would decide in favor of the country making the choice.

There are various methods of setting up the court. Usually each state appoints one member, and these two, or the states themselves, agree upon a neutral third member. Or again, each state chooses one of its own nationals and one neutral, and these agree upon a fifth neutral judge. The joint commission, in which there is no neutral to serve as umpire, does not deserve to be called an arbitral tribunal, although it has its uses. So long as these methods are continued, judges will vote as national representatives rather than as judges, and states will seek to choose judges known to be friendly to their views, thus eliminating many competent persons. Considered from this angle, the criticism that it is difficult to find satisfactory judges is quite true; but what is really sought is a representative rather than a judge.

Even after arrangements have been made in the *compromis* for the personnel of the tribunal, difficulties may arise. A judge may die or quit, and the arbitration may have to be suspended until further agreement can be reached. A state may even refuse to appoint judges after it has agreed to do so—as Bulgaria, Hungary, and Rumania did when complaint was made that they had violated the human rights provisions of the peace treaties. The International Court of Justice, in an advisory opinion, held that the other members of the tribunal were unable to proceed in the face of this refusal.[9] The code of Arbitral Procedure prepared by the International Law Commission attempts to make sure that the tribunal can be constituted in the face of such difficulties. Though its proposals would operate only after states had agreed to arbitrate, there were criticisms of this invasion of the right of a sovereign state to behave as it wishes, regardless of its agreement already made in the *compromis*.[10]

The tribunal usually offers a reasoned opinion in support of its decision, a practice demanded by custom and of great aid in the building of international law. It usually decides by a majority vote, and its decisions are *res judicata*, although the case may be reopened by the consent of both parties. The decision of the arbitral tribunal is binding, for the parties have so agreed—it is for this reason that states hesitate to accept obligatory arbitration, binding them to accept the decision in whatever case may arise in the future.

HISTORY. Although its effective use is quite recent, arbitration has always been known as a means of settling disputes between states. Said Thucydides: "It is wicked to proceed against him as a wrongdoer who is ready to refer the question to an arbitrator." Greece used it often, Rome but little. During the Middle Ages the pope was called upon frequently to serve as arbitrator and so, occasionally, were cardinals or sovereigns. It is hard to distinguish, during this period, between amiable composition and true arbitration. The modern era of arbitration begins with the Jay Treaty between the United States and England in 1794, which set up three boards of arbitration. The *Alabama* Award greatly increased interest and encouraged systematic study and popular support of arbitration. According to Politis, there were seventy arbitrations up to the year 1872; eighty-seven in the following twenty-seven years; and fifty-one from 1899 to 1914. Of these,

[9] *I.C.J. Reports*, 1950, p. 66. It had been agreed that each party would designate a member of the tribunal, that these would name a third person, and that if they could not agree, the secretary-general should name him. The General Assembly asked the court whether, in the face of refusal by one party to designate a member, the secretary-general could name him, after which the truncated tribunal could proceed. The court answered in the negative.

[10] U.N., General Assembly, Seventh Session, *Official Records*, Supp. No. 9, and Sixth Committee debates.

Great Britain participated in seventy-one, the United States in sixty-nine, France in thirty-three, Italy in nineteen, Germany in fifteen (though some half of these were between German states), Russia in three, Austria in two, Japan in two. It should be noted that, under many such agreements for arbitrations, there may be hundreds of cases tried by the tribunal. In the first report of the American Agent before the German-American Mixed Claims Commission, established in 1922, there were listed 12,416 claims; thousands of similar cases were handled by the Mixed Arbitration Tribunals, under bilateral agreements between the various belligerents in the first World War. The report of Fred K. Nielsen, American Agent before the American and British Claims Arbitration Tribunal set up in 1910, discusses a hundred cases tried by the Tribunal. Hundreds of cases have been decided by the Mexican-United States Claims Commission, established in 1923, and there are many other such tribunals.

The somewhat scattered efforts of the previous century were brought together and progress was consolidated in the work of the First Hague Conference, and from that time on the development of pacific means for settling disputes has been rapid. The Convention for the Pacific Settlement of International Disputes was "animated by a strong desire to concert for the maintenance of the general peace," and to that end "desirous of extending the empire of law, and of strengthening the appreciation of international justice." The signatories pledged themselves in Article 1 to use their best efforts to insure the pacific settlement of disputes. They agreed to have recourse "as far as circumstances allow" to the good offices and meditation of friendly Powers; recommended the employment of the International Commission of Inquiry on questions of fact "involving neither honor nor vital interests"; and recognized arbitration as the most efficacious and equitable method of settling questions of a judicial character, and established a code of arbitral procedure.

60. PERMANENT INSTITUTIONS[11]

PERMANENT COURT OF ARBITRATION AT THE HAGUE. So far as it is permanent the old Hague Tribunal consists merely of a registrar and

[11] See as to these institutions, J. Eyma, La cour de justice centro-américaine (Paris, 1928); T. Heyligers, "L'organisation des Tribunaux Mixtes d'Egypte," Hague Acad., 1927, II, pp. 5-107; C. J. B. Hurst, "Wanted! An International Court of Piepowder," B.Y.I.L., 1925, pp. 61-67; D. P. Myers, "The Origins of the Hague Arbitral Courts," A.J., 8 (1914), pp. 768-801, 10 (1916), pp. 270-311; J. B. Scott, "The Evolution of a Permanent International Judiciary," A.J., 6 (1912), pp. 316-58; J. B. Scott, "The Closing of the Central American Court of Justice," A.J., 12 (1918), pp. 458-75; H. Wehberg, The Problem of an International Court of Justice, translation by C. G. Fenwick (Oxford, 1918).

bureau, housed in the sumptuous Peace Palace at the Hague built through the generosity of Andrew Carnegie, and furnished by the gifts of states. The diplomatic corps at the Dutch capital serves as an administrative council. No provision was made for a permanent bench. Each state is entitled to name four persons whose names are included upon the panel of judges of the Court. The *compromis* must be made as usual, and judges selected, though from the panel of the Court. Of the arbitrations pursued since the creation of the Court, a steadily decreasing fraction has been given to the Court. It has been called "neither Permanent nor a Court," "only a phantom, an impalpable ghost." Certainly it has had many deficiencies. It has not had great influence in the development of law; it has not built up much confidence in itself; it has the same faults in the selection of judges as the individual arbitral tribunals; it has not been easily accessible. But for such faults as these its adherents have only themselves to blame. It could not do more than it was given authority to do. It was continued primarily for those states not connected with the League of Nations and has had no cases since the United States joined the United Nations.[12]

PRIZE COURT. The effort of the Second Hague Conference to create an International Prize Court was intended to meet a practical need, and has furnished valuable lessons. By a vote of thirty-six to one with six abstentions, agreement was reached upon a court, to be composed of fifteen members, which should always include judges chosen by the eight Great Powers. It was to have obligatory jurisdiction and to sit permanently at The Hague, and it was to be accessible to individuals as well as to states. Unfortunately, agreement could not be reached upon the law which it was to apply; and it failed to be set up after the vain effort of the London Conference of 1908 to state the law in the Declaration of London.

A COURT OF ARBITRAL JUSTICE. At the Second Hague Conference another effort was made, upon the demand of the United States, to set up a "real" court. Agreement was reached upon a court with a regular bench, sitting permanently, composed of professional judges chosen from the panel of the older Court, with renewable terms of

[12] In the course of a lecture given in 1926, the registrar of the older Court pointed out the following advantages justifying its continued existence: (1) Members of the court are chosen *ad hoc* thus making it possible to secure the type of judge needed for the particular case; (2) states parties to the case choose the judges, thus satisfying public opinion; (3) a state may have its own nationals as judges; (4) statesmen rather than jurists may be chosen for political questions; (5) many disputes involve both political and legal questions and can therefore be better handled by the old Court. These points, it is suggested, are for the most part derogatory of arbitration.

For reports of the cases tried by the Court, see J. B. Scott, *Hague Court Reports* (New York, 1916); for a summary, see Ralston, p. 259 *et seq.*

twelve years. The bureau and administrative council of the older Court were to serve the Court of Arbitral Justice as well. But the project was wrecked by the opposition of Germany and the smaller states, who insisted upon sovereignty. Brazil observed that arbitration means confidence, whereas judicial institutions mean obedience; and each state demanded a judge upon the bench—forty-four in all! Aside from the fact that a judge should not be conceived of as a national agent, the position of the smaller states would seem contrary to their best interests, for of all members of the community, they need to rely upon judicial determination rather than upon sovereign power. The United States continued her efforts to secure a judicial tribunal and a Third Hague Conference was proposed for 1914, which, however, never met.

CENTRAL AMERICAN COURT. Meanwhile, a Central American Court of Justice, which may be called the first real international court ever to be established, was created in 1907. Since there were only five states concerned, the problem of selecting judges was obviated by permitting each state to name one. Disputes of whatever nature were to be submitted to this Court, after diplomacy had failed; and in addition suits by an individual against a foreign state were permitted. In practice, however, it was inclined to proceed too fast, interfering without authority in revolutionary disturbances, and in general displaying zeal rather than discretion. Its last case involved the Bryan-Chamorro Treaty between the United States and Nicaragua, and when the United States showed no inclination to accept the ruling of the Court that the treaty was illegal, the effect was to discourage renewal of the ten-year period for which the Court had been created. Upon the invitation of the United States, a conference was held in December, 1922, which recreated the Court but with greatly limited authority. From a panel of thirty names, three judges are chosen by a minutely regulated process for each case. Its jurisdiction is still obligatory, but all questions which affect sovereign and independent existence are excepted. No cases have been brought before it.[13]

P.C.I.J. The last judicial institution to be established was the permanent Court of International Justice, established under Article 14 of the Covenant of the League of Nations, and now revised as the International Court of Justice. It will be separately considered in a later chapter.

[13] A survey of the Central American Court of Justice may be found in M. O. Hudson, *The Permanent Court of International Justice* (New York, 1943), Chap. iii; and J. B. Scott, "The Closing of the Central American Court of Justice," *A.J.*, 12 (1918), p. 458.

61. OBLIGATORY ARBITRATION

VOLUNTARY ARBITRATION. Arbitration was at first arranged for by special treaty, negotiated for each occasion after the dispute had arisen —if the parties felt so disposed. Obviously, passions might have been inflamed to such a degree that there would be no willingness to effectuate a settlement in this manner. It is clearly better to have a standing agreement beforehand, binding states to submit to peaceful settlement quarrels which might arise in the future, whether or not passions were running high. At this point the legal character of arbitration becomes most evident, for usually states have not been willing to submit to an obligation to arbitrate where they were not sure that there were definite rules of law which the arbiter must follow. States naturally feared that in such circumstances many cases would be left to the discretion or to the idiosyncracies of an arbiter not himself bound by definite legal procedure. An obligation to arbitrate taken in advance would greatly widen the field of arbitration, but to undertake it required much more confidence upon the part of states than existed.

The first step in this direction was taken by the insertion into various types of treaties of a clause (*clause compromissoire*) providing that disputes arising under the treaty in which the clause was included should be arbitrated. The first modern instance of such a clause, according to Hershey, is found in the treaty between the United States and Tripoli in 1796; today it is found in many treaties, such for example as that of the Postal Union, or the Brussels Slave Trade Convention. Of the first thousand treaties registered with the League of Nations, 187 had compromisory clauses. It was an easy first step to take toward obligatory arbitration, for a state bound itself to submit only the type of cases which might arise under the treaty.

OBLIGATORY ARBITRATION. The next step was the making of bilateral treaties of general arbitration. Some such treaties were made during the nineteenth century, and in 1897 the United States attempted to negotiate some of this type, but they were wrecked by the Senate.[14] The first important treaty, the model for many subsequent ones, was that between Great Britain and France in 1903. It provided that "differences which may arise of a legal nature, or relating to the interpretation of treaties existing between the two Contracting Parties, and which it may not have been possible to settle by diplomacy, shall be referred to the Permanent Court of Arbitration estab-

---

[14] See § 65, below.

lished at The Hague by the Convention of the 29th of July 1899, provided nevertheless, that they do not affect the vital interests, the independence, or the honor of the two Contracting States, and do not concern the interests of third Parties." Encouraged by the work of the Hague conferences, and with this treaty as a model, many others were negotiated.

The attempt to secure collective engagements for obligatory arbitration, which represent an advance beyond bilateral engagements, revealed the difficulty of determining which matters states are willing to submit to arbitration. Efforts have been made to solve this problem either by listing the subjects regarded as arbitrable, or by listing exceptions to a general rule of arbitration.[15] At the First Hague Conference an attempt was made to render arbitration obligatory in certain fields, such as pecuniary damages, or the interpretation of treaties concerning submarine cables, money, telegraph and postal communications, railways, rivers and canals, measures, industrial and artistic and intellectual property, sanitary or other matters. The obligations thus assumed were to be subject to the exception of national honor and vital interest; and even so, agreement was impossible. At the conference of 1907, twenty-six subjects were proposed, and of these only eight obtained general acceptance: pecuniary damages, reciprocal free assistance to indigent sick, protection of laborers, prevention of collisions at sea, weights and measures, wages of deceased seamen, protection of literary and artistic property, and tonnage of ships. But even this much agreement was vitiated by Germany, who announced that she accepted the principle for bilateral but not for multilateral treaties. The conference therefore had to content itself with a *voeu* in its Final Act, unanimously approving compulsory arbitration in principle.

This list of subjects of dispute, for the most part innocuous, as well as the clause reserving national honor and vital interest in such cases, is amusing, but nevertheless represents a real difficulty which has not yet been satisfactorily solved. The reservation of national honor and vital interests was especially unsatisfactory, for it was possible through it to reserve any dispute from the obligation to arbitrate, and emphatically those very subjects which most needed pacific means of settlement and which were most apt to lead to war. It represented in fact a setback, for such matters had previously been arbitrated. Sen-

---

[15] See A. Cavalcanti, "Restrictive Clauses in International Arbitration Treaties," *A.J.*, 8 (1914), pp. 723-37; H. Wehberg, "Restrictive Clauses in International Arbitration Treaties," *ibid.*, 7 (1913), pp. 301-14; R. R. Wilson, "Reservation Clauses in Agreements for Obligatory Arbitration," *ibid.*, 23 (1929), pp. 68-93.

ator Sumner, for example, excited over the depredations of the *Alabama*, demanded reparation to the extent of two and a half billions of dollars and the surrender of Canada, besides indirect damages; while England, on the other hand, asserted that "the construction of British statutes could never be submitted to arbitration, that the question involved the honor of the country and so was not appropriate for arbitration." Nevertheless, the matter was arbitrated and the United States was satisfied with a payment of fifteen and a half millions, while English honor was so little hurt that she was able to express her regret at what had happened. Reservations as to sovereignty, political questions, constitutional questions, and the like, were of little assistance in determining which questions should properly be submitted to arbitration.

"DOMESTIC QUESTIONS." An effort more nearly in the right direction was that of reserving "domestic questions" from arbitration. The danger in this direction lies in the assumption that a state, being supreme and irresponsible, can by its own edict designate a matter as within its domestic jurisdiction and therefore not subject to arbitration.[16] On the other hand, it is undoubtedly true that international law makes no effort to control all the activities of a state, very few of them, in fact. There is a large field reserved to the exclusive jurisdiction of the state, and within that field it may legitimately object to interference from the outside, just as member states of the United States resist encroachment by the federal government. But the exercise of a domestic power may produce effects abroad; a state cannot be permitted to decide for itself whether a matter is or is not solely within its domestic jurisdiction. Judicial consideration has been given to the question in cases involving Article 15, paragraph 8, of the Covenant of the League of Nations.[17] The French government claimed that nationality lies within the exclusive domain of sovereignty. The Permanent Court of International Justice replied:

> The words "solely within the domestic jurisdiction" seem rather to contemplate certain matters which, though they may very closely concern the interests of more than one State, are not in principle, regulated by international law. As regards such matters, each State is sole judge. The question whether a certain matter is or is not solely within the jurisdiction of a State is an

[16] As the United States may, under its reservation to its declaration submitting to the compulsory jurisdiction of the court.

[17] "If the dispute between the parties is claimed by one of them, and is found by the Council, to arise out of a matter which by international law is solely within the domestic jurisdiction of that party, the Council shall so report, and shall make no recommendation as to its settlement."

essentially relative question; it depends upon the development of international relations. Thus, in the present state of international law, questions of nationality are, in the opinion of the Court, in principle within this reserved domain.[18]

The Charter of the United Nations goes still further in the effort to protect states against international government. Article 2, paragraph 7, exempts domestic matters from the jurisdiction of the United Nations, but omits two provisions which were in the Covenant of the League: an authority to decide whether or not the matter is one of domestic jurisdiction, and the requirement that decision is to be made according to international law. This drastic statement in Article 2, paragraph 7, as will later be seen, has produced much controversy in United Nations organs.

"JUSTICIABLE QUESTIONS." A vast amount of discussion has been aroused in the effort to determine what are justiciable and what are non-justiciable questions.[19] Some prefer the terms political and legal disputes. If the agreement is to submit to arbitration, which is a judicial process, then national honor or interests or policy should be submitted if questions of law are involved. We have noted the treaty of 1903 between France and Great Britain, in which it was agreed to submit differences "of a legal nature, or relating to the interpretation of treaties." Closer definition was obtained in the treaties negotiated by President Taft in 1911: "international matters in which the high contracting powers are concerned by virtue of a claim of right made by one against the other under treaty or otherwise, and which are justiciable in their nature by reason of being susceptible of decision by the application of the principles of law and equity." Such matters were to be referred to arbitration; all others to a commission of inquiry. This principle has been followed in numerous treaties, and in the so-called "optional clause" (Article 36) of the Statute of the International Court of Justice, it is clearly and specifically stated that the compulsory

[18] P.C.I.J., Series B, No. 4, pp. 23-24. For discussions as to "domestic questions," see J. L. Brierly, "Matters of Domestic Jurisdiction," B.Y.I.L., 1925, pp. 8-19; C. G. Fenwick, "The Scope of Domestic Questions in International Law," A.J., 19 (1925), pp. 143-47; C. J. B. Hurst, "Interpretation of Art. 15, par. 8, of the League of Nations," B.Y.I.L., 1923-24, pp. 175-79; A. Van Deth, Etude sur l'interprétation du paragraphe 8 de l'article 15 du Pacte de la Société des Nations (Amsterdam, 1928). See also pp. 302-3, below.

[19] As to justiciable questions, see T. W. Balch, Legal and Political Questions between Nations (Philadelphia, 1924); R. Y. Hedges, "The Juridical Basis of Arbitration," B.Y.I.L., 1926, pp. 110-20; E. A. Jelf, "Justiciable Disputes," Grotius Society, 7 (1921), pp. 59-72; H. Lauterpacht, "The Doctrine of Non-Justiciable Disputes in International Law," Economica, 1928, pp. 277-317; P. S. Reinsch, "The Concept of Legality and International Arbitration," A.J., 5 (1911), pp. 604-14; D. Schindler, "Les progrès de l'arbitrage obligatoire depuis la création de la Société des Nations," Hague Acad., 1928, V, pp. 237-361.

jurisdiction of the Court covers all or any of the classes of legal dispute concerning:

(a) The interpretation of a Treaty.
(b) Any question of International Law.
(c) The existence of any fact which, if established, would constitute a breach of an international obligation.
(d) The nature or extent of the reparation to be made for the breach of an international obligation.

With this solution most writers appear to be in agreement. Thus Hyde said: "The true test of a justiciable controversy is believed to be whether the principles of international law are sufficiently broad and flexible in their scope and application, and sufficiently well understood, to mark clearly the lawfulness or unlawfulness of the conduct or contentions giving rise to complaint."[20] Some maintain that international law can be extended to cover any possible case which might arise. Sir John Fischer Williams believes "that on a question of rights there is no international conflict possible which, were it referred for decision, the Permanent Court of International Justice would be compelled to declare itself incompetent to decide."[21] It is argued therefore that disputes fall outside arbitration because states are unwilling to submit them, not because international law cannot handle them.

Arbitration finds little favor in the United Nations today, or among its Members. Even when it has been pledged it may be rejected, as India did both with Hyderabad and Pakistan; and the Security Council, in handling disputes, never refers one to arbitration. The trend today is decidedly toward political settlement.

62. CONCILIATION[22]

Two Channels. Resulting from these historical developments it may now be said that there are two main roads for the pacific settlement of disputes, either arbitration (or judicial settlement), or con-

---

[20] Hyde, 1st ed., II, p. 113. On page 112, he spoke of "justiciable, that is, one capable of reasonable adjustment by reference to accepted principles of international law." In Hyde, 2nd ed., II, pp. 1580-82, "arbitrable" replaced "justiciable."

[21] Williams, *Chapters*, p. 50; and see Van Deth, *loc. cit.*, p. 27.

[22] As to conciliation, see P. M. Brown, *La conciliation internationale* (Paris, 1925); F. de la Barra, "La médiation et la conciliation internationale," *Hague Acad.*, 1923, pp. 557-67; Ch. de Visscher, "La procédure de conciliation devant la Société des Nations," *R.D.I.L.C.*, 3rd Series, 4 (1923), pp. 21-36; J. Efremoff, "La conciliation internationale," *Hague Acad.*, 1927, III, pp. 5-146; C. C. Hyde, "The Place of Commissions of Inquiry and Conciliation Treaties in the Peaceful Settlement of International Disputes," *B.Y.I.L.*, 1929, pp. 96-110; A. N. Mandelstam, "La conciliation internationale d'après le Pacte et la jurisprudence du Conseil de la Société des Nations," *Hague Acad.*, 1926, IV, pp. 337-642; S. D. Metzger, "The Settlement of International Disputes by Non-Judicial Methods," *A.J.*, 48 (1954), p. 408.

cilation; and the problem to be solved is the relationship between the two methods. This, it may be suggested, is simply another way of asking which are justiciable and which are non-justiciable questions; but it is important to note that between the two of them pacific settlement is provided for all types of disputes. These channels of development were revealed at the First Hague Conference; they were shaped and deepened through treaties and through use by the League of Nations; they have been made more uncertain now under the Charter of the United Nations, which makes no such clear differentiation as was found in the Covenant of the League of Nations.

FOR CONCILIATION. A proper equilibration between the two methods is hard to find. There are some who maintain that conciliation should come first, whether logically or chronologically. This position is based upon the argument that in the present stage of international society, we cannot safely say *fiat justitia pereat mundus*. What that society most needs now, it is said, is peace and stability; it is more important to obtain a friendly settlement than a just settlement which might leave hard feelings. Conciliation, it is said, on the one hand, gives a safeguard for national sovereignty, and on the other hand, builds up the desire for pacific settlement; when this desire is sufficiently established, it will be time enough to impose justice upon unwilling states. Conciliation represents a great advance over mediation, from which it evolved, in that the inquiry is taken out of the hands of sovereigns who might be suspected of a desire for selfish intervention and turned over to scientific experts from whom sovereignty has nothing to fear. It is to be recalled, too, that arbitration results in a decree and that the decree is binding judicially, while conciliation merely recommends, leaving the state free to accept or reject the recommendation as it pleases, or as it feels the pressure of public opinion. Conciliation therefore harmonizes better, it is said, with a society based upon voluntary cooperation. It permits a state to concede its whole position, for the sake of peace, but without surrendering its principle. Since the conciliation commission is not limited to law, it has a wider range within which to find a solution. Arbitration implies the humiliation of being sentenced at law, whereas conciliation implies friendly adjustment. On the whole, the argument of those who prefer conciliation asserts that an amiable solution is to be preferred to litigation, and that peace weighs more than justice.

FOR ARBITRATION. This argument is undoubtedly valid to a certain extent, or as applied to certain controversies, but it is also true that states should admit the reign of law wherever it can be shown to be effective. International law does apply properly and adequately to some controversies, and in these justice should prevail over conciliation. There is agreement in the community upon some matters as arbitrable, and this agreement needs to be extended as rapidly as possible to other matters. Arbitration, it is maintained, should be regarded as the rule, conciliation as the exception; only so can a society founded upon law and justice be achieved. Conciliation, it is said, offers too wide a margin for abuse by sovereign states, and it should be used only where arbitration cannot be used. Legal questions should always be settled by law and, consequently, conciliation should not necessarily precede arbitration. To submit the question at once to law is to leave sentiment out of it. If, on the other hand, the subject is not one suitable for arbitration, or the court is unable to take jurisdiction, then conciliation should be resorted to. Neither is excluded; on the contrary, both are needed to make up the sum total of pacific settlement which can handle all disputes. The problem is to find a proper relationship between them.

Origins. The origins of conciliation are to be found in the earlier procedure of administration and in the commissions of inquiry provided for in the Convention for the Pacific Settlement of International Disputes at the First Hague Conference. The new method did not get off to a flying start. All questions involving national honor or interests were excepted, even though the report of the commission left the parties entirely free. Inquiry as to facts does not go so far toward proposing a settlement as does mediation. Mediation either secures a settlement or leaves things as they were; inquiry upsets the situation in favor of one party or the other without, nevertheless, providing an answer. It was natural that the power to make recommendations should be added to the power to ascertain the facts; even at the First Hague Conference, it had been vainly proposed that arbitration be made the necessary sequence to the report of a commission of inquiry.

The needed advance was made in the treaties negotiated under President Taft in 1911, which, however, were not approved by the Senate. These treaties made arbitration compulsory, but provided that, upon the demand of either party, the question should first be submitted to a joint high commission of inquiry. The commissioners thus acted as fact-finders, lawyers, or *amiables compositeurs*. Arbitration was employed either if there were no demand for inquiry, or if the commission of inquiry failed to achieve a settlement. These treaties did not go into effect but they furnished an excellent lesson. They were followed by the famous Treaties for the Advancement of Peace, the

Bryan Treaties, which have been discussed above. Under these treaties a permanent commission was instituted, and signatories were obligated to submit to it all questions to which the terms of previous arbitration treaties did not apply or were not applied. Thus conciliation was in principle subordinated to arbitration. No decision was authorized; the commission could make recommendations, but the parties reserved their freedom of action. But every question was to be submitted to a process of peaceable adjustment, and war was at least postponed for a considerable time.

As Used by the League. The Covenant of the League of Nations incorporated these principles, clearly outlining the alternative channels to be followed. Members were, by Article 12, to submit disputes either to arbitration or judicial settlement, or to inquiry by the council, and not to resort to war until three months after the award or recommendation. They might choose between arbitration and conciliation (Article 13), though the matters regarded as justiciable were stated, in terms of Article 36 of the Statute of the Court. While the choice is facultative, and no preference is given to one or the other method, there is no doubt that the makers of the Covenant preferred arbitration, and subsequent efforts were made to amend this article in the direction of making obligatory the arbitration of the matters listed in Article 13, paragraph 2, as, for example, in the Geneva Protocol. It was provided in this agreement (unratified), that if a quarrel were submitted to the council it should propose arbitration. If one party accepted, arbitration was obligatory and the decree binding. If both parties refused, the recommendation of the council was to be binding if unanimous; if not, the question would as a final measure (though there were some exceptions) be submitted to arbitration.

The great advance of the Geneva Protocol lay in finding a solution, by one method or another, which was to be binding upon disputants. Thus the most important defect of conciliation, its impotence to secure obedience, was remedied. The Locarno Pact provided that "any question with regard to which the parties are in conflict as to their respective rights shall be submitted to judicial decision," and all other questions were to be submitted to a conciliation commission. In 1928, the assembly offered a number of model treaties, and collected them into a General Act which was opened for signature. Signatories were bound by it to submit disputes of every nature to conciliation. However, questions in which a right is contested, as described in Article 36 of the Statute of the Court, must be submitted to the Court, unless the parties agree to submit them to arbitral procedure. Disputes not otherwise settled must be arbitrated.[23] When one considers that states may sign the Optional Clause, or the General Act, or a variety of bilateral treaties, the resulting hodge-podge of obligations seems an unnecessary sacrifice to the whims of nations.

63. TREATIES FOR PACIFIC SETTLEMENT

Aside from the work of the League of Nations, a large number of bilateral treaties of arbitration or of conciliation or of both have been signed by various states. A document prepared by the United Nations[24] classifies the treaties for pacific settlement as follows:

(a) Resort to the Court for all types of disputes (20).
(b) Conciliation for all types of disputes, followed in case of failure by resort to the Court (20).
(c) Legal disputes to the Court; all others to arbitration (4).
(d) Resort to the Court for legal disputes and to a commission of conciliation for all other disputes (40).
(e) Conciliation for all disputes; if this fails, legal disputes to the Court, others to arbitration (12).
(f) Legal disputes to the Court; non-legal to conciliation (29).
(g) Conciliation for all disputes; if this fails, legal disputes to the Court (no provision for non-legal) (9).
(h) Conciliation for legal disputes; if failure, resort to the Court, unless parties agree to arbitrate (2).
(i) Declarations under the Optional Clause: resort to the Court for specified legal questions, often with reservations.
(j) Conciliation for all disputes; on failure, to arbitration (3).
(k) All disputes to arbitration (with various reservations) (8).
(l) United States treaties: conciliation for all disputes; if failure, to the Permanent Court of Arbitration (29).
(m) Arbitration for legal disputes (1).
(n) Arbitration for disputes concerning treaties (13).
(o) Conciliation only for all disputes (10).
(p) Varied treaty provisions to settle disputes under the treaty by peaceful means (11).

There are, it thus appears, a surprising number—some two hundred —of bilateral treaties through which states agree, to some extent, and in many varied ways, to settle their deputes peacefully. Many of them

23 The General Act of 1928 was revived by the Interim Committee of the United Nations; few states have ratified the revised act.
24 Systematic Survey of Treaties for the Pacific Settlement of International Disputes, *U.N. Doc.*, Sales No. 1949.V.3, pp. 3-11. The League of Nations issued a similar survey in 1927: *L. of N. Doc.*, 1927.V.29. See also M. Habicht, *Post-War Treaties for the Pacific Settlement of International Disputes* (London, 1931).

are accompanied with reservations.[25] The high tide of such efforts was around 1928-29, after it appeared that a general treaty, such as the Geneva Protocol, or the General Act of 1928, would not receive general support. They represent an advance in the means of settling disputes between states, but not in terms of a general or uniform obligation; in each case, one must study the treaty to see if it is still in effect, what types of disputes are covered, what exceptions are made by reservation. Numerous as they are, they have been little used; practically no cases have been handled by conciliation, and very few by arbitration.

64. ARBITRATION IN THE WESTERN HEMISPHERE[26]

The boast of the Western Hemisphere is that it has always been devoted to the cause of arbitration; indeed, this devotion has been offered as one of the characteristics which distinguish it from the less advanced European states. Arbitration has undoubtedly been much talked about on the American continents. In 1826, Bolivar, a statesman of far vision, succeeded in having signed at the Panama Conference a Treaty of Union and Perpetual Confederation which would have established a real government among the American nations, with pacific settlement for all disputes and a guarantee against aggression. It was ratified only by Bolivar's own state, Colombia. A similar scheme, with more detail, was worked out at a congress at Santiago in 1848; it secured no ratifications whatever. The regular series of Pan-American conferences beginning in 1889 have been little more successful.

[25] These reservations can be put under nine headings: (1) vital interests and independence in 24 treaties, of which only 8 have appeared since 1914; (2) honor in 20, of which only 4 have appeared since 1914; (3) interests of third states in 20, though 9 recent treaties expressly reject this exception; (4) previous disputes in 13, but 11 recent treaties expressly include such disputes; (5) territorial status and frontiers in 8; (6) questions arising from the world war in 7; (7) internal legislation; (8) decisions of national courts except where denial of justice is found—a favorite with South American states; (9) constitutional questions in 2.

[26] As to this topic, see M. Ball, *The Problem of Inter-American Organization* (Stanford University Press, 1944); N. Carbonell, *Las conferencias internacionales americanas* (Habana, 1928); W. R. Manning, *Arbitration Treaties Among the American Nations to the Close of the Year 1910* (New York, 1924); J. O. Murdock, "Arbitration and Conciliation in Pan America," *A.J.*, 23 (1929), pp. 273-91; J. B. Scott, "The Pan American Conference on Conciliation and Arbitration," *A.J.*, 23 (1929), pp. 143-52; F. J. Urrutia, *La evolucion del principio de arbitraje en America* (Madrid, 1920); J. F. Williams, "The Pan American and League of Nations Treaties of Arbitration and Conciliation," *B.Y.I.L.*, 1929, pp. 14-32; *The International Conference of American States on Conciliation and Arbitration 1928-1929* (Washington, Government Printing Office, 1929).

However, sporadic instances of devotion to arbitration deserve approving attention. Brazil, as far back as 1891, included in her constitution a provision requiring arbitration precedent to war, and Venezuela and the Dominican Republic have similar provisions. Argentina and Chile signed in 1902 what is said to be the first compulsory arbitration agreement covering everything, although it excluded constitutional questions. The Central American Court of Justice has been mentioned above. According to Manning, 228 arbitration treaties were made among South American nations to 1910; and according to Carbonell, these nations entered into 120 such treaties between 1909 and 1919. This, however, owing to the South American habit of signing much and ratifying little, gives no fair picture of the actual situation. An authoritative statement sums it up as follows:

Unratified multilateral arbitration treaties and resolutions have been the rule. The first real advance was made through adherence to the Hague Conventions for the Pacific Settlement of International Disputes. Today 19 of the American Republics have ratified or adhered to the Hague Convention of 1907. The Pecuniary Claims Convention and the Gondra Convention of 1923 were the only general multilateral Pan-American treaties providing machinery for arbitration and inquiry up to the time the Conference of 1928 met in Washington. Of course, there are numerous bilateral arbitration treaties between the American Republics. Thirty-six arbitration treaties are in effect between Latin American Republics. Five of the Root arbitration treaties are in force between the United States and American Republics. Eight of the Bryan treaties for the advancement of peace are in effect. A treaty, similar to the Bryan treaties, is in force between the United States and four of the Central American Republics.[27]

While the apparent accomplishments in the field of arbitration are thus much reduced, the resultant figures are well worthy of praise. The Fifth Conference of American States at Santiago in 1923 viewed them with complacence, and upon its suggestion the Commission of Jurists of Rio de Janeiro prepared a project for pacific settlement which was presented to the Sixth Conference at Havana in 1928. This project said nothing of arbitration; but as it was reported out of the Second Commission it included the principle of obligatory arbitration, with free choice of the tribunal desired. Debate arising over this, the conference adopted a resolution which declared "that the American Republics adopt obligatory arbitration as the means which they will employ for the pacific settlement of conflicts between states"—with certain minimum exceptions as to independence and

[27] J. O. Murdock, "Arbitration and Conciliation in Pan America," *A.J.*, 23 (1929), pp. 277-78; see also *Latin American Treaty Developments*, Pan American Union, Law and Treaty Series No. 21 (1947); and a chart, *Status of the Pan American Treaties and Conventions*, revised to 1947, issued by the Pan American Union.

sovereignty—and which provided for a conference to meet at Washington. This conference met from December 10, 1928 to January 5, 1929, with twenty states represented. It agreed upon a General Convention of Inter-American Conciliation, a General Treaty of Inter-American Arbitration, and a Protocol of Progressive Arbitration.[28]

The Seventh Conference of American States (Montevideo, 1933) adopted a "Peace Code," including an American Court of Justice, which was passed on to the Buenos Aires Conference of 1936, and thence to the Eighth Conference (Lima, 1938), and then referred to the Pan American Union for study. The Mexico City Conference (1945) continued the effort to coordinate the numerous peace instruments and referred the problem to the Inter-American Juridical Committee, which had already prepared alternative drafts of a treaty for that purpose. At the Ninth Conference of American States in 1948, the Charter of the Organization of American States was signed, and also the American Treaty of Pacific Settlement, known as the Bogotá Pact.[29] The result of this assortment of treaties, which are interrelated by their own terms, and which have differing groups of signatories, is a very confusing set of obligations upon the American states for the settlement of their disputes. However, in practice little attention is paid to them and such matters as the trouble in Guatemala are handled by consultation rather than by set procedures.

65. UNITED STATES AND PACIFIC SETTLEMENT

It was the United States, as has been observed, which revived the use of arbitration, and during the nineteenth century she could well claim the leadership of the movement for arbitration.[30] But it was the

[28] The treaties may be found in *A.J.*, 23 (1929), Supp., pp. 76-89. See also J. B. Whitton and J. W. Brewer, "Problems Raised by the General Treaty of Inter-American Arbitration," *A.J.*, 25 (1931), pp. 447-68. The United States signed without reservations both treaties, but the Senate added the compromisory clause to the arbitration treaty.

[29] *The International Conferences of the American States: First Supplement, 1933-1940* (Washington, 1940), pp. 50, 161, 244; *Inter American Conference on Problems of War and Peace* (Washington, 1945), p. 68; Inter American Juridical Committee, *Recommendations and Reports* (Rio de Janeiro, 1945). The Bogotá Pact may be found in Dept. of State Pub., No. 3263.

[30] As to the attitude of the United States, see K. Colegrove, *The American Senate and World Peace* (New York, 1944); D. F. Fleming, *The Treaty Veto of the Senate* (New York and London, 1930); J. W. Garner, "The New Arbitration Treaties of the United States," *A.J.*, 23 (1929), pp. 595-602; P. C. Jessup, "The United States and Treaties for the Avoidance of War," *Int. Con.*, No. 239 (1928); J. B. Scott, *Treaties for the Advancement of Peace between the United States and Other Powers* (New York, 1920).

executive which led; the Senate has never been disposed to push arbitration. By the middle of the century it had turned down a number of petitions urging the use of arbitration and declared that it was impracticable and that the sword was the best guarantee of peace. The remarkable success of the Geneva Arbitration aroused widespread interest, and led to the introduction of various resolutions in Congress and finally, in 1874, to the passage of a joint resolution vaguely commending this method of settling disputes. In 1883, Switzerland proposed a general treaty of compulsory arbitration and it was discussed in draft form, but nothing came of it. Agitation in the British House of Commons and in the French Chamber of Deputies led, after some years, to a concurrent resolution calling upon the President to start negotiations for an international tribunal, and finally to work upon an actual treaty.

The treaty as discussed, and as finally signed in 1897, would have arbitrated claims of citizens, but was somewhat uncertain as to disputes involving the state itself. When it was submitted to the Senate what took place was "less a debate than a parliamentary exercise." Every time-killing device was employed, with the result that the treaty was carried over into McKinley's term. Here it was amended to exclude from the obligation to arbitrate, differences "which, in the judgment of either party, materially affect its honor, the integrity of its territory, or its foreign or domestic policy," as well as claims against member states, or the validity of existent treaties; and to provide that when the dispute arose, the agreement to submit (*compromis*) must be approved by a two-thirds vote of the Senate. The Senate then voted to reject the treaty.

During Theodore Roosevelt's term, the approval of the Senate Committee on Foreign Relations having been obtained in advance, Secretary Hay negotiated a number of treaties of arbitration upon the model of the one between England and France in 1903. This time the Senate approved the treaties, with the exception of one word: for "agreement" was substituted "treaty." The result was (bearing in mind the provisions of the Constitution), to use the forceful words of Roosevelt, "to make any one of these so-called arbitration treaties solemnly enact that there shall be another arbitration treaty whenever the two Governments decide that there shall be one," and he refused to proceed with such "shams." Apparently, the determining argument, then as now, was the desire not to decrease, but rather to increase, the prerogatives of the Senate. So said certain members: "The firm grasp upon our relations with foreign governments, placed in the hands of a minority of one-third of the Senate by the Constitution . . . is silently passing . . . into the sole and exclusive power of the President."[31]

However, in 1908, President Roosevelt again negotiated the treaties, retaining the exceptions as to vital interests, independence, and national honor, and allowing the Senate to approve the *compromis*.[32] Some twenty-two of these came into force, though eleven of them were allowed to lapse. They constituted, until around 1928, the only type of arbitration treaties binding the United States. President Taft, who exhibited much interest, attempted in 1911 to make more inclusive treaties, defining justiciable questions and providing conciliation for other questions. Senator Lodge presented the report of the Committee on Foreign Relations, punctuated by objections that "the constitutional powers of the Senate are taken away *pro tanto* and are transferred to a commission upon the composition of which the Senate has no control whatever," and "the Senate could be debarred from passing upon that question."[33] Again the treaties were emasculated by amendments, and Taft let them drop. The Bryan Treaties represented a great contribution to the methods of pacific settlement, and could be accepted by the Senate because they meant no loss of power upon its part, and no binding obligation upon the United States. In 1916, the Naval Appropriations Bill carried the statement that "it is hereby declared to be the policy of the United States to adjudicate and settle its international disputes through mediation or arbitration to the end that war may be honorably avoided." Article II of the Pact of Paris is stated in negative rather than in positive form, and therefore establishes no obligation to settle a dispute.

Until about 1928, no further treaties of arbitration were negotiated by the United States except two of the old type, one with Sweden in 1924 and one with Liberia in 1926. The United States also negotiated a large number of treaties for pacific settlement at about the time of the Pact of Paris. These were a distinct improvement over

[31] Quoted from the report of the minority of the Foreign Relations Committee, in "Arbitration and the United States," *W.P.F.*, IX, Nos. 6-7 (1926), p. 519.

[32] According to D. F. Fleming, *The Treaty Veto of the American Senate*, p. 90, President Roosevelt was induced to agree to these treaties through an expedient devised by Root. This was to submit the *compromis* for the approval of the Senate before it was signed. It was thus not treated as a treaty, nor did it force other nations to make a treaty; but it gave to the Senate the control which it sought.

[33] Of course, the primary purpose of such a treaty is to bind a nation in advance, and to take out of the hands of a legislative body, in which a fire-eating patriotic speech is often regarded as a means of vote-getting, the right to block the peaceful settlement of a dispute. The juridical position of the *compromis* is discussed by Murdock, *op. cit.*, *A.J.*, 23 (1929), pp. 285-86, and by R. R. Wilson, "Clauses relating to Reference of Disputes in Obligatory Arbitration Treaties," *A.J.*, 25 (1931), pp. 469-89.

the earlier ones, but still far behind those concluded by other states. They provided a clearer definition of "justiciable questions" and they omitted the old reservation of national "honor and vital interests," but they introduced other reservations equally as effective. "Domestic questions" were excepted, as was also the Monroe Doctrine. The requirement of Senatorial approval for the *compromis* was retained, thus potentially vitiating the pledge. It was therefore correct to say, before 1946, that the United States was not bound by any treaty for compulsory legal settlement of its disputes. For this the Senate was responsible; public opinion was far ahead of it.

In that year, the Senate approved and the United States accepted the compulsory jurisdiction of the International Court of Justice for disputes of a legal character. It did so, however, with characteristic reservations. One of these, domestic questions "as determined by the United States of America," would make it possible for the United States to refuse to appear before the court in any dispute. It is not probable, however, that the United States would abuse this reservation, and one may say, then, that the United States has changed its long-standing policy and is now prepared to submit its legal disputes to the court for judicial settlement.

CONCLUSIONS. The above rapid survey of the means historically developed for the pacific settlement of disputes between nations takes us up to the League of Nations and the United Nations; the developments under these organizations will be surveyed in later chapters. As in the case of international legislation, the availability of continuing organizations has improved or refined procedures but, as in that case, no fundamental advance has been made because of the unwillingness of states, in these days of free-wheeling sovereignty, to submit to legally binding actions taken without their consent. This is true in spite of the numerous treaties by which almost all states are bound, in one way or another, to means of settling their disputes. Few, if any, settlements have been made by the many commissions set up under the various bilateral treaties.

What is now needed is some consolidation of existing obligations —and, of course, more willingness on the part of state to submit to any sort of obligation. Each state has made such treaties as it liked, and, while this experimentation was desirable, it would seem time now to gather up and systematize the results. Aside from the possible inconsistencies of awards and the lack of authoritative precedents, the various methods in use could result in conflicting obligations. Between the Charter, the Optional Clause of the Court, the collective treaties among American states, and the numerous bilateral treaties of arbitration and conciliation, it may be difficult to determine which obligation is to prevail for a particular state.

The trend today is strongly away from settlement of disputes by an outside authority but, insofar as there is pacific settlement, the trend is definitely for political rather than legal settlement, for conciliation rather than arbitration or judicial settlement. The United Nations does not in practice seek to have disputes between its Members settled by legal procedures or according to law. This trend toward conciliatory processes may be due in part to the difficulty of determining what is a legal dispute and in part to the intrinsic virtues of conciliation for certain types of disputes, but it seems due mostly to the fact that disputes are brought before the Security Council or the General Assembly, and these bodies use only conciliation. Conceivably, a state could refuse to appear before the Security Council to answer charges made against it, but it cannot afford to do so. It is not, however, bound to accept the settlement recommended. Since the Security Council (or Assembly) can only recommend, it is natural that it should seek to work out a compromise acceptable to both parties.

But to put conciliation above arbitration is to put compromise above law and justice. If it is necessary to employ conciliation, upon the ground that peace and stability must be established before justice can gain sway, it should be regarded as a temporary expedient. Arbitration should always be used in cases where it is clear that international law covers the issue, and there should be continuous effort to increase the number of such cases. It is going too far to assert that judicial settlement is impossible, until international law is built up into a complete and well-rounded code; for law is never complete. The problem at present is to find a proper balance between the two methods, and the balance should always weigh upon the side of arbitration. Conciliation represents national sovereignty, unwilling to bow to a decision, and it must doubtless be satisfied for a time; but behind conciliatory processes, there should be a means for imposing a settlement regarded as just and according to law, by the now organized community of nations.

PART IV

We have seen how the growing pressure of interdependence led to the development of rules, procedures, and organs through which needed functions in the community of nations could be performed. These were scattered and largely unrelated arrangements, and the next step to be anticipated would be the establishment of one over-all system.

The terrible potentialities of modern warfare as revealed in the First World War (immeasurably worse today) frightened nations into the creation of the League of Nations; the Second World War frightened the United States into the United Nations. The driving force behind these efforts was the desire to bring war under control, and this clearly called for more than the technical or functional organizations of the past; it demanded an over-all organization, of political character and with coercive functions. The League of Nations was intended to be such a body (as is now the United Nations); and it served both "to provide international cooperation" and "to achieve international peace and security." These two functions we shall consider separately, devoting Part IV to organization and cooperation, and Part V to the effort to bring war under control.

PART IV

Chapter 10

THE LEAGUE OF NATIONS

BACKGROUND

66. EARLIER IDEAS CONCERNING A LEAGUE OF NATIONS[1]

The idea of a league of nations had long been in gestation; its roots reached far back into the past. Isidore of Seville (560-636) thought of a society of nations, of a world which is the "domicile of all mankind." Pierre Dubois (1250-1321) in his work, *De Recuperatione Sanctae Terrae*, written in 1305, proposed that, since the pope is a ruler over souls only and the Emperor merely a national ruler, there should be an *entente* of European princes. Feeling the need for institutions, he urged a union of states, with a council and a court, and his practical political sense added control by France to this plan. Such a plan was fantastic for his day, but it needs to be recalled as the first systematic scheme of this sort ever presented. The imagination of King Podiebrad of Bohemia (or of his advisor, a Frenchman named Marini) went still further. He sought in 1461 a combination of France, Bohemia, and Venice against the infidel Turk, and planned to set up a real world state. Members were to be obliged

[1] A. C. F. Beales, *The History of Peace: A Short Account of the Organized Movements for International Peace* (New York, 1931); M. E. Curti, *Peace or War: The American Struggle, 1636-1936* (New York, 1936); W. E. Darby, *International Tribunals: A Collection of the Various Schemes Which Have Been Propounded; and of Instances in the Nineteenth Century* (London, 1904); R. Y. Hedges, *International Organization* (London, 1935); S. Hemleben, *Plans for World Peace Through Six Centuries* (University of Chicago Press, 1943); C. L. Lange, *Histoire de l'Internationalisme*, I (New York, 1919); J. A. R. Marriott, *Commonwealth or Anarchy? A Survey of Projects of Peace from the 16th to the 20th Century* (Columbia University Press, 1939); J. T. Meulen, *Der Gedanke der Internationalen Organisation in seiner Entwicklung*, 2 vols. (The Hague, 1917-1940); A. Nussbaum, *A Concise History of the Law of Nations* (New York, 1954); J. B. Scott, *Law, the State, and the International Community*, 2 vols. (Columbia University Press, 1939); V. Valentin, *Geschichte des Völkerbundgedankens in Deutschland* (Berlin, 1920); E. Wynner and G. Lloyd, *Searchlight on Peace Plans* (New York, 1949).

to submit to arbitration and to render to each other mutual assistance, even to the point of military execution of orders. There was to be an assembly at Basle, and apparently the three states were to divide the world between them and rule it.

The "Grand Dessein" of Henry IV, really the work of his minister, Sully, was likewise motivated by the crusading spirit, and doubtless also by opposition to the Empire. Sully proposed to redistribute the territory of Europe in order to secure some degree of equality between states, and then reconstitute the Continent into a *république universelle très chrétienne*, composed of fifteen equal units. There was to be a senate of sixty, four from each state, and six local councils. These states were combined in order to maintain the *status quo*, and the maintenance was to be secured through arbitration and a joint army ready to enforce obedience.

Later it gradually came to be denied that even infidels should be excluded from the community of nations. The influence of religion was strong, and writers such as Vitoria, Suarez, Gentili, and others, gave expression to the idea of the unity of the human race and the solidarity of the community.[2] The reformers such as Sir Thomas Moore planned a Utopian community; or like Erasmus, taught the ideal of peace. Theologians, and Grotius as well, taught that it was not proper to fight the Turk simply because of religion; and Francis I not only allied with them, but defended his alliance. An unknown monk, Emeric Cruce, in 1623, wrote *Le Nouveau Cynée*, which is a remarkable forerunner of the League of Nations. His plan called for a mutual guarantee of possessions and provided a council of ambassadors for administrative purposes. The discovery of the New World further widened the horizon and the idea of the community of nations gradually spread beyond Europe to the entire world. William Penn, surprisingly in view of his Quaker beliefs, desired an organization sufficiently strong to arbitrate disputes, and with a military force to back up such decisions. He rejected the principle of conquest and asked for representation based upon population and wealth rather than upon equality.

The famous "Plan for a Perpetual Peace" of the Abbé de St. Pierre probably had more influence than any of these early schemes. By his time, many philosophers were supporting pacifism, were teaching the equality of states, and were seeking in international organization the only legal protection for these equal nations. The Abbé proposed an alliance based upon the Peace of Utrecht, and was therefore subject to the criticism that he merely maintained the *status quo*. This was

[2] See A. Sereni, *The Italian Conception of International Law* (Columbia University Press, 1943).

emphasized by his plan. There was to be a congress of ambassadors, endowed with legislative and judicial power, which could make fundamental changes only by unanimous vote. Pacific procedure was provided for, and disarmament—the latter appearing in but few such plans. The alliance was to back up arbitral decrees, and, like Penn, he proposed to collect the expenses of such an execution from the offending state. The writer detailed an abundance of advantages for his plan; but, as in the case of the Holy Alliance later, its chief result would have been to maintain in power the *beati possidentes*.

During the eighteenth and early nineteenth centuries, a number of philosophers and jurists advocated international organization: Rousseau demanded a European Republic, Wolff a *civitas maxima;* Bentham studied the causes of war and proposed disarmament, the liberation of colonies, and an international tribunal, but he would have no more than moral sanctions; Immanuel Kant explored the conditions for eternal peace, *Der Ewige Friede*, favored republican government, and disarmament, and would have builded public law upon a federation of free states. So the thread of thought, through changing and expanding patterns, was woven into the fabric of international development.

67. DEVELOPMENT OF EXECUTIVE LEADERSHIP

Meanwhile, a related pattern had been developing likewise in the field of practical politics. The society of nations grew from a Christian community united against the infidel into a universal community based upon common human interests, and ceased to be merely a European community. Turkey is no longer ostracized, and was formally admitted to membership in the community in 1856. In the Western Hemisphere two continents of peoples were added as heirs to European civilization; the Far East has added many new states to the United Nations; and Africa is now coming into the world community.

BALANCE OF POWER. When the Peace of Westphalia proclaimed the legality of the separate and independent existence of states, the factual situation remained little changed. It was still true that one state might easily become the prey of another, and that all might be ultimately swallowed up into a universal empire. To meet this possibility, the earliest means of defense offered was the principle of the balance of power. In its application, this principle meant a combination of states against the threat of the strongest aggressive power. Haphazard combinations of this nature doubtless preserved the community of nations against such menaces to its existence as those of Philip of Spain, or Louis XIV, or even Napoleon. In the nineteenth century, a need for more efficient combination was felt, for Napoleon had come perilously near to a complete upset of the equilibrium, and it seemed necessary to have some common leadership against any repetition of the danger.

CONCERT OF EUROPE. The first proposal was made by Alexander I, the fanatic Tsar of Russia, who offered to his fellow sovereigns, at the moment of reviewing the victorious allied troops upon the plains of Vertus, the Act of the Holy Alliance. It bound them in Article I:

> Conformably to the words of the Holy Scriptures which command all men to consider each other as brethren, the Three contracting Monarchs will remain united by the bonds of a true and indissoluble fraternity, and, considering each other as fellow-countrymen, they will, on all occasions, and in all places, lend each other aid and assistance; and regarding themselves towards their subjects and armies as fathers of families, they will lead them, in the same spirit of fraternity with which they are animated, to protect Religion, Peace and Justice.

This proposal was accepted by all, "so to speak, with a shrug of the shoulders," but Castlereagh of England, to whom it was all "verbiage," wished for something more concrete. His purpose, as expressed in the Preamble to the Quadruple Alliance, was "to fix in advance by a solemn treaty the line of conduct which they propose to follow in order to guarantee Europe against the dangers that might yet threaten her." The engagements of the Treaty of Chaumont were renewed, and the actual forces to be provided by each state in case of intervention were specified. The Quadruple Alliance also agreed to "renew at fixed intervals" their previous conferences—"meetings consecrated to great common objects and the examination of such measures as at each one of these epochs shall be judged most salutary for the peace and prosperity of nations and for the maintenance of the peace of Europe."[3]

Thus the Concert of Europe began, purposefully enough. It was based upon the primacy of the Great Powers, upon whom responsibility fell since they alone were strong enough to maintain order.[4] Its principle of action was the maintenance of the balance, the preservation of the *status quo*; it asserted that the public order of Europe was based upon the principle of legitimacy (i.e., the right of the

[3] On this period, see W. A. Phillips, *The Confederation of Europe* (New York, 1914).

[4] A thought recurrently familiar in the discussions concerning the making of the United Nations.

dynasties in power to continue to rule, in contrast to the revolutionary new ideas about the sovereignty of peoples). It worked through the same old alliances; but also through the new method of periodic conferences, concerning which Castlereagh was enthusiastic. It had no secretariat, no formal organization to prepare its meetings. Conferences were held at Vienna in 1815; at Aix-la-Chapelle in 1818; at Troppau and Laibach in 1820 and 1821; and at Verona in 1822. These meetings produced some legislation, such as rules concerning the rank of diplomatic agents, and freedom of navigation on international rivers, and resulted in positive action for the maintenance of rights and order in Europe. The weapon of intervention was actively employed in the name of the Concert to safeguard existing regimes against revolutionary nationalism. Disagreement as to the function of the Quadruple Alliance led to the withdrawal of England at Verona, and Monroe's message of 1823 was directed against this power-grouping. The Holy Alliance hung on, a disembodied spirit, until the Hungarian Revolution of 1849.

Nevertheless, the Concert of Europe, in much broader and more vague grouping, continued its work. Conferences were summoned as crises arose, and by the state most affected or sufficiently interested to take the initiative in calling a meeting. Such action represented the growing feeling of responsibility for maintaining peace in Europe, and it furnished, in most rudimentary form, a sort of an executive direction for Europe.

NINETEENTH CENTURY. Various examples of the control thus exercised can be found in the nineteenth century. The struggle for Grecian independence opened a new phase of the Eastern Question; and that hotbed of war became more than ever a matter of concern to Europe, calling for common action to adjust its affairs. A contest, said Canning, "so ferocious, leading to excesses of piracy and plunder, so intolerable to civilized Europe, justifies extraordinary intervention, and renders lawful any expedient short of positive hostility."[5] As a matter of fact, it produced open hostilities, and after the annihilation of the Turkish fleet at Navarino, the Powers granted independence to Greece and promised her a monarch.[6] From that time on, a close watch was kept over the Balkan peninsula, and no state was permitted to have its own way unsupervised. Regularly the Concert intervened when troubles arose and called conferences to readjust

[5] J. A. R. Marriott, *The Eastern Question*, p. 195.
[6] And in addition opened the Black Sea and the Danube River to neutral vessels, and gave autonomy to the principalities of Moldavia and Wallachia.

the situation, as at the Congress of Paris in 1856,[7] or as when it compelled the revision of the Treaty of San Stefano at the Congress of Berlin in 1878. The neutralization of Belgium, "the cockpit of Europe," and of Luxembourg, are other illustrations of its work. Smaller states were invited to participate on various occasions; and the two Hague peace conferences at the beginning of the twentieth century represented a new phase, both as to universal membership and in the attempt at a legislative solution of the problem of maintaining peace and reducing armaments.

In the present century, four episodes reveal strikingly the growing coherence of the Concert, and its tendency to intervene in matters which would earlier have been considered to be matters of purely national concern. In 1905, Germany demanded that Morocco, over which France had been gradually extending her control, should be placed under international supervision. A conference was assembled at Algeciras in the following year, which resulted in "theoretical acceptance of the German doctrine of internationalization, but a practical disavowal of it by the grant of a privileged position to France and Spain."[8] The dispute was not settled; and when it flared up again with the visit of the German gunboat *Panther* to Agadir in 1911, Lloyd George made a famous speech in which he asserted —as Germany had done herself in 1905—that England could not be omitted from any settlement of the Moroccan question, even though she had no direct political stake in it.[9]

The claim of an international control over troublesome questions was even more strikingly demonstrated in two episodes in the Near East. When Austria, in 1908, annexed Bosnia-Herzegovina, a protest was at once made at such a violation of the public law of Europe, recorded in the Treaty of Berlin, and an international conference was demanded. It was a serious crisis, for Germany "in shining armor" backed up Austria; and the Concert was not operating with sufficient harmony to be able to prevent the violation. The annexation was legalized, but even in this solution the character of international con-

[7] At this Congress, Turkey was admitted "to participate in the public law and concert of Europe," and various territorial rearrangements were made. In addition, the famous Declaration of Paris concerning maritime warfare represented the legislative activity of the Concert.

[8] B. Schmitt, *England and Germany*, p. 237. The conference provided an international police in Morocco, and a self-supporting financial system.

[9] "But if a situation were to be forced upon us by which peace could only be preserved by the surrender of the great and beneficent position Britain has won for centuries of heroism and achievement—by allowing Britain to be treated, where her interests are vitally affected, as if she were of no account in the cabinet of nations— then I say emphatically that peace at that price would be a humiliation intolerable for a great country like ours to endure." Quoted by Schmitt, *loc. cit.*, p. 330,

trol was recognized in that the note through which Serbia unwillingly submitted was addressed to, and in submission to demands from, the Great Powers.[10] When the Balkan War broke out in 1912, the Powers again intervened, even to the extent of a display of naval force; and the Conference at London, in July, 1913, created the independent state of Albania, put Prince William of Wied upon its throne, and established a commission of control, which was responsible for the organization of the new government and for civil and financial administration in Albania.

The concerted action of states is illustrated in less distinctly political action. Thus there has been, in a number of cases, cooperative action to secure financial control, as in Egypt, or Turkey, or China. There have been collective actions for territorial administration, or condominiums, in such cases as Samoa, the New Hebrides, or the puzzling case of Spitzbergen. The joint action taken against Venezuela in 1903 was rewarded by the Hague Tribunal, which gave to the intervening powers a priority in payment, thus giving judicial support to such action.[11] One of the most interesting of these experiments is the international city of Tangier, whose history illustrates how agreement is forced out of conflict. It has been constantly a subject of negotiation, until a revised statute was finally agreed upon in July, 1928. It has an international commission of control, an international legislative assembly, a mixed court, and international administration over such matters as health, navigation, and postal communication. Alongside of this system, and apparently still independent of it, is the Commission for the Cape Spartel Lighthouse, which has functioned successfully for many years.[12]

Whatever one may think of the policies involved or of the decisions taken in these situations, there can be no doubt that the community of nations was taking an increasing interest in all problems that might disturb the peace of nations; that states were demanding participation in community action for this purpose; that the authority of the Concert was admitted; and that it was building precedents and even, at

---

[10] The note is worth quoting: "Serbia recognizes that the *fait accompli* regarding Bosnia has not affected her rights, and consequently she will conform to the decisions that the Powers may take in conformity with the Treaty of Berlin. In deference to the advice of the Great Powers Serbia undertakes to renounce from now onward the attitude of protest and opposition which she has adopted with regard to the annexation since last autumn. She undertakes, moreover, to modify the direction of her policy and to live in the future on good, neighborly terms with the latter." It may be noted that the Austrian ultimatum to Serbia in 1914 claimed a violation of this promise.

[11] J. B. Scott, *Hague Court Reports* (Oxford University Press, 1916), p. 58.

[12] As to Tangier, see D. P. Myers, "Tangier, An International City," *National Municipal Review*, 4 (1915), pp. 60-65; G. H. Stuart, *The International City of Tangier* (rev. ed., Stanford University Press, 1955).

the last, organs for joint action. Its machinery, however, proved totally insufficient when confronted with the ultimatum presented by Austria to Serbia in 1914. It has often been said that had there been any effective international organization whatever, even a means of summoning an international conference, World War I could have been averted; and in view of later developments the assertion does not sound unreasonable. At any rate, the Concert of Europe, with all its precedents of authoritative intervention, lacked the cohesiveness and the organization through which it could respond rapidly and effectively in the emergency which precipitated the war in 1914.

WORLD WAR MACHINERY. The desperate emergencies of the First World War produced a degree of international cooperation which leads one to wonder why such cooperation cannot be attained for the purpose of avoiding war. In 1916, an Allied Supreme War Council was set up to assume general direction over the far-reaching activities of the Allies. An Allied Naval Council, a Maritime Transport Council, and a Blockade Council soon appeared, and also various executives, such as the Wheat Executive, the Petroleum Conference, and sub-committees for many commodities. Their activities extended to neutrals, and the cargo and destination of practically every commercial vessel was directed by the Allied Maritime Transport Council. The success of these organs furnished examples and precedents used in the creation of the League of Nations.[13]

THE LEAGUE OF NATIONS

68. THE MAKING OF THE COVENANT[14]

The efforts looking toward peace and international organization during the war were necessarily scattered and disorganized, but their

[13] S. P. Duggan, *The League of Nations* (Boston, 1919), Chap. iii; Sir Arthur Salter, *Allied Shipping Control, An Experiment in International Administration* (New York, 1921); Cheever and Haviland, pp. 43-46, 53.

[14] On the making of the League of Nations, see R. S. Baker, *Woodrow Wilson and the World Settlement*, 3 vols. (Garden City, 1922); *The Intimate Papers of Colonel House*, 4 vols. (New York, 1926-28); Howard-Ellis, Chaps. i-v; C. A. Kluyver, *Documents on the League of Nations* (Leiden, 1920); David Lloyd George, *Memoirs of the Peace Conference*, 2 vols. (New Haven, 1939); Miller, entire; T. Marburg, *Development of the League of Nations Idea: Documents and Correspondence of Theodore Marburg*, edited by J. H. Latané, 2 vols. (New York, 1932); Morley, Part I; Münch, entire; Ray, Introduction; J. T. Shotwell, *At the Paris Peace Conference* (New York, 1947); Temperley, *passim;* Walters, Part I; F. Wilson, *The Origins of the League Covenant* (London, 1928); *Foreign Relations of the United States: The Paris Peace Conference*, 13 vols. (Washington, 1942-47).

surprising persistence revealed their hold upon the public imagination. In Switzerland, a committee was formed by Professor Nippold in August 1914; a Dutch organization began work in October 1914 and summoned a conference at The Hague which became known as the Organization Centrale pour une Paix Durable; in France La Paix pour la Droit worked for a league endowed with strong sanctions; in Germany such organizations were strictly repressed, but some valuable studies were nevertheless made. Several groups were at work in England: The Union for Democratic Control, the Fabian Society, the Bryce Group, the Phillimore Group, and the League of Nations Society, which was founded in 1915.

Meanwhile, in the United States, and under the leadership of William H. Taft, the League to Enforce Peace had been organized at Independence Hall in January, 1915. It had a program of four points: (1) justiciable questions to be submitted to a tribunal; (2) other questions to a council for inquiry and recommendation; (3) economic and military force to be combined against a state which goes to war before submitting its dispute to settlement; (4) periodical conferences to codify international law. It was a simple and appealing program, although it would delay rather than eliminate war. It met with much support, and also encountered opposition which became organized as the World Court League. The latter body represented the view which finally prevailed in the United States—opposition to sanctions and support for court, conciliation, and codification. In May, 1916, President Wilson spoke to the League to Enforce Peace, supporting the idea of an association of nations to keep the seas free and to prevent war, and favoring a guarantee of territorial integrity and political independence. In his speech to the Senate on January 22, 1917, he added the idea of disarmament. The last of his famous Fourteen Points stated the ideal of a League of Nations: "A general association of nations must be formed under specific covenants for the purpose of affording mutual guarantees of political independence and territorial integrity to great and small States alike."

CONSOLIDATION OF IDEAS. Thus, by the end of the war, the idea of some sort of an association of nations was strong in many countries. The Allied statesmen—Grey in England, Briand in France, Wilson in the United States—as well as Bethmann-Hollweg in Germany were all committed to it, and the neutral states were seriously studying it. Certain common principles appeared. There was content no longer with extemporaneous cooperation; permanent organization was desired. The principle of universality was accepted—all states should be members; and opinion tended toward some mild form of federation rather than toward a superstate. Most plans called for some sort of a representative assembly, for a court, a council, and for a secretariat. Some envisaged military sanctions; the French hoped for an international army and general staff. There was general agreement that it is the duty of every state to accept its share of the collective responsibility for the maintenance of order and systematic cooperation within the association, and to join in against the state which was a menace to peace. The purpose of the organization, in the minds of most, was the diminution of war, though the Anglo-Saxons were not optimistic enough to conceive of more than delaying war, in the sense of the Bryan Treaties. There was a great incidental interest in the limitation and reduction of armaments, and a surprising amount of attention was given to such humanitarian matters as colonies, minorities, and self-determination in general, and to economic problems, all of which were regarded as causes of war and in need of adjustment.

PEACE CONFERENCE. At the plenary meeting of the Paris Peace Conference on January 25, 1919, a resolution was passed, asserting it to be essential "that a League of Nations be created to promote international cooperation, to ensure the fulfillment of accepted international obligations, and to provide safeguards against war"; that it should be created "as an integral part of the general treaty of peace"; and that it should have periodic conferences, a permanent organization, and a secretariat. A commission was appointed, with President Wilson as chairman, to work out the Covenant of the League of Nations. It was composed of two members from each of the five Great Powers and—after a protest by the small states—of nine others representing the smaller states. Suggestions and criticisms poured in from every quarter. Those which came from the United States were of the most importance, not because of their intrinsic merit, but because they revealed an increasing opposition in the Senate, which it would be necessary to placate. The most important of these suggestions concerned "domestic questions," the Monroe Doctrine, the right of withdrawal, unanimity in council and assembly, and the non-obligatory character of the mandates system. These President Wilson supported and they were incorporated into the Covenant. On May 20-21, the neutral states were invited to express their views, and this led to further changes. A text was approved by the Plenary Conference on April 28. Sir Eric Drummond was named as the first Secretary-General, and a committee was appointed to inaugurate the new machinery. While it began work at once, and the League of Nations had its first headquarters in London, the Treaty of

Versailles and therefore the Covenant (which was the first 26 articles of the treaty) did not go into effect until January 10, 1920, when the exchange of ratifications was made.

THE DEFECTION OF THE UNITED STATES. But for the powerful leadership of President Wilson, the Covenant would not have been included in the peace treaties, and quite probably there would have been no League of Nations at all. Thus the League was largely of American origin, yet it was rejected by the United States. Many studies have been made of this situation and it is now possible to speak with confidence as to the facts. "It is as certain as anything in the realm of public opinion can be," says Mr. Bartlett, "that in May, 1919, the majority of the American people favored the ratification by the Senate of the Treaty with the Covenant as it was."[15] A Literary Digest Poll showed newspapers in favor of it, and 32 State Legislatures and 33 governors had endorsed it. Senator Lodge himself, the Chairman of the Senate Foreign Relations Committee, who led the successful fight against the League, explained that since 80 per cent of the American people were for the League, he could not undertake a direct frontal attack but must chip away at it by pointing out dangers and adding "safeguarding" reservations.[16] The attack, though perhaps intensified by Lodge's personal animosity to Wilson, was primarily a matter of political party strategy. The Covenant was seized upon as the best point of attack against the administration in power, and such considerations as the good reputation of the United States or the peace of the world were disregarded in view of the superior needs of the party. Through astute parliamentary strategy, Lodge put himself into the position of being the defender of the Treaty of Versailles (with fifteen reservations attached to it which President Wilson could not accept and which left little of the League of Nations) and put Wilson into the position of voting against his own treaty. Public opinion was apparently changed, though the election of 1920 cannot be regarded as a referendum on this issue,[17] and remained opposed for two decades or

[15] R. J. Bartlett, *The League to Enforce Peace* (University of North Carolina Press, 1944), p. 130; and see T. A. Bailey, *Woodrow Wilson and the Lost Peace* (New York, 1945); C. A. Berdahl, *The Policy of the United States with regard to the League of Nations* (Oxford University Press, 1932); K. Colegrove, *The Senate and World Peace* (New York, 1944), Ch. iv; D. F. Fleming, *The United States and the League of Nations 1918-1920* (New York, 1932).

[16] H. C. Lodge, *The Senate and the League of Nations* (New York and London, 1925); *As I Knew Them: Memoirs of* (Senator) *James E. Watson* (Indianapolis, 1936).

[17] See Berdahl, *loc. cit.*, pp. 47-66; Colegrove, *loc. cit.*, Chap. iv; Fleming, *loc. cit.*, Chap. xviii-xix; Palmer and Perkins, pp. 485-86. Harding, in his campaign for the Presidency asserted that he, too, was for an "association of nations," but this platform promise was forgotten after election.

more. The treaty was not ratified; the United States made a separate treaty of peace with Germany and remained outside the League.

So complete was the reversal of attitude that the Department of State did not dare even to acknowledge communications from the League of Nations for some years. By 1923, American representatives could attend conferences held under the auspices of the League "in an unofficial and consultative capacity"; by 1930, Secretary Kellogg could assert that the United States had sent official delegations to 22 League conferences and unofficial observers to 20 others. Ultimately the United States was taking a larger share in the activities of the League than did 90 per cent of its Members—though without sharing in the overhead cost of the League!

In spite of the increasing sympathy of the United States for the League, its method of unilateral cooperation was so ineffective that the League was unable to do many things which could have been done with the assistance of the United States. Public unions could not be put under the League, as anticipated in Article 24 of the Covenant, because the United States would not belong to them if they belonged to the League. The disarmament effort eagerly supported by the United States depended upon security, but the United States would not contribute to collective security. The Manchurian situation was particularly difficult for the League, since it was of primary interest to the United States and the Soviet Union, and a third Great Power (Japan) was defying the League. In the Ethiopian crisis, economic sanctions could not be effectively applied since the United States was not bound to apply them; and when Japan again attacked China in 1937, coordination of efforts failed though the United States was working in the utmost sympathy with the League. The failure of the League lay in its failure to provide security, and for this failure the absence of the United States was largely responsible.

69. THE NATURE OF THE LEAGUE OF NATIONS[18]

A VICTOR'S PEACE? The League was severely criticized by its opponents in the United States on the ground that it was an organization of victors for the purpose of maintaining the "iniquitous" Treaty of Versailles. The Covenant was, of course, made at the same peace conference which imposed upon Germany the terms of peace, and it was itself a part of the various treaties of peace. The Covenant was, however, a separate instrument; it could be accepted by non-signatories or rejected by signatories of the peace treaty, and a process of amend-

[18] See A. Zimmern, *The League of Nations and the Rule of Law, 1918-1935* (London, 1936); and the works cited in footnote 14 above, especially Walters.

ment was provided independent of the usual procedure for revising a treaty. The League had, of course, a duty to uphold this treaty as any other treaty; but it, like the United Nations later, was excluded from administration or enforcement of political settlements, such as reparations or frontiers.

NOT A SUPERSTATE. It has been observed that the League was evolutionary in origin, being little more than a gathering together, on a broader scale of participation, of the various methods and agencies already long in use. It is not surprising that this first effort at general organization of the community should have restricted but little the freedom of action of its member states. It was a voluntary association of sovereign states, accepting certain common obligations and employing a common machinery of action for certain purposes; it was incapable of creating new law, or imposing new obligations upon a Member, without the consent of the Member. It created a joint responsibility but it respected sovereignty. While it had some personality of its own, it was for the most part merely machinery through which states could cooperate if they so desired—and from this it follows that the failure of the League was the fault of its Members rather than of itself.

COERCIVE POWER. The primary reason for which the League was established was the desire to be secure from war. Such security could be provided only by use of the superior force of the whole community, and the duty of community action against an aggressor was recognized, though not sufficiently implemented. A new theory in relations between states was thus adumbrated, to be compared with the domestic theory of police action. It was not the same, however, for there was no superior authority above states, no independent police force and no automatic action against a law-breaker. If coercive action was to be taken, it must be upon decision by the states themselves, in each separate instance, and through armed forces contributed by Members as they might wish. There was no coercion from an authority above, but there might be joint coercion from outside a state.[19] It was maintained that neutrality was inconsistent with the obligations of the Covenant.

UNIVERSALITY. The admission of former enemy states into the League of Nations destroyed the charge of exclusivity, and its total membership ultimately embraced most of the states of the world. There was never any one time, however, at which all these states were members, nor a time at which all the Great Powers were members; and

[19] Such coercion, of course, had always been possible—i.e., war by another state; now it would emanate from the organized community of nations.

the absence of the United States wrecked any statistical claim of universality. The increasing cooperativeness of the United States made more plausible the claim of the League to speak for the whole community of nations, but the absence from membership of the United States, the withdrawal of Germany, Italy, Japan, and others, and the expulsion of the Soviet Union, left it shockingly weak.

A proposal was made by Argentina at the first Assembly for automatic membership of all states. This might be a desirable objective, but it would have required sufficient authority and strength on the part of the League to compel a recalcitrant state to accept and observe the obligations of membership, and states were not willing to give to it this authority. In practice, the League strove toward universality, and no candidate for membership was ever rejected except entities too small and dependent to assume the responsibilities of membership. Though it never embraced all the states of the world, the League made an important step toward international government when it accepted the principle, *omnium contra unum*. It thereby became the duty of all states to combine, not in particular alliances directed against particular states, but against whatever state happened to be the law-breaker.

A Service Institution. The indispensable and undebated value of the League of Nations lay in its character as a service organ for the community of nations. For the first time, there existed a central agency and machinery to which could be referred practically any question of interest to members. Either the Assembly or the Council could deal "with any matter within the sphere of action of the League or affecting the peace of the world," and while this gave it no authority to make binding decisions, it enabled the League to be of service in many useful ways. This was recognized to such an extent that upon the eve of its downfall it was commonly said that the League must be maintained for this purpose, even if it had failed in its more important political purposes.

Legal Personality. The attempt to define the League of Nations in terms of political science has brought forth many answers. It was clearly not a state; it seems insufficient to call it an association of nations; and its principle, *omnium contra unum*, made it more than an alliance. It has been called a glorified public union but, while it did perform similar administrative functions, it was not limited to one function and it was more than administrative in character. As we have seen, it was not a superstate, nor could it be called a federal system, since the balance of authority did not reside in the central government, nor could that authority reach down to individuals within the member states. Perhaps it most nearly resembled a confederation in which each member retained its sovereignty and most of its autonomy. While there has been some debate in the literature on the subject, most writers seem to admit some degree of legal personality to the League.[20]

70. GENERAL SURVEY[21]

The League of Nations system, in its broadest sense, included three bodies, each founded on a separate instrument and more or less autonomous, but all related to each other in various connections. These were the League itself, the International Labour Organization, and the Permanent Court of International Justice. The International Labour Organization has now become one of the specialized agencies, and will be taken up under that heading; the Permanent Court of International Justice, later revised as the International Court of Justice, will be discussed at the end of this chapter.

THE COVENANT. The Covenant was a self-contained unit, but also embodied the first twenty-six articles of the peace treaties. It represented in every paragraph a hard-won compromise between conflicting views. It also represented the Anglo-Saxon predilection for general principles and broad statements to be worked out in gradual evolution.[22] No organ was given authority to interpret the Covenant. A proposal to give this authority to the Court was rejected on the ground that it would put the Court above the League; and Article 59 of the Statute, which holds a decision of the Court binding only on the parties

[20] On this problem, see Gonsiorowski, I, p. 283; Howard-Ellis, pp. 343, 483; Ray, pp. 63-64; Williams, *Chapters*, Chap. xv; P. E. Corbett, "What is the League of Nations?" *B.Y.I.L.*, 1924, pp. 119-48; O. Hoijer, *Le Pacte de la Société des Nations* (Paris, 1926), p. 12; T. Komarnicki, *La question de l'intégrité territoriale* (Paris, 1923), pp. 135-48; Wm. Martin, "La nature juridique de la Société des Nations," *R.D.I.*, 3 (1929), pp. 403-31; J. Nisot, "La structure juridique de la Société des Nations," *J.D.I.*, 55 (1928), pp. 328-39; R. Redslob, *Théorie de la Société des Nations* (Paris, 1927), pp. 44-48 and *passim*.

[21] The following works are suggested as a short bibliography on the League of Nations: Viscount Cecil, *A Great Experiment* (London, 1941); Cheever and Haviland, Part II; Gonsiorowski, entire; O. Göppert, *Der Volkerhund* (Stuttgart, 1938); Howard-Ellis, entire; Knudson, entire; Miller, *passim;* P. Münch, ed., *Les origines et l'oeuvre de la Société des Nations* (Copenhagen); Morley, entire; Palmer and Perkins, Chap. xiv; W. E. Rappard, *Uniting Europe: The Trend of World Cooperation since the War* (New Haven, 1930); R. Redslob, *Théorie de la Société des Nations* (Paris, 1927); W. Schiffer, *Repertoire of Questions of General International Law before the League of Nations* (Geneva, 1940); G. Schwarzenberger, *The League of Nations and World Order* (London, 1936); Walters, entire; A. Zimmern, *The League of Nations and the Rule of Law* (London, 1941).

Commentaries upon the Covenant: Ray, Schucking-Wehberg; Yepes and da Silva. Yearbooks by Ottlik (*Annuaire*), and by Judith Jackson and Stephen King Hall. H. Aufricht, *Guide to League of Nations Publications* (New York, 1951).

[22] "Probably it was wise to leave the matter vague and uncertain. Complete and final precision in any international document, particularly regarding such a momentous issue, is not always desirable." Miller, I, p. 181.

before it, made judicial interpretation of no final effect. The Council and Assembly were regarded as too much political in character to be allowed to interpret the Covenant. Each Member was thus left free to put his own interpretation upon its words. In practice, debates and resolutions in the Assembly and procedures worked out into accepted interpretations—and these usually constituted limitations upon the authority of the League.

The plan of the Covenant is simple. After a brief Preamble, the first seven articles provide for membership and organization; Articles 8-17 deal with the maintenance of peace; Articles 18-21 are concerned with treaties and regional arrangements; and the remainder, except for Article 26, the amending clause, take care of international cooperation and administration. Before taking up the study of the various parts of the organization, with their functions and interrelations, there are certain matters relating to the League as a whole to be considered.

MEMBERSHIP. Two classes of membership were established by the Covenant. Original Members were those who had signed the Treaty of Peace and were also named in the Annex to the Covenant (thus excluding enemy states), and the thirteen invited neutrals also named in the annex, all of whom accepted membership within the time limit set. The other class was composed of admitted Members.

"Any fully-self-governing State, Dominion, or Colony" could become a Member if approved by a two-thirds vote of the Assembly (Article 1, paragraph 2). The phrase "fully-self-governing" was never defined, but is doubtless to be explained by the inclusion in the annex of the British Dominions and India. Each applicant for membership was required to give "effective guarantees of its intention to observe its international obligations." The actual test of whether qualifications had been met or not was, of course, the vote of the Assembly.[23] The only groups actually denied admission were those considered to be too small for the responsibilities of membership, such as San Marino, Monaco, and some of uncertain political status, such as Georgia and Azerbaijan. The only important state which failed to join the League at all was the United States.

Membership in the League could be terminated in one of three ways: by formal withdrawal upon two years' notice (Article 1, para-

[23] The First Assembly set the following questions to be asked of applicants for admission: (a) Was its application for admission to the League in order? (b) Was the government applying for admission recognized *de jure* or *de facto*, and by which states? (c) Was the applicant a nation with a stable government and settled frontiers? What were its size and its population? (d) Was it fully self-governing? (e) What had been its conduct, including both acts and assurances, with regard to (i) its international obligations; (ii) the prescriptions of the League as to armaments? *Records of the First Assembly*, Second Committee, p. 159.

graph 3); by refusal to accept an amendment (Article 26, paragraph 2); or by expulsion (Article 16, paragraph 4). It was also required that all international and Covenant obligations should have been fulfilled at the time of withdrawal, a provision intended to make it impossible to withdraw for the specific purpose of avoiding an obligation. However, no one called attention to this obligation when Germany, Italy, and Japan withdrew so as to be free to continue to violate the Covenant. A Member which expressed its dissent from an amendment properly adopted automatically ceased to be a Member, though it was not made clear how long a period might elapse before such dissent was expressed. A Member might be expelled for violations of the covenants of the League by a vote of the Council concurred in by all other Members of the League represented thereon. The only case of expulsion was that of the Union of Soviet Socialist Republics, in December 1939, as a result of its attack on Finland.[24]

AMENDMENT. Article 26 provided that "amendment to this Covenant shall take effect when ratified by the Members of the League whose Representatives compose the Council and by a majority of the Members of the League whose Representatives compose the Assembly." While this statement apparently favored the Council, in effect both Council and Assembly were eliminated, since states might ratify the amendment or not, regardless of how their representatives voted in either body. Various uncertainties developed. Should the Council and Assembly act separately or jointly? Was unanimity required for their action (Article 5) though a majority only was required for ratification? Should an amendment not ratified remain open indefinitely? As a result of such problems, the Second Assembly offered an amendment to Article 26 but it was not ratified by a sufficient number of states to put it into effect. A few minor amendments were made but on the whole the Covenant remained practically unchanged.

FINANCES. Like many other new bodies, the early financial situation of the League was precarious.[25] The original provision in Article 6,

---

[24] This, in view of earlier failure to expel Germany, Italy, or Japan, and in view of the wartime Soviet position, now seems a strange procedure. See, as to the procedural question, Leo Gross, "Was the Soviet Union Expelled from the League of Nations?" *A.J.*, 39 (1945), p. 35.

[25] "At one time things reached such a pitch that the Secretary-General and one or two other high officials secretly pooled their month's salary to pay the salaries of the exiguous lower staff." Howard-Ellis, p. 432; and see also H. Ames, *Administration financière et répartition des dépenses de la Société des Nations* (Genève, 1923); H. F. A. Vollmar, *Les Finances de la Société des Nations* (La Haye, 1924); Wertheimer, Chap. xiv; Walters, Chap. xii.

that expenses should be borne "in accordance with the apportionment of the expenses of the International Bureau of the Universal Postal Union," had not been fully considered, and proved inappropriate. For one thing, it provided only for the expenses of the secretariat. For another, the Postal Union scale did not fit a body whose expenses were far greater, and whose members were not so numerous. An amendment was made (which entered into effect in 1924) authorizing the Assembly to decide upon the proportion in which Members should bear the expenses of the League. In 1925, the Assembly set up a scale ranging from one to 105 units. These units were proportioned among Members upon the basis of revenue, population, and other factors.

The budget was in three parts: for the secretariat, for the International Labour Office, and for the Permanent Court of International Justice. Each of these bodies prepared its own budget which was subjected to detailed examination by the Supervisory Commission. The consolidated budget was referred to Members before the meeting of the Assembly, and at the Assembly was handled by the Fourth, or Finance, Committee, whose report was customarily accepted by the Assembly. The first budget called for ten million Swiss francs; in 1939, this had risen to 32,234,012 francs, and the budget of 1943 was for 11,388,376 francs. The attitude of the League toward expenditures was one of severe economy, with the result that the world expended upon its organization for the maintenance of peace and progress among nations, during its entire existence, less than the cost of one modern battleship. While some states were in arrears, dues were on the whole regularly paid, even during World War II.

HEADQUARTERS AND IMMUNITIES. The seat of the League was fixed at Geneva by the peace conference, and while there were occasions on which there seemed to be a possibility of removal, the building of the International Labour Office home and the magnificent League of Nations palace seemed to indicate the intention of remaining at Geneva. Organs of the League could meet elsewhere, but they came to depend so completely upon the secretariat and equipment at Geneva that they rarely met elsewhere than at headquarters.

Complicated negotiations were required with Switzerland with regard to the inviolability of League property and with regard to immunities to be granted to its officials and to the representatives of states. The provision of immunities to delegates to meetings of the Council and Assembly and to numerous conferences, as well as to the officials stationed in Geneva, constituted a unique and heavy responsibility for the state in which headquarters were located.[26]

[26] S. Basdevant, *Les fonctionnaires internationaux* (Paris, 1934); Martin Hill, *Im-*

ORGANS AND FUNCTIONS

71. ASSEMBLY AND COUNCIL

"The action of the League" says Article 2 of the Covenant, "shall be effected through the instrumentality of an Assembly and of a Council, with a permanent Secretariat." The Secretariat was thus legally a subordinated body, though in practice the backbone of the entire system. In addition to these three organs, there developed a number of technical organizations, permanent and temporary commissions, administrative bodies, and institutes, making up a complex system which was in practice tied together through the Secretariat and was actually flexible and adjustable. The table (page 258) presents the system in summary outline.[27]

THE ASSEMBLY. The Assembly of the League was in the nature of a diplomatic conference and, though it developed procedures which gave to it some of the aspects of a parliamentary body, it was not possessed of legislative power.[28] The First Assembly held that the Assembly could not be regarded as possessed of legislative power; on the contrary, delegates to the Assembly "render their decisions as the representatives of their respective states, and in rendering such decisions they have no standing except as such representatives."[29] Delegates were chosen and instructed by their governments and this, though it means political rather than expert consideration, has the advantage that their governments are able to support and put into effect the votes of their delegates. The practice of sending the same delegates from year to year developed personal understanding and produced cooperation rather than diplomatic fencing. The delegates found that they must, if they wished to acquire authority within the organization, take an active part in all of the work of the League, rather than sit back and work only where the interests of their states were involved.

---

munities and Privileges of International Officials (Washington, 1947); J. Secretan, "The Independence Granted to Agents of the International Community in their relations with National Public Authorities," *B.Y.I.L.*, 1935, p. 56. See *L. of N. Doc.* C.555.1926.V.

[27] The table is taken from Ottlik, *Annuaire*, 1938, p. 82, and would not necessarily be accurate for every year.

[28] See, with regard to the Assembly, Margaret E. Burton, *The Assembly of the League of Nations* (University of Chicago Press, 1941); H. R. G. Greaves, *The League Committees and World Order* (Oxford University Press, 1931); Morley, Chaps. xiii-xv; C. Riches, *The Unanimity Rule and the League of Nations* (Johns Hopkins University, 1933).

[29] *Records of the First Assembly* (1920), Plenary, p. 318.

ORGANIZATION OF THE LEAGUE OF NATIONS

I. THE ORGANS

Assembly   *Council*   *Secretariat*

II. AUXILIARY ORGANS

A. Technical Organizations
   Economic and Financial Organization
   Organization for Communications and Transit
   Health Organization

B. Permanent Advisory Commissions
   Military, Naval, and Aerial Questions
   Intellectual Cooperation
   Supervisory Commission
   Mandates
   Control Organ for the Manufacture and Distribution of Drugs
   Advisory Commission for Social Questions
   Opium Commission
   Permanent Central Opium Committee
   Advisory Committee of Experts for Slavery

C. Temporary Advisory Commissions
   Commission for the Study of European Union
   Special Committee on Contributions in Arrears

D. Administrative or Executive Organizations
   Advisory Commission for Refugees
   Commissioner for Bulgarian Refugees (Sofia)

III. AUTONOMOUS ORGANIZATIONS

Permanent Court of International Justice
International Labour Office

IV. SPECIAL ORGANIZATIONS

International Institute of Intellectual Cooperation (Paris)

High Commissioner for Refugees (Jewish and others) from Germany

Institute for the Unification of Private Law (Rome)

International Nansen Office for Refugees

International Center for Study of Leprosy

Each Member was entitled to one vote, though it might have three delegates.[30] The Assembly met regularly once a year and in occasional special sessions, at the seat of the League. The continuity thus established allowed a subject to be carried over from year to year rather than dying at the end of an *ad hoc* conference; on the other hand, it perhaps encouraged procrastination. The agenda was prepared by the Secretary-General and distributed months in advance; the assembly itself could decide whether other items could be added. This agenda always included reports on the work of the Council and the Secretariat, and debates on these afforded an opportunity, during the days when the Assembly was being organized, for speeches to be made upon almost any subject. The Assembly was thus a regular forum for a discussion of world affairs and particularly useful for the smaller states.

The Assembly elected its own president, usually from a smaller state not represented on the council. The six Permanent Committees were then constituted, and six vice-presidents were elected.[31] The six chairmen and the six vice-presidents, with the Chairman of the Agenda Committee, composed the General Committee, a sort of steering committee. No decision could be taken by the Assembly until a committee had acted, though this rule might be dispensed with by a two-thirds vote. Each Member had a representative on each committee. As in all parliamentary bodies, the real work was done in the committees. For each committee, a rapporteur, who had guided the topic through the day, presented the matter to the plenary Assembly. Since each member state was represented on each committee, the committee vote was usually conclusive and there was little debate on the floor of the Assembly.

The work of the Assembly usually issued in the form of a resolution, though it might be as a draft treaty for ratification by Members. The official languages of the League were French and English. A third language could be used but the speaker must furnish his own inter-

---

[30] It was hoped that provision for three delegates would allow representation of different shades of opinion in each member state, but this did not develop in practice. A much larger delegation was actually required. At least six persons were required for the six Permanent Committees, and experts were brought along to deal with the many different subjects under discussion. Four were allowed upon the floor at the same time and it was possible to feed through these four the various experts needed for the different items on the agenda.

[31] The six Permanent Committees were: Legal and Constitutional Questions; Technical Organizations; Reduction of Armaments; Budget and Financial Questions; General and Humanitarian Questions; Political Questions. See M. E. Burton, *The Assembly of the League of Nations* (University of Chicago Press, 1941); H. R. G. Greaves, *The League Committees and World Order: A Study of the Permanent Expert Committees of the League of Nations as an Instrument of International Government* (Oxford University Press, 1931).

preter. Much time was thus consumed in interpretations. The rule of unanimity prevailed in voting, though majority vote was allowed on procedural questions. The Assembly had certain exclusive functions which will be listed below.

THE COUNCIL. The Council was originally to "consist of representatives of the principal Allied and Associated Powers,[32] together with four other Members of the League"; the latter or non-permanent Members being "selected by the Assembly from time to time in its discretion." Thus, while the equality of states was recognized in the Assembly, the actual preponderance and responsibility of the Great Powers was recognized in the Council. The First Assembly recommended that delegates should, in choosing Council members, give consideration to geography, ethnical groups, religious traditions, the various types of civilizations, and the chief sources of wealth. The choice of the non-permanent members of the Council led to jealousies and intrigues for years. In 1922, at the request of the Council, the Assembly increased the number of non-permanent seats to six. This did not satisfy the hunger for prestige, and matters came to a head in 1926 upon the occasion of the admission of Germany, which was to be made a permanent member of the Council. After an amazing display of petty national selfishness, the following procedure was finally accepted: Germany alone of those who demanded permanent seats was made a permanent member; the number of non-permanent members was increased to nine; of these nine, three were to be elected each year by the Assembly for a term of three years each and were not eligible for immediate re-election. By resolution of the Assembly in 1936, the number of non-permanent members was increased to eleven. A practice developed of assigning seats to regional areas, e.g., three seats to Latin America, one to the Little Entente, one to the Scandinavian states.

PROCEDURE. The Council was required by the Covenant to meet at least once a year but actually it met much more often. The anticipated opportunity of such regular meetings was of great psychological importance. States came to send regularly their foreign ministers or prime ministers, who fell into the habit of acting as colleagues in a common cause rather than as rivals. These meetings afforded an opportunity for making many adjustments aside from carrying on the work of the League. The president of the Council was chosen in alphabetical rotation, a practice not always conducive to the best results. It was fortunate, for example, that so competent a person as Briand was president when the Greco-Bulgarian crisis arose in 1924.

[32] The United States of America, the British Empire, France, Italy, and Japan.

The Council was not a legislative body, nor an executive council, though it tended to assume executive functions. Its procedure was very elastic; it might use committees *ad referendum* or with full powers to act, as, for example, in the financial reconstruction of Austria; it might act upon the recommendation of a rapporteur or of the secretariat; it might (as in the case of disputes) do everything itself. It was a political body, and in the settlement of disputes (which function will be discussed later) it sought to achieve agreement rather than to deal out justice. Where legal questions were concerned it could call upon the Permanent Court for an advisory opinion, and it often did so. The rule of unanimity applied in the Council as in all League organs, so that any members, and not only permanent members, could veto. A party to a dispute, under Article 15, however, could not vote in his own case, though he could do so if the dispute were raised under Article 11.

RELATION OF COUNCIL AND ASSEMBLY. No clear differentiation of functions between the Council and the Assembly was written into the Covenant. They could hardly be said to represent the two chambers of a legislative body nor would it be accurate to describe their relation as that of a cabinet to a parliament.[33] They were simply two cogs designed to work closely together in the same machinery. They represented a compromise between the equality of states and the predominance of the Great Powers.

CONCURRENT POWERS. Both the Assembly and the Council were given the right to "deal at their meetings with any matter within the sphere of action of the League or affecting the peace of the world." Article 2 put the two bodies on the same plane and a number of concurrent powers were stated. They shared in the right to increase the number either of permanent or of elective members of the council (Article 4, paragraph 2); together they chose a Secretary-General (Article 6, paragraph 2); "any circumstances whatever" which threatened to disturb the peace could be presented to either body (Article 11, paragraph 2); either might ask an advisory opinion of the Court (Article 14); both participated in the process of amendment (Article 26, paragraph 1). In addition, certain powers were conferred upon the League as a whole without saying whether they be-

---

[33] "It is impossible to consider the Assembly as a Chamber of Deputies and the Council as an Upper Chamber . . .

"It is equally impossible to consider the Council as invested with the executive and the Assembly with the legislative powers . . .

"The truth is that the League of Nations has no analogy in ordinary constitutional law." *Records of the First Assembly* (1920), pp. 318-20.

longed to the Council or the Assembly; and various treaties conferred powers upon both. Thus, by the Statute of the Court, both shared in the election of judges.

POWERS OF THE ASSEMBLY. To the Assembly alone were confided the powers to admit new Members (Article 1, paragraph 2); to elect non-permanent members of the Council (Article 4, paragraph 1); to fix rules concerning the election, terms of office, and conditions of re-eligibility of these members (Article 4, paragraph 2 *bis*); to fix its own rules of procedure and appoint its committees (Article 5, paragraph 2); to control the finances of the League (Article 6, paragraph 5); to handle disputes referred to it from the Council (Article 15, paragraphs 9-10); to advise the reconsideration of treaties (Article 19).

POWERS OF THE COUNCIL. The powers given exclusively to the Council were far more numerous. By Article 5 it regulated its own procedure and committees. It approved staff appointments in the Secretariat (Article 6, paragraph 3); it could move the seat of the League (Article 7, paragraph 2); it had to formulate plans for the reduction of armaments, and had to give its consent before the limits, when agreed upon, could be exceeded (Article 8, paragraphs 4, 5); the Permanent Advisory Commission on armaments was its subsidiary agency (Article 9). It advised upon the means by which the obligations of Article 10 were to be carried out; it was summoned in case of any war or threat of war (Article 11, paragraph 1); it acted as conciliator under Articles 12 and 15; it proposed the steps to be taken when an award was not carried out (Article 13, paragraph 4). It could recommend the military action to be taken under Article 16, and could, under paragraph 4 of the same article, expel from membership in the League; it could set the conditions upon which a non-Member might appear before the League in a dispute, and recommend action to be taken in such a case (Article 17); it exercised such control as the League had over Mandates (Article 22, paragraphs 7-9); it decided whether the expenses of a bureau or commission might be included in the League budget (Article 24, paragraph 3). Various powers were conferred upon the Council by treaties.

RELATIVE POSITIONS. It is doubtless true that the makers of the Covenant favored the Council more than the Assembly, but from this fact, and from the fact that the Council was mentioned some sixty times in the Covenant and the Assembly only twenty-four times, it would be easy to draw wrong conclusions. The Assembly from the beginning represented an international outlook and stood for the idealism and cooperation in which public opinion was interested; it therefore had increasingly the support of the public. Moreover, the Assembly took aggressive action from the start, as, for example, in taking to itself practically entire control over the reduction of armaments. There was ample room for discord, but the use of tact and good sense resulted in a surprising lack of friction between the two bodies.

It is believed, however, that the Assembly gained as compared with the Council. After the First Assembly, the Council regularly made a report to the Assembly on the measures taken by it to execute decisions of the Assembly. This report was critically discussed by the Assembly which thus acquired a sort of supervisory character, which was strengthened by the practice of the Assembly in agreeing upon a line of action and calling upon the Council to carry it into effect. The Assembly had also a certain degree of control over the size and composition of the Council and it controlled the finances of the League. Thus the Council did in practice tend to become a sort of executive body for the League.

On the other hand, if the Council made many concessions to the Assembly, it could afford to do so. In the Council the Great Powers were dominant, regardless of the majority of the small states. Any one of the Great Powers, assured of permanency, had always a veto against anything that it disliked. It was in the Council that the ranking statesmen of the world actually worked. The Council had at least a primary administration of important functions, such as the settlement of disputes, which gave to it great prestige. Behind the scenes it was the Great Powers who directed the affairs of the world. The League could never forget that it was impotent without the Great Powers.

72. THE SECRETARIAT

SECRETARY-GENERAL. A detailed study of the organization and work of the Secretariat would reveal the extent to which it constituted the backbone of the League. The first Secretary-General was Sir Eric Drummond, who was named by the Peace Conference in Annex 2 of the Covenant. Other appointments were to be made by the Council with the approval of the majority of the Assembly (Article 6, paragraph 2). No term of office was fixed by the Covenant, but the first incumbent resigned in 1933, and the Assembly fixed a ten-year term thereafter.

It was not intended, and some regard this as a mistake, that the Secretary-General should be an aggressive character, a statesman or leader.[34] His post was the highest of the League, but it was exclusively an administrative one. Sir Eric Drummond emphasized its administrative character and did not seek to build up the prestige of the post. Only the Secretary-General and his staff represented the organized community of nations, and his authority was not sufficient to shape or define a continuing policy for the League of Nations.

Originally there were four Under-Secretaries-General, but in 1922 the post of Deputy-Secretary-General was established, and in 1932 a second deputy was added. The Under-Secretaries (four in 1919, three in 1920, then two, again three after the entry of Germany) were in practice reserved to the Great Powers and appointed by them;[35] they were, in fact, national representatives though not so in legal function. At the least, they explained to their own governments what was going on in the League; at the most, the German and Italian incumbents sought to direct and control all their own nationals in the secretariat. They had some administrative functions to perform, but were in this respect only slightly differentiated from the directors of sections the rank below them. Continuous struggle and intrigue revolved around these offices, and rivalries concerning them were intense. The problem of the "High Directorate" was never solved by the League.

INTERNATIONAL CIVIL SERVICE. While there was no debate at the Peace Conference as to the need for a permanent Secretariat—on which, indeed, the life of the League depended—there was a divergence of opinion as to whether it should be composed of national delegations, paid by their respective governments and responsible to them as had been the case in previous conferences; or whether it should be constituted as an international civil service, to furnish expert and impartial information in the interests of the community, rather than in the interests of the separate states. Through the insistence of Secretary-General Drummond, the latter view prevailed, and the council report of 1920 laid down the principle that persons once chosen to posts in the Secretariat were no longer in the service of their nations, but exclusively in the service of the League of Nations. Since both Council and Assembly were composed of instructed delegates, the Secretariat was thus the only true international organ of the League.

Nationalistic claims, however, did not die easily. The Italian government supported the rejected principle even to the extent of passing a

[34] F. G. Boudreau, "International Civil Service," in H. E. Davis, *Pioneers in World Order* (New York, 1944), p. 79; C. W. Jenks, "Some Problems of an International Civil Service," *Public Administration Review*, 4 (1943), p. 94; Wertheimer, pp. 48-49; S. M. Schwebel, *The Secretary-General of the United Nations* (Cambridge, 1952), Chap. ix and Appendix.

[35] The organization of the Secretariat in 1938 is shown in the chart on p. 266.

law requiring its citizens holding any posts abroad to report to the Italian government and to surrender their posts when required to do so. The "primordial necessity" was asserted in the Assembly of selecting the members of the Secretariat from those states not well "represented" therein. In 1929 a crisis was imminent because members of the Secretariat felt that their tenure of office was too precarious, and were accepting other positions. The Assembly appointed a Committee of Thirteen which reported that the Secretariat should remain strictly international in character, and should be provided with a staff capable of doing its work with the proper efficiency. It proposed, as the first article of the Staff Regulations: "The officials of the Secretariat of the League of Nations are exclusively international officials, and their duties are not national, but international . . . They may not seek or receive instructions from any Government or other authority external to the Secretariat of the League of Nations."

While an international outlook was regarded as of great importance, other characteristics were equally as important, such as integrity, courage, and technical ability; and among these, paradoxically, the League came to regard as essential that its officials should have strong national roots so that understanding of various national viewpoints could be represented in the Secretariat. The size of the staff varied greatly, beginning with 121 in 1919, rising to 707 in 1931, dropping to 209 in 1940, and to 94 in 1944.

INTERNAL ORGANIZATION. The staff was originally organized in eleven sections; in 1938 there were fifteen sections, as shown on the accompanying table. Some of these were general sections, such as the Central, Political, Legal, and Information Sections, with which should be listed also the Treasury and the Library; others were special sections dealing with the fields shown by their titles. The work was thus organized along functional rather than geographical lines. Each section served not only the Assembly and the Council, but also the other organs and agencies of the League and conferences within their respective fields. Thus all the widespread activities of the League were gathered together through the Secretariat and centralized coordination of activities was maintained.

Not only did the Secretariat furnish coordination; it also furnished continuity, knowledge, and experience behind the shifting personnel of delegates and temporary officials through whom the work of the League was ostensibly done. The rapporteur who worked for a committee, the Council representative who went to investigate a dispute between Greece and Bulgaria, the conference assembled to make a treaty, or other agencies were supplied with information and often

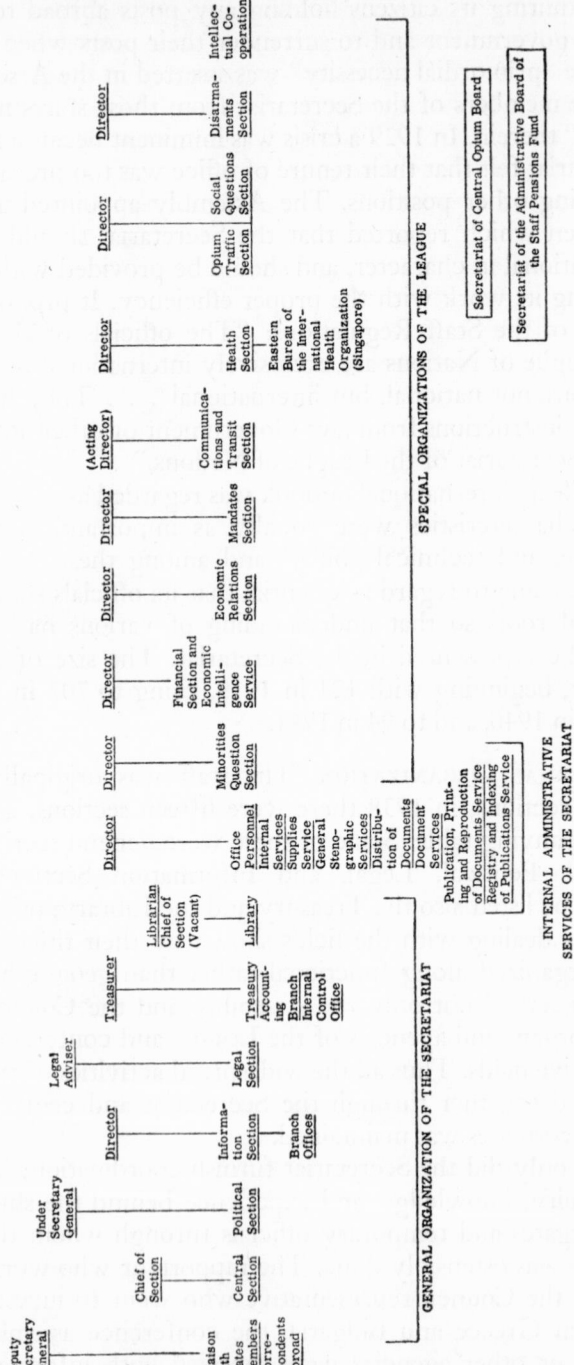

ORGANIZATION OF THE SECRETARIAT—1938

Secretary-General (and Office)
Deputy Secretary-General (and Office)
Under Secretaries-General (and Offices)
Attached to Principal Officer (Official with Rank of Director and Office)

GENERAL ORGANIZATION OF THE SECRETARIAT

SPECIAL ORGANIZATIONS OF THE LEAGUE

Secretariat of Central Opium Board

Secretariat of the Administrative Board of
the Staff Pensions Fund

INTERNAL ADMINISTRATIVE
SERVICES OF THE SECRETARIAT

From E. Ranshofen Wertheimer, *The International Secretariat*, by kind permission of the Carnegie Endowment for International Peace.

with a text drafted by the Secretariat, possible new steps to be taken were whispered into the ears of national delegates who could officially instigate action, and formulae for reconciliation of differences were suggested. The Secretariat did not become, as some had feared, a dangerous international bureaucracy, and it did not actually make policy; but it was, in fact, the permanent part of the League, the agency through which its work was prepared, the backbone of the League.

73. OTHER ORGANS

In addition to these three principal organs of the League, there were various auxiliary organs of differing types making up a system which, as a total picture, appears somewhat intricate, but which was in fact fairly well connected together through the Secretariat. Of these the principal ones were the three technical organizations, more or less autonomous bodies insofar as their own work was concerned, expert in composition and advisory in function, but subject to direction insofar as their activities might engage Members of the League.

The Economic and Financial Organization was set up as the result of a recommendation by the Brussels Financial Conference in 1920. It consisted of an Economic Committee and a Financial Committee, and its function was to advise and to make proposals for submission to the Council or Assembly. It made a number of studies of much value, and issued publications both serial and monograph. Under its auspices were held a number of conferences, among which were the World Economic Conference of 1927, whose recommendations were applauded by everyone but put into effect by no government; the Monetary and Economic Conference of 1933, which the United States helped greatly to wreck; and others dealing with such matters as simplification of customs formalities, treatment of aliens, abolition of import and export restrictions, and so forth. The Financial Committee made possible the financial reconstruction of Austria, Hungary, and other states; and advice as to economic and financial problems was provided at the request of a number of states. The decade following 1930 was not a period of eager economic cooperation, and various changes were made in the effort to achieve more. The Bruce Report of 1939 recommended that the economic and social work of the League should be brought under the supervision of a central committee. Such planning was interrupted by the war, but work in this field was to some extent continued during the war through the transfer of the

Economic, Financial, and Transit Department to Princeton.[36] The Economic and Financial Committees held joint meetings, and decided to continue such pivotal publications as the Statistical Year-Book, the Monthly Bulletin of Statistics, and the World Economic Survey.

The Organization for Communications and Transit originated in Part XII of the Treaty of Versailles and was founded upon a statute provided for it by the Barcelona Conference on Communications and Transit.[37] It was an autonomous body of experts chosen by their own governments which worked upon a technical rather than a diplomatic basis. It had a general conference which met every four years and which drafted treaties; an Advisory and Technical Committee which met twice a year; and it worked through six permanent committees whose titles indicate the field of activity covered: Ports and Maritime Navigation; Inland Navigation; Transport by Rail; Electric Questions; Legal; and Road Traffic. It arranged conferences to deal with such matters as transit cards for emigrants, regime of rivers, road traffic, transmission of electric power, and so forth.

The Health Organization was planned by a conference which met at London in 1920 in accordance with a resolution of the Council of the League. Some delay was encountered because of the unwillingness of the United States to permit the older Health Office at Paris to be included, and a provisional Health Committee at Geneva, in consultation with the Health Office, worked out the plans by which the Health Organization was ultimately set up. The latter body was composed of the Health Committee and the Health Section of the Secretariat, and was assisted by a General Advisory Council chosen by the Health Office of Paris. The Health Organization had a wide and useful field of activity. It drafted a few treaties such as the Sanitary Convention of 1926; most of its work consisted of study of such subjects as cancer, health education, infant mortality, sleeping sickness, and biological and terminological standardization. It maintained an efficient epidemiological service, with staffs in various parts of the world and with printed and radio announcements of the spread of plague; and it assisted various states such as Brazil and China in their public health services.[38]

---

[36] See Report on the Work of the League, *1942-1943, L. of N. Doc.*, General. 1943. I; Henry F. Grady, "World Economics," in Harriet Davis, *loc. cit.*, p. 156; Martin Hill, *The Economic and Financial Organization of the League of Nations* (Washington, 1946).

[37] Found in *L. of N. Doc.*, 1938. VIII. 1.

[38] H. Van Blankenstein, *L'Organisation de L'Hygiène de la Société des Nations* (Purmermend, Holland, 1934); F. G. Boudreau, "International Health Work" in H. E. Davis, *loc. cit.*, p. 193; Mander, Chap. i; C. Vitta, "Le Droit Sanitaire Internationale," *Hague Acad.*, 1930, III.

PERMANENT COMMISSIONS. In addition to the technical organizations, there were a number of permanent commissions, expert and advisory in character. In accordance with Article 9 of the Covenant, a Permanent Advisory Committee on Military, Aerial, and Naval Questions was constituted, though its activities were largely absorbed by other bodies. The Covenant also called for (Article 22, paragraph 9) a Permanent Mandates Commission. It was composed of eleven persons who could have no connection with their own government, but were selected upon their own merit. A Committee of Intellectual Cooperation was established by the Council in 1922 and was part of a rather too widely extended system in this field. Members of the committee were very distinguished persons, each of eminence in some intellectual field as, for example, Dr. Einstein or Mme. Curie. In general, its function was to facilitate intellectual exchange between nations and to encourage collaboration in intellectual activity, and it has been criticized as operating at too high an intellectual level. There was also an Advisory Commission on Opium and Other Dangerous Drugs, a Permanent Central Opium Board, an Advisory Commission for the Protection and Welfare of Children and Young People (later known as the Advisory Commission on Social Questions), and an Advisory Committee of Experts on Slavery.

TEMPORARY COMMISSIONS.[39] Other commissions were set up at different times to meet particular needs, and ended when their task was accomplished. Such, for example, were the Committee for the Progressive Codification of International Law which ended with a conference in 1930, or the Preparatory Commission for the Disarmament Conference, the Commission on Arbitration and Security, and the Temporary Mixed Commission, whose work ended with the Disarmament Conference. Other such bodies were the Inter-Governmental Advisory Commission for Refugees (1928), the Commission of Inquiry for European Union (1930), the Committee on Amendment of the Covenant in order to bring it into harmony with the Pact of Paris (1931), the Wheat Advisory Commission (1933). The Council at times set up special committees such as that on the dispute between Bolivia and Paraguay, or the one on technical cooperation between the League and China.

ADMINISTRATIVE BODIES. The Treaty of Versailles (Article 103) provided for a High Commissioner for the Free City of Danzig to be appointed by the Council of the League, and also for a commission of five members for the government of the Saar Territory. Various agen-

[39] See L. of N. Doc. The Committees of the League of Nations, C.99.M.99. 1945. V.

cies were created to take care of refugees, to serve as trustees for international loans, to conduct military investigations in accordance with the terms of the peace treaties, and other such tasks.

SPECIAL INSTITUTIONS. Three institutes were set up under the supervision of the Council of the League, but located in and supported by individual Members. The Institute of Intellectual Cooperation was located at Paris upon the invitation of the French government after some uncertainty as to whether the League would retain sufficient control over its work. It was a corporation under French law, supported by the French government and nineteen other states, but its governing body was the League Committee of Intellectual Cooperation, and it was served by a section of the League Secretariat. These activities, or part of them, will now be carried on by UNESCO. Upon the invitation of the Italian government, an International Institute for the Unification of Private Law was established in Italy, which contributed one million lire annually for the support of the institute. Its purpose was to secure uniform national laws on various subjects. The Italian government also provided for the International Institute of Educational Cinematography with an annual subvention of 600,000 lire. Its purpose was to study moving pictures with reference to their educational possibilities.

It should be noted in final comment upon the organization of the League that all of these variegated organs were tied together through the appropriate sections of the Secretariat which made possible more coordination than the mere listing of these organs would indicate as possible.

74. ACTIVITIES OF THE LEAGUE

The functions of the League may be classified generally under the two headings of the maintenance of peace and international cooperation. Discussion of the maintenance of peace will be reserved for a subsequent chapter. While it attracted more attention, the task of cooperative effort in many fields engaged far more of the activity of the League, and did much more to justify the existence of such an international organization. Several volumes would be required for study of its activities, and no more can be covered here than a survey of its constitutional functions and something of the work accomplished in the non-political field.

TREATIES. In an effort to avoid secret treaties, a new condition for their validity was established by Article 18—publicity. "Every treaty or international engagement," entered into by any Member after the League had begun its career was to be registered with the Secretariat and published. Just what was meant by "engagements" is not clear, but a memorandum of the Secretary-General, approved by the Council, required registration for ". . . any other international engagement or act by which nations or their governments intend to establish legal obligations between themselves and another state, nation, or government."[40] Registration was a purely formal act, which the Secretary-General performed in a ministerial capacity, and which did not imply approval or support for the document. A treaty could be registered by any or all signatories, and while non-members could not be required to register treaties, any such treaty made with a Member would naturally be registered by that Member, and arrangements were made by which treaties of non-members would voluntarily be entered for publication. All are published in a systematic order in the *Treaty Series* (continued in the U.N. *Treaty Series*), now the most important treaty collection in existence, and a convenience which perhaps justifies Article 18 more than its original purpose.

Article 20 calls for the abrogation of old treaties inconsistent with the terms of the Covenant, and pledges Members not to enter into other inconsistent treaties. Article 21 also deals with inconsistent obligations, for the purpose, however, of excepting some. This article was inserted to cover the Monroe Doctrine, and was stated in general terms because of the general dislike for it—a dislike so great that President Wilson was literally forced to beg for it. The solid reason for accepting it was the fear that without such acceptance the Senate would reject the Covenant. The effort to secure a general wording and at the same time to satisfy the Senate produced the absurdity of calling the Monroe Doctrine a "regional understanding," which it clearly was not. When, in 1927, Costa Rica requested a definition of the Monroe Doctrine as a condition of her re-entry into the League, the Council replied that Article 21 envisages such agreements as they existed, without attempting to define them; that task, it said, belongs to the states which have accepted among themselves such understandings. In the dispute with Paraguay and Bolivia, the Council legitimately asserted its right to intervene and thereby established a valuable precedent; but it as properly accepted the good offices of the Inter-American Conference then in session at Washington.

[40] League of Nations, *Treaty Series*, I, pp. 9-13. See A. Goellner, *La révision des traités sous le régime de la Société des Nations* (Paris, 1925); M. O. Hudson, "The Registration and Publication of Treaties," *A.J.*, 19 (1925), pp. 273-92; J. Lambiris, "L'enrégistrement des traités d'après l'Article 18 du Pacte de la Société des Nations," *R.D.I.L.C.*, 3rd Series, 7 (1926), pp. 697-709; R. Schwab, *Die Registrierung der internationalen Verträge beim Völkerbund* (Berne, 1929).

Article 19 was originally intended to be a corrective to Article 10, which was criticized as perpetuating the *status quo*. It was at first a part of Article 10, but was later detached in order to give to it the separate importance which the French wished it to have. It seemed more useful to discuss the value of this article under the head of international legislation, and it is unnecessary to repeat what has been said there. It did not solve the difficult problem of revising treaties in the absence of consent by all signatories; at most it afforded an opportunity for revealing to public attention the possibility of disputes which might arise from them.

MANDATES.[41] Those territories taken from their former sovereigns and not yet able to stand alone were by Article 22 made "a sacred trust of civilization." The distribution of the territory was not, however, provided in the Covenant. By the various treaties of peace it was surrendered to the Principal Allied and Associated Powers; these, acting through the Supreme Council, parceled out the territory to various states as mandatories and notified the Council of the League of this action; the Council of the League then took over the task of administrative supervision under Article 22. No provision was made for a future transfer or redistribution of territories, and this led into puzzling legal questions when transfer to the United Nations was planned. According to Wright, "The only probable manner of changing the status of mandated territory is through action of the League by amending Article 22, by admitting a mandated community to its membership, or by otherwise recognizing the latter's independence. Thus the League of Nations seems competent and alone competent to change the status of territory now under Article 22."[42]

The mandated territory was to be entrusted to "advanced nations," able to assume the responsibility and willing to accept it. The mandate was exercised "on behalf of the League," and the mandatory was required to (Article 22, paragraph 7) render to the Council an annual report on the territory in its charge. The authority to be exercised

[41] Complete information as to mandates is to be found in the exhaustive work of Q. Wright, *Mandates under the League of Nations* (Chicago, 1930). See also, from the vast literature on the subject, N. Bentwich, "Le système des mandats," *Hague Acad.*, 1929; Davis, p. 121; N. Feinberg, *La juridiction de la Cour Permanente de Justice Internationale dans le système des mandats* (Paris, 1930); B. Gerig, *The Open Door and the Mandates System* (London, 1930); H. Duncan Hall, *Mandates, Dependencies, and Trusteeship* (Carnegie Endowment, 1948); H. Rolin, "La pratique des mandats internationaux," *Hague Acad.*, 1927, IV, pp. 497-628; F. White, *Mandates* (London, 1926); The Mandate System: Origin—Principles—Application, *L. of N. Doc.*, 1945.VI.A.1.

[42] Wright, *Mandates*, pp. 506-7. We shall see that the International Court of Justice has had, on three occasions, to consider this status. See p. 344 below.

by the mandatory state was found in the terms of the mandate.[43] As to the much-disputed problem of sovereignty, Wright's thoroughly considered conclusion is "that sovereignty of the areas is vested in the League acting through the Covenant amending process, and is exercised by the mandatory with consent of the Council for eventual transfer to the mandated communities themselves."[44]

There were three classes of mandates, differing "according to the stage of the development of the people, the geographical situation of the territory, its economic conditions and other similar circumstances." Certain communities which belonged to the Turkish Empire were regarded as having reached such a stage of development that "their existence as independent nations can be provisionally recognized," but subject to administrative advice and assistance until they should be able to stand alone. These were the class A mandates, and included Palestine, Iraq, Syria and the Lebanon, and Transjordan. For other peoples, especially those of Central Africa, the mandatory was given a larger degree of control, but was required to guarantee freedom of conscience and religion, prohibit such abuses as the liquor or arms or slave traffic, prevent fortifications or military training of the natives, and secure equal opportunities for the trade and commerce of other Members. These were the class B mandates, under which were administered the Cameroons, Togoland, Tanganyika, and Ruanda-Urundi. Finally, certain territories "such as Southwest Africa and certain of the South Pacific Islands" could for various reasons "be best administered under the laws of the mandatory as integral portions of its territory" subject to safeguards above mentioned. These were the C mandates. It would appear, from this distribution, that the A mandates might hope for independence—and in fact Iraq, Syria, Lebanon, Palestine (Israel), and Transjordan (Jordan) gained their independence; that the B mandates must remain long in suspense; and that there was little hope of independence for the C mandates.[45]

The authority of the League in this field was exercised by the Council, through the Mandates Commission called for by the Covenant (Article 22, paragraphs 7, 9). Disputes, under the terms of the mandates, were to be referred to the Permanent Court of International

[43] By Article 22, § 8, the authority to be exercised was to "be explicitly defined in each case by the Council." In practice, however, the terms of the mandates were laid down by the Principal Allied and Associated Powers. See Wright, *op. cit.*, p. 109 *et seq.*

[44] Wright, *Mandates*, p. 530.

[45] *The Mandates System*, League of Nations Publication, XI.A. Mandates. 1945. VI.A.1, pp. 19-20, 24. This document gives an authoritative and summary account of the administration of the mandates system under the League. Dates of termination of the various mandates are given in Aufricht, pp. 154-55.

Justice. Mandatories were required to make annual reports concerning the territories under their administration, and the Council provided questionnaires upon which to base these reports. The procedure of the Council allowed also for petitions from inhabitants, which were transmitted through the Mandatory Power. The Commission held hearings at which representatives of a mandatory were present to answer questions, but was not given authority to conduct investigations on the spot. Indeed, the Commission had no authority to do more than offer observations upon the reports concerning conditions within a mandated area, and no sanction except the force of public opinion which it could bring to bear; but it exercised its functions with remarkable success, resulting usually in acquiescence on the part of the Mandatory Power with suggestions offered. The efforts of the Council and Commission were directed principally to three aims: (1) the political and moral education, the improvement of the living conditions and, in general, the protection of the interests of the native population; (2) the application of the principles of non-discrimination in economic matters; (3) the preservation of the legal status, integrity, and individuality of the territory as a distinct international entity. There can be no doubt that the mandates system was a successful experiment in humanitarian advance, and the experiment is now continued in the "trusteeship" system of the United Nations.

OTHER TERRITORIES. Article 103 of the Treaty of Versailles provided for a High Commissioner for the Free City of Danzig, to be appointed by and responsible to the Council of the League of Nations. His chief function was to adjust disputes which might arise from the bizarre relationships created between Poland and Danzig by the terms of the peace settlement. Appeals might be taken from his decisions to the Council, which might refer them to the Court.[46] With the rise of Hitler, Nazis seized political control in Danzig, and a humiliating period followed for the League, ending in the unopposed absorption of Danzig into Hitler's Reich.

The administration of the Saar Territory was more successful. The Treaty of Versailles had provided (Article 50, Annex, Chap. II) for government of this territory by a commission of five, chosen by the Council, and representing the League of Nations. At the end of fifteen years, a plebiscite was to be taken to determine whether the population preferred to live under France or Germany. This plebiscite was duly taken in 1935, and the territory was transferred to Germany.

[46] As was done in the cases of the Polish Postal Service in Danzig, *P.C.I.J.*, Series B, No. 11; Jurisdiction of the Courts of Danzig, Series B, No. 15; Access to or Anchorage in the Port of Danzig of Polish War Vessels, Series A/B, No. 43; Treatment of Polish Nationals, Series A/B, No. 44; and see Series A/B, No. 65.

This was the only case in which the League acted as a governing body over a territory, and it seems generally agreed that it governed with efficiency, and conducted the plebiscite fairly.

REFUGEES.[47] The problem of refugees after the war had led to the establishment of three administrative institutions. The work was due, in the first place, to the generous sympathy of Dr. Nansen, to whom the League originally turned over the problem. Some two million Russians, over a million Greeks, and hundreds of thousands of Armenians, Turks, and others had been dislodged in the maelstrom of war, and the economic situation of Europe was such that it was impossible to find employment for them. Dr. Nansen was appointed high commissioner, and with the aid of relief organizations and after innumerable struggles for funds, he managed to tide over the worst part of the situation. From 1924-1928 the work was put under the direction of the International Labour Office as a problem of employment, but the Ninth Assembly returned it to the League itself. The death of Dr. Nansen in 1930 left a period of uncertainty, until the Nansen International Refugee Office began in 1931, with instructions to complete its work by 1938. This, however, did not take into account the new flood of refugees seeking to escape Hitler, and in 1933 a High Commissioner for Refugees coming from Germany was created but—because of German opposition—operated independently of the League. In 1938, President Roosevelt summoned a conference at Evian, as a result of which the Intergovernmental Committee was established, outside the League. When UNRRA came into being, one of its tasks was the care of refugees. It was estimated that there were in Europe, after World War II, some twenty million displaced persons and, in the Far East, thirty million more. The efforts of the League in this field were marked by uncertainty and tergiversation, which is not surprising in view of the great difficulties involved. A solution may ultimately be found in the legal establishment of human rights so that no country can so mistreat its citizens as to produce a mass refugee problem; but the road to this goal will be long and uphill.

INTERNATIONAL BUREAUX. The desire to secure a more centralized cooperation among states led to the provision, in Article 24, for the inclusion of public unions, or their bureaux, under the auspices of the League. No effort was made to compel the older unions to enter, or to lose their autonomy through entrance but, in the interests of central-

[47] J. G. McDonald, "Refugees," in H. E. Davis, *op. cit.*, p. 208; Sir John Hope Simpson, *The Refugee Problem; Report of a Survey* (London, 1939); Sir Herbert Emerson, "Postwar Problems of Refugees," *Foreign Affairs*, January, 1943, p. 211; International Assistance to Refugees, Report submitted by Sir Herbert Emerson, High Commissioner of Refugees, *L. of N. Doc.*, 1946.XII.B.1. Refer to p. 420, below.

ized administration, new bodies later created were to be placed under the direction of the League. In some cases the absence of the United States has made both provisions difficult. Few of the older unions availed themselves of the opportunity afforded them; nor did the League assert its authority over the newer ones. Whether included or not, the Secretariat of the League was instructed to collaborate and assist such bodies so far as is desirable. Paragraph 3 of Article 24 gave to the Council the authority to include the expenses of any bureau put under the League in the expenses of the League, but the power was actually exercised by the Assembly, which controls the budget.

MINORITIES.[48] One other field of administrative activity remains to be noted, although it is not specifically provided for in the Covenant. The task of protecting minority groups was laid upon the Council of the League by "Minority Treaties" between the Principal Allied and Associated Powers, and Czechoslovakia, Greece, Poland, Rumania, and Yugoslavia. In addition, provisions were inserted into some of the peace treaties, and various declarations and special agreements were made. By these agreements, the states concerned gave certain pledges in behalf of their minorities, such as the right to life, liberty, freedom of worship, civil and political equality, use of language, or equality of opportunity in public employment. The agreements could not be modified except by a majority of the Council, and each state agreed that any members of the Council might bring to the attention of the Council any infraction of an obligation thus contracted. In such a case, the Council could take such action as it might deem proper and effective in the circumstances. Any dispute as to law or fact must be referred to the Permanent Court. Petitions could be submitted by any person or association to the Council and, after observations made by the governments concerned, the Council might make recommendations. Naturally, states thus conditioned in their sovereignty have felt some dissatisfaction, and there has been an effort to generalize the regime of minorities so as to apply to all states. In 1933 a resolution was adopted, and noted by the Council, expressing "the hope that the

---

[48] As to minorities, see P. de Azcarate, *League of Nations and National Minorities, An Experiment* (Washington, 1945); I. Evans, "The Protection of Minorities," *B.Y.I.L.*, 1923-24, pp. 95-123; L. P. Mair, *The Protection of Minorities* (London, 1928); A. Mandelstam, *La protection des Minorités* (Paris, 1925); J. Robinson and others, *Were The Minorities Treaties a Failure?* (New York, 1943); H. Rosting, "Protection of Minorities by the League of Nations," *A.J.*, 17 (1923), pp. 641-60; J. S. Roucek, *The Working of the Minorities System under the League of Nations* (Prague, 1929); J. Stone, *International Guarantees of Minority Rights: Procedure of the Council of the League of Nations in Theory and Practice* (London, 1932); *Ten Years of World Cooperation*, Chap. xi.

States which are not bound by legal obligations to the League with respect to Minorities will nevertheless observe in the treatment of their own racial, religious, or linguistic Minorities at least as high a standard of justice and toleration as is required by any of the treaties and by the regular action of the Council."[49]

The problem of minorities is a very difficult one. Aside from the claim of national sovereignty, the practical difficulties of ascertaining, within a given state, how it treats its minority peoples, are enormous. Complaints are envenomed by prejudice, and may be used by discontented peoples, or by their states of origin, as an excuse for furthering political ambitions. Granted the explosive force of nationalistic ambitions, it is plain that the utmost discretion must be exercised by the Council. On the other hand, the publication of established facts, whether injurious or not to the accused state, has had its value proven in the mandates system. No solution is to be found in shuffling frontiers around until every person is contentedly located in the political system which pleases him most. To take territory away from Czechoslovakia, for example, and give it to Hungary, would mean merely to shift the incidence of the discontent, to present the same problem from another angle.

With minorities, as with refugees, a solution is now being sought on a broader scale, through the statement and protection of certain basic rights for the human being as an individual, wherever he may be found, and regardless of the claims to arbitrary control made by his own state. Progress in this direction will be slow and difficult.

75. TRANSFER OF LEAGUE ACTIVITIES TO THE UNITED NATIONS[50]

The decision to create a new international organization instead of continuing the League of Nations produced a surprising number of questions as to legal succession. There was to be considered not only the obligations of the Covenant and the activities undertaken by the League, but hundreds of treaties which had conferred responsibilities upon the League, and also the relationships between it and the Permanent Court of International Justice and the International Labour Organization.

The problem was studied by the Executive Committee of the

[49] J. Jackson and S. King-Hall, *The League Year-Book* (1934), p. 227.

[50] See The League Hands Over, *L. of N. Doc.*, General. 1946.1; Aufricht, pp. 30-40, 130-33, and Appendix iii; H. Reiff, "Transition from League of Nations to United Nations," *Dept. of State Bull.*, 14 (1946), pp. 691, 739, reprinted as Dept. of State Pub., No. 2542; A. Sweetser, "From the League to the United Nations," *Annals Am. Acad.*, 246 (1946), p. 1.

Preparatory Commission of the United Nations which agreed at the outset that only the League of Nations could arrange for its own dissolution, though the United Nations would assist in every possible way. Most of the Members of the United Nations had been Members of the League of Nations, so that organizational opposition was largely eliminated. It was early agreed, also, that only non-political and technical functions and the material assets of the League should be considered for transfer. After some debate as to whether certain activities should be selected and transferred by designation, it was decided that certain League activities should be excluded and all others transferred *en bloc*. A footnote to the report stated the general limitations:[51]

> The Committee recommends that no political questions should be included in the transfer. It makes no recommendation to transfer the activities concerning refugees, mandates, or international bureaux. The contemplated transfer will not include transfer of personnel. Transfer of assets and liabilities should imply neither profit nor loss for the United Nations. The problem of separating the finances of the International Labour Organization from those of the League is left for later consideration.
>
> The transfer of economic activities is limited to such work in this field as the United Nations might wish to continue; that of the health activities will be subject to any decisions made in the future regarding a new health organisation; and that of the social activities would take place with the understanding that the question as a whole will have to be referred to the competent organ of the United Nations. The transfer of functions arising from treaties is contemplated only as far as is possible and desirable.

The Preparatory Commission refined the report of the Executive Committee somewhat and appointed a Negotiating Committee to work out with the League a "Common Plan" for transfer of the assets of the League, and this was done.[52] The General Assembly, at its first session, set up an *ad hoc* committee to consider the transfer and, on the basis of its report,[53] adopted certain resolutions. On February 12, 1946, it reserved the right not to assume any particular function of power; declared its willingness in principle to assume certain others, such as custody of treaties for which the League had been custodian, and others of a non-political character; and asked the Economic and Social Council to survey the activities of the League and to make recommendations as to those which it might be desirable for the United Nations to assume. It also approved the "Common Plan." On December 14, it authorized the Secretary-General to assume the activities previously performed by the League Secretariat, and the Economic and Social

[51] Report of the Executive Committee, PC/EX/113/Rev. 1, 12 November 1945, p. 108.
[52] *U.N. Doc.* A/18, 28 January 1946; Aufricht, p. 601; Reiff, *loc. cit.*, p. 9, and Appendix ii.
[53] *U.N. Doc.*, A/28, 4 February 1946.

Council to assume and continue the activities previously performed by League committees and commissions, with the exception in each case of those activities exercised pursuant to international agreements and those entrusted to specialized agencies. Other resolutions dealt with opium, health, and the transfer of material assets.[54] The property transfers involved many details, ranging from the proportionate share to which were entitled Members of the United Nations who were or were not Members of the League of Nations, down to the disposition of gifts to the League or the protection of underground mains. No decision was taken as to loans previously made by the League of Nations. The assets of the League as of December 31, 1944 were estimated at about 110 million Swiss francs. It would have been much simpler to continue the old League than to arrange this transfer, but political feelings must be paid for.

Meanwhile, the Assembly of the League of Nations had had a meeting (April 8-18, 1946) to confirm the arrangements for the transfer. Resolutions were adopted terminating the Permanent Court of International Justice on the day after the Assembly ended, which was April 19; transferring to the Secretary-General of the United Nations the original texts of treaties deposited with the League; recommending that the Members of the League should facilitate the assumption by the United Nations or specialized agencies of functions which they were willing to perform; and instructing the Secretary-General of the League to assist in such transfers. A Liquidation Committee was created to transfer material assets at a cost price, the income to be distributed to the Members in proportion to their total contribution to the League. Finally, a resolution was adopted declaring the League of Nations dissolved as of April 19, 1946.[55]

Walters, in his authoritative story of the League of Nations, tells us that there is continuity from it to the United Nations. He observes that nationalists had ridiculed and frustrated the efforts of the League of Nations, yet at the end of World War II, the victorious nations felt it necessary again to set up a world-wide organization for collective security: "In its purposes and principles, its institutions and its methods, the United Nations bears at every point the mark of the experience of the League . . . every specific League function was revived in one form or another; and every one of the new agencies found a continuous thread leading back to the experience of their predecessors."[56]

[54] *Resolutions of the First General Assembly*, First Part, p. 79; see also pp. 35, 78, 81, 96, 139-44.
[55] See *Int. Organ.*, 1 (1947), p. 141, with citations to L. of N. documents.
[56] Walters, II, pp. 812-13.

THE PERMANENT COURT
OF INTERNATIONAL JUSTICE

76. CONSTITUTION OF THE COURT

While the early plans for the League of Nations said little about a court, or referred to the older Permanent Court of Arbitration at The Hague, Article 14 was ultimately put into the Charter. This article instructed the Council to make plans for a Permanent Court of International Justice, competent to determine any international dispute submitted to it and also prepared to offer advisory opinions. The Council therefore summoned a Committee of Jurists which met in the summer of 1920 and elaborated a Statute for the Court. The report of this Committee—which had favored compulsory jurisdiction—was worked over by the Council and the Assembly, and the latter body prepared a protocol by signature of which states would accept the Statute and the Court. It was to come into effect when ratified by a majority of the members of the League, and this was achieved by September 1, 1921.[57]

The Court was thus a body separate from the League, since it was founded upon a separate treaty; but it was closely related to the League and was clearly part of the League of Nations system. Article 14 of the Covenant had provided for it; its judges were elected by the Council and the Assembly of the League; its budget was part of the League budget; the League could ask advisory opinions from it. It was provided with a new name in 1945, with very slight changes in the statute; and the International Court of Justice, which will be considered later, may be regarded as a continuation of the Permanent Court of International Justice.

THE UNITED STATES AND THE COURT. By the end of 1942, fifty-one states had ratified the protocol, and eight others had signed, but not ratified. The protocol had been so worded as to make it possible for the United States to adhere, but, though the traditions of the United States were in favor of judicial settlement of disputes, a small minority of Senators was able, under Senate rules, to block acceptance of the Court.

On February 24, 1923, President Harding asked the Senate to advise and consent to the acceptance by the United States of the Protocol of Accession to the Court, and enclosed a letter from Secretary

[57] The authoritative treatise on the court is M. O. Hudson, *The Permanent Court of International Justice 1920-1942* (New York, 1943). See also A. P. Fachiri, *The Permanent Court of International Justice: Its Constitution, Procedure and Work* (London, 1932); B. de Francqueville, *L'Oeuvre de la Cour Permanente de Justice Internationale,* 2 vols. (Paris, 1928).

of State Hughes suggesting four reservations to cover the demands of the United States. President Coolidge subsequently urged action in each annual message, but it was not until January 27, 1926, that the Senate finally passed a resolution giving its advice and consent to the protocol, with five instead of four reservations. This action of the Senate was communicated by Secretary Kellogg to the Secretary-General of the League, with the notice that the signature of the United States would not be affixed until the signatory governments should "have specified in their writing to the Government of the United States" their acceptance of the reservations, and that toward this end he had addressed each government separately. The Council of the League pointed out the difficulty of separate consideration by states and summoned the Conference of States Signatories to the Protocol of Signature at Geneva in September, 1926, which the United States refused to attend. The conference found no difficulty with any of the five reservations, except the last half of the fifth one: "nor shall it, without the consent of the United States, entertain any request for an advisory opinion touching any dispute or question in which the United States has or claims an interest." This extravagant demand, aside from any desire to concede it, raised legal difficulties. To say that no advisory opinion could be given in a case in which the United States "claims an interest" would be to give it an exceptional position, above that of other signatories. The conference therefore prepared a protocol conceding the demands of the United States upon all except the last point, and guaranteeing her equality on this point, under conditions to be worked out later.

The views of the conference were communicated to the United States. President Coolidge failed to present them to the Senate, and it was not until two years later, at a time when the Senate Committee on Foreign Relations seemed disposed to renew negotiations, that he again took up the matter of the Court. It was doubtless of some relevancy that a committee, of which Elihu Root was a member, was to meet shortly in Geneva to prepare a revision of the Statute.[58] In con-

---

[58] As to the revision of the Statute, see A. Hammarskjold, "Le Règlement revisé de la Cour Permanente de Justice Internationale," *R.D.I.L.C.*, 8 (1927), pp. 322-59; D. F. Fleming, *The United States and the World Court* (New York, 1945); M. O. Hudson, "The Amended Rules of the Permanent Court of International Justice," *A.J.*, 25 (1931), pp. 427-35; Minutes of the Conference regarding the Revision of the Statute . . . and the Accession of the United States, League of Nations, 1929.V.18; Minutes of the Session held at Geneva, March 11th-19th, 1929, Committee of Jurists on the Statute of the Permanent Court of International Justice, League of Nations, 1929.V.5. As to the Root Formula, see P. C. Jessup, "The Root Formula for the Accession of the United States to the Permanent Court of International Justice," *Proc. Am. Soc.*, 1931, pp. 61-67; also *World Court Hearings before the Committee on Foreign Relations*, U.S. Senate, 71st C., 3rd Session.

nection with the work of the committee appointed for this purpose, Mr. Root presented a formula under which the United States might be able to participate. This plan was approved by both Council and Assembly and opened for signature. On December 9, 1929, the three protocols were signed for the United States.[59] No action was taken, however, until 1935, when the Senate rejected all proposals.

SELECTION OF JUDGES. The members of the Court are not states, but the judges. There are fifteen judges, chosen regardless of nationality "from among persons of high moral character, who possess the qualifications required in their respective countries for appointment to the highest judicial offices, or are jurisconsults of recognized competence in international law" (Article 2 of the Statute) and who represent "the main forms of civilization and the principal legal systems of the world" (Article 9). Each national group of persons chosen for the Permanent Court of Arbitration at the Hague, consisting of four persons, is entitled to nominate not more than four judges, not more than two of these of their own nationality. The list of nominees is submitted by the Secretary-General, in their alphabetical order, to the Council and Assembly, which vote upon them independently of each other and by secret ballot. In each body, each candidate must receive an absolute majority; and various provisions guard against deadlock.

The judges regularly elected hold office for nine years and are then eligible for re-election. Thus independence is secured, while at the same time account is taken of the need for change and of the danger that a judge may stay on after he is too old to perform his functions. The Court, however, is always prepared to act, since the judge remains in office in any case until his successor is chosen. A member of the Court cannot be dismissed unless, in the unanimous judgment of the other members, he has ceased to measure up to the required conditions. He may resign by notification to the Secretary-General. Members are entitled to diplomatic privileges and immunities (Article 19).

The Court is located at The Hague, and meets in a dignified room in the Peace Palace given by Andrew Carnegie. The president of the Court is elected by the judges themselves for a three-year term; and he and the Registrar of the Court are required to live at the seat of the Court. Under the original statute, an annual meeting was required, and the president could summon an extraordinary session whenever

[59] The three protocols are: (1) the original protocol of adherence to the Statute; (2) the protocol for the adherence of the United States; (3) the protocol covering the revision of the Statute.

desired; but by the revised Article 23, "the Court shall remain permanently in session except during the judicial vacation," and members, unless on regular leave (six months every three years) or ill, are required to hold themselves permanently at the disposition of the Court. The full Court is ordinarily to sit, but one or more judges may be excused from sitting, provided the number of judges is not thereby reduced below eleven. Nine judges constitute a quorum. Their salaries are fixed by the Assembly upon proposal of the Council, and cannot be changed during the period of office. Provision is made also for travel allowances and for pensions.

Under certain circumstances, there may be additional judges upon the bench. Each nation party to the case before the Court is entitled to have upon the bench a judge of its own nationality, a provision which has caused criticism. A judge is not supposed to be a representative of his own state, but the result of this situation is to make him an advocate for his state, and such an *ad hoc* judge rarely votes against his own country. It might have been desirable, from the viewpoint of an ideal tribunal, to have required the removal from the bench of all nationals of parties to the case, rather than to have added to their number. This concession to national sovereignty apparently has to be made, and various justifications have been offered for it. The judge is able to explain to his colleagues the situation and the law of his own state; and, if his state is defeated, to help frame the opinion of the Court in such fashion as not to wound its susceptibilities.[60]

77. JURISDICTION OF THE COURT[61]

The jurisdiction, or "competence," of the Court is stated in Chapter II of the Statute: "Only States or Members of the League of Nations can be parties in cases before the Court" (Article 34). An individual cannot appear before the Court, although there was a strong feeling in the Committee of Jurists that this should be permitted. International tribunals have, as has been seen, been forced a long way in the direction of recognizing the rights of individuals, but the individual still remains almost entirely at the mercy of the delinquent

[60] Hudson, *Court*, pp. 360-69.

[61] As to the jurisdiction of the court, see P. J. N. Baker, "The Obligatory Jurisdiction of the Permanent Court of International Justice," *B.Y.I.L.*, 1925, pp. 68-102; A. Peaslee, "Obligatory Jurisdiction of the Permanent Court of International Justice," *Proc. Am. Soc.*, 1931, pp. 48-57; H. E. Richards, "The Jurisdiction of the Permanent Court of International Justice," *B.Y.I.L.*, 1921-22, pp. 1-6; Case of the Free Zones of Upper Savoy and the District of Gex, *P.C.I.J.*, Series A, No. 24, dissenting opinion of F. B. Kellogg, reprinted in *A.J.*, 25 (1931), pp. 203-13.

state, or of his own state. The authority of the Court to handle a case put before it derives from the Statute, or from other treaties conferring jurisdiction upon the Court, and if this authority is challenged, the Court decides whether it is competent to take the case.

COMPULSORY JURISDICTION. The most important question which the Committee of Jurists of 1920 had to decide was whether states could be summoned, against their will, before the proposed Court, and they decided unanimously that this was the correct principle. The Council and the Assembly of the League, however, reversed this recommendation—an unfortunate backward step. Consequently Article 36 now reads: "The jurisdiction of the Court comprises all cases which the parties refer to it and all matters specially provided for in treaties and conventions in force." Insofar as the Statute goes, then, no state can be compelled to appear before the Court except of its own volition.

In fact, however, the Court had a certain amount of compulsory jurisdiction, derived chiefly from authority outside the Statute. The peace treaties and others resulting from the war, such as those for mandates, minorities, labor, etc., made provision for the reference of disputes to the Court, and Article 37 authorizes the Court to deal with such matters.

A more important source of compulsory jurisdiction is the famous "Optional Clause" (Article 36) through which states, such as desire to, may agree to submit to a reciprocal compulsory jurisdiction. It may be separately accepted by a "declaration," in which the states "declare that they recognize as compulsory, *ipso facto* and without special agreement, in relation to any other member or state accepting the same obligation, the jurisdiction of the Court in all or any of the classes of legal disputes. . . ." A continually varying number of states (a total of some forty-five) had adhered to the Optional Clause before the Second World War came, some of them, unfortunately, with harmful reservations.

One reason for the hesitation in accepting compulsory jurisdiction had been uncertainty as to what type of question was suitable for arbitration. Article 36 answers this uncertainly by defining matters for arbitration as: "(a) The interpretation of a Treaty. (b) Any question of international law. (c) The existence of any fact which, if established, would constitute a breach of an international obligation. (d) The nature and extent of the reparation to be made for the breach of an international obligation." These terms may be taken to describe the type of case proper to submit to the Court, whether or not the Optional Clause is in question.

LAW APPLICABLE. The Court is authorized to apply international conventions (which are of course applicable only to the states which have signed them); custom, "as evidence of a general practice accepted as law"; the "general principles of law recognized by civilized nations"; and, as a subsidiary means for determining the law, judicial decisions and the teachings of publicists. Judicial decisions of the Court, however, are subjected to Article 59, and the Anglo-American rule of *stare decisis* is not in effect.[62] Thus, the Court may call upon the sources of law which we have considered in Chapter 2—treaty, custom, and general principles. The competence of the Court was made wide, with room for growth through judicial interpretation. The Court was also given power, if the parties so agreed, to judge *ex aequo et bono*, that is, as seems just to the Court; this would cover matters concerning which it might be claimed that there was no established international law.

CONTENTIOUS AND ADVISORY CASES. The questions which come before the Court may be disputes between states, or matters on which the League of Nations, and now the United Nations, could ask the advice of the Court concerning legal phases of subjects under consideration. In the former case, a matter might come before the Court under the Optional Clause or a compromisory clause in a treaty, in which situation one party might require the other to appear; or it might come through voluntary agreement of both parties to submit their question to the Court. In contentious cases, the decision of the Court is binding and final. In advisory cases, however, the opinion of the Court is binding upon no one; it is merely advice. In practice, advisory opinions were asked of the Court frequently—more so than under the United Nations—and have been very helpful. Articles 71-74 of the Rules of Procedure made advisory opinions, so far as judicial procedure is concerned, practically equivalent in legal worth to decisions in contentious cases.[63]

[62] Article 59: "The decision of the Court has no binding effect except between the parties and in respect of that particular case." Nevertheless, great respect is given to previous decisions and they are quoted as properly influential upon a court.

[63] As to advisory opinions, see M. O. Hudson, "The Advisory Opinions of the Permanent Court of International Justice," *Int. Con.*, No. 214, 1925; M. O. Hudson, "Les avis consultatifs de la Cour Permanente de Justice Internationale," *Hague Acad.*, 1925, III, pp. 345-411; A. D. McNair, "The Council's Request for an Advisory Opinion," *B.Y.I.L.*, 1926, pp. 1-13; A. H. Philipse, *Les fonctions consultatives de la Cour Permanente de Justice Internationale* (Lausanne, 1928); C. G. Tenekides, "La compétence de la Cour Permanente de Justice Internationale en matière de procédure consultative," *R.D.I.P.*, 23 (1926), pp. 120-29.

78. PROCEDURE OF THE COURT

If the Court has compulsory jurisdiction, it may take hold of the case upon the demand of either party; if the case is submitted by voluntary agreement, notification to the registrar of the Court is sufficient. If any member considers that it has a right to intervene, it may request permission to do so, and the Court will determine whether or not the request shall be granted. Every state participating in the case is bound by the decision, and the Court may also indicate measures of a provisional nature to protect the rights of the parties (Article 41). Each party is represented by an agent, who is the official representative of his state and who may have the benefit of counsel to aid him before the Court. The presentation of the argument is both written and oral. The written argument consists of "cases, counter-cases, and, if necessary, replies"; and its orderly presentation is arranged for in the Rules of Procedure of the Court. Time limits are fixed for the presentation of each document, and when all have been submitted a date for oral presentation is set. Proceedings are in public, although they may in exceptional cases be private. Witnesses may be heard; the argument of counsel is unfolded; the judges shuffle their papers and ask questions. Experts may also be called upon. If one party fails to appear, the Court may decide against it by default. When the presentation of the case is ended the judges retire for private consultation. A majority of those present is sufficient for a decision, with the president to decide in case of a tie. The judgment of the Court must state the reasons upon which it is based (Article 56), and dissenting judges may utter and have printed their separate opinions. These documents are of the greatest authority in the building up of international jurisprudence. There is no appeal from the judgment, but the Court may construe it upon the request of either party (Article 60), or may proceed to a revision if any new facts are discovered. Each party bears its own costs; the expenses of the Court were provided for in the budget of the League of Nations.

Further consideration will be given to the Court under its new name as part of the United Nations. Little criticism was offered against the Court. Its Statute was revised in 1929,[64] and again in 1945. The Permanent Court of International Justice, as such, gave twenty-one judg-

---

[64] Minutes of the Conference regarding the Revision of the Statute . . . and the Accession of the United States, *L. of N. Doc.*, 1929.V.18; Committee of Jurists on the Statute of the Permanent Court of International Justice, Minutes of the Session held at Geneva March 11-19, 1929, 1929.V.5.

ments in contentious cases, nine more dealing with preliminary questions, and two interpreting previous decisions; and twenty-seven advisory opinions.[65]

[65] O. Lissitzyn, *The International Court of Justice* (Carnegie Endowment, 1951). As to the work of the Court, see Hudson; G. Schwarzenberger, *International Law as Applied by International Courts and Tribunals* (2nd ed., London, 1949); H. Lauterpacht, *The Development of International Law by the Permanent Court of International Justice* (London, 1934).

The opinions and documents of the Court were printed by it in several series. The opinions have been reprinted by M. O. Hudson and the Carnegie Endowment in a number of volumes entitled *World Court Reports*.

There was much discussion of the Permanent Court and the questions connected with it in the Committee of Jurists which met at Washington just before the San Francisco Conference, and again in Committee IV/1 of that Conference. They may be found in the UNCIO documents.

Chapter 11

THE UNITED NATIONS: GENERAL SURVEY

CREATION

79. MAKING THE PEACE

As in the case of World War I, so in World War II many lessons of international cooperation were learned. The Allies worked with more coordination and supplied themselves with more common agencies of action; they exerted even more control than before over the activities of the other nations of the world. Combined boards worked in functional activities which were more unified than cooperative; troops were mixed under one command; Lend-Lease, substituted for the earlier inter-allied loans, made the whole effort seem more of a common enterprise. Much of this experience in international government could have been usefully continued after the war; but it is a fact to be noted with regret that human beings do not seem able to cooperate so well for purposes of peace as for purposes of war.

The procedure by which the peace settlement of 1919 and the building of the League of Nations were accomplished in the same conference has been criticized. The Covenant of the League of Nations thus became part of the "iniquitous" treaties of peace and the butt of attacks made from various viewpoints upon these treaties. A distinction was made in principle at the Paris Peace Conference between the settlement of the past war through treaties of peace and the beginning of the new organization which was to provide for peace in the future; control over the defeated enemy was in principle taken from the League of Nations and it has been debated ever since whether the League was strengthened or weakened by this lack of responsibility.[1] At any rate, a bifurcated international system resulted. The

[1] See W. E. Rappard, *International Relations Viewed from Geneva* (New Haven, 1925), p. 14; L. M. Goodrich, "From League of Nations to United Nations," *Int. Organ.*, I (1947), p. 6.

Supreme War Council continued to function for a short time and then transferred its functions to the Conference of Ambassadors.[2] At the same time, of course, the Council of the League of Nations was beginning to function, and questions arose as to the respective jurisdictions of the two bodies. The Conference of Ambassadors was in general regarded as the agency through which the Allies were to supervise the execution of the terms of the peace, but it was inclined to assume control of other international matters as well. The issue appeared with explosive force at the time of the Corfu episode, in which Italy denied the jurisdiction of the League of Nations and asserted that the Conference of Ambassadors alone had jurisdiction. A Committee of Jurists held that, under Article 15, paragraph 1 of the Covenant, the Council could not take jurisdiction where the dispute was already being handled by another jurisdiction.[3] The result was that Greece was not fairly treated and that the prestige of the League of Nations was badly damaged.

At the end of World War II, a somewhat similar situation appeared, though perhaps more clearly delineated. The making of the Charter and the making of the peace settlements were two quite different processes, but the Charter of the United Nations (Article 107) left to the Big Five complete control over the peace settlements with the defeated states and complete control over the enemy states themselves; and to a large degree (Article 106) it left to the Big Five responsibility for the maintenance of peace and security in the world. The meetings of foreign ministers correspond today to the Conference of Ambassadors, and it may again be debated whether the United Nations would be strengthened or weakened by having the responsibility for the peace settlement.[4] It had been shown, after World War I, that settlement on the basis of nationalistic revenge and reparation was insufficient for the reconstruction needed by the entire community of nations; but the hopes of those who sought a more sensible plan of community reconstruction after World War II were not realized.

[2] The Conference of Ambassadors was a loose organization of the ambassadors living in a given capital. At this time it had a secretariat in the Quai d'Orsay at Paris and its own letterhead. Prime Minister McDonald said that it was to wind up some matters connected with the Treaty of Versailles "and it will be strictly confined to that." See G. P. Pink, *The Conference of Ambassadors* (Geneva Studies, No. 12, 1942).

[3] See *O.J.*, 1923, pp. 1278, 1287, 1294, 1305, and, for 1924, p. 525. That the Conference of Ambassadors was an authoritative body was recognized by the Permanent Court of International Justice in its advisory opinion concerning the Monastery of St. Naoum, *P.C.I.J.*, Series B, No. 9.

[4] It will be seen, in later pages, that the United Nations has considered some questions arising out of the peace settlement, such as the Italian colonies, Trieste, or the Berlin blockade.

The process of putting the pieces together this time was of course a larger and more difficult one. In 1945 as in 1919, the Great Powers exercised control in fact and made the decisions; at both times, the fundamental problem was the same, that of securing agreement among the Great Powers. The general principles upon which the Allies intended to make the peace were stated by President Roosevelt on January 7, 1941, when he said that "we look forward to a world founded upon four essential human freedoms . . . freedom of speech and expression . . . freedom of every person to worship God in his own way . . . freedom from want . . . freedom from fear. . . ." These ideas were given fuller statement in the Atlantic Charter of August 14, 1941, which eschewed territorial aggrandizement, asserted the right of peoples to have their own form of government, planned a system of security in which people would be free from fear and want and under which there would be economic collaboration and free access to trade and materials among the nations of the world. The Declaration by United Nations of January 1, 1942, demanded complete victory so as to preserve human rights and justice; and at Casablanca there were added unconditional surrender, denazification, and punishment of war criminals, but also the promise that the peace would not be a punitive one.

The foreign secretaries of the Soviet Union and the United Kingdom and the Secretary of State of the United States met at Moscow in October, 1943, and issued several statements with respect both to the making of peace and the making of the "general international organization." The heads of states met at Teheran (their second meeting) in November 1943, confirmed the Moscow agreements, and asserted the chief responsibility of the Great Powers for the making of peace. Unconditional surrenders were made by Italy (September 3, 1943), Rumania (August 23, 1944), Bulgaria (September 9, 1944), Finland (September 19, 1944) and Hungary (January 20, 1945); and the Dumbarton Oaks conversations in the fall of 1944 laid the bases of an international organization for security. Another conference of heads of states was held at Yalta, in the Crimea, in February, 1945, at which important decisions were reached, some of which became known only later. Some territorial rearrangements were stated, which would affect Poland, Germany, and China.[5]

After the surrender of Germany in May, 1945, the three heads of states met at Potsdam in July and reached many agreements as to the

[5] Most of the documents for this period may be found in *A Decade of American Foreign Policy: Basic Documents*, issued by the Senate Committee on Foreign Relations, 81st Cong., 1st Sess., Senate Doc. No. 123 (Washington, 1950). See also the annual volumes of *Doc. Am. For. Rel.*

peace settlement, among them that the procedure should be that a Council of Foreign Ministers should outline the settlement, leaving details to be worked out by their deputies in other meetings. This Council found agreement hard to achieve; it could be reached in many instances only by compromises pregnant with trouble for the future— such, for example, as the regime established for Trieste, as lacking in common sense as the earlier regime established for Danzig. Treaties for Bulgaria, Finland, Hungary, Italy and Rumania went into effect on September 15, 1947. Efforts to make a peace treaty for Austria failed and it was not until May 15, 1956, on the initiative of the Soviet Union, that a treaty was agreed upon by which Austria again became a free nation. The peace treaty with Japan was signed at a conference in San Francisco and went into effect on April 28, 1952. The German settlement was more difficult; in 1956 West and East Germany were still separate entities. The Western powers reached agreement with West Germany in 1952, but this was tied to the European Defence Community and failed with it. Late in 1954, revised agreements were made and West Germany became free.

Unanimous agreement by the Great Powers, upon which procedures both for the peace settlement and for the "general international organization" were based, proved a very narrow basis upon which to build. In addition to the usual postwar rivalries, ideological cleavage made issues deeper and more vital, and jockeying for advantageous position was inevitable. We must leave it to the historians to decide whether the methods of reconstructing the world after World War II represent any advance over the past.[6] It was wise, at any rate, that the decision was taken to go on with the making of the international organization without waiting for the conclusion of the peace treaties. To this development we now turn.

80. THE MAKING OF THE CHARTER

The failure of the League of Nations had been discouraging, the more so that this failure had been due to lack of support on the part of the nations of the world. Nevertheless, there seems to have been little doubt at any time that some sort of an international organization would emerge from the clouds of World War II. The need for such an organization was apparent to all, and it was especially important

---

[6] It is not within the purview of this book to consider the peace treaties. As to the procedures in making them, see P. E. Moseley, "Peace-Making, 1946," *Int. Organ.*, I (1947), p. 22; H. Nicholson, *Peacemaking 1919* (Boston, 1933); same writer, "Peace Making at Paris: Success, Failure, or Farce?" *Foreign Affairs*, 25 (1947), p. 190.

that the American people had now swung round to support of the idea. A large degree of unity had been achieved through signature of the Declaration by United Nations; the Atlantic Charter foreshadowed an international organization; the signature of the USSR to the Declaration of Moscow assured it.[7] A great deal of study had been given to the planning of such an organization, both unofficially and officially, and particularly by the Department of State.[8]

The Four Powers who had promised it at Moscow met at Dumbarton Oaks[9] from August 21 to October 7, 1944. The conversations were in two parts, in the first of which the Soviet Union talked with the United Kingdom and the United States, and in the second China talked with them. Each of the Four Powers brought with it a plan. These were discussed and agreement was reached upon an outline of general principles, called the Dumbarton Oaks Proposals. These were widely distributed and criticism was invited. Probably no similar document was ever so thoroughly studied, or subjected to so democratic a procedure of consideration and adoption, as was the document which evolved from these proposals—the Charter of the United Nations.[10]

UNCIO. The United Nations Conference on International Organization assembled at San Francisco on April 25, 1945, with fifty states in attendance, and continued its labors until the signing of the Charter on June 26.[11] It was organized in four commissions and twelve com-

[7] The documents may be found in *Dept. of State Bull.*, VI (1942), p. 3, and IX (1943), p. 307; in *Documents Am. For. Rel.*, IV, p. 203, and VI, p. 229.

[8] The preparatory work done in the Department of State is surveyed, with documents, in *Post-War Foreign Policy Preparation 1939-1945*, edited by Harley Notter, Dept. of State Pub., No. 3580 (1949).

[9] Dumbarton Oaks is an estate in Washington, D.C., owned by Harvard University.

[10] See Appendix for this document. For amendments offered see UNCIO Doc. 2 (collection of amendments officially proposed); *Int. Con.*, No. 405 (1944), and No. 409 (1945).

[11] "It was a large conference, stretching the facilities of that hospitable and interesting city. In all, 282 delegates, representing fifty states, attended, and with their staffs they amounted to 1,726 persons officially working for their states. The International Secretariat, mostly recruited from the United States, numbered 1,058 persons. A total of 2,636 newspaper, radio, etc., representatives were present, and it required the aid of 2,262 Army and Navy boys and girls, 800 AWVS, 400 Red Cross, and 800 Boy Scouts—not to mention 188 telephone and telegraph operators—to service the Conference. The average daily output of documents was about half a million sheets of paper, and on one day 1,700,000 sheets were issued and distributed; seventy-eight tons of papers were used. The total cost of the Conference, aside from expenses of delegations, was some two million dollars, paid by the United States as host," Clyde Eagleton, "The Charter Adopted at San Francisco," *Pol. Sci. Rev.* 39 (1945), p. 935. These figures were provided by the United Nations Information Office.

See also Report to the President, *passim;* "The United Nations Charter," *Int. Con.*, No. 413 (1945), p. 441; W. T. R. Fox, "The Super-Powers at San Francisco," *The Review of Politics*, 8 (1946), p. 115; G. Kirk and L. H. Chamberlain, "The Organization of the San Francisco Conference," *Pol. Sci. Q.*, 60 (1945), p. 321.

mittees, most of the actual work being done in the committees. A coordination committee and a committee of jurists put the pieces together into a final document; there was a steering committee to guide the work and resolve problems; and above all were the Big Five meetings in the penthouse on top of the Hotel Fairmount. The work was arduous and often delayed by the necessity of waiting until the Big Four or Five could reach agreement, but there was little doubt in the mind of anyone that the Conference would succeed in its purpose. The rule of unanimity was abandoned and action was taken by a two-thirds majority; debate was free and unrestricted. The Big Five had their way on the points where they took a firm stand, but this was because of the realization which all had that the system could not work unless the Great Powers were willing to make it work.

The drafting of the Charter was poor, partly because of the desire of various nations to have some of their words recorded in the Charter, partly because the Soviet delegates were unwilling to depart very far from the words of the Dumbarton Oaks Proposals, and partly because those who dominated the conference were inexperienced in such work and impatient with legal terminology; above all, because of the need to compromise on almost every word. There are many uncertainties of meaning and of textual authority, some of which have caused debate and deadlock. The bare bones of the Dumbarton Oaks Proposals were at San Francisco given flesh, somewhat adipose at spots, but the essential principles of the proposals were little modified.

Another document on interim arrangements was signed at the same time, and in accordance with this, the Executive Committee[12] met at London on August 16, 1945, to make proposals for setting up the new organization. The Preparatory Commission itself assembled in London on November 24, 1945, and, with encouraging unanimity and lack of reservations, agreed upon numerous recommendations of measures for establishing the various organs and procedures of the United Nations.[13] These were for the most part adopted by the General Assembly, at the first part of its First Session, at London, January 10 to February 14, 1945. Other steps were taken at the second part, and with these decisions the successor to the League of Nations was launched upon its career.

WHY? The question may be asked at this point: Why was it necessary to build a new organization? Why could not the League of Nations

[12] Report of the Executive Committee to the Preparatory Commission of the United Nations. *U.N. Doc.*, PC/EX/113/Rev.1. November 12, 1945.

[13] Report of the Preparatory Commission of the United Nations, PC/20. December 23, 1945.

have been rebuilt in such fashion as might have been thought necessary? This would have avoided various problems of legal succession and might have saved a great deal of uncertainty and labor. The answer is to be sought in human nature, and even such statesmen as were not themselves troubled with this affliction were nevertheless driven by its effect upon their peoples. It was essential to draw into the international organization the two greatest and most reluctant states of the world and these two were the ones who had been most captious about the Geneva League. American statesmen were afraid that they could not persuade the Senate to accept the League of Nations which it had for so long rejected, and felt that they must present to it a new scheme more American in origin and thinking. The Russians had been expelled from the League of Nations and had a long-standing feud with Switzerland. There were also perhaps some who hoped that a fresh start would bring something stronger than the League had been and less affected by the stigma of failure which, more or less unjustly, rested upon the League.

81. CHARACTERISTICS AND COMPARISONS

A LEAGUE OF VICTORS. Like the League of Nations, the United Nations was conceived in the midst of war and in the fear of war. It was the product of the victors of World War II, and their trade name was carried over to become the name of the universal organization for peace.[14] No states were invited to participate in the San Francisco Conference except those who had signed the Declaration by United Nations;[15] both enemies and neutrals were excluded from original membership. It would seem that the only aggressors whom the makers of the Charter had clearly in mind were the Axis Powers, since the Security Council cannot act against a Big Power aggressor, and its potentially vast strength would not be needed against smaller states. Nevertheless, the United Nations was itself deprived of control over the enemy states, and Article 107 left these states at the disposition of the Five Powers.[16] It was their share in winning the war upon which

[14] The name "United Nations" met with some objection for this reason, and also because of its inconvenience as a name, but it was adopted as a memorial to President Roosevelt. Goodrich and Hambro, p. 58; *UNCIO Doc.* 944, I/1/34 (1).

[15] The Declaration by United Nations pledged joint efforts for the defeat of the Axis. An undignified scramble to sign before the conference met followed this announcement.

[16] The Republic of China, France, the Union of Soviet Socialist Republics, the United Kingdom of Great Britain and Northern Ireland, and the United States of America. See Article 23 of the Charter.

was based the claim of the Five Powers to predominance in the United Nations, and no new state can be admitted without the consent of all five.

While the Great Powers had a position of special importance in the League of Nations, their predominancy in the United Nations is more marked. They have permanent seats on the Security Council, more exclusive than those in the Council of the League, to which the Assembly could elect other members; and only they have a right of veto, a discrimination in their favor as compared with the League Council in which all members had a veto. It is a right which includes not only matters of security but extends in practice to such other matters as admission of new Members, selection of a Secretary-General, or amendment of the Charter. This special position does not depend upon their ability to meet stated criteria; they are arbitrarily named and there is no way to unseat them, even by amendment, without their own consent. They can block almost any action in the Security Council (though not in other organs); on the other hand, when they are in agreement, they should easily be able to influence the two other votes needed to take affirmative action.

Power is further channeled into their hands by Chapter XVII of the Charter. Article 106 authorizes them to take such action "on behalf of the Organization" as they may consider to be necessary for the maintenance of international peace and security; and while the Security Council itself decides when this period of delegation of authority is to be ended, each of the Five has a veto on that decision. By Article 107, entire control over enemy states was given to the Five Powers ("the Governments having responsibility") with no provision as to when or how this control is to be terminated. For an indefinite time, then, the Big Five, rather than the United Nations, were to have legal authority to maintain peace and security throughout the world as they wished, and entire control over the peace settlements and future disposition of the enemy peoples.[17]

REALISM. The position thus given the Five Powers, and particularly the veto, represented what was called a "realistic" viewpoint. This viewpoint maintained that, in the existing exceptional balance, or imbalance, of power among nations, the only hope for the new organization lay in unanimous agreement among these states. If they could agree, their strength would make the United Nations irresistible; if one or more should not agree, it would be hopeless to try to coerce it or them. Such an effort could only mean war upon a vast scale. The

---

[17] A nullity, in fact, for these Powers have been no more able to agree outside than inside the United Nations.

United Nations, therefore, should not, except as a stated legal principle, include among its ambitions that of preventing the use of force by a Great Power; it should be planned so that its strength would be used only against resurgence of the former enemy states or against small aggressors. While it is true that this would deprive each of the Five of the aid of the United Nations against the only aggressors whom each of them need fear, this could not be helped. It would be better to enable it to do what it could do within the range of practical possibility than to wreck the United Nations by putting upon it a load greater than it could carry.[18]

This view prevailed, but there are strong arguments against it. It could be anticipated, and has since been shown, that agreement among the Five Powers is difficult to achieve. If a crisis originating in a Great Power aggression should develop to the point of calling for enforcement action against that Great Power, it would be a crisis dangerous enough to mean war in any case, within or without the United Nations.[19] In such a situation, it would surely be advantageous for the state which must face the aggressor to have upon its side such resources as the obligations put upon Members by the United Nations Charter could provide. These might be sufficient to deter aggression; they might be sufficient to turn the balance against the aggressor; in any case, the United Nations could organize moral support for those who face the aggressor, and the development of such moral support would assist in the long-range task of building a community based upon law and justice. In other words, the use of the veto would not prevent the use of force, if a sufficiently critical dispute should arise; and if force is to be used, it would be better to have it known that the victim of aggression would have the organized community of nations upon its side from the beginning. If it were said that this would disrupt the United Nations, it must also be said that failure on the part of the United Nations even to try to prevent aggression would as effectively disrupt it. This, indeed, is what actually happened to the League of Nations.

Certainly, the result is that no security is provided for the United States or for any other Great Power. The only aggressor whom the American nation has to fear is a Great Power aggressor. Against such a danger the Charter offers protection in principle, but the veto denies it as a practical possibility; and since there is little present likelihood of the United States becoming an aggressor, the veto works to our disad-

---

[18] See Wellington Koo, Jr., *Voting Procedures in International Political Organizations* (New York, 1947).

[19] Enforcement action by the United Nations should not be regarded as war, but as police action. A very important principle is involved in this use of terms. See § 155 below.

vantage in this situation. From the viewpoint of the smaller states, they may be compelled to submit to Security Council decisions (Article 25), while the Great Powers may escape by use of the veto. As a practical consequence, each of the smaller states is compelled to align itself with a Great Power and the rival blocs thus formed have developed on a larger scale than ever before. In general, Five Power control furnishes a quite inadequate base upon which to build a world organization for peace and security.

SOVEREIGNTY. We have spoken earlier of the enormous importance of national sovereignty, even in the limited meaning of a relative freedom from external control, and of the difficulty of building a system of international law upon such a foundation. The Charter bases the United Nations upon the principle of the "sovereign equality of all its Members" and it carefully protects each Member against interference. No organ of the United Nations has legislative authority, and no new rule of law can be issued which is binding upon a Member without its own consent. Only under Chapter VII, in the field of enforcement against an aggressor, may a Member be bound to action without its own consent; and the Security Council can give no final decision, but can only make recommendations, in disputes between Members. Even though no authority is given to legislate, assurance is made doubly sure by Article 2, paragraph 7, which forbids the United Nations to intervene in any matter which is "essentially" a matter of domestic jurisdiction.[20] Finally, a right of withdrawal is apparently understood to exist, though not stated in the Charter.

Potentially, control by the Security Council in cases of breach of the peace is wide-reaching and powerful, much more so than under the Charter; the United Nations is here armed—even if inadequately—with the first of the powers of government, the power to repress the illegal use of force. Aside, however, from this limited interference, which is only in case of the use of force and not for general enforcement of law, national sovereignty remains untouched and is indeed carefully protected. The United Nations is far from being a superstate; like the League, it is an association of states, with each Member free to do as it wishes except for certain limitations upon its right to use force in its international relations. If it can be called "international government" it must be admitted that it is a very weak one.

POLITICAL CHARACTER. It follows from the above that the United Nations is not so much a legal order as a political system. Indeed, the phrase "international law" was not found in the Dumbarton Oaks Proposal (except in the domestic questions clause, from which it was later

[20] See pp. 302-3 below for discussion of this clause.

removed), and as a result of the insistence of many states it was inserted at San Francisco in Article 1, paragraph 1.[21] Here it is limited to the settlement of disputes "in conformity with the principles of justice and international law." The only other reference to international law in the Charter is found in Article 13 which mildly authorizes the General Assembly to "initiate studies and make recommendations for the purpose of: . . . encouraging the progressive development of international law and its codification."

Compulsory jurisdiction was denied to the International Court of Justice as it was to the earlier Court and, consequently, the nearest approach to a requirement that legal disputes be settled in accordance with law is found in Article 36, under which the Security Council may recommend to the parties in a dispute that they should "take into consideration that" legal disputes should, "if the parties so desire," be submitted to the Court. No requirement, beyond the vague reference in Article 1, paragraph 1, is placed upon the Security Council with regard to use of international law; it was given complete freedom in handling disputes or threats to the peace upon a political basis. The Security Council, in the disputes which have thus far been before it, has not felt it necessary to be guided in its decisions by international law, or to refer legal questions to a court.[22] The League made more use of its Court.

COOPERATION. The hope of the United Nations, therefore, as was true also for the League of Nations, lies in the willingness and the ability of its Members to cooperate. This is true even in the one field where authority and governmental power exists, the field of security, for even here the Five Powers must agree before action can be taken. Since no authority beyond recommendation is given to any other organ, a majority vote is sufficient for decisions, and no veto is provided in these organs. Granted cooperation, a wide field of human improvement is opened; but it is in the sense of objectives to be sought through cooperation and not in the sense of authority to act. Adequate facilities for study, planning, and negotiation are provided; whether they will provide progress in the sense of legislative development depends entirely upon the willingness of sovereign states to accept the recommendations made. In practice there has been a fair amount of cooperation; but ratifications of legislative instruments are very slow in coming.

[21] See P. C. Jessup, "Development of International Law of the United Nations," A.J., 39 (1945), p. 754; G. A. Finch, "International Law in the United Nations Organization," Proc. Am. Soc., 1945, pp. 28-40; Eagleton, in G. A. Lipsky, Law and Politics in the World Community (Berkeley, 1953), p. 129.

[22] The Albanian dispute was referred to the court after the Security Council was blocked by a veto.

DECENTRALIZATION. We have observed that the League of Nations under Article 24 of the Covenant sought to bring all international activities under one umbrella, though for various reasons it did not succeed in this effort. The United Nations, on the contrary, encourages the building of separate international organizations, each with its own special function, its own staff, and its own treaty base.[23] These were designated in the Charter as the "specialized agencies"; and it was further provided (Articles 57 and 63) that agreements should be made between each of these and the Economic and Social Council which would bring them into some sort of relationship with the United Nations itself. Thus, the United Nations, though it sought coordination, tended toward decentralization rather than the centralization which the League of Nations attempted. It would be difficult to estimate which institution actually achieved more in coordination of effort.

ORGANIZATION. The Charter provided a much more elaborate organization for the United Nations than did the Covenant for the League of Nations. Three Councils were provided, each with own function to perform; under the League there was only one Council, not greatly differentiated in function from the Assembly. The United Nations system, including the specialized agencies, is much more functionally specialized; but the specialized agencies are independent bodies and, on the other hand, two of the three Councils are subordinated to the General Assembly. The League had an economic organization, but this was elevated in the United Nations into a Council; similarly, the Mandates Commission of the League became the Trusteeship Council of the United Nations. Finally, the Court, which had been a separate institution under the League, became one of the six main organs of the United Nations.

REGIONALISM. The United Nations pays more respect to regional systems than did the League, which had no more in its Covenant than the negative and rather vague statement in Article 21: "Nothing in this Covenant shall be deemed to affect the validity of international engagements, such as treaties of arbitration, or regional understandings such as the Monroe Doctrine, for securing the maintenance of peace." This, indeed, was little more than submission to the United States demand for protection for the Monroe Doctrine. The Charter of the United Nations, however, permits and encourages "regional arrangements and agencies" if consistent with the purposes and principles of the United Nations. Actually, the Charter gives preference to regional

[23] Insofar as there is an umbrella, it is to be found in articles 17(3), 63, and 64.

bodies for the settlement of disputes, and permits them to engage in enforcement action if authorized by the Security Council. Chapter VIII of the Charter is devoted to such regional arrangements.

CONCLUSIONS. To many persons, the Charter of the United Nations was a disappointment. They had hoped for advance beyond the League of Nations, for a system which could provide some degree of security against war; and they had hoped that it might be given sufficient authority to deal more effectively with the more important economic and social causes of war. These hopes were not realized.

It is probably true, however, that the Charter reflected with some accuracy prevailing popular opinion in the world, and particularly in its two most important Members. Certainly, the American people cannot consistently criticize the United Nations, for it was they who made it what it is. The American people have swung from isolation to international organization, but they have not made it clear how far they are willing to go in submitting national sovereignty to the new international order. They could have had as strong a United Nations as they wished, but they did not indicate to their government willingness to pay the price for so strong a system.[24]

In certain respects, the United Nations represents potential gain over the League of Nations; in other respects, it is weaker. In both systems, objectives were stated and machinery was provided, but in both cases progress had to depend upon the voluntary cooperation of its Members rather than on its own authority. It was doubtless a great gain, taking everything into consideration, that the two most powerful and most reluctant states were persuaded to enter the new organization, for without their participation there could be little hope of progress. Though the sharp ideological differences between them present very difficult problems for the United Nations, it is better to have these problems worked out under the jurisdiction of a universal system than for them to be fought out individually. It is a gain, too, that the unanimity rule, so long prevailing in international conferences, is abandoned and that a veto can nowhere be used except in the security field, and that instead of a veto belonging to every Member and to be used in all voting, a veto can now be used only by five states and only in the security field. The authority to require Members to use armed forces

24 American students should keep this in mind as they study the United Nations. It is possible that the President, or the Department of State, underestimated the extent of authority which the American people were willing to give to the United Nations, but they had ample reason for moving cautiously. President Roosevelt kept continuously in mind that one third of the Senate could defeat acceptance of the Charter—which would have been disastrous—and that it had previously done so on other important matters, such as the League of Nations in 1919-20, or the Permanent Court of International Justice in 1935.

against an aggressor is a decided gain over the League of Nations as a legal matter, however weak it may be in its actual operation. There is more provision for action, limited as that action is, in the economic and social field, and the activity in this field is to be continuous rather than occasional. Though the average individual thinks of the United Nations as a security organization, it is weak in this respect, and its greatest achievement will probably be found to lie in other fields.

GENERAL PROVISIONS OF THE CHARTER

With this survey of characteristic features in mind, we may now proceed to examine the system set up by the Charter, taking first those provisions which relate to the organization as a whole, and in later chapters the various organs and their functions.

82. PURPOSES AND PRINCIPLES

The Preamble and Articles 1 and 2 which purport to state the purposes and principles of the United Nations provide an unnecessarily repetitious statement of the aims of the United Nations. The Preamble itself is a conglomeration, the last resting place for various proposals which could not be included in the text, and this raises a question as to the legal force of preambular provisions. International law texts tell us that the preamble to a treaty has no legal validity, but it was asserted at the conference that matters put into the Preamble were as effective as if they had been put into the text.[25] It may be noted also that while the Preamble starts with the words, "We, the peoples," it ends with "our respective Governments . . . have agreed." "Peoples" are not known as subjects of international law, and in some countries only the monarch has the constitutional power to conclude a treaty.

Four paragraphs in Article 1 summarize the purposes of the United Nations, and each was long discussed. Briefly, the four purposes are to maintain international peace and security; to develop friendly relations among nations; to achieve international cooperation in broad fields and to develop the rights of individual human beings; and finally, to provide a common machinery for carrying out these various purposes.

Article 2, which requires the organization and its Members to act in accordance with stated principles, is not so well balanced. Actually, certain paragraphs deal with the organization as a whole, while others deal

[25] Goodrich and Hambro, pp. 54-55, *UNCIO Doc.* 944, I/1/34 (1). The question of *travaux préparatoires* appears in many other places in the Charter, notably in regard to a right of withdrawal.

only with the application of principles; one relates to non-members; the final paragraph is a blanket exception to almost everything in the Charter; and the Article as a whole deals only with security and makes no mention of any other purposes.

Paragraph 1 states the principle of "sovereign equality." Sovereignty is, of course, carefully protected throughout the Charter, and equality of legal rights and voting is assured outside the Security Council. Members agree, by paragraph 2, to fulfill their obligations under the Charter. This, of course, they are already bound by ratification to do, but the paragraph is of importance as stating clearly the important principle that the enjoyment of benefits by some depends upon the performance of duties by all—a lesson which was impressed upon observers by the experience of the League of Nations. The third paragraph requires that international disputes be settled, not only peacefully, but in such a manner as to create no disturbance of the peace, e.g., by injuring third parties. The next paragraph reinforces the requirement of peaceful adjustment by forbidding the use of force inconsistent with the purposes of the United Nations. This marks a definite improvement over earlier prohibitions against "war." The obligation of Members to give each other mutual assistance in enforcement action taken under the Charter is recognized in paragraph 5, which may be regarded as eliminating neutrality, at least insofar as enforcement action by the United Nations is concerned.

Paragraph 6 introduces an important element in the maintenance of peace by subjecting non-members to the power of the United Nations whenever this is necessary for the maintenance of peace and security. No legal obligation was put upon non-members since this could not be done without their consent; they are simply told that they must maintain peace, though they are later provided with opportunity to avail themselves of the procedures of the United Nations for the settlement of their disputes. This, it may be noted, is no more than any state could do to any other state in the past; now it is to be done by the community of nations. The effect of this paragraph is to take a long step toward universal jurisdiction, since it leaves little reason for remaining a non-member; it may be regarded as indispensable for the maintenance of peace throughout the world.

Paragraph 7 is a fundamental and difficult clause, one of the worst examples of several in which the Charter takes away with one hand what was given with the other. In the Dumbarton Oaks Proposals this clause was located in the section on pacific settlement of disputes and applied only to such disputes. At San Francisco it was moved back to become one of the principles applicable to the whole Charter. The restriction had been included in Article 15, paragraph 8, of the Covenant of the League of Nations where, however, decision was to be made by the Council, in accordance with international law, as to whether or not a matter was legally a domestic question. Both these requirements were dropped at San Francisco with the apparent result that each state could, upon its own assertion of domestic jurisdiction, exclude the United Nations from consideration of the matter.[26] The removal of the phrase to Article 2 made it apply, apparently, even to resolutions or recommendations by any United Nations organ, in any field, with the exception of Chapter VII.[27] We shall have a number of opportunities to consider the struggle over the effects of this controversial clause.

These purposes and principles are to some extent elaborated in other parts of the Charter, but they are called upon frequently as controlling directives in decisions. For example, it is nowhere else stated in the Charter that disputes should be settled in accordance with international law and justice. Many of the criticisms of the Dumbarton Oaks Proposals, as represented by proposed amendments, are to be found hidden away in these two articles, and they will probably be recalled by their authors. The only principles enunciated relate to peace and security, and the United Nations was furnished with no principles to guide it in other fields.

83. MEMBERSHIP

Two classes of membership are provided for in Chapter II of the Charter. Article 3 says that "those states which, having participated in the United Nations Conference on International Organization at San Francisco, or having previously signed the Declaration by United Nations," and which have ratified the Charter, shall be original Members. Fifty states participated in the conference and subsequently ratified the Charter; one other signed later.[28] Thus there are fifty-one original Members. Of these, the Byelorussian Republic, the Philippines, Syria, India, and others, might have had difficulty in qualifying under a political science definition of the word "state." It is sufficient to say that they

[26] Some reinforcement for this interpretation was added by Senator Connally's amendment to the Senate's consent to United States adherence to the optional clause of the Statute of the Court, "as determined by the United States."

[27] An amendment at San Francisco changed this exception so that it would not apply to all of what is now Chapter VII, but only to the "application of enforcement measures under Chapter 7."

[28] Poland did not have a recognized government at the time and signed on October 15, 1945.

were invited to attend by the Four Powers who summoned the conference, and that, for the purposes of the Charter, any Member would seem to be a state.

ADMISSION. Any other "peace-loving" state may be admitted to membership if, in the judgment of the Organization, it is able and willing to carry out the obligations which it would accept on becoming a member. The word "peace-loving" met with some criticism and has no clear meaning;[29] and no explanation was given to the word "able and willing." New Members may be admitted by vote of the General Assembly on recommendation of the Security Council. In this vote a veto may be used in the Security Council, and a two-thirds majority of the General Assembly is required. The first applications for membership were debated upon so strictly a political basis and with so little regard to the criteria stated that the General Assembly passed a resolution calling upon the Security Council to re-examine these applications for membership on the basis of their respective merits "as measured by the yardstick of the Charter in accordance with Article 4."[30] Since that time, the General Assembly has annually adopted resolutions calling upon the Security Council to change its ways and to admit applicants.[31] The struggle is entirely a political one, in which the United States and the Soviet Union have more than once reversed their positions to remain opposed to each other.[32] The General Assembly has twice, in its frustration, referred questions concerning admission to the International Court of Justice, with no more result than to embarrass that body, since it was known in advance that no attention would be given to its opinions by the Soviet Union.[33] A Special Committee on

[29] Original Members are apparently *ipso facto* peace-loving, from which it might be concluded that states which were at war with the Axis were peace-loving. By the Potsdam Declaration of August 2, 1945, the Four Powers announced that they would support applications for membership from neutral states with the exception of Spain.

[30] General Assembly Resolution 35 (I). The Roman numeral in parenthesis after an Assembly Resolution number indicates the year in which it was adopted.

[31] The story is too long to be told here. The reader is referred to the Report of the Special Committee on the Admission of New Members, *U.N. Doc.* A/2400, and to Staff Study No. 3, entitled "The Problem of Membership in the United Nations."

[32] On the question of diplomatic recognition of an applicant as a qualification for membership, and with regard to "package deals." The United States originally supported both, but, when they were rejected by the Soviet Union, took the position that each case must be considered separately on its own merits. See the citations in the preceding note; also Brookings, *Organization*, Chap. xi.

[33] In the first request for an advisory opinion, the Court was asked whether admission could be made dependent upon conditions not expressly stated in the Charter; the Court said no. *I.C.J. Reports*, 1948, p. 57.

In the second request, the Court was asked whether admission could be effected by the General Assembly when the Security Council, because of a veto, or because of failure to obtain the requisite majority, made no recommendation? The Court held that the Security Council must make an affirmative recommendation, without which the applicant could not be admitted. *I.C.J. Reports*, 1950, p. 4.

Admission of New Members considered various proposals for ending the deadlock, including some which would interpret the Charter so as to get round the veto, but was unable to find a solution.

MEMBERSHIP IN THE UNITED NATIONS (1956)

ORIGINAL MEMBERS

Argentina	El Salvador	Panama
Australia	Ethiopia	Paraguay
Belgium	France	Peru
Bolivia	Greece	Philippine Commonwealth
Brazil	Guatemala	Poland
Byelorussian Soviet	Haiti	Saudi Arabia
Socialist Republic	Honduras	Syria
Canada	India	Turkey
Chile	Iran	Ukrainian Soviet Socialist Republic
China	Iraq	Union of South Africa
Colombia	Lebanon	Union of Soviet Socialist Republics
Costa Rica	Liberia	United Kingdom
Cuba	Luxembourg	United States of America
Czechoslovakia	Mexico	Uruguay
Denmark	Netherlands	Venezuela
Dominican Republic	New Zealand	Yugoslavia
Ecuador	Nicaragua	
Egypt	Norway	

ADMITTED MEMBERS

Afghanistan (1946)	Iceland (1946)	Pakistan (1947)
Albania (1955)	Indonesia (1950)	Portugal (1955)
Austria (1955)	Ireland (1955)	Rumania (1955)
Bulgaria (1955)	Israel (1949)	Spain (1955)
Burma (1948)	Italy (1955)	Sudan (1956)
Cambodia (1955)	Jordan (1955)	Sweden (1946)
Ceylon (1955)	Laos (1955)	Thailand (1946)
Finland (1955)	Libya (1955)	Yemen (1947)
Hungary (1955)	Nepal (1955)	

APPLICANTS NOT YET ADMITTED

Republic of Korea	Japan	Viet Minh
North Korea	Mongolia	Viet Nam

At the Tenth Assembly, in 1955, the Soviet Union, in an unexpected change of policy, was willing to bargain, and seventeen new Members (including Sudan, admitted at the next Assembly) were added to the list. The bargain did not include all applicants, nor Switzerland and Germany, which are about the only states which have not applied for membership. There are other potential states, so that the General Assembly might have as many as a hundred members. Though this makes for an unwieldy body (already the assembly hall is having to be altered), it means almost complete universality for the United

Nations and in this sense strengthens it far beyond the League of Nations. On the other hand, it raises many questions concerning responsible membership, distribution of voting power, blocs, and balance of power between West and East. Not many of those admitted can contribute much to the United Nations, but it is important to bring as many states as possible within its sphere of operation. Admission to the United Nations is a matter of political bargaining and the qualifications set in the Charter have little to do with it in practice.

SUSPENSION AND EXPULSION. The use of suspension (Article 5) as a penalty is a new idea, not found in the League of Nations. Both its extent and its use are limited; the suspension is not from membership, but from the "exercise of the rights and privileges of membership"; and it can be employed only against a state "against which preventive or enforcement action has been taken by the Security Council." The initial action must be taken upon recommendation by the Security Council and subject to the use of the veto; the General Assembly, by a two-thirds vote, then approves or disapproves the recommendation. Restoration of rights to a suspended Member is, however, given by the Security Council alone. The rights which might be lost by a suspended state would presumably be such as participation, or voting or holding office, in organs of the United Nations.

EXPULSION. A Member may also be expelled, but this penalty is limited to states which have "persistently violated the Principles contained in the present Charter." Since this provision would operate in opposition to the concept of universality held by many, and since the expelled state would no longer be subject to the jurisdiction of the United Nations, there was much opposition to it, but the determination of the U.S.S.R. that it be included prevailed. Neither suspension nor withdrawal has been considered this far.

WITHDRAWAL. There was much debate as to whether a right of withdrawal should be stated in the Charter, and the Charter does not mention it. Nevertheless, it is maintained that there is a right on the part of each Member to withdraw. This is based upon an interpretative resolution adopted by the conference which emphasized heavily the duties of membership, but admitted that the organization would not seek to compel a Member if, because of exceptional circumstances or because of an amendment, that Member should feel constrained to withdraw.[34] This method of statement represented a compromise, since it is probable that neither those who wished to include in the Charter a

[34] *UNCIO Doc.* 1178 I/2/76 (2), quoted in Goodrich and Hambro, pp. 143-44; see also the *Report to the President*, pp. 48-49; Hearings, pp. 232-40, 324-27, 346-48.

statement of a right of withdrawal, nor those who wished to exclude it, could have commanded the necessary two-thirds majority. The result is a problem for the international lawyer, who would usually hold that a signatory state could not be relieved of its obligations under a treaty in the absence of provisions therein by which these obligations could be changed, and who must ask also concerning the extent to which conference proceedings, not included in the text of the Charter (*travaux préparatoires*) and not ratified, can be regarded as expressing the meaning of the Charter.[35]

The Charter is not conceived in terms of universal membership, but in fact it moves a long way in that direction. This is because membership itself means little loss of sovereignty, while on the other hand a non-member may be compelled just as effectively as can a Member to observe the obligations of the Charter with regard to security. The provisions for suspension and expulsion also point in this direction. A suspended Member is in much the same position as an expelled Member, which is to say, as a non-member, since in any of these three cases the United Nations may exercise its security powers over a state, whether or not it is a Member or able to exercise the rights of membership. Very little is to be gained, then, through a refusal of membership; on the contrary, the non-member may wish to participate in the disposition of his own case, and may thereby be encouraged to join.

84. LEGAL CHARACTER

The constitutional system and legal personality of the United Nations is derived from several instruments, and not merely from the Charter itself. Article 104 of the Charter makes it clear, to a greater extent than the Covenant did for the League, that the United Nations is a legal person, having rights and duties under international law. The General Convention on Privileges and Immunities says in Article I: "The United Nations shall possess juridical personality"; and Article I of the agreement with Switzerland (a non-member) concerning the grounds of the Palais des Nations (Ariana Site) is even more definite: "The Swiss Federal Council recognizes the international personality and legal capacity of the United Nations."[36] If any doubt remained after such commitments, it was disposed of by the International Court of Justice, which said (in the case resulting from the assassination of

[35] H. W. Briggs, "Power Politics and International Organization," *A.J.*, 39 (1945), pp. 673-74.

[36] For these and other such instruments, see Handbook on the Legal Status, Privileges and Immunities of the United Nations, *U.N. Doc. ST/LEG/2.*

Count Bernadotte, in which Israel paid damages to the United Nations, according to international law):

> In the opinion of the Court, the Organization was intended to exercise and enjoy, and is in fact exercising and enjoying, functions and rights which can only be explained on the basis of the possession of a large measure of international personality. . . . Accordingly, the Court has come to the conclusion that the Organization is an international person. This is not the same thing as saying that it is a State, which it certainly is not, or that its legal personality and rights are the same as those of a State. Still less is it the same thing as saying that it is a "super-State," whatever that expression may mean. . . . What it does mean is that it is a subject of international law and capable of possessing international rights and duties, and that it has capacity to maintain its rights by bringing international claims.[37]

PRIVILEGES AND IMMUNITIES. It was observed, in an earlier chapter, that one of the commonly accepted prerogatives of the international legal person is the right to privileges and immunities. Article 105 lays down the principle that the "Organization shall enjoy in the territory of each of its Members such privileges and immunities as are necessary for the fulfillment of its purposes"; and provides also that representatives of Members and officials (i.e., of the Secretariat, who are to be distinguished from delegates) shall have privileges and immunities such as "are necessary for the independent exercise of their functions in connection with the Organization." The General Assembly was to work out details, and did so in the General Convention on Privileges and Immunities, which has been accepted by a majority of the Members, but not by the most important one of all, the host state.[38] Delegates and officials must therefore depend, in the United States, upon the International Organizations Immunities Act passed by Congress in 1945—under which the privileges can be withdrawn either by Congress or by the President at will. This act speaks in terms of the older privileges and immunities under international law, whereas the United Nations instruments limit privileges and immunities to those necessary for carrying out the functions assigned. The Headquarters Agreement also has some provisions concerning immunities, and the result is some-

---

[37] In the case of Reparation for Injuries Suffered in the Service of the United Nations, *I.C.J. Reports 1949*, p. 179.

[38] The United States objected to exemption from income tax and from national service for its nationals in the United Nations. The latter raises a question as to the relative importance of service in the United Nations and in a national army. The former objection has resulted in great confusion. Few states have similar income taxes, and if a tax is levied on income, there is a difference in take-home pay. To equalize this, the United Nations assessed its own officials; but since Congress did not exempt Americans from income tax, they now pay two assessments and the United Nations refunds them tax paid to the United States. This refund is taxed, and so on indefinitely —an absurd situation, for which the negligence of Congress is responsible.

what confusing. A few cases have appeared in the courts,[39] but the problem—which involves many persons in a crowded area—has been handled on both sides with common sense and there has been little friction.

Under the General Convention, the United Nations is authorized to issue a *laissez-passer*—a sort of a passport—to its personnel, which signatories are bound to accept; the United States, however, refuses to recognize it. It is interesting to note that most Members have established "permanent missions" at the New York headquarters, a practice which might be compared with the embassies located at national capitals.

HEADQUARTERS. Another fundamental constitutional instrument is the Headquarters Agreement between the United States and the United Nations, which also is conceived of in terms of performance of functions rather than in terms of sovereign right. The headquarters area—roughly between Forty-Second and Forty-Eighth streets and between First Avenue and the East River in New York City—was agreed upon as a result of the gift of John D. Rockefeller, Jr.; and the location in a crowded metropolitan area has been criticized.[40] The United States made an initial loan of sixty-five millions dollars, with which the headquarters buildings were constructed. This area remains part of the United States, and the laws of the United States may operate therein, except insofar as exceptions are made by the Headquarters Agreement and by regulations adopted by the United Nations. Such regulations supersede the law of the United States; only three have been adopted thus far.[41]

On the other hand, no United States official may enter the area in

[39] *Westchester Co. v. Ranallo*, 187 Misc., N.Y.S. 2nd 31; *City of New Rochelle v. Page Sharp*, 91 N.Y.S. 2nd 290; *Tsiang v. Tsiang*, 86 N.Y.S. 2nd 556; *U.S. v. Coplon*, 84 F. Supp. 472 and *A.J.*, XLIII, p. 810.

[40] Political considerations, such as Soviet and United States dislike for Geneva, or desire to maintain the interest of the American people, led to decision to locate headquarters in the United States; its location on the Eastern seaboard was a compromise beween those who wanted Europe and those who wanted San Francisco; it could not be located in the South because of the prevalent prejudice there from which persons of color might suffer. Theoretically, such a headquarters should be an independent unit, entirely independent of any state, such as an island or a peninsula; but this would involve providing, at enormous cost, such needs as public utilities, civil and criminal law facilities, communications, and perhaps munitions factories. See C. W. Jenks, *The Headquarters of International Institutions* (London, 1945); Report of the Headquarters Commission, *U.N. Doc.* A/69, October, 1946.

[41] (1) A social security system for the staff, covering all risks and relieving the United Nations of liability under American laws. (2) The secretary-general to determine qualifications for professional or special occupational services. (3) The secretary-general to control the operation of services, facilities and retail establishments (thus enabling the bar to stay open on American election days!). See G.A. Resolution 604(VI).

official capacity unless invited to do so. If a crime were committed within the area, United Nations guards would doubtless act, but would call in the New York police and turn the criminal over to them for trial in United States courts. The use of American law, courts and police is a convenience; the United Nations would not be justified in setting up its own judicial system for the few matters which it might have to handle. It is, however, independent of control by the United States—with the exception, perhaps, of fire protection and regulations.

The only serious problem under the Headquarters Agreement arose from the concern of the American people over communism around 1950. This led to fears, largely on the part of persons unfriendly to the United Nations, that there might be, among those coming to the United Nations, some Communists whose admission would endanger the existence of the United States. Nothing could be done to stop official delegates—communist nations are Members as well as others—but representatives of nongovernmental organizations, newspaper men, etc., were not so well protected. They were, however, entitled to admission to the United Nations and when several had been refused admission by United States authorities, the Legal Department of the Secretariat issued a memorandum charging the United States with violation of the agreement and suggesting that arbitration would be necessary if the practice were continued.[42] Negotiations seem to have settled the conflict; it arose out of a temporary emotional disturbance of which the American people are already ashamed.

85. BUDGET AND FINANCES

The control of the budget and of the finances of the United Nations in general is wholly in the hands of the General Assembly, thus giving it a large degree of control over other organs. By Article 17, the Assembly apportions expenses among Members, who are obligated to submit to this assessment; an automatic penalty for failure to pay is provided for in Article 19. No state has yet fallen so far into arrears as to be penalized.

It should be noted first that there are several budgets to be taken into consideration in estimating the cost of the whole United Nations system. There is the regular budget of the United Nations itself; there are several others based on voluntary contributions by Members rather than upon assessment; and each specialized agency has its own inde-

---

[42] Debates on this subject took place in the Economic and Social Council for the most part; see the 676th, 678th and 743rd meetings. The Memorandum of the Legal Department is *U.N. Doc.* E/2397.

pendent budget. There is also a Working Capital Fund, used as a reserve from which to draw in case of emergency. The cost of the enforcement action in Korea must be separately estimated.

Members exercise the strictest control and the greatest economy over the finances of the United Nations, as was true with the League of Nations also. The budget is prepared through estimates made by departments, and these are submitted to the Secretary-General for shaping in accordance with his financial policies. The figures submitted by him are examined by an Advisory Committee on Administrative and Budgetary questions, which usually suggests reductions. The General Assembly refers both sets of figures to its Fifth Committee, which consults with the advisory committee. Supplemental estimates may be added. The process is completed by a resolution of the General Assembly adopting the budget. There is also a thorough audit system. The United Nations offers very little opportunity for wasteful extravagance.

The accompanying table seeks to summarize the expenditures of the United Nations and to show the share paid by the United States. The cost of the United Nations itself during the ten years there shown is a little more than $418,000,000; of this the United States has paid something over $130,000,000, a per capita cost to the American taxpayer of seventy-one cents, or seven cents per year. Belonging to the various specialized agencies costs him about four cents more per year. His share of the voluntary contributions to technical assistance and various relief programs amounts to some forty-one cents apiece, on annual average. Thus, the cost to the American citizen of the entire United Nations system, including required assessments and voluntary contributions, is about fifty-two cents per year. To this should be added, by way of striking contrast, the Korean action—also a voluntary action, not part of the budget of the United Nations—which cost him an estimated $37.50 per year (three years only). His required payments for membership in all the various organizations amount to less than twelve cents per year—a pathetic figure for the great organization which he expects to provide him with both peace and prosperity.

In fact, it is true that the presence of the headquarters in the United States brings to this country far more money than it pays to the United Nations. Probably half of the regular budget is spent in this country—which pays about a third of that budget. Aside from this, there is the spending of thousands of persons who are brought to New York to work for the United Nations or to conduct business with it in one way or another. It cannot be maintained that the United States is losing money on the United Nations.

COST OF THE UNITED NATIONS FOR 10 YEARS INCLUDING SHARE PAID BY THE UNITED STATES[43]

(In millions of dollars; * indicates less than $100,000)

	1946	U.S.	1947	U.S.	1948	U.S.	1949	U.S.	1950	U.S.	1951	U.S.	1952	U.S.	1953	U.S.	1954	U.S.	1955	U.S.	Total U.N.	Total U.S.
A. The United Nations	19.3	6.1	27.3	9.1	38.4	10.9	42.6	13.8	43.7	16.6	48.6	13.5	50.2	16.4	49.3	15.4	48.5	15.1	50.2	13.4	418.1	130.3
B. Specialized Agencies																						
ILO	2.7	0.5	3.7	0.4	4.1	0.5	5.0	1.0	5.2	0.8	5.8	1.2	6.4	1.4	6.5	1.5	6.8	1.4	7.1	1.5	53.3	10.2
FAO	0.4	0.6	5.1	1.2	4.1	1.2	4.6	1.2	4.5	1.2	4.6	1.4	4.8	1.3	5.1	1.6	5.5	1.5	6.0	1.6	44.7	12.8
UNESCO	1.0	—	6.2	—	6.7	3.5	7.8	3.6	7.1	2.8	7.9	2.8	8.7	2.7	7.9	2.8	9.0	2.8	9.8	3.1	72.1	24.1
ICAO	0.7	0.1	1.6	0.3	2.3	0.5	2.3	0.5	2.9	0.4	3.0	0.4	3.1	0.7	3.1	0.8	3.1	0.7	3.2	0.8	25.3	5.2
UPU	0.1	*	0.1	*	0.8	*	0.3	*	0.3	*	0.3	*	0.4	*	0.4	*	0.4	*	0.5	*	3.6	*
WHO	0.1	—	1.7	—	4.4	—	4.7	1.8	6.1	1.9	6.2	3.0	7.9	2.4	8.1	2.8	8.1	2.9	9.2	3.0	56.5	17.8
ITU	—	—	—	—	0.8	*	3.0	*	1.6	0.1	1.3	0.4	1.6	0.1	1.5	0.1	1.3	0.1	1.4	0.1	12.5	0.9
WMO	—	—	—	—	—	—	—	—	—	—	0.1	*	0.1	*	0.3	*	0.3	*	0.4	*	1.2	*
Total: S.A.'s	5.0	1.2	18.4	1.9	23.2	5.7	27.7	7.2	27.7	7.2	29.2	9.2	33.0	8.6	32.9	9.6	34.5	9.4	37.6	10.1	269.2	71.0
C. Total: UN & S.A.'s	24.3	7.3	45.7	11.0	61.6	16.6	70.3	21.9	71.4	23.8	77.8	22.7	83.2	25.0	82.2	25.0	83.0	24.5	87.8	23.5	687.3	201.3
D. Voluntary Programs																						
UNTA	—	—	—	—	—	—	—	—	—	—	6.6	12.0	22.3	11.4	22.7	8.2	24.7	8.5	27.8	16.4	104.1	56.5
UNWRA	—	—	—	—	—	—	39.1	8.0	19.2	10.0	42.1	25.4	26.8	50.0	29.2	16.0	29.2	15.0	61.3	16.7	246.9	141.1
UNICEF	—	—	0.8	—	31.5	32.8	46.7	25.4	35.9	15.3	22.6	7.1	13.5	—	12.5	6.6	14.5	9.8	15.0	12.5	193.0	109.5
UNKRA	—	—	—	—	—	—	—	—	0.5	—	4.1	—	53.0	10.0	28.7	40.7	58.1	23.1	17.5	19.0	161.9	92.8
IRO	—	—	75.7	—	132.2	71.0	119.4	70.6	85.4	70.4	—	25.0	—	—	—	—	—	—	—	—	412.7	237.0
ICAO	—	—	—	—	0.6	2.0	1.1	0.9	0.5	1.4	0.6	1.5	0.6	1.6	0.6	1.6	0.6	1.7	0.5		10.7	5.1
Total: Voluntary			76.5	—	163.7	104.4	207.2	105.1	141.9	96.2	76.8	70.1	117.1	72.0	94.7	72.1	128.1	57.0	123.3	65.1	1129.3	642.0
E. Total: Voluntary and Required																					1816.6	843.3

43 These figures are compiled from several tables and are not precise, but they give a sufficiently accurate view of the cost of the United Nations system, and the contributions of the United States thereto. See, *United States Contributions to International Organizations,* 84th Congress, 2d Session, House Doc. No. 337, especially p. 64; and *Staff Study* No. 6.

The percentages of contributions of Members are shown in the following table.

UNITED NATIONS SCALE OF ASSESSMENTS FOR
1956, 1957, 1958

(From Report of the Committee on Contributions, Eleventh Session)

Afghanistan	0.06	Israel	0.16
Albania	0.04	Italy	2.08
Argentina	1.17	Jordan	0.04
Australia	1.65	Laos	0.04
Austria	0.36	Lebanon	0.05
Belgium	1.27	Liberia	0.04
Bolivia	0.05	Libya	0.04
Brazil	1.09	Luxembourg	0.06
Bulgaria	0.14	Mexico	0.70
Burma	0.10	Nepal	0.04
Byelorussian S.S. Republic	0.48	Netherlands	1.15
Cambodia	0.04	New Zealand	0.43
Canada	3.15	Nicaragua	0.04
Ceylon	0.11	Norway	0.49
Chile	0.30	Pakistan	0.55
China	5.14	Panama	0.05
Colombia	0.37	Paraguay	0.04
Costa Rica	0.04	Peru	0.15
Cuba	0.27	Philippines	0.41
Czechoslovakia	0.84	Poland	1.56
Denmark	0.66	Portugal	0.25
Dominican Republic	0.05	Rumania	0.50
Ecuador	0.05	Saudi Arabia	0.07
Egypt	0.36	Spain	1.14
El Salvador	0.06	Sudan	0.12
Ethiopia	0.11	Sweden	1.46
Finland	0.37	Syria	0.08
France	5.70	Thailand	0.16
Greece	0.20	Turkey	0.63
Guatemala	0.07	Ukrainian S.S. Republic	1.85
Haiti	0.04	Union of South Africa	0.71
Honduras	0.04	Union of Soviet S. Republics	13.96
Hungary	0.46	United Kingdom of Great Britain	
Iceland	0.04	and Northern Ireland	7.81
India	2.97	United States of America	33.33
Indonesia	0.51	Uruguay	0.16
Iran	0.27	Venezuela	0.43
Iraq	0.12	Yemen	0.04
Ireland	0.19	Yugoslavia	0.36

Each Member, if all paid the same amount, would contribute about 1.25 per cent of the budget; actually, only thirteen pay this much. Fourteen states pay the smallest amount, 0.04 per cent; sixty states pay less than 1 per cent, and twenty-six of these pay 0.1 per cent or less. This is a matter of importance when one thinks of voting strength, for each state has one vote. The United States pays one third of the budget, but has only one vote; the twenty Latin-American states together pay not quite 6 per cent, but have twenty votes. The five Great Powers pay over 70 per cent, but do not have as many votes as six Arab states who together pay only 0.9 per cent, or as the Asian states, who have eight votes but pay only 8 per cent. Thus the most responsible states—for the apportionment measures strength in various ways—can easily be outvoted by the least responsible; the results of this situation will be seen later.

86. AMENDMENT

The provisions for amending the Charter were much argued at San Francisco and, as adopted, have been much criticized. It is one of the chief lessons of history that change cannot be stayed; a constitution which cannot be changed by regular methods will be changed, or evaded, by irregular methods, or by violence. We shall have occasion to notice the methods of securing change through interpretation or disuse of Charter provisions.

Amendments are negotiated within the General Assembly, where they may be adopted by a two-thirds vote of *all* Members, but they enter into force only when they have been ratified "in accordance with their respective constitutional processes by two-thirds of all the Members, including the five permanent members of the Security Council." It was this extension of the veto to the procedure of amendment which aroused opposition. It was observed that these five states were arbitrarily named and that if one ceased to be a Great Power it could not be unseated, nor could another state which had become a Great Power hope to gain a permanent seat. The difficulty is illustrated by the debate over the seat held by Nationalist China, which is clearly no longer a Great Power, and the suggestion that a permanent seat be given to India which had meanwhile grown in strength. Nor could any part of the special powers given to the Great Powers be taken away from them. It was this situation which produced the clamor for a right of withdrawal; various states felt that they might wish to leave the United Nations if these powers were abused.

In an effort to allay the discontent aroused by this provision, Article 109 was added. This makes it possible to call a conference for general revision of the Charter, whenever two thirds of all Members of the General Assembly and any seven Members of the Security Council approve. In case a conference should not be called before the tenth annual session of the General Assembly, the question is automatically put upon the agenda of that Assembly and the vote as to whether such a revision conference shall be called is in this case by a bare majority of all Members of the General Assembly and any seven Members of the Security Council. The conference method offers little improvement in the situation for, though a conference for proposing amendments can be called without a veto, the veto applies to the ratification necessary to put the amendment into effect. The Great Powers felt that they could not risk their large responsibilities being changed by any sort of a majority of those whose responsibilities are not so great. For this feeling on their part, there is some justification, and the conflict between theory and practicality remains.

Chapter 12

THE UNITED NATIONS: ORGANS

According to Article 7 of the Charter, there are established as the principal organs of the United Nations: a General Assembly, a Security Council, an Economic and Social Council, a Trusteeship Council, an International Court of Justice, and a Secretariat.

THE GENERAL ASSEMBLY

While most emphasis was originally laid upon security and the Security Council, the General Assembly was, and increasingly is, the most important of the organs.[1] It is the only organ to which all Members belong, and they participate in it upon a basis of voting equality. A large majority of Members are small states and in the Assembly they find their opportunity; after some hesitation, they have seized the reins and have been leading the Assembly (in matters in which they have a common interest) at breakneck speed, disregarding the guideposts of the Charter and moving into fields which were intended to be restricted.

87. ORGANIZATION

Members of the General Assembly are not persons, but states, and the persons who participate in its work do so as instructed representatives of member states. Each Member is allowed five delegates upon the floor (though it has only one vote) and provision is made for

[1] Concerning the General Assembly, see John Foster Dulles, "The General Assembly," *Foreign Affairs*, 24 (1945); H. Field Haviland, *The Political Role of the General Assembly* (United Nations Study No. 7, Carnegie Endowment, 1951); L. M. Goodrich, "The Development of the General Assembly," *Int. Con.*, No. 471 (1951); and the annual autumn issue of *Int. Con.* entitled "Issues before the —th Assembly." The *Report to Congress* and the *Annual Review* provide current summaries for each session of the General Assembly.

seating an equal number of advisers behind them. Since most of the work is done in the six main committees, it would appear that at least five persons would be needed by each Member, aside from a working staff behind them. The larger states send delegations of a hundred or more; many of the smaller states cannot afford this and their few representatives must run from one committee to another. Many of them have very few persons trained for this sort of work.

The Assembly elects its president, seven vice-presidents, and seven committee chairmen. These constitute the General Committee, which manages the work of the Assembly, in the sense of arranging the agenda, etc.; actually, the Assembly does not permit centralized control of its activity. There are six main committees: (1) Political and Security; (2) Economic and Financial; (3) Social, Humanitarian and Cultural; (4) Trusteeship; (5) Administrative and Budgetary; (6) Legal. The work of the first committee became so large that an *ad hoc* political committee has been added from year to year. Every Member is represented on all main committees. There are also eight standing committees and some seventy *ad hoc* bodies of various kinds, some of which have been renewed so often that they are almost standing committees. They range from full membership bodies, such as the Interim Committee, to one person, such as the Mediator for Palestine.

88. PROCEDURE

A provisional agenda is prepared by the Secretary-General and circulated some sixty days in advance of the annual meeting; a supplementary list is prepared twenty days ahead; and additional items may be added after the session begins if a majority of Members approve.[2] Any Member may propose an item for the agenda, which has ranged from sixty-five to seventy-eight items per session (after the first and heavier session). The annual meeting (Article 20) is supposed to begin on the third Tuesday after the second day of September, but such factors as a national election in the United States may intervene to affect this date. Four sessions have been adjourned to continue later in the year, and there have been special sessions. This trend toward continuous session seems now to have been slowed down. Another reason for the length of the sessions—the average is ninety-four days—is the difficulty of cutting short long-winded orators. The rules of procedure allow for some control but the chairman rarely

[2] An item is rarely excluded from the agenda even at a late date. The "additional items" are supposed to be of an urgent character, but they have included such things as a Columbus memorial lighthouse, or translation of the classics.

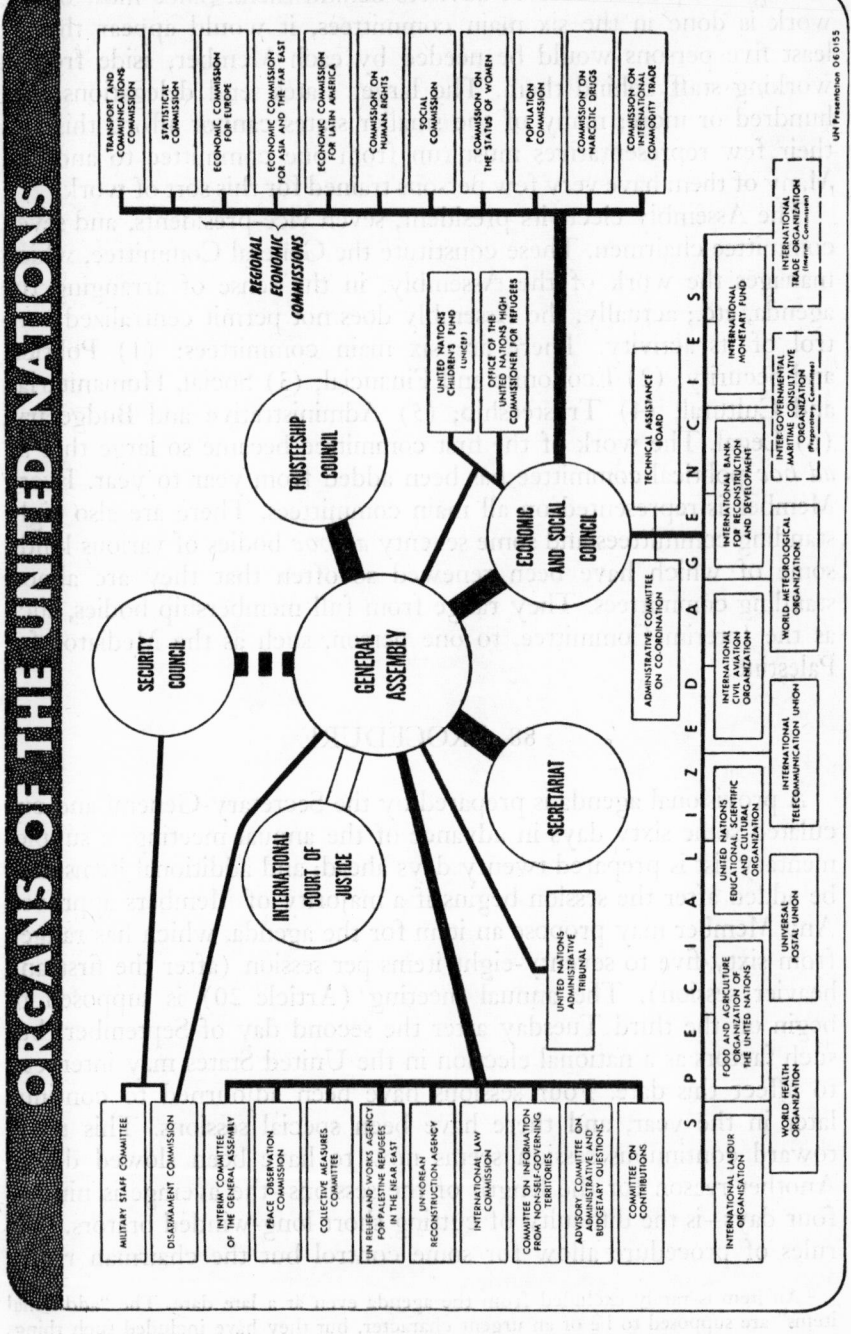

dares to halt the representative of a sovereign state. For plenary meetings, the quorum required is a majority, both for calling the meeting to order and for taking a vote; in committee, the presence of a third of the membership allows work to go on, but a majority must be present before a vote can be taken.

VOTING IN THE GENERAL ASSEMBLY. The rule of unanimity, which prevailed in conferences of the past and in the League of Nations, is abandoned in all organs of the United Nations. For the General Assembly, Article 18 of the Charter requires a majority of those "present and voting." This phrase has been interpreted not to count abstentions and absences; it is thus possible for a motion to be adopted by a single voting Member—all others being absent or abstaining. There have been occasions on which more than half the Assembly were recorded as abstaining. The motivation for abstention varies, but its effect is in general to allow the more determined Members to have their way.

Certain subjects, however, as designated by Article 18 and by the Rules of Procedure, call for a two-thirds majority. These relate to action under Articles 11, paragraph 2; 23; 61; 86, paragraph 1c; 5; 6; 17; Chapters XII and XIII. The Assembly may decide, by a majority, that on a certain measure a two-thirds majority is required. Finally, we may note that the process of amendment of the Charter calls for a two-thirds majority of *all* Members.

Each Member has one vote. The vote of Liberia weighs as much as that of the Soviet Union; 126,000 Icelanders have as much voting power as four hundred million Indians; the population of the Americas below the Rio Grande has twenty times as many votes as the population north of it, almost the same in number. Decisions taken in the General Assembly (except under Article 17 and 19) are not binding upon Members; otherwise, one may feel sure that equality of voting would not be maintained, or else that the larger states would have withdrawn from the United Nations. The decisions taken by the anti-colonial majority have alarmed the larger Members; it is conceivable that a majority of small states—now enlarged by the newly admitted Members—could vote into the regular budget large sums of money for financial assistance to the underdeveloped countries, which sums would have to be paid, for the most part, by the larger states. The situation is one which encourages irresponsibility, for those who have the votes do not have the ability to carry out the decisions taken and the responsibility for them must rest upon a small minority of states who may have opposed the decision. Provisions were put into the Covenant of Human Rights which many of the states which voted for them would be unable to observe, because of their own social or economic habits or financial inability. Sir Carl Berendsen once called attention to this in caustic fashion:

> The Member State sponsoring that resolution was a country that was not a party to such a convention. The representatives will vividly recall the eloquent address of the representative of another nation . . . who began his speech with the frank, honest and manly admission that he was not familiar with the subject; but he did not allow that to deter him from a most vehement and moving admonition to those who were familiar with the subject and who had undertaken certain obligations under the conventions. . . .[3]

There is also a tendency to bloc-voting. The blocs vary in consistency; they are not always geographic, and a state may be in one bloc for one purpose and in another bloc for another purpose. The Latin American bloc is the best organized, often meeting in caucus to decide how to vote on an issue. The Soviet bloc is the most consistent in its voting. A combination of Arab and Asian blocs is often lined up against the NATO bloc; and many Latin American states will line up with the Arabs and Asians to form the anti-colonial majority which has pushed the Assembly into many difficult situations.

As a result of this situation, more consideration is being given to the subject, hitherto considered doctrinaire, of weighted voting. No proposal in this direction has been made; it would be difficult to achieve in the face of the large majority of small states which would be unwilling to give up their present advantage based upon equal votes. It would also be difficult to find a formula which could be agreed upon as fairly representing the weight of a Member in the United Nations. The matter is of some importance in the sense that no strengthening of the powers of the Assembly—e.g., legislative— can be anticipated so long as the present voting situation continues.[4]

LANGUAGES. There are five official languages for the United Nations into which all official records are supposed to be translated: Chinese, English, French, Russian, and Spanish. The two working languages for debate purposes are English and French, and speeches made in any other language must be interpreted into these two languages.[5] This may double or triple the working time of the Assembly or committee. Simultaneous interpretation—a remarkable feat—saves some

[3] General Assembly, Second Session, *Official Records*, 107th Plenary Meeting, p. 695.

[4] As to weighted voting, see Louis B. Sohn, in the Ninth Report of the C.S.O.P., and also in *A.J.*, 40 (1946), p. 71. A proper measure has been sought in population, literacy, military or financial strength, contribution to the budget, etc. Apparently a formula needs to be found which would combine all such elements.

[5] In 1948, the Spanish-speaking group, with the aid of friendly blocs, put through a motion to make Spanish a third working language—at an estimated additional yearly cost of $300,000.

time. As each speech is given, interpreters in the glass-enclosed, sound-proof chambers may be seen hard at work, and the listener may hear through headphones an interpretation in the language he chooses by punching the proper button. A large part of the staff is interpreters and translators and their work and that of those who put it into print consumes a large part of the budget. The efforts to find a common language—such as Esperanto—have never taken hold of peoples' imagination; on the contrary, the strong nationalism of today tends to produce more languages.

89. FUNCTIONS

The Charter gives to the Assembly the widest range of function, and the Assembly has in practice expanded these functions until it feels free to discuss and make recommendations upon practically any subject (Article 10). It can only recommend, however; it has no authority over Members except in the one instance of assessing dues and penalizing for arrears. It is primarily a forum, "the town-meeting of the world," and this is a function of enormous importance. Any point of trouble in the international scene may here be brought out into the open, and when the limelight of public opinion has been focused upon such a matter, even the greatest of states will pay attention. The resolutions of the General Assembly are not legally binding, but they carry much weight, and great pressure may be put behind them.

The Assembly is directly related to all other organs. It receives an annual report from each of them which it may discuss and criticize.[6] To some extent, it distributes work to each of them, though each has its own function. Thus it exercises some degree of supervisory power over all activities of the United Nations; and its budgetary and financial powers enable it to exercise some control over all organs.

In practice, the Assembly has not hesitated to fill any vacuum. The Charter did not provide for all possible contingencies, and the Members claim in the Assembly a reserve power which enables them to take care of such an unanticipated problem as the Palestine mandate. If the Charter omits authorization for the United Nations to make treaties, the Assembly assumes that responsibility; if the Security Council fails in its "primary responsibility" for maintaining peace, the Assembly adopts the Uniting for Peace Resolution; if the meaning of "self-determination" is not clear, the Assembly goes ahead with

[6] It has never taken up the report of the Security Council; it merely "takes note" of its receipt.

its own interpretation of what the Charter intended. There is no doubt that the General Assembly is the most important of all the organs and, insofar as integration is effected among the various organs, it is the achievement of the Assembly.

To many observers, this freedom of action of the Assembly is excellent; it allows the United Nations to "do things," to make progress in the direction which they desire. To others, however, the expanding activity of the General Assembly appears as a violation of Charter restrictions and as a dangerous or offensive invasion into the domestic affairs of member states, made possible by a majority of votes. This controversy will appear in many connections in the following pages; at this point, it may be noted that if Assembly resolutions were binding upon Members, it is probable that more than one Member would have withdrawn, charging that the action taken by the majority was unconstitutional. There is little likelihood that more powers will be given to the General Assembly if that body, through a voting majority, can interpret the Charter in such a way as to evade the restrictions set by the Charter upon its action.

MAINTENANCE OF PEACE AND SECURITY. In the League of Nations, council and assembly were coordinate bodies, each able to do most of what the other could do, such as, for example, handling disputes and maintaining peace. In the United Nations, a clear division of functions between the Security Council and the General Assembly was planned, though by now it is much dimmed. The Security Council was given "primary responsibility for the maintenance of peace and security," but the General Assembly was not excluded from this function. By paragraph 1 of Article 11, the Assembly "may consider the general principles of cooperation in the maintenance of international peace and security"; by paragraph 2, it may discuss specific questions—i.e., a particular dispute—and, with one exception, may make recommendations concerning them. A dispute may, by Article 35, be brought before the General Assembly by a state, Member or not, as well as before the Security Council; and the Assembly, in such a case, can do all that the Council could do, which is to make a recommendation.

There has been some debate, arising out of articles 11, paragraph 2, and 12, as to whether the Assembly may act on a matter which is before the Security Council. The latter article forbids the Assembly to make recommendations with regard to (but not to discuss) any dispute or situation in respect of which the Council is "exercising the functions assigned to it." What does this mean, and who is to judge? If the Council decided that it ought not to consider a case brought before it, would it have exercised its function? The Secretary-General is instructed by Article 12, paragraph 2, to notify the Assembly as soon as the Council ceases to deal with a matter; but it is not clear how the list of such matters is made up by the Secretary-General. However, the Security Council may vote to refer a matter to the General Assembly, as it did in the Spanish case; this is a procedure subject to the veto, and such a proposal was vetoed in the Greek frontier case.[7] On the other hand, a motion to drop a matter from the agenda is a procedural matter, not subject to the veto; and once dropped by the Security Council, the General Assembly is free to take it up—as it did with regard to the Greek frontier case.

DISPUTES. The General Assembly now handles more disputes and situations than does the Security Council.[8] It has a right to consider them, under articles 11, paragraph 2, and 35. No differentiation is made by the Assembly between the handling of disputes and other matters; it has never adopted rules of procedure for disputes. Since it may also deal, under Article 14, with "peaceful adjustment of any situation, regardless of origin, which it deems likely to impair the general welfare or friendly relations among nations," it is hard to tell whether it is settling a dispute or not; it does not follow any legal procedures and, as for any other matter, works out whatever compromise can be agreed upon.

Thus, the Spanish case—which can hardly be called a dispute, since the state principally concerned paid no attention to it—was referred to the Assembly from the Security Council, where action upon it had been blocked by a veto. The General Assembly adopted Resolution 39(I), which called for breaking off diplomatic relations with Spain and for other measures of condemnation. This, it was charged, went beyond the constitutional powers of the Assembly; it violated Article 2, paragraph 7 (for the internal regime of a state has always been considered a domestic matter); and it assumed powers under Article 41 which presumably could be exercised only by the Security Council after it had decided that a threat to the peace existed. It was a foolish effort, in any case, resulting from a vindictive war-feeling led by the Soviet Union; it failed, and the Assembly later revoked its resolution.

[7] "The Security Council resolves that the situation in Spain be taken off the list of matters of which the Council is seized, and that all records and documents of the case be put at the disposal of the General Assembly." Security Council, First Year, Second Series, No. 21, p. 492. See the *Repertory*, I, pp. 386 ff.

[8] The decline of the Security Council apparently began about 1948. Before that year, two-thirds of meetings dealing with peace and security were in the Security Council; after that year, about the same percentage was in the Assembly and its organs.

The question of the treatment of persons of Indian origin in the Union of South Africa was not presented as a dispute, though it later involved a bitter duel between India and South Africa; it was rather an attack on the racial discrimination practiced in the latter country. It has been continued from year to year, with South Africa consistently maintaining that it was illegal, since the treatment by a state of its own citizens in its own territory was a domestic matter. It has accomplished nothing whatever toward inducing South Africa to change its habits.

Similarly, the Palestine question did not originate as a dispute, though it became a bitter one. In this situation, the Assembly sought to have the Council enforce its partition plan and the Council took the position that it was not authorized to use enforcement for anything but a threat to the peace and could not use it merely to carry out an Assembly recommendation. For years now, the Assembly has doggedly sought to hold a lid over the explosive situation in Palestine, and has undoubtedly held violence down to a few border clashes, and also brought into existence the state of Israel.

Colonial questions and demands for "self-determination" are brought before the Assembly rather than before the Security Council, since the anti-colonial majority can assure itself of a hearing there which it would be less likely to obtain before the Council. The Soviet Union finds the Assembly a better sounding board for expressing sympathies with the colonies, or for such of its charges as "Aggression against China by the United States of America." In various ways, then, and for various reasons, most of the situations of discontent and dispute are now being funneled into the General Assembly, and the Security Council has less and less reason for meeting.

ENFORCEMENT ACTION. The General Assembly is not mentioned in Chapter VII of the Charter, but its general powers under articles 10 and 11 enable it to make recommendations in the general field of peace and security. In the Korean affair, the one case where armed enforcement measures were used, it was only a series of lucky chances which enabled action to be taken on this first challenge: the Soviet Union was absent from the Security Council, in protest over refusal to recognize a representative of Communist China; the United States had large forces conveniently at hand in the area and was ready to use them against the aggressor; the United Nations Commission in Korea was there to supply information. The Security Council was thus able to act but, even so, it did not order Members to supply forces for use against North Korea, but merely recommended to Members that they give assistance.

Uniting for Peace. This much the General Assembly could do; and in the realization that on the next occasion so much good fortune might not be available, the Assembly adopted Resolution 377 (V), the famous Uniting for Peace Resolution. It was initiated by the United States and adopted on November 3, 1950 by a vote of fifty-two in favor, two abstentions, and only the votes of the five states in the Soviet bloc against. The resolution clearly recognizes the primary responsibility of the Security Council; it is only when the Council "because of lack of unanimity of the permanent members" fails to do its duty that the Assembly is to make recommendations for action against the aggressor. Provision was made for immediate summoning of the Assembly in case of need; and a Collective Measures Committee was set up to study the means by which the resolution might be implemented in the future.[9] Though undoubtedly not in line with the planning at San Francisco, the resolution cannot be regarded as unconstitutional; on the contrary, the General Assembly could do all that the resolution provides for, even if it had not been adopted. The Assembly does not act until the Security Council has failed to act, because of the veto; and it claims only the right of recommendation to Members. It was intended to provide for an emergency, to fill the vacuum created by the failure of the Security Council; it was a statement of intention and a procedure to be followed. The Assembly was able to carry on against the intervention of Communist China, though awkwardly. The Uniting for Peace Resolution prepared the General Assembly for action in enforcement, extended its functions and responsibility and added greatly to its prestige. Until the veto can be avoided, and until the agreements under Article 43 can be made, the General Assembly can do as much as the Security Council is now able to do, which is to recommend action to Members, rather than to order it.

Peaceful Change and Treaty Revision. Articles 11 to 14 may be regarded as elaboration of the general authority granted to the General Assembly under Article 10. Article 14 stands somewhere in between the maintenance of peace and cooperation for other purposes. It deals with something broader than disputes, that is, with situations calling for what has come to be known as "peaceful change." It corresponds somewhat to Article 19 of the Covenant of the League. The General Assembly has no power to order or enforce any change whatever; it can only "recommend measures for the peaceful adjust-

[9] This resolution, and enforcement in general, will be discussed more fully in §156 below.

ment of any situation, regardless of origin, which it deems likely to impair the general welfare or friendly relations among nations."

The phrase "treaty revision" is nowhere to be found in the Charter, and the Charter reveals no advance over the Covenant of the League with respect to the important problem of revision of treaties. Indeed, it pays less attention to it, though doubtless as much can be accomplished under this article as was possible under Article 19 of the Covenant. The words "regardless of origin" were intended to cover treaty situations.[10] Since the Security Council may deal with "any situation which might lead to international friction or give rise to a dispute," (Article 34) the effect would seem to be to give a coordinate jurisdiction in this field to the Security Council and to the General Assembly. No advance has been made by the General Assembly, beyond the situation described in Chapter IX above, as regards international legislation.

OTHER FUNCTIONS. Certain obligatory functions are laid directly upon the General Assembly by Article 13, which says that it "shall initiate studies and make recommendations" concerning cooperation in the political field, in the development of international law, and in the economic, social, cultural, educational, and health fields, and also for "assisting in the realization of human rights and fundamental freedoms for all without distinction as to race, sex, language, or religion." While the wording of this article is as weak as it is possible to make it, a broad field of endeavor, though not of authority, is opened to the General Assembly by it. Most of this work is carried on through the Economic and Social Council, though final decision rests with the General Assembly as to whether work done should be put into treaty form and submitted for ratification by Members. The work of the International Law Commission, discussed earlier, also derives from Article 13.

In addition to the deliberative functions above described, the General Assembly has other functions of elective, administrative, or supervisory character. It may, after recommendation by the Security Council, admit new Members, suspend or expel Members (Chapter II), or choose the Secretary-General (Article 97). It elects the elective members of the Security Council (Article 23), the Economic and Social Council (Article 61), and the Trusteeship Council (Article

---

[10] Senator Vandenberg, who as a delegate of the United States was chiefly responsible for this article, explained that he had originally intended to refer specifically to revision of treaties, but he had foregone this. UNCIO Doc. 748, II/2/39, p. 2; Hearings, p. 251; Goodrich and Hambro, p. 105. The only case directly calling for treaty revision was the effort by Egypt to change her treaty of 1936 with England, brought before the Security Council in 1947. Nothing was done by the Council.

86), and it shares with the Security Council in the choice of judges of the International Court of Justice (Article 4 of the Statute of the Court). It receives and considers reports from, and thus through the right of criticism exercises varying degrees of supervision over, the Security Council, the Economic and Social Council, and the Trusteeship Council (Article 15), and the International Court of Justice. Its control is complete over the Economic and Social Council (Article 66) and over the Trusteeship Council (Article 85) except for strategic areas. It must approve trust agreements (except for strategic areas, Article 85), agreements with the specialized agencies (Article 63), and agreements as to immunities and headquarters (Article 105). A large field of supervision over United Nations activities is opened to it through complete control over the finances of the United Nations (Article 17), including the court (Article 33 of the statute), and perhaps the specialized agencies (articles 17, 63). The Assembly may request advisory opinions from the court and may authorize other United Nations organs or specialized agencies to request such opinions. It may initiate amendments (Article 108), and may establish such subsidiary organs as it thinks necessary.

THE SECURITY COUNCIL

The primary interest of most persons in the new organization was from the viewpoint of security, and the original emphasis in the drafting of the Charter at Dumbarton Oaks was upon the Security Council. It has not, however, been able to live up to these expectations.

90. ORGANIZATION AND PROCEDURE

The Security Council is composed of the representatives of eleven states, five of which are designated by name in Article 23 to be permanent members.[11] The other six, non-permanent members, are

---

[11] As to the Security Council, see *Report to the President*, p. 66; E. Buehrig, "The Security Council," *Dept. of State Bull.*, 13 (1945), p. 825; H. Kelsen, "Organization and Procedure of the Security Council of the United Nations," *Harvard Law Review*, 59 (1946), p. 1087; R. K. Kane, "The Security Council," *Foreign Affairs*, 24 (1945), p. 12.

The Charter says: "shall consist of eleven Members of the United Nations." The persons who sit in the Security Council are thus representatives of states, instructed and removable by them. The permanent members are the four signers of the Declaration of Moscow, China, the Union of Soviet Socialist Republics, the United Kingdom, and the United States, with France added.

elected by the General Assembly by two-thirds vote, three each year, for a two-year term. Thus the differentiation between Great Powers and other states, recognized in the Council of the League, was continued in the United Nations and somewhat strengthened in that only these five, rather than all Members, were entitled to a veto. There was little opposition to recognition of this factual situation, but much opposition to the extent to which it was carried in the Charter. It was pointed out that these five states were arbitrarily named; that no criteria are established for selection or for change as Great Powers appear or diminish or withdraw; and that the veto in the amending process makes almost impossible any change as to permanent Members. Today, the United Nations is in a quandary as to the permanent seat held by Nationalist China, which is clearly not a Great Power. How can it be replaced?

While the idea of graded representation in United Nations organs received little consideration, an effort was made by Canada to give to states of medium strength a semi-permanent basis, or a longer term. The effort failed, and membership is either permanent or for two years. As a result of this struggle, however, the Charter provides (Article 23, paragraph 1) that the General Assembly shall, in the selection of non-permanent Members, give "due regard," in the first instance, "to the contribution of Members of the United Nations to the maintenance of international peace and security and to the other purposes of the Organization, and also to equitable geographical distribution." The provision that a retiring Member shall not be eligible for immediate re-election further limits the possibility of an intermediate status of longer term. The non-permanent seats are now distributed according to pattern. Two seats go to Latin America and one each to western Europe, eastern Europe, the Middle East, and the British Commonwealth. At first, by a gentlemen's agreement, one of the non-permanent seats was reserved for a state in the Soviet bloc; the United States, however, succeeded in obtaining the election of Greece in 1951 and of Turkey in 1953. In 1955, the United States supported the Philippines against Yugoslavia in an obstinate and undignified contest which had ultimately to be resolved by a gentlemen's agreement that Yugoslavia should be elected, resign at the end of one year, and the Philippines would then be elected for the remaining year of the term. Further trouble came with the admission of seventeen new Members, many from Asia which has not been adequately represented thus far. There is now a demand that the Security Council be enlarged so as to make room for wider representation of blocs and areas.

Little organization is needed for the Security Council. The president is automatically chosen in rotation, serving for one month. His position is one of prestige and some power; the control which he may be able to exercise was well illustrated when the Soviet delegate, Malik, held the Council practically paralyzed for the month he was in office in August, 1950, after the Korean struggle had been initiated in the absence of the Soviet Union. The president may also be called upon to negotiate between the parties to a dispute before the Council. There are two committees which may be regarded as standing committees: the Committee of Experts, and the Committee on Admission of New Members. And, of course, the Council may set up *ad hoc* commissions of various kinds for investigation or conciliation of disputes. The Military Staff Committee, called for by the Charter, is supposed to report to the Security Council, but has been of little service. The Atomic Energy Commission and the Conventional Armaments Commission, later merged into the Disarmament Commission, were set up by the General Assembly to report to the Security Council in connection with its functions concerning regulation of armaments.

PROCEDURE. The anticipated importance of the Security Council is revealed in the provision that it "shall be so organized as to be able to function continuously" (Article 28). It was therefore necessary for each member of the Security Council to maintain a delegate in permanent residence, ready to act in emergency. The Council has never been able to agree on more than provisional rules of procedure, and these allowed the president to call meetings, provided they were not more than fourteen days apart; and he must summon a meeting at the request of any member of the Council, or whenever a dispute or situation is put before the Council for its consideration. The Council may meet wherever it chooses, but experience has shown that it is both costly and inconvenient for any organ to meet elsewhere than at its own headquarters. Article 28, paragraph 2, suggests that there be an occasional special sort of meeting which would be attended by prime ministers and foreign ministers, but this has not been done in practice; such meetings have occurred outside the United Nations.

The record of meetings is a measure of the decline of the Security Council. In 1948, it held 171 meetings; the number dropped to 39 in 1951, and was 43 in 1953. Meetings are now infrequent, in spite of the rule calling for meetings every two weeks. The decline is shown also by the decrease in the number of items on its agenda, from 41 in 1946 to 26 in 1947 and 14 in 1953.

Articles 31 and 32 of the Charter deal with matters in which states, which are not members of the Security Council or not Members of the United Nations, are involved. If a Member's interests are affected in a question brought before the Council, it may participate without vote in the discussion, but the Council decides whether or not it has a proper interest. If a Member, or a non-member, is a party to a dispute it is entitled to participate, without vote. A distinction is thus made between "disputes" and other questions and since this is a matter of constitutional significance,[12] there have been many debates concerning the right to be heard. On the whole, the Council has been very generous, listening even to entities which could not claim to be states, such as the Jewish Agency or the Arab Higher Command.

In general, the procedure of the Security Council is informal, in the sense of not following strict rules, though there have been many long fights over questions of procedure. It is sometimes difficult to ascertain from the debates and records whether a decision has been taken. The Council publishes no collection of resolutions adopted, as the General Assembly does.

91. VOTING IN THE SECURITY COUNCIL[13]

It has been noted that the rule of unanimity was abandoned at San Francisco and that decisions of United Nations organs may be taken by majority vote. In the Security Council, each Member has one vote. Decisions on procedural matters are made by vote of any seven Members; decisions on other matters require a "qualified majority," that is, seven votes including the concurring votes of all the permanent Members. Thus, each of the five permanent Members has a "veto" (though the word is not found in the Charter); and this provision, while clearly an advance over the Council of the League in which every Member had a veto, produced the greatest controversy at San Francisco and since.

---

12 See § 143, below.

13 E. Jiménez de Aréchaga, *Voting and the Handling of Disputes in the Security Council* (United Nations Studies No. 5, Carnegie Endowment, 1950); Wellington Koo, Jr., *Voting Procedures in International Organizations* (New York, 1947); Dwight E. Lee, "The Genesis of the Veto," *Int. Organ.*, 1 (1947), p. 33; Norman Padelford, "The Use of the Veto," *ibid.*, 2, p. 226; J. B. Reston, "Votes and Vetoes," *Foreign Affairs*, 25 (1946), p. 13; F. O. Wilcox, "The Rule of Unanimity in the Security Council," *Proc. Am. Soc.*, 1946, p. 51; *Report to the President*, p. 71.

For the Statement of the Sponsoring Powers, quoted below, see *UNCIO Doc.* 855, III/1/B/2(a), and *Doc.* 852, III/1/37(1).

Many questions were asked at San Francisco concerning the "Yalta formula" which became Article 27 of the Charter, and an elaborate answer was given by the sponsoring Powers, from which the following quotation is taken. The Statement by the Sponsoring Powers distinguished between "procedural" and "other matters," as does Article 27. It then elaborates as follows:

2. For example, under the Yalta formula a procedural vote will govern the decisions made under the entire Section D of Chapter VI. This means that the Council will, by a vote of any seven of its members, adopt or alter its rules of procedure; determine the method of selecting its President; organize itself in such a way as to be able to function continuously; select the times and places of its regular and special meetings; establish such bodies or agencies as it may deem necessary for the performance of its functions; invite a Member of the Organization not represented on the Council to participate in its discussions when that Member's interests are specially affected; and invite any state when it is a party to a dispute being considered by the Council to participate in the discussion relating to that dispute.

3. Further, no individual member of the Council can alone prevent consideration and discussion by the Council of a dispute or situation brought to its attention under paragraph 2, Section A, Chapter VIII. Nor can parties to such dispute be prevented by these means from being heard by the Council. Likewise, the requirement for unanimity of the permanent members cannot prevent any member of the Council from reminding the Members of the Organization of their general obligations assumed under the Charter as regards peaceful settlement of international disputes.

4. Beyond this point, decisions and actions by the Security Council may well have major political consequences and may even initiate a chain of events which might, in the end, require the Council under its responsibilities to invoke measures of enforcement under Section B, Chapter VIII. This chain of events begins when the Council decides to make an investigation, or determines that the time has come to call upon states to settle their differences, or makes recommendations to the parties. It is to such decisions and actions that unanimity of the permanent members applies, with the important proviso, referred to above, for abstention from voting by parties to a dispute.

This statement, however, did not answer all uncertainties. No sufficient definition of "procedure" was given. The Statement of the Sponsoring Powers, however, ends with the assertion that the decision as to whether a matter is procedural or not is to be taken by a vote of seven including the permanent members. After long debate at San Francisco, it was agreed that in decisions under Chapter VI, that is, in the settlement of disputes before the Security Council, the votes of parties to the dispute should not be counted. In early cases before the Security Council, however, the difficulty arose over determining what, under the Charter, constitutes a dispute; who, therefore, would be parties to the dispute; and whether the vote on this question should be regarded as procedural or not. The Statement of the Sponsoring Powers is of course not part of the Charter and its indication of the matters to which the veto is or is not applicable is not binding upon Members. This has frequently been pointed out in debates, but so long as the permanent members continue to accept it, the veto will be employed accordingly. The General Assembly, of course, cannot modify the situation, though it has made various recommendations to this end; the Security Council itself cannot change it, except by agreement among the five permanent members.

ABSTENTIONS. The situation is somewhat alleviated by the practice, initiated by the Soviet Union and now generally accepted, whereby abstentions and, less surely, absences, are not counted as vetoes. This usage reverses the clear wording of Article 27, paragraph 3, which requires the "affirmative vote of seven members including the concurrent votes of the permanent members," but it has made it possible for the Security Council to operate. There have been very few decisions in which all of the permanent members have concurred; by far the greater number of decisions has been possible because of the abstention or absence of a permanent member. It was the absence of the Soviet delegate on June 25, 1950, that made possible the action in Korea.

USE OF THE VETO. Technically, each negative vote by a permanent member would be a veto, but the term applies in usage only to those negative votes which kill a proposal that would otherwise have been adopted. About eighty vetoes have been cast, all but three of them by the Soviet Union; and half or more of its vetoes have been upon individual applications for admission to membership in the United Nations. Consideration must also be given, in estimating the effect of the veto, to actions not pressed for fear of a veto; the United States, for example, threatened to veto the seating of Communist China, and the possibility of a veto in determining whether or not a dispute exists (Article 34) has affected the whole procedure for pacific settlement of disputes.

DOUBLE VETO. The use of the double veto has added to the exasperation. The final words of the Statement of the Sponsoring Powers assert that "the decision regarding the preliminary question as to whether or not such a matter is procedural must be taken by a vote of seven members of the Security Council, including the concurring votes of the permanent members." The double veto, then, includes a vote cast against the decision that a matter is procedural, followed by a veto on the substantive question itself. This is a tricky matter, depending upon how the question is put by the president.[14]

The use of the veto by the Soviet Union is understandable, in its minority position, but it has been carried to ridiculous extremes. While the veto has been obstructive and harmful, it has not been as injurious to the United Nations as many believe it has been. The practice that an abstention or absence is not to be counted as a veto has helped; in the Berlin blockade, though Council action was stopped by a veto, the Soviet nuisance was stopped; though reference of the Greek frontier question to the General Assembly was vetoed, it was dropped from the agenda by a procedural vote and then taken up by the Assembly; though a veto can block the Security Council from ordering action against an aggressor, the Uniting for Peace Resolution provides a means for taking action, etc. It is probable that none of the permanent members would be willing to eliminate the veto.

There has, however, been a constant pressure to modify, at the least, the rule of unanimity. A most thorough study was made by the Interim Committee, which listed some fifty possible actions by the Council which it thought should be decided by procedural vote.[15] Various means for evading or disregarding the veto have been suggested, but the Assembly has not been able to give so liberal an interpretation to Article 27, paragraph 3, as it has with other articles of the Charter. The use of the veto evidences the failure of the concept upon which the United Nations security system was founded, the unanimity of the Great Powers; but there is little chance that it will be abandoned. Its justification lies in the fear of the larger states that they might be forced into costly or dangerous action through a majority vote of irresponsible small states—irresponsible, that is, in the sense that those who voted for an action would not be able to contribute much toward it and the burden would necessarily fall upon the larger states. The conduct of the small state majority in the General Assembly has done nothing to lessen that fear in recent years.

It would be possible however, merely by agreement among the permanent members of the Council, and without amendment of the Charter, to modify use of the veto. The United States had earlier proposed that the possibility of a veto should be eliminated from the proposed control over the atomic bomb; and it now proposes that the veto should be not used in connection with the admission of new

---

[14] See A. W. Rudzinski, "The So-Called Double Veto," *A.J.*, 45 (1951), p. 450; Leo Gross, "The Double Veto and the Four Power Statement on Voting in the Security Council," *Harvard Law Review*, 67 (1953), p. 251. The four cases of the double veto may be found in the *Repertoire*, and in Brookings, *Organization*.

[15] General Assembly, Third Session, *Official Records*, Supplement No. 10 (1948).

Members and with pacific settlement of disputes. This is doubtless all that could be hoped for at present. Until some substitute (weighted representation?) can be found for the veto as a protection for the strong against the weak, it is probable that the militarily strong will reserve the veto at least with regard to the use of their armed forces.

92. FUNCTIONS

The sole function of the Security Council is the maintenance of international peace and security, for which it is given "primary responsibility" by Article 24 of the Charter. The regulation of armaments is included and the Council has the task of formulating plans to this end (Article 26). Thus there is a much clearer differentiation of function than between the Council and Assembly of the League of Nations, and the field of action of the Security Council, though highly important, is much more restricted than that of the General Assembly. It should be noted, however, that the idea of security was stretched to enable the Council to share in, and usually with the veto, the admission of new Members, the suspension or restoration of rights and the expulsion of Members, the procedure of amendment, the election of judges of the Court, the administration of certain trust areas, and the selection of a Secretary-General. While the Security Council thus has a few continuing activities, it is designed for crises, and for one field of activity only. It cannot be regarded as an executive committee for general purposes, as the Council of the League tended to become. It is one of three councils, each limited in function and to some extent dependent upon and supervised by the General Assembly. Of the three, the Security Council is most independent, but it must make annual and special reports to the Assembly (Article 24); it depends upon the Assembly for its financial needs; and the Assembly may review and criticize its actions.

The function of security and the authority and activity of the Security Council in this field will be discussed in a later chapter.

THE ECONOMIC AND SOCIAL COUNCIL

93. CHARTER PROVISIONS

No such organ as the Economic and Social Council was provided in the League of Nations System. Its inclusion in the United Nations is a recognition both of the increasing importance of the work to be done in this field, and of the need of additional international machinery to deal with it.[16] While the emphasis of the Dumbarton Oaks Proposals was primarily upon security, it was recognized that "conditions of stability and well-being" are necessary for friendly relations among nations (Article 55), and that achievement of such conditions would be conducive to peace. The somewhat meagre outlines in the Dumbarton Oaks Proposals were expanded at San Francisco into chapters IX and X of the Charter, and additional references may be found in other parts, such as articles 1 and 14.

This expansion was due to increasing economic interdependence, which had been emphasized by the depression following 1929 and by the problems of World War II. Where the League of Nations was interested from social and humanitarian viewpoints, the United Nations was more interested in the economic phases of life, for millions of people, many of them awakened by war contacts, were beginning to believe that they did not have to live forever in the poverty and degradation to which they had been accustomed for centuries.

In the text of the Charter, however, inconsistencies are found which reflect the conflict between the old ways and the new needs. On the one hand, the Charter insists upon sovereign equality and exclusive domestic jurisdiction; on the other hand, it calls for the United Nations (Article 55) to promote such things as higher standards of living, full employment, respect for human rights and fundamental freedoms, without distinction as to race, sex, language, or religion. These subjects manifestly reach down into the most intimate social habits and legislation of each country. All Members are pledged (Article 56) "to take joint and separate action in cooperation with the Organization for the achievement of the purposes set forth in Article 55." How could this be done in the face of Article 2, paragraph 7, and of national sovereignty?

This inherent conflict has produced much controversy, ranging from one extreme which accepted no more than research and discussion and rejected even efforts to make treaties, to the other extreme

---

[16] *Report of the United States Delegation to the First Part of the First Session of the General Assembly of the United Nations*, Dept. of State Pub., No. 2484; A. Loveday, "Suggestions for the Reform of the United Nations Economic and Social Council," *Int. Organ.*, 7 (1953); L. D. Stinebower, *The Economic and Social Council* (Commission to Study the Organization of Peace, New York, 1946); *The Economic and Social Council of the United Nations. Report to the Secretary of State by the Honorable John G. Winant, United States Representative on the Council, July 15, 1946*, Dept. of State Pub., No. 2600; Annual Reports of the Council.

The "Bruce Report," toward the end of the League of Nations, had recommended a special organ to supervise work in these fields. *L. of N. Doc.*, 1939. General. 3, published also as a Special Supplement to the *Monthly Summary of the League of Nations*, August, 1939.

which claimed what they wanted as "rights" (e.g., financial aid for the internal development) and paid no attention to Article 2, paragraph 7. The situation was complicated by the fact that many of the states which demanded certain measures as "human rights" were unable and even unwilling to put them into effect within their own territories. With regard to some things, such as children's relief or disaster-situations, not much objection is raised; there are certain fields in which need for international action has been recognized, such as slavery, narcotics, health, and perhaps safety and others; and except in extreme demands like the Covenant of Human Rights, there has not been much objection to efforts to make treaties to solve problems— since each state could refuse to ratify the treaty. But each state seeks to advance its own prosperity or stability by internal economic measures and when it is proposed to change these measures, resistance becomes strong. Recommendations of a general character are more acceptable; those addressed to a specific state (e.g., South Africa) arouse resentment. This is a new field into which community action enters and it will require long and patient effort to work out acceptable solutions.

94. ORGANIZATION

There are also constitutional questions concerning the organization of the work in this field. While Article 7 lists the Economic and Social Council as one of the "principle organs," Article 60 puts the Council "under the authority of the General Assembly"; yet Article 62 authorizes it to make recommendations "to the General Assembly, to the Members of the United Nations, and to the specialized agencies concerned." The result has been a great deal of confusion as to functions, authority, and procedure, but in general the Assembly has dominated the field.

COMPOSITION OF THE COUNCIL. The Economic and Social Council is composed of eighteen members elected by two-thirds vote of the General Assembly, six each year for three-year terms (Article 61). No criteria are set for the choice of members; the Assembly has entire freedom in selecting them. In this Council, Members are eligible for immediate re-election and the Assembly may thus continue those states whose participation seems most needed. As in the other councils, each Member is allowed one representative. No special provision for the Great Powers is made here; there are no permanent seats and no veto. This may be due to recognition of the fact that their cooperation is so indispensable in this field that no special privileges were needed for them, or to the fact that there is in this field no authority to take decisions against which a veto might be needed. However, in practice, the five permanent members of the Security Council have been regularly elected to the Economic and Social Council.

Here, as elsewhere, unwritten rules dictate the choice of members. Western Europe and the Soviet bloc formerly held four seats each, but the former has been reduced to three and the latter to two seats. Five seats now go to Asian states. Latin America has four seats, and the British Commonwealth two—or more if India or Pakistan is counted (India has been elected six times and Pakistan four times). Attempts have been made in the past to enlarge the Council and the effort has become stronger with the admission of seventeen new Members.

Article 68 authorizes the Council to set up such commissions as it may need, and specifies that there shall be a commission on human rights. Accordingly, there have been usually eight or nine functional commissions and three regional commissions,[17] some of them with sub-commissions. There are four standing committees, forty or fifty *ad hoc* committees, a few operating bodies, such as UNRRA and UNICEF, and the High Commissioner for Refugees. The organization for economic and social matters is a very complex one, the more so when it reaches out to the specialized agencies and attempts to coordinate their activities with those of the United Nations itself.

RELATIONS WITH OTHER BODIES. We have noted above that the Economic and Social Council is put under the authority of the General Assembly, though specific functions are assigned to it. The Assembly has two of its six main committees assigned to this field: the second committee, for Economic and Financial matters, and the third committee, for Social, Humanitarian and Cultural Matters. In the secretariat, two former departments were combined in 1954 into the Department of Economic and Social Affairs.

The General Assembly is inclined to unload tasks upon, and to interfere with the fulfillment of functions by, the Economic and Social Council. It has, for example, restored subcommissions eliminated by the Council in its efforts to streamline organization; it reversed the decision of the Council that the Commission on the Status of Women should meet only biennially; it ordered inclusion in the Covenant of Human Rights or the "right of self-determination"; it attempted vainly to have the two Covenants of Human Rights combined into one.

[17] See the chart of the United Nations Organs, p. 318.

The Assembly is not so well-equipped as is the Council. The latter body is more apt to include experts, and it is a smaller body within which representation is more balanced, though not by intention equally balanced as in the Trusteeship Council. In the Assembly, and in its committees, delegates speak frequently upon the basis of emotion and without expert knowledge or responsibility, and a majority can frequently be obtained to override the more serious efforts of the Council. As Cheever and Haviland put it, the Assembly "is enthusiastically humanitarian but afflicted with tendencies to be organizationally clumsy, long-winded, over-political, under-expert, and ambitious beyond its means."[18] Thus far, the Economic and Social Council has not found, or has not been given, its proper constitutional position in relation to the General Assembly.

An understanding was reached with the Trusteeship Council in 1947 by which the functions of the Economic and Social Council were to cover trust territories, though no recommendation was to be made for such territories without the approval of the Trusteeship Council. Apparently, the Economic and Social Council has made no such recommendations, but it has asked the Trusteeship Council to include in its questionnaires matters on which the former council desired information. There is an arrangement for reciprocal representation, which does not seem to be used. With the Security Council there has been little relationship, though there has been discussion in the Economic and Social Council as to the right to consider disputes.[19]

The Secretariat, of course, has an important part to play in the work of the Economic and Social Council. Indeed, its suborgans and meetings represent about half the total documentation of the United Nations and about half the budget goes to these functions. A vast amount of work is done by the Secretariat in preparing reports and making researches for the various bodies, and in implementation or checking upon resolutions adopted. Since the most expert knowledge is to be found in the Secretariat, delegates are apt to call upon it and to rely upon its leadership; and this has caused complaint that the Secretariat plays a more important role than its function as a service body justifies.

The Economic and Social Council reaches out also into the work of most of the specialized agencies and plays an important part in the steadily increasing and important work of technical assistance. These relationships will appear in other connections.

[18] Cheever and Haviland, pp. 196-97.
[19] See Brookings, *Organization*, Chapters x and xv.

95. NON-GOVERNMENTAL ORGANIZATIONS[20]

Representation in the Economic and Social Council is somewhat broadened by Article 69, which requires the Council to invite Members that are especially concerned with the topics under discussion. Article 71, however, introduces a novel idea into international government by providing for formal relationships between it and unofficial organizations. The Council originally arranged for A, B, and C categories of these bodies, but later abolished category C and replaced it with a register of organizations which might be able to make significant contribution to some part of the work of the Council. There are now one hundred and fifty-nine non-governmental organizations on the register.

In order to be an "NGO" an organization must deal with matters within the province of the Economic and Social Council; it must be international in character;[21] it must be well enough organized to have a headquarters and be able to speak with the authority of the persons it represents; and it must have standing in its field and represent a respectable proportion of the people interested in that field. Those in category A (now ten) have the right to put an item on the provisional agenda of the council and to submit a two-thousand word statement concerning it (if approved by the council committee on NGOs). Category B includes organizations (now 110 of them) of a more limited or specialized field of interest, and they may submit written statements of five hundred words. All NGOs have the right to attend meetings of the Economic and Social Council and its various bodies, and also meetings of the General Assembly when it is considering economic and social matters.[22]

[20] Lyman White, *International Non-Governmental Organizations* (New Brunswick, N.J., 1951); *Consultation between the U.N. and the Non-Governmental Organizations* (United Nations Studies No. 3, Carnegie Endowment, 1949); *U.N. Doc.* E/C.2/INF/1 and succeeding issues, and E/C.2/374; and the *Yearbook of International Organizations*, issued by the Union of International Associations (Brussels) which also publishes a monthly journal.

[21] But a national organization may be admitted by the Council after consultation with its government, as was done in the case of the United States Chamber of Commerce.

[22] The United States, over-zealously guarding itself against communism, refused to admit certain NGO representatives on the ground that they were authorized only to attend Economic and Social Council bodies, and not the session of the General Assembly. The General Assembly then adopted Resolution 606(VI) which gave this authorization. The United States then pettishly restricted them to a given area of Manhattan. See *U.N. Doc.* E/1291, in which the Legal Department argued that the restrictions were illegal; also, "Report of the Committee for Study of Legal Problems of the United Nations," *Proc. Am. Soc.*, 1954, pp. 164-80.

The purposes of the consultative procedure with the NGOs was stated in Resolution 288(X) of the Council:

on the one hand, for the purpose of enabling the Council or one of its bodies to secure expert information or advice from organizations having special competence . . . and, on the other hand, to enable organizations which represent important elements of public opinion to express their views.

The NGOs can also be of service in informing their members—who amount to millions of persons—concerning what is going on at the United Nations. Two different departments of the secretariat serve the NGOs, the Department of Economic and Social Affairs, and the Department of Public Information. It is difficult to measure the results of the activity of the NGOs, since their representatives sometimes bring influence to bear upon delegates directly, in addition to the usual channels; but the procedure is apparently approved and established, and the peoples of the world have an opportunity both to learn and to be heard in the United Nations.

96. PROCEDURE AND PROBLEMS

A vast range of activity (to be discussed in the following chapter) is given to the Economic and Social Council, and it has increased still more because of interest from various angles in the underdeveloped countries. It would be useless to attempt to survey all its functions; if we exclude political or security matters and those belonging to the Trusteeship Council, there is almost no limit to the subjects which the Council may consider. The activity is increased by the number of pet ideas which are brought forward by delegates and which other delegates are politely unwilling to discourage. The methods of handling so many varied matters is obviously of importance and has occasioned much study.

In the Economic and Social Council itself each member has one vote and decisions are taken by a majority of those present and voting (Article 67). There is no veto and no distinction between procedural and other questions; a decision by bare majority disturbs no one, since it can at most be a recommendation binding upon no Member without its own ratification. Representatives of the specialized agencies are entitled to participate without vote in discussions in the Council and, reciprocally, a representative of the Council may sit in meetings of a specialized agency. The Charter gives to the Council complete freedom as to the numbers and dates of its meetings, except for the requirement that a meeting must be held if requested by a majority of members of the Council.

The methods through which the Council may work are to "make or initiate studies and reports"; to make recommendations; to "prepare draft conventions" or call international conferences (Article 62). The reports issued by the Council and its bodies are for the most part regarded as highly authoritative and useful and would alone justify its existence; but it goes further than this. It is, indeed, the chief source of international legislation today, though the procedure, as has earlier been remarked, is a very limited one. The Council itself may prepare a draft treaty embodying new rules, or it may call a conference for that purpose, but this treaty cannot be submitted for ratification by Members unless approved by the General Assembly (articles 60 and 62, paragraph 3).

Granted the many bodies and the many topics, the procedure for reaching decisions in the economic and social field is difficult and confusing. An item usually originates in the General Assembly which refers it to the Council, which passes it on to a commission or committee, and perhaps it then goes to a subcommittee. Returning, it goes through the commission to the Council and, if approved by the latter, is passed on to the General Assembly. Here it will be considered by the General Committee, then referred to an assembly committee, usually the Second or Third, and, if approved, to the Fifth Committee for consideration of financial consequences. When it comes back to the plenary Assembly, it may be adopted and finished; or it may be referred back to the Council with modifications or instructions, in which case the whole race must be run over again. Not all of this happens on every occasion, of course; but the story explains why the Economic and Social Council has been described as no more than a "post-box," through which pass the documents going from commission to Assembly and back again. It helps also to understand why strong efforts have been made (with some degree of success) to hold down the "proliferation" of suborgans and activities and to reduce the number of items on the agenda. To some extent, perhaps, delegates are realizing that each item, long debates on each, and each new project with its staff, adds to the budget to which every one of them must contribute.

There are various other problems. Should the various bodies in this field—all of which only make preparatory studies and recommendations to the council—be composed of experts, or of representatives of governments? The Soviet Union has consistently upheld the latter view, with the argument that only representatives can commit their states; others have argued that since all the work is prepartory only, it should be done by experts, and then submitted to a higher level of governmental representatives for political decision. However reasonable the latter may sound, most governments seem to prefer to have their instructed representatives, whether they are expert or not, in all bodies.

The Secretariat includes many experts and there is an increasing tendency to call upon it as a body of impartial experts. It has its own problem of organization. Should there be one, or two, or more departments to handle the work? The decision in 1954 was to combine all into one department. The coordination of the efforts of some thirteen hundred employees is quite a problem; but it is only part of the larger problem of attaining coordination between the numerous bodies of the Economic and Social Council, and between them and the specialized agencies. It is a problem frequently complicated by the fact that within one government it may be impossible to achieve coordination and representatives of the same state may take different positions in different bodies, or at different times in the same body. A great deal of study has been made of this problem of coordination, but it was not until the development of the technical assistance work—which had money of its own to distribute—that progress was made.[23]

The greatest problem of the Economic and Social Council is, however, the General Assembly, which has not learned how to conduct itself with efficiency and discipline.

TRUSTEESHIP COUNCIL

97. FROM MANDATES TO TRUST TERRITORIES[24]

It was naturally expected that the mandates system of the League of Nations would be carried over in some form into the United Nations, and one of the results of World War II was to awaken the ambitions of dependent peoples of all sorts, and in various directions. The Dumbarton Oaks Proposals contained nothing on the subject, mostly because in the United States there was a great struggle between the Navy Department, which wished to take over for military purposes the mandated islands of Japan in the Pacific, and the Department of State, which realized that colonialism was approaching its end and

---

[23] See § 121, below; Brookings, *Organization.*
[24] E. H. Armstrong and W. I. Cargo, "The Inauguration of the Trusteeship System of the UN," *Dept. of State Bull.,* 16 (1947); Ralph Bunche, "Trusteeship and Non-Self-Governing territories in the Charter of the United Nations," *ibid.,* 13 (1945); A. K. Bailey, "Dependent Areas of the Pacific: An Australian View," *Foreign Affairs* 24 (1946); P. Fraser, "The Work of the Trusteeship Council," *Int. Con.* (1948); H. D. Hall, *Mandates, Dependencies and Trusteeships* (Washington, 1948); also *Int. Con.,* Nos. 435 (1947) and 458 (1950).

did not wish the United States to stand alone in acquiring colonies as a result of the war.[25] At Yalta, the three Powers agreed that provisions to be put into the Charter should apply only to existing League mandates, to territories detached from the enemy in World War II, and to territory which any state might voluntarily put under trusteeship; and also, that there should be no discussion at San Francisco as to specific assignments of trust territories. Working papers on the subject were prepared by these Powers and, under the leadership of Harold Stassen at San Francisco, evolved into three chapters of the Charter. Chapter XI is a rather remarkable declaration by the colonial powers of certain standards for their colonies which they were willing to pursue; Chapter XII states the purposes of the trusteeship system; and Chapter XIII provides the machinery for its operation.

THE TRUSTEESHIP SYSTEM. The objectives of the trusteeship are stated in Article 76, in terms corresponding to those of Chapter XI, and somewhat broader than those of Article 22 of the Covenant of the League of Nations. They are: (1) to further international peace and security; (2) to promote political, economic, social and educational advancement and development toward self-government or inpendence, each case being a separate one and limited by the terms of the trusteeship to be made; (3) to respect human rights and fundamental freedoms without discrimination as to race, sex, language or religion; (4) equal treatment for all Members of the United Nations in social, economic, and commercial matters and in the administration of justice, but with a reservation as to existing rights (Article 80). These represent an advance over the League system in that they are universally applicable, rather than differentiated between A, B, and C mandates.

The trusteeship system applies to territories in the following categories which are placed under it by trusteeship agreements: (1) territories now held under mandate; (2) those taken from the enemy in World War II; and (3) colonial territories put under the system by the states responsible for them. Thus, no territory is automatically placed under the trusteeship system, and an agreement must be made in each case; it is therefore important to know the parties to such agreements and the method by which the content of the agreements is to be determined. As to this, no more is said than that the agreements are to be made "by the states directly concerned"; and no indication as to these states is given beyond the specific inclusion (Article 79) of the mandatory power in the case of a League mandate. Since the con-

[25] *Post-War Preparation*, pp. 392, 662.

sent of the mandatory state is required, that state in effect had a veto.[26] A solution was found to this problem in the suggestion, accepted by the General Assembly in the second part of its first session, that the agreement should be drafted by the state which wished to be the administering authority. Acceptance by two-thirds of the General Assembly would be regarded as sufficiently caring for the interests of the unknown "states directly concerned."[27] Upon this understanding, eight draft agreements, all of them for former mandated territories, were submitted to and approved by the General Assembly. The debate as to their provisions was a warm one, particularly regarding military use of colonial peoples and territory and over the phrase stating that the trust area could be administered as an integral part of the administering authority.

Of the former mandated territories, only South West Africa now remains outside the trusteeship system. The Union of South Africa asked to annex it and when this was refused, held onto it under the terms of the mandate, denying the United Nations any right in the matter and refusing to deal with the United Nations concerning it. The General Assembly has pressed steadily to have it put under trusteeship and has asked the Court for three advisory opinions concerning the situation. In the first one, the Court replied that South Africa could not be required to put South West Africa under trusteeship but that, on the other hand, her obligations under the mandate and the Covenant of the League were still binding upon her; consequently, she would be unable unilaterally to alter the legal status of the territory, and she must make annual reports concerning it to the United Nations.[28] In a later opinion, the Court advised that the General Assembly, in voting on this situation, did not have to follow the rule of unanimity which prevailed in the League of Nations. In 1956, in reply to another question, it ruled that the Assembly could grant oral hearings to petitioners from South West Africa.[29]

The United States was also unenthusiastic about putting under trusteeship the mandated islands of Japan in the Pacific, which it held under military control after World War II. A compromise was finally

[26] The United States in proposing an agreement for the Japanese mandated islands suggested that, if it were not accepted, the control which she exercised over these areas would automatically be continued.

[27] The Soviet Union fought this procedure as unconstitutional, and for a long time refused to attend meetings of the Security Council. See F. B. Sayre, "Legal Problems Arising from the United Nations Trusteeship System," *A.J.*, 42 (1948), p. 279; and G. V. Wolfe "The States Directly Concerned: Article 79 of the United Nations Charter," *ibid.*, p. 368.

[28] *I.C.J. Reports*, 1950, p. 128.

[29] *I.C.J. Reports*, 1955, p. 67; *ibid.*, 1956, p. 23.

reached, and put into the Charter in Article 82, for a strategic trust area; and an agreement for this area was approved in April, 1947, by the Security Council which, rather than the Trusteeship Council, is made responsible for such areas. This is the only "strategic trust area," and the control over these territories by the United States is almost as complete as ownership; though in practice annual reports have been made to the Security Council, respect has been paid to recommendations made and there has been little criticism of the administration of the area.

It was agreed in the peace treaty for Italy in 1946 that, should the Powers be unable to agree as to the disposition of the Italian colonies, the General Assembly should decide what to do with them. As a result of this authorization from the outside, the General Assembly set up Libya as an independent state, after some tutelage from the United Nations which was not trusteeship; it linked Eritrea with Ethiopia; and in January 1950 it adopted a resolution which made Italy the administering authority over Somaliland for a period of ten years, after which it was to become independent. There was no consideration as to the ability of the area to stand alone, and no inquiry as to whether the inhabitants wished such a status; to the anti-colonial group, independence is the answer for all colonies! One more trust territory was added in November, 1947, when an agreement was approved making the United Kingdom, Australia, and New Zealand jointly administering authority for the island of Nauru.

Thus, there are now eleven trust areas, administered by seven different states: Ruanda-Urundi, by Belgium; Cameroun and Togoland, by France; the Cameroons, Togoland and Tanganyika, by the United Kingdom; Western Samoa by New Zealand; New Guinea by Australia; the Trust Territory of the Pacific Islands, by the United States; Nauru, jointly by the three states named above; and Somaliland, by Italy. This includes all the former mandates except South West Africa (Article 77, paragraph 1a). The noble words of the time of the Atlantic Charter were forgotten, and the only conquered territories put under trusteeship (Article 77, paragraph 1b) were the Pacific Trust Territories and Italian Somaliland, both exceptional cases; there have been no offers under Article 77, paragraph 1c.

The United Nations itself, by Article 81, could be the administering authority for a trust territory, but it has never quite assumed that position. A temporary trusteeship for Palestine was proposed by the United States in 1948, but it did not go through; a proposal for a trusteeship for Korea also failed. Among the proposals concerning Libya in 1949 was one for direct administration by the United Nations, but political rivalries prevented this. In 1950, it was proposed that Jerusalem should be administered by the Trusteeship Council and a statute was actually drawn up, but it was decided that Jerusalem could not be made a trust territory. Jurisdiction was assumed by the Security Council over Trieste, but this was not trusteeship; and proposals have been made, unofficially, for administration by the United Nations of the Antarctic regions, of troubled areas in general and, more recently, of Formosa. It is well to remember that the United Nations is not strong enough to impose a trust regime on Jerusalem, or Formosa, or any other area in which it might have to face military opposition.

98. THE TRUSTEESHIP COUNCIL

When the first eight trusteeship agreements had been made and administering authorities were thus known, it was possible to set up the Trusteeship Council, which held its first meeting in March 1947, about a year after the other organs were in operation. Article 86 of the Charter says that the Trusteeship Council shall consist of the following Members of the United Nations: (1) those Members administering trust territories; (2) any others of the five permanent members of the Security Council which do not administer trust territories; and (3) enough other members, elected by the General Assembly for three-year terms, to ensure that there shall be as many states which do not administer trust territories as there are which do.

The United States was thus a member from the beginning; but when the agreement for the Pacific Trust Territory was approved, she became an administering member, and this required election of two more members by the General Assembly. The Trusteeship Council then consisted of the following twelve members: the two permanent members of the Security Council which did not administer trust territories—China and the Soviet Union; the six states which did administer trust territories; and four other states elected by the General Assembly which, with China and the Soviet Union, made a number equal to the administering states. Italy is an administering authority, but was not a Member of the United Nations until 1955; her admission at that time necessitated election of another non-administering state.

The somewhat complicated arrangements concerning the composition of the Trusteeship Council were due in part to anti-colonial demands that states which had no trust territories ought to share in decisions concerning trusteeship, and partly to insistence by the Soviet Union that all of the Big Five must be on the Council. The balance thus obtained produces tie votes, though the United States often voted on the side of the non-administering members; she does not so often take this position now. As a result of this balanced representation the Council is apt to become deadlocked on political matters and in practice is reduced to consideration of technical matters. Though this does not increase its prestige, it improves its work; its recommendations for new schools, or more hospital beds, are tangible evidence to the peoples affected of the interest which the United Nations takes in them. The Council has thus tended to become an expert body serving as a brake upon the more impetuous and less informed Assembly. Like the Economic and Social Council, it has been weakened by the General Assembly's interference with its activities. It is the least noticed of the main organs.

RELATIONS WITH OTHER ORGANS. According to Article 83, the Security Council was to avail itself of the assistance of the Trusteeship Council in its handling of strategic trust areas, but it has in fact done nothing concerning the reports of the United States, nor has the General Assembly acted directly. Between the two jurisdictions, the United States is in a more fortunate position than other administering authorities. With the Economic and Social Council a liaison committee was established with a view to exchange of information, but little has been accomplished. Apparently there has been more useful intercourse between the Trusteeship Council and some of the specialized agencies. The Secretariat of course is constantly called upon in the trusteeship work. The International Court of Justice has been asked for three advisory opinions concerning trusteeship, but it is to be noted that they were asked for by the General Assembly rather than by the Trusteeship Council. With the Assembly, of course, the Trusteeship Council has ample relationships and its worst problem now is the need for some proper and workable relationship with the Assembly. The latter body is too large, too much occupied with other matters, and too political in its thinking to give to trusteeship matters the expert attention and adequate time which it was intended would be supplied by the Trusteeship Council. The latter body, however, is subject to suspicion because administering authorities have half the votes. Perhaps the League system of a body of experts was better.

99. QUESTIONNAIRE AND PETITIONS

The supervisory work of the Trusteeship Council is performed primarily upon the basis of a questionnaire which Article 86 of the

Charter instructs it to issue, and upon the annual reports from administering authorities which must be based upon this questionnaire. This
inquires as to the political, economic, social, and educational advancement of the inhabitants of each territory. Discussion of the reports is a
large part of the work of the Council. A representative of the administering authority makes a statement, and he is questioned; general debate follows; a committee makes recommendations concerning the
territory under consideration; the Council makes its recommendations
and submits them to the General Assembly, which is usually impatient
with the moderate suggestions of the Council. The Assembly demands
a more detailed questionnaire and asks for special reports; the administering authorities reply that too much work is required of them. The
annual reports themselves are long and detailed documents; the debates are long and tiresome. Doubtless improvement will be made, but
this procedure is typical of the task of the Trusteeship Council.

Another part of the work of the Council is to consider the petitions which, by Article 87b, "the General Assembly and, under its
authority, the Trusteeship Council," may accept. This has been
interpreted to include oral as well as written petitions. As the peoples
concerned have become more aware of this privilege, the number of
petitions has increased enormously—from 27 at the first session to 394
at the twelfth session. Since that time, the number has been cut in half
by letting the visiting missions decide whether a petition should be
considered by the mission itself or passed on to the Council. But the
number of petitions, even thus reduced, was beyond the capacity of
the Council to handle, and it set up a Standing Committee on Petitions,
which works between sessions of the Council. The petition system
presents a difficult problem. It is, on the one hand, an important means
for redress of grievances; on the other hand, many of the petitions are
trivial, such as personal pleas for financial assistance or for means to
complete an education; and petitioners are prone to believe that the
United Nations can remedy any evil, whereas in fact, it can do no more
than make recommendations.

The problem of petitioning is further complicated by oral hearings
and by the attitude of the Fourth Committee of the General Assembly.
In the Trusteeship Council, balanced representation means more expert knowledge and more moderation; in the fourth committee, the
anti-colonial majority refuses to lay down any criteria for deciding on
the petitions to be heard, and may listen to a petitioner before the
Council does, or adopt an attitude toward him different from the one
adopted by the Council. In 1952, for example, the fourth committee
occupied ten meetings in hearing petitions concerning unification of
the Ewe peoples and Togoland. An earnest clergyman, Rev. Michael

Scott, has been the subject of much debate because of his persistent efforts in behalf of African peoples. A great deal of bitterness has developed and the rivalry between the fourth committee, in which the anti-colonials may have their way, and the Trusteeship Council, in which they have at most a tie vote, has injured the Trusteeship Council's status as one of the main organs.

100. VISITING MISSIONS

Another important way in which the functions of trusteeship are exercised is through "visiting missions." These—which the League of Nations did not have—are authorized by Article 87 to make periodic visits to the trust territories. Such visits must be made at times agreed on with the administering authority concerned and they are necessarily to some degree under its guidance, but there has been little complaint of the cooperativeness of the administering authorities in this respect. Here again there was debate whether the missions should be composed of persons or of representatives of states, and a compromise is used in practice, by which certain states are nominated to serve on a mission and this state designates certain persons who must be (but always are) approved by the Council. It is obviously desirable, whether from the viewpoint of the Council and its acquisition of knowledge or from that of the people visited, who should be able to look with respect upon the personnel of the mission, that the Council itself should be represented on the mission; and in fact, almost all the members of missions have been representatives on the Council, or their alternates or advisory experts. Each mission now has four members and there is in addition a larger number of Secretariat officials and, usually, local officials of the administering authority. Such a group is large enough to be expensive to the United Nations, which bears most of the costs. On each mission, it should be noted, there is the same balanced representation as on the Trusteeship Council itself.

Each territory is visited about once in three years, though there has been some argument that not enough change takes place in this time to justify this frequency of visit. The mission visits many places and receives both written and oral petitions; it is a tiring task. The General Assembly, however, has criticized the missions for taking inadequate time and making insufficient reports. Resolution 434(IV) in 1950 asked the Council to do better in this respect; the Council paid little attention to the resolution and the Sixth Assembly again demanded improvement. No agreement has been reached concerning the time which a mission should spend; actually, two to three months are spent in each territory.

A great deal of information is gathered on these trips, which the accompanying Secretariat officials cast into reports. The Secretariat officials have been criticized for exerting undue influence in the whole procedure. The reports are made to the Council, in general terms of recommendation, and the administering authorities often act upon them before the Council does. Each report has separate chapters upon the political, economic, social, and educational situation, and inquires as to the "progressive development towards self-government or independence" (Article 76b). It is this last objective which most interests the Fourth Committee of the Assembly, which debates heatedly and at length such matters as the unification of the Ewe people, hearing petitioners directly, without waiting for the Trusteeship Council to perform its functions.[30] Politicians from local areas have learned to make use of the jealousy between the Council and the fourth committee; it is clear that the United Nations is now familiar to the peoples of the trust territories who, indeed, are coming to rely too heavily upon it. After all, the administering authority has rights under the agreements made, and the United Nations can do no more than make recommendations to it. There is little doubt, however, that the influence of the United Nations is moving the trust peoples more rapidly toward self-government and higher standards.

101. NON-SELF-GOVERNING TERRITORIES

It may seem inappropriate to discuss Chapter XI of the Charter in a chapter dealing with organs, and under the heading of the Trusteeship Council, but there is no connection in which the development can be more conveniently handled. More will be said in the following chapter concerning the colonial problem; here we must note that, through a

[30] The Ewe question occupies many pages of the records. The Ewes were separated by the peace settlement at the end of World War I, part going to the United Kingdom and part to France (British Togoland and French Togoland). There were also many thousands of them in the Gold Coast, which was not a trust territory at all, and which, in fact, had been advanced toward self-government by the British more rapidly than the trust territories had been. The Ewes petitioned for reunification and the General Assembly favored their plea; but there were obvious difficulties of political frontiers, differing political capacity, and adjustment between a trust and a non-trust area. Further, the Ewes themselves were unable to agree on what they wanted.

Similar problems are raised with regard to "administrative unions" in which an administering authority, for convenience sake or perhaps for easier absorption, includes a trust territory in an administrative governmental unit with some other area not under trusteeship.

most remarkable constitutional development, an organ or, at any rate, a means has been provided, which was not anticipated nor found in the Charter, for exercising supervision over colonial areas.

CHARTER PROVISIONS. Chapter XI of the Charter deals with a field not touched in the League of Nations system, and which was carefully differentiated from the trusteeship system of the United Nations. The chapter is headed "Declaration" and creates obligations only for those Members "which have or assume responsibilities for the administration of territories whose peoples have not yet attained a full measure of self-government."[31] These states agreed that "the interests of the inhabitants of these territories are paramount"; and they accepted as a sacred trust the obligation to promote to the utmost the well-being of the inhabitants by (1) respecting the culture of the peoples, ensuring political, economic, social, and educational advancement and protection against abuses, (2) developing self-government according to the circumstances of each, (3) furthering international peace and security, and (4) promoting research and development.

There was, however, no provision whatever for supervision by the United Nations, and no organ or authority was provided for that purpose. The only mention of the United Nations was in the clause by which the administering states agreed to transmit regularly to the Secretary-General "for information purposes" and subject to "security and constitutional considerations," information of various kinds, but from which political matters were carefully excluded. Nothing was said as to what should be done with the information by the Secretary-General. It is to be noted also that, whereas trust territories were to be advanced towards "self-government or independence" (Article 76b), the non-self-governing territories were to "develop self-government" only. There is little doubt that the colonial powers at San Francisco, while recognizing the demand for improvement in the treatment of colonial peoples, thought themselves well protected (also by Article 2, paragraph 7) against interference by the United Nations.

COMMITTEE ON INFORMATION. Nevertheless, the United Nations did interfere, and to a surprising degree. It was natural that it should set up a Committee on Information from the Non-Self-Governing Territories to consider the reports made to the Secretary-General, who did not know what to do with them. Article 10 of the Charter is broad enough to permit discussion and recommendation in this field; how far

---

[31] The term "non-self-governing territories" is in practice a euphemism for colonies. It has been pointed out in debates that it should be applied also to peoples within a metropolitan area (e.g., the Ukraine). The Belgian government has issued many studies of indigenous peoples in many non-colonial states which are not self-governing.

other Charter restrictions might limit this right has been much debated. The colonial powers did not particularly like this development but they submitted and thereafter the pressure upon them steadily increased. The committee was at first *ad hoc*, then "Special"; it was renewed for a year at a time, then for three years at a time; by now, it is practically a standing committee. It has, however, been maintained on the basis of equal representation between colonial and non-colonial powers, though efforts have been made to push the colonial powers out and bring onto the committee indigenous representatives from the colonial peoples.

Chapter XI does not authorize a questionnaire such as the Trusteeship Council issues, but a "standard form" was nevertheless prepared which the colonial powers were expected to answer. It included a section on political information (which had been excluded at San Francisco), but it was noted that answers to this section might be voluntary —thus implying that there was a right to demand answers for requests for other information. To objections against this questioning, the reply was that the colonial powers had promised to supply information. The Secretary-General summarizes the replies; the Committee on Information, with its balanced representation, goes over them; but when its report reaches the General Assembly, the anti-colonial majority takes over. Step by step it has increased its demands and its criticism, and the colonial powers, protesting the unconstitutionality of the procedure and at times withdrawing from meetings in protest, have felt it necessary, in view of mounting anti-colonialism, to accept the demands for the most part.

COMMITTEE ON FACTORS. The development then took another road. Some of the administering states decided that certain of their colonies had advanced to self-governing status and that it was therefore no longer necessary to make reports for these colonies. When the United Kingdom so reported for Malta, there was no objection; by the time that the Netherlands and the United States made such a report, the Assembly was ready to question the right of the colonial power to make this decision. The Fourth Assembly adopted a resolution asserting the right of the United Nations, rather than of the colonial power, to decide when a colony was sufficiently advanced to become self-governing; and it instructed a committee to study the factors which ought to be considered in reaching such a decision. The decision that Puerto Rico should become self-governing was approved; but the Netherlands' statement of decision concerning Surinam and the Antilles was delayed. The Fifth Assembly approved the cessation of information concerning Indonesia; this did not make Indonesia any more independent, but it signified that the right of decision belonged to the United Nations.

With the Sixth Assembly (1951), the acerbity of the controversy increased. Resolution 567 (VI) set up the Committee on Factors, and in various small ways supervision was extended by suggestion. There were seven resolutions in 1952, and the Committee on Factors presented a list of standards which could hardly be reached by any of the sovereign states in existence today. Now, this could have been a step in the direction of overcoming one of the weaknesses in the international system to which we have alluded earlier—the lack of criteria or procedures by which the community of nations could admit a new entity to its membership, as a legal person with rights and duties under international law, recognized by all members and not merely by those states which might choose to give recognition. Unfortunately, this was not the primary purpose of the majority, which thought rather in terms of extracting from the colonial powers as much as possible. The result of this concentration on what the colonial powers ought to do was to set standards for self-government or independence so high that it would be difficult for any colony to attain them. Nevertheless, this is the direction in which the community of nations must move if it is to judge which states qualify as members, and it is to be hoped that effort will be resumed upon a more objective basis. The Committee on Factors was disbanded, but the Committee on Information was instructed to examine reports concerning the colonies with respect to the list of factors which had been approved by the General Assembly.

In terms of organization—with which we are concerned in this chapter[32]—two new organs had been created to serve purposes not stated in the Charter. Only one of these remains, the Committee on Information, but it may now be compared, strange as it sounds, to the Trusteeship Council. In each, representation is equally balanced between colonial and non-colonial Powers; and each can do no more than make recommendations to the General Assembly, which body is more apt to approve or extend the recommendations of the Committee on Information than those of the Trusteeship Council. Earlier thinking had apparently intended that the trust areas should advance more rapidly toward independence than the colonies; indeed, as we have noted, Chapter XI speaks only of self-government as an objective, whereas Chapter XII speaks also of independence. Most of the "non-self-governing territories," however, under the tutelage of their colonial ad-

---

[32] See pp. 69-70 above, § 128 and Appendix IV, below. The important question of interpretation of the Charter is further discussed in the final chapter of this volume.

ministrators, have advanced more rapidly and are more nearly ready for independence than are the trust territories.

During all this increasingly bitter controversy, the colonial Powers maintained that the Charter gave no authorization for such interference in their internal affairs and that, on the contrary, Article 2, paragraph 7, positively forbade it. No authority, however, had been provided which could interpret the Charter, and each organ made its own interpretation. The Eighth General Assembly voted a preambular clause to Resolution 742 (VIII) which asserted that the Assembly was competent under the Charter to act as, under constant challenge, it had been acting for a number of years. The colonial Powers, which have been pushed together in resistance, include the United States, increasingly fearful of intervention into her domestic affairs. Without these Powers, the United Nations could not operate. They have given way steadily before the anti-colonial tide; they recognize the writing on the wall and most of the colonies are being developed toward self-government. They are, of course, not bound by Assembly resolutions, which can only recommend; and they increasingly resent the nagging from the anti-colonial majority. There are elements of cleavage and danger to the United Nations in this situation, and it is to be hoped that pride and vested interest, on the one hand, and historic resentment and desire for retaliation, on the other hand, will give way to a common effort to work out a sensible procedure for determining when a group should have independence and be entitled to membership and legal status in the community of nations.

THE INTERNATIONAL COURT OF JUSTICE

102. A NEW NAME

The Court, as it was under the League of Nations, has been described in an earlier chapter. The Dumbarton Oaks Proposals did not answer the question of whether there should be a new court, nor did the Committee of Jurists, which met at Washington just before the San Francisco Conference for the purpose of studying the Statute of the Court.[33] There was little reason for making a new court, though it was argued that there were many new states and that the court must be

[33] The documents of the Committee of Jurists may be found among the UNCIO documents. The work of this conference was of little value, since it was done all over again in Committee IV(1) of the San Francisco Conference, in which the decisions were made.

fitted into the new organization; the chief reason for giving it a new name was fear that continuation of the old name might produce antagonistic reaction in the Soviet Union and the United States, both of which had rejected the older court. Practically speaking, however, it is the same court with a new name; and the older statute, very slightly modified to fit into the United Nations and with the same numeration of articles, is an "integral part" of the Charter.

CHARTER PROVISIONS. The International Court of Justice is now one of the "principal organs" of the United Nations, and its "principal judicial organ"; and every Member of the United Nations is therefore bound by the Statute. A method of amendment was added (Article 69 of the Statute) which is the same as that for amendment of the Charter. Article 94 of the Charter was an effort to put some strength behind the Court; it not only binds Members to submit to decisions of the Court, but provides a sanction in that, if a party fails to carry out a judgment, the other party may appeal to the Security Council, "which may, if it deems necessary, make recommendations or decide upon measures to be taken to give effect to the judgment." These words, almost the same as those used in Article 39, were explained to mean that the Security Council has no authority beyond that already given to it—i.e., it could take enforcement action only if it had decided that there was a threat to the peace.[34] The method of electing judges was slightly changed, causing some debate at the first election.[35] The right to ask an advisory opinion was given to the Security Council and the General Assembly, and the latter body was authorized to extend the privilege to other organs and to the specialized agencies.[36] Finally, it is to be noted that Article 36, paragraph 3, of the Charter suggests that for legal disputes the Security Council should "as a general rule" recommend to the parties that they refer their dispute to the Court. Weak as these words were, they have been followed only once before the political situation worsened—in the Corfu Channel case; nor has the Security Council ever sought an advisory opinion from the Court to help it settle a dispute, as the Council of the League of Nations frequently did.

[34] Dr. Pasvolsky, in Hearings, pp. 286-87. This, of course, it could do in any case, but usually the judgment of the court would not be expected to lead to a breach of the peace. The Security Council, however, could use this power to back up a court judgment if it wished to do so.

[35] See Brookings, Organization, Chap. iii.

[36] Resolution 91(I) (1947), admitted Switzerland as a party to the Statute, and Resolution 264(III) stated the conditions under which such a non-member party could participate in election of judges. Liechtenstein was admitted by Resolution 363(IV) in 1949; Japan and San Marino by Resolutions 805 and 806(VIII) in 1953.

103. ORGANIZATION OF THE COURT

The court continues to be located at The Hague, in the Peace Palace built by Andrew Carnegie. It elects its own officers—a president, vice-president, and registrar—and has a staff of twenty-five. An excellent library is available in the Peace Palace. A quorum is nine, and five judges may sit as a chamber for summary procedure.

PARTIES. All Members of the United Nations are automatically parties to the Statute of the Court, but non-members may also become parties (Article 93 of the Charter) on conditions determined by the General Assembly upon recommendation of the Security Council. Non-members not parties to the Statute may also appear before the court if they submit to prescribed conditions. Article 34 of the Statute says that "Only states may be parties in cases before the Court"; consequently, no individual can bring a case before the Court, and the United Nations itself cannot do so, though it may appear with regard to advisory opinions.[37]

SELECTION OF JUDGES. The Court consists of fifteen judges,[38] elected by separate and simultaneous vote of the Security Council and the General Assembly, from nominations made by "national groups." The nominating process was intended to operate independently of governments, and geographical distribution is not called for in the choice of judges as it is for other organs. Nevertheless, political and regional influences are felt. The United States has not been above bargaining to give Latin America another judge on the bench (they now have four) in return for their votes to put a non-Communist state on the Security Council. It would be interesting to ascertain how far in practice national groups do act independently of their governments. In any case, even if nominations are independently made, the voting is political and states are not apt to vote against a nominee whose government has indicated favor for him. On the whole, however, the selection has been good, and the quality of judges chosen has been high.

Several ballots are usually required before the separate votings of the

[37] The General Convention on Privileges and Immunities of the United Nations provides (Section XXX) that, in case of dispute between the United Nations and a Member, a request shall be made to the Court for an advisory opinion, and the opinion of the Court shall be accepted as decisive by the parties. Section 21 of the Headquarters Agreement provides that disputes between the United Nations and the United States under that agreement shall be settled by arbitration.

[38] There may be more than fifteen judges on the bench, for the statute allows *ad hoc* judges. States still feel, as they have concerning arbitral tribunals in the past, that they must be "represented"; and if there is no judge from the state of a party to the dispute, that state may name a judge to sit with the court for that case.

Security Council and the General Assembly coincide on fifteen names. The first election became entangled with the procedural question of how many ballots were permissible in one meeting; but fifteen judges were finally chosen, and they drew lots for three-, six-, or nine-year terms. At the end of three years, five judges were elected (in fact, re-elected) for a full nine-year term. In 1952, the six-year terms were ended and five judges were chosen for nine-year terms. The system is now established upon a rotating basis, with five judges elected every three years. Vacancies are filled by the same process of election.

104. JURISDICTION OF THE COURT

The Court may hear "all cases which the parties refer to it," and it decides all questions concerning its own jurisdiction. The case may be brought before it voluntarily, through agreement between the parties, or it may be brought upon demand of one of the parties, if both are bound in some way to compulsory jurisdiction. As of 1955, only three cases could be said to have been brought voluntarily before the Court.[39] The sovereign states of this day are not eager to submit their disputes to legal decision; they show their respect for law by maintaining a Court at a cost of some $600,000 per year, rather than by making use of the Court.

COMPULSORY JURISDICTION. Though a majority of the states at San Francisco favored compulsory jurisdiction, the opposition of the Soviet Union and the United States excluded it, and the compromise made for the earlier court was continued. This is the "Optional Clause" (Article 34, paragraph 2) of the statute, under which states may by declaration agree in advance to submit to the jurisdiction of the court in cases where the other party has also accepted the Optional Clause. We have noted above that some forty-five states had, at one time or another, made this declaration; only thirty-three states do so now. Since three of these are non-members, barely half the Members of the United Nations have shown willingness to submit to being called before the court in cases of the types listed in Article 36 paragraph 2. Two states (Iran and Guatemala) which were brought before the Court under compulsory jurisdiction terminated their declarations, although the Court was favorable to both of them. A state may not, however, terminate its acceptance in order to escape jurisdiction in a particular case.[40]

---

[39] The Corfu Channel and Asylum cases; also in the Minquiers and Ecrehos case, though the parties to this case were under compulsory jurisdiction.

[40] See the Nottebohm Case (Preliminary Objections), *I.C.J. Reports*, 1953, p. 111.

Furthermore, most of the declarations are conditioned by time limits and reservations of various sorts. The most damaging of the reservations was adopted by the Senate of the United States, which excludes from the obligation to submit to compulsory jurisdiction domestic questions "as determined by the United States of America."[41] It is thus possible for the United States to escape jurisdiction in any case by calling the matter a domestic one, whether it is or not. Another reservation made by the United States is incomprehensible, but could be interpreted so as to exclude obligations under the Charter itself, a multilateral treaty. These reservations continue the long opposition of the United States to compulsory settlement of legal disputes, but they nevertheless mark an important advance. It is hardly probable that the United States would expose itself to ridicule by extreme use of the reservations. It would be a great improvement, however, if states would accept the Optional Clause without reservations; indeed, it would thus be possible to establish compulsory jurisdiction without amendment of the statute or Charter.

An additional field of compulsory jurisdiction is to be found in treaties which provide that disputes arising under the treaty must be submitted to the Court. Though the range of application is limited, the total number of treaties (now over two hundred) somewhat increases the compulsory jurisdiction of the Court.[42]

ADVISORY OPINIONS. Article 96 of the Charter provides that either the General Assembly or the Security Council may ask the Court for an advisory opinion "on any legal question," and that the Assembly may authorize other organs, or specialized agencies to do so. The Economic and Social Council, the Trusteeship Council, the Interim Committee, and practically all of the specialized agencies have been so authorized. A state (much less an individual) cannot ask for such advice from the Court, though it might persuade one of the authorized organs to do so. It might be possible thus to bring a dispute before the Court, but the parties would not be bound by an advisory opinion.

105. THE WORK OF THE COURT

The 1954-55 *Yearbook* of the Court lists twenty-nine cases by folio number. Some of these, however, were the same case appearing in different form; and six applications made by the United States and the

---

[41] See F. O. Wilcox, "The United States Accepts Compulsory Jurisdiction," *A.J.*, 40 (1946), p. 699; L. Preuss, "The International Court of Justice, the Senate, and Matters of Domestic Jurisdiction," *ibid.*, p. 720.

[42] For such current information, see the *Yearbooks* of the Court.

United Kingdom in matters not under compulsory jurisdiction were dropped by the Court because of failure of the other party to answer. It might be said, then, that the Court has actually given decisions or opinions in some twenty cases in the first ten years of its existence.

ADVISORY OPINIONS. There were seven advisory opinions, for all of which requests emanated from the General Assembly. Some of these, such as the two concerning admission of new Members, resulted from the frustration of the Assembly itself; they did not help the prestige of the Court at all, since it was known in advance that the Soviet Union would pay no attention to what the Court might say. The same comment might be made concerning the inquiry concerning the procedure of arbitration under the peace treaties.[43]

Three advisory opinions have been given in connection with the status of the mandated territory of South West Africa. The first concerned the legal status of the territory and the relation of the Union of South Africa thereto. The Court advised that South Africa continued to have the same obligations toward the territory and must now report to the United Nations concerning it—which probably prevented absorption of the area into the Union of South Africa, though it did not induce that obstinate state to put it under trusteeship. Later, as the Assembly majority sought to extend its control, the Court was asked whether decisions must be taken as they were in the League of Nations, by unanimity, or whether the two-thirds vote of the General Assembly was sufficient; the Court held that the latter was proper. In 1956, the Court replied, to a third request, that it was permissible for the Assembly to hear oral petitions from persons in South West Africa.[44]

The behavior of the United States in persecuting some of its citizens employed by the United Nations and their consequent dismissal led to an inquiry as to whether a judgment of the Administrative Tribunal of the United Nations could be reviewed by the General Assembly; to this the Court replied that there was no appeal from the Administrative Tribunal.[45]

[43] Conditions of Admission of a State to Membership in the United Nations, *I.C.J. Reports*, 1947-48, pp. 9, 57; Competence of the General Assembly for the Admission of a State to the United Nations," *ibid.*, 1950, p. 4; Interpretation of Peace Treaties with Bulgaria, Hungary and Romania, *ibid.*, 1950, pp. 65, 121, 221.

[44] International Status of South-West Africa, *I.C.J. Reports*, 1949, p. 128; Territory of South-West Africa (Voting Procedure), *ibid.*, 1955, p. 67; Admissibility of Hearings by the Committee on South West Africa, *ibid.*, 1956.

[45] Effect of Awards of Compensation Made by the United Nations Administrative Tribunal, *ibid.*, 1954, p. 46.

Two advisory opinions have been requested on behalf of the Secretary-General—which suggests that the General Assembly might do well to authorize another organ to request advisory opinions. One of these resulted in what is doubtless the most important utterance of the court thus far, that the United Nations is an international legal person and was able to make a claim for reparation for the death of Count Bernadotte. The Assembly asked both the Court and the International Law Commission for opinions concerning reservations to treaties and received divergent answers from them; it approved the one from the Court.[46]

CONTENTIOUS CASES. The first case presented to the Court by parties to a dispute was in 1947, after British warships had been damaged in the Corfu Channel by mines. The United Kingdom charged that Albania was responsible and complained to the Security Council. When a Soviet veto blocked action here, the Council recommended to the parties that they take the matter to the Court. Surprisingly, Albania submitted to the jurisdiction of the Court, though she later challenged it. An award was made to the United Kingdom, but it has never been paid by Albania.[47]

A case of much interest to international lawyers was brought by the United Kingdom in 1949 against Norway, after centuries of dispute over fishing rights. The decision made was in favor of Norway and allowed her control over a wide area of territorial waters within a line drawn generally parallel with her very broken coast line and not required to follow the sinuosities of the coast.[48]

The right of asylum, somewhat questionable in international law but favored in Latin America, came before the court in three different phases in the case of Haya de la Torre, a Peruvian politician who had sought refuge in the Colombian embassy in Peru. He remained there actually for several years, and ultimately Colombia asked the Court for help, appealing to a treaty and to what was claimed to be the particular international law of Latin American states concerning asylum. The Court gave a rather vague answer; Colombia asked for an interpretation of the opinion, and was refused. To a third application by Colombia, the Court replied that that state was not obligated to surrender Haya

[46] Reparation for Injuries Suffered in the Service of the United Nations, *I.C.J. Reports*, 1949, p. 174; Reservations to the Convention on Genocide, *ibid.*, 1951, p. 15.

[47] This case was heard in three phases by the Court: Corfu Channel Case (Preliminary Objection), *I.C.J. Reports*, 1947-48, pp. 7, 15; Corfu Channel Case (Merits), *ibid.*, 1949, p. 4; Corfu Channel Case (Assessment of the Amount of Compensation), *ibid.*, 1949, p. 237.

[48] Fisheries Case, *I.C.J. Reports*, 1951, p. 8.

de la Torre to Peru, but that the asylum ought to be ended; it suggested that the two states should settle the matter between themselves. The fugitive was later permitted to leave the country.[49]

The only case in which the United States has been a party before the Court was one under compulsory jurisdiction, in which France sought an answer concerning the rights of United States nationals in Morocco. It was a complex case, based on outdated treaties and the decision favored each party in certain respects.[50] The Greek government brought a claim against the United Kingdom, to the effect that the latter state was obligated under a treaty to arbitrate a dispute conconcerning one Ambatielos; the Court upheld this claim.[51] France and England submitted to the Court a dispute concerning the tiny islands, Minquiers and Ecrehos, and they were awarded to England. This was a case in which the parties were bound to compulsory jurisdiction, but submitted the case through voluntary agreement.[52]

Nationalization of the oil industry in Iran led the United Kingdom, which suffered greatly thereby, to challenge its legality before the Security Council and the Court. Iran objected that the Court could not take jurisdiction because of reservations made by Iran to her acceptance of the Optional Clause. The Court nevertheless ordered interim measures of protection under Article 41 of the statute; later, it upheld the Iranian claim and denied itself jurisdiction over the merits of the case.[53]

The case of Nottebohm involved a person living in Guatemala who had acquired citizenship in Liechtenstein. This little state—which had just been admitted as a party to the statute and had accepted the Optional Clause—brought a claim in his behalf against Guatemala. The latter state objected that the time limit of its acceptance of the Optional Clause had expired before the case came to trial; the court held, however, that the application of Liechtenstein had been made before the expiration date and that it had jurisdiction until the case was settled. On the merits, the Court asserted that the mere conferring of citizenship did not automatically entitle the state, of which the person had thus become a national, to claim diplomatic protection in his behalf. If this decision stands as a precedent, it could have important consequences in the international law of responsibility of states.

[49] Asylum Case, *I.C.J. Reports*, p. 266; Interpretation of the Judgment in the Asylum Case, *ibid.*, 1950, p. 395; Haya de la Torre Case, *ibid.*, 1951, p. 4.

[50] Rights of Nationals of the United States of America in Morocco, *I.C.J. Reports*, 1952, p. 175.

[51] Ambatielos Case, *I.C.J. Reports*, 1953, p. 10.

[52] Minquiers and Ecrehos Case, *I.C.J. Reports*, 1953, p. 4.

[53] Anglo-Iranian Oil Company Case, *I.C.J. Reports*, 1952, p. 13.

In the intricate case of the *Monetary Gold Removed from Rome in 1943*, the Court felt that it could not take jurisdiction in the absence of Albania. An interesting part of the history of this case was the effort to award the gold, which originally belonged to Albania, to the United Kingdom in payment of the award in the Corfu Channel case.[54]

It cannot be said that the Court has had a great deal of work to do—perhaps two cases per year, advisory and contentious. None of them have dealt with great political issues which could endanger peace; and the important controversies over interpretation of the Charter have not been referred to the Court. That the Court is not more used is of course not its fault; its record is good; it has done its work efficiently and without loss of time and has shown that it can interpret the law fairly and liberally. The record shows rather that Members do not care to settle their disputes by judicial procedures and according to law. Yet the need for a Court is proclaimed by all, and the General Assembly by Resolution 171 (II) urged Members to make use of the Court.

THE SECRETARIAT

The experience of the League of Nations demonstrated the importance of the Secretariat, which the Charter justifiably lists as one of the principal organs of the United Nations. It is the communications- or nerve-center, which holds together the various parts of the system; it is the only organ which represents and works impartially for the whole community of nations.

106. THE SECRETARY-GENERAL[55]

At the head of this organ is the Secretary-General, nominated by the Security Council and elected by the General Assembly. It would be difficult to find a job in the world with which this could be compared. The Secretary-General is primarily an administrator, responsible for preparing the programs of work of the various organs, for organizing a staff of several thousand employees to do this work, and for carrying

[54] *I.C.J. Reports*, 1954, p. 10; see also the Order of July 5, 1951.

[55] Trygve Lie, *In the Cause of Peace* (New York, 1954); Stephen Schwebel, *The Secretary-General of the United Nations: His Political Powers and Practice* (Cambridge, 1952); J. L. Kunz, "The Legal Position of the Secretary-General," *A.J.*, 40 (1946), p. 786; Waldo Chamberlin, "Strengthening the Secretariat: Analysis and Proposition," *Annals*, 296 (1954), p. 131; *United Nations Secretariat* (United Nations Studies No. 4, Carnegie Endowment, 1950); Staff Study No. 12; *Annual Review*, 1954, Chap. vi.

out the decisions of the various organs; at the same time he is looked to as a political leader. He is consulted by Member governments and in this capacity he must be something of a statesman and a diplomat. There is no other person (aside from the staff under his direction) whose primary function is to make the United Nations a success, no one else to personify it and give it dignity in the eyes of the world, no one else to represent it as an institution and to protect its interest as such. But he is not a chief executive; the United Nations has no such officer. He is given very little authority, or none, in his own name; and he has behind him no parliament which can give orders that he can execute against Members, no court that is able to enforce his decisions, no police to back him up. He must depend upon his powers of persuasion and his ability to secure cooperation.

The League of Nations had made its secretary-general a civil servant, and Sir Eric Drummond played that part well. But the experience of the League, and perhaps also the success of the active Albert Thomas in the adjoining I.L.O., led many to believe that the Secretary-General of the United Nations should have a stronger position; and the Conference at San Francisco moved slightly in this direction. While his title was Secretary-General, implying his administrative character, Article 99 gives him specific authority to bring before the Security Council any matter which in his opinion might threaten peace.[56] Since any Member can and should do this, it would be a rare occasion on which he would have an opportunity; only once has he moved in this direction—when the news of the attack upon Korea came. The significance of Article 99 lies rather in its invitation to play a political, in addition to his administrative, role.

The increased importance of the office appears in various minor ways. His nomination is subject to veto in the Security Council; it is in fact negotiated privately among the permanent members of that organ, since they must agree upon him. His term is five years, long enough to give him a chance to prove himself. He is forbidden to accept any national office immediately after leaving his post. He makes an annual report to the General Assembly, in which he has an opportunity to criticize and to suggest policy.

The first Secretary-General, Trygve Lie, was a Norwegian whose socialistic views were acceptable to the Russians and not so strong as to frighten the United States; he had had experience in government and had shared in the making of the United Nations. His administration had both strong and weak points. He had little interest in internal

[56] The rules of procedure of the various organs allow the Secretary-General to participate, not only as regards peace and security, but for other purposes; he has even initiated resolutions.

administration or in the feelings of his staff, which grew increasingly bitter against him because of their uncertainty as to their tenure in office. He left authority with assistant secretaries-general and expected them to handle administrative problems; he did not act as a responsible manager and did not solve personnel difficulties, such as those of temporary and permanent contracts.

He was much more interested in political leadership and in this sense built up the prestige of his office considerably, establishing precedents early. He intervened in the first case before the Security Council (Iran) with a memorandum explaining the constitutional situation under the Charter in a sense which would imply that the Council was acting illegally; and while the Council denied his interpretation, it strongly upheld his right to present his views. When he was instructed to appoint a committee of investigation in the Greek question, he affirmed his right under Article 99 to make independent investigations of his own. With regard to Trieste, he asserted the right of the United Nations to assume responsibility for the administration of the area. In various other ways, such as his annual reports, or visits to Member governments, or his "Twenty-Year Peace Plan," he took an initiative, on behalf of his office and of the United Nations, which was often courageous.

In the end, his troubles piled up till he was ready to resign. He irritated the United States by arguing for the admission of Communist China, and the Soviet Union by his strong leadership against the aggression in Korea. The Soviet Union exasperated him by refusing to address him, or recognize him, as the Secretary-General; the United States put him into a very difficult position by insisting that he dismiss American employees whom it suspected of Communist leanings. At the end of his term, in 1950, the Soviet Union vetoed his reappointment and the United States announced that it would veto the appointment of anyone else. The General Assembly found a way out by extending his term for three years. He offered his resignation in November 1952 and, to the pleased surprise of all, it was found possible to agree upon a successor.

Mr. Dag Hammarskjöld of Sweden was chosen, a civil servant of experience, a member of a well-known family and a capable and attractive person. He gained good will from his staff by visiting every desk at the beginning of his term and he has displayed a more active interest in personnel and administrative matters than did his predecessor—perhaps because he was plunged into a large personnel problem at the outset. He worked quietly and with much consultation, after which he effected a reorganization of the Secretariat, with economies which gained favor for him with Members, and he demanded a stronger control over his staff. All of this the General Assembly approved. The staff, at first pleased, became restive under his increased personal authority, but seem now to have settled down with good morale.

Hammarskjöld has, however, played an increasingly important political role, in quite a different fashion from that of Lie. He prefers "quiet diplomacy" and makes no public announcements of what he is doing. When he was asked to seek the release of the American fliers, he went directly to Peiping and conferred with Mao Tse-tung and no record has been given out concerning these negotiations. He was asked to go to the Middle East when danger flared up again there and he visited the various heads of states and obtained a cease-fire. He did report on this mission, but in terms so generalized and obtuse that little could be learned as to his methods or as to the views of the various parties.[57] Member states apparently feel that he can be trusted to commit no indiscretions at their expense, and he was asked to go back to the Middle East and continue his efforts there. Mr. Hammarskjöld is still a man of mystery to many, but he is increasingly being recognized as the spokesman for the United Nations. The political functions of the Secretary-General are growing.

107. ORGANIZATION AND FUNCTIONS OF THE SECRETARIAT

The work of the Secretariat reaches into many fields calling for expert knowledge. In a library of United Nations documents there is something of interest and value to almost every field of human activity. If one estimates according to the budget, over half the work of the Secretariat is of administrative type. The 1955 budget showed well over fifteen million dollars, out of twenty-eight million dollars, spent on conference services, general services, and common staff costs and services. Almost a third of the staff were employed in economic and social work; some 6 per cent in political and security matters; nearly 3 per cent on trusteeship; 10 per cent on public information; and 2 per cent on legal matters. Looking at it in another way, about half the personnel were engaged in documentation work—keeping the records of meetings, translating, editing, etc.; a fourth were servicing meetings; others were occupied with management, or were out on field missions or other activities. The professional group engaged in study and research is a comparatively small part of the total.[58]

Mr. Lie organized the Secretariat under eight assistant secretaries-

[57] *U.N. Doc.* S/3596.
[58] See Brookings, *Organization.*

general, with an executive office headed by the executive assistant to the Secretary-General, upon whom fell principally the responsibility for coordinating the activities of a staff of some four thousand. Each "ASG" was the head of a department and also an advisor to the Secretary-General. Below this level were eleven directors. The political rivalries over top posts in the League of Nations led to disapproval at San Francisco of the rank of undersecretary-general, and direction of activities was therefore dispersed. Mr. Lie tried, on one occasion, to set up a ninth ASG whose chief task would be administrative coordination, leaving him free for political leadership. The position was anomalous, however, combining equality of rank with power to coordinate, and the effort failed.

Mr. Hammarskjöld effected a large reorganization. He abolished the nineteen top officials and revived the title of undersecretary-general, of whom there are seven, two of them without portfolio. There are also two deputy undersecretaries, five heads of offices, and the Director-General of the Technical Assistance Administration. Officers below the former ASG level were brought more closely into communication with the top command. Hierarchical rank is now somewhat puzzling, and the differing salaries attached to the various jobs add no enlightenment. Apparently, Mr. Hammarskjöld sought for more flexibility in the top administration, more direct contact with lower officials, and some freedom for thought and political assistance on the part of two undersecretaries. Departments were shifted around, some being eliminated as such; and a respectable reduction in costs could be shown.

The Department of Political and Security Council Affairs has declined with the decline of the Security Council, and its posts (including the now useless Military Staff Committee) have diminished from 110 to 93. This department has usually been headed by a Russian and has been as secretive and independent as the Security Council which it serves. It has produced little documentation (credit must be given to it for the *Repertoire*) and has supplied much of the personnel for missions abroad.

The Department of Trusteeship and Non-Self-Governing Territories, on the other hand, has grown steadily and almost doubled in size, corresponding to the increased interest of the Assembly in this field. It now has over a hundred members, including many highly qualified persons, with earlier experience of colonies and mandates. It was an energetic group in its earlier days, but it has been caught between the colonial and anti-colonial forces and, having had its fingers burned, now works with more caution. The department furnishes staffs for the visiting missions.

Whether economic and social matters should be handled together or

STRUCTURE OF THE SECRETARIAT AT HEADQUARTERS 1955

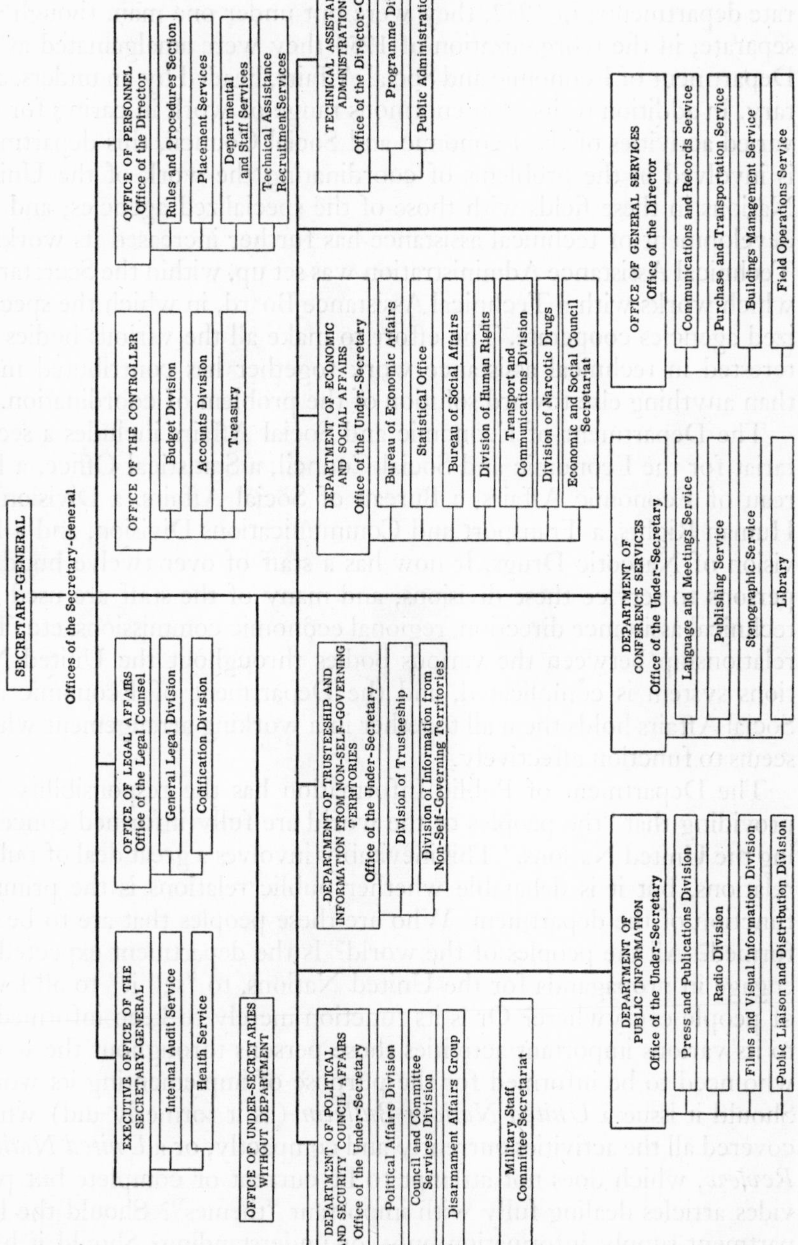

SECRETARY-GENERAL
Offices of the Secretary-General

EXECUTIVE OFFICE OF THE SECRETARY-GENERAL
- Internal Audit Service
- Health Service

OFFICE OF UNDER-SECRETARIES WITHOUT DEPARTMENT

OFFICE OF LEGAL AFFAIRS
Office of the Legal Counsel
- General Legal Division
- Codification Division

OFFICE OF PERSONNEL
Office of the Director
- Rules and Procedures Section
- Placement Services
- Departmental and Staff Services
- Technical Assistance Recruitment Services

OFFICE OF THE CONTROLLER
- Budget Division
- Accounts Division
- Treasury

TECHNICAL ASSISTANCE ADMINISTRATION
Office of the Director-General
- Programme Division
- Public Administration Division

DEPARTMENT OF ECONOMIC AND SOCIAL AFFAIRS
Office of the Under-Secretary
- Bureau of Economic Affairs
- Statistical Office
- Bureau of Social Affairs
- Division of Human Rights
- Transport and Communications Division
- Division of Narcotic Drugs
- Economic and Social Council Secretariat

OFFICE OF GENERAL SERVICES
Office of the Director
- Communications and Records Service
- Purchase and Transportation Service
- Buildings Management Service
- Field Operations Service

DEPARTMENT OF CONFERENCE SERVICES
Office of the Under-Secretary
- Language and Meetings Service
- Publishing Service
- Stenographic Service
- Library

DEPARTMENT OF TRUSTEESHIP AND INFORMATION FROM NON-SELF-GOVERNING TERRITORIES
Office of the Under-Secretary
- Division of Trusteeship
- Division of Information from Non-Self-Governing Territories

DEPARTMENT OF POLITICAL AND SECURITY COUNCIL AFFAIRS
Office of the Under-Secretary
- Political Affairs Division
- Council and Committee Services Division
- Disarmament Affairs Group
- Military Staff Committee Secretariat

DEPARTMENT OF PUBLIC INFORMATION
Office of the Under-Secretary
- Press and Publications Division
- Radio Division
- Films and Visual Information Division
- Public Liaison and Distribution Division

separately has been a matter of controversy from the beginning; together, they constitute the largest part of what is called the "substantive" work of the Secretariat. They were originally handled by separate departments; in 1952, they were put under one man, though still separate; in the reorganization of 1954 they were amalgamated as the Department of Economic and Social Affairs, headed by an undersecretary. In addition to its own enormous range of work in caring for the varied activities of the Economic and Social Council, this department is involved in the problems of coordinating the work of the United Nations in these fields with those of the specialized agencies; and the development of technical assistance has further increased its work. A Technical Assistance Administration was set up, within the Secretariat, which works with a Technical Assistance Board, in which the specialized agencies cooperate. The effort to make all the various bodies interested in technical assistance work together has contributed more than anything else toward solution of the problem of coordination.

The Department of Economic and Social Affairs includes a secretariat for the Economic and Social Council, a Statistical Office, a Bureau of Economic Affairs, a Bureau of Social Affairs, a Division of Human Rights, a Transport and Communications Division, and a Division of Narcotic Drugs. It now has a staff of over twelve hundred persons to service these divisions; and many of the staff are used for technical assistance direction, regional economic commissions, etc. The relationship between the various bodies throughout the United Nations system is complicated, and the Department of Economic and Social Affairs holds them all together in a working arrangement which seems to function effectively.

The Department of Public Information has the responsibility for providing that "the peoples of the world are fully informed concerning the United Nations." This inevitably involves a great deal of public relations, but it is debatable whether public relations is the primary function of the department. Who are these peoples that are to be informed? All the peoples of the world? Is the department expected to engage in propaganda for the United Nations, to "sell it" to all levels of people everywhere? Or is its function merely to keep informed as to its various important activities those persons throughout the world who need to be informed for the purpose of implementing its work? Should it issue a *United Nations Bulletin* (as it formerly did) which covered all the activities currently and compactly, or a *United Nations Review*, which does not attempt to be current or complete but provides articles dealing fully with important "themes"? Should the Department supply information only, or understanding? Should it have the function of interpretation?

Such questions, and others, have made the Department of Public Information a controversial one from the beginning. In any case, its work is manifestly important, taking perhaps ten per cent of the budget,[59] and engaging a staff of almost four hundred. There is a Press and Publications Division, which cares for hundreds of newspaper correspondents from all over the world; they must be properly accredited and their right of entry protected—even though the United States does not like some of them; facilities must be provided for them and information given to them. The quality of the reporting has been high, though the newspapers do not always print what the reporters send in. The Radio Division broadcasts news of the United Nations continuously in twenty-four languages and supplies transcriptions for stations which wish to use them; it is equipped for live television and occasionally meetings of its organs are shown on the networks. There has been debate whether the United Nations should have its own radio network, but thus far it uses local facilities. The Division of Films and Visual Information has a large library of films and photographs from all over the world; it publishes a Catalogue of United Nations Films, from which selection can be made for purchase or rent. They have such titles as *Challenge in the Desert* (Libya), *Rural Nurse* (Salvador), or *Workshop for Peace* (headquarters). The Public Liaison and Distribution Division takes care of visitors to the United Nations, now a million per year, and is in general responsible for spreading information. It has the assistance of over five hundred voluntary educational centers in seventy-four countries and three hundred voluntary speakers' units in fifty-nine countries. The United Nations has twenty-four information centers in different parts of the world. This division is responsible for carrying out an Assembly resolution of 1946 to give to information agencies the fullest possible access to the activities and official documentation of the United Nations. Some two hundred libraries throughout the world (thirty-three in the United States, one in the Soviet Union) are entitled to receive all unrestricted documentary materials,[60] and the division prepares and distributes simple surveys on various subjects. The great problem for the division is to know what are the real needs of the persons to whom this material goes and at what level of intelligence it should be aimed.

The Legal Department was the smallest of the substantive depart-

[59] It is difficult to estimate budget costs. There is a net budget and a gross budget. There are many persons in other departments who contribute to the information function—for example, those who do the reproducing and publishing. The budget allotment for 1955 for this department was a little over three and a half million dollars.

[60] Not every library can afford to receive this material. The amount is large and cumulative; it occupies much space and requires expert staff to organize it and make it usable.

ments, with a staff of hardly fifty. It took care of the legal problems of the organization itself, but was responsible also for the development and codification of international law and for the registration and recording of treaties. It served as secretariat for the International Law Commission and as liaison with the International Court of Justice. It has now ceased to exist as a department, and its activities are carried on by the Office of Legal Affairs in the Office of the Secretary-General.

ADMINISTRATIVE SERVICES. The task of servicing the thousands of meetings and, in general, all the needs of the United Nations requires a large staff and there has been much uncertainty as to how it should be organized. There were for a time a Department of Administrative and Financial Services and a Department of Conferences and General Services; between them a staff of some seventeen hundred was required with numerous temporary employees. Some nine hundred persons work on the recording and preparation of documents and five hundred more are needed to service the fifteen hundred meetings per year. In 1954, a new Department of Conference Services was created to handle this work, and an Office of General Services for other needs.

In this connection should be mentioned the personnel who work for the United Nations away from headquarters. The Geneva Office (in the Palais des Nations of the League of Nations) is a sort of European headquarters. There are information centers, regional economic commissions, the High Commissioner for Refugees, etc. There are also employees in the far-ranging work in technical assistance. A field service takes care of the numerous missions sent out by the United Nations. These missions represent many different parts of the organization and its activities, and a Missions Coordination Committee was established, which attempts to maintain some order and uniformity in their procedures. In the course of technical assistance operations resident representatives were set up in various areas; there is a possibility that they might be developed into functionaries, each to handle the varied activities of the United Nations in his area.

108. INTERNATIONAL CIVIL SERVICE[61]

To recruit, from all over the world, a staff capable of carrying on all the above functions, and to keep them satisfied and dedicated to

[61] See *The United Nations Secretariat* (United Nations Studies No. 4, Carnegie Endowment, 1950); C. W. Jenks, "Some Problems of an International Civil Service," *Public Administration Review*, 3 (1943), p. 93; F. R. Scott, "The World's Civil Service," *Int. Con.*, No. 496 (1954); E. Ranshofen Wertheimer, *The International Secretariat* (Washington, 1945); Walters, *passim*.

their work, is a very difficult task. Officials of the Secretariat are, by Article 101 of the Charter, "appointed by the Secretary-General under regulations established by the General Assembly." "The paramount consideration" in choosing them is the necessity for securing efficiency, competence, and integrity; but due consideration is also to be given to geographical distribution, and the latter is more important in the minds of some Members than the former. The fact that a prospective staff member lives in a certain area does not necessarily make him competent, but it is important from the viewpoint of national pride. Many of the Members of the United Nations do not have many persons of the background and training needed, and positions have sometimes been left unfilled because the director concerned was not satisfied with the qualifications of candidates from states next in order on the basis of geographical distribution.

At the beginning, it was necessary to take on many Americans; almost half the internationally-recruited staff and many more, if lower grades were counted in, were American. A formula was agreed upon in 1948 under which it was held that a country was fairly treated if its percentage of staff members "does not deviate more than 25 per cent from its percentage of total contributions to the budget"; but any Member was entitled to have three of its nationals on the staff. The financial contributions of Members are calculated on the basis of national income, population, economic development and other factors, and is thus a better basis for establishing quotas of "national representation" than population or area alone. This quota system, however, applies only to the upper ranks of the Secretariat, some two-fifths of the total number of employees; it does not apply to clerical and such work, and cannot always be applied where expert knowledge (e.g., in translating) is required. The number of Americans in the Secretariat has been steadily reduced.[62] Various efforts have been made to set up an interne program or to train younger persons for work in the United Nations, but no satisfactory method has yet been found. The Secretariat has also to contend with the tendency of Members to recall for service in their own countries individuals who have acquired some experience through work with the United Nations.

The extent to which governments give information or use pressure to secure or prevent appointment of their nationals cannot be cal-

[62] It is now difficult for an American to obtain a job in the United Nations, not only because of the situation described above, but because of the reduction in staff resulting from Hammarskjöld's reorganization and the wasteful loyalty tests imposed by the United States upon its own nationals who apply. The United Nations cannot afford to wait for months while the FBI investigates an American candidate.

culated. Secretary of State Byrnes, when asked about American candidates, refused information on the very proper ground that he did not wish to interfere with the independence of choice of the Secretary-General. Mr. Lie, however, needed information concerning applicants and found it hard to obtain except through the governments of the applicants—for example, whether an applicant had a police record. A memorandum of working practice with the United States was quietly agreed upon in 1949,[63] but this practice was soon complicated by the anti-Communist excitement, and the claims made then by the United States (discussed below) for control over the employment of its nationals by the United Nations reminded some delegates of the attitude of Mussolini toward the League of Nations. Other states may control their nationals seeking employment through refusal of permission to leave their own countries or in other ways; how. far such measures are actually employed it would be hard to tell. On the other hand, it is usually true that the backing of a candidate by his own state would help him get the job.

TENURE AND SECURITY. It is asking a great deal of a person to leave his established position and friends in his own country, to move into and adjust himself to life in a strange environment, to educate his children in ways different from those which prevail in his home country and, being thus uprooted, to face the risk that his United Nations job may be terminated. And if in addition he is faced with conflict between his national and his international loyalties, even those dedicated to the work, as most of them are, can become discouraged. The United Nations has, with some travail, worked out these problems, apparently with some success.

Appointments to work in the Secretariat, aside from the higher posts and short-time special jobs, are on either temporary or permanent contracts. It was the uncertainty of the many who held the "temporary-indefinite contract" that produced so much dissatisfaction during Mr. Lie's time in office. In 1954, the rule was instituted that an employee on a temporary contract must be evaluated at the end of two years and either separated from U.N. service or given permanent status. Those on a permanent basis are considered every five years by the Review Board. An Appointment and Promotion Board determines tenure and advancement. An employee's connection may be terminated if the post is abolished or the staff reduced (in which case he has priority for other posts), or if his work is

---

[63] Hearings before the Subcommittee to Investigate the Administration of the Internal Security Act: *Activities of United States Citizens Employed by the United Nations*, 82nd Congress, 2nd Session, pp. 330, 414-419. Also, *U.N. Doc.* A/2364.

unsatisfactory or his health is too bad. Also, the Secretary-General may dismiss for serious misconduct. In this, or other disciplinary measures, the employee may go to the Joint Appeals Board and perhaps carry his appeal on up to the Administrative Tribunal. A staff association, with a staff council, seeks to protect and advance the interests of staff members.

The rates of pay are higher than those to which most officials are accustomed in their own countries, but it is soon discovered that they are not too high for living in New York City. Professional posts begin at $4,250 and mount to $18,000 for the under-secretaries, and the higher posts have a "representation allowance" ranging from $3,500 downwards. Service personnel are paid at current union rates, though there are no labor unions in the United Nations. In addition, there are numerous other compensations. Allowances are made for each child and its education. Travel and transportation costs are paid, and there is a repatriation allowance when a person finishes his work and goes back to his own land. Annual leave of six weeks per year is permitted and leave for illness and even for some research purposes is granted. Language training, group life, health insurance, and other advantages are made available.

PRIVILEGES AND IMMUNITIES.[64] Officials of the United Nations have also certain privileges and immunities, more limited than those accorded to diplomats under international law, but such as are necessary for carrying out their functions. They are immune from legal process on account of words uttered or acts performed in official capacity; from taxation upon their income from the United Nations;[65] from the legal restrictions upon immigrants and aliens; and they have certain privileges concerning importation and foreign currency exchange. The Secretary-General and the ASGs (and presumably now the undersecretaries-general) have full diplomatic immunities. The United Nations may issue a travel document, somewhat corresponding to a passport, called a *laissez-passer*, which entitles its bearer to privileges in the Member states through which he passes. The privileges of staff members may be waived by the Secretary-General; and his own may be waived by the Security Council.

[64] See Chapter 11, p. 308, above; and M. Brandon, "The United Nations *Laissez-Passer*," *B.Y.I.L.*, 1950, p. 452; Carol M. Crosswell, *Protection of International Officials Abroad* (New York, 1952); Martin Hill, *Immunities and Privileges of International Officials* (Washington, 1947); J. L. Kunz, "Privileges and Immunities of International Organizations," *A.J.*, 41, (1947), p. 828; Handbook on the Legal Status, Privileges and Immunities of the United Nations, *U.N. Doc.*, ST/LEG/2 (1952).

[65] But see p. 308 above for the United States refusal to accept this.

109. THE PROBLEM OF LOYALTY

The primary loyalty of a United Nations official must be to the organization which he serves; this is clear from Article 100 of the Charter, and from the oath of office which he takes:

I solemnly swear (undertake, affirm, promise) to exercise in all loyalty, discretion and conscience, the functions entrusted to me as an international civil servant of the United Nations, to discharge these functions and regulate my conduct with the interests of the United Nations only in view, and not to seek or accept instructions in regard to the performance of my duties from any government or other authority external to the Organization.[66]

This does not mean, however, that he gives up his nationality or his allegiance to his own country—on the contrary—for the United Nations has nothing corresponding to this relationship to offer him, and it is regarded by the United Nations as important that he maintain connections with his own country and be able understandingly to reflect opinion therein. There is no necessary conflict between the two loyalties, for his own state is as much bound (Article 100) as he is to respect the principles of the United Nations; it has agreed not to seek to influence him in the discharge of his responsibilities. If his own state should, for example, be condemned as an aggressor and the United Nations should undertake action against it, he might have a problem—one made for him by the misconduct of his own state. In any such case, his primary duty would be to the United Nations and if he should prefer to sympathize with his own state, either he or the United Nations could break the connection between them.

Some such situation arose when Communist regimes took over in Czechoslovakia and China and demanded that their nationals in the Secretariat be replaced by others of their own choice. Secretary-General Lie strongly resisted these demands; but he was put into a much more difficult position when the United States, in which most of his staff were located, demanded that he discharge certain Americans in the Secretariat which it accused of being subversive, in the sense of having, or having had, sympathy or connection with Communists. Lie wished here also to preserve the independence of his staff, but he faced the real danger that inflamed American opinion might reduce its financial and other support and thereby imperil the existence of the United Nations.

In the United States, fear of communism had amounted almost to

[66] Staff Regulation 1.9, *U.N. Doc.*, ST/AFS/SGB/94 (1952).

frenzy. The Gubichev case and others seemed to offer justification for their fears, and hundreds of Americans were being forced out of their jobs without due process of law. A federal grand jury, inspired by a ubiquitous henchman of Senator McCarthy, asserted that the continued presence of these disloyal Americans in the United Nations (not one of them proven to be disloyal) was "a menace to our Government." It was a great opportunity for nationalists and those who disliked the United Nations, and it was fanned into a flame of public excitement. A bill was introduced, though fortunately it never became law, which would have made it a crime for an American to take employment with the United Nations until he had first been cleared by American authorities, and Executive Order 10,422 was revised in Executive Order 10,459 to provide standards and procedures for dealing with the United Nations in such matters. Lie complained, however, that no information was given him; he was merely told that the United States did or did not favor the person. Every American on the staff was investigated and Lie was criticized for allowing the premises of the United Nations to be used by the authorities of the United States for this purpose.

All this was very puzzling to Mr. Lie and other Members and, indeed, to many Americans. It was observed that the United States had no law making membership of the Communist Party or the party itself illegal; it was difficult to understand how the Fifth Amendment to the Constitution of the United States, which was supposed to offer protection to a person, should be used instead as an evidence of guilt, or how a person could be regarded as proven guilty merely by association. Bending before the storm, Mr. Lie suspended some of the accused Americans and appointed a Committee of Jurists to advise him. Upon the basis of their report, which has been severely criticized, he discharged some of the Americans on his staff.

A number of the dismissed Americans appealed to the Administrative Tribunal which made awards to some of them as high as $40,000 and amounting in total to almost $180,000. The United States then added to its poor reputation by challenging the awards and demanding that the General Assembly refuse to pay them. The Assembly, fearful of opinion in the United States, found a way out by asking the International Court of Justice whether the Assembly could refuse to give effect to an award of compensation made by the Administrative Tribunal. The Court replied that it had no such right and that the decision of the tribunal was final. The United States then demanded that the Statute of the Administrative Tribunal be revised and this was done, limiting the amount of award which the tribunal could make, and providing a somewhat difficult procedure by which an appeal could be made from the tribunal to the International Court of Justice.[67]

Some questions of law and principle important to the United Nations appeared in this controversy. The independence of the Secretariat was manifestly threatened; if the United States could demand dismissal of its nationals therein on political grounds, any Member could demand—and with every change of administration—that some of its nationals should be dismissed. A Member opposed to a policy adopted by the United Nations cannot be allowed to instruct its nationals in the Secretariat to oppose that policy.

The demands of the United States also raise the question of whether the United Nations must accept the unsupported allegation by one of its Members against a staff member. The United States offered to the Secretary-General no evidence in support of the accusations it made against its nationals; it apparently expected the Secretary-General to accept its statements without allowing him to judge the evidence. Members of the United Nations had much difficulty in understanding why the United States was so concerned with these minor officials when it accepted strong delegations from Communist states, and in understanding what possibilities for espionage existed in the "glass house," the secretariat building; it was much more difficult for them to credit the United States with good faith when it proffered no evidence to show that the dangers which it seemed to fear were real. If every Member could ask of its nationals what the United States demanded, little could remain of the concept of an independent international civil service.

Mr. Hammarskjöld attempted with some success to straighten things out, and was assisted by a cooling-down of American public opinion. Staff Regulation 1(7) was changed to forbid staff members to "engage in any political activities outside the scope of their official duties, other than voting." He negotiated a working agreement with the United States which assured him of some knowledge of the evidence against an accused person, and assured him that any accusation came from a high and responsible United States official. There seem to have been no more important controversies, but it still remains true that an American has a difficult task in getting a position with

[67] The above rather disgraceful story is put together in a report by the Committee for Study of Legal Problems of the United Nations, *Proc. Am. Soc.*, 1954, p. 164; and by Stephen Schwebel, "The International Character of the Secretariat of the United Nations," *B.Y.I.L.*, 1953, p. 71. These contain references to sources of which mention is made here. See *U.N. Doc.*, A/2533 and A/2364.

the United Nations, partly because his own government insists on investigating him and partly because the United Nations regards him as a risk.

Fortunately, the United States did not succeed in establishing a precedent which other Members can follow. While the morale of the Secretariat was badly damaged, the result may have been, in the long run, to strengthen the independence of the Secretariat.

Chapter 13

SPECIALIZED AGENCIES

We have noted above that a number of "specialized agencies" were contemplated by the United Nations, and that they were to be "brought into relationship with" the United Nations.[1] These were to be independent bodies, each founded upon its own treaty and with its own special staff and functions. The League of Nations attempted, under Article 24 of its Covenant, to bring all such activities under one general system, though it did not succeed in doing so; and the Bruce Committee in 1939 recommended that all the economic and social activities of the League should be put under one central agency.

110. CENTRALIZATION OR DECENTRALIZATION?

Those who made the United Nations had therefore to decide whether it should include all international activities in one organization or whether there should be a number of such organizations, each functioning in a limited field. Centralized direction is usually regarded as important in efficient administration. The earlier haphazard creation of international public unions had led to rivalry or overlapping of work; on the other hand, lack of a coordinating direction might leave important matters untouched.

[1] On specialized agencies in general: C. H. Alexandrowicz, *International Economic Organizations* (London, 1952); Louis Hyde, "Specialized Intergovernmental Agencies," *Dept. of State Bull.*, 3 (1945), p. 955, and 17 (1947), p. 1069; D. Mitrany, *A Working Peace System* (Royal Institute of International Affairs, 1943); Szeming Sze, "The Specialized Agencies," in *1950 Annual Review*, p. 113, and *1952 Annual Review*, p. 157; Staff Study No. 10. The Bruce Report is *L. of N. Doc.*, A.23.1939. A bibliography was issued as *U.N. Doc.* Sales No. 1949.I.16.

Documentary information may be found in the U.N. *Yearbooks* and in the publications of each agency; See also Clive Parry, "Constitutions of International Organizations," *B.Y.I.L.*, 1946, p. 394. Current information is recorded in every issue of *International Organization*.

The experience of the League had shown that some of the independent agencies were efficient; that the interconnection between their functions was increasing; that proper coordination of their work was difficult to achieve; that little public interest was aroused by small organizations working remotely in limited fields; and that for each function only a certain number of states could be interested enough to participate actively.

FOR CENTRALIZATION. Those who were seeking to strengthen the economic and social functions of the new United Nations system, as it was being built, had this experience before them, and various theoretical arguments leading in either direction. In favor of a centralized control, it was pointed out that numerous separate institutions mean duplication of staff and expense, requiring also that each member state have a larger staff of its own in order to maintain liaison with the work, and that there were proven dangers of an overlapping jurisdiction with conflicts, on the one hand, and, on the other hand, of omissions of jurisdiction which would result in certain matters having no institution to care for them. Such a matter might be taken up only if some state should have the interest and the initiative to call a conference to deal with it, and the conference would be an isolated affair without staff preparation or sequence. In the Assembly of the League it might have helped if some of the many problems there raised for discussion could have been assigned to existing administrative bodies. Each such body, however, chose its own work and made its own decisions.

Each institution tends to develop its own personality, to seek exclusive control of its field, and to be in jealous rivalry with other similar bodies. Further, since each works in its own corner, lighted only by its own little candle, pressure groups could operate upon it, and there would be no assurance of responsible operation. It was also urged that the various organizations would be separated from the Security Council or other United Nations organs, to which they should be related, and that they would be divorced from the political interests and authorities which alone could breathe life and vigor into them.

FOR DECENTRALIZATION. Strong arguments were adduced, on the other hand, for a decentralized system with various independent units.[2] This really involves a functional approach to international problems, and it is pointed out that this is the prevailing trend in

[2] This argument is largely derived from D. Mitrany, *op. cit.*

domestic government. More reliance, it was said, should be placed upon the technical experts than upon the political representatives of nations.[3]

It was politically easier to establish such institutions as states might be willing to agree upon than to attempt to secure agreement upon one general governmental institution, including all such functions and powers. Their work is largely technical and advisory, and should be separated from the controversies inherent in a political system. To put all authority in one body might mean that political differences and jealousies would limit a particular field of activity which should operate upon an expert basis; it would arouse fears, whereas little danger to national sovereignty would be seen in disparate and limited specialized agencies. If there was danger, it would be lessened by being scattered through the various agencies. States would be willing to grant more authority to institutions of limited function and technical purpose than to an over-all body having political significance, and would cooperate more freely therein.

Furthermore, not all states are interested in all fields; each should be free to join those bodies in which it is interested and not be compelled by membership of the United Nations to share, at greater expense, in all these fields. An inland state might not wish to occupy itself with maritime problems; Ecuador might have little interest in the Rhine river. States work more willingly in those organizations to which they choose to belong; and it would be possible for a small state to acquire more prestige through sheer ability than it could ever acquire in a centralized organization in which the political power of great nations would always dominate. There would thus be less accumulation of power in a few large states. Each institution would tend to become expert in its own field and less subject to political influences. Modern trends of government call for independent commissions whose job is not so much to prohibit and enforce as to administer and assist. Since the work would be done by small staffs of experts, it could be hoped that they would more truly represent the community of nations as a whole and work in its interest rather than, as would delegates to a general assembly, in the interests of their own nations and upon the ancient basis of national honor and vital interests.

RELATION TO THE UNITED NATIONS. For such reasons, and perhaps also in reaction against the League system, the United Nations Charter

---

[3] This trend has been challenged, in the United Nations, by insistence that members even of a committee such as the Commission on Human Rights must be governmental delegates. See Report of the Secretary-General, *U.N. Doc.*, A/65, 30 June, 1946, p. 14. Also A. Loveday, "An Unfortunate Decision," *Int. Organ.*, 1 (1947), p. 279.

provides for a more decentralized system. Various specialized agencies, each with its own constitution and staff, have been and continue to be built up; encouragement is given to this process by Article 59 which authorizes the United Nations itself to initiate negotiations for the establishment of other such agencies. Article 57 says that such agencies "shall be brought into relationship with the United Nations" through agreements made between each of them and the Economic and Social Council. These agreements have been made, and also a number of agreements between the agencies themselves. The problem of coordination is continuously being studied.

We turn now to separate consideration of each agency, only a brief survey being possible; afterwards, we shall consider the relationships which have thus far been established and the extent to which the United Nations and the specialized agencies constitute a system.

THE SPECIALIZED AGENCIES[4]

International Labour Organization (ILO)
Food and Agriculture Organization of the United Nations (FAO)
United Nations Educational, Scientific and Cultural Organization (UNESCO)
International Civil Aviation Organization (ICAO)
International Bank for Reconstruction and Development (IBRD)
International Monetary Fund (IMF)
World Health Organization (WHO)
Universal Postal Union (UPU)
International Telecommunications Union (ITU)
World Meteorological Organization (WMO)
Inter-Governmental Maritime Consultative Organization (IMCO)
Organization for Trade Cooperation (OTC)

Five of the organizations above listed had been put under the direction of the League of Nations; others, such as the Postal Union, had existed independently of the League. The newer bodies carried on functions previously handled by the organs of the League, e.g., UNESCO was preceded by the Institute of Intellectual Cooperation of the League. All these organizations are well rooted in the past.

The now defunct United Nations Relief and Reconstruction Administration (UNRRA) and the International Refugee Organization (IRO) will be mentioned in Chapter 14.

---

[4] It will not be possible to give citations for the documents and literature of each agency; a few will be provided in each case. The fundamental documents can be found in the U.N. *Yearbooks*, in *U.N.T.S.*, in the United States Treaties and International Agreements series, or in *Doc. Am. For. Rel.* Each agency has its own publications and issues an annual report. A useful guide is provided by Aufricht. See also Dept. of State Pub. No. 3655, *International Organizations in which the United States Participates*; and the *Yearbook of International Organizations* (Brussels, 1954).

111. INTERNATIONAL LABOUR ORGANIZATION

The ILO has now become one of the specialized agencies, but it occupied for some years a unique position in international affairs and has much experience behind it.[5] During World War I, a great deal of pressure was exerted by labor to provide an organization which could advance its interests upon an international scale. As a result, Part XIII of the Treaty of Versailles included the charter for a new international organization for labor. It was an independent body which, alongside the similarly independent court, formed part of the League of Nations system. Membership in the League carried with it membership in the ILO, though in practice it proved possible to have separate memberships.[6] Its budget was part of the budget of the League and there were various other connections between the two bodies. They developed different characters, the ILO having the appearance of an industrious business concern, and the League more that of a formal diplomatic body.

During the war, the office was moved to Montreal, where it carried on its work on a much reduced scale; there were no meetings of the conference from 1939 to 1944.[7] In the latter year, the conference met in its twenty-sixth regular session, at Philadelphia, with forty-one states represented. It agreed upon a "Declaration concerning the Aims and Purposes of the International Labour Organization," a restatement of its objectives for the postwar reconstruction era. Meanwhile, it was becoming clearer that the ILO must now adjust itself to the new United Nations, and this process was somewhat complicated by uncertainty as to the attitude of the U.S.S.R. and by the appearance of the World Federation of Trade Unions. At the 1945 conference in Paris, it was decided to "enter into relationship with" the United Nations, and this necessitated some constitutional changes. Amendments, approved at a conference in Montreal, came into force on September 26, 1946; and the agreement with the United Nations came into force by Resolution 50(I) of the General Assembly on December 14, 1946. The headquarters of the ILO have now been returned to its own building in Geneva, Switzerland.

---

[5] The demand for international labor cooperation goes as far back as Robert Owen in 1816. A conference met at Berlin in 1890 and one at Berne in 1906. An International Association for Labour Legislation met annually and the ILO was largely an outgrowth of its effort. See B. E. Lowe, *The International Protection of Labor: International Labor Organization, History and Law* (rev. ed., New York, 1955); J. T. Shotwell, *International Labor Organization*, 2 vols. (New York, 1934).

[6] The United States joined the ILO in 1934, without being a Member of the League. See *P.C.I.J.*, Series B, No. 19.

[7] Except for an extraordinary conference at New York in 1941.

FUNCTIONS. The aim of the ILO is stated in the preamble to its constitution to be the establishment of social justice as the basis of a universal and lasting peace. This meant:

The regulation of the hours of work, including the establishment of a maximum working day and week, the regulation of the labour supply, the prevention of unemployment, the provision of an adequate living wage, the protection of the worker against sickness, disease and injury arising out of his employment, the protection of children, young persons, and women, provision for old age and injury, protection of the interests of workers when employed in countries other than their own, recognition of the principle of freedom of association, the organisation of vocational and technical education and other measures.

According to Article 10 of the constitution, the functions of the International Labour Office, which serves as secretariat for the organization, were to include the collection and distribution of information on all subjects relating to the international adjustment of conditions of industrial life and labor; the framing of conventions and recommendations for adoption by Members; and follow-up and enforcement of measures so adopted.

THE CONFERENCE. The organization of the ILO, according to its constitution, was "to consist of: (1) a General Conference of Representatives of the Members and (2) an International Labour Office controlled by the Governing Body described in Article 393." The most distinctive and famous characteristic of the ILO is its method of tripartite representation, which is carried on even in committees. Each member has four delegates to the conference, of whom two represent the government, one the employers, and one labor; and each delegate is entitled to vote independently. All are designated by governments, but they must be "chosen in agreement with the industrial organisations, if such organisations exist, which are most representative of employers or work-people, as the case may be, in their respective countries." The conference can refuse to admit a delegate whom it deems not to have been nominated in accordance with this article. There have been some difficulties in working out this principle, for in some countries proper organizations did not exist, and in others there was dispute as to which organization should be consulted.[8]

The ILO also broke new ground with regard to conference pro-

[8] See for example, *P.C.I.J.*, Series B, No. 1. The United States opposed admission of the Soviet Union in 1954 on the ground that its employer and employee delegates would actually be representatives of the government. A. Z. Rubinstein, "The U.S.S.R. and the I.L.O.," *Russian Review*, 14 (1955), p. 11.

cedure and international legislative effort. The conference, voting by majority, may take action which eventuates in a recommendation or a draft convention. The former is submitted to members "for consideration with a view to effect being given to it by national legislation or otherwise"; the draft convention is for ratification by members. Each member is obligated to bring the recommendation or draft convention within a year or eighteen months "before the authority or authorities within whose competence the matter lies" for legislative or other action.[9] A special committee (which was reconstituted in 1946) examines and reports upon these actions by members, and the effort to secure ratification is vigorously pushed. Where ratification has been given, the member is obligated to report to the ILO upon the measures taken to put it into effect. Complaint may be made by associations of employers or workers that a state is not observing its obligations. Various means of pressure are provided, and economic sanctions may ultimately be invoked against a member not living up to its obligations. The procedure of the conference, as a legislative process, is well worth study, as are its efforts to solve the problem of revision of treaties.

THE GOVERNING BODY. The executive body for the ILO is called the Governing Body. It originally consisted of thirty-two persons, but the amendment of the charter (now called constitution) increased the number to forty, of which twenty represent governments, ten employers, and ten employees; and the requirement was dropped that six must be non-European states. Of the twenty persons representing governments, ten must be chosen "by the Members which are of the chief industrial importance"; and the criteria laid down for this selection are: total industrial population, including miners and transport workers but excluding agricultural and commerce workers; proportion of industrial to total population; total horsepower, steam, and water; horsepower per inhabitant; length of railways in proportion to area; tonnage of merchant marine. The other government representatives are chosen by member states selected for the purpose by the government delegates to the conference, excluding the states of chief industrial importance. The term of office is three years, and voting is by majority. The Governing Body selects and directs the director, prepares the budget and the agenda

---

[9] This means the body competent to put it into effect. It was thought, for example, that it might be necessary to submit it to the forty-eight state legislatures in the United States. F. O. Wilcox, *The Ratification of International Conventions* (London, 1935), pp. 161-204.

for the conferences, handles complaints, and works upon specific problems of the organization either directly or through committees of experts.

THE INTERNATIONAL LABOUR OFFICE. The secretariat of the ILO is known as the Office (*Bureau*) and was established by the charter at the seat of the League; it has, in fact, a well-equipped building of its own at Geneva, antedating the League palace. Its first Director was Albert Thomas, who made himself a dominant and constructive force in the early development of the work.[10] It collects and distributes information "on all subjects relating to the international adjustment of conditions of industrial life and labor"; it publishes a number of periodicals, of which the *International Labour Review* is most useful to students, a series containing national labor laws, and many special studies of great usefulness. It prepares for the Governing Body the agenda of conferences, and makes such studies as are asked by them, frequently calling conferences of experts to assist in the work.

ACTIVITIES. The work of the International Labour Organization may be summarized under three headings. In the first place, it gathers information, makes studies and issues publications. Since its beginning, it has issued the *International Labour Review, Industry and Labour*, the *Legislative Series*, the *Yearbook of Labour Statistics*, and a series called *Studies and Reports*. It includes such things as the *Report on Forced Labour*, a joint product with the United Nations Ad Hoc Committee on Forced Labour, and studies on *Public Investment and Full Employment* or *International Survey on Social Security*.

Probably the most important effort of the ILO is in securing the adoption and supervising the execution of conventions and regulations. By the end of 1953, a total of 103 conventions and 97 recommendations had been adopted, with a total of 1,413 ratifications. These are known as the International Labour Code and cover all aspects of labor problems—such as employment, wages, general working conditions, holidays, employment of children, maternity protection, night work, migration, maritime labor, and the right to organize.[11]

More recently, the ILO has been offering technical assistance on

[10] E. J. Phelan, *Yes and Albert Thomas* (New York, 1949) is an interesting and useful book. Mr. Phelan worked with Thomas for years and became the first director-general of ILO after its reconstitution.

[11] Originally published by the ILO under the title *International Labour Code 1939: A Systematic Arrangement of the Conventions and Recommendations Adopted by the International Labour Conference 1919-1939*. Subsequent editions have brought materials up to date.

a large scale. It sends teams of experts, when invited, to demonstrate methods of work; it sets up training courses; it grants fellowships and conducts seminars. It has regional offices for these purposes.

112. FOOD AND AGRICULTURE ORGANIZATION[12]

President Roosevelt remarked, in his message to Congress of November 1, 1943: "Food is as important as any other weapon in the successful prosecution of the war. It will be equally important in rehabilitation and relief in the liberated areas, and in the shaping of the peace that is to come." During the war, in 1942, the United States and the United Kingdom set up the Combined Food Board, in order to secure maximum utilization of the food resources of the United Nations for purposes of the war. With these purposes in mind, the United States called a conference on Food and Agriculture, which met at Hot Springs, Virginia, May 18 to June 13, 1943. This conference set up an "Interim Commission" to plan the organization, which came into being on October 16, 1945. The agreement with the United Nations came into force on December 16, 1946. In 1950, Rome was chosen as headquarters, and in April 1951 the organization moved there from Washington, where its main offices had been located since 1946. By August 1955 there were seventy-one members, none of the Soviet bloc being members at that time (Hungary, Czechoslovakia, and Poland had withdrawn).

PURPOSES AND FUNCTIONS. The organization is intended, according to the preamble to its constitution, to raise levels of nutrition and standards of living, to secure "improvements in the efficiency of the production and distribution of all food and agricultural products," to better the conditions of rural populations, and thus to contribute to an expanding world economy. To carry out these aims, the organization is authorized by Article 1 to "collect, analyze, interpret and disseminate information relating to nutrition, food and agriculture"; to recommend and promote national action concerning research in these fields, conservation of natural resources, improvement of processing, marketing and distribution of food and agricultural products; to adopt policies with respect to agricultural commodity agreements; and to furnish technical assistance when requested by governments.

---

[12] See H. Belshaw, "The Food and Agriculture Organization of the United Nations," *Int. Organ.*, 1 (1947), p. 291; G. Hambidge, *The Story of FAO* (New York, 1955); P. Effingham and P. Humphrey, "The Relations between FAO and international non-governmental organizations," *Bulletin NGO-ONG*, 4 (1952), p. 417.

ORGANIZATION. The members are those listed in an annex who accept the constitution within five years, and others who are admitted by two-thirds vote of all members. Withdrawal is permitted after five years. The organization is given legal status, and it and its staff have certain immunities stated in its constitution. An amendment to the constitution which involves new obligations for members must be ratified by two-thirds of the members and binds only those who accept it; other amendments may be made by a two-thirds vote of the conference. Expenses are divided among members as determined by the conference.

The organs of FAO are the conference, to which each member sends a representative, each having one vote; the council, formerly the executive committee, composed of twenty-four persons, chosen by the conference from among qualified persons; and the director-general and his staff. The conference determines policy, makes recommendations or submits draft conventions to members, and arranges for consultation with governments or with other international organizations. The council carries out the instructions of the conference; its members serve not as delegates of their own governments, but on behalf of the whole conference. The director-general has full authority to direct the work of the organization. Various standing advisory committees, such as for nutrition, agricultural production, or statistics, conduct studies and may make proposals. In 1946, at its second session, a provision concerning arrears in payments was added, similar to that in the Charter of the United Nations.

A large part of the work of FAO is carried on through regional offices and in collaboration with other organizations. It has regional offices in various parts of the world; there is a joint FAO/WHO Advisory Committee on Nutrition; and FAO is interested in the work of UNESCO dealing with science abstracting, and other subjects. In member countries, there are national committees, such as UNESCO maintains, to serve as points of contact between FAO and non-governmental organizations.

ACTIVITIES. The urgency of the food situation led FAO into action sooner than anticipated. A conference on urgent food problems met at Washington in 1946, and an International Emergency Food Council was set up. The beginnings of FAO activity were promising. The first director-general, Sir John Boyd Orr, was a bold thinker, and he called for a World Food Board which could buy and sell, build up food stocks, and be able to help in emergency. This idea was apparently accepted at the Copenhagen Conference (1946), but later the United States and others opposed giving the organization the authority needed to operate, and were willing to collaborate only on a voluntary basis. The United States favored commodity agreements and, during 1946-48, sought to build up the International Trade Organization in this respect. The Emergency Food Council was dropped as the economic situation improved, and attention was turned to surpluses. Under another director-general, Norris Dodd, an American, an International Commodity Clearing House was proposed, but this, too was rejected as not leaving enough control to nations —e.g., to administer reserve food stocks. A committee on commodity problems was set up instead, to advise on making intergovernmental agreements. By 1953, food stocks had caught up with needs, and the committee had the problem of balancing encouragement of more production in places where it was needed against disposal of surplus stocks in other places. The problem of economically sound and politically fair distribution of agricultural production around the world has never been solved; potatoes may have to be left to rot on Long Island while in other parts of the world people are starving.

In general, the activities of FAO may be put under five or six headings: agriculture, fisheries, nutrition, forestry, and economics; and to this must be added its participation in technical assistance.

AGRICULTURE. An International Rice Commission resulted from an International Rice Conference held at Baguio in 1948. Asiatic countries furnish most of the members. It attempts to improve techniques of production and distribution and to standardize statistics, and studies the uses of rice—which is the basic food stuff for nearly half the population of the world. Working parties study fertilizers, hybridization, etc. A great deal of teaching is done through meetings and demonstrations; seed samples are sent to be tried in various countries; studies of particular problems are published in a series called "Agricultural Studies"; seminars are conducted on land problems, particularly land tenure; a particular project has been the control of rinderpest in African and Asiatic countries—Ethiopia, Japan, Formosa, India, Thailand, and Afghanistan.

FISHERIES AND FORESTRY. An Indo-Pacific Fisheries Council was set up in 1948 to develop fisheries in that area; a similar body was created for the Mediterranean area in 1952, and one is contemplated for the Latin American region. Advice is given on fishing techniques, marine and inland, on harbors, etc. The 1951 conference adopted a Charter of Principles of Forest Policy and prepared a booklet showing how these principles could be applied. Studies are made of such matters as soil conservation, pulp and paper manufacturing, olive oil, and range management. In 1954, a working party on Logging Techniques and Training of Forest Workers met at Geneva.

NUTRITION. In this comparatively new field, which is regarded as of much importance in areas where health is poor, FAO works closely with WHO. It has helped to increase supplies of milk and, where this cannot be done, to develop foods of high nutritive value. In Indonesia, for example, a soybean "milk" was prepared and tried out. Courses of training in nutrition for both medical and non-medical personnel have been arranged; a three-month course for South East Asia was held at Calcutta in 1951, and a ten-week course for workers from North Africa was held at Marseilles in 1952. There is, of course, much research, and various studies concerning nutrition have been published.

ECONOMICS AND STATISTICS. Aside from fundamental economic policies debated at high levels, FAO does a great deal of work in the statistical field. It has set up training schools for statisticians—in Iraq, for the Middle East, in 1948; in India in 1949; in Nigeria, for West Africa in 1953. The effort is to improve methods of agricultural census taking; various volumes have been published, such as *Methods of Collecting Agricultural Statistics in Different Countries, Yearbook of Fishery Statistics,* and similar yearbooks for forestry and agriculture. A *World Food Survey* was issued in 1946, and another in 1952, both of which have been of much use to governments.

MISSIONS. FAO has sent missions to various countries, both on its own initiative and in connection with the Expanded Technical Assistance Programme. The first was a mission to Greece in 1946, which became overshadowed by the unilateral Truman Doctrine program of the United States. There was one to Poland in 1947, to Siam in 1948, to Nicaragua in 1949; and FAO has participated in missions sent out under the U.N. Technical Assistance Administration, for example, to Somaliland in 1951. As part of technical assistance work it was, during 1953-55, working on improvement of hides and skin-processing in Libya, irrigation in East Pakistan, fisheries development in Chile, and ground water development in Syria. It was reported that, by the middle of 1953, a total of 624 experts from 54 countries were at work in 52 countries; that during 1952, some 227 fellowships were given to persons in 31 nations to study in 53 different countries.[13]

The budget of FAO for 1956 was $6,600,000; for the same year the United States spent on agriculture close to seven billion dollars.

[13] See FAO, *Activities of FAO under the Expanded Technical Assistance,* reports issued for 1950-52, 1952-53, and 1953-54.

113. UNITED NATIONS EDUCATIONAL, SCIENTIFIC AND CULTURAL ORGANIZATION[14]

A figure of speech—"republic of letters"—has long been in use among scholars, to indicate the common interest, transcending political boundaries, of those engaged in intellectual activities. After the First World War, international organization was provided for this "republic" by the League of Nations, in the Institute of Intellectual Cooperation. Its activities were upon a high level, so high that they were criticized because they did not reach the average human being at all.

CREATION. During the war discussions took place among the Allied ministers of education in London, and in the United States unofficial studies were made. In April 1944 a United States delegation headed by Senator Fulbright was sent to London to meet with the Allied ministers, and it presented a draft constitution for an international educational organization which, as modified by the conference, was sent to the United Nations for study. Meanwhile, the Charter of the United Nations included "educational and cultural cooperation"; and the French delegation at San Francisco proposed an international conference which, at the invitation of the British government, met at London on November 1, 1945. The general interest in and support for an education organization led to rapid meeting of minds, and in some sixteen days the conference adopted the Constitution of a United Nations Educational, Scientific and Cultural Organization, to be located at Paris, and an instrument establishing a preparatory commission to set up the new unit. This commission reported in July, and the constitution provided came into force, having received the necessary twenty ratifications, on November 4, 1946. The first session of the General Conference met in Paris, which had been chosen as headquarters for UNESCO, on November 19, and elected Dr. Julian Huxley as the first director-general. The agreement with

[14] From the numerous publications on UNESCO, the following easily available selections are made: Charles S. Ascher, "The Development of UNESCO's Program," *Int. Organ.*, 4 (1950), p. 12; by the same author, *Program-Making in UNESCO 1946-1951: A Study in the Processes of International Administration* (Public Administration Clearing House, Special Publication No. 59, Chicago, 1951); Byron Dexter, "Yardstick for UNESCO," *Foreign Affairs*, 28 (1949), p. 56; Julian S. Huxley, *UNESCO: Its Purpose and Philosophy* (Public Affairs Press, Washington, 1947); R. Niebuhr, "The Theory and Practice of UNESCO," *Int. Organ.*, 4 (1950), p. 3; W. R. Sharp, "The Role of UNESCO: A Critical Evaluation," *Proceedings of the Academy of Political Science*, 24 (1951), p. 101; B. M. H. Tripp, "UNESCO in Perspective," *Int. Con.*, No. 497 (1954); H. E. Wilson, "The Development of UNESCO," *Int. Con.*, No. 431 (1947).

the United Nations came into force on December 14, 1946. By August 1955 UNESCO had seventy-two members, including the U.S.S.R. which, after some years of indifference, joined in April 1954.

PURPOSES. The Purpose of UNESCO is indicated by its name, though the United States delegation made it clear that it was to function not merely in the fields listed in the title, but

in all fields useful to the development of international understanding, including specifically the fields of mass communication between the peoples of the world by press, radio, and moving pictures, the exchange of publications, the access to library holdings on an international basis, international access to the fruits of scholarly and scientific research, cooperation in the advancement of knowledge, and all other means and methods of increasing the sense of the community of human life.[15]

It is, according to Article 1 of its constitution, "to contribute to peace and security by promoting collaboration among the nations through education, science and culture in order to further universal respect for justice, for the rule of law and for the human rights and fundamental freedoms. . . ." Its functions are to advance the mutual knowledge and understanding of peoples through all means of mass communication; to give fresh impulse to popular education and to the spread of culture; and to maintain, increase and diffuse knowledge. Respecting the desire on the part of each nation to maintain its own culture and to preserve the independence of its education, Article 1, paragraph 3, of the UNESCO Constitution forbids intervention "in matters which are essentially within their domestic jurisdiction."

ORGANIZATION. Members of the United Nations have "the right to membership" in UNESCO, and states not Members of the United Nations may be admitted by two-thirds vote of the General Conference, with the approval of the Economic and Social Council. The conference, at its sixth session in 1951, created a new category of associate members for "territories which are not responsible for the conduct of their international relations"; application for such membership must be made by the authority which does have that responsibility. Associate members have the right to propose items for the provisional agenda and to participate, but without voting rights, in the General Conference and its committees. The Montevideo Conference (1954) added a provision to the constitution permitting

[15] *The Defenses of Peace: Documents relating to UNESCO*, Parts I and II, Dept. State Pub., Nos. 2457 and 2475 (1946); *Hearings of the Committee on Foreign Affairs*, House of Representatives, on H. Res. 215 (May, 1945) and on H. J. Res. 305 (April, 1946).

withdrawal on a year's notice.[16] A change, made in 1949, added a provision concerning arrears similar to that in the United Nations Charter.

"The Organization shall include a General Conference, an Executive Board and a Secretariat" (Article 3). The conference is composed of delegates (five each) chosen by their governments "after consultation with the National Commission, if established, or with educational, scientific and cultural bodies." Each delegation has one vote, and decisions are taken by a simple majority except where a two-thirds majority is called for (submission of international conventions, inviting observers, proposal of amendments). The conference, which now meets biennially rather than annually, is the chief organ; it determines policies, summons conferences, submits proposals to members, elects the Executive Board, appoints the director-general, considers reports from member states, and advises the United Nations within its field. A distinction is made between "recommendations," for which a majority vote is sufficient, and "international conventions" submitted for acceptance by states, which require a two-thirds majority. States are obligated to submit both recommendations and conventions to competent national authorities within one year, and to report periodically upon action taken to implement them.

The Executive Board consists of twenty members elected from among the delegates by the conference. They were formerly required to serve as independent experts, but at its eighth session, on proposal of the United States, Article 5 was amended to read: "The Executive Board shall be elected by the General Conference among the delegates appointed by the Member States and shall consist of twenty-two members, each of which shall represent the government of the State of which he is a national." They are chosen for a three-year term and are eligible for only one more term. The Executive Board prepares the agenda for the conference, executes the program of the organization, consults with other organizations, and prepares the annual report.

The conference chooses the director-general, upon nomination by the Executive Board; he is responsible for selecting and instructing the staff. The second director-general, Torres-Bodet, resigned in 1952 in protest against the budget, which he called a "regression." An

---

[16] There are four associate members: Gold Coast, Sierra Leone, British West Indies and British East Indies. In 1952, Poland withdrew because UNESCO had admitted units which Poland disliked; Hungary and Czechoslovakia followed this example. They were asked to reconsider. In April 1954 the Soviet Union and the Byelorussian and Ukrainian republics joined, whereupon Poland, Czechoslovakia and Hungary returned. See UNESCO Report to the U.N., 1952-1953, p. 165; Report of the Director-General, 1954, p. 17.

American, Dr. Luther Evans, Librarian of Congress, was elected in June 1953 and fell at once into the same problem of the loyalty of employees of United States nationality which was plaguing the United Nations.[17] The United States International Organizations Employees Loyalty Board attempted to exercise jurisdiction even in Paris over such persons, and demanded that those who refused to answer their questionnaire be dismissed. Seven of fifteen employees refused to answer, and four of these were informed that their appointments would not be renewed on the ground that their refusal to answer the questionnaire had done disservice to the organization. The UNESCO Board of Appeals advised the director-general to reconsider this decision, but he did not accept the advice.

The budget agreed upon for 1955-56 was $21,617,830, calculated on the scale used by the General Assembly in making its assessments for Members of the United Nations. As a result, the share of the United States was reduced from one-third to 30 per cent. A building of its own is planned for UNESCO in Paris.

NATIONAL COMMISSIONS. Article 7 of the UNESCO Constitution asks each member state to set up a national commission for the purpose of associating the principal national bodies interested in educational, scientific, and cultural matters, such commissions to act in advisory capacity to the respective delegations and to function as agencies of liaison. Up to 1955, sixty-four of the seventy-two member states had formed such commissions.

The United States National Commission for UNESCO was established by the 79th Congress.[18] It is composed of one hundred persons selected by the secretary of state; sixty of these represent national voluntary organizations (such as the American Political Science Association), twenty-five come from national, State, and local officials, and fifteen are appointed at large. It is served by a section in the Department of State called the UNESCO Relations Staff. The National Commission in the United States has been an active body, holding occasional large conferences.

ACTIVITIES. The range of activity of UNESCO is great; it may study the causes of tensions between nations which endanger peace, or nuclear physics, or it may labor to save the frescoes in a small church in Yugoslavia. It has been criticized for diffuseness, for lack of selectivity and practicality in its projects, and is one of the most controversial of the specialized agencies. Some of its work may be

[17] See § 109, above.
[18] Public Law 565, 79 Congress, 2nd Session, 22 U.S.C. 287 ff.

classified as general—the spreading of knowledge—and some of it as specific projects—"putting knowledge to work."

Under the general heading would fall: aiding voluntary organizations which spread knowledge, such as the PEN Club or the Federation of Secondary School Teachers; creating new voluntary organizations, such as the International Political Science Association (founded in 1949); arranging seminars on special subjects, the most famous one, perhaps, being the one on race relations;[19] publishing bibliographies and abstracts, such as the *Index Bibliographicus;* issuing UNESCO sales coupons to enable "soft currency" countries to buy books from "hard currency" countries; arranging an agreement to eliminate customs duties on books and publications;[20] and studying and making recommendations concerning press, radio and film facilities.

Under the heading of projects would fall the most important work of the fundamental education program. It is estimated that half of the population of the world is unable to read or write, and the purpose of this effort is to reach them in a "battle against ignorance." A pilot project was carried on in Haiti in 1948 and one in west China in 1949. There is a Center for Fundamental Education in Mexico City for Latin America and one in Egypt for the Middle East.[21] Advisory missions have been sent when requested, such as to Thailand in 1949, to Burma in 1951, to Libya in connection with Technical Assistance in 1951, and, with UNKRA, to Korea in 1952. UNESCO also assists in the development of libraries. It has made a number of studies in scientific fields; e.g., research in the problems of arid areas, such as the Sahara Desert, Australia, Chile, Arizona or the "European Organization for Nuclear Physics" at Geneva, with a laboratory, under an agreement which went into effect in September 1954.

In the field of the social sciences, there is the famous project on "Tensions Affecting International Understanding,"[22] which inquires

---

[19] It has published a "Statement on Race Relations" (1950) and a "Statement on the Nature of Race and Race Differences" (1952), and a number of scientific studies on the subject.

[20] An agreement to this end went into force in May 1952. See UNESCO, Trade Barriers to Knowledge: A Manual of Regulations Affecting Educational, Scientific and Cultural Materials (1951).

[21] See *Fundamental Education: Common Ground for All Peoples* (Report to the Preparatory Commission, New York, 1947); also W. G. Leland and others in *Harvard Educational Review* (Cambridge, 1950).

[22] In connection with this project UNESCO has published a series of pamphlets entitled "Toward World Understanding." It was apparently one of these, called "The United Nations and World Citizenship" which frightened the American Legion and other such ultra-patriotic bodies into denouncing UNESCO as an agency for world government. A report to the Legion conference in 1955 completely cleared UNESCO of the charge that it advocates world government. But would it be reprehensible or illegal if it did support world government?

concerning (1) influences which lead to international understanding or to nationalistic aggression, (2) population problems, (3) influences of modern technology, and (4) ideas which one people have about themselves and about other peoples. Abstracts and bibliographies are issued for the field, such as the *International Political Science Abstracts* or *Current Sociology*, and an *International Social Science Bulletin* is published.

UNESCO is interested in museums as centers of art and culture and continues to publish the serial, *Museum*, begun by the League of Nations. An effort to translate the great classics of literature moves slowly, but several volumes of an *Index Translationum: International Bibliography of Translations* have appeared.

A conference at the Hague in 1953 adopted a Convention for the Protection of Cultural Property in the Event of Armed Conflict. An important achievement of UNESCO was the adoption of the Universal Copyright Convention, which came into force on September 16, 1954, the United States being among the twelve which had ratified. This may be regarded as the first such agreement having a world-wide jurisdiction.[23]

114. THE INTERNATIONAL CIVIL AVIATION ORGANIZATION

BACKGROUND. We have noted earlier the first efforts to regulate international aviation, which eventuated in the Convention of Air Navigation of 1919 as the foundation for a new system applicable over a large part of Europe. As amended in 1929, the granting of permission by a state to fly over its territory or to land there was made optional rather than mandatory,[24] thereby potentially limiting the opportunity for development of international aviation. Aviation developed on the basis of bilateral or reciprocal arrangements; and the United States airlines, after transoceanic flights became possible, obtained agreements to establish landing privileges in Britain, France,

[23] UNESCO publishes a *Copyright Bulletin* which contains the materials on this important subject. See N. Chediak, "The Progressive Development of World Copyright Law," *A.J.*, 42 (1948), p. 797; J. S. Dubin, "The Universal Copyright Convention," *California Law Review*, 42 (1954), p. 89; F. Honig, "International Copyright Protection and the Draft Copyright Convention of UNESCO," *International and Comparative Law Quarterly*, 1 (1952), p. 217; T. V. Kalijarvi, "International Copyright Protection," *Dept. State Bull.*, 30 (1954), p. 530; "International Copyright Protection and the United States: the Impact of the UNESCO Universal Convention on Existing Law," *Yale Law Journal*, 42, p. 1065; *United Nations Review*, March, 1956, pp. 25-27.

[24] O. J. Lissitzyn, *International Transport and National Policy* (New York, 1942), p. 254.

396   INTERNATIONAL GOVERNMENT

and other European countries. Meanwhile, Great Britain was establishing air routes to her dominions and colonies, and United States airlines were spreading in the Western Hemisphere; thus, the world was being divided among three groups—the continental European countries, Great Britain, and the United States.

World War II produced important changes in this situation. An enormous development of aviation resulted in larger and faster planes, and it was apparent that air transport would be much more reliable and more widely used after the war. The British had during the war concentrated upon the production of combat and training planes, while the United States developed large carriers for long distance transport and gained much experience and knowledge of routes around the world. The British were worried by this handicap, and fearful of the future; they called for international regulation, and an international air authority. The United States, confident in its superiority, forgot its former ideas of protection and was eager for unrestricted competition in the field, though also favoring an international organization.

CHICAGO CONFERENCE.[25] As the defeat of Germany became imminent, the United States extended an invitation to some fifty countries to attend a conference on civil aviation at Chicago on November 1, 1944. An Interim Agreement on International Civil Aviation provided for a provisional organization (PICAO), to be composed of an Interim Assembly and an Interim Council, having its seat in Canada. By Article 8 of the agreement, each state was given "complete and exclusive sovereignty over the airspace above its territory." Each state was to make its own regulations, but apply them without discrimination. The conference also issued a Convention on International Civil Aviation, an International Air Services Transit Agreement, and an International Air Transport Agreement, all of which were to be regarded as drafts for study by member states and by the Interim Organization.

After much disagreement as to freedom or regulation in the air market, a Canadian study broke the problem into separate headings:

[25] The texts of the instruments adopted are in Dept. of State Pub., No. 2282, and *Proceedings of the International Civil Aviation Conference*, Dept. of State Pub., No. 2820 (two volumes). See also *Blueprint for World Civil Aviation, ibid.*, No. 2348; J. Walstrom, "The Chicago Air Conference," *Dept. of State Bull.*, 11 (1944), p. 843; E. P. Warner, *ICAO After Six Years* (Montreal, 1952); D. Goedhuis, "The Development of Rules to Govern International Aviation Communication," *Transport and Communication Review*, 5 (1952), p. 1; Virginia Little, "Control of International Air Transport," *Int. Organ.*, 3 (1949), p. 29; Senate Committee on Foreign Relations, Convention on International Civil Aviation Organization, Hearings, 79 Cong., 1 Sess. (1945).

(1) to fly across a territory without landing (right of innocent passage), (2) to land for non-traffic purposes, (3) to carry traffic taken on in the country of the aircraft's nationality, (4) to take passengers or cargo destined for the country of the aircraft. Of these "four freedoms," agreement was reached upon the first two, but not upon the latter two, thus leaving unsolved the problem of intermediate countries. A "fifth freedom" to cover this by permitting pick-ups en route was suggested by the United States, and a compromise solution provided for two multilateral conventions, one (The International Air Transport Agreement) accepting only the first two "freedoms," the other accepting all five. In the latter instrument, a reservation could be made to eliminate the "fifth freedom." Twenty-eight nations signed the former, and eighteen the latter.

The United States and the United Kingdom met at Bermuda to reconcile their still divergent views, and on February 11, 1946, signed three documents: a Final Act, a Bilateral Agreement, and Heads of Agreement relating to the Civil Use of Leased Air Bases. Both nations had accepted "freedoms one and two" of the Chicago Conference; they now reached agreement that rates would be subject to governmental review, that each country would determine the frequency of operation of its own airlines, that "fifth freedom" traffic could be carried subject to defined principle, and that disputes be referred for advisory opinion to PICAO. On March 27, the Conference on North Atlantic Air Routes at Dublin reached agreement on safety rules for transatlantic flying. With these agreements made between the United States and the United Kingdom, other nations followed and a working solution of the difficult problem of international civil aviation was achieved.

On March 4, 1947, the twenty-sixth state ratified the Convention on International Civil Aviation, which provides for an International Civil Aviation Organization, and thirty days later the permanent organization came into being. The first meeting of the Assembly of ICAO was held at Montreal on May 6, 1947. It was decided to continue the Air Navigation and Air Transport Committees, and to establish an International Law Committee to unify and codify air law.

ORGANIZATION. ICAO has an assembly consisting of all members of the organization. It meets annually on call by the council, decides policies, votes the budget and handles financial and other matters. The council is the executive body, composed of twenty-one members elected by the assembly, which must take into account the chief countries in air transport and the major geographic areas of the world. It supervises the work of committees and makes recommendations to governments. There are three main technical committees: Air Transport Committee; the Air Navigation Commission; and the Legal Committee. There is, finally, a secretariat, headed by a secretary-general chosen by the council.

Field regional offices have been established at Montreal for North America; at Lima for South America; at Paris for Europe and Africa; at Cairo for the Middle East; and at Melbourne for the Pacific and Far East. Various regional meetings have been held.

By August, 1955, there were sixty-four members, including Spain which had previously been barred by a resolution of the General Assembly. An agreement was made with the United Nations, which came into force on May 13, 1947.

ACTIVITIES. ICAO's range of work covers almost everything dealing with aviation.[26] It seeks to ensure the greatest degree of uniformity possible in regulations concerning international civil aviation and to this end has adopted fifteen sets of standards and recommended practices. These deal with aircraft, nationality and registration marks, licensing of personnel, airworthiness, rules of the air, meteorological codes, search and rescue, facilitation of international air transport, etc. A system was established in 1949 under which ten weather stations were established, manned by twenty-five ships. ICAO has done much work in the development of international air law and has completed two conventions, one on International Recognition of Rights of Aircraft (1948) and one on Damages Caused by Foreign Aircraft to Third Parties on the Surface (1952). A large part of the system through which aviation is carried on is in the form of bilateral agreements and national laws, and these are collected and published by ICAO—a thousand of them by January 1952. Such problems as reducing accidents, certificates of airworthiness for new aircraft, aerial collisions, insurance, etc., are being studied.[27]

ICAO also contributes to the Expanded Technical Assistance Programme of the United Nations through training and giving expert advices, e.g., to Ethiopia and Iran concerning meteorological service, and to Afghanistan in setting up a civil aviation authority. The *ICAO Bulletin* gives full information concerning the activities of the organization.

[26] The commercial aspects of air transport have been the subject of conventions, beginning with the Warsaw Convention of 1929. See Sibert, I, p. 841; Sir Arnold McNair, *The Law of the Air* (2nd ed., London, 1953).

[27] There was a fascinating discussion of the problems of the upper air space, such as satellites and guided missiles, reported in the 1956 *Proc. Am. Soc.*

115. INTERNATIONAL MONETARY FUND (IMF)

The abandonment by the major countries of the gold standard during the 1930's, the financial uncertainties of the depression period, and the ruthless methods of economic warfare instituted by Germany furnished ample warning that international financial cooperation and institutional aid would be needed after World War II if the great task of postwar reconstruction was to be accomplished.[28]

In 1943, the United States released a plan by H. D. White for an International Stabilization Fund, and almost at the same time the British issued a plan for an International Clearing Union prepared by Lord Keynes. The two were widely compared and discussed by technical experts from thirty countries; this led to a "Joint Statement by Experts" which was the base of discussion for the United Nations Monetary and Financial Conference which assembled at Bretton Woods, New Hampshire, July 1-22, 1944, on the invitation of the United States.[29] Two related, though separate, institutions were provided for at this conference, an International Monetary Fund and a Bank for Reconstruction and Development.

PURPOSES. The purposes of the Monetary Fund, as stated in Article 1 of the agreement, may be summarized as follows: To promote international monetary cooperation; to facilitate the expansion and balanced growth of international trade and to contribute thereby to high levels of employment and real income; to promote exchange stability; to maintain orderly exchange arrangements among members and to avoid competitive exchange alterations; to assist in the establishment of a multilateral system of payments and in the elimination of foreign exchange restrictions; to encourage confidence by making the resources of the Fund available to members; and thus to shorten the duration and lessen the degree of disequilibrium in international balances of payments.

ORGANIZATION. While states are members, the Fund will deal only with the member's designated fiscal agency, such as its treasury or cen-

[28] The economic and financial problems involved cannot, of course, be discussed here. Reference is made, out of a vast literature, to *International Currency Experience: Lessons of the Inter-War Period* (League of Nations, 1944); W. A. Brown, Jr., *The International Gold Standard Reinterpreted, 1914-1934*, 2 vols. (New York, 1940); G. N. Helm, *International Monetary Cooperation* (Chapel Hill, North Carolina, 1945).

[29] *Proceedings and Documents of the United Nations Monetary and Financial Conference*, Dept. of State Pub., No. 2866 (Washington, 1948); *Documents Am. For. Rel.*, VI (1943-44), pp. 331-98; *Int. Organ.*, 1 (1947), p. 124; J. P. Young, "Developing Plans for an International Monetary Fund and a World Bank," *Dept. of State Bull.*, November 13, 1950.

tral bank. Each member's subscription, payable in gold and local currency, equals its quota. The quota is determined by reference to the member's population, volume of trade, national income, gold, and foreign exchange reserves. The total is 8.8 billions of U. S. dollars. The subscription of the United States was 2.75 billion dollars, as compared to 1.3 billions for the United Kingdom, or a half million for Panama. These quotas are subject to revision, a four-fifths majority being required for the purpose (Article 4, section 2).

The primary obligations of members, after they have joined the Fund are to collaborate with the Fund to "promote exchange stability, to maintain orderly exchange arrangements with other members, and to avoid competitive exchange alterations" (Article 4, section 4a). To this end a member is generally required: (1) to define, in agreement with the Fund, its currency unit in terms of gold or U. S. dollar of the weight and fineness as of July 1, 1944; (2) not to change the par value of its currency, except with the approval of the Fund; (3) to take appropriate measures to ensure exchange transactions between its currency and the currencies of other members only within the margins prescribed under Section 3 of the Fund Agreement; (4) to consult the Fund annually, beginning on March 1, 1952, on the further retention of specified exchange restrictions; (5) not to impose exchange restrictions in respect of current international transactions, nor introduce multiple currency practices or discriminatory currency arrangements, except with the approval of the Fund, nor to restrict the convertibility of foreign-held balances. These requirements apply to members which have undertaken the obligations of Article 8, sections 2, 3 and 4.

The Fund is given "full juridical personality," and is entitled to immunity from judicial process, search, taxation, or appropriation. Membership is open to other states on terms prescribed by the Fund; and a member may withdraw upon notice, settling its accounts in accordance with Schedule D of the Appendix. A member which fails in its obligations may be declared ineligible to use the Fund, or required to withdraw.

Voting power is distributed in accordance with the financial contribution made, each having 250 votes plus one more for each one hundred thousand U. S. dollars contributed, and decisions are taken by a majority of the votes cast (Article 12, section 5). Amendments may be suggested by a member, a governor, or the executive directors and, if approved by the board, are submitted by circular letter or telegram to members; they come into force when approved by three-fifths of the members having four-fifths of the voting power. For certain changes, acceptance by all members is required (Article 17). The headquarters are located in the member having the largest quota, now the United States. In relation to non-members, members agree to do nothing contrary to the purposes of the Fund.

"The Fund shall have a Board of Governors, Executive Directors, a Managing Director and a staff" (Article 12, section 1). Each member appoints one governor and one alternate, to serve five years. All powers of the Fund are vested in the board of governors which may, however, delegate to the executive directors any powers except those listed in Article 12, section 2, paragraph 6. The board of governors, composed mostly of ministers of finance and presidents of central banks, meets annually to review activities and determine policies. The executive directors are responsible for general operations of the Fund. The executive directors are in continuous session. Each appointed member is entitled to cast the number of votes allotted to the member state which appointed him; each elected director may cast the number of votes which counted toward his election. There is also a managing director, chosen by the executive directors, who selects and manages the staff and conducts the ordinary business of the Fund. Questions as to the interpretation of the agreement are referred to the executive directors, and may be appealed to the board of governors whose decision is final. Article 10 contains the usual provision for cooperation with other international organizations.

A meeting was held at Wilmington Island, Savannah, Georgia, on March 8, 1946, to establish the Fund and the Bank; the first meeting of the executive directors was held on May 6 and the first meeting of the board of governors at Washington on September 27. Formal operation was begun on March 1, 1947.

ACTIVITIES. In general, the Fund operates through buying, selling, and controlling exchange. To assist members in temporary deficits, the Fund is to sell foreign exchange against the national currency of that member. A member is entitled to buy the currency of another member in exchange for its own currency or gold to an annual amount not to exceed 25 per cent of its quota, though the Fund authorities may waive this limitation. A charge is made for this service by the Fund, not only because it is a service, but also to discourage too frequent or too extensive use of the Fund. Members are expected to repurchase their own currency from the Fund when the emergency is over (Article 5, section 7) and their monetary reserve position is strong enough to permit it. The general purpose is to provide temporary assistance, and there are provisions to discourage use of the money "contrary to the Purpose of the Fund" (Article 5, section 5). In these "transactions," from

March 1, 1947, through November 30, 1955, the Fund sold currencies equivalent to $1,216.4 millions; during the same period $859.8 millions were repaid.

The Fund serves also as a center for the collection and exchange of information on monetary and financial problems. It took over from the League of Nations publication of the *Balance of Payments Yearbook*, and publishes the monthly *International Financial Statistics*. It has also rendered technical assistance in money, banking, and finance, through missions to countries and through training courses.

In general, the Fund is intended to facilitate the expansion of, and to promote, financial stability; it has, it may be noted, special powers and functions in relation to GATT. How far it achieves its purposes is a matter of controversy. A United Nations subcommission on Employment and Economic Stability criticized it as being afflicted with a policy of "safety first" and reported that it and the Bank were defied by states bent on economic nationalism; others have accused it of being merely the handmaiden of "dollar diplomacy" and as being overly restrictive in its interpretation of its charter provisions relating to the use of its resources. The Fund replied that its members had not been nationalistic and had supported it in its efforts to prevent competitive import restrictions and currency devaluation.

116. INTERNATIONAL BANK FOR RECONSTRUCTION AND DEVELOPMENT (IBRD)[30]

The Bank, we have noted, was created at the same time as the Fund, though as a separate institution, under a separate agreement.

PURPOSES. The Bank is intended (Article 1) to assist in reconstruction and development by facilitating investment of capital for productive purposes; to promote private foreign investment by means of guarantees or participation, and to supplement private funds when necessary; to encourage international investment for development of productive resources of members (thereby assisting in raising productivity, the standard of living, and conditions of labor in their territories); to establish a priority of urgency and usefulness in projects; and to bring about smooth transition from wartime to peacetime economy. In an economically insecure world the private lender may be unable or unwilling to take risks with his money, though the need for the money might be great. The Bank may lend its own money as

---

[30] *Documents Am. For. Rel.*, VI (1943-44), pp. 373-98; *Int. Organ.*, 1 (1947), pp. 126, 354; *The International Bank for Reconstruction and Development* (IBRD, Baltimore, 1954).

either a whole loan or a share in a loan; or it may guarantee loans by private investors for productive reconstruction and development. The borrower may be a government or a private concern supported by his government and the private lender is reassured in the sense that he may rely upon both the borrower's government and the Bank.

ORGANIZATION. The Bank, like the Fund, is given juridical personality and similar immunities and exemptions. Members of the Bank must be also members of the Fund; provisions for admission, withdrawal, and supervision are similar. The authorized capital was ten billions in United States dollars divided into a hundred thousand shares of a par value of ten thousand dollars apiece. Each original member subscribed to a minimum number of shares as set forth in Schedule A. A capital stock of $9,100 million was envisaged, and of this the United States pays 3,175 million. Each member is entitled to 250 votes, plus one for each share of stock, (which gives the United States a third of the voting power) and decisions are usually by majority vote. In 1954, Israel, Korea, and Afghanistan were accepted as members, raising the total to fifty-nine members.

The Bank, like the Fund, has a board of governors consisting of a representative from each member (who is usually the finance minister or president of a central bank), each having a voting power proportionate to its shares of stock; a board of executive directors of fourteen, five appointed by the five members owning the most shares and eleven others elected by the governors of the other members; and a president, who directs the staff of over four hundred.

ACTIVITIES. The Bank was slow in getting into operation, and cautious in its undertakings, as befits such an institution but, by June, 1955, the gross amount loaned by the Bank from the beginning was about two and a third billion dollars. This was distributed in 124 loans made in thirty-seven countries.

A subcommission, on economic development, of the U.N. Economic and Social Council criticized the Bank as not affording sufficient help to the less developed countries; it observed that the Bank did not have enough money and that the terms on which it made loans were too strict. The Bank replied that it would not be deflected from the principles laid down in its charter and that its loans must be productive ones. In its Fourth Annual Report, the Bank stated that it could not be expected to cure all the ills of the world, such as, for example, the dollar shortage. It noted that the less well-developed countries would not be able to utilize their capital imports to their best advantage unless these imports could be integrated into a well-planned investment and development program.

The Bank has furnished technical assistance to members by sending to them general survey missions, by helping them to draw up long range plans for increasing production, by assisting in the establishment of special financial institutions, and through a traineeship program. It plans to open in 1956 an Economic Development Institute which will offer six month seminar courses to broaden the knowledge of administrators and to permit exchange of experience between them.

Examples of loans made by the Bank are: to a Brazilian company for purchase of electrical equipment to furnish electric power; to Colombia for railways; to KLM to re-equip its air fleet; to Peru to improve the port of Callao; to Pakistan for a natural gas line; to Norway to expand its merchant fleet. The Bank takes particular interest in the development of rivers for purposes of power, irrigation, and flood control; through such aid, the Bank may contribute to settlement of disputes such as the difficulty between India and Pakistan over the waters of the Indus River.

INTERNATIONAL FINANCE CORPORATION. On April 11, 1955, the Bank approved, for submission to governments, Articles of Agreement for an International Finance Corporation. The proposal for this body had originated out of discontent with the difficulty of borrowing from the Bank, and the General Assembly, by Resolution 823(IX) had requested the Bank to prepare a statute for such a body. The corporation is to have a capital of one hundred million dollars to be subscribed by Members in the proportion of their quotas in the Bank. It is to be affiliated with the Bank, having the same executive directors, but to have its own president and to be a separate entity from the Bank. It has more latitude in financing private enterprises than is permitted to the Bank; it may make loans without governmental guarantee. It is to go into effect as soon as at least thirty governments have subscribed at least seventy-five million dollars to its capital.

The Bank and the Fund stand out somewhat distinctively among the specialized agencies. They have to be especially cautious and, because of this and doubtless also because of the weight of the United States in them, their agreements with the United Nations give them a more independent position. They do not feel obligated, as other agencies are, to consider items put upon their agenda by the United Nations nor to admit representatives of the United Nations to directors' meetings. Each is free to determine its own budget and is not obligated to submit this budget, as are other agencies, to the United Nations for examination and recommendation by the General Assembly under Article 17, paragraph 3, of the UN Charter.

117. WORLD HEALTH ORGANIZATION (WHO)

For many years past, there has been more international cooperation and less political interference in the field of health than in other international activities. The reorganization of health work after World War II was similarly nonpolitical and successful. An International Health Conference, called by the Economic and Social Council, met at New York during June and July 1946 and adopted four instruments, signed by sixty-one states.[31] An interim commission of eighteen states set to work to build the new organization, which was to take over the League of Nations Health Organization, the International Office of Public Health at Paris, and some of the work of UNRRA. Regional health organizations, such as the Pan American Sanitary Bureau, were to be integrated by mutual agreement. The permanent World Health Organization came officially into existence on September 1, 1948, which has since been celebrated as "World Health Day."

PURPOSES. The Preamble to the Constitution of WHO defines health as "a state of complete physical, mental, and social well-being and not merely the absence of disease or infirmity," and regards the highest attainable standard of health as a right of every human being, fundamental to peace and security. Its objective is stated in Article 1 as "attainment by all peoples of the highest possible level of health," and a long list of functions is set forth in Article 2. Among these are "to act as the directing and coordinating authority on international health work"; to assist governments and the United Nations in various ways; to maintain epidemiological and statistical services; to promote nutrition, housing, sanitation, etc.; and to encourage cooperation among scientific groups and advance research.

ORGANIZATION. Membership in WHO is open to all states, and those who were not initial members may be admitted by majority vote of the Health Assembly. No provision for withdrawal or for reservations was included, but the United States made a reservation (which was accepted) for withdrawal on a year's notice. Members who fail to meet their financial obligations may have their voting privileges and services suspended. Provision is made for admission of non-sovereign territories as associate members (Article 8). The Health Assembly decides upon

[31] The Final Acts of the International Health Conference are in *U.N. Doc.*, E/155; it contains the constitution, the "Arrangement" setting up the interim commission, and the protocol taking over the International Office of Public Health in Paris. See also the articles by H. V. Z. Hude, in *Dept. of State Bull.*, 15 (1946), pp. 453 and 756; W. R. Sharp, "The New World Health Organization," *A.J.*, 41 (1947), pp. 509.

the budget and apportions expenses among members. Each member has one vote; decisions on important matters (listed in Article 60) require a two-thirds majority of those present and voting, and other decisions a bare majority. Provisions as to legal status and immunities are as stated in the terms of the United Nations Charter. Amendments must be adopted by two-thirds of the Health Assembly and accepted by two-thirds of the members. Disputes as to the interpretation or application of the constitution are to be referred to the International Court of Justice.

The organs provided are the World Health Assembly, an executive board, and a secretariat. Each member may send three delegates to the Health Assembly, who should be technically qualified and preferably represent the national health administration. The assembly meets annually and in various countries. It determines policies, decides upon members to be represented in the board, appoints the director-general, instructs the board as to action to be taken, supervises budget and finance, brings matters of health to the attention of members (through the board or director-general), considers recommendations bearing on health made by other organizations, promotes research, etc. It may adopt conventions or agreements for submission for ratification by members, and members are obligated to act upon them within eighteen months. It is given authority to make regulations with regard to sanitary and quarantine requirements and other procedures to prevent the spread of disease; to adopt nomenclature with regard to disease, causes of death, and public health practices; to adopt standards with regard to diagnostic procedures and with regard to safety, purity, and potency of biological and pharmaceutical products moving in international commerce, and concerning labeling and advertising of such products. Such regulations are binding upon members unless they reject them within the time limit stated in the notice. In no other organization has as much legislative power been granted or as much expert representation asked—though sovereignty remains fully respected.

The executive board is composed of persons designated by eighteen states selected by the assembly and technically qualified in the field of health. Their term of office is three years, and they may be re-elected. The board acts as executive organ, carries out functions assigned by the Health Assembly, submits proposals to and prepares agenda for the assembly; and it is authorized to take emergency measures to combat epidemics and to share in health relief in calamities. The director-general is appointed by the Health Assembly on nomination of the board. He is the chief technical and administrative officer of WHO; he prepares the budget, and appoints the staff. He is authorized to arrange with members a procedure of direct access to their various health administrations and organizations, to other organizations, and to the regional offices.

A unique chapter is devoted to regional arrangements. The Health Assembly may define areas and, with the consent of members in such an area, establish there a Regional Committee and Office. Such regional organizations are integral parts of WHO, and their rights and duties are to be determined by the Health Assembly in consultation with members in the area. The Latin American states preferred regional organization and were not easily persuaded to coordinate the work of the Pan American Sanitary Bureau with that of WHO. There are now six regional offices, located at New Delhi for South-East Asia; Alexandria for the eastern Mediterranean; Manila, for the western Pacific; Washington (Pan American Sanitary Bureau); Brazzaville for Africa below the Sahara; and temporarily, for Europe, Geneva, which is headquarters for WHO.

The agreement with the United Nations came into force on July 10, 1948. The organization has had a total of eighty-one members and three associate members (Morocco, Tunisia, and the Federation of Rhodesia and Nyasaland), but the states in the Soviet bloc announced withdrawal. Since there is no provision for withdrawal, the organization expressed hope that they would resume active participation.[32]

ACTIVITIES.[33] WHO offers advisory services to those who desire it. This includes training of personnel for combating diseases such as malaria, tuberculosis, venereal diseases, maternal and child troubles, and diseases in connection with nutrition. Demonstration teams are sent out on specific projects. Some twenty projects for control of malaria have been conducted in Burma, India, Iran, Lebanon, and Pakistan; about as many against tuberculosis in Costa Rica, Egypt, Iran, Iraq, Libya, Turkey, etc. DDT was in such demand that it became difficult to obtain, and research became necessary as mosquitoes developed resistance to it.

A great deal of technical work is done. The important task of disseminating epidemiological intelligence—which may be credited with having stopped the great plagues of the past—is continued. Special research on various diseases is carried on. A new international health regulation, codifying various health measures applicable to travel, was

[32] C. E. Allen, "World Health and World Politics," *Int. Organ.*, 4 (1950), pp. 27-43.
[33] See C. S. Ascher, "Current Problems in the World Health Organizations Program," *Int. Organ.*, 4 (1952), p. 27; N. H. Goodman, *International Health Organizations and Their Work* (London, 1952); A. Mudaliar, "World Health Problems," *Int. Con.*, No. 491 (1953); C. E. A. Winslow, "International Cooperation in the Service of Health," *Annals*, 283 (1951), p. 192. The annual reports of the director-general, of course, are the best source of information.

brought into operation in October 1952. The first *International Pharmacopeia*, establishing international standards of purity and strength for medicines, was published in 1951. There are various other publications which inform national health administrations concerning progress in public health, such as the *Bulletin of the World Health Organization* and the *Chronicle of the World Health Organization.*

WHO has, of course, participated in the technical assistance work of the United Nations. It is responsible for a five-year model health demonstration in El Salvador; it has established a children's hospital in Bolivia with the support of the International Children's Emergency Fund; and it has helped various countries to organize and coordinate public health programs. It has given emergency aid to countries in time of disaster, such as to Thailand after a plague, to El Salvador after an earthquake, or to Palestine refugees.

International cooperation and organization in the field of health have advanced rapidly, doubtless more so than in any other field, though they still fall far short of what is needed. The budget of WHO is only a small fraction of the public health expenditures of the United States, yet members constantly endeavor to diminish it.

118. UNIVERSAL POSTAL UNION (UPU)

The Postal Union, one of the oldest of the public unions, was described in Chapter 7. The Economic and Social Council called a meeting of postal experts in 1946 to consider bringing UPU into relationship with the United Nations. A draft agreement was approved in 1947 but did not come into effect until July 1, 1948, when a revised postal convention entered into force. Under this convention, there is a congress, as in the past, which meets about every five years; a permanent Executive and Liaison Committee consisting of twenty members elected by the congress on a geographical basis and meeting once a year; and the International Bureau at Berne, which is the secretariat of the new specialized agency. The congress is the policy making and legislative body; the committee controls the bureau, maintains working relations with other bodies, and makes studies and recommendations; and the bureau supervises the system, publishes information, and acts as a clearing house for settlement of accounts. The United Nations was authorized to set up a separate postal administration without becoming a member of UPU. The UN unit, mostly for philatelists, adds over half a million dollars per year to the income of the United Nations.

There were, in 1955, ninety-three members of the UPU. This excluded Germany, which was authorized to notify its accession when the circumstances which debarred it were ended. Under the new convention, new members do not enter by notification, as before, but must be admitted by a vote of two-thirds of the members.[34]

119. INTERNATIONAL TELECOMMUNICATIONS UNION (ITU)

The Economic and Social Council on March 28, 1947, authorized negotiations to bring the ITU into agreement with the United Nations. The United States had previously organized a conference, which met at Atlantic City on July 1, 1947. Its chief purpose was to revise the Madrid Convention of 1932. The agreement with the United Nations, setting up the new International Telecommunication Convention as a specialized agency, went into effect on January 1, 1949.

In general, the purpose of the ITU is to encourage cooperation in the use of telecommunications; more particularly, it attempts to maintain some order in the atmosphere by allocating radio-frequencies; it seeks to establish the lowest possible rates for service; it works upon measures for ensuring safety of life through telecommunications; and it makes studies and publishes information.

ORGANIZATION. The revised ITU has a Plenipotentiary Conference of all members, including associate members, and administrative conferences, all of which meet quinquennially. It has six permanent organs: the Administrative Council; the General Secretariat; the International Frequency Registration Board; the International Telegraph Consultative Committee; and the International Radio Consultative Committee. Its work is too technical for description here, but its importance can easily be recognized.[35]

120. WORLD METEOROLOGICAL ORGANIZATION (WMO)

The origins of this new specialized agency reach back as far as 1853, when a conference met at Brussels to discuss the collection of meteorological information. The International Meteorological Organization was established in 1878. This was not an intergovernmental body, but was composed of the directors of the various national services. It held a

---

[34] *L'Union Postale Universelle, sa fondation et son developpement, 1874-1949, Mémoire* (UPU, Berne, 1950).

[35] See G. A. Codding, Jr., *The International Telecommunications Union* (Leiden, 1952), with full bibliography.

number of conferences and developed much standardization. In 1939, it decided to convert itself into an official body, with states as members. The twelfth Conference of Directors, meeting at Washington in 1947, drew up a convention creating the World Meteorological Organization, which came into force on March 23, 1950. The agreement with the United Nations came into force on December 20, 1951.

The purposes of WMO are to establish a network of stations throughout the world which could rapidly exchange weather information; to promote standardization of meteorological observations and ensure uniform publication of information; to further the application of the science to aviation, shipping, agriculture, and in other useful ways; and to encourage research in meteorology. The importance of this work has been realized by millions through newspaper forecasts of hurricanes with feminine names.

ORGANIZATION. Membership is of various kinds. Members of the United Nations or states represented at the conference become members simply by acceding to the convention. Trust territories could become members when the United Nations applied the convention to them. Annexed to the convention is a list of other territories which could become members through accession by the states responsible for their international relations. Other states and territories may become members upon approval by two-thirds of the member states (not territories).

The World Meteorological Congress, composed of the directors of the national services of members (as chief delegates), meets once a year, determines policies, and adopts technical regulations by a two-thirds vote. The Executive Council is composed of the president and vice-presidents of WMO, elected by the congress, the presidents of the regional associations, and an equal number of directors of national services elected by the congress. The executive body sees that resolutions are carried out; it makes studies and recommendations and offers counsel to members. There is also a permanent secretariat and six regional associations; for Europe, for Asia, for Africa, for North and South America, and for the south-west Pacific. There are a number of technical commissions composed of experts.

ACTIVITIES. The work of the WMO is interesting and far-reaching. It is now engaged in preparing a new code for reporting observations by reconnaissance flights (RECCO code), an International Cloud Atlas, and a guide for air crews in making observations. It works with the International Union of Geodesy and Geophysics, with ICAO in a study for the detection of thunderstorms, with ITU on meteorological telecommunications, with the United Nations on its arid zone development program, and helps the technical assistance program by training personnel and organizing national services.

121. ORGANIZATION FOR TRADE COOPERATION (OTC)

Trade between nations is essential; in a world of interdependence and specialization, life and prosperity depend upon it. It is perhaps because of this very importance that nations have kept trade under severe national restrictions, but the results of such restrictions have been disastrous. For many years, efforts have been made toward better regulation of such trade but, while experts could and did agree upon recommendations, nations would not put them into effect. The Atlantic Charter proposed "to further the enjoyment by all states, great or small, victor or vanquished, of access on equal terms, to the trade and to the raw materials of the world"; and in the Lend-Lease agreements made with the United States there was a commitment to eliminate discriminatory treatment and to reduce tariffs and trade barriers. Within the United States, the long struggle over the reciprocal trade agreements illustrated the controversial character and difficulty of the problem.

The United States had devoted a great deal of study to this problem, and in November 1945 had prepared "Proposals for Expansion of World Trade and Employment."[36] This noted that international trade is kept small by four things: (1) restrictions imposed by governments; (2) those imposed by private combines and cartels; (3) fear of disorder in the markets for primary commodities; and (4) irregularity in production and employment. Recommendations were made for each of these situations, and a conference was suggested to meet in 1946. The Economic and Social Council of the United Nations called for such a conference in February 1946, and set up a preparatory committee to plan for it. For this meeting, the United States revised its earlier proposals into a Suggested Charter for an International Trade Organization,[37] which served as a basis of discussion for the first meeting of the preparatory committee in London in October 1946. The report of this meeting accepted a very large part of the United States proposals,

[36] Dept. of State Pub., No. 2411; see articles in the *Dept. of State Bull.*, 14 (1946), pp. 403, 509, 561, 616, 630, 647.

[37] Dept. of State Pub., No. 2598; summarized in *Dept. of State Bull.*, 15 (1946), p. 585.

and added a new chapter on economic development, which laid down various principles of governmental aid and international cooperation. The second session of the preparatory committee met in Geneva in 1947, completed the draft Charter for an International Trade Organization, and called a Conference on Trade and Employment for the fall of that year.

This conference met at Havana on November 21, 1947, and was attended by representatives of fifty-six nations. The issues there were largely between the industrially developed countries and the underdeveloped countries, on such matters as measures for promotion of economic development, safeguards for foreign investment, or the voting system in the executive board. The charter was signed on March 24, 1948 by fifty-three countries; it has never been ratified by enough states to put it into effect. The Congress of the United States split badly over ratification, and in December 1950 the Department of State announced that the charter would not be resubmitted to Congress. Thus, the organization was for all practical purposes dead, killed by the hand that made it.[38] The story of ITO is still of interest, however, as an essential part of subsequent development; it is related also to the work on "Restrictive Business Practices" and to that on International Commodity Arrangements.

GATT. At the same time that the charter was drafted in 1946-47, a draft General Agreement on Tariffs and Trade was prepared; this was signed on October 30, 1947 by twenty-three countries.[39] The original schedules cover more than forty-five thousand tariff items. Article 25

[38] For the text of the "Havana Charter" see United Nations Conference on Trade and Employment . . . Final Act and Related Documents, *U.N. Doc.*, E/CONF.2/78, Sales No. 1948.II.D.4; it is found also in the Dept. of State Pub., No. 3206 (1948). Among the many comments upon it: *Analysis of the Geneva Draft of the Charter for an International Trade Organization* (U.S. Tariff Commission, Washington, 1947); H. S. Piquet and H. Ficker, *The Havana Charter for an International Trade Organization* (Library of Congress, Legislative Reference Service, 1950) containing arguments *pro* and *con;* H. Feis, "The Geneva Proposals for an International Trade Organization," *Int. Organ.*, 11 (1948), p. 39; P. W. Bidwell and W. Diebold, "The United States and the International Trade Organization," *Int. Con.*, No. 449 (1949); Clair Wilcox (who directed negotiations for the United States), *A Charter for World Trade* (New York, 1949).

[39] For GATT, see GATT, Final Act Adopted . . . Conference on Trade and Employment, in four volumes, *U.N. Doc.*, Sales No. 1947.II.D.10; Hearings before the House Ways and Means Committee, 80 Cong., 1 Sess. (1947), and Hearings before the Senate Finance Committee, 80 Cong., 1 Sess. (1947); *The General Agreement on Tariffs and Trade (GATT): An Explanation of its Provisions and the Proposed Amendments*, Dept. of State Pub., No. 5813 (1955); W. Willoughby, "The Annecy Conference on Tariffs and Trade," *Dept. of State Bull.*, 21 (1949), p. 774; C. H. Alexandrowicz, "International Trade and Tariffs at Torquay," *World Affairs* (1951), p. 211; R. Vernon, *America's Foreign Trade Policy and GATT* (Princeton, 1954).

made provision for organizations, and GATT began its existence on January 1, 1948 through an undertaking between eight of the leading trading countries—the United States, the United Kingdom, Canada, France, and the Benelux countries. The tariff schedules have been renegotiated several times. Thirty-four countries, accounting for 80 per cent of the world trade, now participate.

The General Agreement on Tariffs and Trade is a complex, detailed and technical instrument. It includes a code of rules under which trade relations are to be conducted: no discrimination, commitments to give effect to negotiated concessions on specified products, and prohibitions against use of quotas limiting imports and exports. There are lists, separate ones for each country, of the products on which tariffs are fixed; and the agreement provides for periodic meetings for the settlement of mutual problems and the operation of the system.

ORGANIZATION FOR TRADE COOPERATION. During the ninth of meetings, the system was thoroughly debated. The United States had made trouble by subsidizing orange exports and putting quantitative restrictions on dairy products imports; a resolution was adopted censuring it for such actions and permitting other states to take retaliatory action. Other states felt justified in setting restrictions upon imports from the United States because of her subsidies and her import controls; they were not enthusiastic about its desire to sell everywhere without limit, and to limit buying from other countries. GATT was due to expire in the middle of 1955.

An agreement was signed on March 21, 1955, which was to come into force on the thirtieth day following the day on which governments representing 85 per cent of the trade under GATT accepted it.[40] On coming into force, the new organization (OTC) was to become one of the specialized agencies, through an agreement with the United Nations. Existing tariff schedules were extended until January 1958 and amendments to GATT strengthened provisions for international review and consultation.

The function of the new organization is to administer GATT and to study, negotiate, and make recommendations concerning problems of trade and commercial policy. It is to have an assembly composed of all members; an executive committee, elected by the assembly, with seventeen members, of which five should represent countries of chief economic importance; and a director-general.

[40] The agreement for OTC is in *Dept. of State Bull.*, 32 (1955), p. 579. President Eisenhower recommended membership but hearings were postponed on H. R. 5550 until the second session of the 84th Congress in 1956. See *Dept. of State Bull.*, 33 (1955), p. 188.

122. A COHERENT SYSTEM?

At the beginning of this chapter there was a discussion of the general question of centralization as against decentralization in international organization. Having surveyed briefly the structure and functioning of the various specialized agencies, we may now inquire as to the extent to which, when considered together with the United Nations itself, all these various international institutions may be regarded as constituting a coherent or unified whole.

CHARTER PROVISIONS. The Charter of the United Nations manifestly contemplated the separate existence of certain international bodies "having wide international responsibilities, as defined in their basic instruments, in economic, social, cultural, health, and related fields"; indeed, Article 59 authorizes the United Nations to initiate new ones. It was as clearly intended that these bodies should be coordinated in some way. Article 57 provides that they "shall be brought into relationship with the United Nations"; Article 58 that the organization "shall make recommendations for the coordination of the policies and activities of the specialized agencies." This is to be accomplished largely through agreements to be entered into between the Economic and Social Council and each agency (Article 63). The Economic and Social Council is in general made responsible for such coordination, "under the authority of the General Assembly" (Article 60); it may coordinate these activities through consultation and recommendation, through reports from each agency, through comments to the General Assembly upon such reports (Article 64), through reciprocal representation (Article 70), and in other ways to be laid down in the agreements.

At its first session, then, the Economic and Social Council set up a negotiating committee, and invited five of the agencies to set up corresponding committees to conduct negotiations. The Bank and the Fund, not being sufficiently organized and being in any case in an exceptional situation, were not ready to make such an agreement; ILO, FAO, and UNESCO did make agreements, which were approved by the General Assembly. Since then, agreements have been made with all the agencies, and between various agencies themselves. These agreements are all similar, and their contents have been summarized in an official United States report as follows:

(1) those establishing the fundamental relationship between the United Nations and the agencies, which include the articles recognizing the competence of the agencies in their particular fields; reciprocal representation;

membership; proposal of agenda items; recommendations of the General Assembly and the Council; exchange of information and documents; relationship to Security Council, Trusteeship Council, International Court of Justice; budgetary and financial arrangements; and inter-agency agreements;

(2) those providing for administrative and technical cooperation, which include the articles on statistical services; headquarters and regional offices; personnel arrangements; administrative and technical services; financing of special services; liaison; and

(3) those establishing the status of the agreements themselves, which include articles on implementation of the agreements; revision; and entry into force.[41]

A resolution offered by the United States and adopted by the council on September 21, 1946 established a committee on coordination "to insure the fullest and most effective implementation of the agreements entered into between the United Nations and the specialized agencies."

It was soon apparent that the specialized agencies were not eager to be brought into any close relationship with the United Nations. The proposal that the United Nations should control the budgets of all, though still upheld by many, has made no headway; such an arrangement would give to the United Nations control over all, and subject them to political pressures. The Preparatory Commission for an International Civil Service Commission was not followed; instead, an International Personnel Advisory Board was set up to consult concerning standards. No provision was made for common hiring or for transfer of personnel from one organization to another. Each agency tends to be jealous of its own autonomy. The problem is increased by the differing memberships of each, and the difficulty is compounded by the lack of coordination within each member. A delegate may urge centralization or the undertaking of more projects in the Economic and Social Council or in the General Assembly, while the delegate of the same state to another body is standing up for the independence of an agency or preaching reduction of the budget.

A committee was set up in 1946, later called the Administrative Committee on Coordination, and the Secretary-General could report in 1949 increasing cooperation of the agencies with the regional commissions, though not with each other. Resolution 310(IV) called attention to proliferation of bodies and projects, attempted to set some priorities and urged greater efforts at coordination. It should be noted that not merely the specialized agencies and some other inter-

---

[41] *The Economic and Social Council of the United Nations,* Dept. of State Pub., No. 2600 (1946). The agreements are collected in Agreements between the United Nations and the Specialized Agencies, *U.N. Doc.,* ST/SG/1, Sales No. 1951.X.1. See C. W. Jenks, "The Conflict of Law-Making Treaties," *B.Y.I.L.,* 30 (1953), p. 401.

governmental bodies constituted the problem; the Commission of the Economic and Social Council and even the departments of the Secretariat were involved.[42]

Little progress was made until around 1950, when the Expanded Technical Assistance Programme came into being. This had a budget independent of the agencies and separate from the United Nations budget. With the opportunity to obtain money the resistance of the agencies diminished and more coordination was achieved. The Secretary-General, who had been asked to make recommendations concerning the program, emphasized the desirability of attack upon the problem by combined efforts of the agencies rather than a piecemeal and unrelated approach. This viewpoint prevailed.

Control over the technical assistance work was retained by the Economic and Social Council, which exercises it through a Technical Assistance Committee. The projects are administered through a Technical Assistance Board composed of the Secretary-General and the directors of the participating agencies (or their representatives). It thus became possible to establish common standards for salaries and conditions of employment and for estimating costs and priorities, etc. The board (TAB) seeks to reach agreement rather than decision through voting, and, if it cannot agree, the committee (TAC) decides.

The problem of coordination reaches down into each beneficiary state, which must organize itself so as to be able to carry on the project which is to help it; toward this end, the United Nations sends Resident Technical Assistance Representatives to various areas, to assist in coordinating technical assistance activities within a state or an area. One result has been to encourage improvement in governmental organization and public administration in some states. On the other hand, there is the more delicate problem of avoiding conflict or overlapping with national technical assistance programs, such as the United States Point Four effort, or regional efforts, such as the Colombo Plan. The United States expends ten times as much on its own technical assistance work as the United Nations has to spend; and the question is often asked whether it would not be better to combine all such efforts in one coordinated system under the United Nations.

Mr. Winant, in his report, said: "It is to be anticipated that by way of these agreements an integrated pattern of economic and social en-

42 W. R. Sharp, "The Specialized Agencies and the U.N.: Progress Report," *Int. Organ.*, 1 (1947), p. 460, and 2 (1948), p. 247; *U.N. Doc.*, E/740, Report of the Council Committee on Matters Relating to Co-ordination or Co-ordination Machinery; *Doc.* E/1076, Fourth Report of the Administrative Committee on Co-ordination; and *Doc.* E/1141, Report of the Secretary-General on General Co-ordination Matters; C. W. Jenks, "Co-ordination: A New Problem of International Organization," *Hague Acad.*, 77 (1950), p. 189.

deavor will be evolved which, while achieving coordination and unity of purpose, will allow a desirable measure of flexibility and decentralization of responsibilities."[43] This expectation is apparently being realized, at any rate so far as technical assistance work is concerned, and this leads into integration of efforts in other fields. Like the member states of the United Nations itself, each of the agencies in the broader United Nations system seeks to reserve independence and is unwilling to be submitted to control. Here, as elsewhere, the United Nations must strive to obtain agreement and consent from its component units; it is an association and is far from being a super-state.

[43] *The Economic and Social Council of the United Nations: Report by the Honorable John G. Winant, July 15, 1946.* Dept. of State Pub., No. 2600, p. 25.

Chapter 14

ADVANCEMENT OF HUMAN WELFARE

Like the League of Nations, the United Nations has two chief purposes, one the maintenance of peace and security and, the other, in the words of the preamble to the Charter, "to employ international machinery for the promotion of the economic and social advancement of all peoples." To the former purpose Part V of this volume will be devoted. The latter purpose, to be surveyed in this chapter, has been developed on a far broader range than in the League of Nations. The activities of the United Nations, in this period of revival for some nations and awakening for many, cover an enormous range, and we can only outline here the efforts and trends.

123. RELIEF AND RECONSTRUCTION

It was natural that the first preoccupation of the nations devastated and exhausted by World War II should be recovery and reconstruction. Several of the leading industrial countries had a large part of their plant destroyed and had to begin all over again; agricultural production had been badly injured and the food supply for the world was uncertain; and there were millions of uprooted people who had to be relocated and for whom work had to be found, not only for their own sakes but for the world economy.[1] Only the United States had surpluses for export and this resulted in a flow of dollars to it from other nations, which created a great problem of financial exchange. Other states, with little or nothing to export, were unable to acquire dollars and became dependent to a large degree upon the

[1] For a survey of the situation, see Economic Report, Salient Features of the World Economic Situation, *U.N. Doc.*, Sales No. 1948.II.C.1. Also, *Cheever and Haviland*, Chaps. ix, xviii, and elsewhere.

policies of the United States. And many small states had been caught in the swirling vortex of war and encouraged to desire more for themselves.

UNRRA. These needs had been foreseen, and there was a meeting of Allied states toward the end of 1943 which set up the United Nations Relief and Rehabilitation Administration.[2] This was an improvement over previous postwar efforts, both in the sense of organized joint effort and in the amount of money made available; its range and effects were wide; it employed a staff six times as large as that of the United Nations. It assisted in maintaining health and preventing epidemics which had followed wars in the past; it contributed greatly to the restoration of communications, public utilities, and agricultural production; it kept many people alive. It was, however, beset with vicissitudes, the chief one being the unwillingness of nations to continue to support it. This was particularly true of the United States, which suspected that it was giving too much aid to Communist peoples, and which preferred in general to control its own national giving rather than to leave to international administration the use of its money. Owing to the insistence of the United States, UNRRA came to an end in 1947. It had raised and expended nearly four billion dollars, of which three quarters had been contributed by the United States.

There was much regret at the premature demise of UNRRA, and its work was picked up in various ways. The Food and Agriculture Organization held a meeting on Urgent Food Problems in 1946, looking ahead to future needs; it made bold plans, but member states were not willing to give to it the authority which it needed. By 1947, the International Bank was beginning, in its slow and cautious ways, to make some loans which aided reconstruction; and in that year the General Assembly provided for an Economic Commission for Europe (ECE) and a similar one for Asia and the Far East (ECAFE). The former has done effective work in securing cooperation between governments in such matters as distribution of supplies, or aiding transportation, or, with more difficulty, building up trade between East and West Europe.

The Marshall Plan, of course, was a very important contribution to reconstruction; it was proposed in 1947, and in the following year the Economic Cooperation Administration was set up. This was a unilateral project of the United States, which might better have been carried on through the United Nations; but states were too eager for

[2] The history of UNRRA has been written by George Woodbridge, entitled *UNRRA*, 3 vols. (New York, 1950).

aid to fight over this—though the Soviet bloc denounced it and refused to participate in it. The "European Recovery Program" (ERP) undoubtedly advanced Europe toward stability, and it also contributed to the efforts toward European unity.[3] It came to an end on the last day of 1951, though the work has been carried on in some respects under other names—Mutual Security Administration, Foreign Operations Administration, etc.

RELIEF AND REFUGEES. The International Refugee Organization was set up in 1947 by eighteen states. It increased the food supply for the needy, improved health, and built up legal protection for refugees; its especial work was repatriation of those who wished to return to their own countries, and resettlement for those who did not—meanwhile keeping them all alive. Over a million were resettled in other countries. There was constant dispute over this work, particularly as to the definition of "refugee"; and the Soviet Union continually demanded return, willy-nilly, of her nationals. The effort to provide legal protection led to establishment of an *ad hoc* committee to deal with statelessness and related problems, which sought to draw up a consolidated convention on the status of refugees; in July 1951 a conference met to sign a Convention on Refugees and Stateless Persons. The latter part of the job was not accomplished, but a Convention on the Status of Refugees was adopted. The question of statelessness was later referred to the International Law Commission, and alternative plans for "elimination" or "reduction" of statelessness were prepared.[4] Legal problems were also touched upon in the final act of the Conference on Declaration of Death of Missing Persons in 1950, which declaration, however, has received but few acceptances.

Those who supported the International Refugee Organization were unwilling to carry it beyond 1951, and it came to an end with half a million persons not settled. The United Nations was not willing to assume the burden, but it did authorize a High Commissioner of Refugees, giving him money for a staff, but leaving it to him to find money for the refugees. He succeeded sufficiently to justify the continuance of his office, but of course, he cannot meet all the needs.

UNICEF. Another great effort for relief was the United Nations International Children's Emergency Fund (UNICEF). The program

---

[3] On the Marshall Plan: Reports of the Office of European Economic Cooperation; *The Marshall Plan: Where We Are and Where We Are Going,* issued by the Economic Cooperation Administration, 1950; Howard S. Ellis, *The Economics of Freedom* (New York, 1950); *Int. Con.,* No. 447 (1949), on "European Recovery," and No. 488 (1953) on "European Integration."

[4] General Assembly, Ninth Session, *Official Records,* Supp. No. 9 (A/2693), Report of the International Law Commission, Sixth Session.

has dramatic appeal and has drawn money from private sources as well as from governments. The General Assembly decided in 1953 to continue it, on a separate budget, and made its staff part of the Secretariat. The United Nations has, more directly, financed a Relief and Works Agency for Palestine Refugees—close to a million of them; and in 1950 it set up a United Nations Commission for Relief and Rehabilitation of Korea, which was implemented by the United Nations Korean Reconstruction Agency (UNKRA). Most of the contributions for this were from the military command; other contributions, like those for all relief agencies, have been slow and small.

124. TECHNICAL ASSISTANCE

Another activity, and by now the most important and continuing of all the efforts at reconstruction and development, is what is known as "technical assistance."[5] It was not an unknown idea, but it has been developed and focused to a remarkable degree by the United Nations; and it has in turn contributed much to the reputation and even to the effective operation and coordination of United Nations machinery. Perhaps the most important characteristic of this development is its recognition of the need for assisting the "underdeveloped" countries to a higher level of living and of production; it is not charity, but "helping others to help themselves" and in the long run benefiting the whole community of nations.

The General Assembly, by Resolution 52(I) in 1946, asked the Economic and Social Council to study means of furnishing expert advice to member nations which might desire such assistance.[6] The underdeveloped countries complained that attention should be given to

---

[5] This is a fascinating subject, worth reading outside this volume. See U.N., Technical Assistance for Economic Development: Plan for an Expanded Cooperative Programme through the United Nations and the Specialized Agencies, *U.N. Doc.*, Sales No. 1949.II.B.1.; B. F. Hoselitz, *The Progress of Underdeveloped Areas* (Chicago, 1952); W. R. Sharp, *International Technical Assistance* (Chicago, 1952); P. G. Franck and D. Seelye, "Implementation of Technical Assistance," *Int. Con.*, No. 468 (1951), and *Int. Con.*, No. 479 (Bolivia); Stacy May, "Folklore and Fact about Underdeveloped Areas," *Foreign Affairs*, 22 (1955), p. 212; W. R. Brown and R. Opie, *American Foreign Assistance* (Washington, 1953).

[6] This resolution was initiated by Lebanon, and it is of significance that a United States amendment which would have included assistance from Members was rejected. The interested states were opposed to bilateral arrangements which would, they feared, make them dependent upon other states—i.e., the United States. It was their purpose in introducing the proposal to substitute for such arrangements assistance through an international organization. See G.A. I/2, *Official Records*, Plenary, pp. 1387, 1581-82. The United States has preferred to provide most of its funds on a unilateral basis, thus keeping control and prestige for itself.

them as well as to war-devastated countries, and they sought to guard themselves against economic exploitation by other states. The Secretary-General was authorized to send out teams, but no money was provided. The Third Assembly (1948), by Resolution 200(III), which carefully guarded the independence of the states to be assisted, appropriated something under $300,000 and gave further impetus to the plan.

A great impetus was added when, in January 1949, President Truman put forward his "Point Four" program. The United States argued for a more comprehensive plan, and for larger appropriations by Members. Such a plan was prepared, and thus began the "expanded program" of technical assistance which, at small cost, has stirred life into many countries and aroused the interest of millions in the United Nations.

Exchange of knowledge between peoples the world over has made possible the civilization that we now have; technical assistance is such an exchange, more purposed, more widely organized. It goes further than the printed page, or word of mouth; persons and utensils are sent, and the skills and the tools are personally demonstrated. The experts are found and sent and arrangements are made by the United Nations, but these arrangements must be satisfactory to the recipient country (how far should experts from the Soviet Union be considered acceptable?), and those who are sent must work under the direction of that country. There is no control from the outside, no liens to give an exploiting country a foothold, no charity; everyone contributes something to a common cause.

Technical assistance is, indeed, a most remarkable cooperative endeavor. Nations are learning to exchange their knowledge and skills, and an amazing "cross-fertilization" is taking place. The examples which could be given are innumerable: A Netherlands expert studying low cost housing for India; a Peruvian expert calculating that Ethiopia could raise fifty thousand acres of cotton; and a Swiss expert teaching telecommunication to Ethiopians. A ceramics expert aids that industry in Yugoslavia, and an expert from Iceland, which uses hot springs for heat and power, is studying the possibilities of such use in Mexico. The capacity of the port of Aqaba (Jordan) was doubled. Every country is able to provide some knowledge and expert assistance. The specialized agencies, of course, are essentially interested; the Bank plans development of rivers for power and irrigation; WHO sprays DDT and eliminates malaria, or in other ways regulates prevalent diseases and makes available more working people and more work from each; FAO helps with agricultural methods—the story goes that one expert sent back a telegram: "Send me a hoe"! There are close to a thousand separate projects now being carried on; they involve twenty-five hundred experts, from sixty-four countries, and two thousand fellowships.

It is probably true that never in history has there been so much improvement made at so low a cost. The United Nations has usually had a fund for technical assistance of about twenty million dollars; for 1955 it went up to about twenty-four millions. About three-fifths of this is contributed by the United States, which, however, provides ten times that amount for its own Point Four work. Each state contributes as it wishes—in 1953 the Soviet Union for the first time made a contribution; and each recipient country pays local costs which, in 1953, amounted in total to thirty-eight million dollars. India, for example, received aid to the amount of $1,045,000 and paid $275,000; Brazil gave $459,000 and received $495,000.

The operation of the program has improved steadily. In 1954, procedures were put into effect for comprehensive and coordinated programs for each country. In each country, resident representatives coordinate the activities of the various United Nations agencies. The funds available are handled so as to enable continuing projects. An illustration of coordination on the part of recipient countries is the pooling of requests by the five countries of Central America for developing answers to common needs; they plan training in public administration and industrial research. Another by-product of technical assistance is study of land reform, concerning which ECOSOC adopted a resolution in 1952. A questionnaire was sent to governments and the answers will provide knowledge concerning land tenure upon which to plan for the future. The ramifications of technical assistance seem without end, and the possibilities for future development illimitable. Perhaps a new profession is being developed.

125. ECONOMIC DEVELOPMENT

The underdeveloped countries, now beginning to see possibilities for themselves, were not content with advice; they wanted money with which to develop. They could not obtain it from the International Bank, which can loan only for enterprises from which there would be a safe return; it could not, for example, lend money to build a highway. The weaker countries, then, demanded an institution which could lend money more freely, at greater risk. They made little headway for several years, since the countries which had the money were opposed, particularly the United States; but their pressure steadily increased.

FINANCIAL AID. The fundamental problem of the United Nations —nationalism—was well illustrated at the Seventh Assembly, where a resolution was proposed by Uruguay to affirm the right of each country to nationalize and freely exploit its own natural resources; the debate revealed the feeling of some countries that whatever was in their own country, even if owned by foreigners, belonged to them and could be taken by them. This position raises some interesting philosophical questions, but it was inconsistent with the desire of these same countries to obtain capital from abroad; a foreign investor would not be attracted to put his money into a country which claimed the right to seize it because it was in that country. It was pointed out that such seizure would be contrary to international law, which, however, does not deny the right to nationalize with compensation. As finally adopted, General Assembly Resolution 626(VII) recommended member states, "in the exercise of their right freely to use and exploit their wealth and natural resources wherever deemed desirable by them for their own progress and economic development, to have due regard, consistently with their sovereignty, to the need for maintaining the flow of capital in conditions of security, mutual confidence and economic cooperation among nations"; and recommended that states refrain from acts which might impede the exercise of the sovereignty of a state over its natural resources.

There were three methods proposed to provide capital at the time of the Eighth Assembly in 1953. One was the Special United Nations Fund for Economic Development (SUNFED—a better abbreviation than UNFED, but nevertheless susceptible to various jokes); another was the International Finance Corporation; and the third was the encouragement of private investment. The United States, more interested in the last, was still opposed to putting up money for the other two, and suggested that when there could be some disarmament, then money could be made available. The Assembly thereupon adopted a resolution calling for disarmament and the constructive use of the money thus saved. This solved no immediate problems; and the report of the Special Rapporteur (Raymond Scheyven) asserted that the time was not yet ripe for creation of the two finance bodies.[7] At the Ninth Assembly, a resolution was adopted continuing Mr. Scheyven in his office and asking him to prepare a detailed report on the form, functions and responsibilities of the proposed SUNFED. On November 11, the United States, reversing its position, announced

[7] This report is U.N. Doc., E/2599. The above development can be traced through the issues of International Organization and, in less detail, in the Annual Report by the President on U.S. Participation in the U.N. See §115, above.

that it would support and contribute to an International Finance Corporation, and a resolution was adopted asking the Bank to draft a statute for an IFC. A third resolution recommended to countries seeking foreign capital that they re-examine their domestic policies and legislation with a view to improving the investment climate, and suggested a number of things which could be done by capital-importing and -exporting countries.

OTHER ECONOMIC ACTIVITIES. According to Article 62 of the Charter, the Economic and Social Council may make or initiate studies, and may make recommendations concerning "international economic, social, cultural, educational, health, and related matters." There is very little, then, outside the political field, in which it does not have a function to perform. It has no legislative authority, but its studies and recommendations are not to be demeaned. Its reports not only provide reliable information on which to build for the future, and which is useful in business everywhere, but they arouse interest in possibilities and dangers of which states were not aware. The various ECOSOC bodies issue special reports, such as "National and International Measures for Full Employment" (1949), or more regular publications, such as the *World Economic Report*, or the *Statistical Yearbook*. There were so many activities that it was thought necessary to publish an annual *Catalog of Economic and Social Projects*, unfortunately now discontinued.

The Economic and Social Council may also make recommendations, not only to the General Assembly, to which it is responsible, but also to Members and to specialized agencies; its work is closely interrelated with that of the agencies. The implementation of these recommendations is at the pleasure of each Member, but each is pledged (Article 56) "to take joint and separate action in cooperation with the Organization." A continuing pressure may be applied which states find hard to resist; thus, Resolution 290(XI), mentioned below, is regularly reviewed, and it has been pointed out that the United States has not done as well as others in carrying out its recommendations. In general, it may be observed that the enterprising United States has been conservative in this field and unenthusiastic about bold international planning for the future.

Another procedure open to the Council is the calling of conferences, and not a day goes by which has not included one or more meetings on economic or social matters. Some of these are very large conferences, such as the Scientific Conference on Conservation and Utilization of Resources (1949), which resulted in seven useful volumes, or the 1955 conference on peaceful uses of atomic energy; others consist of small groups of experts. Some of them are attended only by governmental representatives, some by experts, some by both.

The purpose of such meetings, of course, is to reach agreement; and, if there is sufficient agreement, a convention may be drafted which, if approved by the General Assembly, will be submitted to states for ratification. This activity, as has been noted above, is the largest part of the international legislation produced by the United Nations. Economic interdependence and the consequent necessity of multilateral agreements are now recognized, even though nationalism pulls back at each agreement. The political atmosphere has sometimes influenced decisions which should have been made on purely economic grounds; on the other hand, there is growing realization that the solution of economic problems is an important part of clearing the political atmosphere and avoiding war.

It would be impossible here to cover all the economic activities of the United Nations, but a few of the more important ones may serve for illustration.

FULL EMPLOYMENT. There was much interest in, and debate over, the term "full employment" at San Francisco; its meaning is wider than it appears to be. Other states have never forgotten the disastrous economic depression in the United States in 1929 and its effect upon them. Discussion of the means of assuring "full employment" reaches out into trade, finance, and development. In 1946, the council appointed an Economic and Employment Commission, which made a report in 1949. The International Labour Organization also prepared a report, and the Communist viewpoint was presented through proposals by the World Federation of Trade Unions. A committee of experts submitted a report on *National and International Measures for Full Employment*,[8] and on the basis of this report, ECOSOC Resolution 290(XI) was adopted. It asked each state to publish its economic planning, to cooperate in achieving balance of payments, in removal of trade restrictions (this was what the United States emphasized, though with some inconsistency), in building gold reserves, promoting investment, and refraining from actions injurious to others.

A committee of experts appointed by the Secretary-General made a report in 1952 on *Measures for International Economic Stability*, which suggested commodity agreements as part of the solution,[9] and urged more liberal policies on the part of the International Bank and

[8] *U.N. Doc.*, Sales No. 1949.II.A.3.
[9] *U.N. Doc.*, ST/ECA/13. Later it issued a report entitled *Commodity Trade and Economic Development*.

the International Monetary Fund. These views were generally accepted, though weaker states wished a broader stabilization of the relation between prices of the raw materials which they sold and of the manufactured products which they imported. For each commodity, separate arrangements were to be made, initiated by whatever state was sufficiently interested. In 1953, the Economic and Social Council set up an Interim Coordinating Committee for International Commodity Arrangements. In that year, agreements were reached concerning wheat, sugar, and tin, and there was some consideration of rubber and cotton. These agreements attempt to maintain price levels.

RESTRICTIVE BUSINESS PRACTICES. The effort to avoid crises of unemployment led also to study of business practices such as cartels, barriers to trade, and limitation of competition in general. In 1951, the United States asked for a study, and an *ad hoc* Committee on Restrictive Business Practices was set up. It made a report in 1953 proposing an agreement to limit harmful cartel practices affecting international trade. Under this agreement, complaint could be made against a government, which must reply to it with facts; the parties to the agreement would decide whether the practice was harmful to others and, if so, would request the government to take remedial action. A draft convention was prepared, but did not meet with acceptance when considered in 1955.

TRADE. The effort to remove trade barriers is of long standing, and was renewed as part of postwar reconstruction. The situation was changed. The British were no longer the champions of free trade, and the United States felt strong enough to engage in competition—though lobbies maintained quite a lot of protectionism. The smaller states, eager for industrial growth, wanted to be free to control trade in ways which they thought would benefit them. The situation was complicated by the greatly increased range of governmental participation in business, ranging from complete nationalization, as in the Soviet Union, to scattered government enterprises and controls in nations which claimed to believe in free competition, such as the United States.

Under the pressure of the United States, reluctantly followed by the United Kingdom, whose economic distress was great, the Economic and Social Council set up a committee which met in 1947 and negotiated a large number of tariff schedules and a General Agreement on Tariffs and Trade (GATT), which in some degree provided a code of conduct and a system for future negotiations.[10] In 1947-48 a World

---

[10] See § 121, above.

Conference on Trade and Employment assembled at Havana and struggled through warm debates and innumerable proposals to adopt a Charter for an International Trade Organization. This achievement was due to the careful preparation and determined leadership of the United States, and it was ironical that a resurgence of protectionism prevented ratification. There seems little chance that life can be breathed into the ITO, but some of its principles have been taken over by GATT, which holds regular meetings. GATT examines the conduct of parties and makes allowances for exceptions to the rules. For example, when the dairy lobby in the United States cut down the import of cheese, to the detriment of Italy, Denmark, and other countries, these countries were authorized to reduce their imports from the United States, and the United States was asked to repeal Section 104 of the Defense Production Act (which considered it vital to our defense that importation of cheese be limited!). In general, GATT can hardly hold its own, especially in the face of United States policies, and there seems little hope at present of loosening trade barriers among nations.

126. SOCIAL ADVANCE

The activities of the United Nations in the social field are as wide-ranging as those in the economic field, and it is not always easy to classify such activities under either heading. The specialized agencies contribute greatly in both fields, as does also technical assistance. The Social Commission of the Economic and Social Council is the starting-point and core of this activity, which, however, ranges far beyond this organ.

SOCIAL WELFARE. Under this heading fall a number of things inherited from UNRRA and the League of Nations. The demands for assistance steadily increased until by 1950 the United Nations felt it desirable to establish certain activities in the field of social welfare on a permanent basis. These activities are in connection with family and child welfare, rehabilitation of the handicapped, social security, social defense (meaning prevention of crime and improvement of penal methods), housing, town and country planning, etc. Much of this is done through technical assistance. Fellowships, seminars, and training for social welfare in general constitute an important part of the program.

NARCOTIC DRUGS.[11] Since 1912 there has been steady advance in the

[11] See H. L. May, "The International Control of Narcotic Drugs," *Int. Con.*, No. 441 (1948); also *ibid.*, "Narcotic Drug Control," No. 485 (1952).

control over narcotic drugs, and the League of Nations supervision of this control had been praised. The war, however, resulted in a setback; production increased, especially in China, but also in Near Eastern countries. The United Nations took up the task of control, operating through a Commission on Narcotic Drugs, the Permanent Central Opium Board, which checks observance of the various treaties, and a Drug Supervisory Body, which studies the actual needs of each nation. An important part of the problem is to decide which drugs should be brought under control, for synthetic drugs constitute a new danger. In 1949 a convention was agreed upon and widely accepted authorizing the World Health Organization to make this decision. An effort has been made to draft a convention to include all the existing conventions into one system, a very difficult job which is not yet completed. In June 1953, a protocol limiting cultivation of the poppy plant and production and trade in opium was opened for signature. This was signed by a large number of states, though it has not yet come into force.

OTHER MATTERS. A Population Commission studies methods of obtaining information on and making forecasts about the growth of population, and of developing an international census. It publishes a *Demographic Yearbook* and provides statistics as to migration and mortality rates. The United States in 1949 proposed a commission of inquiry concerning forced labor; it was said that there were ten million people in forced labor camps in the Soviet Union. The committee, set up in the following year, reported in a carefully documented statement in 1953 that forced labor was an essential part of the economy of the Soviet Union and could be found elsewhere in the world. A resolution was adopted by the General Assembly on December 7, 1953, condemning forced labor as a violation of human rights. The Secretary-General set up a committee of experts in 1949 to survey the problem of slavery. It made a report in 1951, and sought more information thereafter. The Eighth General Assembly, at the suggestion of the United States, adopted a protocol transferring to the United Nations the functions formerly performed by the League of Nations under the International Slavery Convention of 1926, and urged states to adhere to that convention. It was decided in 1948 that the United Nations should carry on the preventive work of the League of Nations with regard to traffic in women and children and with regard to obscene publications. A Convention on Suppression of Traffic in Persons and of the Exploitation of the Prostitution of Others went into force in July 1951. It is aimed at those who carry on the traffic rather than at the victims of the traffic themselves.

HUMAN RIGHTS. The revolutionary movement for the statement and protection of the rights of individual human beings has been discussed in Chapter 5; while it was moved along too rapidly and suffered setbacks, it must still be regarded as one of the greatest contributions made by the United Nations.

There have been a number of corollary or related efforts. A subcommittee of the Commission on Human Rights, on Freedom of Information and of the Press, met at Geneva in March 1949 and asserted that its topic was the touchstone of all the freedoms to which the United Nations is dedicated. Its life has been characterized by considerable disagreement and it has made little progress. A Conference on Freedom of Information met at Geneva in 1948 and adopted three draft conventions: (1) on the gathering and transmission of news (sponsored by the United States); (2) on the right of correction of false information (sponsored by France); and (3) on freedom of information, meaning freedom to seek and express information (sponsored by the United Kingdom). There was no agreement, however, as to the meaning of freedom of information. The Soviet Union and doubtless other states wished freedom to control the press in their countries; the United States wanted none or few restrictions; in between, a great many states wished to be able to limit the press for certain purposes. A Rapporteur (Lopez) was appointed and submitted a report in 1953 which favored few limitations and these to be enforced by press associations.[12] The Economic and Social Council did nothing about the report, and was criticized for its inaction by the Ninth General Assembly, which felt that it should take up the burden. Resolutions were adopted concerning technical assistance for freedom of information. These requested the Economic and Social Council to prepare the convention on freedom of information, for consideration by the Eleventh session and approved the transfer to the United Nations of the League of Nations functions under the 1936 Convention concerning the Use of Broadcasting in the Cause of Peace. An effort to provide a code of honor for journalists collapsed when they displayed little interest in a conference to draft the code.

Human Rights is a broad field, and could embrace many UN activities carried on by other organs. The Genocide Convention doubtless belongs under this heading; so do the efforts concerning forced labor, slavery and prisoners of war. In no field of United Nations work has there been so much activity and so much interest. Advance will be slow, for long-standing folk habits and psychological outlooks must be changed.

[12] The Lopez Report is *U.N. Doc.*, E/2462; see C. Binder, "Freedom of Information and the United Nations," *Int. Organ.*, 6 (1952), p. 221.

STATUS OF WOMEN. Originally a subcommission of the Commission on Human Rights, the Commission on the Status of Women demanded and obtained independent status. It has been an industrious and aggressive body, working in general for equality between the sexes. It has demanded equal educational opportunities, equal pay for equal work, equal chance at government jobs (and high posts in the United Nations), and funds for technical assistance to improve the condition of women. It has opposed laws forbidding mixed marriages and laws forbidding a woman to leave her own country to go with her husband. It has also produced studies on the nationality of women and on conflicts of law which affect them. A Convention on the Political Rights of Women, approved by the assembly in 1952, has been signed by a number of states but ratified by very few. In this connection there might be mentioned, though it was not the work of the commission, the draft Convention on Recognition and Enforcement of Maintenance Obligations Abroad, which would require a man resident abroad to maintain his family as if he were at home.

127. DEPENDENT PEOPLES

Another field of great activity, really another phase of the same revolutionary struggle for human rights, concerns dependent peoples, in which intense interest is displayed. The effort in their behalf is, thus far, an anti-colonial movement; it shows no interest in oppressed or minority groups other than those in colonies and has been limited to attacks upon and demands from colonial powers. It is characterized by intense feeling and has formed a line of international cleavage similar to that produced by the cold war.

This is not the place to consider the debate over imperialism, but there is no doubt that colonial enterprisers have outrageously exploited and humiliated other peoples, leaving behind them a compressed resentment not only against the colonial powers, but against the whole white race. It does little to assuage this resentment to point out that many white men were opposed to and increasingly diminished such abuses; or that colonial peoples were educated toward higher standards of living and learned something of self-government, and were indeed thus made aware of and ambitious for improvement; or that, since World War II, half a billion people or more have achieved self-government or independence. It is of little avail to point out, on the other hand, that individuals may be found in any race or nation who have no hesitation in exploiting their fellows for their own gain. These reflections do not alter the fact that these long-repressed feelings are now breaking forth in strength which cannot be disregarded.

The United Nations is thus confronted with an enormous and very difficult problem, and it is to be hoped that the statesmen in the United Nations may approach it with reason rather than with emotion, constructively rather than negatively. This is much to ask, for resentment is deep and justified. It is a new problem in the sense that it is now up to the community of nations to decide the question of who is to judge, and on what criteria, which groups should have independence. International law has provided no answer to these questions;[13] in the past, each group has had to fight its way to independence with whatever assistance it might be able to obtain. The principle of "self-determination" was widely asserted, but it was not law and, indeed, could not be implemented as law until the community of nations was strongly enough organized to make and enforce decisions. It was, however, stated in vague terms in Article 1, paragraph 2, of the Charter of the United Nations and is often referred to in debates.

This desire for national independence has been a leavening force since the American and French revolutions, through the days of Kossuth and Mazzini; it produced an opposition to colonialism which led to the mandates system of the League of Nations and the trusteeship system of the United Nations. In the United Nations, however, Chapter XI was added containing certain principles for the treatment of "Non-Self-Governing Territories"—a euphonious term for colonies; and we have noted the remarkable extension by the United Nations of its claims to supervision over these areas. This has arisen partly from appeals from some of the territories to the United Nations, but much more from appeals made in their behalf by states newly released from colonial domination and still smarting from it. The point of the development is that appeal is now made to the United Nations—it is no longer *self*-determination, but United Nations determination. The United Nations was not authorized or equipped to deal with such claims.

There were thus two roads of development within the United Nations, and we turn to a brief survey of the operation and achievement of the Organization along these roads.

TRUST TERRITORIES. The trusteeship system was an advance over the mandates system in several ways. The League had no more than a commission to administer its work, while one of the main organs of the United Nations performs this function. The League classification into three types, of which only the first could have much hope for independence, is replaced by the objective of "self-government or independence" for all alike. Visiting missions are authorized, and have

13 See pp. 69-70 above, and pp. 440 ff. below.

proved of much value; and the right of petition is given more respect. On the other hand, the "strategic trust area"—for which the United States is responsible—provides for a control about as complete as actual ownership; and the right to make military use of the area is retrogressive, even though called "playing its part in maintaining peace and security" (Article 84).

The Trusteeship Council operates for the most part in regard to three requirements stated in the Charter. The first of these is the annual report required for each trust territory from the administering authority. The discussion of these reports provides opportunity for criticism and for making recommendations to the administering authority. Secondly, there is the right of petition to the United Nations, which is part of a territory's training in self-reliance. Anyone may present such a petition, either orally or in writing. The petitions are an original and useful source of information. Thirdly, there are the visiting missions authorized by the Charter. An effort is made to have a mission visit each territory regularly, and the reports of these missions evidence to the peoples visited the United Nations interest in their problems.

Various large problems have arisen from these sources. One of these is the "administrative union," in which a trust territory is combined for administrative purposes with another territory of the administering authority. This has been attacked as leading away from the objective of self-government or independence. The Third General Assembly feared that the combination of Tanganyika with Kenya and Uganda by the United Kingdom, or of Papua and New Guinea by Australia, might lead to the loss of the identity of the trust territory. The Fourth Assembly adopted resolutions asking the administering authority to notify the Council in advance of such combinations and suggesting that, if precise information were not given, the United Nations should exercise supervision over the entire administrative union. The Assembly insisted also that the trust territory be kept distinct in boundaries and have its own separate organs, and that opportunity must be given for expression of the wishes of the people therein. An administrative union, however, is not necessarily bad; participation with a more advanced colonial unit may save administrative costs, mean economic gain for the inhabitants, and move the people more rapidly toward self-government—which is the essential aim. Such arrangements were permitted by the trusteeship agreements. The Council, through its Committee on Administrative Unions set up in 1950, has, therefore, contented itself with watching carefully the operation of such arrangements.

A somewhat similar problem derives from the fact that some peoples were long ago divided between the colonial areas of European powers. The best example of this is the Ewe people, who were divided between the political units of French Togoland, British Togoland, and the Gold Coast. At the beginning of the Council's work, a petition was received asking for unification of all the Ewe people under one administration, with a plebiscite to determine who should be the the administering authority. There were a hundred and forty such petitions by the time of the Seventh Assembly. A visiting mission to the Ewes reported that there was a real national movement, but was unable to offer recommendations because of differing views among the people themselves. Its report led to Assembly Resolution 652(VII), which recommended a joint council of all segments of the population and the development of opinion so as to enable the people to express the political destiny they desired. The Eighth Assembly adopted similar resolutions. There was some pressure for unification, but, since the Ewes themselves could not agree, the emphasis was shifted to their political education. It should be noted that the administering authorities were cooperative and responsive, setting up joint councils and aiding in various ways; none, however, volunteered to include under trusteeship their own areas which were part of the administrative union involved in the problem.[14]

Aside from such general problems as these, the Trusteeship Council is occupied usually with small problems—the number of beds in a certain hospital, the number of teachers for a school, whether corporal punishment should be permitted, whether the United Nations flag should be flown in a trust territory.[15] Hundreds of petitions on such matters are received each year. It is clear that most of the trust territories are far from being ready for self-government or to "stand by themselves in the strenuous conditions of the modern world" (Article 22 of the League Covenant). Efforts have therefore been directed primarily at education and improvement of social standards. But there is little provision for more than primary education for the natives. The recommendations to the administering authorities emphasize political education and more participation by inhabitants in governmental proc-

14 This rather critical remark calls for some qualification. It is not at all sure that more progress would be made toward self-government under trusteeship than as a colony. This would depend upon the government in charge: rapid advance has been made under the United Kingdom and New Zealand; not so much under other countries; the strategic trust area of the United States is given much education and assistance, but has little prospect of independence.

15 The resolution calling for display of the United Nations flag in trust territories was disliked by administering authorities because it signified in the mind of its proponents that these territories were United Nations territories. Apparently, the strategic trust territory under the United States is the only one in which the flag is regularly flown. See 1953 Annual Review of United Nations Affairs, p. 53.

esses; they ask also for improvement along economic lines, which also largely involves education and training in skills. One of the difficulties is that natives do not always see the need for living up to "civilized standards." The administering authorities have in general followed the recommendations made by the Council. New Zealand, in its administration of Western Samoa, is a shining example of this. The much more enlightened treatment of inhabitants began under the pressure of public opinion before the United Nations was born. It is hard to say how much this pressure has contributed to further development in the direction of preparing backward peoples for participation in the complicated and rapid life of our times. There is little doubt, however, that it has helped. If the pressure has been too great and ill-considered at times, it has, nevertheless, put the administering authorities upon their good behavior, and they find it difficult to ignore criticism offered in the glaring publicity of the United Nations. Progress is necessarily slow; it is not always desired by natives to the extent affirmed in orations in the General Assembly. The habits of centuries cannot be changed in a few years, and the experience necessary for independent national existence cannot be so rapidly acquired.

The work of the Trusteeship Council is slow and unspectacular; it rarely attracts the attention of the newspapers. It makes its progress slowly and in realistic fashion, and this arouses the impatience of many delegates in the General Assembly. The administering authorities have rights under the Charter and under the agreements, and they disregard the efforts of the Assembly to reach beyond these rights; for example, they disregard the question in the questionnaire which asks them how soon their trust territory can expect to have independence. Most of the trust territories are not so well prepared for self-government as most of the colonies, but ambition is now stirring in many of them and, as they become increasingly aware of the support they can obtain from the United Nations, they are gaining in self-confidence.

128. NON-SELF-GOVERNING TERRITORIES

Part of the same movement, but far more sensational, has been the controversy aroused by the efforts of the General Assembly to extend its sway over colonial territories. The story has been summarized above from the viewpoint of organization and function.[16] We have now to consider it not only as an emotional drive based on resentment, but also in relation to the way in which the United Nations operates

16 See § 101, above.

and the effect of this development upon international law and the United Nations. The problem here raised is one of fundamental importance to the United Nations.

Chapter XI of the Charter was thought of at San Francisco as a unilateral "declaration" by colonial powers, in which they accepted certain obligations toward their colonies. The United Nations was given no supervisory powers, such as it was given over the trust territories; reports were to be made to the Secretary-General. Yet the colonies were, for the most part, further advanced toward self-government than were the trust areas; the latter included less than twenty million people, while the colonial populations amounted to ten times as many —even after half a billion had gained their independence during the decade of the 1940s. Indeed, colonies had, before World War II, included half the area of the world and a third of its population; they amounted to twenty times the area of the states which owned them.[17] It was not surprising, then, that there should be more interest in the colonies than in the trust territories.

Examination of the resolutions[18] adopted during the years 1947-55 reveals not only the extent of the United Nations interest in non-self-governing territories, but also a number of different lines of attack on the problem. Proposals which were not adopted reveal other approaches.

The Secretary-General asked the advice of Members as to the areas which he should regard as non-self-governing and suggested that Members who might wish to do so could contribute information concerning their territories. The United States was the first to respond, reporting on six areas.[19] Eight states reported on a total of seventy-four non-self-governing territories; these were not questioned and a list was thus established. The First Assembly, in 1946, adopted two resolutions. One of these instructed the Secretary-General to analyze the information received and to submit it to an *ad hoc* committee for examination. The administering states objected to this assumption of a right of supervision, but it was not unreasonable to handle the information in this manner, and they submitted under protest. The other resolution indicated more clearly the attack which was to come; toned down from the original proposal for a world conference of representatives from colonies, it called upon the administering authorities to convene representatives of their colonies in conferences.

[17] See *Palmer and Perkins*, pp. 248, 1177.

[18] The Second Assembly adopted five resolutions; the Third, five; the Fourth, ten; the Fifth, five; the Sixth, seven; the Seventh, seven; the Eighth, seven; and the Ninth, seven.

[19] Including the Canal Zone, against which Panama at once protested as a violation of her sovereignty. It was withdrawn from the list.

INFORMATION. The opening wedge for the remarkable development which was to follow was the Committee on Information from the Non-Self-Governing Territories. The opposing views may be summed up in excerpts from the Report of the United States Mission to the United Nations: [20]

Many of the states now administering such areas, while recognizing the need of change and development in the administration of dependent areas, desire that such progress come through a process of increasing political experience and that the competence of the United Nations under Chapter XI of the Charter shall not be enlarged upon through interpretation of the Charter at this time. Some other powers, such as China, the Philippines, and India, desire that progress be made more rapidly and that the responsibilities of the United Nations in connection with the political developments of those areas be enlarged wherever possible.

. . . The United States . . . has taken the position that the many steps that can be taken for the political, economic and social advancement of dependent peoples and their attainment of self-government or independence should be energetically encouraged but that the process must be one within the framework set by the provisions of the Charter of the United Nations.

. . . It was argued throughout the discussions that the administration of dependent areas as at present existing is unjust to the dependent peoples; that the resources of those areas are used for the benefit of the administering states rather than of the inhabitants; and that those areas are used as a source of cheap labor. Counterarguments were advanced by administering states that their territories are soundly evolving toward self-government or independence and that in fact under existing progress these areas enjoy greater freedom than obtains in the metropolitan areas of some Members of the United Nations. Some of the administering states have held that these territories are under their sovereignty or jurisdiction and that any interference savors of an intrusion on their rights and is thus contrary to the domestic-jurisdiction clause of the Charter.

. . . The administering Members stressed the special character of Chapter XI of the Charter as a unilateral declaration of intention on their part . . . they logically held that the Charter did not envisage any machinery for the examination of this information or for the making of recommendations with respect to it . . . that the framers of the Charter . . . deliberately excluded the transmission of political information.

The nonadministering Members, on the other hand, took the position that Chapter XI was a treaty obligation, not a mere unilateral obligation. They contended for a permanent committee of the General Assembly with unlimited powers to examine the information and make recommendations to those administering non-self-governing territories. Further (they) . . . contended that political information should be transmitted.

The Second Assembly renewed the *ad hoc* committee as a special committee, retaining its balanced representation, and authorized it to seek information from other sources than the reports made. Resolution 142 (II) set forth a "Standard Form" according to which reports

[20] Report to the Congress (1947), pp. 127-29.

should be made. The first part of this was designated as an "optional category" and included political information; the other parts referred to social, educational, and economic conditions.[21] A third resolution (for which the United States was also responsible) authorized the Secretary-General to gather supplemental information and to make comparisons between the colonial areas and independent states—the purpose being to show that the peoples in some colonial areas were better off than in some sovereign states. A fourth resolution encouraged Members voluntarily to supply political information; the effort of the Soviet Union, India, and others to make this a requirement failed. This resolution had been excluded at San Francisco, but it was argued with some reasonableness that since the colonial Powers had obligated themselves to advance their colonies politically, they should report on what they had done. The resolution called on the specialized agencies to assist in analyzing the information.

All these resolutions related to information, which was the foundation upon which to build. The Third Assembly adopted resolutions of the same character, and continued for another year the Special Committee on Information—a compromise between those who wished to abolish it completely and those who wanted to make it a permanent organ comparable to the Trusteeship Council. The Fourth Assembly began to cut down the optional category in the Standard Form, leaving political information upon a voluntary basis but calling on Members as usual to supply it. Another resolution called for periodic publication of the information received. The special committee was renewed, this time for three years. The Fifth Assembly, to the dissatisfaction of the United States, cut down the authority of the Secretary-General to compare colonies with independent states. The states which formed the majority in the Assembly did not like to be compared with colonies and they limited the comparison to that between the colony and its mother country. The Sixth Assembly adopted a revised Standard Form, which omitted the optional category; it approved the work of the special committee and removed the word "Special" from its title. At the Seventh Assembly, after warm debate between those who wished to abolish the committee entirely and those who wished to continue it "for as long as there exist territories whose peoples have not yet attained a full measure of self-government," agreement was

---

[21] This was prepared by the United States, which was at first on the anti-colonial side and willing to interpret the Charter broadly. It always insisted, however, that action should be in accordance with the Charter and later became concerned over the way in which it was being disregarded. For this reason, and also through need for keeping allies, it swung round more to the side of the colonial Powers.

reached upon its renewal for another three-year term. It has by now become almost a standing committee, though that name is denied to it.

The General Assembly had thus taken the one item of Chapter XI which referred to the United Nations, that is, the reports to the Secretary-General. Upon this item it has built rights to take, analyze, and publish the information in the reports; to acquire further information including that of a political nature; and to make comparisons between conditions in a colony and its mother country, though not between a colony and other independent countries. It has also called on the specialized agencies to assist in acquiring and analyzing information.

SUBSTANTIVE RECOMMENDATIONS. Meanwhile, the attempt to exert control over colonies was proceeding along other lines. In 1949, the Assembly began to make recommendations concerning what should be done in the colonies; to the colonial Powers, this was an impertinence which they regarded as illegal under Article 2, paragraph 7, of the Charter and without authorization from any part of the Charter.[22] The United States supported the Assembly, however, so long as recommendations were addressed to states in general and not to any particular state. Resolutions were adopted in that year concerning equal treatment in education, use of native languages in schools, eradication of illiteracy, and provision for technical training. In the following year, the Committee on Information followed the policy of making a report on one phase, and reported only on education in the non-self-governing territories. This policy was approved by the General Assembly, which also adopted a resolution calling on administering states to report upon the implementation of human rights within their territories. A report was made to the Sixth Assembly on economic conditions and to the seventh on social conditions. The Seventh Assembly also adopted resolutions concerning racial discrimination in colonies and laid down educational, economic, and social policies for the colonial territories.

Efforts were made along other lines to extend control over the colonies. As early as 1947, India had proposed a resolution asserting that the Charter had intended that all colonies be placed under trusteeship and calling upon the colonial Powers to do so; the resolution was adopted in the Fourth Committee, where a bare majority is all that is needed, but failed to get the required two-thirds in the plenary As-

[22] Said the Australian representative: "This is a fine company to teach France the rights of man, to give lessons to England in the ways of parliamentary democracy, to enjoin liberalism on Belgium, and to tell the mighty republic forged by Washington, Jefferson and Lincoln how to educate people in the arts of self-government." Quoted in Brookings, *Organization*.

sembly. On another occasion, India tried to exclude the colonial powers from any participation in the Committee on Information. Other resolutions, of various origin, called for more participation by representatives of indigenous populations in the work of the United Nations concerning non-self-governing territories, and offered technical assistance to the colonial Powers in carrying out the recommendations of the Assembly as to what should be done in their colonies. Ample advice was offered to the colonial Powers, and, though they have steadily insisted that all this was unconstitutional, they have apparently attempted to show in their reports how they have met the criticisms and recommendations made.

THE MEANING OF SELF-GOVERNING. Originally, the non-self-governing territories were simply those so designated by their administering states, and the number varied from year to year as these states included or did not include certain areas. Thus, the United States ceased to include the Panama Canal Zone; France omitted several areas after the French Union was formed; England declared that Malta was self-governing so far as Article 73e was concerned, though not in other ways. A question was raised concerning this practice in 1948, and Resolution 222 (III) asserted that the United Nations ought to be informed concerning any proposed change which might lead to the cessation of transmission of information. The United States voted for this, claiming that it did not affect the rights of the administering states. Resolution 334 (IV) asserted that it was within the responsibility of the General Assembly to express its opinion upon the principles which might guide a Member in claiming self-governing status for one of its territories, and it asked the Committee on Information to examine the factors which should be taken into account in making such a decision.

This began an important new phase, not only in interpreting the powers of the United Nations under the Charter, but also in finding an answer to the hitherto unanswered question: How does one judge whether a group of people is self-governing or independent, or deserving to be so rated, and who has the authority to decide? The special committee reported a list of factors to the Sixth Assembly, which set up an *ad hoc* Committee on Factors to study and report further. In 1950, Resolution 448 (V) approved the cessation of information from the Netherlands on Indonesia, which had become independent; this implied that the Assembly had a right to pass judgment on such matters. In 1951, the Assembly reserved judgment upon the announcement of the Netherlands that Surinam and the Netherlands Antilles had become self-governing, and did so again in the following year. Finally, the Eighth Assembly, in Resolution 742 (VIII), voted for a preambular statement which asserted its competence to act upon such matters. Its right to tell Members what they should do concerning colonial territories had been challenged on every occasion, but this was the first time the Assembly had by vote interpreted the Charter in support of this right. The resolution went on to say that the list of factors should be used so that "a decision may be taken by the General Assembly on the continuation or cessation of transmission of information required by Chapter XI of the Charter." In the same year, the Assembly accepted the statement of the United States that Puerto Rico was self-governing, but again questioned the action of the Netherlands—which seems to be regarded by the Assembly as a whipping-boy for the colonial Powers. The Netherlands has disregarded the resolution. Other colonial Powers have walked out of meetings in protest against action proposed or taken, and tension has increased steadily.

The Committee on Factors made a final report (see Appendix IV) which, approved by the General Assembly, is attached to Resolution 648 (VII). It deserves a great deal of study, though it may not be much used in United Nations practice. It is the beginning of the necessary effort which the United Nations must make to establish criteria for "self-determination." If this effort was successful, it would fill a lacuna in international law and would be an important step in developing international government.

The report classifies factors under three headings: those indicative of attainment of independence; those indicative of other separate systems of self-government; those indicative of free association on equal terms with the state of which it is an integral part. There are two ways of looking at the factors listed under these headings: (1) from the viewpoint of what the colonial Powers are expected to concede to their colonial peoples—in which case the standards would be set high by the anti-colonial Powers; or (2) from the viewpoint of criteria according to which the United Nations should determine whether a group deserved to be called self-governing or independent—after which determination the United Nations could no longer claim supervision over that group. Actually, the standards are set so high that few sovereign states could measure up to them; so high that colonial groups would have a long way to go before they could be recognized as self-governing or independent.

CONCLUSIONS. Whatever the motives of delegates might have been in issuing this list of factors, it is only a beginning; there is much confusion, and many questions remain unanswered. Independence has long been an accepted goal, but is there any assurance that independence is necessarily good for every group? And do some of the groups for which speeches are made really want independence? Is there any assurance that such a group, made independent, would be able to maintain itself against aggrandizement or in an economic sense? Or that it would not be better off as part of a strong state? The two thus far set up as independent states through United Nations efforts—Indonesia and Libya—have not been very successful. Can a people feel sure that they will not be more exploited by their own leaders than by colonial administrators? There are states in which the mass of people are worse treated than the people in some colonies. However, the Committee on Information was instructed not to make such comparisons. The reply to such questions tends to be emotional; we would rather be exploited by our own people than by outsiders; we would rather be poor and independent than prosperous under domination.

From the viewpoint of the community of nations there are also important questions. If a group made independent by the United Nations is unable to support itself, must the United Nations support it? It is much to be doubted whether those Members which voted for a state's independence would be willing to add to their financial or military contributions to the United Nations for the purpose of such support. Is it desirable to splinter the world into many small and weak states? What would be the effect of this upon voting in the United Nations? One effect, probably, would be that those states which have the veto would retain it.

There are some quirks of human nature which affect this situation. It is a strange fact that a group which has claimed self-determination and fought its way to national independence, will not permit self-determination when claimed against it. An example is India, long a champion of self-determination and still so in the United Nations when her own interests are not concerned, which swallowed up groups, sometimes by force (Hyderabad), and which has conducted a cold war to take over the French and Portuguese colonies in India. India does not take these cases to the United Nations on the plea of self-determination. Again, Indonesia has rejected pleas of self-determination by the Republic of South Moluccas, which did not wish to be absorbed in the unitary state into which Indonesia converted herself. Another quirk is the limitation of United Nations action to colonies; no interest is shown in the indigenous peoples of non-colonial states, or in minorities, or in other groups now as cruelly oppressed as in any colony.[23]

Colonialism, in the sense of exploitation, is dead, but it leaves behind it many difficult questions. The United Nations has made a beginning

---

[23] Belgium, particularly, has brought this point forth, and has published much material concerning indigenous peoples and their treatment in many states of the world. This viewpoint has become known as the "Belgian thesis" in the United Nations.

in dealing with them, but it has, as with human rights, sought to move too rapidly, and it has been inspired by emotion rather than by reason. The colonial, and now other, states, assert that the action is not permitted by, or is contrary to, the provisions of the Charter. To this it is replied that Article 10 and other articles give the Assembly the right to make recommendations upon practically any matter. This viewpoint is looked upon with increasing alarm; it has helped to push the United States over to the side of the colonial Powers. A cleavage has been produced in the United Nations, and it remains to be seen how far it will go. Without the colonial Powers, the United Nations could not exist, and they might well have left it by now had the resolutions adopted by the majority been more than recommendations. It is to be hoped that this problem can be studied as the new problem that it is, and not upon the basis of past legal rights or upon the basis of vindictiveness.[24]

129. PEACEFUL CHANGE[25]

Rules of law, or legally binding agreements, or long-accepted situations, often become outmoded and are not adapted to current needs, and this gives rise to controversies and discontent. The community of nations has never provided adequate means for dealing with such situations; this deficiency has been noted in several connections above. Peaceful change is one of the most important functions of any society, and it is regrettable to have to say that the Charter of the United Nations shows no advance toward "provision for peaceful change." These words are not found in the Charter; they are used by writers in the very broad sense of means of taking care of such situations as described above. "Peace," says Professor Jessup, "will never be secure if progress is confined to putting an international lid on a national boiling pot."[26]

[24] As to the above, see Thomas R. Adam, *Modern Colonialism: Institutions and Policies* (Doubleday Short Studies in Political Science, New York, 1955); C. Eagleton, "Excesses of Self-Determination," *Foreign Affairs*, 31 (1953); B. Rivlin, "Self-Determination and Dependent Areas," *Int. Con.*, No. 501 (1955).

[25] On peaceful change, see: E. H. Carr, *The Twenty Years' Crisis 1919-1939* (London, 1940); C. R. M. F. Crutwell, *A History of Peaceful Change in the Modern World* (New York, 1937); J. F. Dulles, *War, Peace and Change* (New York, 1939); F. S. Dunn, *Peaceful Change: A Study of International Procedures* (Council on Foreign Relations, New York, 1937); J. L. Kunz, "The Problem of Revision in International Law," *A.J.*, 33 (1939), p. 33; G. Scelle, *Théorie juridique de la revision des traités* (Paris, 1936); W. E. Stephens, *Revisions of the Treaty of Versailles* (New York, 1939); Bryce Wood, *Peaceful Change and the Colonial Problem* (New York, 1940); *Peaceful Change: Proceedings of the Tenth International Studies Conference* (L. of N., Institute of Intellectual Cooperation, Paris, 1938).

[26] Jessup, p. 160.

The chief provisions of the Charter for peaceful change are to be found in Articles 13 and 14, though the problem is implicit in many other articles, such as those in Chapter VI. If the parties can agree on a change, well and good. Though compromise may not furnish the best answer, it may be the only answer. For the purpose of securing agreement, the United Nations is well equipped. It can supply meeting places, preparatory studies, expert assistance; and it can focus upon the parties the mediatory pressure of the organized community of nations.

Where such agreement is lacking, resort has been had to inadequate means of settling disputes, or to use of force; these are to be considered in Part V below. Revision of treaties has been one of the most difficult problems, for the party having an advantage is usually reluctant to give it up. We have considered the doctrine of *rebus sic stantibus* and related efforts to solve the problem (Chapter VIII), and later the vain efforts of the League of Nations. At San Francisco the problem reappeared; the victors would permit nothing which might allow a change in the peace treaties. But the General Assembly may recommend measures for the adjustment of "any situation, regardless of origin" (these words were included in Article 14 on the insistence of Senator Vandenberg), and thus for revision of treaties.

The usual method of peaceful change within a state is legislative, backed by the enforcement agencies of the government; but the United Nations is founded on the "sovereign equality" of all its Members and can adopt no new rule of law binding upon one of them without its own consent. No organ is authorized to make law, or to produce change in a legal situation, unless the parties consent to it; even in the case of enforcement action the Security Council is not authorized to impose terms of settlement, though in practice it would doubtless do so.[27] The sanctions of the United Nations are merely to halt aggression, and not for the enforcement of law. At San Francisco, there were numerous demands to make more provision concerning international law and legislation, but the Great Powers, with Dulles as their spokesman, reduced them all to insignificance in the Charter.[28]

The weak words of Article 13, paragraph 1a, reflect this lack of interest: "The General Assembly shall initiate studies and make recommendations for the purposes of: . . . encouraging the progressive development of international law and its codification." The law of nations is, however, being slowly developed in several ways under the United Nations.

[27] See pp. 501-2 below.
[28] The situation is now reversed. The smaller states now seek to push law aside in order to get the changes they want; the larger states call upon law to protect their vested interests.

INTERNATIONAL LAW COMMISSION. The General Assembly performed its task under the above clause by setting up the International Law Commission. Various hindrances have affected its work. Its members are supposed to be independent experts, and the commission has in fact included some of the most famous international lawyers; but half of them are delegates of their nations to other bodies of the United Nations and regard their work on the commission as incidental. A meeting of two months per year is not time to accomplish much, and even international lawyers must have time to make a living; it is a financial sacrifice for them to give up two months of income and to devote further time when called upon to serve as Rapporteurs. The General Assembly has tended to unload upon the commission subjects of little interest to the latter; probably half its time is devoted to such topics, for which the Assembly frequently asks priority. The commission can choose its own topics only for "codification"; for "development" (i.e., making new law) it must have the approval of the Assembly. Its drafts must go out to governments for comment, and most governments do not bother to reply.[29] The draft convention must then be approved by the General Assembly, and finally sent out for ratification by states.

It is not surprising, then, that no new law has been made as a result of the work of the commission. It has completed a draft text on arbitral procedure, which does not add to the obligation of a state to submit to arbitration; it merely provides a procedure for tribunals to follow once states have agreed to arbitrate. Nevertheless, objections were raised to some of its provisions as invasions of sovereignty, and it has not yet been acted upon; nor has any other of the commission's work. For such slow work, the Members and the Assembly are responsible. Incomplete as it is, the work of the commission, as found in its annual reports and other documents, is of great interest and usefulness to lawyers and courts; even unratified, it helps to build international law.

LEGISLATIVE TREATIES. We have earlier observed that the only sources of international law are custom and treaties, and that the treaty is a much overburdened and inadequate instrument for this purpose. Yet it is the only means of making new international law, aside from the slow growth of customary law (this is a problem which faces the International Law Commission). The Charter gives no legislative

[29] See Brookings, *Organization;* H. Briggs, in *A.J.,* 48 (1954), p. 603. The request of the commission for information may in fact mean much work for a government; France replied that it would involve "tons of archives." It would help if each government would set up its own national body to cooperate with the commission. The work of the commission may be followed in its annual Reports to the General Assembly.

power to any organ. At San Francisco, even a proposal to authorize the United Nations to draft legislative treaties was defeated. But the right to prepare such treaties was given to the Economic and Social Council, and it may be implied for other organs in other articles of the Charter; it is not forbidden by the Charter.

A convention may be initiated in various ways; by an individual, as in the case of the Genocide Convention, or by an organization, such as the International Chamber of Commerce, or by the Secretariat. In any case, it must be proposed by a Member. A conference may be called at which to secure agreement upon a text. There is no systematic way of deciding that a certain treaty is needed, nor any procedure for drafting it in proper form.[30] But the chief obstacle to progress is of course the need for ratification of a treaty by states.

The chart issued by the Secretariat in connection with its record of treaties and action upon them (ST/LEG/3) shows that some seventy-five treaties have advanced far enough to be submitted for approval of Members or of other states. Though two or three of them—such as the agreement concerning the World Health Organization—have been approved by many states, on the average, no treaty has been acted upon by as many as half the Members. The Arab states, on the average, act on about one fourth of them; the record of the Latin American states is only slightly better. The Netherlands has the highest record, and the western European states in general have done well. The United States has ratified less than twenty, though she has signed others. The record seems to show that Members have little interest in international legislation, and less in improving procedures therefor.

Nevertheless, the preparation of legislative treaties is necessarily a large and constant part of the activity of the United Nations. The seventy-five treaties listed indicate a tremendous amount of effort and some achievement. It is often necessary to break a subject down into several treaties, so that some states at least will accept all the proposals; thus, there are seven conventions for road traffic. Progress is slow and difficult, but some is being made; and it would be far more difficult if the United Nations did not exist. But it should also be said that the United Nations has not recognized the need for, nor initiated studies concerning, improved methods for making new laws, which would greatly aid peaceful change.

---

[30] See the interesting article by Jenks, referred to in footnote 4, Chap. 8, above. Treaties made by the various bodies vary widely as to form and phraseology, leaving uncertainty as to meaning. The Secretariat has attempted to help by preparing a Handbook of Final Clauses, for reference. See also Resolution 684(VII) of the Assembly.

RESOLUTIONS. The General Assembly adopts some resolutions which may be regarded as binding upon those to whom they are addressed (e.g., the Trusteeship Council, or the Secretariat), but the only case in which its action binds Member states is with regard to the assessment of dues. Nevertheless, an Assembly resolution may have great weight, and may contribute to the building of international law. The Declaration of Human Rights is doubtless the best example of this. While the Declaration has no legally binding force, rights are claimed under it and national courts are being called upon to decide its effect. There is no authority in the Charter for the United Nations to detach territory and set up new states, but this has been done for Israel and Indonesia, as well as Libya. Great pressure can be put behind a resolution which represents a consensus of opinion; it can be maintained that it is more effective than treaty-law.

However, the record of implementation of resolutions is not good in general. It is difficult to measure implementation with accuracy. An effort was made to have states report upon their own implementation of Economic and Social Council resolutions, but under half of them replied. Naturally, resolutions relating to administrative matters are best observed; next, perhaps, are those relating to collective measures to be taken; worst observed are resolutions relating to the development of international law. Speeches are made calling upon Members to "obey" resolutions, and a resolution may be repeated from year to year; thus pressure is built up behind a recommendation which is hard to resist. But it is hard to make sovereign states conform; and while resolutions do contribute in some degree to the development of international law, it is not an imposing contribution.

PEACEFUL ADJUSTMENT. Peaceful change through legislative procedures is, then, a difficult problem for the United Nations. Article 14 also authorized the General Assembly to recommend "peaceful adjustment" of situations "likely to impair the general welfare or friendly relations among nations." Such situations are apparently less urgent than those found under Chapter VI of the Charter, "which might lead to international friction or give rise to a dispute"; and these situations are still less important than a dispute, "the continuance of which is likely to endanger the maintenance of international peace and security." The settlement of disputes is part of the process of peaceful change, but it is to be handled by a special procedure according to the Charter. It is, however, very difficult to draw a line between these gradations. The treatment of Indians in South Africa was not brought up as a dispute, though it has become a very bitter one, nor could the condemnation of the Franco regime in Spain be regarded as a dispute.

On the other hand, the desire of Egypt for revision of her 1936 treaty with England was presented as a dispute. Both the Security Council and the General Assembly prefer to disregard Charter procedures and restrictions, which, indeed, are vague and often confusing, and to adjust the situation in whatever way they can; the General Assembly, in fact, has no rules of procedure for dealing with disputes. The process of peaceful adjustment is one of finding agreement in whatever way is possible.

While the above is discouraging as to procedures and achievement, something has been achieved. Such situations as those in Palestine or Indonesia have been adjusted with a minimum of fighting. Seventy-five treaties accepted, even by small numbers of states, is evidence, in the light of the difficulties stated above, of distinct gain. While these treaties rarely deal with important political or economic matters, they are of cumulative importance in readjusting the community of nations to new needs; even those which have not so far been adopted contribute to the slow process of education. If the United Nations were, as is sometimes said, no more than machinery through which sovereign states can negotiate and solve their problems, it would be worthwhile for what it has accomplished, in face of great obstacles, in this respect alone.

PART V

We have recorded the slow and frequently unconscious development toward government in the community of nations. We have seen law slowly evolving through custom and treaty, and methods and agencies developed by sovereign states for carrying on the increasingly needed intercourse between them. We have noted the effort to establish the League of Nations as an over-all and centralized body and seen that it was a skeleton of government which was not given the lifeblood of authority to make and enforce law.

None of these developments brought war under restraint; yet it is the primary purpose of law and government to control the use of force among its subjects. The problem of control over war remains the most pressing of the many which today confront harassed humanity. To uproot so ancient and established an institution as war is no easy task; it will require much study, much psychological adjustment, approach from various directions, and wide reconstruction of the society of nations.

We have, therefore, reserved for separate study the problem of the control of war. We shall first attempt to analyze the problem in relation to the various proposals and efforts heretofore made; then consider the experience of the League of Nations in this respect; then study the United Nations security system; and finally survey briefly current trends of thought looking toward world government.

Chapter 15

THE PROBLEM OF WAR

130. WHAT IS WAR?[1]

International lawyers have never been able to provide a satisfactory definition of war. The earlier writers thought of it as a means for settling a dispute as to rights; the path of approach in the minds of these writers was the "just war." It was with the problem of the justice of the war, rather than its definition, that Grotius was concerned; and Vitoria and Suarez, followed by Vattel and others, asserted that the justifiable cause of war was a wrong received. International lawyers, called upon by national sovereignty to justify its actions, but unwilling to legalize immoral acts, abandoned the attempt to say what is a just or a legal war, and accepted war as a sad fact. International law neither acknowledged nor denied war; it was simply a happening beyond the power of law to control, like an earthquake or fire. The law of nations has contented itself, until our own day, with efforts to ameliorate the horrors of war by making rules for its conduct.

In the popular sense, war is simply the use of force between states. It has been beyond law, and was therefore incapable of legal definition. Clausewitz, the master of military science, described it as means, a political instrument, through which a state seeks to achieve its purposes. It is a weapon, which may be used for good purposes or for bad purposes, and international law, not being competent, raised no question as to the legitimacy of its purpose or of its use. It might be a defense of a legal right; it might be a brutal act of aggression. But international law was forced to take into account its existence and its results, and has tried to circumscribe it in various ways, such as regu-

[1] See Wm. B. Ballis, *The Legal Position of War: Changes in its Practice and Theory from Plato to Vattel* (The Hague, 1937); C. Eagleton, "The Attempt to Define War," *Int. Con.*, No. 291 (June, 1933); Lothar Kotzsch, *The Concept of War in Contemporary History and International Law* (Geneva, 1956); F. Grob, *The Relativity of War and Peace* (New Haven, 1949); Wright, *Study of War*.

lation of the methods to be employed once war is started or by attempting to regulate the effects of war upon neutrals or belligerents and their nationals. Thus, the law of war and neutrality was developed.

A LEGAL STATUS. It may be said, therefore, that a legal status was created by the existence of war. When a war was begun, many changes in the law between nations automatically took place. The law of war and the law of neutrality to a large extent replaced the law of peace. Insurance or other contracts might become operative or inoperative; rules as to contraband and blockade went into effect; ordinary acts of trade could become illegitimate and subject to heavy penalties. Individuals or states stood to gain or lose because of the incidence of the new rules. It matters a great deal, for this and other reasons, to know the exact moment when the legal status of war begins and ends.

But international lawyers have not been very successful in saying when this metamorphosis occurs. Professor Wright, in his exhaustive treatise on war, defines war in its broadest sense as *"violent contact* of *distinct* but *similar* entities," and its narrower and more useful sense as "the *legal condition* which *equally* permits two or more *hostile groups* to carry on a *conflict* by *armed* force."[2] According to Hyde, war "may be fairly described as a condition of armed hostility between states,"[3] and this definition is more in harmony with the actual facts than many definitions, narrower in scope. But is every status of armed hostility to be called war? "There must be," says Wright, "at least two parties to a war, and in law one or both of them must have intended war. A state of war can not, in legal contemplation, flow from accident or negligence."[4] Is intent, then, an essential part of a legal definition of war? It may be asked, in this connection, whether a declaration of war is necessary. Except possibly for states bound by the third Hague Convention of 1907, the answer must be negative. There is no general rule of international law which forbids a surprise attack. Failure to acknowledge intent to make war might mean certain advantages resulting from the inapplicability of the laws of war.[5] Apparently, declaration by one party is sufficient to create a legal

[2] Wright, *Study of War*, I, p. 8.

[3] Hyde, III, § 597; See also A. D. McNair, "The Legal Meaning of War and the Relation of War to Reprisals," *Grotius Society*, 10 (1925), pp. 29-50.

[4] In Q. Wright, "Neutrality and Neutral Rights following the Pact of Paris for the Renunciation of War," *Proc. Am. Soc.*, 1930, p. 79. See also C. Eagleton, "The Form and Function of the Declaration of War," *A.J.*, 32 (1938), p. 19; Q. Wright, "Changes in the Conception of War," *ibid.*, 18 (1924), p. 765.

[5] For this reason, states sometimes prefer to describe their forceful action as "intervention" rather than as war.

status of war, though it does not seem reasonable to burden the community of nations with the consequences of the status of war simply upon the declaration of one party.[6]

If a declaration of war, or other manifestation of intent, is not decisive, how can one determine that the legal status of war exists? Important as that question is, no satisfactory answer has yet been found. European states accepted the blockade of Southern ports by the United States as sufficient evidence that the Civil War was war in the legal sense, and they consequently assumed the position of neutrals. But the action of the U.S. Marines in Nicaragua in 1912 was not regarded as war; the bombardment and seizure of Corfu by Italy in 1924 was denied by Italy to be war, nor did Greece allege it to be war; and no one was willing to designate the Japanese invasion of Manchuria in 1937 a war.

Nor is it possible to find an answer in judicial decisions, which are inconsistent and confusing. An English court, at the beginning of the Spanish American War, considered the capture of one Spanish vessel as proof of the existence of war;[7] an American court, however, refused to call the long and bloody naval struggle with France at the end of the eighteenth century a war.[8] For certain purposes, the courts have held a short Indian attack in New Mexico to be war, and also the Boxer Expedition to Peiping. The conflict in Korea has brought greater confusion; the courts have split badly over clauses in insurance contracts referring to war.[9]

The Korean situation was unique in that it was the first time that

---

[6] Or, for that matter, upon the declaration of both parties. The status of war may apparently be found where the declaration is accompanied by no warlike measures whatever. Thus a number of states which declared war against Germany offered little if any military or naval aid against her in either of the world wars.

[7] "I will state why it is a fact that a state of war then existed. An act of hostility had been committed on April 22 by American men-of-war against Spanish traders, or, at all events, against one Spanish trader, which act, in my opinion, was only consistent with the existence of a state of war. Further, on April 22, the American President issued a proclamation in which he declared a general blockade of Cuba . . ." *U.S. v. Pelly,* 4 Commercial Cases 100 (1899).

[8] "It is urged that the political and judicial departments of each Government recognized the other as an enemy; that battles were fought and blood shed upon the high seas; that property was captured by each from the other and condemned as prize; that diplomatic and consular intercourse was suspended, and that prisoners had been taken by each Government from the other and 'held for exchange, punishment or retaliation, according to the laws and usages of war.'" The Supreme Court held that such acts did not constitute public war, "but limited war in its nature similar to a prolonged series of reprisals." *Wm. Gray, Administrator, v. U.S.,* 21 Ct. Cl. 340 (1886).

[9] See, for example, *Weissman v. Metropolitan Life Ins. Co.,* 112 F. Supp. 420; *Stanberry v. Aetna Life,* 98 A 2nd 134; *Beley v. Penn Mutual Life,* 95 A 2nd 221; *Stankus v. New York Life,* 44 N.E. 2nd 687; *Rosenhau v. Idaho Mutual Benefit Assn.,* 145 P 2nd 227.

the community of nations had employed military force against an offender. Is such an enforcement action to be regarded as war? Should the law of war be binding upon the United Nations in such an action?[10] One of the few elements in a definition of war, of which one can feel sure, is that, in the past, it has been a contest between states, both having equality of legal status; but in principle, there can be no equality between the United Nations and an aggressor. Likewise, it would seem that no Member of the United Nations could properly claim the legal status of neutral.

It may be that, with the fearsome weapons of modern war, nations will hesitate to conduct war in the future as they have in the past. New ways of achieving national purposes with little or no use of force are being employed, and we now have "cold war," which brings new problems. But it can hardly be hoped that nations, any more than individuals, will relinquish entirely the use of force. It may be possible to say that war is now illegal, or that there will be no more war, but this is a matter of definition. If one is to "outlaw" or control war, it is of primary importance to know what war is. The end of preventing the use of force between states will not have been attained if war is prohibited but defined in a narrow sense; on the other hand, it is not desirable or possible to eliminate every use of force. Either the law must be stated in terms of forbidding war, in which case war must be clearly and broadly defined; or else the law must abandon the term war and state which uses of force are to be illegal. The latter course would seem preferable.

Even so, there are difficulties, and one of these is "self-defense," to which reference has already been made. The defense of a right has always been regarded as justifiable; unfortunately, the community of nations has provided no authority, such as exists within a state, to determine whether or not the right of self-defense was legitimately exercised. Much attention has been directed toward the opposite concept, aggression, but without result. A special committee of the Temporary Mixed Commission came to the conclusion that "no satisfactory definition of what constitutes an act of aggression could be drawn up."[11] It is manifest that if the dictionary definition of first attack is accepted, the party seeking to uphold its right might frequently be the aggressor. Even the military sanctions of the com-

---

[10] See the Report of the Committee to Study Legal Problems of the United Nations, in *Proc. Am. Soc.*, 1952, p. 216.

[11] L. of N., *Records of the Fourth Assembly*, 1923, p. 184. See C. Eagleton, "The Attempt to Define Aggression," *Int. Con.*, No. 264 (1930); *Research in International Law*, Rights and Duties of States in Case of Aggression (1939); Q. Wright, "The Concept of Aggression in International Law," *A.J.*, 29 (1935), p. 373.

munity of nations might in such case be regarded as aggression. There are numerous cases in which the claim of self-defense should be deemed illegal, and many in which aggression might be regarded as not only legal but a duty.

In spite of thorough study by the League of Nations, with quite negative results, the effort continues to define aggression. It was rejected at San Francisco, where an attempt was made to put it into the Charter as a guide for the Security Council; it has now been revived in the United Nations where a special committee was set up (after the International Law Commission had shown little interest in it) on the Question of Defining Aggression.[12] This continuing interest is part of the problem we have been discussing: what uses of force should be made illegal? An arbitrary political vote in the Security Council to decide upon the aggressor is not satisfactory to many who wish to have some legal criteria according to which the decision would be made.

131. ANALYSIS OF THE PROBLEM OF WAR[13]

It is only within the last half-century that people have begun to think seriously of the possibility of eliminating the scourge of war. For centuries, the average person accepted war as the peasants of the *ancien régime* accepted their hard lot, regarding it as a providential visitation to be compared with plague or flood or fire. But these things have been brought by human intelligence under a large degree of control; why cannot the same be done for war? The terrible cost of modern war, of which we have spoken earlier, has spurred on the effort. The lessons of the two world wars, whose cost can never be repaid, was final proof of the argument advanced by Norman Angell that there is no gain possible in war.[14] Earlier efforts were, however, misdirected, and much energy was wasted on ill-considered and fantastic proposals. It is not enough to teach hatred for war, for war will not disappear simply because it is hated. Nor is it enough to say that hate produces war, for the opposite is more true; nor that war is due to love of glory and martial fanfare, and that soldiers should therefore be dressed in brown derbies; nor that munitions makers, or bank-

[12] For its report, see General Assembly, Ninth Session, *Official Records*, Supp. No. 11(A/2638). Refer in general to pp. 80-82 above and 525-27 below.

[13] The material for this discussion is drawn largely from C. Eagleton, *Analysis of the Problem of War* (New York, 1937).

[14] Norman Angell, *The Great Illusion* (4th Am. ed., New York, 1916).

ers, or other scapegoats should be put into the first ranks of battle; nor that it must be disregarded and left to die. There are no such single solutions; the problem is far wider and far deeper.

WHY WAR? The first point to note is that war is not an end in itself. Few if any persons or nations instigate war solely for the purpose of making war. War is a means for achieving an end, a weapon which can be used for good or for bad purposes. Some of these purposes for which war has been used have been accepted by humanity as worthwhile ends; indeed, war performs functions which are essential in any human society. It has been used to *settle disputes*, to *uphold rights*, to *remedy wrongs;* and these are surely functions which must be served. They may, indeed, be stated as the primary functions of government, but no government has been provided among nations, nor any other means, except war, for serving these fundamental needs. One may say, without exaggeration, that no more stupid, brutal, wasteful, or unfair method could ever have been imagined than war for such purposes, but this does not alter the situation. Intelligent human beings have provided no other method, and they have only themselves to blame.

From the above, the conclusion inescapably follows that war will not cease until a substitute for it is in operation, which can, at least as satisfactorily as war, perform these necessary functions. A state cannot be expected to give up the use of war, nor would its people permit it to do so, unless there were some other adequate means by which that state could settle its disputes, uphold its rights, and remedy its wrongs. The whole purpose of the state is to protect and advance the interests of its people. Its people would not permit it to surrender the means at its disposal, incompetent as they may be, until other satisfactory means of caring for their interests have been put into operation.

We must go deeper into the problem than this, for it reaches into the fundamental values of human life. The question is sometimes asked: is war ever worth while? is there anything more important than peace? The answer which history gives is that there are certain things for which human beings have always been willing to fight. We may sum them up in the word "justice"; and immediately the question arises, what is justice? Without debating this abstractly, the answer relevant to this discussion is that justice is whatever the organized community, through its laws and courts, says that it is. In the absence of such a decision in the community of nations, it may be expected that each nation will continue to make war to gain what it regards as justice for itself.

Thus, what is involved is much more than the mere prevention, or absence, of war; the mere elimination of war would not accomplish what human beings desire. Force seems to be an essential part of life, at least until that happy day arrives, dreamed of by philosophical anarchists, when each person will know and respect the rights of others, and force will not be used among men. Until that happy day, the problem will be one of controlling the use of force among nations so that it will be used for desirable rather than undesirable ends. The solution to that problem as between individuals has been to make force a monopoly belonging to the organized community; they have preferred this to continuous fighting, but they do not think the same way in their capacity as nations.

There are thus many approaches to the problem of war, and all must be taken into consideration. If war is now an assurance of security, then confidence in security must be provided in some other way. If war is a means of self-defense, then other means of defense must be provided. If war is rooted in human psychology, it must be slowly uprooted. If justice is to be obtained only by war, some other way of guaranteeing justice must be found. If the existence of war is part of the economic system, it must be removed with due consideration for economic effects.[15] And if war has legal bases, the necessary legal consequences of its elimination must be studied. The task is not merely one of destruction, the abolition of war. That would leave a vacuum which must be filled; substitutes must be found for the services which it performs. It is precisely this constructive aspect of the problem that has so far frustrated human agreement.

132. EFFORTS AT A SOLUTION

Various proposals have been offered or attempted in the effort to get rid of war. It will help to understand the problem if we examine some of these proposals and test them against the analysis above made. We shall then be better able to reach conclusions as to the manner in which war can be brought under control.

THE CAUSES OF WAR. It is frequently observed that war can be eliminated only by removing the causes of war, and to many people international organization and law therefore seem useless. No plan has ever been proposed to accomplish this worthwhile end, and it may safely be assumed that those who advance the idea have not thought it

---

[15] As to war in its economic effects, see E. Silberner, *The Problem of War in Nineteenth Century Economic Thought* (Princeton, 1946).

through. It is an idea urged most strongly by those who are convinced that substitution of another system for the capitalistic economy would automatically remove the causes of war, those causes being economic ones.

It is of course most desirable to remove the causes of war, but this is no easy task, to be accomplished by saying *"Presto change."* Much dispute exists in the first place as to what are the causes of war,[16] and this raises a question as to the authority which is able to determine them. Each party to a dispute would doubtless insist that his cause was real, while that of his opponent was unreal. Assuming that the causes of war could be ascertained, it would appear that they could be removed only by an authority of overwhelming strength. If communism were declared to be a cause of war, it would not be lightly surrendered by those who believe in it; nor would capitalism. And if, by some providential intervention, all causes of war were removed today, a thousand new causes would develop tomorrow, for the causes of strife are ever changing.

One must conclude that the causes of war can be eliminated only by a powerful international government, continuously at work, able to decide authoritatively what is a cause of war, to legislate or otherwise provide a remedy, and to enforce its decisions upon those who disagree. So long as nations exist, there will be causes of strife between them, and this would be true of the most perfect communistic theory; and when there are no longer nations, causes of strife and the use of force as between individuals will still have to be handled by law and government. It is always one of the primary functions of government to remove causes of strife, but the mere statement, without implementation, that the causes of war must be removed is no solution to the problem of war.

EDUCATION. The same sort of an answer must be given to those who say that education is the only answer. Education to what? If it is intended to teach people to dislike war, it is a work of supererogation, since practically everyone already dislikes war and, in any case, war will not cease merely because it is disliked. If it is intended to train every human being, or nation, to such a point that war will not be needed, we are again approaching philosophical anarchy. This would mean omniscience and infallibility on the part of each, so that there would always be agreement as to rights and justice; it would mean also that each would respect the conclusion reached. Not all the

[16] See Wright, *Study of War*, II, Chap. xix, and elsewhere. Professor Wright concludes that the cause of war is the absence of law and organization to control war.

preachers and teachers and philosophers, or even the mighty power of government, have been able to raise human beings to such a level of perfection.

There is a further question: who is to decide what is to be taught? The only possible answer, and it is a dangerous answer, is that an international authority should decide upon the curriculum and should do the teaching. No nation would agree to such control. Such an authority could not be established, and if it were established, it would be confronted with the question of what to teach. Thus, we are back where we started. Education, like the removal of the causes of war, is something much to be desired, but a uniform education could only be achieved through international government. It is a problem in itself, not a solution of the problem of war.

PASSIVE RESISTANCE.[17] A few years ago there was strong support for the proposition that the way to eliminate war is to refuse to support war. Students, preachers, and others took formal pledges never to support another war; various organizations worked to this end. The tide of interest in this concept has now diminished greatly, but the concept itself must be examined.

It should be said, in the first place, that those who live up to their pledge and refuse to fight in war (conscientious objectors) cannot be dismissed as cowards. On the contrary, they face disgrace, ostracism, even execution. The quarrel is not with their character or their courage, but with their judgment. In these cases, the individual claims a right to decide for himself what is right and what is wrong; he rejects the community decision, and does not accept its law. He decides for himself that war is bad, or that he is not willing to kill his fellow men. If enough persons should accept this view, in all countries, there would be no war; but also, there would be no solution. Passive resistance destroys the means—granted that they are stupid means and of uncertain result—but offers no substitute for war as a means of upholding rights or remedying wrongs. It puts peace above justice, and this attitude has always been rejected by human beings. It is a negative, rather than a constructive, approach to a solution. It leaves force supreme, if the other party uses force; if both parties refrain from force, it leaves the situation as it is, however bad that may be.

Some passive resisters, dissatisfied with this result, have sought a more positive approach through mass passive resistance, or "non-violent coercion." Their inspiration is derived from the success of Gandhi

[17] See Devere Allen, *Pacifism in the Modern World* (New York, 1929); Merle Curti, *The American Peace Crusade, 1815-1860* (Durham, 1929); A.J. Muste, *Non-Violence in an Aggressive World* (New York, 1940); J. E. Stoner, *S. O. Levinson and the Pact of Paris* (Chicago, 1943).

in India, who was able not only to resist superior force, but to compel it to accept his wishes. Through organized effort, they would say, passive resistance can be a powerful instrument, a constructive force. But if this be true, then it is a weapon, a means to an end, just as war is; it could be used for purposes as unworthy as those of which war is accused. It would be necessary to ask who is its leader, and what ends does he pursue? He might be a Hitler or a Huey Long, rather than a Gandhi. He cannot be made to order for each occasion.

The difficulty with the pacifist position is that it is an individualist position, taken precisely in that field for which law and government were created. It is impossible to permit each individual to decide what is justice for himself; that must be a community judgment, at least in those fields where force is threatened. We must conclude, then, that passive resistance does not offer a substitute for war; it does not provide the means for upholding rights and for remedying wrongs which humanity demands should be upheld and remedied even if this involves the use of war.

DISARMAMENT. The greatest effort so far put forward for the purpose of escaping the burden of war is doubtless the idea of disarmament.[18] The American people and government have for long supported this as a panacea; the League of Nations made intensive studies and exhaustive efforts to reach agreement, all of which were fruitless. For this, there were two general reasons: the technical difficulties, and the inconsistency in principle of the proposal. Space cannot be taken here for discussion of the technical problems involved; it is uncertain whether they could have been solved if other difficulties could have been overcome.

Worse than the technical problems, however, is the matter of logic and principle involved. To disarm is to put the cart before the horse. No state can afford to disarm so long as war is the only means by which it can uphold its interests as against other nations. If war were not used, there would be no need for arms, and disarmament would be automatic and doubtless precipitate, for no state wishes to spend three-quarters of its taxes upon arms; but so long as war exists, armaments must be maintained, at whatever cost. That this is a vicious circle was proved by the experience of the disarmament effort. The First Hague Peace Conference (1899) was called to reduce "the staggering burden of armaments"; instead, it issued the Convention for the Pacific Settlement of International Disputes, and established the Permanent Court of Arbitration. The Second Hague Conference (1907) was sought for the same purpose, but disarmament was finally dropped from its

---

18 The disarmament effort is more fully discussed at §§ 136 and 156 below.

agenda. The Covenant of the League of Nations called for reduction of armaments (not disarmament), and the League held hundreds of meetings in an impressive effort to reach agreement. Yet its whole history can be summed up in the change of the name of one of its committees, which started as a committee on Reduction of Armaments, and ended as a committee on Arbitration, Security, and Disarmament. The latter order of words represents the evolution of the thinking of the League.

There were two approaches to the problem: the direct method, at first pursued by the United States and later by the Soviet Union, which held that the way to disarm is to disarm; and the indirect method, which regards disarmament as dependent on security. This latter principle, logically inevitable, dominated all subsequent efforts, and made agreement impossible at the Conference on Reduction and Limitation of Armaments (1932), even though the draft treaty there proposed invited states to write in whatever limits they were willing to state.

Arms do not cause war; it is war which produces arms. The effort to regulate the private trade in arms, so popular in the United States in the 1930's, is still further away from the mark. The effort may be worth while from the viewpoint of such financial saving as could be effected by minor reductions, or from the psychological viewpoint of encouraging confidence among nations. But disarmament, even if complete, would not solve the problem of war; it would provide no means for settling disputes, for upholding rights, or for remedying wrongs. Men would still fight with fists and sticks and stones. If war is to remain the means by which intelligent human beings are to serve these purposes, then it will be the duty of each state to build its warmaking power to the greatest strength possible.

133. OUTLAWRY OF WAR

Another approach to the problem, very popular in the United States, was the movement to outlaw war; and it has some positive achievement to its credit. It is a surprising thing that not until around 1921 had the idea occurred to anyone that war should be declared illegal. One reason for this was, doubtless, that an outlaw is presumed to be in flight from government; but there was in the community of nations no government, no sheriff which might set a posse in pursuit of the outlaw state. The movement in the United States, however, opposed the idea of an international government with power to act against the state which illegally went to war. It was content to issue a *fiat,* and to have a court which could declare that a state was an outlaw, and it fought bitterly against any further authority in the international system. It had the important result, however, of leading into the so-called Kellogg Pact or Pact of Paris, more properly, the General Treaty for the Renunciation of War.

PACT OF PARIS. On April 6, 1927, the anniversary of American entrance into World War I, M. Briand, then Foreign Minister of France, announced in a newspaper interview that "France would be willing to subscribe publicly with the United States to any mutual engagement tending to outlaw war, to use an American expression, as between these two countries." No official answer was returned, and on June 20 the French government submitted a draft treaty for consideration, which was considered for six months. Meanwhile public opinion was pressing for action, and on December 28, 1927, Secretary Kellogg answered with the proposal that, instead of a bilateral treaty, an effort should be made to obtain the adherence of all the principal powers of the world to a declaration renouncing war as an instrument of national policy. After some negotiation, during which Secretary Kellogg uttered certain important interpretations of the treaty,[19] it was signed on August 27, 1928, in a historic ceremony at the Quai d'Orsay, and ratifications subsequently poured in until they numbered sixty-four. It is a brief document, containing the following two articles of substance:

Article 1. The high contracting parties solemnly declare in the name of their respective peoples that they condemn recourse to war for the solution of international controversies, and renounce it as an instrument of national policy in their relations with one another.

Article 2. The high contracting parties agree that the settlement or solution of all disputes or conflicts of whatever nature or of whatever origin they may be, which may arise among them, shall never be sought except by pacific means.

The two articles are complementary. Technically, war is not outlawed; it is condemned and renounced, but it is not declared to be illegal. Moreover, it is renounced only as an instrument of national policy. The meaning of this phrase is not clear, but it is of importance as leaving free the use of war for an *international* policy, and thus permitting the use of forcible sanctions which, however, are of course not provided for by the treaty.

[19] *Notes Exchanged between the United States and Other Powers on the subject of a Multilateral Treaty for the Renunciation of War* (Washington, Government Printing Office, 1928), p. 33. The correspondence is printed also in *Int. Con.*, No. 243 (October, 1928) and in D. P. Myers, *Origin and Conclusion of the Paris Pact, W.P.F.,* 12, No. 2 (1929). Mr. Kellogg's speech containing the interpretations is in the *Proc. Am. Soc. Int. Law,* 1928, p. 141. See J. T. Shotwell, *War as an Instrument of National Policy* (New York, 1929); Q. Wright, "The Outlawry of War and the Law of War," *A.J.,* 47 (1953), p. 365.

The second article is the more important of the two, and, so far as the wording of the treaty goes, more nearly makes war illegal than does Article 1. The statement is broad and covers every type of dispute, but it is a negative form of statement, and creates no positive obligation to seek a settlement. If a settlement is sought, it must be by pacific means, but one state may be satisfied to leave things as they are and refuse to take any steps whatever toward a settlement. Thus the state which desires to maintain the *status quo* has a distinct, and perhaps unjust, advantage.

The real meaning of the treaty, however, is not so much to be found in its actual wording as in the explanations concerning it communicated by Secretary Kellogg to the other signatories and accepted by them—explanations which greatly limit its meaning. The most important of these interpretative statements was that concerning self-defense.

There is nothing in the American draft of an antiwar treaty which restricts or impairs in any way the right of self-defense. That right is inherent in every sovereign state and is implicit in every treaty. Every nation is free at all times and regardless of treaty provisions to defend its territory from attack or invasion and it alone is competent to decide whether circumstances require recourse to war in self-defense.

Secretary Kellogg had rejected the French proposal to outlaw only "aggressive war," yet his interpretation admitted that the treaty applies only to wars of aggression, since it does not exclude wars of self-defense. The exception of self-defense may be said to admit almost any war; it does so unquestionably when each state "alone is competent to decide whether circumstances require recourse to war in self-defense." In modern days no state would admit that it was fighting an aggressive war, but reasons of self-defense can always be found so long as each state is its own judge. The legal effect of the treaty is undoubtedly much weakened by this exception.

It is unfortunately true that the Pact of Paris, of itself, has little legal effect,[20] but it states a vitally important principle. It could have been made highly effective if certain legal rules or certain machinery had been adopted to implement it. If, for example, there were a positive obligation to arbitrate disputes, there could be said to be a violation of the treaty when arbitration was refused. Or, if a definition of aggression had been agreed upon, it might be possible to say when the treaty

[20] When added to the Covenant of the League, however, it produced important legal effects for those bound by the Covenant, and the League made efforts to harmonize it with the Covenant. See Report of the Committee for the Amendment of the Covenant of the League of Nations in order to Bring It into Harmony with the Pact of Paris, 1930.V.2. See also *Records of the Eleventh Assembly*, First Committee, pp. 131-32.

had been violated. But no definition of aggression has thus far been found, and each state was left free by Secretary Kellogg to make its own definition for its own purposes.

It does not follow, however, that the treaty was insincere, or an idle gesture. On the contrary, it is one of the most important documents in human history. Never before had public opinion arrived at a stage at which it dared to deliver a frontal attack upon war. Never before had humanity dared affirm, even in principle, that war is illegal. Regardless of legal uncertainties, the pact has made its impression upon the mind of the world; it has been accepted by public opinion everywhere; and it became one of the bases of the Nuremburg trial, whose affirmation by the United Nations would seem to accept as a rule of customary law that aggressive war is illegal.

Thus, the outlawry-of-war movement made a contribution toward solution of the problem of war but, like the Pact of Paris, which was its fruit, it was incomplete. The mere declaration that war, or a certain type of war, is illegal is not sufficient to stop war. There must be an agency with authority to decide that the law has been violated, and strength sufficient to stop the aggressor.

134. NEUTRALITY

It may be said that a discussion of neutrality is irrelevant to the problem of controlling war, and there would be much truth in the assertion. While it has been argued that the law of neutrality restricts the spread of war, it cannot well be argued that neutrality is a method by which war could be eliminated. It nevertheless deserves some consideration, partly because of its historical importance in relation to war, and partly because it brings to a head the issue between national and international action, between isolation and collective security.

FUNDAMENTAL PRINCIPLES. War, we have noted, creates a certain legal status. Any state has the right to go to war; it has equally a right to remain neutral. The neutral state announces no judgment upon the issue; it takes no part in the conflict; it displays its impartiality by refraining from any act injurious or favorable to either belligerent. There are two legal positions to be considered: the belligerent has certain rights and duties; and the neutral has certain rights and duties. The problem of international law has been to find a proper equilibration between them.

On the one hand, the belligerent state has the right to make war against its opponent, and this implies a right to take certain repressive measures against that opponent, even though these measures result in injury to neutral states. On the other hand, the neutral state, though it must respect belligerent rights, cannot legally be compelled to suffer too much from a quarrel in which it has no concern. In this sense, neutrality has been of much value: it has set limits to unlicensed warfare. But the conflict between belligerent and neutral reached a breaking point. A belligerent, fighting for what it conceives to be its very existence, is disposed to disregard the rights of neutrals. In such a conflict the neutral is at a decided disadvantage in comparison with its prepared opponent, and in the long struggle to balance the rights of belligerent and neutral, the neutral has lost steadily.

In the first place, the neutral must not participate in the conflict, even in an impartial manner. It cannot, officially, express its sympathy for either side. According to the Convention Concerning the Rights and Duties of Neutral Powers in Naval War, signed at the Second Hague Conference, "The supply, in any manner, directly or indirectly, by a neutral Power to a belligerent Power, of warships, ammunition, or war material of any kind whatever, is forbidden." Loans could not be made to either belligerent, nor credits extended. A neutral could not allow its territory to be used as a base of operations against an enemy. Permission to a belligerent for its troops to cross neutral territory must be refused. The duty to prevent the construction of a warship for a belligerent, in a neutral state, was illustrated by the famous case of the *Alabama*. Except for emergency, captured ships could not be taken to neutral ports; nor could a belligerent set up a prize court in a neutral state,[21] nor could a belligerent warship take refuge in a neutral port for longer than a specified time.[22] A capture could not be made in neutral waters; during the Civil War the United States apologized to Brazil for the capture of the *Florida* within her territorial limits. Certainly a neutral state could expect, and had a duty to do all that was reasonably necessary to assure, that its territory should not be made the scene of military operations, as Belgium did in two world wars.

But a neutral state had no duty to prevent the sale of munitions of war by private individuals from within its borders, and at this point the rights of belligerents began to appear. If a neutral state had no duty to prevent this trade, the trade was nevertheless illegal, and the belligerent

[21] *The Appam*, 243 U.S. 124 (1917). In general as to the duties of neutrals, see Bishop, pp. 651-85; Briggs, pp. 1026-45; Fenwick, Chap. xxix-xxxii; Hackworth, *Digest*, VII, Chap. xxiv; Hudson, *Cases*, pp. 1428-65; Hyde, III, Title K; Moore, *Digest*, VII, Chap. xxviii.

[22] For this reason, the *Alabama* went bravely forth to destruction from a French port during the Civil War.

state had a right to stop it and to penalize it.[23] On the other hand, if a belligerent were able to avail itself of this source of supply, it would have a great advantage over the belligerent which was unable to do so. Thus England, during the world wars, was able to draw needed materials from the United States and elsewhere, while at the same time preventing Germany from doing so. The burden was upon the belligerent to prevent such supplies from reaching his enemy, and in the interplay of rights and duties thus created is to be found the most fertile cause for friction.

For the most part this situation was covered by the laws of contraband and blockade, and the question thus presented was: how far should a belligerent be permitted to interfere with the ordinary trade and intercourse between private individuals in neutral states and the enemy state and persons therein? Originally, the belligerent had no compunctions in seizing anything destined for his enemy, but gradually his rights were restricted. There grew up lists of articles to be regarded as contraband, and therefore as subject to capture by a belligerent. In legal theory, the basis of this list was the usefulness of the articles for purposes of warmaking, but what articles deserved to be placed upon the list was an extremely and increasingly difficult problem, dependent upon the nature of the article and the uses to which it might be put from one period to another, and upon the changes in the methods of warfare. If contraband lists were settled for one war, or agreed upon by convention, new discoveries in warmaking would cause the limits thus set to be disregarded, with the argument that certain articles had now become of direct use in military operations.[24] By the time of the Second World War, practically everything was included in the Allies' contraband list.

The other important weapon by which the belligerent defended himself against supplies going to his enemy was blockade. The declaration of a blockade meant cutting off all access to the blockaded districts, regardless of whether the goods carried were contraband or not. The Declaration of Paris in 1856 laid down the rule that a blockade to be binding upon neutrals must be effective—must be able, that is, actu-

---

[23] Article 7 of the above-quoted Hague Convention says: "A neutral Power is not bound to prevent the export or transit, for the use of either belligerent, of arms, ammunition, or, in general, of anything which could be of use to an army or fleet."

[24] Since the time of Grotius, a three-fold classification of contraband has been attempted: (1) articles of use only in war (absolute contraband); (2) those of no use in war (not contraband at all); (3) those of use both in war and in peace (conditional contraband). But the result is simply to make the problem more intricate, as the belligerent shifts articles from one group to another. The story of neutrality is told in P. C. Jessup and F. Deak, *Neutrality: Its History, Economics and Law*, 4 vols. (New York, 1935-36); and see C. G. Fenwick, *American Neutrality: Trial and Failure* (New York, 1940).

ally to stop access to the enemy. On the other hand, rather than provide naval strength to meet this requirement, belligerents might extend the lists of contraband until, without blockade, they could claim to capture everything within sight. During the two world wars, blockade was extended to cover not merely one port, but the entire continent of Europe, and to prevent export from, as well as import into, that area.

In order to guard themselves against violations of their rights, belligerents maintained the right of visit and search. A neutral vessel suspected of contraband carriage or of blockade running could be stopped and searched upon the high seas; if it resisted, whether innocent or not, it could be sunk. This practice, always a source of abuse and friction, has been extended to cover the world. Contraband, blockade, and visit and search were stretched into a system which controlled the movements of practically every ship in the world.

It was not difficult in earlier days to pick out the articles essential to warfare, for their number was limited. In a modern war, however, far more than guns and powder are needed; indeed, there is little for which war does not call. The vast size of modern armies makes such things as clothing and food primarily military supplies; indeed, the civilian population is put upon rations so that the armies may be supplied. The change is much more fundamental than this, however. It raises the whole question as to the distinction between combatants and noncombatants. Hitherto, war had been conducted against combatant forces, and the law of war carefully protected the civilian population. But now it could be argued that the activities of civilians at home were an essential part of warmaking; and it could be said with very good reason that a girl manufacturing shells in a munitions factory was doing as much to win the war as the infantryman at the front.[25]

FAILURE OF THE LAW OF NEUTRALITY. Thus the law of neutrality broke down completely in the First World War. No effort was made to revive it, and little attention was paid to it during the Second World War. The position of the neutral had become untenable in the face of modern war. If he wished to maintain his rights as a neutral, he found that he must fight for them, but then he was no longer a neutral. This was the experience of the United States in the First World War; and a strong opinion, reflected in the Neutrality Legislation of 1935, asserted that if the maintenance of neutral rights leads to war, then we should not maintain those rights. But this means simply surrender and encouragement to the aggressor, and it led to Pearl Harbor in 1941. The conclusion is inevitable that neutrality leads to war, rather than discourages war.

[25] See § 3, above.

But the lesson is deeper than this. Neutrality in effect disavows desire to stop war; it rejects any share in the community responsibility for preventing war. To surrender to the aggressor, as the United States did before Pearl Harbor, allows the aggressor to grow in strength until the day when he is strong enough to devour the unprepared neutral. Neutrality has been shown to be both immoral and unpracticable, and its failure has cleared the thinking of many, and permitted a more sensible attitude toward the problem of war.[26] Certainly, neutrality served in no way as a substitute for war in settling disputes, in upholding rights, or in remedying wrongs.

135. CONCLUSIONS: COLLECTIVE SECURITY

From the above brief survey of ideas and efforts to limit war, certain conclusions may be drawn. It is probably as untrue to say that war can be completely eliminated as to say that the use of force can be eliminated from life; the effort must be made to find substitutes which can serve the functions which war now performs. Such a substitute should be able to perform at least the three functions mentioned above, and to do this a strong international organization is needed. None of the proposals above considered fulfill these functions. Disarmament might reduce the cost of war, in blood or money, but it offers no solution and no security, and cannot therefore be accepted. Both education and the removal of the causes of war are highly desirable, but both beg the question; neither can be accomplished except through international authority. Passive resistance, in an individual sense, means surrender to injustice; in the mass sense, it presents the same problem as war, since it is also a weapon which must be controlled. War cannot be outlawed unless there is a sheriff to handle the outlaw; the warmaker can be stopped only by a force superior to him, and the only way to provide such a force is through the collective action of the community of nations.

Thus, we are forced back always to the need of international organization—though we are far from a final solution when we have said this. Modern interdependence calls pressingly for limitations upon national freedom of action; those limitations must be set by law, and the law must be made by the community. Modern war, from which no one escapes, faces a nation with the choice between continuous fight-

---

[26] It has, however, been revived today by India and other states in the idea of "neutralism." It represents a natural feeling, with which Americans can sympathize historically, but these nations will doubtless learn, as Americans learnt, that it is no solution.

ing to uphold or achieve its desires, and collective action which can assure those of its desires which are approved by the community. Every state gains by the collective protection of those rights agreed upon by the community; as to other claims or ambitions which a state has, it may be recalled that the road of history is strewn with the wrecks of states which have sought to have their own way.

The inescapable conclusion is that states must accept responsibility for organized community action, and submit to the law of the community. But this they will not do, and should not do, until the community can give them at least as much assurance of justice and security as war has given them. The international organization, then, must have behind it sufficient authority and physical force to prevent wrongful use of force by one state against another; and this is the great issue which faces the peoples of the world today. The pressure of great forces pushes the world toward international government; ancient tradition and loyalties to the sovereign state resist these pressures. International organization, as we have seen, has been steadily developing. The first effort to control war through international organization was the League of Nations, and this effort toward "collective security" must now be studied.

Chapter 16

THE LEAGUE OF NATIONS AND WAR

The Covenant of the League of Nations attacked war from various angles. One of the two functions of the League, as stated in the preamble, was "to achieve international peace and security"; but the other function, to "promote international cooperation," was not dissociated from this purpose. The Covenant contains no general statement that war was thereby made illegal. Its provisions, however, postponed war in every case, made it illegal in some situations, and adopted in legal principle, if not in practical possibility, sanctions against the illegal warmaker. An effort was made to guarantee independence and territory. There were excellent provisions for the peaceful settlement of disputes, and it might be said that the general principle underlying the Covenant was that there should be no war until there had been at least a preliminary effort at settlement in accordance with the procedures prescribed. Reduction of armaments was also to be undertaken.

The provisions for the maintenance of peace are to be found in Articles 8-17 of the Covenant, and we will examine the experience of the League of Nations with regard to control of war in the order of these articles.

136. REDUCTION OF ARMAMENTS[1]

The League did not at first regard disarmament as an important step toward elimination of war. The Covenant does not call for disarma-

[1] From the vast literature concerning disarmament, the following references are taken: *Armaments Year Book* (annual) of the League of Nations; P. J. N. Baker, *Disarmament* (London, 1926); C. Loosli-Usteri, *Geschichte der Konferenz für die Herabsetzung und Begrenzung der Rüstungen 1932-1934* (Zurich, 1940); S. de Madariaga, *Disarmament* (New York, 1929); D. P. Myers, *World Disarmament: Its Problems and Prospects* (Boston, 1932); Th. Niemeyer, *Handbuch der Abrüstungsprobleme*, 3 vols. (Berlin-Grunewald, 1928); N. Sloutzky, *The World Armaments Race, 1919-1939* (Geneva Studies, XII, No. 1, July 1941); M. Tate, *The Disarmament Illusion* (New York, 1942); J. W. Wheeler-Bennett, *The Pipe Dream of Peace* (New York, 1935).

ment, but for reduction of arms, and no obligation was imposed upon Members by articles 8-9 except the contingent obligation that if and when a limit of armaments had been set, no Member could thereafter exceed that limit except by permission of the Council.[2] There was simply the statement that the reduction of armaments was desirable, and the criteria for such reduction were to be, on the one hand, national safety, and, on the other hand, a strength sufficient for "the enforcement by common action of international obligations." Consideration was also to be given to the geographic situation and special circumstances of each state. The Council was not authorized to compel reduction; it could only formulate plans, upon which Members must agree. It was affirmed that the private manufacture of munitions was "open to grave objections"; and Members agreed to exchange "full and frank information" concerning the scale of their armaments, military programs, and war industries. Article 9 provided for a permanent committee, of military character, to advise the Council.

DIRECT METHOD. The Council set to work at once along the lines of what was called the "direct method," which asserted that the way to disarm is to disarm. The Permanent Advisory Commission asserted that reduction was impossible until (1) integral execution of the military, naval, and aerial clauses of the treaty of peace had been accomplished, (2) this execution was assured by international supervision, and (3) the League of Nations was organized for rapid emergency action. The Assembly, dissatisfied with this lack of constructive proposal, demanded a committee not composed of military experts, and set up the Temporary Mixed Commission. A scheme was put forward by Lord Esher which called for a mathematical coefficient, or "yardstick," which he set at thirty thousand military and air force men, and which assigned (for example) six units to France, four to Italy and Poland, and three to Great Britain. It was rejected on the ground that numbers alone do not measure military strength, and that such factors as material and financial strength must be taken into consideration.[3] The direct method failed partly because of the political problem, to which we shall turn in a moment, but also largely because of the enormous technical difficulties involved. These were later summed up in one of the numerous questions in a questionnaire sent out by the League of Nations Preparatory Commission for the Disarmament Conference of 1932: "By what standards is it possible to measure the arma-

[2] It was therefore important to reach agreement upon such limits, so that the Council might acquire jurisdiction; and this helps to explain the laborious and continuing effort to arrive at a treaty.

[3] Report of the Temporary Mixed Commission, *L. of N. Doc.*, A. 31. 1922, C.T.A. 173.

ments of one country against the armaments of another—e.g., numbers, equipment, expenditures, etc.?"[4] Who is a soldier—regular army, trained reserves, National Guard, merchant marine, policeman, Boy Scouts? What is an instrument of war[5]—a gun mounted on a truck, and therefore the truck, the wheels, the axle grease? How is it possible to measure naval and air force as against land forces? What are the relative needs of each nation in each military category? When the Soviet Union, at the Disarmament Conference, suggested total disarmament, the British delegate replied that this would leave Russia with the largest armed force, since her vast area would require more police, customs, and frontier guards than any other country would have. How can mobilization of men be measured against mobilization of industry? Today, the technical problems are far greater; we shall have occasion to mention them later.

INDIRECT METHOD. From the very beginning, the question of security had been raised, particularly by France. In 1922, on the basis of proposals by Lord Robert Cecil, the Assembly adopted the famous Resolution XIV, which became the foundation of later disarmament efforts. It is summarized as follows:

> No scheme for the reduction of armaments can be successful unless it is general. In the present state of the world, the majority of Governments could not carry out a reduction of armaments unless they received satisfactory guarantees for the safety of their respective countries; such guarantees should be of a general character. And, finally, there can be no question of providing such guarantees except in consideration of a definite undertaking to reduce armaments.[6]

Thus disarmament became linked with security, and security involved arbitration and many other elements, so that the efforts of the League were necessarily directed toward building up a coherent system for the whole matter of peace.

During 1922 and 1923 the Temporary Mixed Commission prepared a draft Treaty of Mutual Assistance which was communicated to the various governments by the Fourth Assembly. Its first article declared that "aggressive war is an international crime"; but a war waged by a state which had accepted a judgment according to the proper proce-

---

[4] Report of the Preparatory Commission, quoted in *Ten Years of World Cooperation* (League of Nations, 1930), pp. 83-84.

[5] "The Commission examined the matter and penetrated into a regular labyrinth of subtleties and distinctions with the result that they declared that while the steel and wood necessary to manufacture a rifle were war material, the complete rifle, if stored up in an army depot and not in actual service, ceased to be war material and became an inoffensive object of peace." Madariaga, p. 200.

[6] *Ten Years of World Cooperation*, p. 57; see also p. 59, and *Records of the Third Assembly*, Plenary, p. 291.

dure was not to be regarded as aggressive if it did not violate Article 10 of the Covenant. Sweeping powers were given to the Council for the purpose of preventing war. On the one hand, signatory states were obligated to come to the aid of one of their number when the Council decided that it was the object of aggression, provided the latter had reduced its armaments as stipulated. On the other hand, if hostilities actually broke loose, the Council was to determine within four days which was the aggressor state, and put into motion against it the machinery of the treaty. Regionalism was recognized in the provision that no state need exert itself beyond its own continent. The theory behind the treaty was that it would furnish enough security to induce states to reduce their armaments; but the treaty did not actually give this assurance.

The great difficulty was to determine when aggression had appeared. Over this problem League bodies had already been struggling, and a special committee which had been set to work upon it had produced a detailed "Commentary on the Definition of a Case of Aggression," in lieu of an agreed definition. The Permanent Advisory Commission had, insofar as it was able to agree at all, reported that it was "impossible to decide, even in theory, what constitutes a case of aggression," and that the former double test of mobilization or violation of the frontier had quite lost its value. The special committee accepted this view and reported that all that could be done was to endow the Council with complete discretion in deciding which was the aggressor. A committee of jurists which studied the treaty considered that it would be better to substitute the word "war" for the word "aggression," since the latter could not be defined.[7] This was the chief cause for the failure of the treaty, but there were other objections to it. The Council was not trusted for the exercise of so important a function; and there was still a fundamental dislike for assuming responsibility for collective sanctions.

Conference for the Reduction and Limitation of Armaments. The Sixth Assembly set up a preparatory commission to prepare for a general conference on disarmament. For four years it worked exhaustively on the subject, in an effort to prepare an acceptable draft treaty. Naval limitation now entered into the picture, there having been several conferences dealing with it.[8] There was disagreement at every point. The United States, Great Britain, Germany, and others demanded that reduction should apply to all armed forces, including

---

[7] This debate is summarized, with pertinent quotations, in *Int. Con.*, No. 264 (1930). The Treaty of Mutual Assistance is given in *ibid.*, No. 201 (1924).

[8] Conferences on naval armaments were held at Washington, 1921-22, at Geneva in 1927, and at London in 1931.

trained reserves, and all materials available for immediate mobilization; this was opposed by other countries as negating the advantage of rapid mobilization, and as favoring states with most industrial strength. Should navies be limited by total tonnage, or by categories of vessels? Should limitation of air armaments apply to civil aviation? Should there be one general treaty, or separate ones for naval questions? Could budgetary limitation serve as an adequate measure? Should inspection and enforcement be authorized, or should reliance be placed on the good faith of nations? The entry of Russia brought in a new problem, for Litvinov proposed absolute and universal disarmament within four years. Germany demanded that a conference be called and that the general disarmament promised in the peace treaties be provided.

A draft convention was finally prepared, as of December 9, 1930, calling for limitation and, so far as consistent with national safety, reduction of armaments. Tables were provided for different categories, with blank spaces to be filled in by each member as it wished. The conference assembled on February 2, 1932, with sixty states represented (including the United States). The Russian proposal for general and immediate disarmament, and its alternative proposal for progressive and proportional reduction, were not accepted. The French proposed an international police force, which Germany opposed as intended to maintain the inequalities of the peace treaties. President Hoover proposed reduction by one third, with specific statement for various categories. The British also had suggestions for "qualitative" reduction. Most agreement was reached with regard to reduction of weapons of offense; tentative agreement was also given on July 23, 1932, to budgetary limitation, control of arms manufacture, supervision by a disarmament commission, prohibition of both chemical warfare and aerial bombardment of civilians. Practical implementation of these principles produced difficulty, and no agreement could be had as to naval limitation.

In general, it was impossible to reconcile the French demand for security, the Russian and American demands for direct disarmament, and the German demand for equality. Germany, indeed, withdrew, and the Conference was able to reconvene in 1933 only after the Five Powers had approved equality for her. Meanwhile, the political situation in Europe was becoming disturbed, and Mr. Ramsay MacDonald laid new proposals before the conference. The United States went so far as to agree to consult with other states in case of aggression and, if she agreed as to the aggressor, to take no action which would interfere with the efforts of other states to maintain peace. By now, however, Germany was under Hitler and was rearming, and France was seeking alliances. In October, 1933, Germany withdrew and the conference met no more. Studies and negotiations continued and the General Commission met in May, 1936; but the air was filled with political thunder, and the effort was fruitless. Twelve years of intensive effort had failed; they remain as lessons for the future.

137. TERRITORIAL INTEGRITY

Article 10, according to President Wilson, was the "backbone of the whole Covenant," and around it many battles have been waged.[9] Generally speaking, the principle which it embodied was one which we have earlier discussed, that title by conquest is to be denied; but the article had other far-reaching implications. Some feared that the Treaty of Versailles, or the *status quo* in general, would be guaranteed by Article 10; others feared that American mothers would be called upon to sacrifice their sons in faraway corners of the world in which the United States had no interest. After such portentous expectations as these, a study of Article 10 as it developed is something of an anticlimax.

By Article 10, Members "undertake to respect and preserve as against external aggression the territorial integrity and existing political independence of all Members of the League." How far Article 10 imposed a legal obligation upon Members to support by arms an attacked state was a subject of theoretical debate. President Wilson asserted that it was only a moral obligation, since each state was free to make its own decision as to which was the aggressor; and it was held that the sanctions of Article 16 were not applicable to Article 10. The Council could only advise; it could give orders to no state. Nor could it advise except by unanimous agreement, so that any Member of the Council which refused to cooperate could block the entire recommendation. The obligation assumed was only "as against external aggression." Again we encounter the difficulty of explaining what is meant by aggression. There would seem to be no doubt that self-defense would be permitted under this rule; but if the defending state should

[9] See as to Article 10, J. C. Baak, *Der Inhalt des modernen Völkerrechts und der Ursprung des Artikels 10 der Völkerbundsatzung* (Berlin, 1926); S. Engel, *League Reform: An Analysis of Official Proposals and Discussions 1936-1939* (Geneva Studies, XI, 1940); H. Kelsen, *Legal Technique in International Law* (Geneva Studies, X, Dec. 1939), pp. 67-81; T. Komarnicki, *La question de l'intégrité territoriale dans le Pacte de la Société des Nations (l'Article X du Pacte)*, (Paris, 1923); Ray, *Commentaire*, pp. 343-71; A. Rolin, "L'article 10 du Pacte de la Société des Nations," *Münch*, II, pp. 453-88; A. A. H. Struycken, "La Société des Nations et l'intégrité territoriale," *Bib. Viss.*, 1 (1923), pp. 91-156; B. Williams, *State Security and the League of Nations* (Baltimore, 1927); Yepes and da Silva, I, pp. 278-310. For League documents, see list in Aufricht, pp. 48-50.

win the war, could it seize territory from its adversary? There was little force to the argument that Article 10 was simply a guarantee of the peace settlement, and perpetuated the *status quo* in general. There was clearly room for legitimate change; the only change forbidden was that accomplished by violence.

Within the League itself, two opposing currents of interpretation appeared at once, the one fearing infringement upon the freedom of national action, the other fearing that weakening of Article 10 would weaken that security which attracted so many states to the League. The former attitude was represented by a Canadian amendment, offered at the First Assembly, to abolish Article 10. This was later modified into an interpretative resolution, limiting the application of the article without destroying its principle. The other viewpoint was emphatically represented by Persia, who cast the only negative vote against the proposed resolution—although there were twenty-two states absent or not voting.[10] The chairman declared the motion neither adopted nor rejected and there was thus no official change. Nevertheless, the current opinion within the League did not favor effective use of Article 10, and it was little called upon.

138. SETTLEMENT OF DISPUTES

Articles 8-10 deal with special problems; with Article 11 we enter upon a coherent system for the maintenance of peace. This article serves as an introduction to the system; it is followed by four articles which provide for the pacific settlement of disputes and which lead up to the determination of aggression. Article 16 provides sanctions, and Article 17 deals with non-members.

PREVENTION OF WAR. Article 11 endowed the League with a wide competence for considering any question capable of disturbing the peace. "Any war or threat of war" was a matter of concern to the entire League, and could no longer be reserved as a matter of national

---

[10] The significant portions of this resolution are as follows:

"It is for the constitutional authorities of each Member to decide, in reference to the obligation of preserving the independence and the integrity of the territory of Members, in what degree the Member is bound to assure the execution of this obligation by employment of its military forces.

"The recommendation made by the Council shall be regarded as being of the highest importance, and shall be taken into consideration by all the Members of the League with the desire to execute their engagements in good faith."

The Canadian efforts seem to have been due partly (they were officially so explained) to their desire to satisfy the United States and secure her entry into the League; and for the same reason many states reluctantly voted affirmatively (e.g., France), and others refrained from voting. *Records of the Fourth Assembly*, Plenary, pp. 73-87.

sovereignty. A meeting of the Council was required upon the request of any Member. The purpose of Article 11, as indicated by its position in the text and as stated by the Assembly in 1928, was to forestall future wars; decision of a dispute upon its merits and actual repression of war were provided for in later articles.

It could not be said that Article 11 gave to the Council the power to arrive at a decision binding upon disputants, and the Council was itself bound by the rule of unanimity with, in this article, no exception made for the votes of the disputants. Nevertheless, the Council was remarkably successful in preventing war, even though it did not always achieve a satisfactory settlement. More disputes were brought up under Article 11 than under other articles, though if the dispute became serious it might be transferred to Article 15, under which the vote of the disputant was not counted. It was possible to intervene under the broad terms of Article 11, even though it might not be possible to do so under other articles.

RENUNCIATION OF WAR. While Article 11 may be regarded as prophylactic in purpose, the following articles put upon Members an obligation to substitute pacific settlement for war as a means of settling disputes, and provided for common action against a Member which failed to observe this obligation. Article 12 required Members to submit all disputes, without exception, to one or the other of the methods of settlement formulated, and "in no case to resort to war until three months after the award by the arbitrators, or the judicial decision, or the report by the Council." They might choose between three (really two) methods of settlement: arbitration, judicial settlement, or inquiry by the Council (conciliation).[11] The result was not so much to proscribe war as to prescribe pacific settlement. Some wars were licit, most became illicit; but the criterion was not sought in the nature of the dispute or the justice of the cause. The test was simply whether an attempt had been made to secure peaceful settlement; and the obligation was to refrain from war against the state which had accepted the results of that settlement. The right of self-help was not taken away finally from the claimant, as it is within a state, but he must now wait for a decision upon the merits of the case. Whatever the situation, the winning party could not undertake a war of execution until three months after the award or recommendation.

[11] Both arbitration and judicial settlement call for decision according to law, and differ only as to machinery. The phrase "judicial settlement" was added after the court was created and refers to settlement by the court, while arbitration implies a tribunal created by the parties. It may now be observed that the Covenant combined into a comprehensive and obligatory system the methods of arbitration and conciliation, whose development was separately traced in an earlier chapter.

ARBITRATION. The methods of pacific settlement suggested in Article 12 were developed in detail by Articles 13-15, and the consequences of failure to live up to these obligations were stated in Article 16. Arbitration (which term for our present purposes will be used to include judicial settlement) was not itself compulsory, but was one of two alternatives. The parties themselves must agree that the dispute is "suitable for submission to arbitration"; they were not bound to submit cases of the types listed in the following paragraph, although the presumption was that these types should be submitted to arbitration. If arbitration were chosen, a decision was inevitable, and there was no loophole for escape. Such a decision was based upon law, and Members were obligated to carry out in full good faith the award announced. If they did this, they could not be legally attacked; but if a state refused to accept the award, the Council "shall propose what steps should be taken to give effect thereto." Here war was possible, for any state was free to go to war against the state which rejected the award. There was no assurance that the Council could guarantee execution to the state in whose favor an award had been announced, and its only recourse might be to go to war against the state whom it had defeated in court.

INQUIRY BY COUNCIL. If the disputants did not agree upon arbitration, they were bound by Article 15, paragraph 1, to submit the matter to the Council. The dispute must be one "likely to lead to a rupture," but a refusal of the Council on this ground to hear the case would encourage the rejected applicant to take violent measures so as to produce a rupture. For the purposes of the dispute, the disputant states might be given special representation on the Council. The Council could seek advice from a committee of jurists, or from the Permanent Court, or could appoint a committee from its own membership, with one member as Rapporteur. The duty of the Council was to "endeavor to effect a settlement of the dispute," and it had a range of action limited only by its own powers of imagination as applied to the opposing desires of the disputants. It was actually very successful in finding a settlement satisfactory to all disputants, until the last great clashes with the fascist states.

If the dispute was not settled to the satisfaction of all parties, and thus ended, the Council was required to publish a report, and to make "recommendations which are deemed just and proper with regard thereto." This process was one of compromise based not necessarily upon rules of law, and states are not usually so willing to accept the conclusions of such a process as binding as in the case of an arbitral award. Whether the recommendation of the Council was or was not unanimous became therefore a matter of some importance. If the decision was unanimous (votes of disputants excepted), Members of the League were obligated not to go to war against the state accepting this unanimous "recommendation." Several possibilities present themselves at this point. Both parties might accept the recommendation, and the Council made every effort to achieve this ideal end, even to postponing action for several months. Or, one party might refuse while the other accepted. In this case, the party which accepted was assured against attack from other Members, and was free to proceed against its foes, as was also any other Member; while, on the other hand, the foe was obligated not to go to war against the Member which accepted the unanimous recommendation of the Council, and subjected itself to the threat of Article 16 even if it acted in self-defense. Finally, the recommendation might be rejected by both parties, in which case it would appear that there were no restraints at all—except, of course, the ever-present obligation not to go to war for three months.

In case of failure to agree unanimously upon a recommendation (a situation surprisingly rare) "the Members of the League reserve to themselves the right to take such action as they shall consider necessary for the maintenance of right and justice." This was the notorious "fissure" in the Covenant, perhaps its weakest spot. The delay of three months would still apply but, aside from that, war would seem to be unrestrained. Another well-known gap in the Covenant, found in Article 15, paragraph 8, reappears now in the U.N. charter.[12] This clause deprived the Council of jurisdiction if the matter was one which "by international law is solely within the domestic jurisdiction" of the party claiming it. As to whether it was such a matter the Council had the right to decide; but if the Council should admit that it was a domestic question, it could make no recommendation, and states were again free to make their own decisions and, after the three months' delay, to resort to war.

NON-MEMBERS. By Article 17, in case of a dispute between a Member and a non-member, or between non-members, an invitation could be extended to the non-members to accept the obligations of the League for the purposes of that dispute, under conditions laid down by the Council. The non-member state was free to accept or to decline the invitation, as it saw fit.[13] If, however, the non-member rejected the invitation and resorted to war against a Member, the sanctions of

---

[12] Refer to pp. 302-3, above.

[13] This was made quite clear by the Permanent Court, in the Eastern Carelia Case: "The submission, therefore, of a dispute between them and a Member of the League for solution according to the methods provided for in the Covenant, could take place only by virtue of their consent." *P.C.I.J.*, Series B, No. 5, pp. 26-27.

Article 16 were automatically released against the non-member. If the invitation was accepted, the provisions of Articles 12 to 16 were applicable, with such modifications as were deemed necessary by the Council, although, according to Article 17, paragraph 2, the Council could proceed with an inquiry from the moment the invitation was issued. A non-member was, of course, not juridically bound by Article 17, but in practical effect the theory of consent was overruled in this respect.

LICIT WARS. It has been observed that the Covenant did not pretend to outlaw all wars. On the contrary, in a number of cases war was permitted, either because it seemed a necessary act of justice, or because of the insufficiency of the organization of the League. In seven cases, it would appear, war was licit: (1) When one disputant refused to abide by the arbitral award or unanimous recommendation of the Council, war against it was permitted to all other Members. (2) When both refused, there seemed to be no limitation at all upon the right to make war. (3) When the Council was unable to reach a unanimous decision, freedom of action was reserved. (4) If the Council conceded that the matter was one which by international law was solely within domestic jurisdiction, it had no control. (5) Civil wars, in which belligerency is recognized, were wars under international law, but were not covered in the Covenant. (6) If the arbitral award or recommendation of the council was not given within a reasonable time, the state involved would appear to recover its liberty of action. (7) States not Members of the League, not bound by the Covenant, could claim the right to wage war in accordance with the international law existent before the creation of the League.[14]

139. SANCTIONS

ILLICIT WARS. We have sketched the obligations of Members of the League for the maintenance of peace: preliminary submission of disputes to pacific settlement; choice between arbitration and conciliation, with the latter as the necessary final resort; no war in any case for three months; no war at all against the party accepting the award or the unanimous recommendation of the Council. We have noticed that there were several gaps in the Covenant leaving war legal. We may now list four cases in which war was made illegal: (1) war commenced without submission to arbitration or judicial settlement, or to the Council (Article 12, paragraph 1); (2) war commenced without

[14] This list, as well as the following list of illicit wars, is taken from J. B. Whitton, "La neutralité et la Société des Nations," *Hague Acad.*, 1927, II, Chaps. ii-iv.

waiting until three months after the award or recommendation (Article 12, paragraph 2); (3) war against a state which accepted the award or unanimous recommendation of the Council (Article 13, and Article 15, paragraph 6); (4) war by a non-member under Article 17.

What penalties were provided against states which engaged in wars of these types? At this point we arrive at the heart of the problem of war, the question of sanctions, and it is important to note that the principle of collective action against offenders, as a duty resting upon members of the community of nations, was recognized for the first time in history by Article 16. The advance made was in the recognition not only of a right—an advance in itself—but of a duty on the part of members of the community to assume responsibility for the maintenance of order.

ECONOMIC SANCTIONS. It is to be observed, in the first place, that the sanctions of Article 16 were applicable only as against a state which had actually gone to war, and to war in violation of the obligations mentioned above, and were not applicable to any other obligations under the Covenant.[15] And it should be noted further that the state which went to war in disregard of its covenants under Articles 12, 13, or 15 "shall *ipso facto* be deemed to have committed an act of war" against all other Members. But this act of war did not create a state of war unless the challenge flung down was taken up by another state.

Various questions arose at this point. To define war is itself a difficult legal question; who could say that a state had resorted to war, and in disregard of these particular articles of the Covenant? Once decided, how and by whom were the sanctions to be put into effect? To answer such questions the Blockade Committee was set up and, on the basis of its report, the Second Assembly adopted interpretative resolutions which admitted that the League itself could not decide these questions, since "such a power would not be consistent with the sovereign rights of the various states." It was therefore the duty of each Member to decide for itself who was the aggressor. If and when it made such a decision, it was then obligated to break off economic intercourse with that aggressor.[16]

[15] Aside from the last clause of Article 16, which deals with expulsion. See as to Article 16, P. Barandon, *Das Kriegsverhütungsrecht des Völkerbondes* (1933); L. de Brouckère, "La Prévention de la guerre," *Hague Acad.*, 50 (1934); A. E. Highley, *The First Sanctions Experiment: A Study of League Procedures,* (Geneva Studies, IX, No. 4, July 1938); N. Petrascu, *Les mésures de contrainte qui ne sont pas la guerre* (Paris, 1927); N. Politis, "Les représailles entre états Membres de la Société des Nations," *R.D.I.P.*, 33 (1924), pp. 5-16; W. Schiffer, *L'Article 16 du Pacte de la Société des Nations* (Paris, Geneva Research Centre); Stone, Chap. vi; C. G. Tenekides, "L'évolution de l'idée des mésures coercitives et la Société des Nations," *R.D.I.L.C.*, 3rd Series, (1926), pp. 398-418.

[16] *Records of the Second Assembly, Third Committee*, p. 385.

The automatic economic action apparently intended by Article 16 was obviously weakened, if not destroyed, by this interpretation. There was no League organ which could organize these economic sanctions or lead those Members willing to apply them, and apparently no provision for suspending some rather than all economic intercourse. The potentialities of the economic weapon are enormous in this interdependent world, and enough to daunt any aggressor if they could be properly concentrated against him; but their application is very difficult. There is required detailed knowledge of the economic needs of the aggressor, and also of each prosecuting Member in its economic relation to him. If any important state fails to join in, the aggressor may be able to supply his needs from this state. Universal action is called for. In each application, the burden will fall unequally upon various Members, and arrangements must be made for equalizing this burden, which in some cases might be dangerously heavy.[17] Similarly, within each state the burden would fall unequally upon individuals—upon oil dealers in the case of Italy, upon silk dealers in the case of Japan—which would require equalization within each state. Finally, certain states might be attacked by the aggressor if they engaged in economic measures against him; the Italo-Ethiopian affair made it clear that economic sanctions cannot be effective unless backed by sufficient military force.

The observations above help to explain the difficulties and the complicated procedure followed in the only case in which the League attempted to use economic sanctions. It remains uncertain whether it can properly be said that the League itself applied sanctions, though the initiative undoubtedly came from the League.[18] It seems clear that the League action was recommendatory, and that Members decided for themselves the extent of their actions. Some refused to cooperate from the beginning; others terminated their participation without waiting for collective decision. While cooperation was surprisingly well maintained, the experience shows the necessity of advance study and planning, and of a central authority to direct the effort. This, however, is difficult to achieve in a system which recognizes the sovereignty of its Members.

MILITARY SANCTIONS. While economic sanctions were supposedly automatic under the Covenant, the obligation of Members to contribute

---

[17] This duty was recognized in Article 16(3) but without implementation. The Eleventh Assembly adopted a Convention for Financial Assistance to States Threatened with Aggression, but its signature was to be delayed until the disarmament treaty was signed.

[18] For a thorough discussion of the action taken, including the above point, see A. E. Highley, *The Actions of the States Members of the League of Nations in Application of Sanctions Against Italy, 1935/1936* (Thesis, University of Geneva, 1938).

to military action against an aggressor was not clearly stated, and was not accepted in practice. The Council was given the duty, in case economic measures had failed, to "recommend to the several Governments concerned what effective military, naval or air force the Members of the League shall severally contribute to the armed forces to be used to protect the covenants of the League." Apparently the makers of the League contemplated unwillingly the necessity for military action, and made slight provision for it, in the hope that economic pressure would be sufficient. When the matter of preparing in advance these military measures was brought before the assembly in 1927 the "Rutgers Memorandum" displayed a fear that such measures would shake mutual confidence among Members; others retorted that if there could be greater security, there would be greater confidence. The Covenant, it may be said, recognized military coercion as a matter of principle, but did not implement it. The machinery was available, and the right stated, if Members cared to make use of either; but on no occasion was any effort made by Members to employ military sanctions.

140. EFFORTS TO STRENGTHEN THE LEAGUE

Members did not fail to recognize that the League did not offer as much security and confidence as had been desired, and they attempted in many directions to make improvements. We have noted, in connection with the disarmament effort, the proposed Treaty of Mutual Assistance, which appeared as a result of the growing consciousness that reduction of arms depended upon security.

GENEVA PROTOCOL. In spite of the failure of this treaty, efforts were still continued upon the theory that security must precede disarmament. A draft treaty by an American committee was submitted, and rejected, which defined the aggressor state as the one which refused arbitration. By now it was becoming realized that provisions for maintaining peace must be positive as well as negative—that states could not simply sit by and allow peace to arrive. If states are to give up war and arms, there must be means provided for determining and protecting rights. The Treaty of Mutual Assistance had emphasized security; attention was now directed toward Article 12 of the Covenant, and thus the trilogy was completed—arbitration, security, and disarmament. Following this orientation, the Fifth Assembly devoted itself to strengthening arbitration, and prepared the Protocol for the Pacific

Settlement of International Disputes, the famous "Geneva Protocol." It was called a protocol to avoid the implication of being a movement outside of the Covenant, and its purpose was to close up the "fissures" of the Covenant. "The Protocol may be defined in one sentence as being an attempt to promote disarmament by creating security, to create security by outlawing war, to enforce the outlawry of war by uniting the world against the would-be aggressor, and to base this union of mutual protection upon the fundamental principle of compulsory arbitration."[19]

The connection with the Covenant was emphasized both in the preamble and in Article 1. By the latter, signatory states undertook to make every effort to amend the Covenant along the lines of the protocol. By Article 2, they renounced war against a state which accepted the obligations of the protocol, except "in case of resistance to acts of aggression," or when enforcing the Covenant or protocol. Provisions for pacific settlement were strengthened, and compulsory arbitration became the backbone of the system; the jurisdiction of the Permanent Court became compulsory *ipso facto* for cases included in Article 36 of the statute. In other cases, arbitration could be had if the parties so agreed, but if no agreement were made the Council was to take up the case and report upon it. If the recommendation of the Council was unanimous, it was final; if not, the Council would refer the case to a special arbitral tribunal, whose decision would be final. Thus a decision was achieved, either by the judgment of the court, or by the unanimous recommendation of the Council, or by the award of the special tribunal. The gaps of the Covenant were closed.

But the protocol also provided sanctions against a state which violated its obligations. An ingenious test for determining the aggressor was set up by Article 10. In case of hostilities, that state was presumed to be the aggressor which (1) had failed to submit to the specified procedure of pacific settlement or to accept the decision, or which (2) had disregarded a decision that the dispute arose from a matter solely within the domestic jurisdiction of the other state, or which (3) had violated the provisional measures enjoined by the council under Article 7. The automatic presumptions thus set up might be overcome by unanimous vote of the Council. Aside from these cases, if the Council did not succeed in determining the aggressor it should decree an armi-

[19] W. E. Rappard, *International Relations as Viewed from Geneva* (New Haven, 1925), p. 156. See as to the protocol, P. J. N. Baker, *The Geneva Protocol for the Pacific Settlement of International Disputes* (London, 1925); D. H. Miller, *The Geneva Protocol* (New York, 1925); H. Wehberg, "Le Protocole de Genève," *Hague Acad.*, 1925, II, pp. 5-149.

stice, and the state which violated the terms of this armistice was held to be the aggressor. The aggressor state having been determined, each state was bound by the obligations of Article 16 of the Covenant, which "shall be interpreted as obliging each of the signatory States to cooperate loyally and effectively ... in the degree which its geographical position and its particular situation as regards armaments allow" (Article 11 of the protocol). Thus the system seemed complete, and no way open by which war was legally possible.

It needs to be recalled that the original purpose of all this work was the reduction of armaments. The Geneva Protocol was in a sense preparatory to disarmament, and it consequently provided that if the conference on disarmament, called for by Article 17 of the protocol, did not succeed in making an acceptable plan of disarmament, the protocol should not go into effect. Under this condition, of course, it would not yet be in effect; actually, however, it failed at once. It was adopted by the Assembly and signed by a large number of states, but it was ratified by none. At the Council meeting in March, 1925, Sir Austen Chamberlain gave it the *coup de grâce*. His speech displayed dislike for the increase of responsibility resulting from compulsory arbitration and from compulsory sanctions. But the position of Britain was due also to her unwillingness to assume obligations calling for the use of its navy in enforcing sanctions in face of the possible maintenance by armed force, on the part of the United States, of the rights of neutrality.

The protocol revealed more clearly the weaknesses of the Covenant, and in attempting to remedy them made important progress in the study of the means of controlling war, such as the lesson of the futility of attempting to define aggression. As M. Branting of Sweden remarked, it is preferable to speak of "the suppression of war contrary to the Covenant," rather than in terms of aggression or self-defense. While the protocol is open to criticism in some parts, it marks the greatest advance made by the community of nations toward the elimination of war. There are many who believe that any final settlement of the problem of war will involve a return to these principles.[20]

THE LOCARNO TREATIES. In the same speech in which Sir Austen Chamberlain pronounced the doom of the protocol, he suggested that obligations, which seemed too onerous for general acceptance, might be arranged by limited special agreements among groups which have

[20] See, in the *Records of the Sixth Assembly*, Plenary, pp. 117-25, the remarks of Paul-Boncour; *Records of the Eighth Assembly*, Third Committee, pp. 16-17 (de Brouckère) and p. 31 (Politis); also Madariaga, pp. 113-14; D. H. Miller, *The Geneva Protocol* (New York, 1925), p. 112.

special common interests or face common perils. "The best solution," he said, "would be to supplement the Covenant, with the cooperation of the League, by making special arrangements in order to meet special needs." Negotiations were soon initiated by Germany, looking toward greater security along her frontiers, and these efforts were approved by the Sixth Assembly. At the end of 1925, seven treaties were signed which, together with a Final Act and a letter to the German delegation with regard to interpretation of Article 16 of the Covenant, make up the Locarno system.

The most important of these was the Rhine Pact. By it, the signatory Powers collectively and severally guaranteed the territorial status with regard to the frontiers between Germany and Belgium and between Germany and France, established by the Treaty of Versailles. And Germany and Belgium, and Germany and France, mutually agreed not to resort to war against each other, except in self-defense or in execution of League sanctions, or for action taken under Article 15, paragraph 7, of the Covenant. They were obligated to pacific settlement in accordance with treaties signed at the same time. If the treaty should be violated, appeal was to be made to the Council; and if the Council was satisfied that there had been a breach, the signatory Powers promised to come to the aid of the state attacked. In case of "flagrant violation" they need not wait upon the Council decision, although they must submit to it when later given. The treaty was to go into effect as soon as Germany had entered the League, and to remain in effect until the Council by two-thirds vote should assert that it was no longer necessary and that the League could give sufficient protection.

The provisions for pacific settlement were more extensive than those of the Covenant, and represented a high stage of development in the use of arbitration and conciliation.[21] "All disputes of every kind" which involve a dispute as to rights were to be submitted to arbitration, with the exception of disputes arising in the past. The parties might first, however, by mutual agreement, submit the dispute to a Permanent Conciliation Commission, created by the same treaty. If no agreement was reached before this body, the dispute must go to arbitration. Other questions, not settled by judicial decision, must be submitted to the Conciliation Commission, and if no agreement was reached through it, they were to be taken over by the Council and handled under Article 15 of the Covenant.

The eastern frontier of Germany was also included in the Locarno system, but not upon the same basis of guarantee. Similar treaties of

[21] See N. Politis, "Les accords de Locarno," *R.D.I.L.C.*, 3rd Series, 6 (1925), pp. 713-21; K. Strupp, "Die Verträge von Locarno," *R.D.I.* (Genève), 3 (1925), pp. 303-41.

arbitration were obligatory but, if they were violated, the guarantee was found in alliances between France and Poland and between France and Czechoslovakia. The Pact of Locarno was a regional agreement and, within its geographical limits, it carried on the principles of the Covenant and the Geneva Protocol.

GENERAL ACT OF 1928. The defeat of the Geneva Protocol represented a distinct check in the development of the Covenant, and efforts were directed toward regional agreements, which were encouraged by the praise accorded to the Locarno system. A period of uncertainty and confusion followed. Some states favored more study of arbitration; others wished to speed up disarmament. It had long been recognized that the two were inseparable. In September, 1925, the Assembly passed a resolution "declaring afresh that a war of aggression should be regarded as an international crime," and proposing to work for peace "by the sure methods of arbitration, security, and disarmament." Shortly thereafter, the Preparatory Commission for the Disarmament Conference was set up, and study was again directed toward filling up the "fissures" of the Covenant.

At the Eighth Assembly, a resolution was passed that "all wars of aggression are, and shall always be, prohibited"; and M. Loudon and Politis asserted that the necessary next step was to condemn "not only wars of a certain category, such as wars of aggression, but in general all wars." The Assembly resolution of October 14, 1921, was brought up for reconsideration, and the question asked whether the right was really given to each state to decide for itself when the Covenant had been broken. The Dutch proposal to resume study of the Geneva Protocol, however, frightened Sir Austen Chamberlain, and it was toned down to "study the principles of disarmament, security, and arbitration which are expressed in the Covenant." Accordingly, the important Committee on Arbitration and Security was set up, which made three reports to the Assembly. The general introduction to all called attention to the significant fact that "the Covenant itself creates a measure of security which needs to be appreciated at its full value, and that its articles are capable of being applied in such a way that in the majority of cases they can prevent war"; that "the will for peace can be exercised effectively within the framework of the Covenant"; and that regional pacts of security should be regarded as supplementary guarantees, available for those states which do not consider that the Covenant affords them a sufficient degree of security.

The Committee on Arbitration and Security also offered a series of model treaties in varying degrees of completeness. There were three of them: one exclusively for conciliation; one providing for conciliation and also for the compulsory jurisdiction of the Permanent Court where questions of right were involved; and one submitting all disputes whatever either to arbitral settlement or to the Court. The Assembly collected the three instruments into one "General Act" containing one chapter for each of the above texts, and a fourth chapter combining them all.[22] At the same time there were offered a treaty of collective mutual assistance, a collective treaty of non-aggression, and a bilateral treaty of non-aggression.

The Assembly recommended the General Act for signature, with some explanation of its purposes. In the first place, the system was intended to be elastic enough to meet the needs of different states. This was achieved by (1) allowing a choice between the General Act or bilateral treaties; (2) allowing choice between three methods of settlement; (3) permitting reservations. In the second place, in spite of its elasticity, the system was intended to assure obligations of equal force, by providing that failure to agree on a *compromis* should not stop the arbitral process, by excluding certain reservations, and by interpretation of the General Act by the Permanent Court. Whereas the bilateral treaties were merely guides, the General Act was thrown open for signature, with provision for total or partial adhesion, denunciation, and reservations. It was to go into force upon receiving two adhesions, which Norway and Belgium at once gave. By 1938, twenty-two states had ratified the General Act. It was revived by the United Nations, but without noticeable effect.

This offering could fairly be described as "one of the most considerable efforts so far made to organize peace." It had a sample to suit the taste of every state. But the variety itself of the offering was disconcerting and aroused a division of opinion. In general, it was argued that such a variety of obligations led too far away from the purposes and from the control of the League.[23] On the other hand, it was argued that the numerous efforts to strengthen the Covenant had failed, and that the only hope for advance lay in agreement between states which were willing to advance; that such agreements were rigidly in line with the Covenant; that they filled some, at least, of the gaps in the Covenant;

---

[22] See *L. of N. Doc.* C.356.M.163.1928. IX.

[23] "Why," asks Professor Brierly, "in view of the conciliation functions of the Council of the League, is this system of a multiplicity of separate conciliation commissions recommended to us at all? . . . If we are to multiply them in the wholesale fashion contemplated by the Act and to give them a priority over a tried machinery already existing for the same purpose, we are entitled to ask for reasons." *B.Y.I.L.*, 1930, pp. 120-21, 124.

and that by affording a greater degree of security to certain states, these states will be encouraged to a greater degree of responsibility and participation in the work of the League.

OTHER PROPOSALS. Mention may be made of a few other efforts and proposals. A plan for European Union was put forward by Premier Briand of France in 1929, and a commission of inquiry worked until 1937 on the matter, without result.[24] A Convention on Financial Assistance for a victim of aggression was signed in 1930, but received few ratifications. In 1931 a Convention to Improve the Means of Preventing War was adopted, but failed with the Disarmament Conference. The French government proposed, in 1932, an international police force, and concerted action by signatories of the Pact of Paris in case of threat to the peace. Attention was diverted from League reform by the Four Power Pact of March 1933.[25] After the collapse of the disarmament effort, and with growing tension in Europe, a Committee on the Organization of Collective Security was set up in 1935, and in 1936, after the Italo-Ethiopian affair, a Committee of Twenty-Eight to study Application of the Principles of the Covenant, rather than reform of the Covenant. This committee inquired how to secure the cooperation of non-members, which led to an interesting report by Lord Cranborne[26] and to the withdrawal of Chile because of failure to accept her ideas as to universality and non-coercive character for the League. At the next Assembly, the issues thus raised were further discussed, and it was clear that Members were unwilling to accept obligations concerning military, or even economic, sanctions. After a communication from the United States revealed willingness to cooperate in the non-technical work of the League, the "Bruce Committee" made recommendations concerning economic and social cooperation, including establishment of a Central Committee for Economic and Social Questions. The Bruce Report was approved at the twentieth session of the Assembly, in December, 1939, and an organizing committee was appointed.[27] It thus appears that the coercive authority of the League was diminishing in the minds and support of its Members, and that it was tending, in its final hours, to become machinery for cooperation rather than an agency for the maintenance of security.

[24] As for the European Union, see § 167, below.

[25] J. W. Wheeler-Bennett, *Documents on International Affairs, 1933* (London, 1934), p. 242.

[26] Report of the Special Committee Set up to Study the Application of the Principles of the Covenant, *L. of N. Doc.*, A.1938.VII, also in *O.J.*, Special Supp., No. 180.

[27] The Bruce Report is *L. of N. Doc.* A.23.1939. It prepared the way for the Economic and Social Council of the United Nations.

141. SURVEY OF DISPUTES HANDLED BY
THE LEAGUE

Space does not permit study of the various cases before the League,[28] but a brief survey will perhaps disclose something as to its procedures and its success. The first case before the Council (as later before the Security Council of the United Nations) was between Russia and Persia, and was settled by Russian withdrawal from the town of Engeli, on the Caspian Sea.

AALAND ISLANDS. Great Britain brought before the Council on July 11, 1920, under Article 11, paragraph 2, a dispute between Sweden and Finland concerning the Aaland Islands. The latter state was not a Member, and Article 17 was applied. There being as yet no court, a committee of Jurists was called upon to decide whether the issue was a "domestic question," and the committee decided that it was not. A commission was sent to the Islands, and on its report, the Council confirmed Finnish sovereignty and suggested certain safeguards for the Swedish inhabitants, and also neutralization. Both parties accepted the recommendations.

POLAND-LITHUANIA. A long-drawn-out struggle over borders between Poland and Lithuania was brought up in September, 1920, also under Article 11. Efforts at a settlement continued for a decade or more, and while fighting was not entirely prevented, war was to some extent smothered. No satisfactory settlement was ever attained.

ALBANIAN BOUNDARY. The unsettled frontiers of Albania led to conflicts with neighbors, and Albania appealed to the Council under Article 11 in April and June, 1921. Debate in the Council as to use of economic sanctions, and support of Albania by Italy, led to acceptance by Yugoslavia of boundaries as delimited by the Conference of Ambassadors.

UPPER SILESIA. The area of Germany known as Upper Silesia was, under the Treaty of Versailles, to hold a plebiscite to determine to whom it should belong. The plebiscite showed preference for German rule, but agreement could not be reached upon a boundary. The Conference of Ambassadors requested assistance from the Council, which

---

[28] Citations for each of these may be found in Aufricht, pp. 306-28, who lists forty-two incidents. See also Cheever and Haviland, Chap. xiv; R. J. Bartlett, *The League to Enforce Peace* (University of North Carolina Press, 1944); J. T. Shotwell and Marina Salvin, *Lessons on Security and Disarmament from the History of the League of Nations* (Carnegie Endowment, 1949); Sir Alfred Zimmern, *The League of Nations and the Rule of Law* (London, 1936).

appointed a committee of neutrals to study the matter, and suggested a boundary and also certain economic and social adjustments. These were accepted by the parties.

HUNGARIAN OPTANTS. There was involved in this dispute expropriation by the Rumanian government of the property of Hungarians transferred by the peace settlement. Hungary presented their case to the Council in March 1923 and it remained upon the Council Agenda until 1930. It was brought up under Article 11, under which the votes of the disputants are not excluded. A Rapporteur was appointed and arguments were heard. Settlement was reached in connection with the reparations settlement in 1930, and Hungary withdrew the case.

CORFU. One of the most famous cases before the League resulted from the murder of an Italian member of a commission of the Conference of Ambassadors which was seeking to establish the boundary between Greece and Albania. Italy issued an ultimatum to Greece, and seized the island of Corfu. Greece appealed to the Council in September 1923, under articles 12 and 15 of the Covenant, and a conflict of jurisdiction arose as between the Council and the Conference of Ambassadors. The Council made certain recommendations, and communicated them to the Conference of Ambassadors, which assessed penalties against Greece. Italy gave up Corfu, but her position as a Great Power resulted in satisfaction of most of her claims. The League could not claim credit (or discredit) for the settlement, but lost in reputation by surrendering the case to the Conference of Ambassadors.

MOSUL. Great Britain, having failed to agree with Turkey as to boundaries in the Mosul area, appealed to the Council in March 1924. Since the Treaty of Lausanne was involved, an advisory opinion was asked from the Court, which replied that the Council had jurisdiction, and should act under Article 15. A boundary line was then agreed upon by the parties in a treaty of June 5, 1926.

GRECO-BULGARIAN AFFAIR. This was another famous case, from which the League emerged with enhanced reputation. It was a case in which war was clearly averted, since orders to attack had been issued by Greece. The controversy arose over a border shooting, and the president of the Council at once dispatched a telegram calling upon both states to observe their obligations to retire their troops behind their own frontiers. An extraordinary meeting of the Council was summoned, which demanded confirmation that troops had been withdrawn. This was given and, hostilities having been forestalled, a commission was sent to investigate on the spot. It was preceded, in fact, by representatives of the Secretariat, who obtained the information sought and prepared recommendations for the commission. The Council held Greece responsible, and required an indemnity from her. The League thus showed itself able to act promptly and decisively, and an important precedent was established.

CHACO. No such brilliant success attended the efforts to resolve the dispute between Bolivia and Paraguay over the territory known as the Gran Chaco. Both states preferred settlement of their own, by arms, and the Council intervened on its own initiative in December, 1928. The affair was made delicate by the fact that both the United States and a conference of American republics were at the same time attempting to settle the controversy, and the Council refrained from action. In 1932, Paraguay appealed to the Council under articles 10 and 11, and the Council, after waiting for approval by the United States, sent a commission of inquiry. A truce was arranged, but failed, and Bolivia then appealed under Article 15. The dispute was transferred to the Assembly and an embargo on munitions against both states was agreed to. Paraguay announced her withdrawal from the League, and the American republics again attempted a settlement, with the approval of the Assembly. A settlement was reached at last (1938), probably due mostly to the exhaustion of the disputants.

MANCHUKUO. Japanese troops, in 1931, seized the town of Mukden in Manchuria, and on September 21, the Chinese appealed to the council under Article 11. It was a difficult situation for the League, involving a Great Power, faraway and lying between two other Great Powers, who were the most interested parties but not Members of the League. The Council was concerned as to the participation of the United States, which took the unprecedented step of authorizing its consul at Geneva to sit with the Council. The United States was willing to invoke the Pact of Paris, to which it was a signatory, but this treaty had no sanctions behind it. The Council was further weakened when the United States withdrew from the Council and would consult only at Paris, a ridiculous situation. The Council sought first to limit hostilities by asking Japan to withdraw her troops, by proposing a neutral zone, and in various other ways. On the contrary, the Japanese continued to advance. It was then decided to send a commission of inquiry (Lytton Commission) which made fair and impartial recommendations. Japan, however, organized "Manchukuo" as an independent state. Meanwhile, the United States, on January 7, 1932, announced the "Stimson Doctrine," a sort of a negative sanction, refusing to recognize a change in a legal situation brought about by the use of force contrary to treaty obligations.[29] China transferred her appeal to Article 15, and to the Assembly, which adopted a resolution condemning Japan. Japan thereupon gave notice of withdrawal from the League. The League had failed in this difficult case, and with this failure, disorder increased in the world, and aggressors became more daring.[30] It was a gain, however, that the situation could be brought before a world forum, and that world opinion was concentrated against Japan.

THE LETICIA DISPUTE. On September 1, 1932, armed Peruvians occupied the town of Leticia, in Colombia, and Colombian forces were sent to repel the "aggression." Peru disclaimed official participation, but asserted that she must protect her citizens, and fighting ensued. Peru appealed to the Permanent International Conciliation Commission under the Havana Treaty of 1929; Colombia replied that it was a domestic matter, but later called first upon the signatories of the Pact of Paris, and then upon the League of Nations. Meanwhile, the Brazilian government attempted to mediate, without success. The Council of the League in January asked both parties for information, reminded them not to use force, and appointed a Committee of Three. Both parties refused arbitration. The Council proposed an international commission to take charge of the disputed territory, and this was agreed to. The League thus administered the territory until a settlement was reached between the two parties in a treaty of May 24, 1934. The United States had supported both Brazilian and League efforts. The case may be regarded as one of the League's successes.

ITALO-ETHIOPIAN AFFAIR. A clash of troops of Italy and Ethiopia occurred at Wal-Wal in December 1934, and both governments referred the matter to the Council, which encouraged direct negotiations, and then arbitration. In September, 1935, Ethiopia appealed under Article 15 and a Committee of Five was appointed, and later, a Committee of Thirteen, to prepare a report under Article 15, paragraph 4. Italy attempted to block all action by the League, and moved her troops forward. On October 7, the Council held that Italy had resorted to war contrary to Article 12, thus bringing Article 16 into play, and called upon the Assembly to cooperate in arranging economic sanctions.

[29] This principle was approved by the Assembly on March 11, and other precedents allow argument that it is now part of customary international law.

[30] See M. O. Hudson, *The Verdict of the League: China and Japan in Manchuria* (World Peace Foundation, Boston, 1933); Sara S. Smith, *The Manchurian Crisis: A Tragedy in International Relations* (New York, 1948); H. L. Stimson, *The Far Eastern Crisis* (New York, 1936); W. W. Willoughby, *The Sino-Japanese Controversy and the League of Nations* (Baltimore, 1935).

The Assembly, with the exception of Albania, Austria, Hungary, and, of course, Italy, approved, and established a complicated set of committees to arrange for the economic measures to be taken.[31]

Various difficult problems arose. An embargo on arms, measures to prevent financial resources reaching Italy, and prohibition of importation of Italian goods were agreed to at once. The problem of mutual assistance among the sanctioning states was not so easy. It was difficult to measure losses suffered, to divert trade routes and substitute other markets, or to manage a mutual aid fund. Some states had difficulty with their national laws, others who were dangerously close to Italy (Albania, Austria, Hungary, Switzerland) sought special exemptions. The cooperation of several non-members was needed if Italy was to be deprived of supplies, and mere parallel action was not enough. If the United States Neutrality Legislation incidentally deprived Italy of some items, it also injured Ethiopia. There were political angles as well, as manifested by the notorious "Hoare-Laval deal," which would have surrendered much Ethiopian territory to Italy, but which was killed by public opinion. Meanwhile, Italy proceeded to conquer all of Ethiopia, breathing threats of military action against any state which might interfere, and thus raising a question as to the ability of the League to protect a Member which might be attacked by Italy. In July, 1936, the Assembly conceded failure, and lifted sanctions. At the same time, it refused to recognize the conquest, and later admitted Ethiopian representatives.

The failure of the League was due to various reasons, a chief one being inability to secure cooperation of the United States. At the same time, the rise of Hitler, German rearmament, and the seizure of the Rhineland preoccupied statesmen with the vision of greater dangers to come. There were now three Great Powers acting in defiance of the League, and tending to combine their opposition. It would have been almost impossible for the League to stop Japan in 1931, but the weakness then revealed encouraged others to aggression. A stronger stand was attempted against Italy, but the League did not have enough authority and was not universal enough to succeed. France and England, for political reasons, did not wish strong action against Italy; having failed here, it was too late when they anxiously sought its help against Germany. The existence of the League machinery, however, had focused attention and concentrated public opinion, so that when the inevitable crisis developed, the world was already opposed to the Axis combine.

[31] See Highley, *op. cit.*

CIVIL WAR IN SPAIN. The terrifying tide of events pushed its way next into Spain, where the fascist forces of Franco sought to overthrow the constituted government.[32] Franco was recognized and was assisted by Germany and Italy, and the republican government appealed to the Council under Article 11. On the other hand, France and England had organized twenty-seven European states into a non-intervention committee, to prevent intervention or shipment of arms by foreign powers. The Council approved this effort in a special meeting on December 10, but left responsibility to the non-intervention committee. The failure of the League to act can be explained by the fact that Spanish Civil War was regarded as a domestic struggle over which the League had no jurisdiction under the Covenant. The success of Franco was, however, another step on the road to war.

SINO-JAPANESE WAR. At Liukuchiao, in July, 1937, the latent struggle between China and Japan flamed up into open hostilities. China first notified the signatories of the Nine Power Treaty[33] of what she alleged to be a violation of that treaty. On September 12, she appealed to the Council under articles 10, 11, and 17 (Japan having withdrawn from the League) of the Covenant. A Far East Advisory Committee was given charge of the question. Its first step was to condemn aerial bombardment of open towns by the Japanese; the United States concurred, but by parallel action, through its non-voting representative on the committee. A resolution was later adopted by the Assembly to invite a conference of the signatories of the Nine Power Treaty. This action was due in the first place to the fact that Japan was not a Member and that the League was not prepared to apply sanctions as might have been necessary had Article 17 been invoked; it was due also to the hope that Japan would feel it necessary to attend such a conference, and to the fact that the United States could participate directly, whereas it would not so participate in a League action.

The conference met at Brussels on November 3. Japan refused to attend, the U.S.S.R. and Germany were especially invited, and the former did attend. Nothing was accomplished at the conference, beyond restatement of moral principles. The Chinese addressed an appeal to the hundredth session of the Council which passed a resolution deploring the situation. Actually, the trend of events was beyond control. The signature of the Anti-Comintern Pact by the Axis Powers in the midst of the Brussels Conference made hopeless efforts at con-

---

[32] N. J. Padelford, *International Law and Diplomacy in the Spanish Civil Strife* (New York, 1939).

[33] *League of Nations Treaty Series*, 38 (Geneva, 1925), p. 278; Hudson, *International Legislation*, II, p. 823.

ciliation. The League had no authority to provide military sanctions, and especially in the degree now needed; and the United States still sought to "keep out of war." Reason, intelligence, and cooperation appeared after the attack on Pearl Harbor; the community of nations had not learned how to use them for purposes of peace.

142. CONCLUSIONS

The League of Nations was the first organized effort of the community of nations to regulate the use of force among nations, and it was to be expected that it would be weak, both in constitutional authority and in support from its Members. It proved to be of much use in conciliation of disputes between states which were willing to reach a settlement, and can also be credited with generating enough pressure to induce some unwilling states to submit to settlement. In a few cases, though this is largely conjectural, it is reasonable to believe that war was prevented, and in others hostilities were ended. The cases above surveyed are only a part of those handled, and it is to be observed that Great Powers, and not merely small states, submitted to League recommendations. For most cases, the League worked effectively; it failed in the case of Great Power aggressors of the most obstinate type. It might have succeeded here had Members been willing in the earlier conflicts to back the League with military action which the League itself had not the authority to take, though it would have been embarrassed by the non-participation of the United States, the U.S.S.R., and others. Lessons may be drawn from this experience as to the need of universality and of wholehearted support by Members; without the latter, no association of sovereign states can hope to succeed.

While impatience was often expressed at the slow and often roundabout methods employed, the flexibility of League methods deserves consideration. It did not seek to arrogate power to itself; it was willing to turn a matter over to the states most directly concerned, such as the American republics or the signatories of the Nine-Power Treaty; it called in non-members who had an interest involved; it sought the maintenance of peace in every way possible. Disputes between nations are often complicated and difficult, involving strong popular emotions; they cannot be rushed too rapidly to a solution.

Granted the rule of unanimity, it is surprising how often the Council and Assembly were able to act; it would be almost correct to say that it never failed. Of course, matters on which there was no hope might not be brought to a vote; and other matters had to be watered down to a common level of acceptance. The ability to transfer a case from the

Council to the Assembly made possible a broader base of support and pressure toward a solution; at the least, it concentrated the attention of the world upon the problem being considered in this forum.

The primary weaknesses of the League were lack of authority to bind Members by its decision as to the aggressor, lack of machinery and authority for effective use of economic sanctions, and entire absence of authority to use armed force against an aggressor. The failure of the League in these respects was of course the failure of its Members; but states would doubtless be more prepared to offer physical support if they were in a system in which they were obligated to do so. The final lesson from the League experience with sanctions is that such an organization must be able to call upon sufficient physical force to overcome aggressors.[34]

[34] As to the record of the League, see Max Beer, *The League on Trial* (Boston, 1933); H. Butler, *The Lost Peace* (New York, 1942); Viscount Cecil, *A Great Experiment: An Autobiography* (London, 1941); H. Schiffer, *The Legal Community of Mankind* (New York, 1954); and Stone and Walters.

Chapter 17

THE UNITED NATIONS: SETTLEMENT OF DISPUTES

The failure of the League of Nations was disappointing to the world, even to the complacent American people who had rejected responsibility for it. The destructive potentialities of a war implemented by modern science, alarmingly apparent after World War II, made increasingly urgent the desire to bring war under control. It was the hope of a "security organization" able to guard them against war which brought about the conversion of the American people from isolation into active leadership and planning of the United Nations; it was such a hope among all peoples that assured from the beginning the establishment of that institution. We have noted above the structure and characteristics of this new organization; we turn now to more detailed study of its functions as a security system. It is the "primary responsibility" of the Security Council to maintain international peace and security, and this task includes the settlement of disputes among states as well as the prevention or repression of aggression.

143. CHARTER PROVISIONS[1]

It can be debated whether the Charter of the United Nations represents any advance over the methods for the settlement of disputes of

[1] Jiménez de Aréchaga, *Voting and Handling of Disputes in the Security Council* (U.N. Studies, No. 5, Carnegie Endowment, 1950); C. Eagleton, "The Jurisdiction of the Security Council over Disputes," *A.J.*, 40 (1946), p. 513; P. Hasluck, *Workshop of Security* (Melbourne and London, 1948); L. M. Goodrich, "The United Nations: Pacific Settlement of Disputes," *Pol. Sci. Rev.*, 39 (1945); J. N. Hyde, "Peaceful Settlement: A Survey of Studies in the Interim Committee of the General Assembly of the United Nations," *Int. Con.*, No. 444 (1948); Kelsen, *passim*; W. Koo, Jr., *Voting Procedures in International Organizations* (New York, 1947); Yuen-li Liang, "The Settlement of Disputes in the Security Council: The Yalta Voting Formula," *B.Y.I.L.*, 1947; Use by Organs of the United Nations of Measures and Procedures of Pacific Settlement, *U.N. Doc.*, A/AC.18/61 (1948); Brookings, *Peace and Security*; Staff Studies No. 5.

the League of Nations, and especially as regards legal or judicial settlement. It was hoped that the "gaps" of the League Covenant would be filled in the new system, but there is actually in the Charter no requirement of a final settlement between parties in a dispute. The Security Council has a wide freedom of recommendation, within which it is little bound by law or definition of aggression or other standard of guidance, but it can do no more than recommend; it has no power to impose a final settlement upon parties.[2] And, of course, hanging round its neck like millstones are the veto and the "domestic jurisdiction" clauses.

MEANS OF THEIR OWN CHOICE. The key to the procedure for the settlement of disputes as provided for in the Charter is to be found in Article 33, which asserts that the "parties to any dispute, the continuance of which is likely to endanger the maintenance of international peace and security, shall, first of all, seek a solution" by means of their own choice. Certain methods are listed in this article but this listing does not exclude other means; for example, the parties could doubtless agree among themselves to submit their dispute to the Security Council, though the Council is not included among the means therein named.[3] The obligation imposed upon Members to settle their disputes exists only for a certain type of dispute, as described in the unwieldy words above quoted. The text emphasizes that it is the right, as well as the duty, of Members to settle their disputes by means of their own choice; indeed, five of the six articles in Chapter VI relate to settlement by the parties themselves, and the participation of the Security Council in the settlement is stringently limited.

In the first stage of settlement, two possible situations appear. The dispute may be one not regarded as likely to endanger peace, and as to which, therefore, no obligation to settle exists. The parties may nevertheless wish to settle it, and they are of course free to do so by whatever procedure they may wish to follow. The other situation is one which might be regarded as dangerous to future peace, but which has not yet been so designated by the Security Council. In this situation, an obligation to settle does exist, and the parties are actually trying to settle it between themselves. In either case, action belongs to the parties and the Security Council does not have jurisdiction for more than discussion. Not until the Council has determined that the matter is one

[2] The Dumbarton Oaks Proposals did not even authorize the Security Council to recommend terms of settlement. The United States opposed this, in fear of the Senate, but was forced to give way at San Francisco and Article 37 was amended to include "terms of settlement." See *UNCIO Doc.* 2, G/29, p. 4.

[3] Article 38 authorizes this, but was really intended to make possible the reference to the Council of disputes which Members are not obligated to settle.

"the continuance of which is likely to endanger the maintenance of international peace and security" does it have jurisdiction to make formal recommendation to the parties, either of procedures or of terms of settlement. Article 34 authorizes it to make this decision.

WHAT IS A DISPUTE? The procedure usually to be expected would begin with Article 35, under which a state, Member or not, may bring a dispute or a situation to the attention of the Security Council or of the General Assembly. The matter could also be brought before the Security Council by the Secretary-General (Article 99), or by reference from the General Assembly (Article 11, paragraph 2); and the Security Council could refer a matter to the General Assembly. It is important to note, however, that the Security Council may intervene in any dispute or situation and may conduct an investigation to determine whether or not it is of the type which, under Article 33, obligates the parties to seek a settlement. The Council may take this action upon its own initiative, without awaiting a complaint from another source.

The intention of the Charter was, apparently, that the Security Council *must* decide, under Article 34, that the matter is one "the continuance of which is likely to endanger the maintenance of international peace and security," before the Council itself would be able to take jurisdiction for the purpose of making recommendations, whether of procedure or settlement. Otherwise, it would be possible for one party, by its own mere assertion that the dispute was one of the type creating the obligation, to compel the Council to take up the dispute. This would deprive the Council of the independent right of decision given it by Article 34. On the other hand, either party might assert that the dispute was not one of the required type, and thus by its mere allegation—unless the Security Council made the decision—exclude the Council from jurisdiction and escape its own obligations.

The Council has not, in practice, usually undertaken to decide whether or not a dispute did exist, apparently because of uncertainty as to whether the veto could be used in that decision; and it has been unable to draw up more than provisional rules of procedure. A party to a dispute cannot, under Article 27, vote in its own dispute, but if it can veto the decision that a dispute exists, it has blocked action more effectively than if it could use the veto in voting on the dispute itself. In theory, the Council cannot make recommendations until it is known that there is a dispute which the parties are obligated to settle. Of course, it cannot be known who are the parties to a dispute, and therefore who is entitled or not to vote, until it has been decided that there is a dispute.

Since such things as voting procedure, or invitation to non-members, as well as other issues, depend upon decision whether or not a dispute exists, there has been frequent controversy. The situation appeared first in the second Iranian case (see below), in which no decision was taken that a dispute existed, but the Council nevertheless adopted a resolution. The Soviet Union protested strongly, and the Secretary-General sent in a memorandum suggesting that the procedure was illegal. In only one case, and in this almost incidentally, has the Security Council labeled an issue as a "dispute"—in the Kashmir dispute between India and Pakistan. The Council has, in fact, proceeded in whatever way was necessary to procure the required number of votes, paying little attention to the procedures set down in Chapter VI. If it had followed the Charter in this respect, it would doubtless have been often blocked by a veto applied against the determination that a dispute existed, thereby preventing any consideration of the issue brought before it. Here, as in other situations, there is debate between those who think that the law of the Charter should be followed, and those who are willing to interpret the Charter liberally, or push it aside, rather than have it block possibility of achievement. And, it will be observed, states are quite inconsistent as to this; which side of a controversy a state will take depends upon whose ox is being gored.

TERMS OF SETTLEMENT. Under the theory of Chapter VI, after the Council had acquired jurisdiction by deciding that a dispute or situation of the proper type is before them, two further stages of action are open to it, neither of which would necessarily arrive at the stage of a final settlement. It may first (Article 36) recommend "appropriate procedures or methods of adjustment," a right which is three times stated in Chapter VI, and which appears again in Article 39. It may (Article 33, paragraph 2) "call upon the parties to settle their disputes" by the means suggested in Article 33; it may (Article 36, paragraph 1) recommend a specific procedure of settlement; it may choose again to recommend a procedure rather than terms of settlement (Article 37); and it is again given an opportunity to recommend a procedure of settlement rather than enforcement measures under Article 39. It is of course most desirable that disputants should settle their own disputes, but the great emphasis laid upon their right to do so, and upon exhortation rather than decision by the Council, are other evidences of the intent of the makers of the Charter, and primarily of the United States, to protect the sovereignty of Members. This is further shown in the last two paragraphs of Article 36: the Security Council must, in recommending procedures, respect the choice of the parties themselves; and it cannot itself refer legal disputes to the Court—it can only recommend to the parties that they refer their dispute to the Court.

The final stage appears (Article 37) when the parties have failed to reach a settlement by means of their own choice, including perhaps the procedures recommended to them by the Council. They must, in this case, refer the dispute to the Security Council, which may again recommend further procedures of adjustment, or now, and not until now, recommend terms of settlement.[4] The Council can only recommend terms of settlement, and the parties are not obligated to accept them.[5] Thus, there is no final settlement provided in the Charter, and in this respect no advance beyond the League of Nations procedure. It is nevertheless true, as shown in the experience of the League of Nations, that such recommendations have great force. They bring a great pressure of public opinion to bear upon recalcitrant states, and few states dare to defy the pressure.

One possibility remains to be noted. The procedure of pacific settlement itself is exhausted by the stages above described, but the Security Council may, under the enforcement action of Chapter VII, decide that a situation constitutes a breach of the peace and may then employ the sanction of Chapter VII to correct the situation. The Council might, then, decide that the failure of one of the parties to accept its recommendation under Chapter VI was a threat to the peace, and take action against it on that basis. It is to be expected that efforts to settle a dispute would continue even while enforcement action is being undertaken. The two procedures would thus become commingled and confused, but they rest upon different grants of authority and are different procedures.

144. EARLIER CASES[6]

Before the Security Council had organized itself or provided itself with rules of procedure, a flurry of cases descended upon it. Some of

[4] The explanation was made in Committee III/2 that if one party does not refer the dispute to the Council, the other may do so. UNCIO Doc. 433, III/2/15.

[5] This was clearly understood and expressed in the debates at San Francisco. UNCIO Doc. 433, III/2/15, p. 2, and Doc. 498, III/2/19, p. 2. Testimony before the Senate Foreign Relations Committee indicated that the Security Council could not impose terms of settlement even after enforcement action was taken. Hearings, pp. 275-79.

[6] The reader may trace these cases further through the Repertoire, and the detailed analysis and citations therein. A "Tabulation of questions submitted to the Security Council, 1946-1951" is provided at pp. 403-9. Analysis of procedures may also be found in Brookings, Peace and Security.

these were initiated, and all were procedurally affected, by the political or propaganda purposes of the states concerned; few of them were worthy of the attention of the Council. There was much debate and uncertainty, but precedents of some sort were established through which the Council was able to operate.

IRAN. The government of Iran, in a note of January 19, 1946, charged that Soviet interference in Iranian affairs, backed by the continued presence of Soviet forces, had produced a situation likely to lead to international friction. The Soviet Union replied that a solution could be reached through bilateral negotiations between the parties and that, in fact, such negotiations were proceeding; consequently, the Security Council had no basis upon which to intervene. The Soviet delegates were willing to debate procedure, but not discuss the case on its merits. The Council agreed that the negotiations in process should be continued and requested the parties to inform the Council as to the result of these negotiations.

GREECE. Apparently by way of reprisals, the Soviet Union, on January 21, asked for discussion of the continued presence of British forces in Greece. The Soviet delegate, forgetting the procedural questions which he had raised in the Iranian dispute, took up the case on its merits and attacked the United Kingdom through many pages of the *Journal*. Mr. Bevin, in his eagerness to have the charges against his country disculpated, also disregarded procedure and discussed the case on its merits. The delegate of the United States, who had argued that the Iranian matter should be a continuing concern of the Council until a settlement had been reached, now argued that the Council had no authority to make recommendations since it had not found that a dispute existed. The matter was informally closed by permitting the president of the Security Council to issue a statement which took note of what had been said, neither condemned nor approved, and declared the matter closed.

INDONESIA. The Ukrainian delegate on the same date made various extreme accusations with regard to the presence of British troops in Indonesia, and demanded that a commission be appointed to investigate and "establish peace in Indonesia"—a task obviously beyond the authority of the Council under Chapter VI. The Ukrainian proposal was defeated.

SYRIA AND LEBANON. A note of February 4 brought to the attention of the Security Council a "matter which might give rise to serious disputes," concerning the continued presence of French and British troops in Syria and Lebanon. The two countries jointly asked for the "total and simultaneous evacuation" of these troops. Since neither of these states had a seat on the Security Council, both were invited to sit with it but on the understanding that the invitation did not constitute a recognition that a dispute existed. Various delegates insisted that it was the right and duty of the Council, and not of the complainant, to say whether a dispute existed within the meaning of the Charter. Long and involved efforts were made by the Soviet group to induce the Council to make recommendations. Britain and France volunteered to withdraw their troops and to abstain from voting so as to arouse no questions of procedure. Seven votes were obtained for this solution, but the Soviet delegate objected that without his vote the resolution was not carried. The British and French, not content with this strange way of escape offered them, promised to withdraw their troops and did so.

IRAN AGAIN. It seems appropriate to designate the renewal on March 18 of the Iranian case as another case, since it was raised this time upon a different Charter footing, as a dispute rather than as a situation. The ensuing debate was warm and difficult to comprehend, and eventuated in a question of fundamental procedural importance. The United States was represented by Secretary of State Byrnes who was now taking a more firm attitude against the Soviet Union. The Council had not decided that there was a dispute before it, and Mr. Gromyko (Soviet Union) charged that the United States was acting as if the communication from Iran was alone sufficient to compel the Security Council to deal with the substance of the dispute. Mr. Byrnes denied this, claiming still to be on a procedural basis—that is, debating whether it was a dispute over which the Council could take jurisdiction. Nevertheless, the resolution which he offered on April 4 took note of statements that the Soviet troops were to be withdrawn and that no conditions were to be attached to their withdrawal, and asked that both parties report by May 6 as to whether they had been withdrawn. This could be interpreted merely as a request for information from the parties; it could also be interpreted as an ultimatum. The Soviet Union took the latter viewpoint. Its delegates had already refused to attend meetings of the Council because its request for a few days' delay had been refused, and they now demanded that the Iranian question be removed from the agenda as being in conflict with the Charter.

Meanwhile, the Secretary-General had intervened with a memorandum, which maintained that the matter could not be on the agenda properly unless the Council had found that it was a dispute of the type referred to in Article 33—which had not been done. The Council overrode this objection as too narrow; it seemed to argue that its authority under Article 24 was superior to procedural limitations set by the

Charter. The Soviet delegate did not appear on May 6, the date set for report, but Soviet troops were withdrawn—and possibly would have been withdrawn in any case. The case constituted an important precedent, and thereafter the Council did what it could with cases brought before it, without stopping to determine whether it was a dispute in which it had jurisdiction.

THE EGYPTIAN COMPLAINT. Egypt complained, on July 8, 1947, of the presence of British troops in Egypt and in the Sudan, asserting that this was contrary to the wishes of the people and that it was impairing the unity of the Nile Valley—neither of which complaints seemed to have relevance either to the Charter or to international law. She referred to Articles 35 and 37 of the Charter and asked that the Council direct the immediate and total evacuation of British troops. This was beyond the power of the Council. The doctrine of *rebus sic stantibus* was raised in connection with the treaty of 1936. The Egyptian demands were extravagantly presented and aroused no sympathy; nothing was done by the Council.

GREEK FRONTIER. On August 24, 1946, the Ukrainian Republic, referring to Articles 34 and 35, charged that the Greek government was provoking border incidents along its Albanian frontier and that the presence of British troops in Greece was the principal factor in producing this situation. The representative of the Netherlands appealed to the Council to maintain its dignity and not allow itself to become the "sounding board of unsubstantiated grievances"; and the British delegate objected to putting on the agenda "for extraneous and irrelevant purposes, frivolous counter-charges designed to distract attention from real issues." After several weeks of heated discussion a number of resolutions were all defeated, including a proposal for a committee of investigation, which was vetoed by the Soviet Union.[7]

A few weeks later, however, on December 3, 1946, the Greek government submitted a plea, based on Articles 34 and 35, alleging that guerilla warfare was being waged against her by her neighbors, Albania, Bulgaria and Yugoslavia. A proposal by the United States to send a commission of investigation to the Balkans was this time not opposed, and a commission composed of representatives of all members of the Security Council was dispatched in January, 1947. It was not only to investigate, but "to make any proposals that it may deem wise for averting a repetition of border violations and disturbances in that area."

[7] In connection with this proposal, the Secretary-General asserted an independent right to conduct his own investigation of such a situation. Security Council, *Official Records*, First Year, Second Series, No. 16, p. 404. The statement was approved by the president of the Council (Soviet Union) and was challenged by no one.

This was criticized as going beyond the purposes of Article 34, and as delegating to a suborgan powers which should be exercised only by the Council itself. The unanimity thus displayed was much jarred by announcement of the "Truman Doctrine."[8] The Soviet representative proposed a resolution to assure that outside aid should be administered in the real interests of the Greek people. Resolutions proposed by the United States were vetoed, among them one for a supervisory commission, and one to hold that a threat to the peace existed. Finally, a resolution was adopted to take the matter off the list of items of which the Security Council was seized and to place the records of the case at the disposal of the General Assembly.

The Assembly, thus free to act, adopted Resolution 109 (II), in terms similar to the resolution defeated in the Security Council, and set up the United Nations Special Committee on the Balkans (UNSCOB) to keep an eye on the situation. Long resolutions were adopted in the two following years, calling upon the neighbors of Greece to behave; they were uncooperative, however, and refused to allow UNSCOB in their territories. By 1950, the effects of the Truman Doctrine were being felt, and the defection from the Communist bloc of Yugoslavia, which thereupon resumed normal relations with Greece, relieved some of the pressure. The continuing supervision of the United Nations undoubtedly had some effect in this situation, but how much, in comparison with other pressures, it would be hard to determine.

ALBANIA. British warships were damaged by mines in the Corfu Channel and the British government, charging the Albanian government with having caused the damage, brought the matter before the Security Council under Article 35, on January 10, 1947. Albania was invited to send a representative, and one arrived after a few weeks delay and assured the Council that Albania knew nothing whatever about the mines and that the United Kingdom was carrying on "organized and consecutive provocations." A resolution having been

---

[8] The Security Council was officially informed on March 28, 1947, of a proposal by the United States to provide some $400 million for aid to Greece and Turkey. This offer had been made in a message by President Truman on March 12. He included military aid because "it must be the policy of the United States to support free peoples who are resisting attempted subjugation by armed minorities or by outside pressures." He asserted that the situation was one of immediate urgency, and that "the United Nations and its related organizations are not in a position to extend help of the kind that is required." *Dept. of State Bull.*, 16 (1947), p. 534. Senator Vandenberg, representing a public opinion somewhat shocked at this disregard of the United Nations, led Congress to adopt a resolution under which the aid provided should cease whenever the Security Council or General Assembly should by majority vote find that such aid is unnecessary or undesirable.

vetoed by the Soviet Union, it was agreed to recommend to the parties (Article 36, paragraph 3) that they should refer the matter to the International Court of Justice.[9]

Four controversies which had their beginnings in 1946-47 deserve fuller treatment because of their significance in the development of the methods of handling disputes by the United Nations. It would be hard to classify them all as disputes, but their handling by organs of the United Nations indicates that these organs were not greatly concerned as to the distinctions made or the procedures set by the Charter according to which the situations should be considered.

145. SPAIN

The delegate of Poland, in a note of April 9, 1946, called the attention of the Security Council to the "international friction" arising from the existence of the Franco regime in Spain and suggested action under Article 34. He maintained that the situation in Spain could not be regarded as an internal matter, and that Article 2, paragraph 6, enabled the Council to deal with non-members. A committee was appointed to ascertain whether or not the Spanish situation actually endangered international peace and security; it made a long report which admitted that there was no threat to the peace under Article 39, but claimed that the Franco regime did endanger peace and security. It was a strange situation, in which there were no parties to a dispute and where the state principally concerned paid no attention whatever to the uproar. The debate was largely whether the matter was one of domestic jurisdiction. The United Kingdom regarded it as undeniable that the governmental regime within a country was a matter of domestic jurisdiction, and there was much support for this view, including some from Latin American states, on the ground of non-intervention. Mr. Evatt of Australia, chairman of the subcommittee, said:

. . . Article 2, paragraph 7 of the Charter does not say that the United Nations shall not intervene in any matter which does not fall within Chapter VII. What it does say is that the United Nations shall not intervene in a matter essentially within the domestic jurisdiction of a state.[10]

The strong passions against the accomplice of the Axis Powers would have prevailed, except that the Soviet Union thought that the resolution proposed did not go far enough and therefore cast a veto. Its dele-

[9] See p. 360 above. This is the only instance in which the Security Council recommended that the parties have recourse to legal settlement of their disputes.

[10] Security Council, *Official Records*, First Year, First Series, p. 317 (44th Meeting).

gate insisted that the Franco regime was a threat to the peace and therefore not excluded by Article 2, paragraph 7. Finally, the Council dropped the matter from its agenda.

This left the way open for the General Assembly to act, and after long debate it adopted Resolution 39(I) which excluded Spain from membership in specialized agencies—an action for which the Assembly had no authority. It also requested Members to break off diplomatic relations with Spain; this is one of the sanctions mentioned in Article 41, to be applied by the Security Council after determination that a threat to the peace exists. The Assembly further suggested that, if a democratic government were not set up within a reasonable time in Spain, the Security Council should consider what ought to be done. All this was done out of loss of temper and resentment against Spain, and it set a bad precedent of disrespect for the Charter. The suggestion that the Court be asked whether the proposed action was legitimate received no support. The effort was a failure; Members were not enthusiastic about breaking off diplomatic relations, and the Fourth Assembly rescinded the action taken.

146. SOUTH AFRICA

India complained, beginning on June 22, 1946, of the treatment of persons of Indian origin (though South African nationals) in South Africa. The matter was not submitted as a dispute, but India charged that the actions by South Africa were contrary to the Capetown agreement and to the provisions of the Charter concerning human rights. She asserted that the mistreatment of these persons impaired friendly relations within the meaning of Article 14. Marshal Smuts, representing South Africa, replied that the persons concerned were nationals of South Africa and legitimately under its control; that the so-called Capetown agreement was not an international legal instrument but a mere statement of policy; and that the General Assembly could not constitutionally deal with such a domestic matter. He proposed that the question of the competence of the Assembly to deal with the matter be referred to the International Court of Justice. This was rejected by vote of thirty-one to twenty-one, with two abstentions, and Resolution 44(I) was adopted, asserting that friendly relations had been impaired and expressing the hope that the treatment of the Indians in South Africa would be made to conform with international obligations. This singled out a particular state for criticism; Assembly resolutions are usually in general terms.

Thereafter, almost every session produced a resolution directed against South Africa. The Assembly took no notice of the claim, consistently and inflexibly maintained by South Africa, that the resolutions were illegal because of Article 2, paragraph 7. The tide of sentiment against South Africa overran respect for the Charter. Belgium and a few other states insisted upon referring the question to the Court; the United States was on both sides, but increasingly turned toward respect for Charter provisions; most of the other states were impatient with Charter restrictions. The Mexican delegate felt that it was wrong to invoke legalistic reasoning against the express provisions of the Charter concerning human rights. The Philippine delegate asserted that reference to the Court would beg the moral question. Pakistan asked how legal arguments on competence could be invoked to divert attention from so tragic a situation. The Soviet delegates claimed that the fact that the Assembly had acted was sufficient proof that it had a right to do so; if not, the Assembly would not have adopted the resolutions!

All this pressure had no effect upon South Africa, except perhaps to push it into worse measures of racial discrimination (*apartheid*). This opened a new line of attack against her, and the Sixth Assembly adopted a resolution requesting South Africa to suspend enforcement of her Group Areas Act; this carried intervention still further by concentrating on a specific item of internal legislation. The Seventh Assembly was asked by thirteen states to consider the race conflict in South Africa, and again South Africa raised the question of competence. The president ruled in accordance with Rule 80 of procedure that the question must be voted on immediately; he was overruled by a vote of forty-one to ten, with eight abstentions. South Africa raised the question in the *ad hoc* Political Committee and was voted down; she raised it again in plenary Assembly, asking specifically that the Assembly declare that it was unable to adopt the proposed resolution. It was voted down, forty-three to six, with nine abstentions; and the Assembly had thus, for the first time, voted that it was not incompetent to do the things it had been doing for seven years, in the face of continuous challenges to its competence.

Two resolutions were adopted at this seventh session. Resolution 616(A) established a Commission on the Racial Situation in South Africa to study and report back;[11] Resolution 616(B) was not addressed specifically to South Africa, but called upon all Members to bring their policies into consonance with their obligation to promote

---

[11] The report of this commission (A/2505) contains the strongest argument officially made to show that Article 2(7) should not stand in the way of the action proposed.

human rights. By now, alarm was beginning to be shown at the continuous expansion of Assembly action through majority vote. The former resolution, adopted by thirty-five in favor and one against, had twenty-three abstentions; the latter was adopted by twenty-four to one, with the surprising number of thirty-four abstentions. The Eighth and Ninth Assemblies adopted resolutions no stronger than before; the Tenth Assembly adopted resolutions in still milder terms, and discontinued the commission.

This controversy, and that over Spain, brought out clearly the inherent conflict in the Charter between the restriction in favor of domestic jurisdiction and the obligation of the United Nations and its Members to promote human rights and fundamental freedoms. It would be difficult to imagine a more clearly domestic matter than the internal legislation of South Africa concerning its own citizens; at the same time, the policies of South Africa gave good ground for the accusation that it was not respecting human rights—even though the Charter does not say what are the human rights. The anti-colonial majority could obtain some sympathy for its accusations, and the states which wished to uphold what they regarded as the law of the Charter were embarrassed to oppose them. Increasingly, these states resorted to abstentions; some even said that they regarded the proposal as unconstitutional but, since the matter had not been referred to the Court for decision, they would abstain. This was a convenient way out, and left the majority free to do what they wished. Many of the resolutions adopted by the General Assembly could not have been adopted but for abstentions.

Again, as in the case of Spain, the extreme effort resulted in nothing. The Charter was pushed aside and the majority had its way, but it had no effect upon South Africa, convinced of the illegality of the action against it, except to build up resentment and push it farther away from the United Nations; in the last sessions, its delegates refused to participate in discussion of its situation. There seems now to be a slight trend toward support of Article 2, paragraph 7, or toward less extreme interpretation of it, and an increasing unwillingness to direct action against a particular state.

147. INDONESIA[12]

When the Japanese withdrew from the Indonesian islands in August 1945 there was a confused situation. British forces arrived first in the territory, and it was their embarrassing responsibility to maintain order. A Republic of Indonesia had been set up, of debated back-

12 J. F. Collins, "The United Nations and Indonesia," *Int. Con.*, No. 459 (1950).

ground, but the Dutch, whose colony it was, were not present. We have noted above the Ukrainian complaint concerning British forces in Indonesia.

The Indonesian situation was brought up again, however, in more serious fashion, by Australia and India, at the end of July 1947. A long struggle followed, of both constitutional and political importance to the United Nations. Australia raised the question under Article 39, as a threat to the peace; India contented herself with referring to Article 35. By this time the Netherlands had resumed control over the islands, but had encountered much resistance. In March 1947, carrying further her earlier plans for a commonwealth of her colonies, the Netherlands had, by the Linggadjati agreement, recognized the Republic of Indonesia as *de facto* sovereign of the territory it controlled, and agreed to set up a federal system for the various Indonesian units. This did not work out satisfactorily, and there was armed conflict. It was this situation which disturbed Australia and India to the point of bringing the matter before the Security Council.

The representative of the Netherlands argued, in consonance with past colonial practice, that this was only a quarrel between a colony and its parent country, and not a dispute between states; further, that Article 2, paragraph 7, forbade the United Nations to intervene in such domestic matters; and that there was no quarrel, no threat to the peace, of an international character. Australia maintained that the Netherlands, by making the Linggadjati agreement, had recognized the Republic of Indonesia as a sovereign state, and insisted that there was conflict between two sovereign states, though one of them was not a Member of the United Nations. Article 2, paragraph 6, covered that situation. The early discussion was with regard to the competence of the Council to consider the case. Belgium insisted upon a vote on this matter, but none was ever taken; later, it was on several occasions remarked that the question of competence had never been decided. Mr. Van Kleffens (Netherlands) plaintively asked: If the majority of the members of the Council indicated that they intend to do as they please, why have any Charter?

There was no doubt in the statement of Mr. Gromyko (Soviet Union) that there was a threat to the peace and that the Council must act. Various others felt as did the Indian representative, who asserted that the Council must take care that attempts to defeat international justice under the guise of legalism should not be encouraged. The United States was on the fence, but seemed to think that if there was shooting, something ought to be done about it. The Soviet Union asked for a commission of investigation, but this was vetoed by France. It was agreed instead to set up a commission composed of the consuls of those members of the Council which had consuls in Batavia —thus neatly excluding the Soviet Union. The Council also offered its good offices and set up a commission to assist. A truce was agreed upon in January 1948; it was negotiated on the neutral ground of the U.S.S. *Renville* and was therefore called the Renville agreement. During the months which followed, there were various resolutions urging the parties to the dispute to find a peaceful settlement—though it had never been decided that there was a dispute. In January 1949, the two bodies above mentioned being ready to give up, the Council established the United Nations Commission for Indonesia, and called upon the Netherlands to set up a "federal, independent and sovereign United States of Indonesia." By this time, no one bothered about the authority of the United Nations to make such a demand.

Meanwhile, the Dutch had proposed a "round table conference" at The Hague, and the Council's commission furnished assistance. It was agreed at this conference that the Netherlands would transfer sovereignty unconditionally to the Republic of the United States of Indonesia, and this was done on December 27, 1949. The Security Council had thus shown strength, whether in harmony with the Charter or not; but some credit must also go to the economic pressure exerted by the United States, and some to internal Dutch troubles. It was a remarkable feat to deprive a state of its rich colonies in this fashion, with no authority whatever to do so.

An epilogue may be added. Insatiable nationalism went at once to work in its autophagous fashion. The Indonesian federation, agreed upon at the Round Table Conference, was at once dissolved into a unitary state, and other units, who had expected autonomy within the system, rather than submission to the Indonesian Republic, claimed the same right of self-determination which it had claimed. Such claims were resisted by force, and the struggle was maintained by the "Republic of the South Moluccas" and others. In both the political sense and the economic sense, the new state—it was admitted to the United Nations in 1950—has had a struggle to maintain itself. Neverthless, it now reaches out to claim "Irian," or Western New Guinea.

148. PALESTINE

In the Near East, many changes occurred during and after World War I. Parts of the Turkish Empire became mandated territories under the League of Nations, among them Palestine, for which the mandatory power was Great Britain. At varying times, a number of units appeared as independent Arab states. Great Britain had said, in the Balfour Declaration of 1917, that she favored making a national home for the Jews in Palestine. Jews began to move in, especially after Nazi persecution, and this brought strife with the Arabs and put Britain into a difficult situation. In 1947 Britain called a special session of the General Assembly, and passed the problem over to it. This could hardly be called a dispute—it was brought up under Article 10—though it later developed into a bitter one. The Arab states fought against putting it on the agenda, but the General Assembly appointed a Special Committee on Palestine (UNSCOP), which reported with a Plan for Partition with Economic Union, with autonomy for the holy city of Jerusalem. A United Nations Commission was to administer the scheme, and Jerusalem would be put under the Trusteeship Council. Resolution 181(II), which incorporated this plan, barely received the necessary two-thirds majority.

This resolution also requested the Security Council to implement the plan and to "determine as a threat to the peace, breach of the peace, or act of aggression, any attempt to alter by force the settlement envisaged by this resolution." The Security Council took up the request in December 1947 and after much debate decided that it did not have the authority to enforce a recommendation of the Assembly—that is, not until it had decided that there was a threat to the peace. Instead, it called upon the parties to avoid violence and called for another special session of the assembly. The United States proposal for a trusteeship regime met with no support. Instead, the Assembly decided in May, 1948 to appoint a mediator, and Count Bernadotte of Sweden acted in this capacity with some success, until he was unaccountably assassinated in Israel in September. He had achieved a temporary truce, but could not effect a settlement. On July 15, then, the Security Council, after two or three previous refusals, determined "that the situation in Palestine constitutes a threat to the peace within the meaning of Article 39 of the Charter." It then ordered the parties to cease fighting, which, for a time, they did.

The work of Count Bernadotte was carried on by Ralph Bunche, of the Secretariat, with great success; indeed, a large part of whatever success the United Nations had in Palestine should be credited to the Secretariat. The Third Assembly, by Resolution 194(III), set up a conciliation commission, and Dr. Bunche, working with patience, persistence, and tact, was able to announce that an armistice had been arranged, to be supervised by a United Nations Truce Supervision Organization. Israel had abruptly been recognized, *de facto*, by the United States on May 14, 1948, and it was admitted to the United Nations on May 11, 1949.

The armistice, unfortunately, did not lead to a final settlement. Jerusalem remains divided, and the fact that Israel moved its capital to that city did not help to produce good feeling. Almost a million Arab refugees have had to be fed by the United Nations, and there have been sporadic outbursts of violence along the frontiers. The Arab states have never been willing to recognize the existence of Israel as a state and have refused direct negotiations with it. Egypt has been particularly hostile, claiming that a state of war exists; and in 1954, Israel complained to the Security Council concerning the blockade maintained by Egypt. Later, Egypt released a captured Israeli vessel and crew, but has maintained the blockade. By the summer of 1955 tension had increased alarmingly and the United States offered to join with Britain and France to guarantee frontiers and to help financially in the resettlement of refugees. This could hardly be called United Nations action, and the Soviet Union was naturally unenthusiastic about it. Supply of arms to Egypt by Czechoslovakia increased the danger and, early in 1956, the Security Council requested the Secretary-General to use his good offices. He consulted with the leaders of the various states concerned and was successful to the extent of securing agreement to another uneasy truce. He had made no effort to obtain a final settlement and urged that the parties be left to work this out among themselves.

The above brief sketch does not begin to show the effort which the United Nations has exerted in this problem, the various organs concerned, the numerous approaches and methods tried. The struggle is a bitter one, and the United Nations cannot claim to have settled it; but it can claim with some pride that it has prevented an outright war, which would undoubtedly have been a bloody one.

149. INDIA

When Great Britain gave up India, she did so through the India Independence Act of 1947, which set up as independent the Hindu state of India and the Moslem state of Pakistan, and allowed the hundreds of other "princely states" to choose between joining one of these two, or remaining independent. Most of them joined India, some of them under pressure, but a few were unwilling; two such cases came before the Security Council. Kashmir, in between India and Pakistan, had a Hindu ruler, although most of the population belonged to the Moslem faith. Hyderabad, in the center of India, had a Moslem ruler, with 85 per cent of the population Hindu.

KASHMIR. The struggle over Kashmir led to use of both Pakistani and Indian troops, and on January 1, 1948, India took this "situation" to the Council; a fortnight later, Pakistan brought it up as a "dispute."[13] The Council at once adopted several resolutions, calling for withdrawal of armed forces (which was not done), establishing a commission to investigate, and—since India had asserted that it would not take Kashmir without a plebiscite favoring it—appointing Admiral Nimitz as plebiscite administrator. But the parties were unable to agree upon terms of demilitarization, with particular regard to the number of troops each should be allowed to have in Kashmir. This would manifestly affect the conduct of a plebiscite, and the difficulty effectively prevented a solution. It is one of those situations in which there is generous agreement *en principe*, and obstinate inability to agree on details.

Many methods were followed by the Council in its effort to reach a satisfactory settlement. The commission above mentioned reported failure, and recommended that one man continue the effort. The president of the Security Council tried; in 1950, Sir Owen Dixon tried and failed; and, in 1951, Dr. Frank Graham began patient and tenacious efforts. He was able to report some gains in 1953, as a result of which a conference was held at Geneva—in vain. No final solution has been reached, though Kashmir is steadily being absorbed into India; the Security Council, however, may here also claim to have prevented bloody war. There are other causes of friction—communal, religious rivalry, claims arising out of the separation, and the control by India over waters of the Indus River needed for irrigation in Pakistan. In the fall of 1955, a step toward reconciliation was made through a trade agreement helpful to both states.

HYDERABAD. There was a somewhat similar situation, quickly ended, when one of the princely states, Hyderabad, fearing invasion by India, appealed to the Council under Article 35.[14] A "stand-still" agreement had been made, and an agreement to arbitrate; but the Security Council had barely begun discussion when news came that Indian forces had seized Hyderabad, and the Nizam of Hyderabad instructed his representative to withdraw the complaint. This he refused to do, and the Council, apparently suspecting that the instruction had been given under duress, kept the matter on its continuing agenda. Further than this, the Council did nothing, though Pakistan brought the case before it again in the following year. Members were unwilling to offend India,

---

[13] Later, both sides called it a dispute and it was so recognized in the preamble of a Security Council resolution of April 21, 1948. This is the only case in which the Council determined, even indirectly, that a dispute existed. See Security Council, Third Year, *Official Records*, 286th Meeting.

[14] Taxaknath Das, "The Status of Hyderabad During and after British Rule in India," *A.J.*, 43 (1949), p. 57; C. Eagleton, "The Case of Hyderabad before the Security Council," *A.J.*, 44 (1950), p. 277.

which might become Communist. And, it was argued, Hyderabad was in fact geographically part of India. The case is interesting because of the questions it raised. Could a non-member of the United Nations enter a complaint? India asserted that Hyderabad was not a state. Could India exclude discussion on the ground that it was a domestic question? This barrier had not held her back with regard to South Africa or Indonesia. Could the claim be continued after the ruler had withdrawn it? The Council asserted its jurisdiction by keeping it on the agenda; even though doing nothing about it. This was the most clear case of aggression which the Council has faced, and its inaction represents its most complete failure.

150. LATER CASES

When the Communists took over Czechoslovakia by a *coup d'état* in 1948, Chile asked the Security Council to investigate. The Soviet Union maintained that it was a domestic question, and Czechoslovakia refused to participate. A proposal to appoint a committee to investigate was defeated by a double veto.

BERLIN. In the case of the Berlin blockade in 1948, identic notifications were sent by France, the United Kingdom, and the United States complaining that no settlement had been possible under Article 33 and that the situation constituted a threat to the peace under Article 39. The Soviet representative replied that there was no threat to the peace and that the Council, because of Article 107, had no jurisdiction over the case. The veto prevented adoption of any resolution; but the "airlift" maintained at some cost by the United States relieved Berlin. The United Nations could claim little more credit in this situation than making possible the meeting between Jessup and Malik which led to agreement to end the blockade.

FAR EASTERN PROBLEMS. The Korean situation will be discussed in the following chapter, but there arose out of it several matters to keep the Security Council occupied. The month of August, 1950, was a memorable one; it was the month of the presidency of the Soviet Union in the council. The Soviet representative, Mr. Malik, whose previous absence had made possible the action in Korea, involved the Council in parliamentary maneuverings for the entire month. On August 24 the Peoples' Republic of China charged the United States with aggression against Taiwan (Formosa). The debate was largely over inviting a representative of Communist China, but a Soviet resolution condemning the United States was defeated. Three days later, another charge was made, of invasion of the air sovereignty of Communist

China by the United States; the United States proposed a commission to investigate, and this was vetoed by the Soviet Union. The United States brought to the Council, on September 8, 1954, the charge that Russian jet planes had attacked an American aircraft over the high seas near Siberia. Mr. Vyshinsky denied the charge and asserted that his government would pay no attention to a Council directive. Mr. Lodge (United States) reinforced his case by citing thirty-nine instances of similar attacks by "trigger-happy" Communists. In the General Assembly, it was agreed on November 2 to consider Soviet charges that the United States had committed aggression against Communist China and that Nationalist China had committed acts of piracy on the high seas by seizing vessels destined for the mainland. The latter charge was referred to the International Law Commission.[15] In December, the United States, together with fifteen other nations which had fought in Korea, presented a resolution calling for the release of eleven soldiers illegally imprisoned by Communist China. The Secretary-General flew to Peiping to discuss this; later, the prisoners were released.

The danger of collision around Formosa increased, as it appeared that Communist China was preparing to seize from the Nationalists some offshore islands. The Security Council in January 1955 invited the Communists to come and discuss the matter, but they refused unless the representatives of Nationalist China "were driven out" of the Council, and unless first consideration were given to the resolution condemning the United States for its aggression. Later in that year, a changed Soviet attitude gave hope that there would be no further war and that a settlement might ultimately be reached.

ANGLO-IRANIAN OIL CO. A strong upsurge of nationalism in Iran led to the assumption of power by the fanatical Mossadegh, and to a law nationalizing the oil industry of that country, including the great British refinery at Abadan, held by the British under an agreement made in 1933. Mossadegh maintained that his unilateral termination of this agreement was a domestic question. The British attempted to negotiate the issue—as did also Averell Harriman on behalf of the United States —in vain, and then appealed to the International Court of Justice which ordered provisional measures. Iran denied the right of the Court to issue such orders and forced the British out; whereupon the British appealed to the Security Council. Political cross-currents were at work here, and the Council decided to wait until the court made a pronouncement. The Court, however, denied that it had jurisdiction, in view of the reservation which Iran had attached to its acceptance of

---

[15] Which referred to its article on piracy, in its draft code on the Regime of the High Seas, G.A. X, *Official Records*, Supp. No. 9, pp. 6-7.

the Optional Clause. Thus Britain found no relief; on the other hand, Iran was on the verge of bankruptcy. Finally, Mossadegh was forced out of power by internal pressure, and a joint international group of oil producers took over the handling of the Iranian oil.[16]

NORTH AFRICA. The same nationalistic and anti-colonial tide, which flowed throughout Asia and the Near East, brought trouble to France in North Africa. Six Arab states put before the General Assembly in 1951 the charge that France was violating human rights in Morocco. France took a strong stand against interference by the United Nations with her domestic problem and the Council did not take up the charge. A few months later, eleven Arab and Asian states brought before the Security Council the "alarming situation" in Tunisia, which, they said, constituted a threat to the peace; the Council, in April 1952, refused to put the item on its agenda. The General Assembly, in the practically identical resolutions 611(VII) and 612(VII), hoped and urged that "the parties" (was it a dispute?) would negotiate their differences successfully; the Ninth Assembly postponed consideration of the items. At the Tenth Assembly, Algeria was added to the complaints, and France indignantly withdrew from the Assembly, with hints that it might withdraw from the United Nations. As a result, the Assembly resolved that it was no longer seized of the Algerian question, and decided also to postpone the Moroccan item again.

The check thus put upon the anti-colonial drive was due partly to the strong stand by France against what it asserted was illegal interference in its domestic affairs (South Africa had also withdrawn her delegates); partly to increasing concern shown by the majority for restrictions set in the Charter, and partly to a political situation which called for support of France by her NATO allies. Nevertheless, France was forced to make concessions to her territories in North Africa. The Indian attempt to push the Portuguese out of Goa and other possessions in that subcontinent, the violence in Cyprus and the Indonesian claims to "west Irian," all testify to the continuing strength of anti-colonialism.[17]

GUATEMALA. One other incident may be mentioned, which illustrates the meaning of "regional arrangements" in Chapter VIII of the Charter. Guatemala, on June 20, 1954, charged that open aggression had been perpetrated against her by Honduras and Nicaragua; the

[16] See p. 361 above, for the case before the Court. Both countries were bound to compulsory jurisdiction by acceptance of the Optional Clause, but Iran claimed that her reservation denied jurisdiction to the Court in this matter, and the Court upheld the claim. If the Court had no jurisdiction, did it have a right to order provisional measures? Iran said no, and withdrew her acceptance of the Optional Clause.

[17] For further consideration of the drive for self-determination, and against colonialism, see pp. 436-43 above.

charge, as explained by her representative to the Security Council, made the United States almost as guilty a party. There was no doubt that the United States, fearful that the Communists might be taking over Guatemala, played an energetic role in the situation. She and other states felt that it was a matter which ought to be referred to the Organization of American States (OAS), but the Soviet Union cast its sixtieth veto against this. A resolution was adopted calling on the parties to refrain from bloodshed and upon Members to refrain from giving assistance to any of the parties. Another urgent session of the Council met on June 25, but could not reach agreement.

Meanwhile, the Inter-American Peace Committee, notified by Guatemala, had begun to consider the matter; Guatemala objected, but Honduras and Nicaragua asked it to investigate. When the Security Council did not act, Guatemala agreed to receive a fact-finding committee from the American body. By the time it had arrived, however, the controversy had, with the overthrow of the existing government in Guatemala, ceased to exist. The situation here was much confused and it is doubtful whether it established a precedent for determining whether the Security Council or the OAS should take jurisdiction when appeals are made to both.

151. CONCLUSIONS

The methods employed by the United Nations for the peaceful settlement of disputes among its Members, or other states, have for the most part been *ad hoc* and opportunistic, with little adherence to the rules or procedures provided in the Charter, or even in the rules of procedure. We have earlier observed that two main methods for the settlement of disputes had been historically developed. They may be called legal methods, including arbitration and judicial settlement, and political methods, meaning efforts of various kinds to persuade the two parties to reach agreement between themselves.

The former method, so far as the United Nations has been concerned, may be disposed of briefly, for no organ of the United Nations has been inclined to refer disputes to legal settlement. Though Article 36, paragraph 3, is supposed to encourage reference by the parties to the Court, the Security Council has done this but once—in the Corfu Channel case. It has once or twice (India-Pakistan, Indonesia) suggested arbitration to the parties, but without avail.

Practically all peaceful settlement efforts, then, have been by the method of political adjustment, that is, conciliation between the parties. Since the United Nations cannot require parties to submit to legal settlement, in which the award is binding, and can act only through methods which require the consent of the parties, it is forced to study refinements and niceties of procedure which seem trivial to the average person (the same person, it may be noted, who is unwilling to allow his state to submit to a settlement imposed from the outside). These refinements, or various methods of procedure, are too numerous to be studied in detail here.[18] In general, the Security Council has been inclined to follow the procedure suggested by the parties. The first step is usually to urge the parties to refrain from hostile action or to cease fire if shooting has begun, and to seek agreement through direct negotiations between themselves. It may then undertake an investigation, through hearing the parties or by appointment of a commission for the purpose—though in practice such commissions never report on the purpose, according to Article 34, for which they are created, which is to determine whether the dispute is one of the type which gives to the Council the right to take jurisdiction over it. The commissions are in fact of various kinds; some of them are authorized to engage in efforts at conciliation between the parties. It would seem, however, that the most successful efforts at conciliation have been carried out by a single person acting as mediator. The Secretary-General has been employed, but in the lesser, though important, function of "good offices."

Beyond conciliation, the organs of the United Nations can go no further. It is dealing with sovereign nations whom it has no authority to command, and whom it can only persuade. Its resolutions are recommendations only.

During its ten years, the United Nations has dealt with perhaps twenty-five cases which could be regarded as disturbances of the peace. It is difficult to classify them since neither the Council nor the Assembly ever decides that a matter is a dispute "the continuance of which is likely to endanger the maintenance of international peace and security"; and it is difficult to distinguish between such a dispute and other matters calling for adjustment, such as Palestine or Trieste. In few of these cases has a permanent and satisfactory settlement been achieved; and this is not surprising, granted the lack of authority given to the United Nations. It has, however, been able to prevent any large scale fighting, except in Korea. It has been successful in carrying out the task stated in Article 1, "to maintain international peace and security" or, in the words of the preamble, "to save succeeding generations from the scourge of war."

This achievement has been made in the midst of confusion, both external and internal. Externally, the bi-polar political world and the

---

[18] Four pages of fine print in the *Repertoire* classify in detail the various methods actually used by the Council, pp. 297-300.

tide of nationalism and anti-colonialism have worked heavily against it. Internally, there has been no consistent interpretation and application of the Charter, and the irresponsibility and inconsistency of Members has not helped it. The Charter speaks in terms of gradations of seriousness: in Article 14, "likely to impair the general welfare or friendly relations among nations"; in Article 33, "likely to endanger the maintenance of international peace and security"; in Article 34, as to situations, "which might lead to international friction or give rise to a dispute"; in Article 39, "threat to the peace, breach of the peace, or act of aggression." In practice, Members have paid little attention to such differentiations, except as to Article 39, and it is often not possible to determine under which article of the Charter a decision has been taken. Little attention has been paid to the procedures laid down in Chapter VI, or to the limitation in Article 2, paragraph 7.

The veto, while abused, has proved to be not so great a hindrance as was believed. A procedural vote permits a matter to be dropped from the agenda of the Security Council and left for the Assembly to handle; and the practice of not counting abstentions as vetoes has enabled many decisions to be taken. Complaints have been generously heard; non-members and even non-states have been listened to. The duty of peaceful adjustment and peaceful settlement has been widely interpreted, and organs have been patient in listening to trivial complaints and to long-winded and vituperative speeches.

It was originally intended that the Security Council should handle disputes, though it was made possible for the Assembly to act in a reserve capacity; but the cold war and the veto have weakened it and reduced its prestige greatly. Where in 1946 it had fifteen cases before it, in 1953 there were only three, and the number of its meetings has diminished until it no longer keeps up with its stated schedule, which requires that there be no period longer than two weeks between meetings. The trend has been to bring issues before the General Assembly which, after all, can do as much as can the Council concerning disputes —that is, to hear them and make recommendations concerning them. The Uniting for Peace Resolution prepared the Assembly for greater responsibility in this regard.

All this flexibility in practice makes apprehensive those who would like to see the United Nations more of a legal order; it is praised by others as making achievement possible. Some degree of liberal interpretation is doubtless needed in view of the lack of authoritative statement, the conflicting provisions of the Charter, and the political maelstrom in the world outside. Little hope for improvement can be seen until states are more willing than they are at present to have their disputes settled by an authority outside themselves.

Chapter 18

THE UNITED NATIONS: CONTROL OF WAR

Within the people of each nation there is a yearning for an international order capable of giving to them the protection which they want against war, and, at the same time, there is a reluctance to submit to any controls from the outside.[1] As a result of the former feeling, too much was doubtless expected from the "International Security Organization" set up in 1945. The result of the latter feeling has been to hold back rather than develop the potentialities of that organization. Even so, the Charter was a definite advance over the League of Nations, in principle and even in practice.

PREREQUISITE DETERMINATION

152. CHARTER PROVISIONS

Governmental responsibilities for handling disputes and the use of force are usually quite different functions, dealt with by different organs. The policeman who stops a fight on the street does not pause to decide who is right and who is wrong; it is not his task to determine the aggressor, but only to prevent the use of force between the parties; a court will later pass on the claims of the disputants. In the United Na-

[1] On the problem in general, see E. M. Borchard, "The Impracticability of Enforcing Peace," *Yale Law Journal*, 55 (1946); Lord David Davies, *The Problem of the Twentieth Century: A Study in International Relationships* (London, 1930); F. S. Dunn, *War and the Minds of Men* (New York, 1950); F. Haviland, *The Political Role of the General Assembly* (U.N. Studies No. 7, Carnegie Endowment, 1951); *International Sanctions* (Royal Institute of International Affairs, London, 1938); P. C. Jessup, *International Security: The American Role in Collective Action for Peace* (New York, 1935); Kelsen, *passim*; J. MacLaurin, *The United Nations and Power Politics* (London, 1951); E. Rappard, *The Quest for Peace* (Cambridge, 1940); W. Schiffer, *The Legal Community of Mankind* (New York, 1954); Julius Stone, *Legal Controls of International Conflict* (New York, 1954); Staff Studies No. 7.

tions, the Security Council and, as things have developed, the General Assembly as well, have responsibility for both these functions; but they are different functions, represented by the differentiation between Chapter VI and Chapter VII of the Charter. At least in principle, the United Nations is given more authority to prevent the use of force between states than to give decisions as to the merits of a dispute or to impose a settlement upon the parties. The measures of enforcement given to the Security Council are limited to use in cases of a "threat to the peace, breach of the peace, or act of aggression" (Article 39) and cannot be used as a sanction to require performance of a settlement recommended under Chapter VI.

PRIMARY RESPONSIBILITY. The Security Council has more definite authority within its limited field of action, and its decisions are in principle more binding upon Members, than was the case with the Council of the League of Nations. By Article 24, it is given "primary responsibility" for the maintenance of international peace and security, but this, as will be seen, is not an exclusive responsibility, and the General Assembly stands ready to assume the responsibility when the Council fails. The only limitation set upon the Council is that it should "act in accordance with the Purposes and Principles of the United Nations"; but no authority was provided to judge whether it does so or not. Since there is no central authority to interpret the Charter, each Member may apparently decide for itself whether the decision taken was in accordance with the Charter and, therefore, whether it is bound by the decision. An effort has been made to extend the meaning of articles 24 and 25 by asserting that any decision (i.e., vote) is binding upon those concerned.[2]

In respect of sanctions, the Charter is, at least in theory, an advance over the Covenant of the League, in that it puts an obligation upon Members to contribute armed forces and other assistance to the United Nations for use in a disturbance of the peace, when called upon by the Security Council to do so. This obligation, in the case of the League, was limited to economic sanctions and there was no provision for the Council to call upon members to participate; a resolution early adopted interpreted this to mean that each Member of the League could decide for itself whether it was called upon to act. A decision by the Security

[2] This view, which depends upon the meaning to be given to the word "decision," has not prevailed. See, for instance, Brookings, *Peace and Security*, pp. 180-82. On the other hand, see the stand taken by the Security Council in overruling the memorandum of the Secretary-General in the Iranian case (p. 517-18 above). It is to be observed that no decisions of the General Assembly in this field can have the same binding effect upon Members as some decisions of the Security Council are supposed to have.

Council, on the contrary, calls for immediate obedience and response by all Members, or by "some of them as the Security Council may determine" (Article 48); they are bound also to afford "mutual assistance" (Article 49), a phrase the meaning of which has not been developed. While these provisions in theory confer upon the Security Council great authority, its ability to act is in practice so limited as to make decision impossible and action ineffective in most cases of enforcement. As things have developed, Members are about as free to decide whether to help or not as they were under the League of Nations. This situation is due, aside from current political factors, to the veto, to Article 43 and its uncertainty as to supply of forces, and to various technical problems.

153. THE DECISION TO ACT

Article 39 takes us a step beyond Chapter VI, though a connection remains; even after the Council has decided that enforcement action is in order, it may still make a recommendation. This might be another recommendation to settle the trouble, or it might be a recommendation, rather than an order, to Members to help with enforcement. At any rate, the Council is required to "determine the existence of any threat to the peace, breach of the peace, or act of aggression"; and, having reached such a decision, it must then decide what measures should be taken. The former determination is prerequisite to enforcement action; it is a vital decision, one not easy to make. It is subject to the veto, for it was clearly understood at San Francisco that the enforcement action of the United Nations could not be directed against one of the Great Powers. Each has a veto which can be employed to prevent action against itself; it can also be employed to prevent action against a friend, or for any other reason, or for no reason. Enforcement action against a Great Power, it was said, would simply mean a world war and wreck the United Nations; that institution should have no such ambition and must be content with holding down wars between smaller states, if and when the five permanent members of the Council agree to do so. The required unanimity would in ordinary times be difficult to obtain, and the development of the "cold war" has made it increasingly difficult.

Only three times has the determination been made, twice by the Security Council and once by the General Assembly. On July 15, 1948, the Council finally decided that the situation in Palestine was a "threat to the peace"; on June 25, 1950, in the fortunate absence of the Soviet Union, the attack by North Korea on South Korea was held to be a "breach of the peace"; and the General Assembly, on February 1, 1951, adopted Resolution 498(V), which held that the intervention of Communist China constituted "aggression." The determination by the General Assembly could not have the effect of obliging Members to act, but, since the Council gave no such order in either of its decisions, there has been in fact little difference between a determination by the Assembly and one by the Council.

In various other instances a determination has been called for but not given; e.g., in the cases of Spain, of Indonesia, and of Berlin. It is not a decision lightly to be made; it has been observed on a number of occasions by speakers that Members should not vote for a determination unless they are prepared to back it up by use of their national armed forces. The assertion has been made, and was indeed urged at San Francisco, that the Council must reach a decision when a charge is put before it; the Charter says "shall determine." There have been cases (e.g., Hyderabad), however, in which the Council took no action whatever; and there is no way to compel the Council to act. Its failure to determine that peace was disturbed could be taken as showing its belief that there was no such disturbance.

There seems to be little difference of meaning in the three terms used in Article 39. "Threat to the peace" is a very broad term; in the Spanish case, the Polish delegate observed that any threat to the peace is potential in nature and, when no longer potential, is actual aggression.[3] It has been insisted, however, that the threat must be a threat to international peace, and this might exclude civil war (the Soviet Union claimed that the Korean affair was an internal struggle of Korea), or a colonial fight (e.g., Indonesia). This also involves Article 2, paragraph 7. As regards "threat to the peace" and "breach of the peace," it is possible to take action against either or both parties without having to determine first, as was the case with the League of Nations, which party is the aggressor. "Act of aggression" in Article 39 would appear to involve a more serious decision than in the case of the other two terms, since it amounts to judging one party guilty.

DEFINITION OF AGGRESSION. The decision that a "threat to the peace, breach of the peace, or act of aggression" exists is a prerequisite to the ability of the Security Council to order enforcement action. For making this determination, the Charter provides no rules of law or criteria for guidance to the Council, beyond the vague words in articles 24 and 25. It was felt that the Security Council should be left completely free

---

[3] Security Council, *Official Records*, First Series No. 2, p. 370. See Kelsen, pp. 933-35. The Uniting for Peace Resolution (see below) did not provide that the General Assembly should determine the existence of a "threat to the peace" as it did for the other two terms.

to meet disturbances of the peace in whatever form they might appear, for the methods of Hitler and of the Soviet Union were fresh in the minds of all.

There was at San Francisco, however, some criticism of this freedom and an unsuccessful effort was there made to add to Article 39 the words "in conformity with international law." There was also a strong effort to include a definition of aggression. This was something the League of Nations had studied on various occasions;[4] one of its bodies reported that it was "impossible to decide, even in theory, what constitutes a case of aggression"; another thought that it would be better to substitute the word "war" for the word "aggression," since the latter could not be defined. To define aggression, it was said, would furnish a guide for those who wished to commit aggression, and be a trap for the unwary, who would think themselves protected by the definition.[5]

Though the attempt to include in the Charter a definition of aggression failed, the effort has been renewed. It represents a deep-seated feeling that a decision condemning aggression ought to be made in accordance with rules or principles. The Soviet Union, at the Fifth Assembly, offered a definition which was criticized as not covering "devious methods of infiltration, intimidation and subterfuge." The problem was referred to the International Law Commission, which disposed of it by including it in the draft code of Offences against the Peace and Security of Mankind.[6] The matter was debated in the Assembly's Sixth Committee, where some favored enumeration of acts which should be regarded as aggression, others favored a general statement which would leave more discretion to the Security Council, and a large number opposed any attempt to provide a definition.

The strong drive behind this effort finds some explanation in Resolution 559(VI) which, considering, *inter alia*, "that it would be of defi-

[4] For a summary of this effort, with citations to documents, see C. Eagleton, "The Attempt to Define Aggression," *Int. Con.*, No. 264 (1930). As to the problem in general, *Research in International Law*, Rights and Duties of States in case of Aggression; Q. Wright, "The Concept of Aggression in International Law," *A.J.*, 29 (1935), p. 373; W. Komarnicki, "La Definition de l'Aggresseur dans le Droit International Moderne," *Hague Acad.*, 75 (1949), p. 5. See also pp. 454-55, 484-85 above.

[5] The general result of the League debates was to give to the word "aggression" the connotation: "any use of force which the organized community of nations ought to stop." This has become its popular meaning, though the dictionary provides no such definition.

[6] This reads: "Any act of aggression, including the employment by the authorities of a state of armed force against another State for any purpose other than national or collective self-defence or in pursuance of a decision or recommendation by a competent organ of the United Nations." Report of the International Law Commission, General Assembly, Sixth Session, *Official Records*, Supp. No. 9, p. 11.

nite advantage if directives were formulated for the future guidance of such international bodies as may be called upon to determine the aggressor," asked the Secretary-General to prepare a report for the next session. At that session, Resolution 688(VII) set up a special committee to submit "draft definitions of aggression or draft statements of the notion of aggression" to the Ninth Assembly. The report of this committee considered a general definition, an enumerative definition, and a combination of both. It discussed the Charter meaning of the term and a number of acts which might be listed as aggression (e.g., armed aggression, threat to use force, intent, indirect aggression, economic and even ideological aggression). It debated also whether a definition was possible or desirable, and whether the Assembly could give it binding effect.[7] It made no recommendations, however, and the Ninth Assembly set up another special committee to report with a definition to the Eleventh Assembly. By now, the effort to find a definition, extremely difficult at any time, is caught up in the reckless wave of extremism characteristic of the majority which now dominates the Assembly, and which has brought both the concepts of human rights and of self-determination to confusion and defeat.

ENFORCEMENT ACTION

154. POSSIBLE ACTIONS

Having determined that a "threat to the peace, breach of the peace, or act of aggression" exists, the Security Council has a wide range of possible action open to it. The Charter allows for graduated steps of pressure to be employed. Starting with recommendations of procedure or for settlement under Chapter VI, it may move on (Chapter VII) to renewal of previous recommendations, or it may impose provisional measures. It may proceed to non-military measures (Article 41) or to military measures (Article 42), and it may call upon Members for assistance of various kinds. These steps may be taken in any order desired by the Council.

PROVISIONAL MEASURES. Article 40, added at San Francisco, was intended to prevent a threat of war from developing into actual war. To delay actions which might aggravate a situation is the natural first step in any dispute. The International Court of Justice is similarly empowered, by its Article 41, to indicate provisional measures. A very large part of the procedures actually used for settling disputes has been

---

[7] General Assembly, Ninth Session, *Official Records,* Supp. No. 11 (A/2638).

to arrange "cease-fires" and truces. Presumably Article 40 would not go into effect until a determination had been made under Article 39, but, in practice, little distinction has been made between Chapter VI and Chapter VII in calling for provisional measures.[8] It is understood that provisional measures do not affect ultimate decision on the merits of the case; on the other hand, the Council "shall duly take account of failure to comply with such provisional measures."

NON-MILITARY MEASURES. Article 41 authorizes the Security Council to call upon Members for "measures not involving the use of armed force," but it has not made use of this power. It debated the matter in the Spanish case, but resolutions were not adopted. The General Assembly then took it up and recommended that Spain be debarred from participation in international organizations and conferences, and that Members break off diplomatic relations with the Franco regime. This effort, as we have seen, was a failure. The Assembly recommended in 1949 an embargo on the export of war materials to Albania and Bulgaria. The Korean conflict happened so abruptly that military measures were at once employed. In 1951, by Resolution 500(V), the Assembly recommended that some categories should be embargoed, but left it to each state to determine what it should halt.[9]

We have observed in an earlier chapter the difficulties in the use of economic sanctions. They require preliminary preparation adjusted to each situation, universal participation, careful coordination, and the backing of force. The Charter makes no such provision for economic sanctions as it did in providing a Military Staff Committee for military measures; and the United Nations has since made no such preparation. After the Korean affair, the Collective Measures Committee made a study with recommendations along these lines, but no action has been taken to carry them out.[10]

MILITARY MEASURES. The Security Council may, under Article 42, require Members to participate with their own "air, sea or land forces" if the measures under Article 41 are inadequate. This, however, is a contingent obligation; before it becomes effective, each state must

---

[8] *The Repertoire of Security Council Practice*, p. 423, says: "Decisions explicitly under Chapter VII of the Charter have been exceptional. . . . No distinction of procedure would appear to have been introduced to differentiate proceedings under Chapter VI from proceedings under Chapter VII of the Charter." See also P. Mohn, "Problems of Truce Supervision," *Int. Con.*, No. 478 (1952); Kelsen, pp. 739-44.

[9] Actually, an embargo had already been laid, in large part through pressure from the United States, including an Act of Congress which forbade assistance to be given to any nation which refused to join in. See the "Third Report on the Battle Act," *Dept. of State Bull.*, October 27, 1953, p. 57.

[10] See its Report in General Assembly, Sixth Session, *Official Records*, Supp. No. 13 (A/1891).

have made a formal treaty with the Security Council "in accordance with their respective constitutional processes" (Article 43), governing "the numbers and types of forces, their degree of readiness and general location, and the nature of the facilities and assistance to be provided." The Military Staff Committee was supposed to plan and direct such measures, but has been impotent. The chief problem with regard to military measures is the supply of forces.

155. THE PROBLEM OF THE SUPPLY OF FORCES

When one recalls the long, intensive, and completely futile efforts of the League of Nations, extending over fifteen years, to reach any agreement whatever as to the limitation or reduction of armaments, one is left with a great deal of pessimism with regard to the much more difficult task of making the agreements called for under Article 43. In addition to the former task of establishing a limitation upon the armed forces which a state may have, there is now the task of setting a minimum of forces below which a Member cannot go, that is to say, of maintaining enough forces to contribute to the needs of the United Nations. Articles 26 and 43 of the Charter are inextricably tangled together. On the one hand, the willingness of Members to reduce their armaments will depend upon a supply of forces adequate to give them security; on the other hand, the number of forces needed to put down aggression will depend upon the extent to which potential aggressors are disarmed. In addition to this, new technical difficulties have appeared out of the new ways of waging war, and shifts in the balance of power have upset previous ways of thinking. Finally, the lesson of the League of Nations was that the disarmament effort is linked with collective security. Consequently, the making of the agreements under Article 43 involves not only supply of forces for the use of the Security Council, but regulation of armaments (including nuclear weapons) and the whole matter of international security.

The technical difficulty is to be found largely in the question: what criteria, or measures, can be devised to serve as a basis of comparison so as to get a fairly proportioned distribution of contributions from Members? The disarmament discussions of the League of Nations showed that it was difficult to define a soldier or a weapon of war; and the problem is far more difficult today because scientific instruments and machines have become more important than men. How, for example, is the atomic bomb to be measured against men? If the United States should contribute to the UN one atomic bomb, would that be equal to the contribution of, say, a million men by another state? would it be a sufficient contribution for Switzerland to provide services of hospitalization, for Belgium to provide rights of passage and transportation, for a South American country to provide food? These are essential "facilities" in warmaking. If a state can contribute essential industrial production and financial aid, which other states cannot give, should it be called upon also to supply manpower? Would it be fair to say that the cost of killing one soldier, or of maintaining one soldier, should be taken as a unit of measurement, and that for each financial unit so contributed, a state need provide one less person? Should persons be counted equally, when one is trained in the scientific use of radar or the atomic bomb and the other has only physical ability? Is the girl who works in a munitions plant to be counted? These questions illustrate the great difficulty of working out the agreements; and behind them lies the question of whether states could be induced to accept a scientific formula of comparison if it could be found.

The Military Staff Committee reported in 1948 that it was not able to make progress toward conclusion of the special agreements required by Article 43.[11] For our purposes, the possible methods of obtaining the forces to be used by the United Nations may be grouped under three headings: (1) an independent international force maintained by the United Nations, (2) contingents of national forces, and (3) compromise methods.

INTERNATIONAL POLICE.[12] There is nothing in the Charter to prevent the United Nations from creating an independent military force of its own, if the General Assembly is willing to appropriate the vast sums of money needed and if Members are willing to accept and support it. However, the popular concept of a powerful world police force, analogous to domestic police, is not as simple or as satisfactory as many of its advocates think that it might be. In the first place, it implies a much stronger governmental system behind it than the United Nations was planned to be. And the American people, as well as most nations, have shown themselves fearful of anything which approaches a "superstate."[13] So strong a force as this, sufficient to overwhelm any aggressor

[11] See *U.N. Doc.*, S/956; for the full report, *U.N. Doc.*, S/336 (1947).

[12] On this subject see: Fourth Report of the Commission to Study the Organization of Peace, reprinted in *Int. Con.*, 396 (January, 1944); de Rusett, pp. 26 ff.; P. C. Jessup, "Force under a Modern Law of Nations," *Foreign Affairs*, 24 (1946), p. 90; Grayson Kirk, "The Enforcement of Security," *Yale Law Journal*, 55 (1946), p. 1083; *International Sanctions* (Royal Institute of International Affairs, New York, 1938); J. M. Spaight, *An International Airforce* (London, 1932); H. Wehberg, *Theory and Practice of International Policing* (London, 1935); and the publications of the New Commonwealth Society (London).

[13] A recent study, however, indicates that "most Americans do not automatically recoil from the extremely internationalist idea of an IPF." *An International Police Force and Public Opinion* (Publication No. 3 of the Center for Research on World Political Institutions, Princeton, 1954).

or probable combination of aggressors, would be dangerous. If a Napoleon or a Hitler could gain control of such a force, he might be able much more easily to accomplish his purposes of world domination than if he used his own national forces. Granted the present weakness of the United Nations, or granted the uncertainties which would exist if it were made stronger, responsible statesmen cannot afford to abandon their own national forces and to depend entirely upon the international force; this might prove to be more of a danger than a protection. The development would have to be gradual, national forces being diminished in the measure that the international system proved more and more able to guarantee security.

Objections of a technical nature are also raised. How would recruits be obtained? Would enough be secured through volunteering, or would it be necessary to resort to drafting, and if the latter, what constitutional problems would be raised within Member states? International bases and administration would be required for the maintenance of these forces, which would call for a stronger United Nations than was created. If the international police was to be sufficiently independent, would it have to maintain its own plants for the production of munitions and other needs? This would mean not only vast industrial enterprises, but complicated problems of access to materials, transportation, and competition with private enterprise. There are numerous other technical problems, such as command, distribution according to nationality, use of men against their own countries, or necessary scientific research.

It was for such reasons as these, and particularly because the concept did not harmonize with the weak United Nations system planned, that the idea of an independent international police force was rejected at Dumbarton Oaks. On the other hand, there are various theoretical arguments in favor of such a force. It is undoubtedly the strongest system of security which could be devised, granted that its dangers could be brought under control; if it calls for a stronger United Nations to administer it, this in itself could be regarded as a gain. It would be a more efficient military instrument than a congeries of national forces; it could strike more rapidly and decisively and with the advantage of unified command. If the required numbers could be obtained by volunteering—as might be reasonably expected if states were disarmed and pay and conditions of service made sufficiently attractive —then the need for drafting soldiers within each state would be eliminated. Member nations would be relieved of a great burden of anxiety as to the financial cost of maintaining large military establishments and as to the conscription and training of their personnel. Bases could be found, and the location and transportation of armed forces would not be so difficult in an air age. If atomic and other modern weapons could be reserved for the international force, it would have an enormous advantage; scientific weapons might make unnecessary the maintenance of huge armies of men. All this, of course, assumes that national armaments would be greatly restricted; it assumes also the willing cooperation and support of member states, of which there is little indication at present.

NATIONAL CONTINGENTS? At the other extreme of thinking with regard to supply of forces for the United Nations, there would be no international or independent forces whatever, and such forces as would be needed by the United Nations would be supplied from the national armies of Members. The arrangements which might be made in this way could vary considerably. At the lowest, there would be no obligation upon Members to contribute forces, and they would do so by *ad hoc* agreement for each need as it might arise.[14] There might, as a next stage, be a general obligation to contribute, but in whatever way each Member might decide for itself. Again, the obligation might be to contribute specified amounts. Finally, each Member might be obligated to contribute whatever amounts were required of it by the Security Council, or the international military staff. Questions of command, and of reduction of national armaments would be important and difficult in connection with any of these proposals.

The argument against reliance upon national contingents is that such a method is ineffective and unreliable. There would be uncertainty as to whether certain national contingents would be forthcoming, and as to how well trained and equipped they would be; it would take time to assemble them, and it would be difficult to establish a unified command or a discipline under which they could operate jointly. States would not trust such a system to provide security and would therefore remain armed, thereby making both disarmament and suppression of aggression more difficult. States are not eager to contribute where their own interests are not directly affected and even when obligated to contribute they will argue as to proportionate amounts and interpret obligations as restrictively as possible. Furthermore, such a system implies a continuation of the methods of power politics rather than development toward an international governmental order.

On the other hand, it is argued that it is better to take short steps than to attempt too long a jump; that nations are as yet too uncertain as to the new system to risk such submission as a strong police would mean; that each nation by the method of national contingents reserves

[14] This, as will be said below, is the actual situation of the United Nations.

armed strength for its own protection; that such a reserve of national strength is needed as a protection against the danger of, or in place of, an international police which might seek to dominate the world. States would naturally be glad to reduce their armed strength to the extent that the new system proved itself able to protect national security. And, finally, the idea of a super-state implicit in the international police is not yet acceptable to peoples who still think in terms of sovereign nations; consequently, the system of military action, like the rest of the United Nations system, should be planned in terms of the associated action of sovereign states.

OTHER METHODS. In between these extremes of thought there are other approaches to the problem. An ingenious scheme has been proposed by Ely Culbertson, combining both ideas. This would divide up the total armed strength of the world in such a measure that the United Nations would have, say, 22 per cent of that force and no one nation would have more than, say, a maximum of 20 per cent, with others shading down into smaller percentages. Thus, he argues, the United Nations alone would be able to deal with any single aggressor and could call for help from its Members if more than one aggressor was involved. On the other hand, nations would reserve to themselves sufficient strength, by combination of their resources, to counterbalance the danger of seizure of world control by the international police itself.[15]

Various other compromise proposals have been suggested. The Soviet Union upheld at Dumbarton Oaks the idea of an international air force. A small force, not necessarily air forces alone, has been advocated as providing a spearhead force able to act quickly and perhaps able to prevent by itself some uses of force. It might also have a deterrent effect, particularly if armed with the atomic bomb; and it might serve as the experimental beginning of a larger international police.[16] Suggestions have been made for regional forces, to take care of regional disturbances, in addition to whatever provisions might be made by the United Nations. This would raise questions as to their relationship to the United Nations, and they would be subject to the same questions as raised above. The least form of international control would be an international staff to direct national contingents.

UNITED NATIONS GUARD FORCE. Secretary-General Lie, in an address at Harvard in June 1948, asserted the need of the United Nations

[15] Ely Culbertson, *Total Peace* (New York, 1943), pp. 280-84 and *passim*.

[16] C.S.O.P., Fourth Report, p. 14; see also Fifth Report, p. 20, and Seventh Report, p. 25.

for a "force to back up its decisions," and suggested that a small beginning might be made in that direction "through the establishment of a comparatively small guard force, as distinct from a striking force." He later made a formal report to the General Assembly, which set up a special committee to study the matter. Under his proposal, the functions of this force were to be confined to providing protection for United Nations missions and property in disputed areas under United Nations supervision. The cost was estimated at some four million dollars. Mr. Lie was discouraged by the debate in the committee and reduced his proposal to a field service of three hundred; this was further reduced by the General Assembly into a field service and a panel of field observers. Resolution 297 (IV) left no characteristic of an international police in the proposal.[17]

REGIONAL SUPPLY. Another approach to the supply of forces is through regional arrangements for collective action, as provided for in Chapter VIII of the Charter. Military action of this type, however, finds a better base in Article 51. The Rio Treaty, NATO, SEATO, and other such groupings, as well as the mutual assistance treaties of the Soviet Union, may be cited as examples. All such agreements assert that they are intended to support the United Nations, and that they are subordinated to obligations under the Charter; Article 103 would assure this in any case. Since Article 53 requires authorization by the Security Council before a regional group can engage in military action, such agreements are not made in terms of regional arrangements, but rather in terms of collective self-defense under Article 51. This leaves uncertain the extent to which such groups could act independently of the United Nations, and some criticisms have been made concerning their incompatibility with the Charter.[18] The Soviet bloc, of course, condemns them as unconstitutional.

COMMAND AND DIRECTION. No provision is made in the Charter for the command of the diverse national contingents of armed forces which Members are expected to provide; according to Article 47, paragraph 3, such questions were to be worked out subsequently. A Military Staff Committee was provided. Its functions are to advise and assist the Security Council in the making of "plans for the application

[17] The original request of the Secretary-General is in *U.N. Doc.*, A/656; the report of the committee is found in Supplement No. 13 of the *Official Records* of the Fourth General Assembly (1949). The subject is surveyed in C.S.O.P., United Nations Guards and Technical Field Services (September, 1949).

[18] See C.S.O.P., Eighth Report; Sir Gladwyn Jebb, "The Free World and the United Nations," *Foreign Affairs*, 31 (1953), p. 385.

of armed force" (Article 46), and on "all questions relating to the Security Council's military requirements for the maintenance of international peace and security, the employment and command of forces placed at its disposal, the regulation of armaments, and possible disarmament." And it is also made responsible for "the strategic direction of any armed forces placed at the disposal of the Security Council." The Military Staff Committee is composed of the chiefs of staff of the five Great Powers and should therefore be an expert group, competent to give direction—provided they can agree. Each, however, represents his own nation and *ex officio* is primarily responsible for guarding the interests of that country. It can hardly be expected that they would contribute knowledge of new weapons or military improvements, or reveal information to their national disadvantage for purposes of United Nations enforcement action. It is possible that one of them might some day be called an aggressor! Each of them has a number of friends, which might also include an aggressor. In such a situation, the Great Power would be in the strange position of helping direct a campaign against itself or its friend, and of knowing the strategy to be used by the United Nations. Of course, it has a veto to forestall any such development.

The United Nations is, in fact, without the means for providing an efficient military command or, more important, for providing political direction for its military action. These deficiencies were apparent in the one instance of military action, and some lessons were learned from the Korean experience.

A number of other questions can be asked concerning the supply of forces and the participation of Members in enforcement action. On the improbable assumption that the agreements under Article 43 could be made, would reservations to these treaties be permissible? For example, could the United States stipulate that the forces and facilities which she supplies can only be used in the Western hemisphere?[19] What is meant by availability: organized units trained for the purpose and ready to leave at a moment's notice, or simply regular and reserve forces? Who is to pay for the maintenance of these forces while under United Nations direction: does each contributing state pay for its own, or should the United Nations pay for all?[20] What is meant by "facilities" or by "assistance"? And does the United Nations pay for them? Speaking in terms of the United States, what effect would her obligations have upon her military system? Would they result in con-

[19] Mr. Dulles gave an affirmative answer to the Senate Committee on Foreign Relations. Hearings, p. 653.

[20] At San Francisco, this was left for later decision. *UNCIO Doc.* 681, III/3/46.

scription and military training in peacetime? Would Congress have to approve each separate sending of troops at the call of the Security Council?[21]

It is manifest that enforcement action by the United Nations is not a simple and easy procedure. The Military Staff Committee made little progress toward answering questions such as those above. Implicit in its report[22] was the understanding that the armed forces of the UN could not be employed against one of the Big Five. Members would not be expected to train and keep available special contingents; on the contrary, the forces supplied to the Security Council would be drawn from "normally maintained" national forces. Agreement was not reached as to the over-all strength which would be needed by the UN, as to the amount to be contributed by each Member, or as to bases to be put at the disposal of UN forces. The Big Five "shall contribute initially the major portion of these forces"; other states would be permitted to add to these forces if they so wished. It was agreed that contributions of other states might be in the form of facilities and assistance, rather than of forces. The Soviet Union stood firmly for quantitative equality of contribution, in over-all strength and in composition, though no way has yet been discovered of measuring the comparative strength of national forces, and equality would reduce the strength of the United Nations to the level of the lowest contributor. Neither the Committee nor the Council could state the principles upon which the agreements under Article 43 should be made. Since 1948, the Military Staff Committee has been moribund, a useless expense to the United Nations.

156. REGULATION OF ARMAMENTS

We have noted above that the supply of armed forces by Members for enforcement action is inextricably related to the problem of limiting the armed forces of states. The United Nations has been no more successful than was the League of Nations in dealing with disarmament, though the urgency of the need is now far greater in view of weapons which could destroy civilization.

According to the Charter (Article 26), responsibility for establishment of "a system for the regulation of armaments" rests upon the Se-

---

[21] By the United Nations Participation Act of 1945, Congress authorized the President to make available to the Security Council, on its call, forces within the terms of the agreement to be made; but the agreement was never made. Public Law 264, 79th Cong.; 59 Stat. 619-21, quoted in Zeydel and Chamberlin, pp. 2-6.

[22] *U.N. Doc.* S/336 (1947).

curity Council; but the General Assembly (Article 11) may consider and make recommendations concerning "the principles governing disarmament and the regulation of armaments." The atomic bomb was not known—much less the hydrogen bomb—at the time of the making of the Charter; what effect it might have had upon that instrument it is interesting to speculate. It is clear, however, that the new weapons must be studied as part of the general problem of disarmament and security, and that they do not constitute a separate and independent problem. The vast menace which they represent justifies priority and emphasis for their study, however, and the first act of the General Assembly was to adopt Resolution 1(I) setting up a Commission on Atomic Energy. In February, 1947, a Commission for Conventional Armaments was established and the two worked separately until January 1952, when they were combined into the Disarmament Commission.[23]

CONTROL OF ATOMIC ENERGY. The Atomic Energy Commission was composed of persons from each state represented on the Security Council, plus Canada. It was instructed to make proposals for extending to all nations basic scientific information for peaceful ends; for control of atomic energy so that it would be used only for peaceful purposes; for the elimination of atomic weapons from national armaments; and for safeguards to protect states against violations of agreements made. Finally, the resolution required that the work of the commission proceed by "separate stages, the successful completion of each of which will develop the necessary confidence of the world before the next stage is undertaken."[24]

Since the United States possessed the secret of the bomb, it was necessary for her to take leadership with regard to its international control. A Department of State committee was set up in January, 1946, which issued what became known as the Acheson-Lilienthal Report, in which it was boldly proposed that an international Atomic Development Authority be set up to control all activities with regard to atomic energy. It called for strong measures of inspection, and listed stages of progress according to which information would be released (thus

[23] See the *Official Records* of the Atomic Energy Commission of the United Nations; *Report on International Control of Atomic Energy*, Dept. of State Pub., No. 2498; also, Nos. 2661 (*Technical Information*) and 2702 (*Growth of a Policy*); Brookings, *Proposals*, Chap. vii; Brookings, *Peace and Security*, Part V; M. W. Boggs, "Regulation and Reduction of Armaments: Action of the General Assembly," *Dept. of State Bull.*, February 23, 1947; J. M. Ludlow, "The Establishment of the Commission for Conventional Armaments," *ibid.*, April 27, 1947.

[24] Resolution of the General Assembly, No. 1 (I), p. 9. See also *Report of the United States Delegation to the First Part of the First Session of the General Assembly of the United Nations*, Dept. of State Pub., No. 2484, pp. 18, 33.

assuring national security) until finally, when adequate guarantees had been provided, existing bombs would be destroyed and no new ones made. When Mr. Baruch became the United States representative on the Atomic Energy Commission, his staff made further studies, and he presented a resolution much along the lines of the earlier report, but rejecting the use of the veto in connection with control over the new weapon. A few days later (June 19), the Soviet delegate proposed that a treaty be made under which the use of atomic weapons would be outlawed and existing stocks destroyed within three months; thereafter, national legislation for control of atomic energy would be passed. A fundamental divergence of approach to the problem was thus presented. In neither plan was provision made for enforcement action which might be needed to back up inspection or prevent violations.

The United States then presented three memoranda which suggested the content of a treaty establishing the Authority, and outlined its functions and the relations between it and the United Nations organs. The Authority was to be autonomous and related to the Security Council in such manner as to leave to the latter its general function of maintaining peace and at the same time enable action to be taken without hindrance from the veto. It was suggested that Article 51 of the Charter might be called upon, and that collective self-defense could be used against a state which was preparing to use the atomic bomb. The Soviet representatives opposed these ideas, including inspection, and preferred national to international controls. Attention was then turned with more profit to technical discussions, and from this viewpoint it appeared that controls were technically possible. The commission reported to the Council that an international control agency was needed.

Meanwhile, Mr. Molotov had, on October 29, 1946, proposed a plan for reduction of armaments, which would include prohibition of the use of atomic energy for military purposes. This was consistent with the earlier support given by Russia at Geneva to direct disarmament. The suggestion was supported by the United States on condition of adequate provision for inspection and control, including the implementation of Article 43 and others also emphasized that Article 43 must be considered in connection with Article 26. Thus, the old lessons were being restated; it was clear that regulation of armaments was part of the general problem of assuring security to states.

In the very complicated debates which followed, four points were at issue and were finally compromised into a resolution adopted by the General Assembly on December 14, 1946. In the first place, the Soviet Union made advance possible by two concessions: that there should be inspection to see whether a nation was living up to its obligations as to armaments, and that in the organs to be created for this purpose the veto would not be used—though of course, it could be used, in their view, in the Security Council, where final decisions would be made. In the second place, the United States insisted strongly that control of the atomic bomb was the most pressing issue and that it must be handled separately through the Atomic Energy Commission. The resolution adopted called on the Security Council to formulate measures "according to their priority," and asserted that nothing therein altered the resolution of January creating the Atomic Energy Commission. It provided also for establishment "within the framework of the Security Council" of an international system, operating through special organs, "which organs shall derive their powers and status from the convention or conventions under which they are established."[25] In the third place, the problem of procedure was worked out by urging the Atomic Energy Commission to "expeditious fulfilment" of its task; by urging that the Security Council expedite consideration of the report of that commission and prepare draft conventions for creation of a system of inspection and control, which should include prohibition of atomic and other weapons of mass destruction; and by calling upon the General Assembly to submit these conventions, after consideration in special session for the purpose, to Members for ratification under Article 26. In the fourth place, the resolution recognized that the problem of security is closely connected with that of disarmament, and urged the Security Council to accelerate the making of the agreements under Article 43 so that forces would be at its disposal. It also asked Members to withdraw their troops stationed in other countries as rapidly as possible and to undertake reduction of national armed forces.

In December, Mr. Baruch pressed for adoption of his proposals. Meanwhile, the subject of general disarmament had come before the General Assembly. Concessions made by the Soviet Union, with regard to inspection and to the use of the veto, aided agreement, and on December 17, 1946, the Commission on Atomic Energy adopted the United States proposals and approved a report to the Security Council. Some progress had apparently been made, but later developments showed it to be illusory.

Discussion of the AEC report showed differences concerning (1) use of the veto, (2) the safeguards needed for control over atomic energy, and (3) methods for the establishment of the international

[25] Thus reassuring the Russians that control remained with the Security Council and at the same time making clear that the organs created under separate conventions would not be bound by the Charter rules for voting.

control and the right of the international body to conduct research. By January 1948, efforts were deadlocked and in 1950 the Soviet representative withdrew from the commission. The United States reopened the effort on UN Day, 1950, and the General Assembly, by Resolution 502(VIII), combined the two bodies into one disarmament commission with the same membership as before.

The stalemate over control of atomic energy continued, and in December 1953, President Eisenhower made a new and more modest approach. In an address to the General Assembly he proposed that an International Atomic Energy Agency be set up, and that contributions of fissionable materials be made to it by nations which could do so. The purpose would be to use this material "to serve the peaceful pursuits of mankind." The "atoms for peace" proposal had nothing directly to do with control of atomic weapons, though indirectly and ultimately it might lead in that direction. The Ninth General Assembly adopted Resolution 810(IX) calling for an "International Atomic Energy Agency" and for a conference to explore peacetime uses of atomic energy. This conference met at Geneva in 1955, with much success; various nations, including the Soviet Union, contributed important knowledge and many valuable papers were presented.[26]

On the general question, the Disarmament Commission considered various constructive proposals more hopefully. Private conversations were held in London in 1954 between Canada, France, the Soviet Union, the United Kingdom, and the United States, during which an Anglo-French memorandum was discussed.[27] This sought to relate, in stages of development, reduction of armaments and prohibition of atomic weapons to safeguards and controls over them. Once an effective control was established it would then be possible gradually to reduce armaments at a rate commensurate with confidence in the operation of the system to provide security. At the General Assembly, the Soviet delegate did not insist, as before, that atomic weapons must first be abandoned, and to some extent he accepted the idea of stages of control and reduction. Hopes again rose, particularly after the change of government and apparently of policy in the Soviet Union, and the "summit conference" at Geneva in 1954, but in 1956 agreement upon a workable system had not been achieved.

This experience has demonstrated again that diminution of armed strength by nations depends upon the establishment of international strength and controls, which can assure these nations of security. Much as they may want security and peace, these nations are not willing to

---

[26] The address by the President is printed in *Dept. of State Bull.*, 29 (1953), p. 850.
[27] *The Record on Disarmament*, Dept. of State Pub., No. 5581 (1954).

submit themselves to international controls for this purpose. Not even the fright occasioned by the dangerous new weapons of war—weapons which could wipe mankind off the face of the earth—has induced nations to consider that national strength is insufficient for protection against modern war, and that national security might better be provided through a strong international order. Until they learn this lesson, there can be little hope for regulation of armaments, which is necessarily linked with collective security.[28]

157. THE KOREAN EXPERIENCE

On June 25, 1950, the Secretary-General was awakened from his sleep with the news that North Korea had invaded South Korea. The Allied Powers had agreed, in the Cairo Declaration of 1943, that Korea should become independent. At the end of the war with Japan, however, the part of Korea above the 38th parallel was occupied by Soviet forces, and the part below that line by United States forces. The Russians refused to withdraw and rapidly converted the area into a Communist stronghold; and the United States brought the matter before the General Assembly in September, 1947. The Assembly recommended withdrawal of both Soviet and American forces, and that a free election be held in Korea, supervised by the United Nations. The Soviet Union, however, refused to admit the representatives of the United Nations into their occupied area, and elections could be held only in the southern part. As a result of these elections, a Republic of Korea was set up, with Dr. Syngman Rhee as President. This government was recognized by the General Assembly in December, 1948, as the lawful and only government in Korea; and the deadlock continued until the North Korean army, well trained by the Russians, without notice invaded South Korea.[29]

BREACH OF THE PEACE. While the United Nations had talked of enforcement action on other occasions, it had never before undertaken it. In the Korean situation, a fortunate combination of circumstances led to action. In the first place, the United States had strong forces conveniently at hand and, more important, was willing to use them; it was fortunate that its desire to halt the spread of communism coin-

[28] In April, 1955, President Eisenhower created the post of Presidential Assistant for Disarmament and appointed Harold Stassen to concentrate upon the problem.

[29] See *U.S. Policy in Korea*, Dept. of State Pub. 3922 (1950); L. Goodrich, "Korea: Collective Measures Against Aggression," *Int. Con.*, No. 494 (1953); Kelsen, pp. 927-50; Stone, Discourse No. 11; Q. Wright, "Collective Security in the Light of the Korean Experience," *Proc. Am. Soc.*, 1951, p. 165.

cided with the United Nations desire to halt aggression. In the second place, a United Nations Commission was in Korea and was able to provide authoritative information from the spot. Most fortunate, the Soviet representative to the Security Council, sulking in his tent because a representative of Communist China had not been seated, was not present at the meeting of the Council to cast a veto.[30] The Council was thus able to adopt a resolution on June 25, determining the situation to be a breach of the peace, calling for immediate cessation of hostilities, and asking Members to "render every assistance to the United Nations in the execution of this resolution." It did not require, or ask for, military action by Members, but the word "assistance" might be interpreted to include such action. At any rate, the United States, on the next day, ordered its forces to assist South Korea and to "neutralize" Formosa against an attack from Communist China. On the following day, June 27, another Security Council resolution recommended, rather than ordered, that Members "furnish such assistance to the Republic of Korea as may be necessary to repel the armed attack and to restore international peace and security in the area." Thus, the unilateral action of the United States was approved; previously it had been criticized.

CONDUCT OF OPERATIONS. The Council had, in effect, asked for voluntary contribution from Members in the effort to repel the North Korean aggression. Fifty-three Members were willing to help; sixteen of these sent armed forces (in some cases, the offer of armed forces was refused); others contributed in various ways, such as sending a hospital ship, or food or other supplies, or transport.[31]

A Security Council resolution of July 7 authorized a "unified command under the United States," with the right to fly the flag of the United Nations; on the next day, President Truman appointed General Douglas MacArthur as the commanding general of all forces put under the unified command. The channels of authority and even of communication above him were not made clear; there was, indeed, no organ of the United Nations which could give him political direction, much less military direction. Communications went awkwardly through the Secretary-General to the United States Mission to the United Nations, and from it through American agencies to the com-

[30] The practice had been established, and, indeed, on the initiative of the Soviet Union, that abstention or absence should not count as a veto.

[31] The United States and Korea of course furnished the greater part: of ground forces, the United States about half and Korea two-fifths; of naval forces, the United States 96%; of air forces, the United States about 93%. Most other states were unable, in a military or in a financial sense, to contribute more. France, for example, had 800,000 soldiers in Indo-China. See the U.N. *Yearbook* for 1951, p. 226; Report to Congress, 1952, p. 227.

mand in Korea. The United States negotiated agreements with each state contributing forces. In general, the function of command was about the same as if all the forces had been United States forces; the need of a single authority for military purposes was recognized.

Political direction, however, did not work so well, as became evident over the question of crossing the 38th parallel (and later of crossing the Yalu River), which raised in the minds of some Members the spectre of intervention by Communist China or the Soviet Union. Representatives of the sixteen contributing states met weekly with the Department of State in Washington, but they merely received information; they did not constitute a body competent to give leadership or to determine policy. Some questions were referred by the United States to the General Assembly or to participating governments; the replies to these, and speeches made, served to hold down hotheads in the United States who were apparently willing to take on Communist China and the Soviet Union as well. In this connection, it needs to be remarked that, as the wording of the June 27 resolution shows, it is not the function of the United Nations to win a "victory," but merely to halt aggression and restore peace.

INTERVENTION OF COMMUNIST CHINA. In October 1950 Communist China entered the fray, thereby making both the military task and the political problems much greater. The Soviet representative had returned to the Security Council and his veto rendered it impotent. The United States therefore turned to the General Assembly, which displayed uncertainty. Arab-Asian states, though they were not in favor of communism, had little sympathy for intervention by the larger powers in Asian affairs. Some delegates felt that Communist China could sincerely regard her action as necessary for self-defense and therefore ought not to be condemned for aggression; some felt that United States leadership had brought this added danger, and many were afraid that it might develop into a world war. A commission was set up to bring about a cease-fire, but the Chinese, who at the moment were pushing the United Nations forces back, refused to negotiate. This helped turn opinion against them and as the United Nations regained lost ground, the General Assembly, by Resolution 498(V), on February 1, 1951, declared that China had engaged in aggression, and set up the Additional Measures Committee to see what should be done about it. As a concession to the doubtful delegates, a Good Offices Commission was also created. Neither of these bodies achieved anything. It was some months before the Assembly was convinced that Communist China was implacable; it then adopted Resolution 500(V), under which an embargo was set up against the aggressor.

TERMS OF SETTLEMENT. How to make a settlement after an enforcement action was another matter for which the United Nations was not prepared. The Charter gave no authority to impose a settlement and the Security Council was certainly not, in this situation, the body to attempt such a settlement. The purpose of the United Nations was merely to halt aggression; it had no desire to invade and conquer China, and if it had sought such an objective, this would probably have brought the Soviet Union in. This was not a United Nations action, in the sense of a decision and order having come from the Security Council; it was rather a joint venture by a small group of its Members, though acting under the recommendation of the Council.

This situation raises an interesting question: should enforcement action by the United Nations be regarded as war, or as a police action by the community of nations?[32] The UN command demanded that Communist China respect the law of war, certainly as regards prisoners of war. Communist China regarded the United Nations simply as an enemy, and not as a superior authority, able to dictate terms as a government does to its subjects who violate its laws. War, we have noted elsewhere, is a status in which both belligerents have equal rights; if the Korean situation were war, then the United Nations should negotiate on equal terms with the aggressor which had violated its laws. At any rate, the United Nations did not seek to beat the aggressor to its knees, and was ready to work out a settlement with it when possible. In this case, should the United Nations, as an institution, be a party to the settlement, or should it leave it to the states which were actually engaged?

Resolution 489(V) had laid down the principle that as soon as the aggression was repelled, military action should be stopped and negotiations begun; but Communist China refused to consider the principles stated in this resolution. Peiping insisted that political concessions must be made to them before they would cease fire; the United Nations replied that it would not negotiate under duress. As the United Nations forces were more and more successful, the Soviet Union in a broadcast suggested a cease-fire; but it was not until July 27, 1953 that an armistice was signed. Carrying out the terms of the armistice was a continuous struggle, and in 1956 the United Nations ended the Neutral Nations Commission which had been attempting to supervise the operation, with the statement that Communist authorities

---

[32] See the Report of the Committee for Study of Legal Problems of the United Nations, *Proc. Am. Soc.*, 1952, p. 216.

would not permit them to operate in North Korea and that strong military forces and installations were being established there in violation of the armistice.

158. UNITING FOR PEACE

Realizing that the good fortune which had made it possible for the Security Council to act against aggression in Korea would probably not be present on future occasions, the General Assembly girded itself for action by adopting Resolution 377(V), commonly called the Uniting for Peace Resolution. The Assembly had earlier taken a step in this direction by setting up the Interim Committee, whose purpose was in part to watch over disputes and aid in their settlement;[33] now, the Assembly was preparing itself for enforcement action.

In the Korean action, the Security Council did no more than recommend to Members that they act, and this much the General Assembly can do under Articles 10 and 11 of the Charter. Section A of the Uniting for Peace Resolution states its purposes. It recognized that the Security Council had primary responsibility for maintaining peace and security, and it did not attempt to substitute the Assembly for the Council in this responsibility; it provided that the Assembly should take over only when the Council was unable to act for the specific reason of "lack of unanimity of the permanent members." In such a case, the Assembly would recommend collective measures which might include, "in the case of a breach of the peace or act of aggression," the use of armed force. By implication, then, the Assembly could determine the existence of a breach of the peace or act of aggression (but not a threat to the peace) and recommend enforcement action. Provision was made for quickly calling the Assembly into emergency session, and the Assembly Rules of Procedure were adjusted to the new situation.

Section B of the resolution set up a Peace Observation Commission to report on tension in any area which might endanger peace. Unfortunately, it was given no independence; it could act only if called upon by the Council, the Assembly, or the Interim Committee; and it could not enter any state without permission from that state. Consequently, it has been of little service, though potentially it could be quite useful. Section C recommended that each Member survey its own resources and inform the United Nations of the amount of armed force which

[33] The Interim Committee was established by Resolution 111(II); its documents are found under the designation A/AC.18/—. See especially A/AC. 18/114. The committee did active work during 1948 and 1949 and produced some useful studies, one in particular, concerning voting in the Security Council. Since 1950, it has been inactive, largely because of the opposition of the Soviet Union.

it would be willing to hold available for use when called upon; and it provided a panel of experts to advise Members concerning the training and equipment of such forces. Section D established a Collective Measures Committee to study and report upon methods for strengthening peace and security.

LEGALITY. The Uniting for Peace Resolution was of course denounced by the Soviet bloc as unconstitutional, and others have had their doubts.[34] It was certainly not in line with the viewpoint which prevailed at San Francisco as to the dominant position of the Security Council; but the Council was not given exclusive responsibility, and its failure to carry out its primary function forced the United Nations to fall back upon the reserve powers of the General Assembly. The resolution respects the position of the Council and permits the Assembly to act only when a veto has blocked action by the Council. There is no doubt that articles 10 and 11 give to the Assembly a broad range of recommendation in this field. The central question is whether the Council alone (Article 12) can decide whether or not it is dealing with a matter, or whether decision on this point is open to the Assembly. If the Council, through a veto, decides against action in a certain case, has it thereby acted or has it failed to act? Any seven members may drop an item from the Security Council agenda, and the Assembly is not apt to act without that much support. The Uniting for Peace Resolution has undoubtedly helped to hold up the sagging principle of collective security; but it does so through recommendation rather than through order, and collective security has thus in practice been set back to the level of the League of Nations.

159. COLLECTIVE MEASURES COMMITTEE

The extent of this setback is further shown by the response to the reports of the committee which was set up to study measures for implementing the Uniting for Peace Resolution. Its reports are the most serious studies yet made of the role and capacity of the United Nations for maintaining peace, but they have received little support from Members.[35]

The committee report emphasized the duty of each Member to participate in the maintenance of international peace and security, and

[34] See C.S.O.P., Seventh Report (1951); and Kelsen, pp. 953-86.

[35] The first Report of the Collective Measures Committee is Supplement No. 13 to the *Official Records* of the Sixth Assembly (A/1891), and is reprinted in Staff Studies, Collection, pp. 606-70; the second report is Supplement No. 17 to the *Official Records* of the Seventh Assembly.

recommended that each survey its resources and examine its legislation so as to be able to take the legal and administrative steps which might be needed when called upon to participate.[36] Under political measures which might be undertaken it included appeals to or denunciations of parties in a conflict, collective diplomatic representations, severance of diplomatic relations, suspension or expulsion from international organizations, and non-recognition of changes brought about through the use of force. Coordination of such measures would be needed, but this would have to be arranged individually for each situation.

Under economic and financial measures, the committee considered in some detail embargoes, suspension of economic and financial intercourse and of communications, and sequestration of property. It pointed out the need for each state to have ready the legislation under which such measures could be taken, and the need for equitable distribution of losses sustained and for assistance to those who might suffer from the application of such measures. The second report showed how the specialized agencies might be brought into the action. Again, coordination would be very difficult and the committee could hope for no more than that a committee for this purpose should be set up *ad hoc* in each situation, though it hesitantly recommended future consideration of international machinery or the use of existing international bodies.

As to military measures, the committee concluded, in its second report, that it was impracticable from administrative, financial, or military viewpoints to develop an independent United Nations force, and suggested rather that measures be prepared in advance for the utilization of contingents from national forces. For the purpose of making the decisions necessary in an enforcement action it proposed an executive military authority, composed of one state or a group of states; one part of its work would be to negotiate (i.e., beg for!) armed forces and "ancillary assistance" from Members. The General Assembly or Security Council should be responsible for general policies. The report was careful to reserve to Members the right to use their forces under articles 51 and 53, and suggested that regional forces and facilities might be employed to help the United Nations effort.

[36] Even this simple suggestion to "make ready and amend their laws" was attacked by Mexico, which "regarded the amendment of its laws as a sovereign right not liable to subordination or compromise of any sort." General Assembly, Sixth Session, *Official Records*, First Committee, p. 141. It may be noted that Mexico found no difficulty in supporting a resolution calling for similar action (against racial discrimination) from the Union of South Africa. Every Member has been guilty of similar inconsistency, and this raises discouraging questions as to their sincerity in upholding the purposes of the United Nations.

The principle was accepted, as it had also been accepted by the Military Staff Committee, that each Member should contribute according to its ability; and a contribution of food, transportation, medical aid, etc., could be regarded as sufficient from some states not so well prepared as others for military measures.

RESPONSE. These suggestions received little support, though some of them were specifically recommended by the General Assembly in Resolution 503(VI). When the Secretary-General inquired of Members what provision they had made for making available armed forces and assistance, the replies were decidedly noncommittal. Thirty-eight Members answered, four of these being simply acknowledgment of the receipt of the inquiry. A few, such as India, expressed dissent or opposition; most replied sympathetically, and would "keep the matter under constant review," but found that their contributions in Korea, or NATO, or elsewhere, were sufficient contribution for the present. The replies from the specialized agencies were equally noncommittal. Adding to these replies the experience with sanctions in Spain and Korea, the conclusion seems to be clear that Members still reserve complete freedom to decide whether they shall act, and when, and to what extent, when called upon by the Security Council or General Assembly; and that they reject authoritative direction established in advance and will only decide after the occasion arises. The Korean action indicates that some Members are willing in this way to contribute to an enforcement action; but upon such a foundation it is difficult for the United Nations to anticipate whether and how it can handle an action against an aggressor.

160. COLLECTIVE SELF-DEFENSE

The above survey of the unwillingness of Members to accept responsibility for maintaining peace and security evidences the wisdom of those who insisted upon putting Article 51 into the Charter—however much of a setback this may be to those who wish a strong system of collective security.[37] The Latin American states at San Francisco were unwilling to subordinate the regional arrangements for security, upon which they were working, to prior decision by a Security Council in which one voice might be able to deny the region the right to act. Article 53 still requires approval by the Security Council for en-

---

[37] ". . . a loophole that perhaps more than anything else betrays the frontier character of the international community. Like Janus, the Charter faces in two directions —forward to the organization of force on an over-all basis that is at least suggestive of world government, and backward to the present fragmentation of power which seems to spell international anarchy," Cheever and Haviland, pp. 140-41.

forcement action by a regional group, but, at the insistence of these states, a statement of the right to act in self-defense was pushed back into the Chapter on enforcement action. Self-defense is of course a generally recognized legal principle, but it is broadened in the Charter by addition of the concept of "collective self-defense," which makes it possible for a group to combine against an aggressor even though the Security Council takes no decision.

Collective defense is not necessarily regional in character; it is based more upon political considerations than upon geography. It has developed into a number of groupings, beginning with the Brussels Treaty (March 17, 1948) in which five European states joined; it is doubtless most fully represented in the North Atlantic Treaty Organization (NATO) set up on April 4, 1949; it has spread into the South Pacific (ANZUS) and South East Asia (SEATO) and elsewhere.[38] These instruments proclaim that they are in harmony with the Charter of the United Nations. Taking NATO as an example, Article 1 pledges the signatories not to use force "in any manner inconsistent with the purposes of the United Nations." They agree (Article 5) that an armed attack against one of them will be considered an attack against all and each of them, and that "in the exercise of the right of individual or collective self-defense recognized by Article 51 of the Charter" they will assist the attacked party. The attack and the measures taken are to be reported to the Security Council and are to be terminated when the Council "has taken the necessary measures to restore and maintain international peace and security."

Even so, the relationship of NATO to the United Nations is a problem. It is far stronger than the United Nations itself and it goes its way independently of the United Nations. The charge has been uttered against it that it was intended to sidestep the United Nations and this was doubtless true, though not necessarily in a bad sense. The United States would argue that NATO enables action to be taken on behalf of the United Nations which that institution is unable to take itself. It has been suggested that it would have been better if the treaty had been opened for signature by any Member of the United Nations which wished to participate;[39] and to this it is replied that such a development would destroy the effectiveness of NATO as a military instrument. NATO has, at least indirectly, aided the United Nations by preparing a trained and organized body of soldiers from various national forces, which could possibly be put at the service of the United Nations on

[38] See the chart in Brookings, *Proposals*, p. 146, and accompanying discussion; also, Staff Studies, Collection, pp. 676-706, where some of the agreements are printed; Cheever and Haviland, Chap. xxiv; Palmer and Perkins, Chap. xxi.

[39] See C.S.O.P., Sixth and Eighth Reports.

occasion, there being no other such body available. It has set a remarkable example of an organization in which national sovereignty is subordinated to centralized direction.

But NATO also illustrated the point that states are inclined to make such a submission to international organization only where they feel that their national safety is involved. Some statesmen and experts therefore feel that it is only through such small groupings of interested parties, and not in the universality of the United Nations, that support for collective security is to be found. It is probably true that many people feel safer because of NATO, and equally true that their respect for the United Nations is correspondingly diminished. If the Members of the United Nations are unwilling to give it the authority and strength to assure security for themselves, they must expect other systems to appear to meet particular interests. The result is inevitably the creation of rival groups, such as NATO against the Soviet bloc, with the prospect of "bigger and better" wars. It is a hard choice.[40]

161. CONCLUSIONS AS TO COLLECTIVE SECURITY

The high hopes for an effective international security organization of which the papers were full at the time of the United Nations Conference on International Organization in 1945 have not been realized; indeed, say Goodrich and Simons:

> The United Nations system in practice is even looser than that of the League of Nations system, for not only has there been an absence of any central determination of measures that Members of the United Nations must take, but there is no legal duty placed on any Member to take any measures in the absence of such a determination.[41]

The common failure in all the different approaches surveyed above has been the unwillingness of states to commit themselves in advance even to a measure of their own choice, much less to submit to orders to engage in an effort to maintain peace. As much as ever in history, states reserve to themselves freedom of decision. The striking advance of the Charter was the ability of the Security Council—contingent as it was—

[40] "It must be clearly recognized, however, that the world organization is not being strengthened by the multiplication and tightening of these regional security arrangements . . . if the United Nations as an organization to maintain international peace and security becomes effective, such regional arrangements should decline in importance and be subordinated in operation to the responsible organs of the United Nations." L. M. Goodrich, *Columbia Journal of International Affairs*, 3 (1949), pp. 19-20, quoted in Palmer and Perkins, p. 810.

[41] Brookings, *Peace and Security*, p. 450.

to require cooperation from Members and submission from aggressors; in practice, this power has been diminished to recommendation and usually to inability even to make a recommendation.

The terrible new weapons—atomic, hydrogen, bacterial—while sensational topics for a time, have not been frightening enough to peoples to induce them to submit to agreements under which these weapons could be brought under control. To control them is in fact an essential part of the problem of providing enough security for a nation to justify it in giving up, or reducing, what it regards as the present protection afforded by its national armaments.[42] After centuries of traditional belief that security can be provided for a nation only through its own armed strength, it is hard for a people to believe that a better means of security can be had, and that, indeed, their own weapons may destroy them. Yet, until this better means is found and accepted, national armaments will not be much reduced; and collective security cannot make much headway until these powerful national forces are reduced. This is the vicious circle within which disarmament swings.

There is no support for an independent United Nations force for use against an aggressor. A beginning could be made with a small force to guard a truce area, or a small air force; but even the thought of a few guards to protect United Nations missions in the field—i.e., within the territory of some state—has been enough to frighten Members. The United Nations cannot even plan the use of national forces, for it cannot know, in the present mood of Members, what forces, if any, they will put at its disposal. This, of course, affects decisions to act, for the United Nations would be in a foolish position if it voted to take action and then was unable to do so.

It was not intended that the function of maintaining peace should be taken away from the Security Council, but the principle of unanimity upon which it must operate was too narrow a base upon which to build; the cold war has wrecked it and left the Council with little ability to act. The General Assembly has attempted to take over, but it is not equipped for enforcement action; it is a slow, cumbersome, and often divided body which finds it hard to act decisively—e.g., with regard to the aggression by Communist China. And Members have been no more willing to promise national contingents for the use of the Assembly than for the Security Council.

Nor was it intended that Article 51 would have to support the function of collective security through groupings of limited character which much resemble the old style alliances. Even in these arrange-

---

[42] As a matter of fact, there are not more than three or four nations in the world capable of giving to themselves any measure of security, and any of them could face annihilation in war.

ments, as with the United Nations, states reserve to themselves the right to decide when to act and how large a contribution they shall make.

The record of the United Nations for providing security for its Members against the use of force is thus rather discouraging; but its record is nevertheless a great advance over the past. It is inadequate, but far from useless; without it, one may be sure that much more blood would have been shed. While nations are unwilling to give up their independence of decision, they manifest great eagerness to avert war and exert great joint pressure to this end through the machinery of the United Nations, which can focus the pressure so intensely as to discourage actions endangering peace. Furthermore, states have shown that, even though not committed, they may be willing to contribute armed forces and make large sacrifices against aggression. In this respect, it is of much importance that the United States, abandoning its past neutrality and isolation, has shown itself willing to take strong leadership in such a cause. There is some progress toward collective security, both in the willingness of peoples to contribute to it and in the pressures exercised by the United Nations. If the United Nations cannot do more than it has, the fault lies with the Members who made it and operate it, and who, it seems, still prefer the tooth and the fang to international law and order.

Chapter 19

PLANS, PROBLEMS, AND TRENDS

The Charter of the United Nations of course did not satisfy everyone in 1945. Many groups had been working during the war on plans for reorganization of the community of nations, and their ambitions had not been realized. And there were earnest young veterans who had seen enough of war, atomic scientists fearful of the results of their discoveries, and others doubtful that the new organization was strong enough to ensure the world against another war. Enthusiasm for a stronger world order was high, so high that much of the thinking was impractical and has since been submerged beneath hard facts. Most of the thinking, however, has been on a higher plane of understanding of the problems involved than some of the unreal concepts mentioned in Chapter 15 above. It will not be possible to examine them all here, but we may get an idea of the various approaches and then evaluate their possibilities, with regard to particular proposals, against the trends shown in the development of the United Nations, and in terms of revision of the Charter. The result of this survey will show that the title of this book has become perhaps less justified, and that "world government" still lies in the unseen future.

The proposals offered may be summarized under three approaches: (1) world government, (2) regional or other interest groups (as opposed to, or combined with, a universal system), and (3) gradual improvement of the present Charter.

162. WORLD GOVERNMENT[1]

The most far-reaching proposals for improvement are those which envisage what may be called a *"supra*-national," as differentiated from an *"inter*-national," system. The former calls for authority above

---

[1] On world government see the following, some of which will be useful throughout the chapter: "World Government," *Annals,* 264 (1949); H. W. Briggs, The Problem of World Government," *A.J.,* 41 (1947), p. 111; B. Brodie, "The Atomic Dilemma," *Annals,* 249 (1947); *Toward an Integrated World Order: A Joint Report* (Catholic

states, which can be imposed upon a state regardless of its own consent. (International law and government now rest upon the consent of each state, individually given.) To put it in the usual terms, world government plans call for subordination, in varying degrees, of national sovereignty; they would make it possible, contrary to centuries of tradition, to submit a state without its consent individually given, to rules and decisions made by the community of nations through certain organs or procedures. Most such plans would enable the world government to reach down to the individual—another invasion of sovereignty. It is, indeed, difficult to see how such a system could operate unless the world government were able, within its range of authority, to require obedience from or give protection to individual human beings.

It is conceivable that world government could be provided by the conquest of the world by one state—by a Caesar or a Napoleon.[2] None of the plans, however, makes such a proposal; they think rather in terms of federal organization. In the United States, a number of groups, which thought along these lines, combined in 1947 at a meeting in Asheville, N. C., into the United World Federalists, who constitute the most active group in this country. It adopted the following policy statement for 1955:

The continuing threat of total warfare imperils the God-given rights of all men to life, liberty and the pursuit of happiness.

War must be eliminated and universal disarmament must be enforced under proper safeguards through a system of world law applicable to all nations and to all individuals.

Only under such a system can world order be developed, a just and lasting peace achieved, and the necessary resources provided to meet human needs at home and throughout the world, enabling all peoples to achieve responsible self-government and to realize their legitimate aspirations for a better life.

All men everywhere must now support the United Nations and seek such amendments to its Charter as will strengthen it into a world federation having powers limited to the prevention of aggression and the control of armaments.

The Committee to Frame a World Government, headed by the former president of the University of Chicago, issued what was stated to be an

---

Association for International Peace, 1950); Jessup, *passim;* W. Levi, *Fundamentals of World Organization* (Minneapolis, 1950); G. J. Mangone, *The Idea and Practice of World Government* (New York, 1951); Cord Meyer, *Peace or Anarchy?* (Boston, 1947); D. Mitrany, "The Functional Approach to World Government," *International Affairs,* 24 (1948); R. Niebuhr, "The Illusion of World Government," in *Christian Realism and Political Problems* (1953); E. Reves, *The Anatomy of Peace* (New York, 1945); A. De Rusett, *Strengthening the Framework of Peace* (London, 1950); F. L. Schuman, *The Commonwealth of Man: An Inquiry into Power Politics and World Government* (1952); Sohn, *passim;* Staff Studies in general; R. A. Taft, *A Foreign Policy for Americans* (1951); Q. Wright, *The World Community* (Chicago, 1948); E. Wynner, *World Federal Government* (1954).

[2] J. Burnham, *The Struggle for the World* (1947), p. 53.

ideal, rather than a practicable, plan.[3] The most serious and careful studies along these lines have been made by Grenville Clark and Louis Sohn.[4] There are other national organizations, and a world conference on world government was held at Copenhagen in 1953. The so-called ABC plan of Ely Culbertson was directed mostly toward building a force to suppress aggression, and also against the Soviet Union; it had a limited federal character.[5] The Congress of the United States interested itself in 1950, and many resolutions were introduced in the House and Senate and in state legislatures. But the Senate Foreign Relations Committee felt that fundamental and constitutional issues were involved and that no position should be taken until there had been more discussion and consensus of opinion among the people. In the following years debates over the Bricker Amendment and other issues revealed a powerful vocal minority against the United Nations; this faded away by 1955, and the polls show that a majority of the people were in favor of at least as much international government as now exists.

The proposed schemes, varied as they are, have certain common principles. They contemplate universality, all states being necessarily submitted to the world government. Implicit in all of them is the rule of law, without which there could not be government. The Clark-Sohn proposals assert that "if war is to be prevented in the modern age, *all* countries and *all* individuals must at *all* times be bound by world law against the use of violence between nations." Disarmament, or reduction of armaments, is essential; the Clark-Sohn proposals are built round this. Most of the plans are federal in character, and draw upon the Constitution and experience of the United States. Most of them call for some sort of a legislature, either representing states or directly elected by the peoples of the world; its powers are much limited, usually to those essential to maintaining peace, though some recognize that the world government must be able to raise money. All other powers are reserved to the sovereign states. The legislature would have power to reach binding decisions by some sort of a majority vote, and even states which had not approved would be bound. This raises the question, considered at length by some, of weighted or graded representation; this would reject the long established principle of "sovereign equality" in voting, and would give to each state a number of votes

[3] R. M. Hutchins and others, *Preliminary Draft of a World Constitution* (Chicago, 1948). Other materials concerning this effort were published in a periodical entitled *Common Cause.*

[4] Grenville Clark and Louis B. Sohn, *Peace Through Disarmament and Charter Revision: Detailed Proposals for Revision of the United Nations Charter* (prelim. print. July 1953; supp., Feb. 1956). Printed by the authors.

[5] See p. 533 above.

corresponding to its actual weight in the affairs of the community of nations. A strong, independent police force is usually called for, and it is recognized that this means a strong executive department. Of course, if the system is to be based on law, there must be a court with compulsory jurisdiction. A Bill of Rights is frequently included.

A key feature of all proposals is the ability on the part of the world government to reach down to individuals within a state. This is of course characteristic of a federal system, within which both the national government and the member states have each a certain defined jurisdiction over individuals. The difficulty of achieving world government may be measured in terms of this principle. It has long been maintained that international law deals only with states, and that only states may deal with individuals—though, as we have seen earlier, this assumption has been much weakened in practice. Much more difficult than legal theory, however, is the matter of popular attitude and established popular loyalties. It would be novel and probably disliked if a United Nations inspector entered with authority into an American city or factory, searching for an individual who, for example, was illegally using atomic energy, and arrested that individual within the jurisdiction of the United States. The other side of the picture is the protection which the United Nations might be called upon to give to an individual as against his own state, and the loyalty which might be required of an individual to the United Nations. Could the United Nations, for example, protect a citizen who reported to it that his own state was preparing to use the atomic bomb for illegal purposes? Could it protect an individual whose own state had violated his rights under an International Bill of Rights?

It is manifest that the proposals for world government are far-reaching and fundamental. There is little doubt that they move in the right direction; the question is: How fast is it wise to move? A poll conducted in 1946 by the Columbia University Bureau of Applied Social Research produced almost unanimous agreement among the experts consulted that thinking must be in the direction of world government and equal agreement that progress toward it must be made by and through the United Nations. The experts disagreed greatly as to whether such a change could be accomplished in a short or a long time. These were experts; the decision, however, must be made by the people. It is impossible in a democracy to take such rapid steps until the people are prepared to move, and there is little indication of such a desire on the part of the mass of the American people. The suggestion that an international legislature should be able to change a tariff which protects an American citizen would probably evoke an instant reaction against the whole idea. The attitude of other states, as revealed in the United Nations debates, shows no enthusiasm for strengthening that institution in the direction of world government. On the contrary, national sovereignty is insisted upon to an extreme degree and little interest is shown in law or courts.

It does not follow from this current situation that the study of world government is useless. Every strengthening of the United Nations is a step towards world government. Occasionally, circumstances appear which force states to seek a solution, and perhaps one day that solution will be found in world government plans. The behavior of the present majority in the General Assembly is now, for example, leading to serious study of plans for weighted representation.

Earlier proposals to abolish the United Nations and to substitute for it a more complete and powerful system have now been modified, and it seems to be agreed that progress must be sought through revision of the Charter of the United Nations rather than *de novo*. The difference between the first, seeking immediate change, and third, visualizing a slower rate of change, of the approaches above mentioned would seem to lie, then, in the speed of progress sought.

163. REGIONALISM[6]

A more cautious approach is that of preliminary, if not ultimate, organization by geographical areas. There had been some development along this line earlier, and it was recognized in the Charter. Since that time the concept has been broadened and blurred by the development of groupings based on interests other than geography, such as the collective defense groupings mentioned in the preceding chapter. We shall look first at the arguments *pro* and *con* regionalism; then survey, rather hastily, existing arrangements; and, finally, consider their relationship to the United Nations.

ARGUMENTS FOR. The following arguments have been offered in favor of regionalism:

1. Development should be attempted gradually, rather than in one jump toward world government. Such a world system could be better built after experience with smaller and closer interest groups.

2. A threat to security is most apt to originate between neighboring

[6] On the general subject, see Brookings, *Regional Security; Regionalism and World Organization* (Public Affairs Press, 1944); C.S.O.P., Eighth Report; G. Bebr, "Regional Organizations: A United Nations Problem," *A.J.*, 49 (1955), p. 66; Crane Brinton, *From Many One* (Cambridge, 1948); H. F. Armstrong, "The World is Round," *Foreign Affairs*, 31 (1953); E. N. Van Kleffens, "Regionalism and Political Pacts," *A.J.*, 43 (1949); "Regional Organizations: Their Role in the World Community," *Columbia Journal of International Affairs*, 3 (1949).

states; the peoples in that area are the ones most affected and consequently the ones most willing to undertake security measures. Outside states, on the other hand, would be less willing to send their soldiers to be used in the settlement of distant quarrels in which they have little interest.

3. Action against an aggressor would be undertaken not only more willingly, but with more dispatch and efficiency by those within a region. There would be delay and uncertainty if it were necessary to await action by faraway states with long distances to traverse.

4. Aside from aggression, many other problems are local ones and should be handled by local people, since outsiders have neither the interest nor the knowledge to solve them. Neighbors can work together.

5. In each region there would be a dominant Great Power, thus constituting a balance of power under the deserved leadership of the Great Powers.

6. Homogeneity of interests of various kinds, such as language, culture, or economic interests, produce a natural trend toward regional groupings.

ARGUMENTS AGAINST. Equally strong reasons for opposition to regionalism may be offered:

1. International problems are today world-wide in scope and can be solved only by a universal system. This is the result of increasing economic and other interdependence.

2. If decentralization is desired, it would be better to plan it upon a functional rather than upon a geographical basis.

3. While disputes may originate between neighboring states, they tend to develop into global wars, and the universal community of nations must therefore take an interest in every dispute, and make sure that it does not produce general conflagration.

4. Regional groupings are simply enlarged alliances, leading to "bigger and better" wars. The possible regions vary so much in industrial and military power that it could not be expected that there would be a balance of power between them, and it would hardly be possible to organize an artificial balance.

5. In such regional systems, smaller states would be submitted to the domination of the Great Power within the area, and the region would not be able to control the Great Power. This could only be done from the outside, by other Great Powers. If there were more than one Great Power in the region, the problem would simply be more complicated.

6. There is little more reason to hope that nations in a given region could work together with more cooperation and efficiency than could all nations in a universal system.

7. If security enforcement were attempted through regional systems, authority and power would be divided and the potential strength which could be massed against an aggressor would be much smaller. Economic sanctions could not be used within a region, since they must be universal to be effective.

164. ORGANIZATION OF AMERICAN STATES[7]

The earliest movement toward regionalism was in the Western Hemisphere, where the famous South American statesman, Simon Bolivar, summoned a conference which met at Panama in 1826 and adopted a "Treaty of Perpetual Union." In 1889 Secretary Blaine summoned the first of a series of Conferences of American States which have continued ever since. The Pan American Union was created at that time, though it was not given legal status or a clear definition of function until 1929.

A great deal of waste motion has characterized the development of the system. Many treaties were negotiated and never put into effect, or never used; special conferences were held which produced little; administrative institutions were created (such as the Pan American Postal Union, or the Trade-Mark Bureau) which duplicated existing institutions or developed little in the way of actual accomplishment. There was a long effort to build up an "American International Law," an American court of justice, an American League of Nations. Such ideas came into conflict, when the League of Nations appeared, with the idea of universal international organization. At the Havana Conference of 1929, these separatist ideas appear to have been defeated, and American regionalism was accepted as part of and subordinate to a world organization.

The American republics became much alarmed by the extension of Nazi influence and by the aggressiveness of Mussolini and Hitler, and they drew together under that danger into a somewhat more coherent

[7] See Margaret Ball, *The Problem of Inter American Organization* (Stanford, 1944); A. Guani, "La solidarité internationale dans l'Amérique latine," *Hague Acad.*, 1925, III, pp. 207-337; Alberto Lleras, "The American Regional System," *Bulletin of the Pan-American Union*, 81 (1947); J. R. de Orue y Arrequi, "Le régionalisme dans l'organisation internationale," *Hague Acad.*, 1935, III, pp. 7-94; W. Sanders, "Bogotá Conference: Ninth International Conference of American States," *Int. Con.*, No. 442 (1948); J. B. Scott (ed.), *International Conferences of American States, 1889-1928* (New York, 1931), and *First Supplement, 1933-1940* (New York, 1940); A. P. Whitaker, "Development of American Regionalism," *Int.Con.*, No. 469 (1951); J. M. Yepes and Pereira da Silva, *Commentaire théorique et practique du Pacte de la Société des Nations et des Statuts de l'Union Pan Américaine*, 3 vols. (Paris, 1934); Yuen-li Liang, "Regional Arrangements and International Security," *Grotius Society*, 1946, p. 216; and, in general, *Annals of the Organization of American States*.

system. They had hitherto tended to draw away from the United States and to safeguard themselves against Yankee imperialism in the League of Nations. Now, the "Good Neighbor Policy" enunciated by President Roosevelt and his rejection of intervention on the part of the United States, together with the diminishing strength of the League of Nations, all operated to bring them into closer cooperation in the Western Hemisphere. The United States, on the other hand, striving to keep out of war and at the same time to build up defenses against Hitler, was eager to cooperate with them. The manifest dangers revealed by the war, and the increased cooperation with the United States, led to more definite efforts to organize the Western Hemisphere into a security system. At the Mexico City Conference (February 21-March 8, 1945) a resolution was adopted On the Establishment of a General International Organization (Resolution XXX) which approved in general of the Dumbarton Oaks Proposals but suggested a number of changes in them. At the same time, two other resolutions were adopted which raised important questions as to the relationship with this "general international organization." One was Resolution VIII, known as the Act of Chapultepec, which bound the American republics to resist aggression from amongst themselves and from the outside as well. The other was Resolution IX, Reorganization of the Inter American System, which stated some of the steps in such a reorganization, but called for a conference to be held in the following year to work out a comprehensive charter for the American regional system.[8]

In accordance with these preliminary decisions, a conference met at Rio de Janeiro in 1947, and on September 2 the Inter American Treaty of Reciprocal Assistance was signed, known as the Rio Treaty. The signatories agreed that "an armed attack by any State against an American State shall be considered an attack against all American States," and each undertook to assist against the aggressor in the exercise of the right of self-defense under Article 51 of the Charter. The treaty indicates that it is a regional arrangement under the United Nations, though it refers to Article 51 as well as to Chapter VIII.

At the Ninth Conference of American States at Bogotá, a Charter was adopted for the Organization of American States (OAS), Article 104 of which asserts that it is not to be construed in any respect as impairing rights or obligations under the Charter of the United Nations. The system thus set up comprises the Inter American Conference, which is the authoritative body, the Meeting of Consultation of Foreign Ministers, the council, and the Pan American Union, which is the

[8] The resolutions of the Mexico City Conference may be found in *Inter American Conference on Problems of War and Peace* (Pan American Union, Washington, 1945).

secretariat of the new body. It has its own specialized agencies, as well as an Inter American Economic and Social Council, a Cultural Council, and a Council of Jurists. It is the Meeting of Foreign Ministers which is called in emergency. At the same conference, the Pact of Bogotá was signed, a treaty for pacific settlement of disputes, which attempted to put together into a systematic arrangement the numerous and variegated treaties of the past; it is consequently a somewhat complicated instrument itself. All this definitely improved and gave more substance to the Latin American "regional arrangement," and it is now doubtless the best example of what was originally contemplated by that term.

165. THE ARAB LEAGUE[9]

An Arab nationalist movement began to take shape after the Turkish Revolution of 1908, and definite gains toward independence in various areas resulted from the political exigencies of two world wars. There are now seven new Arab states which, with Israel, fill the Middle East area.

Upon the initiative of Egypt, exploratory conversations with regard to Arab unity were begun, and in September, 1944, delegates of the Arab states held a meeting which debated full union as against federal union, and agreed upon a League of Arab States. The agreement was signed by Syria, Transjordan, Iraq, Saudi Arabia, the Lebanese Republic, Egypt, and Yemen, and opportunity is offered to any other independent Arab group to enter the League. It provides a council, a permanent secretariat, and a committee for each of the following stated purposes: economic and financial matters; communications; cultural matters; matters connected with nationality, passports, extradition, and execution of judgments; social welfare; health. In case of disputes not involving sovereignty and territorial independence, the decision of the council is final; for other disputes, the council is to conciliate. The council is also to determine the measures necessary to be taken to repel aggression, acting in this case by unanimous (except for

---

[9] See G. Antonius, *The Arab Awakening* (London, 1938); Philip W. Ireland, *The Near East: Problems and Prospects* (Chicago, 1942); H. Kohn, *History of Nationalism in the East* (London, 1929). The Pact of the League of Arab States, signed at Cairo, March 22, 1945, may be found in *UNCIO Doc.* 72, III/4/1. See also Charles Issawi, "The Bases of Arab Unity," *International Affairs*, 31 (1955); M. Khadduri, "The Arab League as a Regional Arrangement," *A.J.*, 40 (1946), p. 756; same author, "Towards an Arab Union: The League of Arab States," *Pol. Sci. Rev.*, 40 (1946), p. 90; L. Seabury, "The League of Arab States: Debacle of a Regional Arrangement," *Int. Organ.*, 3 (1949).

disputants) vote. Withdrawal is permitted on a year's notice; amendments require the approval of two-thirds of the members, and those who do not accept the amendment may withdraw.

Thus, some clarification began to appear in the tangled politics of the Near East. Five of the seven members were invited to the UNCIO, and became Members of the United Nations; Yemen and Transjordan did not adhere to the Declaration by United Nations. These five formed a bloc at the San Francisco Conference and have done so in the United Nations since then. They sought but did not obtain a seat on the Security Council; they displayed interest in Palestine; and they were instrumental in obtaining Article 80, paragraph 1, of the Charter. Later, however, they did not agree so well; Egypt took a strong stand against Israel, which Jordan would not follow, and Iraq was not sympathetic with Egypt. In 1950, a collective security pact was signed by all but Jordan. A secretariat is maintained at Cairo, and conferences are held; but the Arab League, torn internally, cannot be regarded as a successful regional arrangement.

166. BRITISH COMMONWEALTH OF NATIONS

The concept of regionalism accepted at San Francisco was sufficiently broad to cover mutual assistance and nonaggression pacts but, as we have noted, the concept has now been so extended that it seems to cover almost any group of nations, not necessarily having a common geographic base, but having common military or even economic and cultural interests.

This being so, it is perhaps permissible to include under this topic the unique grouping known as the British Commonwealth of Nations. It is composed of former British colonies which have gradually and constitutionally advanced to self-government and independence, without cutting themselves off entirely from the parent country. They illustrate the remarkable talent of the British for training their peoples in the art of self-government and of giving way to their wishes for independence when the time comes, without violent disruption (since the American Revolution!). Gradually, over the years, Australia, Canada, New Zealand, South Africa, and Eire became independent and separate members of the League of Nations. They did not, as Members of the League, constitute or act as a bloc. When Sir Cecil Hurst in 1925 appeared to speak in the name of these nations, he was challenged by the representatives of Eire and Australia.[10]

[10] L. of N. Doc., Records of the Third Assembly (1922), Plenary, p. 146; Records of the Sixth Assembly (1925), Plenary, pp. 24-45.

After World War II, India and Pakistan became free, and this caused some change in the pattern. Dominion status had implied that all had a common monarch—not the monarch of all, but of each separately; but the Indian states rejected allegiance to the Crown. The flexible Commonwealth was nevertheless stretched to admit them as republics, to whom the monarch was merely the Head of the Commonwealth. Ceylon also joined; Burma preferred to go its own way; and in 1949 Eire broke away. There are thus eight states—Australia, Canada, Ceylon, India, New Zealand, Pakistan, and South Africa, and of course the United Kingdom—which constitute the British Commonwealth of Nations.

What this Commonwealth is it would be hard to say. It has no constitution, no organization, no headquarters. For a time, there were more or less regular Imperial Conferences, of which the one in 1926 was perhaps the most important. Discussion of the relationship between these states there led to a report agreed to by all and enacted into the Statute of Westminster in 1931, which stated this principle:

. . . first, that each member of the Commonwealth must determine its own foreign policy and, second, that it is a conventional rule of the Commonwealth association that every effort should be made to obtain agreement among the members on the fundamental principles of foreign policy.[11]

The members do not maintain formal diplomatic relations with each other, but they maintain representatives at the other capitals. There is no secretariat or council, but the prime ministers occasionally come together and discuss matters of common interest. It is a most intangible sort of an organization, but one probably as effective as the OAS; it sets a high standard of cooperation between separate and independent states.[12]

167. EUROPEAN UNION[13]

The idea of combining the states of Europe into some sort of a system goes back for many years. An organized movement in this direc-

[11] *The British Empire* (Royal Institute of International Affairs, London, 1938), p. 230. See also P. J. Noel-Baker, *The Present Juridical Status of the British Dominions in International Law* (London, 1929); W. Y. Elliott, *The New British Empire* (New York, 1932); R. B. Stewart, *Treaty Relations of the British Commonwealth of Nations* (New York, 1939).

[12] The reservations to their acceptance of the Optional Clause of the Statute of the Court exclude from compulsory jurisdiction disputes between members of the Commonwealth.

[13] As to European Union, see Documents relating to the Organization of a System of European Federal Union, *L. of N. Doc.*, 1930, VII. 4, found also in *Int. Con.*, Special Bulletin, June, 1930, and No. 265, December, 1930; R. N. Coudenhove-Kalergi, *Pan Europe* (New York, 1926); same author, *Crusade for Pan Europe* (New York, 1943); E. Herriot, *Europe* (Paris, 1930).

tion was initiated by Count Coudenhove-Kalergi in 1926, and a number of conferences were held. It became a practical and formal proposal when Premier Briand offered it as such to the representatives of twenty-seven European states in 1929. This effort resulted from discussion in the League of Nations and, in the memorandum which he was charged to prepare, M. Briand stated as the purpose of the proposed union the creation of "some kind of a federal bond" between European nations which would encourage them to "study, discuss and settle problems likely to be of common interest." He insisted that such a formula for European cooperation should be in conjunction with and subordinate to the League of Nations, and he argued that the economic problem should be subordinated to the political problem. The machinery proposed was simple: a regular "European Conference," a permanent political committee acting through special technical committees, and a secretariat. It was not to be used as an economic weapon against outside states.

Replies to this proposal were received from twenty-six governments; all agreed that more cooperation in Europe was essential, but as to methods and principles there was much divergence. Some did not want the League of Nations to suffer; some feared that it might lead to intercontinental rivalries; some disagreed with the proposition that political questions should precede economic ones. Meanwhile, the economic situation became worse, fears of the Soviet Union were appearing, and with the rise of Hitler, interest in European Union faded away.

During the Second World War, the idea was revived. Churchill proposed union with France, but it was too sudden; in a speech in 1943, he spoke of a Council for Europe and a Council for Asia. After the war, the weakness of Europe and the desire of the United States to build up its strength was added to the existing fear of the Soviet Union. A congress at The Hague in 1948, of various groups, set the movement on foot. The French and Belgians apparently wanted a supra-national system, with a parliamentary body; the British, more cautious, favored a council which would not be so much in the public view. Compromises were made and in May, 1949 ten states signed the Statute of the Council of Europe, and it came into force on August 3, 1949. Other states later became members.[14]

The foreign ministers of the members constitute the Committee of Ministers, and there is a Consultative Assembly chosen as the govern-

[14] The preparatory work was done by the council under the Brussels Pact. To the members of this pact were added Eire, Denmark, Italy, Norway, and Sweden; Greece, Turkey, and Iceland joined in 1949; Germany in 1950. Only Portugal, Spain, Switzerland, and Yugoslavia, aside from Soviet-controlled countries, remained outside the union in 1953.

ment of each wishes; in practice, it is elected by parliaments in numbers corresponding to populations. There is a secretary-general, with a staff of some two hundred. The system was a hybrid combination of popular representatives and government officials, who came into conflict at once. The former sought to set up a real political authority for all of Europe—a supra-national body; the latter naturally opposed this, since such an authority would dictate to their governments. They proposed instead to work on specific functions, and some useful—though not sensational—work has been done. The Thirteenth Session of the Committee of Ministers signed conventions concerning patent applications, social security, equivalence of examinations for admission to universities. Studies are made as to a European army, passports, and integration in general. Britain and the Scandinavian states were not willing to give up any sovereignty, so the Schuman Plan states set up their own constitution. All were eager to cooperate, and the movement was pushed along by the agreement of France, the United Kingdom, and the United States to support a European army, admitting Germany.

Along with this more or less parliamentary development there were various movements which brought the long separatist states of Europe into more common action. The Marshall Plan money led to the Organization for European Economic Cooperation (OEEC). Belgium, Luxembourg and the Netherlands had formed a customs union earlier (BENELUX) and this was expanded into the treaty of Brussels on March 17, 1948. This was a security pact, including Britain and France, with headquarters, a Council of Foreign Ministers, and with Field Marshal Montgomery to head the military forces. This was expanded into NATO, with twelve members including the United States, its principal supporter; and later others were admitted—Portugal, Iceland, Norway, Denmark, Italy, Greece, and Turkey. This heterogeneous collection stretched considerably the concept of regional arrangement, but it constituted a very strong international organization, raising the question in the minds of some why it had not been opened to membership by all Members of the United Nations who cared to join.[15]

Such events as the Communist coup in Czechoslovakia and the Berlin blockade had helped to further the above developments; and the attack on Korea expedited the idea of a European Defence Community (EDC). The United States became eager to rearm Germany as an additional defense against communism, and this agitated the French, to

---

[15] NATO is not here regarded as a "regional arrangement" under the Charter, but rather as a means of "collective self-defence." See § 160 above.

whom Germany was a worse enemy than was the Soviet Union. France would not hear of a German army but supported the Pleven Plan, which proposed to abolish national armies and create a European army into which all would be absorbed; there would thus be no German army. On May 27, 1952 a treaty was signed constituting the European Defence Community, with a council of ministers and a parliamentary assembly. The guarantees of NATO were extended to EDC, and this seemed to reassure the French, though the organizations were by now becoming tangled and confused with each other. There were many questions to bother the French; for example, concerning Britain and the United States, who were not members and might drop out. Attempts to meet her fears failed and in September 1952 she refused to ratify, and EDC was wrecked.

The long effort to achieve a supra-national organization for Europe had thus failed, though there remained a number of bodies working toward European integration. "Western Union" is a confused collection of organizations rather than a regional arrangement, but nevertheless it is a remarkable development in international organization. The process of regional arrangements will doubtless continue, for the European states are no longer the strong leaders of the world and must work together; they cannot afford the separate independent attitudes of the past.[16]

SOVIET REGIONALISM. The Soviet regional system, if it can be called that, is based upon a set of bilateral mutual assistance agreements; there is no multilateral instrument, no constitution, no central organization —except in the sense that Moscow efficiently provides direction. The Third Communist International (Comintern) had been dissolved during the war; in 1947, in answer to the Marshall Plan, the Cominform was set up. It was supposed to be an information office for the Communist states but it apparently worked in such a way as to hold in line the "independent" satellite states. Yugoslavia was lost by defection, and there remained in the grouping Albania, Bulgaria, Czechoslovakia,

[16] A few references are given here, as an entering wedge into the mass of materials. Documentary: Documents Relating to the North Atlantic Treaty, *Senate Doc.* No. 48, 81 Cong., 1 Sess.; *Documents on European Recovery and Defense* (Royal Institute of International Affairs, 1949); Dept. of State Pub. No. 4173 (Schuman Plan); No. 4630 (NATO); No. 4492 (Council of Europe). The Council of Europe has its own publications.

Other materials: J. Goormatigh, "European Integration," *Int. Con.*, No. 488 (1953); H. J. Hilton, "Benelux—A Case Study in Economic Union," *Dept. of State Bull.*, 23 (1950), p. 183; P. Reynaud, *Unite or Perish* (New York, 1951); F. L. Schuman, "The Council of Europe," *Pol. Sci. Rev.*, 45 (1951); D. U. Stikker, "The Functional Approach to European Integration," *Foreign Affairs*, 29 (1951); W. A. Surrey, "Emerging Structure of Collective Security Arrangements," *Dept. of State Bull.* 22 (1950), p. 792.

Hungary, Poland, and Rumania, along with the U.S.S.R. Perhaps there should also be listed on the one hand Finland, which cannot be entirely independent, and the Ukrainian and Byelorussian republics, which are separate members of the United Nations. All, excepting Finland, were cut off by the "iron curtain" about the beginning of 1949 when the "Molotov Plan" barred the Eastern European states from the trade and culture of the world and sought to make them dependent on the Soviet Union. In appearance at least, an effort was being made to build an integrated Eastern Europe to match the effort being made to build an integrated Western Europe. Granted the uncertain meaning of the term "regional arrangement," the Soviet grouping could doubtless qualify as well as some others.

168. REGIONALISM IN THE PACIFIC AREA

Development along regional lines has been slower in Asia and the Pacific Ocean area. There have been great discrepancies in these areas between the various political entities, as to weight in the community of nations, governmental development, industrial production, and other factors. Large areas of the Pacific and the Far East belong to or are under the influence of states far away from the area. Vast distances, huge population, political rivalries and emotions are involved, making the problem of regional organization extremely difficult.

The Institute of Pacific Relations, which cannot be regarded as a regional organization of official nature, has served as a medium of cooperative study of problems, including the problem of regionalism. The Nine Power Treaty, made at the Washington Conference of 1921-1922, proposed a Board of Reference to adjust questions arising under the treaty, but the board was never established. At an IPR conference in 1933, Japanese delegates proposed a regional organization backed by a nonaggression treaty, and other such proposals were studied at later conferences. One such study envisaged three groupings: (1) Netherlands Indies, Philippines, Burma and British Malaya, to include, after the war, Thailand (Siam) and Indo-China in an "Indonesian Union"; (2) a "Far Eastern Group" of China, Manchuria, Japan, the "Indonesian Union" and India; and (3) a "Pacific Association" to include the United States, Canada, Australia, and New Zealand, the western coast of South America, and the "Far Eastern Group."[17]

A broader viewpoint was taken by Dr. Chow. He points out the particular need of such an organization in the Far East because of its

[17] K. Mitchell and W. L. Holland, *Problems of the Pacific 1939* (New York, 1940), p. 127.

remoteness and because of unfamiliarity of outsiders with its problems, because of coming colonial emancipation and rising nationalism, and because of shifts in the balance of power and in the degree of freedom from external control. He would include in a "Pacific Association of Nations" China, Soviet Russia, India, the United States, Canada, Australia, Philippines, Great Britain, the Netherlands and, after peace had been made, Japan and Siam. Korea might in due time be included. These states would be bound by a nonaggression pact, and a regional organization with its own military forces, distributed at strategic points, would be prepared to act against an aggressor. The organization would be composed of a general conference, a Pacific council, a court, a military staff, and a permanent secretariat, and it should work positively to advance the interests of the area as well as negatively to prevent the use of force. It would be subordinated to the United Nations, but with the general principle that matters of purely local concern should be left to the regional system.[18]

With the growth of nationalism in Asia, and the thrust of communism there, it was inevitable that attempts should be made at closer cooperation. The presidents of the Philippines, of Korea, and of Nationalist China sought more security through closer association; Nehru of India was less enthusiastic, but could not keep out. Danger in southeast Asia spurred interest in that area. The conference on Indonesia called by India in 1949 favored regional organization in a vague way. In May 1950 a conference, which met at Baguio in the Philippines, included Australia, Ceylon, India, Indonesia, Pakistan, the Philippines, and Thailand; Burma was unable to attend. It was for general discussion, and no resolutions or plan for organization were adopted, though Romulo, as president of the conference, was asked to study possibilities.

The United States at first indicated that NATO engaged all of her interest, and France and the United Kingdom held similar positions. But by 1951 the United States had made security pacts in the Pacific area with the Philippines, and with Australia and New Zealand (the latter being called ANZUS). There had been, during the war, a Pacific War Council and the ANZAC agreement for regional security; after the war, the South Pacific Commission was set up to advance economic and social welfare. It has been an active body.

In 1954, after preliminary negotiations, a conference met at Manila, at which Australia, France, New Zealand, Pakistan, the Philippines,

18 S. R. Chow, *Winning the Peace in the Pacific* (New York, 1944). See also N. Peffer, *Basis for Peace in the Far East* (New York, 1942); *War and Peace in the Pacific* (Institute of Pacific Relations, New York, 1943), and other publications of the institute.

Thailand, the United States, and the United Kingdom were represented. These states, on September 8, signed the South-East Asia Collective Defense Treaty (known as SEATO). It is not nearly so strong an arrangement as NATO; and a number of states which were sought as members did not join, some for "neutralist" reasons. The signatories agreed to settle disputes by peaceful means, to develop ability to resist attack, and to promote economic progress. By Article 55, they may, in unanimity, designate an area, and if armed attack is made against that area, or against any signatory, each agrees to "act to meet the common danger in accordance with its constitutional processes." Cold war methods are taken into account by agreement to consult if danger threatens from other than armed attack. Other states may be invited to join, by unanimity. A council was provided for planning as to situations which might develop; it held its first meeting at Bangkok in February 1955.

169. FEDERAL UNION

Clarence Streit, as the Geneva correspondent of the *New York Times*, had for many years watched the struggles and the failures of the League of Nations, and had concluded that a stronger system was desirable. He proposed[19] that an international government be established upon the model of the American federal union, and his arguments were persuasively presented in terms of the experience of the United States. He regarded the League of Nations as patchwork, extending rather than controlling the concept of national sovereignty; he compared it with the Articles of Confederation in American history and asserted that with regard to the League, as in the case of the confederation, mere amendment was not enough. He proposed to start with fifteen democracies (the Anglo-Saxon and western European democracies), which furnished a combination of the greatest power with the strongest natural bonds. These were to constitute a nucleus, but the ultimate goal was a universal system, and states would be admitted as they became sufficiently democratic. Enforcement action, he argued, is possible only against individuals, not against nations; consequently, the system must be a union rather than a league, and the central government should be able to reach down to and control individuals. Furthermore, states should be represented, not on the usual basis of equality of voting, but upon the basis of population, and the

[19] C. K. Streit, *Union Now* (New York, 1939).

delegates should be chosen directly by the people in each nation. Representation by population would be checked, as in the United States, by a bicameral legislature. Under this apportionment, the smallest state would have four representatives, and the United States would have 136.

The powers of the union would be limited but would include the right to grant citizenship, to make treaties, to raise forces and provide for the common defense, to regulate commerce, to issue and regulate money, to own and operate the postal and other communications services, and to issue patents and copyrights. Other powers than those delegated to the central government would be reserved to the states. His illustrative constitution begins with a Bill of the Rights of Man. Instead of a president, there was to be a board of five and a premier.

An organization was established to propagate the idea of federal union, and it gained many adherents. Objection was raised, however, to the narrow membership, which would exclude the Latin American states, the Far and Near Eastern states, and the Soviet Union. There were some who disagreed with the practical possibility of international control over individuals, and some who were uncertain as to the scheme of representation and of direct popular election. The movement therefore broke up into several groups, all, however, advocating some form of federal world government. Mr. Streit later spoke of "Atlantic Union," and the course of events has led the Western democracies in the direction of his proposals, though they are far from being fully realized. The movement, which has many eminent men among its supporters, claims to help the United Nations rather than to oppose it. Both the movement and the following plan are much influenced by opposition to the Soviet Union.

THE ABC PLAN. A quite different scheme was proposed by Ely Culbertson.[20] He rejected the idea of a strong central government and a closely knit union of states and asked no more than an association of eleven regional federations, artificially created, in each of which only the most populous state could be a member of the world federation, and would speak therein for its group. A Provisional Council of Temporary Trustees was to make peace, bring relief to the liberated states, and establish a "World Police" on an ingenious "quota force" principle. According to this principle, the armed strength of the world would be divided as follows: 22 per cent to an independent international police; 20 per cent to the United States; 15 per cent each to Britain and the Soviet Union; 6 per cent each to the French and Chi-

[20] Ely Culbertson, *Total Peace* (Garden City, 1943).

nese; 3 per cent each to Germany, Poland, Turkey, and India; 2 per cent each to Malaysia and Japan. As a result of this distribution of power, the world government would be able to deal with any single state, and could presumably expect help from other states against a combination of aggressors; on the other hand, the danger of an all powerful international police force would be countered by the possibility of the combination against it of national forces. There was to be also a World Supreme Court, and this would be the authority which would call for economic or military measures against aggression. While the quota force idea has received sympathetic consideration, the scheme as a whole does not seem to have gained many supporters.

The famous Vandenberg Resolution, which was adopted by the Senate on June 11, 1948 and which laid down Senate approval of certain fundamentals of foreign policy, supported regional arrangements, but insisted that they be in consonance with the Charter of the United Nations. Mr. John Foster Dulles in 1952 seemed to think that regional security agreements had to some extent harmed the United Nations, but as Secretary of State he said that "security may have to be achieved primarily through regional organizations which are authorized by the United Nations Charter, but which to some extent function outside the scope of the United Nations direct authority."[21] The Commission to Study the Organization of Peace admits regional security pacts, in the weakness of the United Nations, but warns against permitting any one of them to be more powerful than the United Nations. Political developments have brought about more regional organizations, and there is debate as to whether they help or hurt the United Nations.

170. REGIONALISM AND THE UNITED NATIONS[22]

Nothing in the Charter, says Article 52, precludes the existence of regional arrangements for matters appropriate for regional action, provided they are "consistent with the Purposes and Principles of the United Nations." The term regional arrangements, it should be noted, was intended to cover pacts of mutual assistance, such as the British-Soviet treaty, as well as arrangements for definite areas. The articles of the Charter, as written, represent a compromise between the advocates

21 *Dept. of State Bull.*, 28 (1953), p. 403.
22 W. P. Allen, "Regional Arrangements and the United Nations," in *Organizing the United Nations*, Dept. of State Pub., No. 2573 (1946); *Report to the President*, pp. 101-08; V. Belaunde, *La Conferencia de San Francisco* (Lima, 1945); Goodrich and Hambro, Chap. viii; Palmer and Perkins, pp. 808-14; the UNCIO documents of Committee III/4.

of these types of arrangements, and between conflicting claims of regional autonomy, universalism, and Security Council control through the veto.

Insofar as the settlement of disputes is concerned, the Security Council and Members are urged to employ regional methods where possible, and "resort to regional agencies or arrangements" was included among the means of settlement listed in Article 33. The rights of the Security Council under articles 34 and 35, however, were not impaired, and this means that Members may refer disputes to the Council and that it may investigate and decide whether a dispute exists which the Members are obligated to settle. Having so decided (in theory, for in practice it does not so decide), however, the Security Council is obligated to "encourage" settlement through regional agencies, either on the initiative of the parties themselves or by "reference from the Security Council." Since the Security Council is not elsewhere given the authority to refer a dispute to any method of settlement, and since under Chapter VI it can do no more than recommend a procedure to the parties, it cannot require parties to submit to regional means of settlement if they do not desire to do so. If the regional agreement requires that disputes between members of the regional system be submitted to regional procedures for adjustment, there would seem to be no conflict of jurisdiction, since Members of the United Nations are free under Chapter VI to choose such procedure as they may wish. If and when such efforts have failed, it would appear that the Security Council would be able to recommend terms of settlement under Article 37.

There have been a few illustrations in practice. In December, 1948, Costa Rica notified the council of the OAS of invasion from Nicaragua. The council met at once and sent a committee of investigation, which reported that each side was stirring up trouble in the other, and called upon both to prevent expeditions from their territories. A committee was appointed to see that these decisions were carried out. The action was duly notified to the Security Council under Article 54 of the United Nations Charter. The Dominican Republic in the same year notified the Security Council that it had complained to the Inter-American Committee of OAS that Cuba was permitting on its territory the organization of forces for the purpose of overthrowing the Dominican government, and later reported that in accordance with the recommendation of the above committee it was negotiating with Cuba. In the Guatemalan affair, mentioned in the preceding chapter, the Security Council refused to handle the case, thereby leaving it to the OAS. In practice, the Security Council has followed Article 52 and encouraged settlement through regional arrangements; there has been no precedent of action by the Council itself in a dispute within a regional system.[23]

The provision of sanctions by a regional system raises more difficult questions. Article 53 of the Charter makes it clear that no regional enforcement action may be taken by a regional arrangement, except against former enemy states, without the prior authorization of the Security Council. As a result, it would be possible for a Great Power outside the region to prevent by veto measures of enforcement or of resistance to aggression by a regional group. Objection was reasonably taken to this situation at San Francisco, as well as to the situation in which the veto would make it impossible for the Council itself to act; and such objections led to the inclusion of Article 51 in the Charter and since then to the collective defense agreements above mentioned. The North Atlantic Treaty makes no reference to Chapter VIII; if it were limited by Article 53 it would be impotent. The Charter does not give to the United Nations the right to designate a group as a "regional arrangement" and require it to submit to Chapter VIII. There seems then to be little meaning left to Article 53. The right of nations to defend themselves, individually or collectively, has always been and must be admitted; and it is doubtless true that collective security may be sought through regional organization in this sense and regardless of Article 53. The reserve power behind collective security, as provided in Chapter VII, seems to stem from Article 51 rather than from Article 53.

171. GRADUALISM

We have looked at two of the three approaches mentioned above for strengthening the United Nations, or putting something better in its place: world government, as to particular details of which we shall have more to say; and regionalism, subordinated to the United Nations, but spreading out from under its control. The third approach is the attempt to shape the development of the United Nations in more gradual and usual ways. A constitution may be changed not only by amendment but by interpretation and usage. This approach may best be considered by reference to some of the more frequent proposals for change, measuring their possibilities against the trends of practice and viewpoint which have appeared in the first decade of experience of the United Nations.

[23] These episodes can most conveniently be found in the issues of *International Organization*.

CHARTER REVIEW.[24] Article 109, representing a compromise made at San Francisco, makes a special arrangement for considering a general revision of the Charter. Many states, already dissatisfied with the Charter which was then emerging, were discouraged by the fact that the veto could be used in the amending process and saw little hope of future improvement against this veto. The Great Powers, very generously, gave them a chance to call a conference for revision with no veto allowed to block the call; and they put upon the agenda of the Tenth Session of the General Assembly the question whether a conference should be called. This was as far as their generosity went, for still no amendment could go into effect unless ratified by two-thirds of the Members including all the permanent members of the Security Council.

A great deal of interest has been shown, and some important studies made concerning revision of the Charter, on the outside of the United Nations; within the United Nations, there has been much hesitation and uncertainty. Few states were willing to commit themselves for or against a conference,[25] and not even preparatory studies could be authorized, for fear that governments, therein taking a position, would be committed to such positions, making it more difficult to reach agreement later. Some understanding of their timidity may be gleaned from the following pages; it is very much a question whether such a conference would help or hurt the United Nations.

The Tenth Assembly, having the question automatically on its agenda, adopted Resolution 992(X) which in its preamble recognized that it was desirable to review the Charter in the light of experience, but also that such a review "should be conducted under auspicious international circumstances." It therefore set up a Committee consisting of all Members to consider the time, place, organization and procedure for such a conference, its report to be made to the Twelfth Assembly. It was not authorized to recommend changes in the Charter, so con-

[24] See especially Brookings, *Proposals*, and Brookings, *Organization*, final chapter. Also, Staff Studies, in general; *Charter Review Conference*, Ninth Report of the Commission to Study the Organization of Peace, with accompanying papers; The Future of the United Nations: Issues of Charter Review, *Annals*, November, 1954; *The United States Stake in the United Nations: Problems of United Nations Charter Review* (Fifth American Assembly, Arden House, August, 1954); *Report of Committee on Review of the Charter of the United Nations* (International Law Association, Edinburgh Conference, 1954); Ernest A. Gross, "Revising the Charter: Is it Possible? Is it Wise?," *Foreign Affairs*, 32 (1954), p. 203; Trygve Lie, *In the Cause of Peace* (New York, 1954), Chap. xxiii; Yuen-li Liang, "Preparatory Work for a Possible Revision of the United Nations Charter," *A.J.*, 48 (1954), p. 83; Jacob Robinson, "The General Review Conference," *Int. Organ.*, 8 (1954), p. 316.

[25] The United States announced that it would favor such a conference, regarding it as in the nature of a pledge made at San Francisco.

sideration of such changes cannot begin before 1958. Whether the committee will wish to call such a conference then will depend upon the attitudes revealed by Members, and also upon the possibilities and needs which we will consider in the following pages.

UNIVERSALITY. In the various world government plans, as differentiated from those based on regionalism, universality of membership is demanded. This is the logical consequence of the concept of "world" government, which seeks to bring all nations under the jurisdiction of the organized community of nations. Whether this can be achieved depends upon whether the United Nations can be strengthened in other ways, for the proposal implies ability on the part of the United Nations to coerce a dissident state. If, for example, the United States should not wish to belong, it would be beyond the present capacity of the United Nations to compel it to membership.

The United Nations, as Secretary-General Hammarskjöld once remarked, should not be regarded as a club, in which applicants for membership can be blackballed, or members expelled for misconduct; good or bad, democratic or undemocratic, say those who favor universality, all states should be members and under such control as the organization can exert. The Charter provisions for admission by political vote, however, make membership depend upon the liking which Members have or have not for the applicant; thus, the American people refuse to admit Communist China because they do not like it, and some of them would push out the Soviet Union. The result of such thinking would be to set up a rival organization, free to do as it wished. Membership, it is said, should be automatic.

This statement, however, does not solve the problem, for the community of nations has never provided itself with means for determining whether an applicant is a state, or deserves to be called one; we have raised this question earlier, in connection with "self-determination." The United Nations has made some study of the factors which should enter into such a determination, but they have not been accepted nor has the United Nations been authorized to apply them. Until such criteria and authority are provided, in a form according to which a court could decide, it is difficult to think of "automatic" membership. The decision in such matters has always been reserved to each state individually, and has always been a political decision; this is the case, it might be noted, with regard to the admission of Alaska and Hawaii in the United States as States of the Union.

Within the United Nations itself, speeches have often been made stating universality as the proper goal, but present practice is far from that goal. It could be achieved to some extent in practice if Members would vote for admission of applicant states; if they are not willing to do this, they would probably not be willing to change the Charter in this respect.

PACIFIC SETTLEMENT OF DISPUTES. Chapter VI of the Charter has been much criticized and, in fact, provides a quite inadequate system for settling disputes between Members. The success which has been achieved in this field has been through methods pursued in disregard of the procedures of Chapter VI. The Security Council has in fact as much freedom as it could desire in all but one respect—it has no power to impose settlement of a dispute upon the parties. This power was carefully kept out of the Charter by the United States at San Francisco, and it may be doubted whether the Senate of the United States would approve including it in a current revision of the Charter.

There are, as we have seen earlier, two methods which can be followed to the settlement of a dispute. One is the method of conciliation, or political compromise, through the Security Council—or now, perhaps, more often through the General Assembly. These organs can only make a recommendation, not binding on the parties. Some advance could be made if those states sufficiently interested would agree among themselves to be bound by such a recommendation, or to one emanating from a commission of experts set up for the purpose. But it is discouraging concerning such a proposal to recall that many such treaties, with permanent commissions named, were signed in the past, and that practically no disputes have been handled under them. States dislike to have a political decision imposed upon them, and this is especially true with a body in which a fair settlement can be blocked by a veto, or in which an irresponsible majority can impose an inequitable settlement for prejudiced reasons.

The other method is judicial determination and this looks more promising in the sense that the way is open without amendment of the Charter. A state may, by accepting the Optional Clause (Article 36 of the Statute) submit itself to the compulsory jurisdiction of the International Court of Justice for defined types of legal disputes. The outlook does not appear so promising when one discovers that barely half of the Members have submitted themselves in this fashion, and these with reservations; and that the number of those who had earlier done so has been decreasing. Again, the trouble is with the Members, rather than with the Charter or Statute.

ENFORCEMENT. A similar situation exists with regard to the ability of the United Nations to prevent the use of force among nations. It would not be necessary to amend the Charter to provide an independent police force for the United Nations; that is within the power of the Members at the present moment. All that is necessary is to vote the money and agree upon how it is to operate. A supplementary pact in this direction was proposed in Senate Resolution 52, in 1950, by Senators Douglas and Thomas; it would have pledged the United States to use force against any nation adjudged to be an aggressor by two-thirds vote of the General Assembly, including three of the permanent members of the Security Council.[26] Thus far, however, Members have not been willing to consider even a small guard force or a small air force. Though the Charter in principle requires Members to contribute from their armed forces when called upon by the Security Council, this has been ineffective in practice; and they have refused even to pledge in advance, in whatever amounts or kind they might wish, to have forces readily available for use when needed by the United Nations.

With regard to supply of forces to maintain peace, then, the record shows that Members have gone backward rather than forward. Apparently, the most that can be expected is a voluntary contribution, made if the Member feels like it, after the occasion has arisen; and a collective security system cannot effectively operate on so uncertain a foundation as this. With this attitude prevalent, there could be little hope for amendment of the Charter to put upon Members stronger obligations than now exist; on the other hand, if Members wish, they can build up effective collective security under the terms of the Charter as it now stands.

THE VETO. The most frequent demand for change in the Charter is to abolish the veto in the Security Council. This feeling, in the United States, is largely due to resentment against abuse of the veto by the Soviet Union, and it disregards the possibility that there might someday be a majority against the United States such as the Soviet Union now has to face. This is indeed a possibility, for there is in the General Assembly an anti-colonial majority of small states, most of them physically unable to contribute to the support of actions which they wish to have taken, but able and willing to push through proposals calling upon the larger Powers for action.[27] This majority, of course, cannot

---

[26] See the Hearings before a subcommittee of the Senate Committee on Foreign Relations, entitled *Revision of the United Nations Charter*, 81 Cong., 2 Sess. (1950); also, C.S.O.P., Sixth Report (1948).

[27] It was the extremism shown by this group which frightened Senator Bricker and others into proposing to amend the Constitution to limit the treaty-making power, and which led the United States to refuse to accept the Covenant of Human Rights.

operate in the Security Council, but it can elect the nonpermanent members of that body; and it is conceivable that it could so constitute that body that, with the aid of the Soviet Union and perhaps China, it could order the United States to send armed forces to drive the French out of Morocco—assuming that there were no veto available to the United States to block the action. A majority can abuse power as much as can one state with the veto, and the few great military states must have protection against abuse of power by such a majority. Proposals to confer upon the General Assembly the right to make use of the armed forces of Members would for similar reasons not meet with favor, unless some equivalent of the veto were provided to protect Member states.

Some means have already been found for evading the veto, such as abstention, the Uniting for Peace Resolution, or collective defense pacts; and the Interim Committee made a detailed study of the problem, with constructive proposals, some of which were embodied in Assembly Resolution 267 (III) in 1949. The United States—which has never used its veto, though it has at least twice threatened to do so— would not be willing to give up the veto entirely, but has announced that it favors modification in its use, particularly as regards Chapter VI of the Charter, and with regard to admission of new Members; perhaps also with regard to control of atomic weapons. This could be done through agreement among the permanent members of the Council; and if they could not agree in this fashion, no amendment would be possible, since each could veto such an amendment.

WEIGHTED REPRESENTATION. A possible substitute for the veto, offered in various forms, would deny equality of voting and give to each Member a number of votes corresponding to its actual weight in the affairs of the community of nations. One proposal would give votes in proportion to population, which would probably satisfy no one except India and China. Mr. Dulles tried to find a better balance by requiring two votes on important issues, one based on sovereign equality, the other on some formula for weighted voting. Other proposals have suggested as bases for estimating the votes of each Member, education, income, production, military strength, contribution to the United Nations budget, or some combination of these factors. One proposal, with surprising results, would take the square root of population, budget, etc., each for a different type of action.[28]

---

[28] See "The Role of the General Assembly and the Problem of Weighted Voting," by Louis B. Sohn, and "A Proposal for Weighting Votes in the UN General Assembly," in C.S.O.P., Ninth Report, with attached papers. Weighted representation is used in some of the functional international organizations.

Aside from finding a substitute for the veto, the idea of weighted representation has direct importance in relation to the desire to give more power to the General Assembly. The larger Powers are not likely to agree to extend the powers of the Assembly, unless they have a share in the voting commensurate with the responsibility which they would have to assume as a result of the voting. On the other hand, it would be too much to expect from human nature that the smaller states would willingly give up the equality of votes which they now have. The dilemma is a political one; it would not be impossible to find a formula for representation which would fairly represent each Member in the system, but it would be a more difficult task to persuade Members to accept it.

LEGISLATIVE POWER. We have noted above the importance of providing procedures for making new international law in a changing world; most of the world government plans call for legislative power, more or less within a strictly limited range. Our earlier consideration of current attitudes was discouraging. Member states show no interest in giving up, even in part, their right of individual consent to a legislative treaty before being bound by it, and then for the most part they do not proceed to ratification. They have made no study of the problem from the viewpoint of the United Nations, as to the fields in which legislative power might be granted, or the methods by which it would be exercised. They have not considered the proposal, which would not deprive them of the right of individual consent, under which a legislative instrument adopted by some majority vote would be considered as binding upon each Member unless within a given time it announced its rejection. The possibility of obtaining improvement in the legislative field depends upon other factors, such as weighted representation, provision for judicial determination, or the attitudes of Members. The last gives little hope that any forward steps can be taken, badly as they are needed.

The above discouraging survey must be blamed upon Members, rather than upon the Charter of the United Nations. The Charter is a very flexible instrument, and much advance could be made under it toward some of the proposals above considered, if Members were willing. Where there is no provision in the Charter, a supplementary treaty might be made by those Members willing to move. In other cases, amendment of the Charter would be required, and in the present nationalistic mood of Members there seems little hope for amendment. If the tensions of the cold war and the anti-colonial drive can be relaxed and more confidence built up among nations, leadership might develop which is now lacking; meanwhile, progress will be slow and gradual.

172. LEGAL ORDER

Yet it is doubtless true that the peoples of the world desire a world governed by law. Every President of the United States since World War II has asserted this; many speeches in the United Nations call for respect for law. But the practice of the United Nations shows little regard for law, and a definite preference for political decision. International law was almost omitted from the Charter, and no provision was made for making new law, or requiring that disputes be settled in accordance with law. In practice, compulsory jurisdiction for the Court is refused by half the Members, and they rarely take a dispute to the Court by voluntary agreement.

INTERPRETATION OF THE CHARTER. Probably the best illustration of this dislike for legal processes is to be found in the debates over the meaning of the Charter; the procedures followed and the conclusions reached—insofar as there are any—may affect greatly the character of the United Nations. Whether one regards the Charter as a constitution or as a treaty, it is a legal instrument proper for judicial interpretation. The conference which made it, however, rejected suggestions that a body be authorized to interpret it, and contented itself with saying that doubtless each organ would interpret its rights for itself. Since such decisions by organs are not binding on anyone, the practical result is that each Member is free to interpret the Charter as it wishes, and may walk out, or refuse to observe a decision, on the ground that it was unconstitutional.

In practice, interpretation has been by political vote or, rather, by implication from political vote. Usually, the organ disregards the challenge to competence when it is raised, though Rule 80 of the General Assembly Rules of Procedure requires immediate decision on such a challenge. It then asserts that an action taken established the constitutional authority of the organ to take that action. Only three times has the plenary Assembly formally voted on its own competence: once after seven years of resolutions concerning race relations in South Africa, to affirm its competence to adopt the resolutions already adopted; once to assert its competence to define "self-governing," in relation to the non-self-governing territories, which it had already been doing; and once with regard to the relation of Italy to the Trusteeship Council. In every case in which an organ voted itself incompetent, it was with regard to something proposed by the Soviet Union; and in every case in which it voted itself competent, it was with regard to an action eagerly desired by the anti-colonial majority. These decisions were clearly political ones, taken without regard to legal interpretation; indeed, they were asserted so to be by the only body which, in the United Nations, has studied interpretation of Article 2, paragraph 7.[29]

DOMESTIC QUESTIONS. The principle embodied in Article 2 is a key point in any government, and is of especial importance in the building of international government, where national sovereignty demands the utmost respect. Where is the line to be drawn between the authority of the government and the rights of the individual member? Article 2, paragraph 7, was severely criticized as restricting the authority of the United Nations to act; but, as it has developed in practice, it serves as very little restriction upon action by the United Nations, and various states object that it does not give sufficient protection to them. It would be hard to conceive of more domestic a question than that of the internal regime of Spain, or the application of South African laws to its own nationals or—in terms of earlier law and practice—the treatment of a colony, such as Indonesia, by the parent country. Yet the Assembly has for years passed resolutions on these matters, and in only two instances (two of the three mentioned above) has it bothered to answer the numerous charges that it had no authority to intervene in such domestic matters. One result of this practice was to make the United States fearful that the Charter was being too much overlooked, and to push it over from the anti-colonial to the colonial side. On various occasions, motions were made to refer the question of competence under Article 2, paragraph 7, to the Court, but all were refused.

The reasons offered for this attitude are that there must be a liberal interpretation of the Charter if the United Nations is to achieve its purposes; that Article 2, paragraph 7, could not have been intended to prevent development and protection of human rights, so much emphasized in other parts of the Charter; and that law should not be allowed to stand in the way of human progress. It is quite true that strict construction of the clause could be disastrous, halting human rights and economic development. It is equally true that too much interference with the internal affairs of states may turn them against the United Nations in which they thought they were protected by the Charter. A balance will have to be found between these extremes, and it is to be doubted that it can be provided in a new text of the clause. It will have to come, as it has come in the United States, through interpretation and usage and agreement—a slow and difficult process.

[29] Report of the United Nations Commission on the Racial Situation in the Union of South Africa, U.N. General Assembly, Eighth Session, *Official Records,* Supplement No. 16(1953), p. 22. See Brookings, *Organization.*

PEACEFUL CHANGE. One reason for the unwillingness to submit to Charter restrictions is that many new or weak states are dissatisfied with an international law, made in the past by the Christian and Western world, in which they had no share. Changes and additions are badly needed, but the United Nations has not made provisions for accomplishing peaceful change. It can and does make important studies and recommendations, but it cannot put them into effect. It is not surprising, in these days of economic interdependence and revolutionary change in all fields, that many states should react against restrictions which uphold the vested interests of a few states, but give no help to many others who need it. This feeling, very strong in many small nations, has had its share in producing such interpretation of the Charter as has been made.

There is, then, no interpretation by judicial process, and very little interpretation by formal political vote. In practice, it is assumed that, if a proposal is voted by the proper majority, it is constitutional; this, of course, would mean that anything that an organ wishes to do, it can do—if it has sufficient votes. With such an interpretation, it would be more proper to regard the United Nations as conference machinery than as an institution; certainly, there would be little of legal order left to it.

However, it is to be doubted that the actions taken so far have established a stable interpretation of the Charter, if for no other reason than the inconsistency shown by Members. There is hardly one of them which has not voted both for and against application of the domestic jurisdiction clause, depending upon its political interests on that occasion. A number of the larger states, including the United States, are now taking a stronger stand against such loose procedures and interpretation. Protests against disregard for law have been uttered, particularly by the United Kingdom, but also by other states. The tide is beginning to turn toward more respect for the Charter.

There is no doubt that the United Nations is a political order, but as Mr. Feller and others have pointed out: "The United Nations is a legal order and can not tear itself loose from the specific restrictions of the Charter, irksome though they may be from time to time to one interest or another."[30] This is true of any governmental system. The game of politics is always being played, and the importance of law is that it furnishes the rules within which the game must be played. At the present moment the rules of the game are not well observed in the United Nations, and, until they can be better observed, the United

[30] A. H. Feller, *United Nations and World Community* (Boston, 1952), p. 43.

Nations will not be able to progress, as people desire that it should, toward becoming a strong legal order and an effective international government.

The trouble is not with the United Nations, but with nations and peoples themselves. Until sovereign states are willing to accept limitations upon their freedom of action, a strong international system cannot be built; and until peoples are ready to submit to international law and government, their states cannot act. This is a matter of particular import to the American people, who are the leaders of the world today; and it is with this lesson that this book ends.

APPENDICES

APPENDIX I

COVENANT OF THE LEAGUE OF NATIONS [1]

THE HIGH CONTRACTING PARTIES,

In order to promote international cooperation and to achieve international peace and security.

by the acceptance of obligations not to resort to war,

by the prescription of open, just and honourable relations between nations,

by the firm establishment of the understandings of international law as the actual rule of conduct among Governments, and

by the maintenance of justice and a scrupulous respect for all treaty obligations in the dealings of organised peoples with one another,

Agree to this Covenant of the League of Nations.

ARTICLE 1

1. The original Members of the League of Nations shall be those of the Signatories which are named in the Annex to this Covenant and also such of those other States named in the Annex as shall accede without reservation to this Covenant. Such accession shall be effected by a Declaration deposited with the Secretariat within two months of the coming into force of the Covenant. Notice thereof shall be sent to all other Members of the League.

2. Any fully self-governing State, Dominion or Colony not named in the Annex may become a Member of the League if its admission is agreed to by two-thirds of the Assembly, provided that it shall give effective guarantees of its sincere intention to observe its international obligations, and shall accept such regulations as may be prescribed by the League in regard to its military, naval and air forces and armaments.

3. Any Member of the League may, after two years' notice of its intention so to do, withdraw from the League, provided that all its international obligations and all its obligations under this Covenant shall have been fulfilled at the time of its withdrawal.

ARTICLE 2

The action of the League under this Covenant shall be effected through the instrumentality of an Assembly and of a Council, with a permanent Secretariat.

---

[1] The Covenant is given with annotations as found in *Ten Years of World Co-operation*. Amendments in force are included in the text in italics; other proposed amendments have been added in footnotes. The paragraphs are given as officially numbered by an Assembly resolution of September 21, 1926.

Article 3

1. The Assembly shall consist of Representatives of the Members of the League.

2. The Assembly shall meet at stated intervals and from time to time as occasion may require at the Seat of the League, or at such other place as may be decided upon.

3. The Assembly may deal at its meetings with any matter within the sphere of action of the League or affecting the peace of the world.

4. At meetings of the Assembly, each Member of the League shall have one vote, and may have not more than three Representatives.

Article 4

1. The Council shall consist of Representatives of the Principal Allied and Associated Powers,[2] together with Representatives of four other Members of the League. These four Members of the League shall be selected by the Assembly from time to time in its discretion. Until the appointment of the Representatives of the four Members of the League first selected by the Assembly, Representatives of Belgium, Brazil, Spain and Greece shall be Members of the Council.

2. With the approval of the majority of the Assembly, the Council may name additional Members of the League, whose Representatives shall always be Members of the Council;[3] the Council with like approval may increase the number of Members of the League to be selected by the Assembly for representation on the Council.[4]

2 bis.[5] *The Assembly shall fix by a two-thirds majority the rules dealing with the election of the non-permanent Members of the Council, and particularly such regulations as relate to their term of office and the conditions of re-eligibility.*

3. The Council shall meet from time to time as occasion may require, and at least once a year, at the Seat of the League, or at such other place as may be decided upon.

4. The Council may deal at its meetings with any matter within the sphere of action of the League or affecting the peace of the world.

5. Any Member of the League not represented on the Council shall be invited to send a Representative to sit as a member at any meeting of the Council

---

[2] The Principal Allied and Associated Powers are the following: The United States of America, the British Empire, France, Italy, and Japan (see Preamble of the Treaty of Peace with Germany).

[3] In virtue of this paragraph of the Covenant, Germany was nominated as a permanent Member of the Council on September 8, 1926.

[4] The number of Members of the Council selected by the Assembly was increased to six instead of four by virtue of a resolution adopted at the third ordinary meeting of the Assembly on September 25, 1922. By a resolution taken by the Assembly on September 8, 1926, the number of Members of the Council selected by the Assembly was increased to nine.

[5] This amendment came into force on July 29, 1926, in accordance with Article 26 of the Covenant.

during the consideration of matters specially affecting the interests of that Member of the League.

6. At meetings of the Council, each Member of the League represented on the Council shall have one vote, and may have not more than one Representative.

ARTICLE 5

1. Except where otherwise expressly provided in this Covenant or by the terms of the present Treaty, decisions at any meeting of the Assembly or of the Council shall require the agreement of all the Members of the League represented at the meeting.

2. All matters of procedure at meetings of the Assembly or of the Council, including the appointment of Committees to investigate particular matters, shall be regulated by the Assembly or by the Council and may be decided by a majority of the Members of the League represented at the meeting.

3. The first meeting of the Assembly and the first meeting of the Council shall be summoned by the President of the United States of America.

ARTICLE 6

1. The permanent Secretariat shall be established at the Seat of the League. The Secretariat shall comprise a Secretary-General and such secretaries and staff as may be required.

2. The first Secretary-General shall be the person named in the Annex; thereafter the Secretary-General shall be appointed by the Council with the approval of the majority of the Assembly.

3. The secretaries and staff of the Secretariat shall be appointed by the Secretary-General with the approval of the Council.

4. The Secretary-General shall act in that capacity at all meetings of the Assembly and of the Council.

5.[6] *The expenses of the League shall be borne by the Members of the League in the proportion decided by the Assembly.*

ARTICLE 7

1. The Seat of the League is established at Geneva.

2. The Council may at any time decide that the Seat of the League shall be established elsewhere.

3. All positions under or in connection with the League, including the Secretariat, shall be open equally to men and women.

4. Representatives of the Members of the League and officials of the League when engaged on the business of the League shall enjoy diplomatic privileges and immunities.

5. The buildings and other property occupied by the League or its officials or by Representatives attending its meetings shall be inviolable.

ARTICLE 8

1. The Members of the League recognise that the maintenance of peace requires the reduction of national armaments to the lowest point consistent with

---

[6] This paragraph came into force August 13, 1924, in accordance with Article 26.

national safety and the enforcement by common action of international obligations.

2. The Council, taking account of the geographical situation and circumstances of each State, shall formulate plans for such reduction for the consideration and action of the several Governments.

3. Such plans shall be subject to reconsideration and revision at least every ten years.

4. After these plans shall have been adopted by the several Governments, the limits of armaments therein fixed shall not be exceeded without the concurrence of the Council.

5. The Members of the League agree that the manufacture by private enterprise of munitions and implements of war is open to grave objections. The Council shall advise how the evil effects attendant upon such manufacture can be prevented, due regard being had to the necessities of those Members of the League which are not able to manufacture the munitions and implements of war necessary for their safety.

6. The Members of the League undertake to interchange full and frank information as to the scale of their armaments, their military, naval and air programmes, and the condition of such of their industries as are adaptable to warlike purposes.

ARTICLE 9

A permanent Commission shall be constituted to advise the Council on the execution of the provisions of Articles 1 and 8 and on military, naval and air questions generally.

ARTICLE 10

The Members of the League undertake to respect and preserve as against external aggression the territorial integrity and existing political independence of all Members of the League. In case of any such aggression or in case of any threat or danger of such aggression the Council shall advise upon the means by which this obligation shall be fulfilled.

ARTICLE 11

1. Any war or threat of war, whether immediately affecting any of the Members of the League or not, is hereby declared a matter of concern to the whole League, and the League shall take any action that may be deemed wise and effectual to safeguard the peace of nations. In case any such emergency should arise the Secretary-General shall on the request of any Member of the League forthwith summon a meeting of the Council.

2. It is also declared to be the friendly right of each Member of the League to bring to the attention of the Assembly or of the Council any circumstance whatever affecting international relations which threatens to disturb international peace or the good understanding between nations upon which peace depends.

ARTICLE 12 [7]

1. The Members of the League agree that if there should arise between them any dispute likely to lead to a rupture they will submit the matter either to arbitration *or judicial settlement* or to enquiry by the Council and they agree in no case to resort to war until three months after the award by the arbitrators *or the judicial decision* or the report by the Council.

2. In any case under this Article, the award of the arbitrators *or the judicial decision* shall be made within a reasonable time, and the report of the Council shall be made within six months after the submission of the dispute.

ARTICLE 13 [7]

1. The Members of the League agree that whenever any dispute shall arise between them which they recognise to be suitable for submission to arbitration *or judicial settlement,* and which cannot be satisfactorily settled by diplomacy, they will submit the whole subject-matter to arbitration *or judicial settlement.*

2. Disputes as to the interpretation of a treaty, as to any question of international law, as to the existence of any fact which, if established, would constitute a breach of any international obligation, or as to the extent and nature of the reparation to be made for any such breach, are declared to be among those which are generally suitable for submission to arbitration *or judicial settlement.*

3. *For the consideration of any such dispute, the court to which the case is referred shall be the Permanent Court of International Justice, established in accordance with Article 14, or any tribunal agreed on by the parties to the dispute or stipulated in any convention existing between them.*

4. The Members of the League agree that they will carry out in full good faith any award *or decision* that may be rendered, and that they will not resort to war against a Member of the League which complies therewith. In the event of any failure to carry out such an award *or decision,* the Council shall propose what steps should be taken to give effect thereto.

ARTICLE 14

The Council shall formulate and submit to the Members of the League for adoption plans for the establishment of a Permanent Court of International Justice. The Court shall be competent to hear and determine any dispute of an international character which the parties thereto submit to it. The Court may also give an advisory opinion upon any dispute or question referred to it by the Council or by the Assembly.

ARTICLE 15

1.[8] If there should arise between Members of the League any dispute likely to lead to a rupture, which is not submitted to arbitration *or judicial settlement* in accordance with Article 13, the Members of the League agree that they will

---

[7] The amendments printed in italics relating to these articles came into force on September 26, 1924, in accordance with Article 26 of the Covenant.

[8] The amendment to the first paragraph of this article came into force on September 26, 1924, in accordance with Article 26 of the Covenant.

submit the matter to the Council. Any party to the dispute may effect such submission by giving notice of the existence of the dispute to the Secretary-General, who will make all necessary arrangements for a full investigation and consideration thereof.

2. For this purpose the parties to the dispute will communicate to the Secretary-General, as promptly as possible, statements of their case with all the relevant facts and papers, and the Council may forthwith direct the publication thereof.

3. The Council shall endeavour to effect a settlement of the dispute and, if such efforts are successful, a statement shall be made public giving such facts and explanations regarding the dispute and the terms of settlement thereof as the Council may deem appropriate.

4. If the dispute is not thus settled, the Council either unanimously or by a majority vote shall make and publish a report containing a statement of the facts of the dispute and the recommendations which are deemed just and proper in regard thereto.

5. Any Member of the League represented on the Council may make public a statement of the facts of the dispute and of its conclusions regarding the same.

6. If a report by the Council is unanimously agreed to by the Members thereof other than the Representatives of one or more of the parties to the dispute, the Members of the League agree that they will not go to war with any party to the dispute which complies with the recommendations of the report.

7. If the Council fails to reach a report which is unanimously agreed to by the members thereof, other than the Representatives of one or more of the parties to the dispute, the Members of the League reserve to themselves the right to take such action as they shall consider necessary for the maintenance of right and justice.

8. If the dispute between the parties is claimed by one of them, and is found by the Council, to arise out of a matter which by international law is solely within the domestic jurisdiction of that party, the Council shall so report, and shall make no recommendation as to its settlement.

9. The Council may in any case under this Article refer the dispute to the Assembly. The dispute shall be so referred at the request of either party to the dispute provided that such request be made within fourteen days after the submission of the dispute to the Council.

10. In any case referred to the Assembly, all the provisions of this Article and of Article 12 relating to the action and powers of the Council shall apply to the action and powers of the Assembly, provided that a report made by the Assembly, if concurred in by the Representatives of those Members of the League represented on the Council and of a majority of the other Members of the League, exclusive in each case of the Representatives of the parties to the dispute, shall have the same force as a report by the Council concurred in by all the members thereof other than the Representatives of one or more of the parties to the dispute.

Article 16

1.[9] Should any Member of the League resort to war in disregard of its covenants under Articles 12, 13 or 15, it shall *ipso facto* be deemed to have committed an act of war against all other Members of the League, which hereby undertake immediately to subject it to the severance of all trade or financial relations, the prohibition of all intercourse between their nationals and the nationals of the covenant-breaking State, and the prevention of all financial, commercial or personal intercourse between the nationals of the covenant-breaking State and the nationals of any other State, whether a Member of the League or not.

2. It shall be the duty of the Council in such case to recommend to the several Governments concerned what effective military, naval or air force the Members of the League shall severally contribute to the armed forces to be used to protect the covenants of the League.

3. The Members of the League agree, further, that they will mutually support one another in the financial and economic measures which are taken under this Article, in order to minimise the loss and inconvenience resulting from the above measures, and that they will mutually support one another in resisting any special measures aimed at one of their number by the covenant-breaking State, and that they will take the necessary steps to afford passage through their territory to the forces of any of the Members of the League which are co-operating to protect the covenants of the League.

4. Any Member of the League which has violated any covenant of the League may be declared to be no longer a Member of the League by a vote of the Council concurred in by the Representatives of all the other Members of the League represented thereon.

---

[9] The following proposal for the amendment of paragraph 1 of Article 16 now awaits ratification:

"Should any Member of the League resort to war in disregard of its covenants under Articles 12, 13 or 15, it shall *ipso facto* be deemed to have committed an act of war against all other Members of the League, *which hereby undertake immediately to subject it to the severance of all trade or financial relations and to prohibit all intercourse at least between persons resident within their territories and persons resident within the territory of the covenant-breaking State and, if they deem it expedient, also between their nationals and the nationals of the covenant-breaking State, and to prevent all financial, commercial or personal intercourse at least between persons resident within the territory of that State and persons resident within the territory of any other State, whether a Member of the League or not, and, if they deem it expedient, also between the nationals of that State and the nationals of any other State whether a Member of the League or not.*

"*It is for the Council to give an opinion whether or not a breach of the Covenant has taken place. In deliberations on this question in the Council, the votes of Members of the League alleged to have resorted to war and of Members against whom such action was directed shall not be counted.*

"*The Council will notify all Members of the League the date which it recommends for the application of the economic pressure under this Article.*

"*Nevertheless, the Council may, in the case of particular Members, postpone the coming into force of any of these measures for a specified period where it is satisfied that such a postponement will facilitate the attainment of the object of the measures referred to in the preceding paragraph, or that it is necessary in order to minimise the loss and inconvenience which will be caused to such Members.*"

It is proposed also to delete the words "in such case" in the following paragraph.

Article 17

1. In the event of a dispute between a Member of the League and a State which is not a Member of the League, or between States not Members of the League, the State or States not Members of the League shall be invited to accept the obligations of membership in the League for the purposes of such dispute, upon such conditions as the Council may deem just. If such invitation is accepted, the provisions of Articles 12 to 16 inclusive shall be applied with such modifications as may be deemed necessary by the Council.

2. Upon such invitation being given the Council shall immediately institute an enquiry into the circumstances of the dispute and recommend such action as may seem best and most effectual in the circumstances.

3. If a State so invited shall refuse to accept the obligations of membership in the League for the purposes of such dispute, and shall resort to war against a Member of the League, the provisions of Article 16 shall be applicable as against the State taking such action.

4. If both parties to the dispute when so invited refuse to accept the obligations of membership in the League for the purposes of such dispute, the Council may take such measures and make such recommendations as will prevent hostilities and will result in the settlement of the dispute.

Article 18

Every treaty or international engagement entered into hereafter by any Member of the League shall be forthwith registered with the Secretariat and shall as soon as possible be published by it. No such treaty or international engagement shall be binding until so registered.

Article 19

The Assembly may from time to time advise the reconsideration by Members of the League of treaties which have become inapplicable and the consideration of international conditions whose continuance might endanger the peace of the world.

Article 20

1. The Members of the League severally agree that this Covenant is accepted as abrogating all obligations or understandings *inter se* which are inconsistent with the terms thereof, and solemnly undertake that they will not hereafter enter into any agreements inconsistent with the terms thereof.

2. In case any Member of the League shall, before becoming a Member of the League, have undertaken any obligation inconsistent with the terms of this Covenant, it shall be the duty of such Member to take immediate steps to procure its release from such obligations.

Article 21

Nothing in this Covenant shall be deemed to affect the validity of international engagements, such as treaties of arbitration or regional understandings like the Monroe doctrine, for securing the maintenance of peace.

ARTICLE 22

1. To those colonies and territories which as a consequence of the late war have ceased to be under the sovereignty of the States which formerly governed them and which are inhabited by peoples not yet able to stand by themselves under the strenuous conditions of the modern world, there should be applied the principle that the well-being and development of such peoples form a sacred trust of civilisation and that securities for the performance of this trust should be embodied in this Covenant.

2. The best method of giving practical effect to this principle is that the tutelage of such peoples should be intrusted to advanced nations who, by reason of their resources, their experience or their geographical position, can best undertake this responsibility, and who are willing to accept it, and that this tutelage should be exercised by them as Mandatories on behalf of the League.

3. The character of the mandate must differ according to the stage of the development of the people, the geographical situation of the territory, its economic conditions and other similar circumstances.

4. Certain communities formerly belonging to the Turkish Empire have reached a stage of development where their existence as independent nations can be provisionally recognised subject to the rendering of administrative advice and assistance by a Mandatory until such time as they are able to stand alone. The wishes of these communities must be a principal consideration in the selection of the Mandatory.

5. Other peoples, especially those of Central Africa, are at such a stage that the Mandatory must be responsible for the administration of the territory under conditions which will guarantee freedom of conscience and religion, subject only to the maintenance of public order and morals, the prohibition of abuses such as the slave trade, the arms traffic and the liquor traffic, and the prevention of the establishment of fortifications or military and naval bases and of military training of the natives for other than police purposes and the defence of territory, and will also secure equal opportunities for the trade and commerce of other Members of the League.

6. There are territories, such as Southwest Africa and certain of the South Pacific islands, which, owing to the sparseness of their population, or their small size, or their remoteness from the centres of civilisation, or their geographical contiguity to the territory of the Mandatory, and other circumstances, can best be administered under the laws of the Mandatory as integral portions of its territory, subject to the safeguards above mentioned in the interests of the indigenous population.

7. In every case of mandate, the Mandatory shall render to the Council an annual report in reference to the territory committed to its charge.

8. The degree of authority, control or administration to be exercised by the Mandatory shall, if not previously agreed upon by the Members of the League, be explicitly defined in each case by the Council.

9. A permanent Commission shall be constituted to receive and examine the annual reports of the Mandatories, and to advise the Council on all matters relating to the observance of the mandates.

ARTICLE 23

Subject to and in accordance with the provisions of international conventions existing or hereafter to be agreed upon, the Members of the League:

(*a*) will endeavour to secure and maintain fair and humane conditions of labor for men, women, and children, both in their own countries and in all countries to which their commercial and industrial relations extend, and for that purpose will establish and maintain the necessary international organisations;

(*b*) undertake to secure just treatment of the native inhabitants of territories under their control;

(*c*) will entrust the League with the general supervision over the execution of agreements with regard to the traffic in women and children and the traffic in opium and other dangerous drugs;

(*d*) will entrust the League with the general supervision of the trade in arms and ammunition with the countries in which the control of this traffic is necessary in the common interest;

(*e*) will make provision to secure and maintain freedom of communications and of transit and equitable treatment for the commerce of all Members of the League. In this connection, the special necessities of the regions devastated during the war of 1914-1918 shall be borne in mind;

(*f*) will endeavour to take steps in matters of international concern for the prevention and control of disease.

ARTICLE 24

1. There shall be placed under the direction of the League all international bureaux already established by general treaties if the parties to such treaties consent. All such international bureaux and all commissions for the regulation of matters of international interest hereafter constituted shall be placed under the direction of the League.

2. In all matters of international interest which are regulated by general conventions but which are not placed under the control of international bureaux or commissions, the Secretariat of the League shall, subject to the consent of the Council and if desired by the parties, collect and distribute all relevant information and shall render any other assistance which may be necessary or desirable.

3. The Council may include as part of the expenses of the Secretariat the expenses of any bureau or commission which is placed under the direction of the League.

ARTICLE 25

The Members of the League agree to encourage and promote the establishment and co-operation of duly authorised voluntary national Red Cross organisations having as purposes the improvement of health, the prevention of disease and the mitigation of suffering throughout the world.

ARTICLE 26 [10]

1. Amendments to this Covenant will take effect when ratified by the Members of the League whose Representatives compose the Council and by a majority of the Members of the League whose Representatives compose the Assembly.

2. No such amendment shall bind any Member of the League which signifies its dissent therefrom, but in that case it shall cease to be a Member of the League.

ANNEX

I. ORIGINAL MEMBERS OF THE LEAGUE OF NATIONS, SIGNATORIES OF THE TREATY OF PEACE

United States of America	Haiti
Belgium	Hedjaz
Bolivia	Honduras
Brazil	Italy
British Empire	Japan
Canada	Liberia
Australia	Nicaragua
South Africa	Panama
New Zealand	Peru
India	Poland
China	Portugal
Cuba	Roumania
Ecuador	Serb-Croat-Slovene State
France	Siam
Greece	Czechoslovakia
Guatemala	Uruguay

---

[10] The following amendment has been offered to replace Article 26, and now awaits ratification:

"*Amendments to the present Covenant the text of which shall have been voted by the Assembly on a three-fourths majority, in which there shall be included the votes of all the Members of the Council represented at the meeting, will take effect when ratified by the Members of the League whose Representatives composed the Council when the vote was taken and by the majority of those whose Representatives form the Assembly.*

"*If the required number of ratifications shall not have been obtained within twenty-two months after the vote of the Assembly, the proposed amendment shall remain without effect.*

"*The Secretary-General shall inform the Members of the taking effect of an amendment.*

"*Any Member of the League which has not at that time ratified the amendment is free to notify the Secretary-General within a year of its refusal to accept it, but in that case shall cease to be a Member of the League.*"

States Invited to Accede to the Covenant

Argentine Republic
Chile
Colombia
Denmark
Netherlands
Norway
Paraguay

Persia
Salvador
Spain
Sweden
Switzerland
Venezuela

II. First Secretary-General of the League of Nations

The Honorable Sir James Eric Drummond, K. C. M. G., C. B.

APPENDIX II
PROPOSALS FOR THE ESTABLISHMENT OF A GENERAL INTERNATIONAL ORGANIZATION

THERE should be established an international organization under the title of The United Nations, the Charter of which should contain provisions necessary to give effect to the proposals which follow.

CHAPTER I. PURPOSES

The purposes of the Organization should be:

1. To maintain international peace and security; and to that end to take effective collective measures for the prevention and removal of threats to the peace and the suppression of acts of aggression or other breaches of the peace, and to bring about by peaceful means adjustment or settlement of international disputes which may lead to a breach of the peace;

2. To develop friendly relations among nations and to take other appropriate measures to strengthen universal peace;

3. To achieve international cooperation in the solution of international economic, social and other humanitarian problems; and

4. To afford a center for harmonizing the actions of nations in the achievement of these common ends.

CHAPTER II. PRINCIPLES

In pursuit of the purposes mentioned in Chapter I the Organization and its members should act in accordance with the following principles:

1. The Organization is based on the principle of the sovereign equality of all peace-loving states.

2. All members of the Organization undertake, in order to ensure to all of them the rights and benefits resulting from membership in the Organization, to fulfill the obligations assumed by them in accordance with the Charter.

3. All members of the Organization shall settle their disputes by peaceful means in such a manner that international peace and security are not endangered.

4. All members of the Organization shall refrain in their international relations from the threat or use of force in any manner inconsistent with the purposes of the Organization.

5. All members of the Organization shall give every assistance to the Organization in any action undertaken by it in accordance with the provisions of the Charter.

6. All members of the Organization shall refrain from giving assistance to any state against which preventive or enforcement action is being undertaken by the Organization.

The Organization should ensure that states not members of the Organization act in accordance with these principles so far as may be necessary for the maintenance of international peace and security.

CHAPTER III. MEMBERSHIP

1. Membership of the Organization should be open to all peace-loving states.

CHAPTER IV. PRINCIPAL ORGANS

1. The Organization should have as its principal organs:
   a. A General Assembly;
   b. A Security Council;
   c. An international court of justice; and
   d. A Secretariat.

2. The Organization should have such subsidiary agencies as may be found necessary.

CHAPTER V. THE GENERAL ASSEMBLY

Section A. Composition

All members of the Organization should be members of the General Assembly and should have a number of representatives to be specified in the Charter.

Section B. Functions and Powers

1. The General Assembly should have the right to consider the general principles of cooperation in the maintenance of international peace and security, including the principles governing disarmament and the regulation of armaments; to discuss any questions relating to the maintenance of international peace and security brought before it by any member or members of the Organization or by the Security Council; and to make recommendations with regard to any such principles or questions. Any such questions on which action is necessary should be referred to the Security Council by the General Assembly either before or after discussion. The General Assembly should not on its own initiative make recommendations on any matter relating to the maintenance of international peace and security which is being dealt with by the Security Council.

2. The General Assembly should be empowered to admit new members to the organization upon recommendation of the Security Council.

3. The General Assembly should, upon recommendation of the Security Council, be empowered to suspend from the exercise of any rights or privileges of membership any member of the Organization against which preventive or enforcement action shall have been taken by the Security Council. The exercise of the rights and privileges thus suspended may be restored by decision of the Security Council. The General Assembly should be empowered, upon recommendation of the Security Council, to expel from the Organization any member of the Organization which persistently violates the principles contained in the Charter.

4. The General Assembly should elect the non-permanent members of the Security Council and the members of the Economic and Social Council pro-

vided for in Chapter IX. It should be empowered to elect, upon recommendation of the Security Council, the Secretary-General of the Organization. It should perform such functions in relation to the election of the judges of the international court of justice as may be conferred upon it by the statute of the court.

5. The General Assembly should apportion the expenses among the members of the Organization and should be empowered to approve the budgets of the Organization.

6. The General Assembly should initiate studies and make recommendations for the purpose of promoting international cooperation in political, economic and social fields and of adjusting situations likely to impair the general welfare.

7. The General Assembly should make recommendations for the coordination of the policies of international economic, social, and other specialized agencies brought into relation with the Organization in accordance with agreements between such agencies and the Organization.

8. The General Assembly should receive and consider annual and special reports from the Security Council and reports from other bodies of the Organization.

Section C. Voting

1. Each member of the Organization should have one vote in the General Assembly.

2. Important decisions of the General Assembly, including recommendations with respect to the maintenance of international peace and security; election of members of the Security Council; election of members of the Economic and Social Council; admission of members, suspension of the exercise of the rights and privileges of members, and expulsion of members; and budgetary questions, should be made by a two-thirds majority of those present and voting. On other questions, including the determination of additional categories of questions to be decided by a two-thirds majority, the decisions of the General Assembly should be made by a simple majority vote.

Section D. Procedure

1. The General Assembly should meet in regular annual sessions and in such special sessions as occasion may require.

2. The General Assembly should adopt its own rules of procedure and elect its President for each session.

3. The General Assembly should be empowered to set up such bodies and agencies as it may deem necessary for the performance of its functions.

CHAPTER VI. THE SECURITY COUNCIL

Section A. Composition

The Security Council should consist of one representative of each of eleven members of the Organization. Representatives of the United States of America, the United Kingdom of Great Britain and Northern Ireland, the Union of Soviet Socialist Republics, the Republic of China, and, in due course, France, should have permanent seats. The General Assembly should elect six states to fill the non-permanent seats. These six states should be elected for a term of two years, three retiring each year. They should not be immediately eligible for reelection. In the first election of the non-permanent members three should be chosen by the General Assembly for one-year terms and three for two-year terms.

Section B. Principal Functions and Powers

1. In order to ensure prompt and effective action by the Organization, members of the Organization should by the Charter confer on the Security Council primary responsibility for the maintenance of international peace and security and should agree that in carrying out these duties under this responsibility it should act on their behalf.

2. In discharging these duties the Security Council should act in accordance with the purposes and principles of the Organization.

3. The specific powers conferred on the Security Council in order to carry out these duties are laid down in Chapter VIII.

4. All members of the Organization should obligate themselves to accept the decisions of the Security Council and to carry them out in accordance with the provisions of the Charter.

5. In order to promote the establishment and maintenance of international peace and security with the least diversion of the world's human and economic resources for armaments, the Security Council, with the assistance of the Military Staff Committee referred to in Chapter VIII, Section B, paragraph 9, should have the responsibility for formulating plans for the establishment of a system of regulation of armaments for submission to the members of the Organization.

Section C. Voting

(NOTE.—The question of voting procedure in the Security Council is still under consideration.)

Section D. Procedure

1. The Security Council should be so organized as to be able to function continuously and each state member of the Security Council should be permanently represented at the headquarters of the Organization. It may hold meetings at such other places as in its judgment may best facilitate its work. There should be periodic meetings at which each state member of the Security Council could if it so desired be represented by a member of the government or some other special representative.

2. The Security Council should be empowered to set up such bodies or agencies as it may deem necessary for the performance of its functions including regional subcommittees of the Military Staff Committee.

3. The Security Council should adopt its own rules of procedure, including the method of selecting its President.

4. Any member of the Organization should participate in the discussion of any question brought before the Security Council whenever the Security Coun-

cil considers that the interests of that member of the Organization are specially affected.

5. Any member of the Organization not having a seat on the Security Council and any state not a member of the Organization, if it is a party to a dispute under consideration by the Security Council, should be invited to participate in the discussion relating to the dispute.

CHAPTER VII. AN INTERNATIONAL COURT OF JUSTICE

1. There should be an international court of justice which should constitute the principal judicial organ of the Organization.

2. The court should be constituted and should function in accordance with a statute which should be annexed to and be a part of the Charter of the Organization.

3. The statute of the court of international justice should be either (a) the Statute of the Permanent Court of International Justice, continued in force with such modifications as may be desirable or (b) a new statute in the preparation of which the Statute of the Permanent Court of International Justice should be used as a basis.

4. All members of the Organization should *ipso facto* be parties to the statute of the international court of justice.

5. Conditions under which states not members of the Organization may become parties to the statute of the international court of justice should be determined in each case by the General Assembly upon recommendation of the Security Council.

CHAPTER VIII. ARRANGEMENTS FOR THE MAINTENANCE OF INTERNATIONAL PEACE AND SECURITY INCLUDING PREVENTION AND SUPPRESSION OF AGGRESSION

Section A. Pacific Settlement of Disputes

1. The Security Council should be empowered to investigate any dispute, or any situation which may lead to international friction or give rise to a dispute, in order to determine whether its continuance is likely to endanger the maintenance of international peace and security.

2. Any state, whether member of the Organization or not, may bring any such dispute or situation to the attention of the General Assembly or of the Security Council.

3. The parties to any dispute the continuance of which is likely to endanger the maintenance of international peace and security should obligate themselves, first of all, to seek a solution by negotiation, mediation, conciliation, arbitration or judicial settlement, or other peaceful means of their own choice. The Security Council should call upon the parties to settle their dispute by such means.

4. If, nevertheless, parties to a dispute of the nature referred to in paragraph 3 above fail to settle it by the means indicated in that paragraph, they should obligate themselves to refer it to the Security Council. The Security Council should in each case decide whether or not the continuance of the particular dispute is in fact likely to endanger the maintenance of international

peace and security, and, accordingly, whether the Security Council should deal with the dispute, and, if so, whether it should take action under Paragraph 5.

5. The Security Council should be empowered, at any stage of a dispute of the nature referred to in paragraph 3 above, to recommend appropriate procedures or methods of adjustment.

6. Justiciable disputes should normally be referred to the international court of justice. The Security Council should be empowered to refer to the court, for advice, legal questions connected with other disputes.

7. The provisions of paragraph 1 to 6 of Section A should not apply to situations or disputes arising out of matters which by international law are solely within the domestic jurisdiction of the state concerned.

Section B. Determination of Threats to the Peace or Acts of Aggression and Action With Respect Thereto

1. Should the Security Council deem that a failure to settle a dispute in accordance with procedures indicated in paragraph 3 of Section A, or in accordance with its recommendations made under paragraph 5 of Section A, constitutes a threat to the maintenance of international peace and security, it should take any measures necessary for the maintenance of international peace and security in accordance with the purposes and principles of the Organization.

2. In general the Security Council should determine the existence of any threat to the peace, breach of the peace or act of aggression and should make recommendations or decide upon the measures to be taken to maintain or restore peace and security.

3. The Security Council should be empowered to determine what diplomatic, economic, or other measures not involving the use of armed force should be employed to give effect to its decisions, and to call upon members of the Organization to apply such measures. Such measures may include complete or partial interruption of rail, sea, air, postal, telegraphic, radio and other means of communication and the severance of diplomatic and economic relations.

4. Should the Security Council consider such measures to be inadequate, it should be empowered to take such action by air, naval or land forces as may be necessary to maintain or restore international peace and security. Such action may include demonstrations, blockade and other operations by air, sea or land forces of members of the Organization.

5. In order that all members of the Organization should contribute to the maintenance of international peace and security, they should undertake to make available to the Security Council, on its call and in accordance with a special agreement or agreements concluded among themselves, armed forces, facilities and assistance necessary for the purposes of maintaining international peace and security. Such agreement or agreements should govern the numbers and types of forces and the nature of the facilities and assistance to be provided. The special agreement or agreements should be negotiated as soon as possible and should in each case be subject to approval by the Security Council and to ratification by the signatory states in accordance with their constitutional processes.

6. In order to enable urgent military measures to be taken by the Organization there should be held immediately available by the members of the Organization national air force contingents for combined international enforcement action. The strength and degree of readiness of these contingents and plans for their combined action should be determined by the Security Council with the assistance of the Military Staff Committee within the limits laid down in the special agreement or agreements referred to in paragraph 5 above.

7. The action required to carry out the decisions of the Security Council for the maintenance of international peace and security should be taken by all the members of the Organization in cooperation or by some of them as the Security Council may determine. This undertaking should be carried out by the members of the Organization by their own action and through action of the appropriate specialized organizations and agencies of which they are members.

8. Plans for the application of armed force should be made by the Security Council with the assistance of the Military Staff Committee referred to in paragraph 9 below.

9. There should be established a Military Staff Committee the functions of which should be to advise and assist the Security Council on all questions relating to the Security Council's military requirements for the maintenance of international peace and security, to the employment and command of forces placed at its disposal, to the regulation of armaments, and to possible disarmament. It should be responsible under the Security Council for the strategic direction of any armed forces placed at the disposal of the Security Council. The Committee should be composed of the Chiefs of Staff of the permanent members of the Security Council or their representatives. Any member of the Organization not permanently represented on the Committee should be invited by the Committee to be associated with it when the efficient discharge of the Committee's responsibilities requires that such a state should participate in its work. Questions of command of forces should be worked out subsequently.

10. The members of the Organization should join in affording mutual assistance in carrying out the measures decided upon by the Security Council.

11. Any state, whether a member of the Organization or not, which finds itself confronted with special economic problems arising from the carrying out of measures which have been decided upon by the Security Council should have the right to consult the Security Council in regard to a solution of those problems.

Section C. Regional Arrangements

1. Nothing in the Charter should preclude the existence of regional arrangements or agencies for dealing with such matters relating to the maintenance of international peace and security as are appropriate for regional action, provided such arrangements or agencies and their activities are consistent with the purposes and principles of the Organization. The Security Council should encourage settlement of local disputes through such regional arrangements or by such regional agencies, either on the initiative of the states concerned or by reference from the Security Council.

2. The Security Council should, where appropriate, utilize such arrangements or agencies for enforcement action under its authority, but no enforcement action should be taken under regional arrangements or by regional agencies without the authorization of the Security Council.

3. The Security Council should at all times be kept fully informed of activities undertaken or in contemplation under regional arrangements or by regional agencies for the maintenance of international peace and security.

CHAPTER IX. ARRANGEMENTS FOR INTERNATIONAL ECONOMIC AND
SOCIAL COOPERATION

Section A. Purpose and Relationships

1. With a view to the creation of conditions of stability and well-being which are necessary for peaceful and friendly relations among nations, the Organization should facilitate solutions of international economic, social and other humanitarian problems and promote respect for human rights and fundamental freedoms. Responsibility for the discharge of this function should be vested in the General Assembly and, under the authority of the General Assembly, in an Economic and Social Council.

2. The various specialized economic, social and other organizations and agencies would have responsibilities in their respective fields as defined in their statutes. Each such organization or agency should be brought into relationship with the Organization on terms to be determined by agreement between the Economic and Social Council and the appropriate authorities of the specialized organization or agency, subject to approval by the General Assembly.

Section B. Composition and Voting.

The Economic and Social Council should consist of representatives of eighteen members of the Organization. The states to be represented for this purpose should be elected by the General Assembly for terms of three years. Each such state should have one representative, who should have one vote. Decisions of the Economic and Social Council should be taken by simple majority vote of those present and voting.

Section C. Functions and Powers of the Economic and Social Council

1. The Economic and Social Council should be empowered:
   a. to carry out, within the scope of its functions, recommendations of the General Assembly;
   b. to make recommendations, on its own initiative, with respect to international economic, social and other humanitarian matters;
   c. to receive and consider reports from the economic, social and other organizations or agencies brought into relationship with the Organization, and to coordinate their activities through consultations with, and recommendations to, such organizations or agencies;
   d. to examine the administrative budgets of such specialized organizations or agencies with a view to making recommendations to the organizations or agencies concerned;

    e. to enable the Secretary-General to provide information to the Security Council;

    f. to assist the Security Council upon its request; and

    g. to perform such other functions within the general scope of its competence as may be assigned to it by the General Assembly.

Section D. Organization and Procedure

1. The Economic and Social Council should set up an economic commission, a social commission, and such other commissions as may be required. These commissions should consist of experts. There should be a permanent staff which should constitute a part of the Secretariat of the Organization.

2. The Economic and Social Council should make suitable arrangements for representatives of the specialized organizations or agencies to participate without vote in its deliberations and in those of the commissions established by it.

3. The Economic and Social Council should adopt its own rules of procedure and the method of selecting its President.

CHAPTER X. THE SECRETARIAT

1. There should be a Secretariat comprising a Secretary-General and such staff as may be required. The Secretary-General should be the chief administrative officer of the Organization. He should be elected by the General Assembly, on recommendation of the Security Council, for such term and under such conditions as are specified in the Charter.

2. The Secretary-General should act in that capacity in all meetings of the General Assembly, of the Security Council, and of the Economic and Social Council and should make an annual report to the General Assembly on the work of the Organization.

3. The Secretary-General should have the right to bring to the attention of the Security Council any matter which in his opinion may threaten international peace and security.

CHAPTER XI. AMENDMENTS

Amendments should come into force for all members of the Organization, when they have been adopted by a vote of two-thirds of the members of the General Assembly and ratified in accordance with their respective constitutional processes by the members of the Organization having permanent membership on the Security Council and by a majority of the other members of the Organization.

CHAPTER XII. TRANSITIONAL ARRANGEMENTS

1. Pending the coming into force of the special agreement or agreements referred to in Chapter VIII, Section B, paragraph 5, and in accordance with the provisions of paragraph 5 of the Four-Nation Declaration, signed at Moscow, October 30, 1943, the states parties to that Declaration should consult with one another and as occasion arises with other members of the Organization with a view to such joint action on behalf of the Organization as may be necessary for the purpose of maintaining international peace and security.

2. No provision of the Charter should preclude action taken or authorized in relation to enemy states as a result of the present war by the Governments having responsibility for such action.

NOTE

In addition to the question of voting procedure in the Security Council referred to in Chapter VI, several other questions are still under consideration.

WASHINGTON, D. C.
October 7, 1944

APPENDIX III

CHARTER OF THE UNITED NATIONS

We the peoples of the United
Nations determined

to save succeeding generations from the scourge of war, which twice in our lifetime has brought untold sorrow to mankind, and
to reaffirm faith in fundamental human rights, in the dignity and worth of the human person, in the equal rights of men and women and of nations large and small, and
to establish conditions under which justice and respect for the obligations arising from treaties and other sources of international law can be maintained, and
to promote social progress and better standards of life in larger freedom,

and for these ends

to practice tolerance and live together in peace with one another as good neighbors, and
to unite our strength to maintain international peace and security, and
to ensure, by the acceptance of principles and the institution of methods, that armed force shall not be used, save in the common interest, and
to employ international machinery for the promotion of the economic and social advancement of all peoples,

have resolved to combine our
efforts to accomplish these aims.

Accordingly, our respective Governments, through representatives assembled in the city of San Francisco, who have exhibited their full powers found to be in good and due form, have agreed to the present Charter of the United Nations and do hereby establish an international organization to be known as the United Nations.

CHAPTER I

Purposes and Principles

Article 1

The Purposes of the United Nations are:

1. To maintain international peace and security, and to that end: to take effective collective measures for the prevention and removal of threats to the

peace, and for the suppression of acts of aggression or other breaches of the peace, and to bring about by peaceful means, and in conformity with the principles of justice and international law, adjustment or settlement of international disputes or situations which might lead to a breach of the peace;

2. To develop friendly relations among nations based on respect for the principle of equal rights and self-determination of peoples, and to take other appropriate measures to strengthen universal peace;

3. To achieve international cooperation in solving international problems of an economic, social, cultural, or humanitarian character, and in promoting and encouraging respect for human rights and for fundamental freedoms for all without distinction as to race, sex, language, or religion; and

4. To be a center for harmonizing the actions of nations in the attainment of these common ends.

Article 2

The Organization and its Members, in pursuit of the Purposes stated in Article 1, shall act in accordance with the following Principles.

1. The Organization is based on the principle of the sovereign equality of all its Members.

2. All Members, in order to ensure to all of them the rights and benefits resulting from membership, shall fulfil in good faith the obligations assumed by them in accordance with the present Charter.

3. All Members shall settle their international disputes by peaceful means in such a manner that international peace and security, and justice, are not endangered.

4. All Members shall refrain in their international relations from the threat or use of force against the territorial integrity or political independence of any state, or in any other manner inconsistent with the Purposes of the United Nations.

5. All Members shall give the United Nations every assistance in any action it takes in accordance with the present Charter, and shall refrain from giving assistance to any state against which the United Nations is taking preventive or enforcement action.

6. The Organization shall ensure that states which are not Members of the United Nations act in accordance with these Principles so far as may be necessary for the maintenance of international peace and security.

7. Nothing contained in the present Charter shall authorize the United Nations to intervene in matters which are essentially within the domestic jurisdiction of any state or shall require the Members to submit such matters to settlement under the present Charter; but this principle shall not prejudice the application of enforcement measures under Chapter VII.

CHAPTER II

Membership

Article 3

The original Members of the United Nations shall be the states which, having participated in the United Nations Conference on International Organization at San Francisco, or having previously signed the Declaration by United Nations of January 1, 1942, sign the present Charter and ratify it in accordance with Article 110.

Article 4

1. Membership in the United Nations is open to all other peace-loving states which accept the obligations contained in the present Charter and, in the judgment of the Organization, are able and willing to carry out these obligations.

2. The admission of any such state to membership in the United Nations will be effected by a decision of the General Assembly upon the recommendation of the Security Council.

Article 5

A Member of the United Nations against which preventive or enforcement action has been taken by the Security Council may be suspended from the exercise of the rights and privileges of membership by the General Assembly upon the recommendation of the Security Council. The exercise of these rights and privileges may be restored by the Security Council.

Article 6

A Member of the United Nations which has persistently violated the Principles contained in the present Charter may be expelled from the Organization by the General Assembly upon the recommendation of the Security Council.

CHAPTER III

Organs

Article 7

1. There are established as the principal organs of the United Nations: a General Assembly, a Security Council, an Economic and Social Council, a Trusteeship Council, an International Court of Justice, and a Secretariat.

2. Such subsidiary organs as may be found necessary may be established in accordance with the present Charter.

Article 8

The United Nations shall place no restrictions on the eligibility of men and women to participate in any capacity and under conditions of equality in its principal and subsidiary organs.

CHAPTER IV

The General Assembly

COMPOSITION

Article 9

1. The General Assembly shall consist of all the Members of the United Nations.

2. Each Member shall have not more than five representatives in the General Assembly.

FUNCTIONS AND POWERS

Article 10

The General Assembly may discuss any questions or any matters within the scope of the present Charter or relating to the powers and functions of any organs provided for in the present Charter, and, except as provided in Article 12, may make recommendations to the Members of the United Nations or to the Security Council or to both on any such questions or matters.

Article 11

1. The General Assembly may consider the general principles of cooperation in the maintenance of international peace and security, including the principles governing disarmament and the regulation of armaments, and may make recommendations with regard to such principles to the Members or to the Security Council or to both.

2. The General Assembly may discuss any questions relating to the maintenance of international peace and security brought before it by any Member of the United Nations, or by the Security Council, or by a state which is not a Member of the United Nations in accordance with Article 35, paragraph 2, and, except as provided in Article 12, may make recommendations with regard to any such questions to the state or states concerned or to the Security Council or to both. Any such question on which action is necessary shall be referred to the Security Council by the General Assembly either before or after discussion.

3. The General Assembly may call the attention of the Security Council to situations which are likely to endanger international peace and security.

4. The powers of the General Assembly set forth in this Article shall not limit the general scope of Article 10.

Article 12

1. While the Security Council is exercising in respect of any dispute or situation the functions assigned to it in the present Charter, the General Assembly shall not make any recommendation with regard to that dispute or situation unless the Security Council so requests.

2. The Secretary-General, with the consent of the Security Council, shall notify the General Assembly at each session of any matters relative to the maintenance of international peace and security which are being dealt with by the Security Council and shall similarly notify the General Assembly, or the Members of the United Nations if the General Assembly is not in session, immediately the Security Council ceases to deal with such matters.

Article 13

1. The General Assembly shall initiate studies and make recommendations for the purpose of:

a. promoting international cooperation in the political field and encouraging the progressive development of international law and its codification;

b. promoting international cooperation in the economic, social, cultural, educational, and health fields, and assisting in the realization of human rights and fundamental freedoms for all without distinction as to race, sex, language, or religion.

2. The further responsibilities, functions and powers of the General Assembly with respect to matters mentioned in paragraph 1 (b) above are set forth in Chapters IX and X.

Article 14

Subject to the provisions of Article 12, the General Assembly may recommend measures for the peaceful adjustment of any situation, regardless of origin, which it deems likely to impair the general welfare or friendly relations among nations, including situations resulting from a violation of the provisions of the present Charter setting forth the Purposes and Principles of the United Nations.

Article 15

1. The General Assembly shall receive and consider annual and special reports from the Security Council; these reports shall include an account of the measures that the Security Council has decided upon or taken to maintain international peace and security.

2. The General Assembly shall receive and consider reports from the other organs of the United Nations.

Article 16

The General Assembly shall perform such functions with respect to the international trusteeship system as are assigned to it under Chapters XII and XIII, including the approval of the trusteeship agreements for areas not designated as strategic.

Article 17

1. The General Assembly shall consider and approve the budget of the Organization.

2. The expenses of the Organization shall be borne by the Members as apportioned by the General Assembly.

3. The General Assembly shall consider and approve any financial and budgetary arrangements with specialized agencies referred to in Article 57 and shall examine the administrative budgets of such specialized agencies with a view to making recommendations to the agencies concerned.

VOTING

Article 18

1. Each member of the General Assembly shall have one vote.

2. Decisions of the General Assembly on important questions shall be made by a two-thirds majority of the members present and voting. These questions shall include: recommendations with respect to the maintenance of international peace and security, the election of the non-permanent members of the Security Council, the election of the members of the Economic and Social Council, the election of members of the Trusteeship Council in accordance with paragraph 1 (c) of Article 86, the admission of new Members to the United Nations, the suspension of the rights and privileges of membership, the expulsion of Members, questions relating to the operation of the trusteeship system, and budgetary questions.

3. Decisions on other questions, including the determination of additional categories of questions to be decided by a two-thirds majority, shall be made by a majority of the members present and voting.

Article 19

A Member of the United Nations which is in arrears in the payment of its financial contributions to the Organization shall have no vote in the General Assembly if the amount of its arrears equals or exceeds the amount of the contributions due from it for the preceding two full years. The General Assembly may, nevertheless, permit such a Member to vote if it is satisfied that the failure to pay is due to conditions beyond the control of the Member.

PROCEDURE

Article 20

The General Assembly shall meet in regular annual sessions and in such special sessions as occasion may require. Special sessions shall be convoked by the Secretary-General at the request of the Security Council or of a majority of the Members of the United Nations.

Article 21

The General Assembly shall adopt its own rules of procedure. It shall elect its President for each session.

Article 22

The General Assembly may establish such subsidiary organs as it deems necessary for the performance of its functions.

CHAPTER V

The Security Council

COMPOSITION

Article 23

1. The Security Council shall consist of eleven Members of the United Nations. The Republic of China, France, the Union of Soviet Socialist Republics, the United Kingdom of Great Britain and Northern Ireland, and the United States of America shall be permanent members of the Security Council. The General Assembly shall elect six other Members of the United Nations to be non-permanent members of the Security Council, due regard being specially paid, in the first instance to the contribution of Members of the United Nations to the maintenance of international peace and security and to the other purposes of the Organization, and also to equitable geographical distribution.

2. The non-permanent members of the Security Council shall be elected for a term of two years. In the first election of the non-permanent members, however, three shall be chosen for a term of one year. A retiring member shall not be eligible for immediate re-election.

3. Each member of the Security Council shall have one representative.

FUNCTIONS AND POWERS

Article 24

1. In order to ensure prompt and effective action by the United Nations, its Members confer on the Security Council primary responsibility for the maintenance of international peace and security, and agree that in carrying out its duties under this responsibility the Security Council acts on their behalf.

2. In discharging these duties the Security Council shall act in accordance with the Purposes and Principles of the United Nations. The specific powers granted to the Security Council for the discharge of these duties are laid down in Chapters VI, VII, VIII, and XII.

3. The Security Council shall submit annual and, when necessary, special reports to the General Assembly for its consideration.

Article 25

The Members of the United Nations agree to accept and carry out the decisions of the Security Council in accordance with the present Charter.

Article 26

In order to promote the establishment and maintenance of international peace and security with the least diversion for armaments of the world's human and economic resources, the Security Council shall be responsible for formulating, with the assistance of the Military Staff Committee referred to in

Article 47, plans to be submitted to the Members of the United Nations for the establishment of a system for the regulation of armaments.

VOTING

Article 27

1. Each member of the Security Council shall have one vote.

2. Decisions of the Security Council on procedural matters shall be made by an affirmative vote of seven members.

3. Decisions of the Security Council on all other matters shall be made by an affirmative vote of seven members including the concurring votes of the permanent members; provided that, in decisions under Chapter VI, and under paragraph 3 of Article 52, a party to a dispute shall abstain from voting.

PROCEDURE

Article 28

1. The Security Council shall be so organized as to be able to function continuously. Each member of the Security Council shall for this purpose be represented at all times at the seat of the Organization.

2. The Security Council shall hold periodic meetings at which each of its members may, if it so desires, be represented by a member of the government or by some other specially designated representative.

3. The Security Council may hold meetings at such places other than the seat of the Organization as in its judgment will best facilitate its work.

Article 29

The Security Council may establish such subsidiary organs as it deems necessary for the performance of its functions.

Article 30

The Security Council shall adopt its own rules of procedure, including the method of selecting its President.

Article 31

Any Member of the United Nations which is not a member of the Security Council may participate, without vote, in the discussion of any question brought before the Security Council whenever the latter considers that the interests of that Member are specially affected.

Article 32

Any Member of the United Nations which is not a member of the Security Council or any state which is not a Member of the United Nations, if it is a party to a dispute under consideration by the Security Council, shall be invited to participate, without vote, in the discussion relating to the dispute. The Security Council shall lay down such conditions as it deems just for the participation of a state which is not a Member of the United Nations.

CHAPTER VI

Pacific Settlement of Disputes

Article 33

1. The parties to any dispute, the continuance of which is likely to endanger the maintenance of international peace and security, shall, first of all, seek a solution by negotiation, enquiry, mediation, conciliation, arbitration, judicial settlement, resort to regional agencies or arrangements, or other peaceful means of their own choice.

2. The Security Council shall, when it deems necessary, call upon the parties to settle their dispute by such means.

Article 34

The Security Council may investigate any dispute, or any situation which might lead to international friction or give rise to a dispute, in order to determine whether the continuance of the dispute or situation is likely to endanger the maintenance of international peace and security.

Article 35

1. Any Member of the United Nations may bring any dispute, or any situation of the nature referred to in Article 34, to the attention of the Security Council or of the General Assembly.

2. A state which is not a Member of the United Nations may bring to the attention of the Security Council or of the General Assembly any dispute to which it is a party if it accepts in advance, for the purposes of the dispute, the obligations of pacific settlement provided in the present Charter.

3. The proceedings of the General Assembly in respect of matters brought to its attention under this Article will be subject to the provisions of Articles 11 and 12.

Article 36

1. The Security Council may, at any stage of a dispute of the nature referred to in Article 33 or of a situation of like nature, recommend appropriate procedures or methods of adjustment.

2. The Security Council should take into consideration any procedures for the settlement of the dispute which have already been adopted by the parties.

3. In making recommendations under this Article the Security Council should also take into consideration that legal disputes should as a general rule be referred by the parties to the International Court of Justice in accordance with the provisions of the Statute of the Court.

Article 37

1. Should the parties to a dispute of the nature referred to in Article 33 fail to settle it by the means indicated in that Article, they shall refer it to the Security Council.

2. If the Security Council deems that the continuance of the dispute is in fact likely to endanger the maintenance of international peace and security, it shall decide whether to take action under Article 36 or to recommend such terms of settlement as it may consider appropriate.

Article 38

Without prejudice to the provisions of Articles 33 to 37, the Security Council may, if all the parties to any dispute so request, make recommendations to the parties with a view to a pacific settlement of the dispute.

CHAPTER VII

Action With Respect to Threats to the Peace, Breaches of the Peace, and Acts of Aggression

Article 39

The Security Council shall determine the existence of any threat to the peace, breach of the peace, or act of aggression and shall make recommendations, or decide what measures shall be taken in accordance with Articles 41 and 42, to maintain or restore international peace and security.

Article 40

In order to prevent an aggravation of the situation, the Security Council may, before making the recommendations or deciding upon the measures provided for in Article 39, call upon the parties concerned to comply with such provisional measures as it deems necessary or desirable. Such provisional measures shall be without prejudice to the rights, claims, or position of the parties concerned. The Security Council shall duly take account of failure to comply with such provisional measures.

Article 41

The Security Council may decide what measures not involving the use of armed force are to be employed to give effect to its decisions, and it may call upon the Members of the United Nations to apply such measures. These may include complete or partial interruption of economic relations and of rail, sea, air, postal, telegraphic, radio, and other means of communication, and the severance of diplomatic relations.

Article 42

Should the Security Council consider that measures provided for in Article 41 would be inadequate or have proved to be inadequate, it may take such action by air, sea, or land forces as may be necessary to maintain or restore international peace and security. Such action may include demonstrations, blockade, and other operations by air, sea, or land forces of Members of the United Nations.

Article 43

1. All Members of the United Nations, in order to contribute to the maintenance of international peace and security, undertake to make available to the Security Council, on its call and in accordance with a special agreement or agreements, armed forces, assistance, and facilities, including rights of passage, necessary for the purpose of maintaining international peace and security.

2. Such agreement or agreements shall govern the numbers and types of forces, their degree of readiness and general location, and the nature of the facilities and assistance to be provided.

3. The agreement or agreements shall be negotiated as soon as possible on the initiative of the Security Council. They shall be concluded between the Security Council and Members or between the Security Council and groups of Members and shall be subject to ratification by the signatory states in accordance with their respective constitutional processes.

Article 44

When the Security Council has decided to use force it shall, before calling upon a Member not represented on it to provide armed forces in fulfillment of the obligations assumed under Article 43, invite that Member, if the Member so desires, to participate in the decisions of the Security Council concerning the employment of contingents of that Member's armed forces.

Article 45

In order to enable the United Nations to take urgent military measures, Members shall hold immediately available national air-force contingents for combined international enforcement action. The strength and degree of readiness of these contingents and plans for their combined action shall be determined, within the limits laid down in the special agreement or agreements referred to in Article 43, by the Security Council with the assistance of the Military Staff Committee.

Article 46

Plans for the application of armed force shall be made by the Security Council with the assistance of the Military Staff Committee.

Article 47

1. There shall be established a Military Staff Committee to advise and assist the Security Council on all questions relating to the Security Council's military requirements for the maintenance of international peace and security, the employment and command of forces placed at its disposal, the regulation of armaments, and possible disarmament.

2. The Military Staff Committee shall consist of the Chiefs of Staff of the permanent members of the Security Council or their representatives. Any Member of the United Nations not permanently represented on the Committee shall be invited by the Committee to be associated with it when the efficient discharge of the Committee's responsibilities requires the participation of that Member in its work.

3. The Military Staff Committee shall be responsible under the Security Council for the strategic direction of any armed forces placed at the disposal of the Security Council. Questions relating to the command of such forces shall be worked out subsequently.

4. The Military Staff Committee, with the authorization of the Security Council and after consultation with appropriate regional agencies, may establish regional subcommittees.

Article 48

1. The action required to carry out the decisions of the Security Council for the maintenance of international peace and security shall be taken by all the Members of the United Nations or by some of them, as the Security Council may determine.

2. Such decisions shall be carried out by the Members of the United Nations directly and through their action in the appropriate international agencies of which they are members.

Article 49

The Members of the United Nations shall join in affording mutual assistance in carrying out the measures decided upon by the Security Council.

Article 50

If preventive or enforcement measures against any state are taken by the Security Council, any other state, whether a Member of the United Nations or not, which finds itself confronted with special economic problems arising from the carrying out of those measures shall have the right to consult the Security Council with regard to a solution of those problems.

Article 51

Nothing in the present Charter shall impair the inherent right of individual or collective self-defense if an armed attack occurs against a Member of the United Nations, until the Security Council has taken the measures necessary to maintain international peace and security. Measures taken by Members in the exercise of this right of self-defense shall be immediately reported to the Security Council and shall not in any way affect the authority and responsibility of the Security Council under the present Charter to take at any time such action as it deems necessary in order to maintain or restore international peace and security.

CHAPTER VIII

Regional Arrangements

Article 52

1. Nothing in the present Charter precludes the existence of regional arrangements or agencies for dealing with such matters relating to the maintenance of international peace and security as are appropriate for regional action, provided that such arrangements or agencies and their activities are consistent with the Purposes and Principles of the United Nations.

2. The Members of the United Nations entering into such arrangements or constituting such agencies shall make every effort to achieve pacific settlement of local disputes through such regional arrangements or by such regional agencies before referring them to the Security Council.

3. The Security Council shall encourage the development of pacific settlement of local disputes through such regional arrangements or by such regional agencies either on the initiative of the states concerned or by reference from the Security Council.

4. This Article in no way impairs the application of Articles 34 and 35.

Article 53

1. The Security Council shall, where appropriate, utilize such regional arrangements or agencies for enforcement action under its authority. But no enforcement action shall be taken under regional arrangements or by regional agencies without the authorization of the Security Council, with the exception of measures against any enemy state, as defined in paragraph 2 of this Article, provided for pursuant to Article 107 or in regional arrangements directed against renewal of aggressive policy on the part of any such state, until such time as the Organization may, on request of the Governments concerned, be charged with the responsibility for preventing further aggression by such a state.

2. The term enemy state as used in paragraph 1 of this Article applies to any state which during the Second World War has been an enemy of any signatory of the present Charter.

Article 54

The Security Council shall at all times be kept fully informed of activities undertaken or in contemplation under regional arrangements or by regional agencies for the maintenance of international peace and security.

CHAPTER IX

International Economic and Social Cooperation

Article 55

With a view to the creation of conditions of stability and well-being which are necessary for peaceful and friendly relations among nations based on respect for the principle of equal rights and self-determination of peoples, the United Nations shall promote:

a. higher standards of living, full employment, and conditions of economic and social progress and development;

b. solutions of international economic, social, health, and related problems; and international cultural and educational cooperation; and

c. universal respect for, and observance of, human rights and fundamental freedoms for all without distinction as to race, sex, language, or religion.

Article 56

All Members pledge themselves to take joint and separate action in co-operation with the Organization for the achievement of the purposes set forth in Article 55.

Article 57

1. The various specialized agencies, established by intergovernmental agreement and having wide international responsibilities, as defined in their basic instruments, in economic, social, cultural, educational, health, and related fields, shall be brought into relationship with the United Nations in accordance with the provisions of Article 63.

2. Such agencies thus brought into relationship with the United Nations are hereinafter referred to as specialized agencies.

Article 58

The Organization shall make recommendations for the coordination of the policies and activities of the specialized agencies.

Article 59

The Organization shall, where appropriate, initiate negotiations among the states concerned for the creation of any new specialized agencies required for the accomplishment of the purposes set forth in Article 55.

Article 60

Responsibility for the discharge of the functions of the Organization set forth in this Chapter shall be vested in the General Assembly and, under the authority of the General Assembly, in the Economic and Social Council, which shall have for this purpose the powers set forth in Chapter X.

CHAPTER X

The Economic and Social Council

COMPOSITION

Article 61

1. The Economic and Social Council shall consist of eighteen Members of the United Nations elected by the General Assembly.

2. Subject to the provisions of paragraph 3, six members of the Economic and Social Council shall be elected each year for a term of three years. A retiring member shall be eligible for immediate re-election.

3. At the first election, eighteen members of the Economic and Social Council shall be chosen. The term of office of six members so chosen shall expire at the end of one year, and of six other members at the end of two years, in accordance with arrangements made by the General Assembly.

4. Each member of the Economic and Social Council shall have one representative.

FUNCTIONS AND POWERS

Article 62

1. The Economic and Social Council may make or initiate studies and reports with respect to international economic, social, cultural, educational, health, and related matters and may make recommendations with respect to any such matters to the General Assembly, to the Members of the United Nations, and to the specialized agencies concerned.

2. It may make recommendations for the purpose of promoting respect for, and observance of, human rights and fundamental freedoms for all.

3. It may prepare draft conventions for submission to the General Assembly, with respect to matters falling within its competence.

4. It may call, in accordance with the rules prescribed by the United Nations, international conferences on matters falling within its competence.

Article 63

1. The Economic and Social Council may enter into agreements with any of the agencies referred to in Article 57, defining the terms on which the agency concerned shall be brought into relationship with the United Nations. Such agreements shall be subject to approval by the General Assembly.

2. It may coordinate the activities of the specialized agencies through consultation with and recommendations to such agencies and through recommendations to the General Assembly and to the Members of the United Nations.

Article 64

1. The Economic and Social Council may take appropriate steps to obtain regular reports from the specialized agencies. It may make arrangements with the Members of the United Nations and with the specialized agencies to obtain reports on the steps taken to give effect to its own recommendations and to recommendations on matters falling within its competence made by the General Assembly.

2. It may communicate its observations on these reports to the General Assembly.

Article 65

The Economic and Social Council may furnish information to the Security Council and shall assist the Security Council upon its request.

Article 66

1. The Economic and Social Council shall perform such functions as fall within its competence in connection with the carrying out of the recommendations of the General Assembly.

2. It may, with the approval of the General Assembly, perform services at the request of Members of the United Nations and at the request of specialized agencies.

3. It shall perform such other functions as are specified elsewhere in the present Charter or as may be assigned to it by the General Assembly.

VOTING

Article 67

1. Each member of the Economic and Social Council shall have one vote.

2. Decisions of the Economic and Social Council shall be made by a majority of the members present and voting.

PROCEDURE

Article 68

The Economic and Social Council shall set up commissions in economic and social fields and for the promotion of human rights, and such other commissions as may be required for the performance of its functions.

Article 69

The Economic and Social Council shall invite any Member of the United Nations to participate, without vote, in its deliberations on any matter of particular concern to that Member.

Article 70

The Economic and Social Council may make arrangements for representatives of the specialized agencies to participate, without vote, in its deliberations and in those of the commissions established by it, and for its representatives to participate in the deliberations of the specialized agencies.

Article 71

The Economic and Social Council may make suitable arrangements for consultation with non-governmental organizations which are concerned with matters within its competence. Such arrangements may be made with international organizations and, where appropriate, with national organizations after consultation with the Member of the United Nations concerned.

Article 72

1. The Economic and Social Council shall adopt its own rules of procedure, including the method of selecting its President.

2. The Economic and Social Council shall meet as required in accordance with its rules, which shall include provision for the convening of meetings on the request of a majority of its members.

CHAPTER XI

Declaration Regarding Non-Self-Governing Territories

Article 73

Members of the United Nations which have or assume responsibilities for the administration of territories whose people have not yet attained a full measure of self-government recognize the principle that the interests of the inhabitants of these territories are paramount, and accept as a sacred trust the obligation to promote to the utmost, within the system of international peace and security established by the present Charter, the well-being of the inhabitants of these territories, and to this end:

a. to ensure, with due respect for the culture of the peoples concerned, their political, economic, social, and educational advancement, their just treatment, and their protection against abuses;

b. to develop self-government, to take due account of the political aspirations of the peoples, and to assist them in the progressive development of their free political institutions, according to the particular circumstances of each territory and its peoples and their varying stages of advancement;

c. to further international peace and security;

d. to promote constructive measures of development, to encourage research, and to cooperate with one another and, when and where appropriate, with specialized international bodies with a view to the practical achievement of the social, economic, and scientific purposes set forth in this Article; and

e. to transmit regularly to the Secretary-General for information purposes, subject to such limitation as security and constitutional considerations may require, statistical and other information of a technical nature relating to economic, social, and educational conditions in the territories for which they are respectively responsible other than those territories to which Chapters XII and XIII apply.

Article 74

Members of the United Nations also agree that their policy in respect of the territories to which this Chapter applies, no less than in respect of their metropolitan areas, must be based on the general principle of good-neighborliness, due account being taken of the interests and well-being of the rest of the world, in social, economic, and commercial matters.

CHAPTER XII

International Trusteeship System

Article 75

The United Nations shall establish under its authority an international trusteeship system for the administration and supervision of such territories as may be placed thereunder by subsequent individual agreements. These territories are hereinafter referred to as trust territories.

Article 76

The basic objectives of the trusteeship system, in acordance with the Purposes of the United Nations laid down in Article 1 of the present Charter, shall be:

a. to further international peace and security;

b. to promote the political, economic, social, and educational advancement of the inhabitants of the trust territories, and their progressive development towards self-government or independence as may be appropriate to the particular circumstances of each territory and its peoples and the freely expressed wishes of the peoples concerned, and as may be provided by the terms of each trusteeship agreement;

c. to encourage respect for human rights and for fundamental freedoms for all without distinction as to race, sex, language, or religion, and to encourage recognition of the interdependence of the peoples of the world; and

d. to ensure equal treatment in social, economic, and commercial matters for all Members of the United Nations and their nationals, and also equal treatment for the latter in the administration of justice, without prejudice to the attainment of the foregoing objectives and subject to the provisions of Article 80.

Article 77

1. The trusteeship system shall apply to such territories in the following categories as may be placed thereunder by means of trusteeship agreements:

a. territories now held under mandate;

b. territories which may be detached from enemy states as a result of the Second World War; and

c. territories voluntarily placed under the system by states responsible for their administration.

2. It will be a matter for subsequent agreement as to which territories in the foregoing categories will be brought under the trusteeship system and upon what terms.

Article 78

The trusteeship system shall not apply to territories which have become Members of the United Nations, relationship among which shall be based on respect for the principle of sovereign equality.

Article 79

The terms of trusteeship for each territory to be placed under the trusteeship system, including any alteration or amendment, shall be agreed upon by the states directly concerned, including the mandatory power in the case of territories held under mandate by a Member of the United Nations, and shall be approved as provided for in Articles 83 and 85.

Article 80

1. Except as may be agreed upon in individual trusteeship agreements, made under Articles 77, 79, and 81, placing each territory under the trusteeship

system, and until such agreements have been concluded, nothing in this Chapter shall be construed in or of itself to alter in any manner the rights whatsoever of any states or any peoples or the terms of existing international instruments to which Members of the United Nations may respectively be parties.

2. Paragraph 1 of this Article shall not be interpreted as giving grounds for delay or postponement of the negotiation and conclusion of agreements for placing mandated and other territories under the trusteeship system as provided for in Article 77.

Article 81

The trusteeship agreement shall in each case include the terms under which the trust territory will be administered and designate the authority which will exercise the administration of the trust territory. Such authority, hereinafter called the administering authority, may be one or more states or the Organization itself.

Article 82

There may be designated, in any trusteeship agreement, a strategic area or areas which may include part or all of the trust territory to which the agreement applies, without prejudice to any special agreement or agreements made under Article 43.

Article 83

1. All functions of the United Nations relating to strategic areas, including the approval of the terms of the trusteeship agreements and of their alteration or amendment, shall be exercised by the Security Council.

2. The basic objectives set forth in Article 76 shall be applicable to the people of each strategic area.

3. The Security Council shall, subject to the provisions of the trusteeship agreements and without prejudice to security considerations, avail itself of the assistance of the Trusteeship Council to perform those functions of the United Nations under the trusteeship system relating to political, economic, social, and educational matters in the strategic areas.

Article 84

It shall be the duty of the administering authority to ensure that the trust territory shall play its part in the maintenance of international peace and security. To this end the administering authority may make use of volunteer forces, facilities, and assistance from the trust territory in carrying out the obligations towards the Security Council undertaken in this regard by the administering authority, as well as for local defense and the maintenance of law and order within the trust territory.

Article 85

1. The functions of the United Nations with regard to trusteeship agreements for all areas not designated as strategic, including the approval of the terms of the trusteeship agreements and of their alteration or amendment, shall be exercised by the General Assembly.

2. The Trusteeship Council, operating under the authority of the General Assembly, shall assist the General Assembly in carrying out these functions.

CHAPTER XIII

The Trusteeship Council

COMPOSITION

Article 86

1. The Trusteeship Council shall consist of the following Members of the United Nations:

a. those Members administering trust territories;

b. such of those Members mentioned by name in Article 23 as are not administering trust territories; and

c. as many other Members elected for three-year terms by the General Assembly as may be necessary to ensure that the total number of members of the Trusteeship Council is equally divided between those Members of the United Nations which administer trust territories and those which do not.

2. Each member of the Trusteeship Council shall designate one specially qualified person to represent it therein.

FUNCTIONS AND POWERS

Article 87

The General Assembly and, under its authority, the Trusteeship Council, in carrying out their functions, may:

a. consider reports submitted by the administering authority;

b. accept petitions and examine them in consultation with the administering authority;

c. provide for periodic visits to the respective trust territories at times agreed upon with the administering authority; and

d. take these and other actions in conformity with the terms of the trusteeship agreements.

Article 88

The Trusteeship Council shall formulate a questionnaire on the political, economic, social, and educational advancement of the inhabitants of each trust territory, and the administering authority for each trust territory within the competence of the General Assembly shall make an annual report to the General Assembly upon the basis of such questionnaire.

VOTING

Article 89

1. Each member of the Trusteeship Council shall have one vote.

2. Decisions of the Trusteeship Council shall be made by a majority of the members present and voting.

PROCEDURE

Article 90

1. The Trusteeship Council shall adopt its own rules of procedure, including the method of selecting its President.

2. The Trusteeship Council shall meet as required in accordance with its rules, which shall include provision for the convening of meetings on the request of a majority of its members.

Article 91

The Trusteeship Council shall, when appropriate, avail itself of the assistance of the Economic and Social Council and of the specialized agencies in regard to matters with which they are respectively concerned.

CHAPTER XIV

The International Court of Justice

Article 92

The International Court of Justice shall be the principal judicial organ of the United Nations. It shall function in accordance with the annexed Statute, which is based upon the Statute of the Permanent Court of International Justice and forms an integral part of the present Charter.

Article 93

1. All Members of the United Nations are *ipso facto* parties to the Statute of the International Court of Justice.

2. A state which is not a Member of the United Nations may become a party to the Statute of the International Court of Justice on conditions to be determined in each case by the General Assembly upon the recommendation of the Security Council.

Article 94

1. Each Member of the United Nations undertakes to comply with the decision of the International Court of Justice in any case to which it is a party.

2. If any party to a case fails to perform the obligations incumbent upon it under a judgment rendered by the Court, the other party may have recourse to the Security Council, which may, if it deems necessary, make recommendations or decide upon measures to be taken to give effect to the judgment.

Article 95

Nothing in the present Charter shall prevent Members of the United Nations from entrusting the solution of their differences to other tribunals by virtue of agreements already in existence or which may be concluded in the future.

Article 96

1. The General Assembly or the Security Council may request the International Court of Justice to give an advisory opinion on any legal question.

2. Other organs of the United Nations and specialized agencies, which may at any time be so authorized by the General Assembly, may also request advisory opinions of the Court on legal questions arising within the scope of their activities.

CHAPTER XV

The Secretariat

Article 97

The Secretariat shall comprise a Secretary-General and such staff as the Organization may require. The Secretary-General shall be appointed by the General Assembly upon the recommendation of the Security Council. He shall be the chief administrative officer of the Organization.

Article 98

The Secretary-General shall act in that capacity in all meetings of the General Assembly, of the Security Council, of the Economic and Social Council, and of the Trusteeship Council, and shall perform such other functions as are entrusted to him by these organs. The Secretary-General shall make an annual report to the General Assembly on the work of the Organization.

Article 99

The Secretary-General may bring to the attention of the Security Council any matter which in his opinion may threaten the maintenance of international peace and security.

Article 100

1. In the performance of their duties the Secretary-General and the staff shall not seek or receive instructions from any government or from any other authority external to the Organization. They shall refrain from any action which might reflect on their position as international officials responsible only to the Organization.

2. Each Member of the United Nations undertakes to respect the exclusively international character of the responsibilities of the Secretary-General and the staff and not to seek to influence them in the discharge of their responsibilities.

Article 101

1. The staff shall be appointed by the Secretary-General under regulations established by the General Assembly.

2. Appropriate staffs shall be permanently assigned to the Economic and Social Council, the Trusteeship Council, and, as required, to other organs of the United Nations. These staffs shall form a part of the Secretariat.

3. The paramount consideration in the employment of the staff and in the determination of the conditions of service shall be the necessity of securing the highest standards of efficiency, competence, and integrity. Due regard shall be paid to the importance of recruiting the staff on as wide a geographical basis as possible.

CHAPTER XVI

Miscellaneous Provisions

Article 102

1. Every treaty and every international agreement entered into by any Member of the United Nations after the present Charter comes into force shall as soon as possible be registered with the Secretariat and published by it.

2. No party to any such treaty or international agreement which has not been registered in accordance with the provisions of paragraph 1 of this Article may invoke that treaty or agreement before any organ of the United Nations.

Article 103

In the event of a conflict between the obligations of the Members of the United Nations under the present Charter and their obligations under any other international agreement, their obligations under the present Charter shall prevail.

Article 104

The Organization shall enjoy in the territory of each of its Members such legal capacity as may be necessary for the exercise of its functions and the fulfillment of its purposes.

Article 105

1. The Organization shall enjoy in the territory of each of its Members such privileges and immunities as are necessary for the fulfillment of its purposes.

2. Representatives of the Members of the United Nations and officials of the Organization shall similarly enjoy such privileges and immunities as are necessary for the independent exercise of their functions in connection with the Organization.

3. The General Assembly may make recommendations with a view to determining the details of the application of paragraphs 1 and 2 of this Article or may propose conventions to the Members of the United Nations for this purpose.

CHAPTER XVII

Transitional Security Arrangements

Article 106

Pending the coming into force of such special agreements referred to in Article 43 as in the opinion of the Security Council enable it to begin the exercise of its responsibilities under Article 42, the parties to the Four-Nation Declaration, signed at Moscow, October 30, 1943, and France, shall, in accordance with the provisions of paragraph 5 of that Declaration, consult with one another and as occasion requires with other Members of the United Nations with a view to such joint action on behalf of the Organization as may be necessary for the purpose of maintaining international peace and security.

Article 107

Nothing in the present Charter shall invalidate or preclude action, in relation to any state which during the Second World War has been an enemy of any signatory to the present Charter, taken or authorized as a result of that war by the Governments having responsibility for such action.

CHAPTER XVIII

Amendments

Article 108

Amendments to the present Charter shall come into force for all Members of the United Nations when they have been adopted by a vote of two thirds of the members of the General Assembly and ratified in accordance with their respective constitutional processes by two thirds of the Members of the United Nations, including all the permanent members of the Security Council.

Article 109

1. A General Conference of the Members of the United Nations for the purpose of reviewing the present Charter may be held at a date and place to be fixed by a two-thirds vote of the members of the General Assembly and by a vote of any seven members of the Security Council. Each Member of the United Nations shall have one vote in the conference.

2. Any alteration of the present Charter recommended by a two-thirds vote of the conference shall take effect when ratified in accordance with their respective constitutional processes by two thirds of the Members of the United Nations including all the permanent members of the Security Council.

3. If such a conference has not been held before the tenth annual session of the General Assembly following the coming into force of the present Charter, the proposal to call such a conference shall be placed on the agenda of that session of the General Assembly, and the conference shall be held if so decided by a majority vote of the members of the General Assembly and by a vote of any seven members of the Security Council.

CHAPTER XIX

Ratification and Signature

Article 110

1. The present Charter shall be ratified by the signatory states in accordance with their respective constitutional processes.

2. The ratifications shall be deposited with the Government of the United States of America, which shall notify all the signatory states of each deposit as well as the Secretary-General of the Organization when he has been appointed.

3. The present Charter shall come into force upon the deposit of ratifications by the Republic of China, France, the Union of Soviet Socialist Republics, the United Kingdom of Great Britain and Northern Ireland, and the United States of America, and by a majority of the other signatory states. A protocol of the ratifications deposited shall thereupon be drawn up by the Government of the United States of America which shall communicate copies thereof to all the signatory states.

4. The states signatory to the present Charter which ratify it after it has come into force will become original Members of the United Nations on the date of the deposit of their respective ratifications.

Article 111

The present Charter, of which the Chinese, French, Russian, English, and Spanish texts are equally authentic, shall remain deposited in the archives of the Government of the United States of America. Duly certified copies thereof shall be transmitted by that Government to the Governments of the other signatory states.

IN FAITH WHEREOF the representatives of the Governments of the United Nations have signed the present Charter.

DONE at the city of San Francisco the twenty-sixth day of June, one thousand nine hundred and forty-five.

STATUTE OF THE INTERNATIONAL COURT OF JUSTICE

Article 1

THE INTERNATIONAL COURT OF JUSTICE established by the Charter of the United Nations as the principal judicial organ of the United Nations shall be constituted and shall function in accordance with the provisions of the present Statute.

CHAPTER I

Organization of the Court

Article 2

The Court shall be composed of a body of independent judges, elected regardless of their nationality from among persons of high moral character, who possess the qualifications required in their respective countries for appointment to the highest judicial offices, or are jurisconsults of recognized competence in international law.

Article 3

1. The Court shall consist of fifteen members, no two of whom may be nationals of the same state.

2. A person who for the purposes of membership in the Court could be regarded as a national of more than one state shall be deemed to be a national of the one in which he ordinarily exercises civil and political rights.

Article 4

1. The members of the Court shall be elected by the General Assembly and by the Security Council from a list of persons nominated by the national groups in the Permanent Court of Arbitration, in accordance with the following provisions.

2. In the case of Members of the United Nations not represented in the Permanent Court of Arbitration, candidates shall be nominated by national groups appointed for this purpose by their governments under the same conditions as those prescribed for members of the Permanent Court of Arbitration by Article 44 of the Convention of The Hague of 1907 for the pacific settlement of international disputes.

3. The conditions under which a state which is a party to the present Statute but is not a Member of the United Nations may participate in electing the members of the Court shall, in the absence of a special agreement, be laid down by the General Assembly upon recommendation of the Security Council.

Article 5

1. At least three months before the date of the election, the Secretary-General of the United Nations shall address a written request to the members of the Permanent Court of Arbitration belonging to the states which are parties to the present Statute, and to the members of the national groups appointed under Article 4, paragraph 2, inviting them to undertake, within a given time, by national groups, the nomination of persons in a position to accept the duties of a member of the Court.

2. No group may nominate more than four persons, not more than two of whom shall be of their own nationality. In no case may the number of candidates nominated by a group be more than double the number of seats to be filled.

Article 6

Before making these nominations, each national group is recommended to consult its highest court of justice, its legal faculties and schools of law, and its national academies and national sections of international academies devoted to the study of law.

Article 7

1. The Secretary-General shall prepare a list in alphabetical order of all the persons thus nominated. Save as provided in Article 12, paragraph 2, these shall be the only persons eligible.

2. The Secretary-General shall submit this list to the General Assembly and to the Security Council.

Article 8

The General Assembly and the Security Council shall proceed independently of one another to elect the members of the Court.

Article 9

At every election, the electors shall bear in mind not only that the persons to be elected should individually possess the qualifications required, but also that in the body as a whole the representation of the main forms of civilization and of the principal legal systems of the world should be assured.

Article 10

1. Those candidates who obtain an absolute majority of votes in the General Assembly and in the Security Council shall be considered as elected.

2. Any vote of the Security Council, whether for the election of judges or for the appointment of members of the conference envisaged in Article 12, shall be taken without any distinction between permanent and non-permanent members of the Security Council.

3. In the event of more than one national of the same state obtaining an absolute majority of the votes both of the General Assembly and of the Security Council, the eldest of these only shall be considered as elected.

Article 11

If, after the first meeting held for the purpose of the election, one or more seats remain to be filled, a second and, if necessary, a third meeting shall take place.

Article 12

1. If, after the third meeting, one or more seats still remain unfilled, a joint conference consisting of six members, three appointed by the General Assembly and three by the Security Council, may be formed at any time at the request of either the General Assembly or the Security Council, for the purpose of choosing by the vote of an absolute majority one name for each seat still vacant, to submit to the General Assembly and the Security Council for their respective acceptance.

2. If the joint conference is unanimously agreed upon any person who fulfils the required conditions, he may be included in its list, even though he was not included in the list of nominations referred to in Article 7.

3. If the joint conference is satisfied that it will not be successful in procuring an election, those members of the Court who have already been elected shall, within a period to be fixed by the Security Council, proceed to fill the vacant seats by selection from among those candidates who have obtained votes either in the General Assembly or in the Security Council.

4. In the event of an equality of votes among the judges, the eldest judge shall have a casting vote.

Article 13

1. The members of the Court shall be elected for nine years and may be re-elected; provided, however, that of the judges elected at the first election, the terms of five judges shall expire at the end of three years and the terms of five more judges shall expire at the end of six years.

2. The judges whose terms are to expire at the end of the above-mentioned initial periods of three and six years shall be chosen by lot to be drawn by the Secretary-General immediately after the first election has been completed.

3. The members of the Court shall continue to discharge their duties until their places have been filled. Though replaced, they shall finish any cases which they may have begun.

4. In the case of the resignation of a member of the Court, the resignation shall be addressed to the President of the Court for transmission to the Secretary-General. This last notification makes the place vacant.

Article 14

Vacancies shall be filled by the same method as that laid down for the first election, subject to the following provision: the Secretary-General shall, within one month of the occurrence of the vacancy, proceed to issue the invitations provided for in Article 5, and the date of the election shall be fixed by the Security Council.

Article 15

A member of the Court elected to replace a member whose term of office has not expired shall hold office for the remainder of his predecessor's term.

Article 16

1. No member of the Court may exercise any political or administrative function, or engage in any other occupation of a professional nature.

2. Any doubt on this point shall be settled by the decision of the Court.

Article 17

1. No member of the Court may act as agent, counsel, or advocate in any case.

2. No member may participate in the decision of any case in which he has previously taken part as agent, counsel, or advocate for one of the parties, or as a member of a national or international court, or of a commission of enquiry, or in any other capacity.

3. Any doubt on this point shall be settled by the decision of the Court.

Article 18

1. No member of the Court can be dismissed unless, in the unanimous opinion of the other members, he has ceased to fulfil the required conditions.

2. Formal notification thereof shall be made to the Secretary-General by the Registrar.

3. This notification makes the place vacant.

Article 19

The members of the Court, when engaged on the business of the Court, shall enjoy diplomatic privileges and immunities.

Article 20

Every member of the Court shall, before taking up his duties, make a solemn declaration in open court that he will exercise his powers impartially and conscientiously.

Article 21

1. The Court shall elect its President and Vice-President for three years; they may be re-elected.

2. The Court shall appoint its Registrar and may provide for the appointment of such other officers as may be necessary.

Article 22

1. The seat of the Court shall be established at The Hague. This, however, shall not prevent the Court from sitting and exercising its functions elsewhere whenever the Court considers it desirable.

2. The President and the Registrar shall reside at the seat of the Court.

Article 23

1. The Court shall remain permanently in session, except during the judicial vacations, the dates and duration of which shall be fixed by the Court.

2. Members of the Court are entitled to periodic leave, the dates and duration of which shall be fixed by the Court, having in mind the distance between The Hague and the home of each judge.

3. Members of the Court shall be bound, unless they are on leave or prevented from attending by illness or other serious reasons duly explained to the President, to hold themselves permanently at the disposal of the Court.

Article 24

1. If, for some special reason, a member of the Court considers that he should not take part in the decision of a particular case, he shall so inform the President.

2. If the President considers that for some special reason one of the members of the Court should not sit in a particular case, he shall give him notice accordingly.

3. If in any such case the member of the Court and the President disagree, the matter shall be settled by the decision of the Court.

Article 25

1. The full Court shall sit except when it is expressly provided otherwise in the present Statute.

2. Subject to the condition that the number of judges available to constitute the Court is not thereby reduced below eleven, the Rules of the Court may provide for allowing one or more judges, according to circumstances and in rotation, to be dispensed from sitting.

3. A quorum of nine judges shall suffice to constitute the Court.

Article 26

1. The Court may from time to time form one or more chambers, composed of three or more judges as the Court may determine, for dealing with particular categories of cases; for example, labor cases and cases relating to transit and communications.

2. The Court may at any time form a chamber for dealing with a particular case. The number of judges to constitute such a chamber shall be determined by the Court with the approval of the parties.

3. Cases shall be heard and determined by the chambers provided for in this Article if the parties so request.

Article 27

A judgment given by any of the chambers provided for in Articles 26 and 29 shall be considered as rendered by the Court.

Article 28

The chambers provided for in Articles 26 and 29 may, with the consent of the parties, sit and exercise their functions elsewhere than at The Hague.

Article 29

With a view to the speedy despatch of business, the Court shall form annually a chamber composed of five judges which, at the request of the parties, may hear and determine cases by summary procedure. In addition, two judges shall be selected for the purpose of replacing judges who find it impossible to sit.

Article 30

1. The Court shall frame rules for carrying out its functions. In particular, it shall lay down rules of procedure.

2. The Rules of the Court may provide for assessors to sit with the Court or with any of its chambers, without the right to vote.

Article 31

1. Judges of the nationality of each of the parties shall retain their right to sit in the case before the Court.

2. If the Court includes upon the Bench a judge of the nationality of one of the parties, any other party may choose a person to sit as judge. Such person shall be chosen preferably from among those persons who have been nominated as candidates as provided in Articles 4 and 5.

3. If the Court includes upon the Bench no judge of the nationality of the parties, each of these parties may proceed to choose a judge as provided in paragraph 2 of this Article.

4. The provisions of this Article shall apply to the case of Articles 26 and 29. In such cases, the President shall request one or, if necessary, two of the members of the Court forming the chamber to give place to the members of the Court of the nationality of the parties concerned, and, failing such, or if they are unable to be present, to the judges specially chosen by the parties.

5. Should there be several parties in the same interest, they shall, for the purpose of the preceding provisions, be reckoned as one party only. Any doubt upon this point shall be settled by the decision of the Court.

6. Judges chosen as laid down in paragraphs 2, 3, and 4 of this Article shall fulfil the conditions required by Articles 2, 17 (paragraph 2), 20, and 24 of the present Statute. They shall take part in the decision on terms of complete equality with their colleagues.

Article 32

1. Each member of the Court shall receive an annual salary.

2. The President shall receive a special annual allowance.

3. The Vice-President shall receive a special allowance for every day on which he acts as President.

4. The judges chosen under Article 31, other than members of the Court, shall receive compensation for each day on which they exercise their functions.

5. These salaries, allowances, and compensation shall be fixed by the General Assembly. They may not be decreased during the term of office.

6. The salary of the Registrar shall be fixed by the General Assembly on the proposal of the Court.

7. Regulations made by the General Assembly shall fix the conditions under which retirement pensions may be given to members of the Court and to the Registrar, and the conditions under which members of the Court and the Registrar shall have their traveling expenses refunded.

8. The above salaries, allowances, and compensation shall be free of all taxation.

Article 33

The expenses of the Court shall be borne by the United Nations in such a manner as shall be decided by the General Assembly.

CHAPTER II

Competence of the Court

Article 34

1. Only states may be parties in cases before the Court.

2. The Court, subject to and in conformity with its Rules, may request of public international organizations information relevant to cases before it, and shall receive such information presented by such organizations on their own initiative.

3. Whenever the construction of the constituent instrument of a public international organization or of an international convention adopted thereunder is in question in a case before the Court, the Registrar shall so notify the public international organization concerned and shall communicate to it copies of all the written proceedings.

Article 35

1. The Court shall be open to the states parties to the present Statute.

2. The conditions under which the Court shall be open to other states shall, subject to the special provisions contained in treaties in force, be laid down by the Security Council, but in no case shall such conditions place the parties in a position of inequality before the Court.

3. When a state which is not a Member of the United Nations is a party to a case, the Court shall fix the amount which that party is to contribute towards the expenses of the Court. This provision shall not apply if such state is bearing a share of the expenses of the Court.

Article 36

1. The jurisdiction of the Court comprises all cases which the parties refer to it and all matters specially provided for in the Charter of the United Nations or in treaties and conventions in force.

2. The states parties to the present Statute may at any time declare that they recognize as compulsory *ipso facto* and without special agreement, in relation to any other state accepting the same obligation, the jurisdiction of the Court in all legal disputes concerning:

    a. the interpretation of a treaty;

    b. any question of international law;

c. the existence of any fact which, if established, would constitute a breach of an international obligation;

d. the nature or extent of the reparation to be made for the breach of an international obligation.

3. The declarations referred to above may be made unconditionally or on condition of reciprocity on the part of several or certain states, or for a certain time.

4. Such declarations shall be deposited with the Secretary-General of the United Nations, who shall transmit copies thereof to the parties to the Statute and to the Registrar of the Court.

5. Declarations made under Article 36 of the Statute of the Permanent Court of International Justice and which are still in force shall be deemed, as between the parties to the present Statute, to be acceptances of the compulsory jurisdiction of the International Court of Justice for the period which they still have to run and in accordance with their terms.

6. In the event of a dispute as to whether the Court has jurisdiction, the matter shall be settled by the decision of the Court.

Article 37

Whenever a treaty or convention in force provides for reference of a matter to a tribunal to have been instituted by the League of Nations, or to the Permanent Court of International Justice, the matter shall, as between the parties to the present Statute, be referred to the International Court of Justice.

Article 38

1. The Court, whose function is to decide in accordance with international law such disputes as are submitted to it, shall apply:

a. international conventions, whether general or particular, establishing rules expressly recognized by the contesting states;

b. international custom, as evidence of a general practice accepted as law;

c. the general principles of law recognized by civilized nations;

d. subject to the provisions of Article 59, judicial decisions and the teachings of the most highly qualified publicists of the various nations, as subsidiary means for the determination of rules of law.

2. This provision shall not prejudice the power of the Court to decide a case *ex aequo et bono,* if the parties agree thereto.

CHAPTER III

Procedure

Article 39

1. The official languages of the Court shall be French and English. If the parties agree that the case shall be conducted in French, the judgment shall be delivered in French. If the parties agree that the case shall be conducted in English, the judgment shall be delivered in English.

2. In the absence of an agreement as to which language shall be employed, each party may, in the pleadings, use the language which it prefers; the decision of the Court shall be given in French and English. In this case the Court shall at the same time determine which of the two texts shall be considered as authoritative.

3. The Court shall, at the request of any party, authorize a language other than French or English to be used by that party.

Article 40

1. Cases are brought before the Court, as the case may be, either by the notification of the special agreement or by a written application addressed to the Registrar. In either case the subject of the dispute and the parties shall be indicated.

2. The Registrar shall forthwith communicate the application to all concerned.

3. He shall also notify the Members of the United Nations through the Secretary-General, and also any other states entitled to appear before the Court.

Article 41

1. The Court shall have the power to indicate, if it considers that circumstances so require, any provisional measures which ought to be taken to preserve the respective rights of either party.

2. Pending the final decision, notice of the measures suggested shall forthwith be given to the parties and to the Security Council.

Article 42

1. The parties shall be represented by agents.

2. They may have the assistance of counsel or advocates before the Court.

3. The agents, counsel, and advocates of parties before the Court shall enjoy the privileges and immunities necessary to the independent exercise of their duties.

Article 43

1. The procedure shall consist of two parts: written and oral.

2. The written proceedings shall consist of the communication to the Court and to the parties of memorials, counter-memorials and, if necessary, replies; also all papers and documents in support.

3. These communications shall be made through the Registrar, in the order and within the time fixed by the Court.

4. A certified copy of every document produced by one party shall be communicated to the other party.

5. The oral proceedings shall consist of the hearing by the Court of witnesses, experts, agents, counsel, and advocates.

Article 44

1. For the service of all notices upon persons other than the agents, counsel, and advocates, the Court shall apply direct to the government of the state upon whose territory the notice has to be served.

2. The same provision shall apply whenever steps are to be taken to procure evidence on the spot.

Article 45

The hearing shall be under the control of the President or, if he is unable to preside, of the Vice-President; if neither is able to preside, the senior judge present shall preside.

Article 46

The hearing in Court shall be public, unless the Court shall decide otherwise, or unless the parties demand that the public be not admitted.

Article 47

1. Minutes shall be made at each hearing and signed by the Registrar and the President.

2. These minutes alone shall be authentic.

Article 48

The Court shall make orders for the conduct of the case, shall decide the form and time in which each party must conclude its arguments, and make all arrangements connected with the taking of evidence.

Article 49

The Court may, even before the hearing begins, call upon the agents to produce any document or to supply any explanations. Formal note shall be taken of any refusal.

Article 50

The Court may, at any time, entrust any individual, body, bureau, commission, or other organization that it may select, with the task of carrying out an enquiry or giving an expert opinion.

Article 51

During the hearing any relevant questions are to be put to the witnesses and experts under the conditions laid down by the Court in the rules of procedure referred to in Article 30.

Article 52

After the Court has received the proofs and evidence within the time specified for the purpose, it may refuse to accept any further oral or written evidence that one party may desire to present unless the other side consents.

Article 53

1. Whenever one of the parties does not appear before the Court, or fails to defend its case, the other party may call upon the Court to decide in favor of its claim.

2. The Court must, before doing so, satisfy itself, not only that it has jurisdiction in accordance with Articles 36 and 37, but also that the claim is well founded in fact and law.

Article 54

1. When, subject to the control of the Court, the agents, counsel, and advocates have completed their presentation of the case, the President shall declare the hearing closed.

2. The Court shall withdraw to consider the judgment.

3. The deliberations of the Court shall take place in private and remain secret.

Article 55

1. All questions shall be decided by a majority of the judges present.

2. In the event of an equality of votes, the President or the judge who acts in his place shall have a casting vote.

Article 56

1. The judgment shall state the reasons on which it is based.

2. It shall contain the names of the judges who have taken part in the decision.

Article 57

If the judgment does not represent in whole or in part the unanimous opinion of the judges, any judge shall be entitled to deliver a separate opinion.

Article 58

The judgment shall be signed by the President and by the Registrar. It shall be read in open court, due notice having been given to the agents.

Article 59

The decision of the Court has no binding force except between the parties and in respect of that particular case.

Article 60

The judgment is final and without appeal. In the event of dispute as to the meaning or scope of the judgment, the Court shall construe it upon the request of any party.

Article 61

1. An application for revision of a judgment may be made only when it is based upon the discovery of some fact of such a nature as to be a decisive factor, which fact was, when the judgment was given, unknown to the Court and also to the party claiming revision, always provided that such ignorance was not due to negligence.

2. The proceedings for revision shall be opened by a judgment of the Court expressly recording the existence of the new fact, recognizing that it has such a character as to lay the case open to revision, and declaring the application admissible on this ground.

3. The Court may require previous compliance with the terms of the judgment before it admits proceedings in revision.

4. The application for revision must be made at latest within six months of the discovery of the new fact.

5. No application for revision may be made after the lapse of ten years from the date of the judgment.

Article 62

1. Should a state consider that it has an interest of a legal nature which may be affected by the decision in the case, it may submit a request to the Court to be permitted to intervene.

2. It shall be for the Court to decide upon this request.

Article 63

1. Whenever the construction of a convention to which states other than those concerned in the case are parties is in question, the Registrar shall notify all such states forthwith.

2. Every state so notified has the right to intervene in the proceedings; but if it uses this right, the construction given by the judgment will be equally binding upon it.

Article 64

Unless otherwise decided by the Court, each party shall bear its own costs.

CHAPTER IV

Advisory Opinions

Article 65

1. The Court may give an advisory opinion on any legal question at the request of whatever body may be authorized by or in accordance with the Charter of the United Nations to make such a request.

2. Questions upon which the advisory opinion of the Court is asked shall be laid before the Court by means of a written request containing an exact statement of the question upon which an opinion is required, and accompanied by all documents likely to throw light upon the question.

Article 66

1. The Registrar shall forthwith give notice of the request for an advisory opinion to all states entitled to appear before the Court.

2. The Registrar shall also, by means of a special and direct communication, notify any state entitled to appear before the Court or international organization considered by the Court, or, should it not be sitting, by the President, as likely to be able to furnish information on the question, that the Court will be prepared to receive, within a time limit to be fixed by the President, written statements, or to hear, at a public sitting to be held for the purpose, oral statements relating to the question.

3. Should any such state entitled to appear before the Court have failed to receive the special communication referred to in paragraph 2 of this Article, such state may express a desire to submit a written statement or to be heard; and the Court will decide.

4. States and organizations having presented written or oral statements or both shall be permitted to comment on the statements made by other states or organizations in the form, to the extent, and within the time limits which the Court, or, should it not be sitting, the President, shall decide in each particular case. Accordingly, the Registrar shall in due time communicate any such written statements to states and organizations having submitted similar statements.

Article 67

The Court shall deliver its advisory opinions in open court, notice having been given to the Secretary-General and to the representatives of Members of the United Nations, of other states and of international organizations immediately concerned.

Article 68

In the exercise of its advisory functions the Courts shall further be guided by the provisions of the present Statute which apply in contentious cases to the extent to which it recognizes them to be applicable.

CHAPTER V

Amendment

Article 69

Amendments to the present Statute shall be effected by the same procedure as is provided by the Charter of the United Nations for amendments to that Charter, subject however to any provisions which the General Assembly upon recommendation of the Security Council may adopt concerning the participation of states which are parties to the present Statute but are not Members of the United Nations.

Article 70

The Court shall have power to propose such amendments to the present Statute as it may deem necessary, through written communications to the Secretary-General, for consideration in conformity with the provisions of Article 69.

APPENDIX IV

FACTORS INDICATIVE OF THE ATTAINMENT OF INDEPENDENCE OR OF OTHER SEPARATE SYSTEMS OF SELF-GOVERNMENT[1]

FIRST PART

FACTORS INDICATIVE OF THE ATTAINMENT OF INDEPENDENCE

A. International status

1. *International responsibility.* Full international responsibility of the territory for acts inherent in the exercise of its external sovereignty and for the corresponding acts in the administration of its internal affairs.

2. *Eligibility for membership in the United Nations.*

3. *General international relations.* Power to enter into direct relations of every kind with other governments and with international institutions and to negotiate, sign and ratify international instruments.

4. *National defense.* Freedom of the territory to enter into arrangements concerning its national defence.

B. Internal self-government

1. *Form of government.* Complete freedom of the people of the territory to choose the form of government which they desire.

2. *Territorial government.* Freedom from control or interference by the government of another State in respect of the internal government (legislature, executive, judiciary and administration of the Territory).

3. *Economic, social, and cultural jurisdiction.* Complete autonomy in respect of economic, social and cultural affairs.

SECOND PART

FACTORS INDICATIVE OF THE ATTAINMENT OF OTHER SYSTEMS OF SELF-GOVERNMENT IN CONTINUING ASSOCIATION WITH THE METROPOLITAN COUNTRY OR IN OTHER FORMS

A. General

1. *Political advancement.* Political advancement of the population sufficient to enable them to decide upon the future destiny of the territory with due knowledge.

2. *Opinion of the population.* The opinion of the population of the territory, freely expressed by informed and democratic processes, as to the status or change in status which they desire.

---

[1] Taken from the Report of the *Ad Hoc* Committee on Factors (Non-Self-Governing Territories), *U.N. Doc.*, A/2428, Eighth Session of the General Assembly (1953). The document contains also an account of the work of the Committee and the way in which the factors were developed.

3. *Voluntary limitation of sovereignty.* Degree to which the sovereignty of the territory is limited by its own free will when that territory has attained a separate system of self-government. Degree of evidence that the attribute or attributes of sovereignty which are not individually exercised will be collectively exercised by the larger entity thus associated.

B. *International status*

1. *General international relations.* Degree or extent to which the territory exercises the power to enter freely into direct relations of every kind with other governments and with international institutions and to negotiate, sign and ratify international instruments freely. Degree or extent to which the metropolitan country is bound, through constitutional provisions or legislative means, by the freely expressed wishes of the territory in negotiating, signing and ratifying international conventions which may influence conditions in the territory.

2. *Eligibility for membership in the United Nations.*

C. *Internal self-government*

1. *Territorial government.* Nature and measure of control or interference, if any, by the government of another State in respect of the internal government, for example, in respect of the following:

Legislature: The enactment of laws for the territory by an indigenous body whether fully elected by free and democratic processes, or lawfully constituted in a manner receiving the free consent of the population;

Executive: The selection of members of the executive branch of the government by the competent authority in the territory receiving consent of the indigenous population, whether that authority is hereditary or elected, having regard also to the nature and measure of control, if any, by an outside agency on that authority, whether directly or indirectly exercised in the constitution and conduct of the executive branch of the government;

Judiciary: The establishment of courts of law and the selection of judges.

2. *Participation of the population.* Effective participation of the population in the government of the territory: (*a*) Is there an adequate and appropriate electoral and representative system? (*b*) Is this electoral system conducted without direct or indirect interference from a foreign government?[4]

---

[4] For example, the following questions would be relevant: (i) Has each adult inhabitant equal power (subject to special safeguards for minorities) to determine the character of the government of the territory? (ii) Is this power exercised freely, i.e., is there an absence of undue influence over and coercion of the voter and of the imposition of disabilities on particular political parties? Some tests which can be used in the application of this factor are as follows:

(*a*) The existence of effective measures to ensure the democratic expression of the will of the people;

(*b*) The existence of more than one political party in the territory;

(*c*) The existence of a secret ballot;

(*d*) The existence of legal prohibitions on the exercise of undemocratic practices in the course of elections;

3. *Economic, social and cultural jurisdiction.* Degree of autonomy in respect of economic, social and cultural affairs, as illustrated by the degree of freedom from economic pressure as exercised, for example, by a foreign minority group which, by virtue of the help of a foreign Power, has acquired a privileged economic status prejudicial to the general economic interest of the people of the territory; and by the degree of freedom and lack of discrimination against the indigenous population of the territory in social legislation and social developments.

Third Part

FACTORS INDICATIVE OF THE FREE ASSOCIATION OF A TERRITORY WITH THE METROPOLITAN OR OTHER COUNTRY AS AN INTEGRAL PART OF THAT COUNTRY

A. General

1. *Political advancement.* Political advancement of the population sufficient to enable them to decide upon the future destiny of the territory with due knowledge.

2. *Opinion of the population.* The opinion of the population of the territory, freely expressed by informed and democratic processes, as to the status, or change in status which they desire.

3. *Geographical considerations.* Extent to which the relations of the territory with the capital of the central government may be affected by circumstances arising out of their respective geographical positions, such as separation by land, sea, or other natural obstacles.

4. *Ethnic and cultural considerations.* Extent to which the population are of different race, language or religion or have a distinct cultural heritage, interests or aspirations, distinguishing them from the peoples of the country with which they freely associate themselves.

5. *Constitutional considerations.* Association (*a*) by virtue of the constitution of the metropolitan country; or (*b*) by virtue of a treaty or bilateral agreement affecting the status of the territory, taking into account (i) whether the constitutional guarantees extend equally to the associated territory, (ii) whether there are powers in certain matters constitutionally reserved to the territory or to the central authority, and (iii) whether there is provision for the participation of the territory on a basis of equality in any changes in the constitutional system of the State.

B. Status

1. *Legislative representation.* Representation without discrimination in the central legislative organs on the same basis as other inhabitants and regions.

(*e*) The existence for the individual elector of a choice between candidates of differing political parties;

(*f*) The absence of "martial law" and similar measures at election times.

(iii) Is each individual free to express his political opinions, to support or oppose any political party or cause, and to criticize the government of the day?

2. *Citizenship*. Citizenship without discrimination on the same basis as other inhabitants.

3. *Government officials*. Eligibility of officials from the territory to all public offices of the central authority, by appointment or election, on the same basis as those from other parts of the country.

C. *Internal constitutional conditions*

1. *Suffrage*. Universal and equal suffrage, and free periodic elections, characterized by an absence of undue influence over and coercion of the voter or of the imposition of disabilities on particular political parties.[5]

2. *Local rights and status*. In a unitary system equal rights and status for the inhabitants and local bodies of the territory as enjoyed by inhabitants and local bodies of other parts of the country; in a federal system an identical degree of self-government for the inhabitants and local bodies of all parts of the federation.

3. *Local officials*. Appointment or election of officials in the territory on the same basis as those in other parts of the country.

4. *Internal legislation*. Local self-government of the same scope and under the same conditions as enjoyed by other parts of the country.

---

[5] For example, the following tests would be relevant:

(*a*) The existence of effective measures to ensure the democratic expression of the will of the people;

(*b*) The existence of more than one political party in the territory;

(*c*) The existence of a secret ballot;

(*d*) The existence of legal prohibitions on the exercise of undemocratic practices in the course of elections;

(*e*) The existence for the individual elector of a choice between candidates of differing political parties;

(*f*) The absence of "martial law" and similar measures at election times;

(*g*) Freedom of each individual to express his political opinions, to support or oppose any political party or cause, and to criticize the government of the day.

INDEX

Secretary-General: of League of Nations, 263; of United Nations, 362-64

Security Council: *See* United Nations: Organs, Security Council

Self-defense: collective (Article 51 of U. N. Charter), 534, 538, 549, 560; legal right, 80-82; under Pact of Paris, 463

Self-determination: revival in United Nations, 25, 51, 70, 324, 432, 441-43; Woodrow Wilson, in Fourteen Points, 58

Self-governing, meaning of: 440-41, Appendix IV

Self-help: 49

Self-preservation, as fundamental right: 80

Serbia: 245, 246

Servitudes: 98

Siam: *See* Thailand

Slavery: 176-77

Smuggling: 104

Sokoloff v. National City Bank: 37

Somaliland: 345

South Africa: *See* Union of South Africa

South East Asia Treaty Organization (SEATO): 549, 569

South Pacific Commission: 568

South West Africa: 344

Sovereignty: Bodin, 4; compared to individual liberty, 23-24; discussed and rejected, 21-26; doctrine of, 22-23; modifications of, 23, 43; relative, 24, 64, 65; strong today, 25; in United Nations, 42

Spain: civil war, 495; and United Nations, 305, 313, 323, 507-8

Specialized Agencies: listed, 381; problem of coordination, 414-17; as a system, 378-81; and Technical Assistance, 416; and United Nations, 380-81 (*See also* specific agencies)

Special United Nations Fund for Economic Development (SUNFED): 424-25

Spheres of Influence: 58

Sponsoring Powers, statement of: 331, 332

Stanberry v. Etna Life Ins. Co.: 453

Stankus v. New York Life Ins. Co.: 452

State: as basic unit, 19-20; definition of, 63; classification of, 63-69; continuing personality, 77; inadequate today, 12, 26; origins of, 4, 71

State succession: 78-79

Stateless person: 134-35, 420

Statute of International Court of Justice: Appendix III

Stimson Doctrine of nonrecognition: 57, 76

Stowell, Lord: 39

Straits: 60

Strategic Trust Territory: 342-43, 344-45

Strathearn S.S. Co. v. Dillon: 93

Streit, C. K.: on Federal Union, 569

Suarez: 30, 240, 451

Sudan: 305, 313

Sugar Union: 174-75

Sully, and "Grand Dessein": 240

Surinam: 352

Sweden: 490

Switzerland: League of Nations headquarters, 256; party to Statute of Court, 355

Syria: mandate, 273; in United Nations, 303, 503

Taiwan (Formosa): 516

Tanganyika: 273, 345, 433

Tangier: 58-69, 245

Tariffs: 10, 87, 411-13

Technical Assistance: beginnings, 421; expanded program, 422; and Technical Assistance Administration (TAA); and Technical Assistance Board (TAB), 368; U. S. Point Four program, 422

Telecommunications: 167-68, 409

Territorial integrity, in Covenant of League of Nations: 475-76

Territorial waters: boundaries, 59-61; codification, 104; continental shelf controversy, 39, 106; jurisdiction over, 60, 95-96

Territorial Waters Jurisdiction Act (1878): 96

Territory: acquisition and title, 55-58; boundaries, 59-62; jurisdiction over, 93-102

Territory of South West Africa (Voting Procedure): 359

Terrorism: 13, 113

Texas, state succession of: 78

Thailand: 305, 313

Thalweg: 61

Thomas, Albert: 363

"Threat to the peace": Charter meaning, 523-26; in Palestine, 523

Three Friends, The: 72

Tinoco Claim: 71

Togoland: 273, 345, 348, 350

Trade: barriers, 8, 10, 87; efforts to improve, 411-13; necessity of, 7, 8

Trail Smelter Case: 94

Transportation: by air, 166-67; by rail, 165-66; by river, 162-64; by sea, 100-3, 165-67

Treatment of Polish Nationals: 274

United States: (*Continued*)

—— disputes in United Nations: Anglo-Iranian, 517; Greek frontier, 505; Guatemala, 519; Indonesia, 511; Iranian, 504; Korea, 541-43; Palestine, 513; South Africa, 511

—— foreign policy: aid to Greece and Turkey, 506; anti-colonial struggle, 352, 354; good neighbor policy, 560; neutrality, 465, 466, 467; neutrality legislation, 494; NATO, 549, 565-66; opposition to communism, 304, 310, 374-75, 519; Point Four and Technical Assistance, 416, 422; recognition policy, 74; recovery for Europe, 419, 420, 564-65; SEATO, 569

—— League of Nations: defection of United States, 249-50, 251-52, 254, 267, 268, 494; Manchuria, 495; peace planning, 247; Paris Peace Conference, 248-49

—— Specialized Agencies: FAO, 386, 387, 389; IBRD, 403; ICAO, 395-96; ILO, 383; IMF, 399, 401; ITU, 409; OTC, 411, 412, 413, 414; UNESCO, 390-91; UNRRA, 419; WHO, 405

—— United Nations: admission to and representation in, 304; Charter review, 574, 577; choice of Secretary-General, 364; creation, 290-91, 292, 294; domestic jurisdiction, 509, 511, 581; economic development, 424, 427; GATT, 427-28; headquarters, 309-10; human rights, 122-23; loyalty of Americans in Secretariat, 371-72; loyalty pressure by U. S., 375-77; membership and dues, 305, 311, 313; no security for U. S., 296; non-self-governing territories, 354, 436, 437, 438, 439-40; privileges and immunities, 308-9; Puerto Rico, 352; Security Council elections, 328, 356; selection of Secretariat officials, 372, 374-77; strategic trust area, 342-45, 347; Uniting for Peace Resolution, 325, 545-46; veto, 296-97, 332, 364, 578; voting, 314, 319

—— World Court: 280-82, 303, 355, 357, 358, 359, 361

U. S. v. Arjona: 45, 116

U. S. v. Bowman: 107

U. S. v. Coplon: 309

U. S. v. Pelly: 453

U. S. v. Percheman: 79

U. S. v. Prioleau: 98, 101

U. S. v. Rauscher: 110

Uniting for Peace Resolution: 325, 333, 521, 545-46

Universal Postal Union: 168-70, 408-9

Upper Silesia: 490-91

Vandenberg, Senator A. H.: 326, 571

Vatican City: 67-68

Vattel: 31-32, 451

Vavasseur v. Krupp: 101

Venezuela: 305, 313

Venezuelan Preferential Claims: 83, 245

Veto: in conferences, 191; double, 332-33; in United Nations, 295, 297, 330-34, 500, 573, 577-78

Vienna school of international law: 42

Virginius, The: 104

Visit and search: 104, 467

Vitoria: 240, 451

Voting: in conferences, 190-93; in League of Nations, 192, 260; at Paris Peace Conference, 192; in public unions, 192; in United Nations, 193, 319-20, 330-33; in UNCIO, 193

Waddington (Carlos) Case: 146

Wal-wal arbitration: 493

Walters, F. P.: on continuity of League of Nations, 279

War: analysis of problem of, 455-57; causes of, 457-58; cost of, 17-18; definition of, 451-55; declaration of, 452-53; effects of, 13-18; League of Nations efforts to control, 480-81; law of, 15, 32-33; military exigency, 15; modern dangerous character, 13-18; noncombatants, 14, 15; outlawry of, 454, 461-64; private property in, 15; range of, 16; totalitarian character, 13, 16-18 (*See also* United Nations: Maintenance of peace and security)

Weighted Voting: *See* Representation, graded or weighted

Weights and measures: 172

Weissman v. Metropolitan Life Co.: 453

West Germany: 291

Westlake, J.: 41

Westphalia, Treaty of: 5, 241

West Rand Central Gold Mining Co. Case: 79

Wildenhus Case: 95

William Gray, Administrator, v. U. S.: 453

Williams, Sir John Fischer: 225

Williams v. Bruffy: 71

Wilson, Woodrow: creation of League of Nations, 247-50; as mediator, 212;